THE**GREEN**GUIDE
Great Britain

Grenadier Guards at Buckingham Palace, ©Peter Phipp/World Pictures/Photoshot

General Manager   Cynthia Clayton Ochterbeck

THEGREENGUIDE **GREAT BRITAIN**

Editor	Jonathan P. Gilbert
Principal Writer	Paul Murphy
Production Manager	Natasha G. George
Cartography	John Dear, Josyane Rousseau, Evelyne Girard, Michèle Cana
Photo Editor	Yoshimi Kanazawa
Proofreader	Liz Dalby
Interior Design	Chris Bell
Cover Design	Chris Bell, Christelle Le Déan
Layout	Anna Gatt, Natasha G. George, John Heath
Cover Layout	Michelin Apa Publications Ltd.
Contact Us	The Green Guide Michelin Maps and Guides One Parkway South Greenville, SC 29615 USA www.michelintravel.com Michelin Maps and Guides Hannay House 39 Clarendon Road Watford, Herts WD17 1JA UK ℘01923 205240 www.ViaMichelin.com travelpubsales@uk.michelin.com
Special Sales	For information regarding bulk sales, customized editions and premium sales, please contact our Customer Service Departments: USA 1-800-432-6277 UK 01923 205240 Canada 1-800-361-8236

Note to the reader Addresses, phone numbers, opening hours and prices published in this guide are accurate at the time of press. We welcome corrections and suggestions that may assist us in preparing the next edition. While every effort is made to ensure that all information printed in this guide is correct and up-to-date, Michelin Apa Publications Ltd. accepts no liability for any direct, indirect or consequential losses howsoever caused so far as such can be excluded by law.

HOW TO USE THIS GUIDE

PLANNING YOUR TRIP

The blue-tabbed PLANNING YOUR TRIP section at the front of the guide gives you **ideas for your trip** and **practical information** to help you organize it. You'll find tours, practical information, a host of outdoor activities, a calendar of events, information on shopping, sightseeing, kids' activities and more.

INTRODUCTION

The orange-tabbed INTRODUCTION section explores Great Britain's **Nature** and geology. The **History** section spans from Roman times through Empire to the modern day. The **Art and Culture** section covers architecture, art, literature and music, while the **Country Today** delves into modern Great Britain.

DISCOVERING

The green-tabbed DISCOVERING section features Principal Sights by region, featuring the most interesting local **Sights**, **Walking Tours**, nearby **Excursions**, and detailed **Driving Tours**. Admission prices shown are normally for a single adult.

ADDRESSES

We've selected the best hotels, restaurants, cafes shops, nightlife and entertainment to fit all budgets. See the Legend on the cover flap for an explanation of the price categories. See the back of the guide for an index of hotels and restaurants.

Sidebars

Throughout the guide you will find blue, orange and green-colored text boxes with lively anecdotes, detailed history and background information.

A Bit of Advice

Green advice boxes found in this guide contain practical tips and handy information relevant to the sight in the Discovering section.

STAR RATINGS★★★

Michelin has given star ratings for more than 100 years. If you're pressed for time, we recommend you visit the ★★★, or ★★ sights first:

★★★ **Highly recommended**
★★ **Recommended**
★ **Interesting**

MAPS

⊚ National Driving Tours map, Places to Stay map and Sights map.
⊚ Region maps.
⊚ Maps for major cities and villages.
⊚ Local tour maps.

All maps in this guide are oriented north, unless otherwise indicated by a directional arrow. The term "Local Map" refers to a map within the chapter or Tourism Region. A complete list of the maps found in the guide appears at the back of this book.

PLANNING YOUR TRIP

INTRODUCTION TO GREAT BRITAIN

DISCOVERING GREAT BRITAIN

CONTENTS

5

Welcome to Great Britain

Three unique countries and dozens of different cultures and landscapes make up Great Britain and its surrounding isles. The largest island in the United Kingdom has only been politically unified since 1707, which given over 700,000 years of modern and early human occupation gives an idea of the variety to be found here. Modern Great Britain is an island where heritage, history and high culture play a continuing role, but nothing stands still for long.

British Museum

Y. Kanazawa/Michelin

LONDON *(p92–129)*

London is one of the most cosmopolitan, dynamic, fashionable and cultural cities on earth. It is also home to so many quintessential images of Britain: Big Ben, Tower Bridge, red double-decker buses, Buckingham Palace and bear-skinned guards. For visitors who want a crash course in British history and culture it holds some of the world's finest museums, galleries and performance venues.
An indispensable first stop.

SOUTHEAST *(p130–181)*

Exploring the Southeast of England is much more than a day trip to Windsor Castle. The most affluent region in

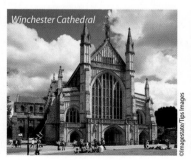
Winchester Cathedral

©Imagestate/Tips Images

the country is home to a rich vein of diverse historical attractions, within easy reach of the capital and set in lovely countryside. Further afield, towns like Winchester, Canterbury and, above all, Oxford, repay an overnight stay. The New Forest, Chiltern Hills and Surrey Hills are just a sample of the great outdoors enjoyed by walkers and others, while the coast traces the epic history of maritime Britain and includes the classic seaside resort of Brighton.

Eden Project, Cornwall

Tamsyn Williams/Eden Project

SOUTHWEST *(p182–258)*

The Southwest has long been Great Britain's holiday playground, though the region offers much more than just buckets and spades by the seaside. Devon is one of England's most beautiful counties with contrasting coastlines, delightful inland and coastal villages, wild moorland, and many unspoiled seaside retreats. Cornwall offers similar pleasures, with a more untamed beauty. Bath's Georgian and Roman heritage and Bristol's maritime past are historic highlights of the West Country, while further north are the gentle rolling hills of the Cotswolds.

Dovedale, Peak District, Derbyshire

EAST ANGLIA (p258–275)

East Anglia is a peaceful, bucolic region, and a favourite of Constable for landscape painting. Its canvas is still splashed with a green and pleasant land, devoid of relief but full of traditional seaside resorts, preserved medieval towns and villages, extensive waterways and England's second oldest university town.

MIDLANDS (p276–315)

A mix of industrial conurbations and bucolic countryside, the Midlands begins around 50 miles north of London and meanders north, south east and west. The very essence of Englishness is to be found here: thatched black-and-white Shakespeare properties; Robin Hood's Sherwood Forest; and the unlikely birthplace of the Industrial Revolution, Ironbridge, nestling among the peaceful hills of beautiful Shropshire.

NORTH (p316–377)

The North is Britain's fastest growing, region. Manchester, Leeds and Liverpool boast cutting-edge galleries, revitalised museums, 21C architecture, and the finest shopping, eating and nightlife. York is a repository of English history, and its Dales and Moors are surpassed only by the rolling fells and pikes of the Lake District to the west, overlooking glittering lakes, slate houses and green pastures.

SCOTLAND (p378–439)

In Scotland you will find all of the old cliches of kilts and tartans, shortbread, whisky, bagpipes, castles and golf, alongside a modern country re-inventing itself. Visit Edinburgh for its setting and history, but don't miss Glasgow for its unique cultural scene. Beyond lie some of the most remote parts of Britain, with breathtaking scenery, ancient history, and a way of life a thousand miles from Edinburgh's Royal Mile. Bring weatherproof clothing and a sense of adventure.

Walking in Cairngorms, Highland

WALES (p440–467)

Like Scotland, Wales offers some of Britain's most dramatic mountain scenery and a very different historical and cultural perspective on being British. Wales is easily the least densely populated nation in Britain and away from the cities; four-legged creatures far outnumber people. Fairy-tale castles, magnificent golden beaches and a fascinating industrial heritage await.

Barafundle Bay near St Goven's head, Pembrokeshire

7

Snowdon Horseshoe, Wales
© WILLIAM/MICHELIN

Michelin Driving Tours

GRAND TOURS

These tours are highlighted on the map on the next page.

Driving in Wales

© Harvey Hudson/Fotolia.com

SOUTHERN ENGLAND

1010mi/1630km. 14 days including a day in Bath, Oxford and Taunton.

(1) Thames Valley to Cheltenham: Follow the leafy river north to the dreaming spires of Oxford, past magnificent Blenheim, through idyllic Cotswolds villages to the elegant spa town of Cheltenham. **(2) Bath to Exmoor**: Bath is the most graceful provincial city in England, while Somerset include the natural delights of Cheddar and Exmoor. **(3) North Devon**: The coast road passes through the popular resort of Ilfracombe, the market town of Barnstaple and the picture-postcard village of Clovelly. **(4) Cornish Coast**; This is lined with classic English seaside towns, villages and fishing ports. **(5) South Devon to Stonehenge**: Leave Devon via southern Dartmoor and head east to the legendary stone circle, via Stourhead, one of England's finest gardens. **(6) Winchester and the South East**: Winchester is an ancient town with a wonderful cathedral, and a night in Brighton should not be missed. Charming backwater Rye contrasts with mighty Dover Castle and ecclesiastical Canterbury.

MIDLANDS AND E. ANGLIA

630mi/1010km. 10 days including a day in Cambridge.

(1) St Albans to Lichfield: First stop north from London is the old Roman town of St Alban's. Pay your respects to Shakespeare in Stratford-upon-Avon then visit the cathedrals in Coventry and Lichfield. **(2) Stoke-on-Trent to Stamford**: Potter around Stoke-on-Trent, then onto the Peak District to England's finest country house and estate, Chatsworth. Lincoln is a superbly sited little city, while Stamford is a little-known gem. **(3) East Anglia**: The cathedrals of Peterborough and Ely loom above the flat East Anglian fenlands. Follow the unspoiled coast to the boating playground of the Broads, and Norwich, the characterful historic regional hub. **(4) Cambridge and stately homes**: Spend a day exploring the city and colleges, then head back south via the grand estates of Audley End and Hatfield House.

NORTHERN ENGLAND

580 mi/930km. 7 days including two nights in York.

(1) York and North York Moors: Historic York is a good base for exploring the Moors, the seaside town of Whitby and aristocratic Castle Howard **(2) Northern cities**: Leeds, Manchester and Liverpool are just a few miles from each other, but you'll want to linger, maybe a night in each, to see their varied sights, art galleries, stunning contemporary buildings, football, Beatle-mania, and sample the nightlife. **(3) West coast and Lake District**: After the bustle of the city, simply relax, or go walking amid England's finest mountain-and-lake scenery. The quintessentially English resort of Blackpool is a cheery summer distraction. **(4) Hadrian's Wall to the Dales**: From Carlisle follow the old frontier – created by the Roman Emperor, Hadrian, some 1,900 years ago – east to Durham, England's most perfectly sited cathedral city. Head south through the splendour of the Yorkshire Dales, taking in the glorious remains of Fountains Abbey and the genteel spa town of Harrogate.

SCOTLAND

1110 mi/1770km. 13 days including a day in Edinburgh, Glasgow and Skye.
(1) Edinburgh to St Andrews: Explore the capital (at least two days) then cross the awe-inspiring Forth Bridge to enter the kingdom of Fife; explore its history at Culross and its fishing traditions along the picturesque East Neuk coast. St Andrews is a delightful university town and the home of golf. **(2) Perth to Inverness**: The city of Perth is a fine base for the scenic Southern Highlands and its many adventure sports opportunities. Continuing north east, the Grampians is castle and whisky country; Aberdeen, makes a good base. **(3) The Northern Highlands & Skye:** This is picture-postcard Scotland with majestic scenery, awesome wild places and towering mountains. Cross the water to "bonnie" Skye and spend a night savouring its atmosphere. **(4) Loch Ness to Stirling**. Hire a boat and go "monster spotting" before heading south via the Trossachs, enjoying more quintessentially Scottish scenery. Stirling is a fine compact historic city. **(5) Glasgow & the Borders**: Glasgow is Scotland's most vibrant metropolis, with a whole raft of cultural attractions. Head back to Edinburgh via the peaceful lowland Borders country.

WALES AND THE MARCHES

590mi/950km. 7 days.
(1) Severn Bridge to Swansea: Enter Wales in style via the Severn Bridge and spend a night in the revitalised capital, Cardiff, to sample its buzz and culture. Swansea is another South Wales city on the up, while just to the west, the Gower Peninsula is a chain of superb beaches and cliff scenery. **(2) Pembrokeshire**: Tenby is a beautifully sited typical British seaside resort, also surrounded by wonderful beaches. St David's, Britain's smallest city, is the Principality's little gem. **(3) Aberystwyth to Portmeirion**: Aberystwyth is Wales' most complete seaside resort with a scenic hinterland known as the Welsh Lake District.

Harlech is renowned for its castle, while Portmeirion is a delightful Italianate village created "to celebrate life and architecture…". **(4) Snowdonia and North Wales**: Mount Snowdon is the highest point in England and Wales with scenery and walks not to be missed. Around the area are mighty castles and fascinating industrial heritage. **(5) The Marches:** Historic Chester, with its Roman and medieval walls, is the finest of the Marches (border) towns, but also to be enjoyed are Ludlow, Hereford and Monmouth, all very close to unspoiled natural beauty.

LOCAL DRIVES

Discover Britain's hidden routes:

SOUTHEAST
- **Thames Valley**
  Windsor to Oxford

SOUTHWEST
- **Truro**
  South Cornish Coast
  Truro to St Michael's Mount

MIDLANDS
- **Cotswolds**
  Cirencester to Chipping Campden
- **Wye Valley**
  Ross-on-Wye to Chepstow

NORTH
- **Lake District**
  Lakeland Poets Tour
  Eskdale via Wrynose Pass
  Keswick and Northern Lakes
  Kendal and Furness

SCOTLAND
- **Isle Of Arran**
- **Tweed Valley**
- **Wester Ross**
  Kyle of Lochalsh to Gairloch
  Gairloch to Ullapool

WALES
- **Pembrokeshire Coast**
  Tenby's to St David's
  St David's to Cardigan

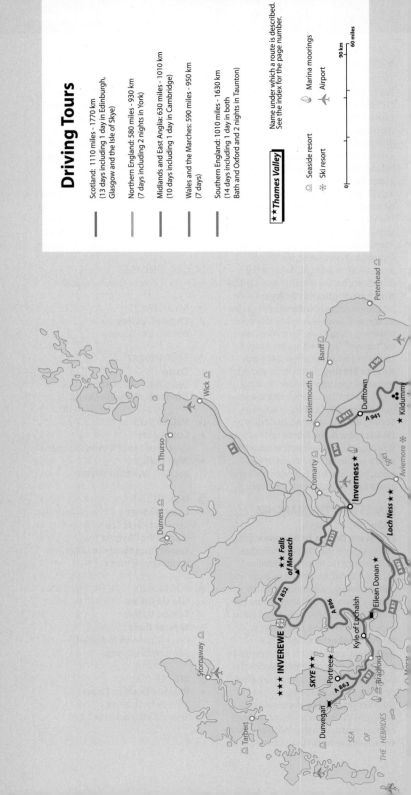

Driving Tours

Scotland: 1110 miles - 1770 km
(13 days including 1 day in Edinburgh,
Glasgow and the Isle of Skye)

Northern England: 580 miles - 930 km
(7 days including 2 nights in York)

Midlands and East Anglia: 630 miles - 1010 km
(10 days including 1 day in Cambridge)

Wales and the Marches: 590 miles - 950 km
(7 days)

Southern England: 1010 miles - 1630 km
(14 days including 1 day in both
Bath and Oxford and 2 nights in Taunton)

★★ Thames Valley Name under which a route is described.
See the index for the page number.

⚓ Marina moorings
✈ Airport

⌂ Seaside resort
❄ Ski resort

0 | 90 km
0 | 60 miles

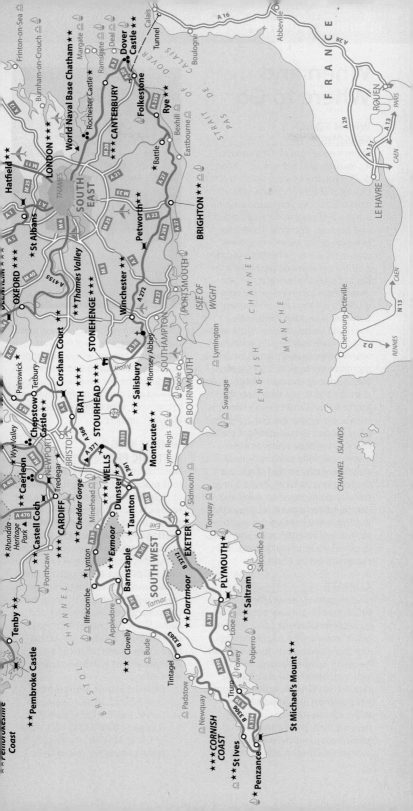

When and Where to Go

WHEN TO GO
SEASONS

There is no season of the year when it's too hot, too cold, too wet or too dry for you to enjoy the sights, but the changeable British climate lives up to its reputation. Spring and autumn are the best seasons for visiting parks and gardens, when the flowers are in bloom or the leaves are turning colour; most stately homes and other country sights are closed from October to Easter. In **spring** as the days grow longer and warmer, the light is glorious, but showers are frequent. **Summer** is unpredictable with moderate temperatures; in July and August there may be occasional heat waves in the southern areas, when the thermometer tops 30°C, or the days may be cloudy and cool. **Autumn** can start dry and sunny, with clear skies and beautiful sunsets, while the air is crisp and invigorating. But as the days grow shorter, the temperature usually lowers. In **winter**, southern areas can remain fairly mild until Christmas. There may be cold snaps, but the temperature rarely drops below freezing point. However, wind and dampness can make it feel very cold. Autumn and winter are the best time for visiting museums or for shopping, as places are less crowded, except in the weeks before Christmas.

CLIMATE

Chatting about the weather is a great British tradition, if only because it is so unpredictable and rain is seldom unaccompanied by brighter spells. The moist and breezy oceanic climate has many compensations. Stressful extremes of either heat or cold are rare, so that outdoor activity of some kind is almost always possible. Although the western mountains receive the highest amount of precipitation, which on some summits reaches an astonishing

Spring - Bluebells in the woodland
© John Woodworth/iStockphoto.com

200in/5,000mm, it is in the west that the tempering effects of the **Gulf Stream** are felt and where sub-tropical plants can flourish in sheltered locations. The drier, sunnier climate of the east and south is more continental in character, with colder winters and warmer summers.

WHERE TO GO
HISTORIC PROPERTIES

Many country houses, gardens, historic monuments and ruins are owned or maintained by the following organisations, which offer free admission to their members. The **Great British Heritage Pass** (valid for 4, 7, 15 days or one month, and valid for 6 months from date of purchase) gives access to over 580 properties throughout Great Britain under the care of the National Trust, English Heritage, National Trust for Scotland, Historic Scotland, and Cadw. See www.britishheritagepass. com for more details. It is available from major tourist offices in the UK and may also be purchased online.

- ◆ **Cadw (Welsh Historic Monuments)**
  Over 125 properties: Cadw, Plas Carew, Unit 5/7 Cefn Coed, Parc Nantgarw, Cardiff CF15 7QQ, Wales. ✆01443 336 000. www.cadw.wales.gov.uk

◆ **English Heritage**
Exists to protect and promote England's spectacular historic environment and ensure that its past is researched and understood. Over 400 properties:
Customer Services Department, PO Box 569, Swindon SN2 2YP. ℘0870 333 1181.
www.english-heritage.org.uk

◆ **Historic Scotland**
An executive agency of the Scottish Government, responsible for historic monuments in Scotland. Over 300 properties:
Longmore House, Salisbury Place, Edinburgh EH9 1SH, Scotland. ℘0131 668 8600.
www.historic-scotland.gov.uk

◆ **Manx National Heritage**
National organisation for the Asle of Man responsible for eight principal sites and 4000 acres:
Douglas, Isle of Man, IM1 3LY. ℘01624 648000.
www.gov.im/mnh

Membership of some of the above organisations entitles discounted admission to sites owned by another.

◆ **National Trust**
One of the largest landowners in the United Kingdom. Owns many heritage properties and natural beauty spots
England and Wales:
PO Box 39, Warrington WA5 7WD. ℘0844 800 1895.
www.national trust.org.uk
Scotland
28 Charlotte Square, Edinburgh EH2 4ET. ℘0844 493 2100.
www.nts.org.uk

There are reciprocal arrangements between these Trusts and similar overseas Trusts.

◆ **The Royal Oak Foundation,**
American public charity affiliated with the National Trust to promote the preservation of Anglo-American heritage. Royal Oak members automatically receive the rights and privileges of full National Trust (England and Wales) members.
35 West 35th Street, Suite 1200 New York, New York 10001-2205, USA. ℘212-480 2889 or 800-913-6565. www.royal-oak.org

BEER

◆ **Campaign for Real Ale**
Protects traditional draught beer and traditional pubs, organises beer festivals and produces the annual *Good Beer Guide.*
230 Hatfield Road, St Albans, Herts, AL1 4LW. ℘01727 867 201.
www.camra.org.uk

ARTS

◆ **British Arts Festivals Association**
Provides advance information on leading annual arts festivals in the United Kingdom.
2nd Floor, 28 Charing Cross Road, London, WC2H 0DB.
℘20 7240 4532.
www.artsfestivals.co.uk

BATTLES

◆ **The Sealed Knot**
Organises re-enactments of the battles of the English Civil War.
Burlington House, Botleigh Grange Business Park, Southampton, Hampshire SO30 2DF.
www.thesealedknot.org.uk

GARDENS

Formal gardens attached to grand country houses to delightful small cottage gardens, all attest to the British passion for gardening. Plants are sometimes for sale.

◆ **The National Gardens Scheme**
Publishes an annual guide – *The Yellow Book* – to private gardens that open to the public for a limited period in aid of charity.
Hatchlands Park, East Clandon, Guildford, Surrey GU4 7RT.
℘01483 211 535. www.ngs.org.uk

What to See and Do

OUTDOOR FUN

The temperate climate of Great Britain has helped to make it the home of many outdoor sports and games. There are few days in the year when outdoor activities are impossible and the long coastline, the rivers and lakes, the mountains and lowlands provide opportunities for a great variety of sports. The mild and moist climate has fostered the development of many games played on a flat grass surface – football (both 'Soccer' and Rugby), hockey and lacrosse in winter and croquet, bowls, lawn tennis and cricket in summer. Every weekend (weather permitting) from May to September cricket matches are played on club fields and village greens. The English Tourist Board publishes an annual guide listing contact addresses for many sports.

CYCLING

The Cyclists Touring Club (CTC) publishes brochures with detailed itineraries, useful maps and addresses, main sights etc. Air lines, ferry companies and the rail network will transport accompanied bicycles. Most local Tourist Information Centres will give advice on hire and routes.

* **Cyclists' Touring Club**
  Parklands, Railton Rd,
  Guildford, Surrey, GU2 9JX.
  01483 238 337. www.ctc.org.uk

HORSEBACK RIDING

Trekking and trail riding are good ways of discovering the countryside. There are some 600 approved establishments throughout the country, which offer hacking (transport by horse, rather than show jumping etc...) and pony trekking, usually in groups.

* **Association of British Riding Schools**
  Queens Chambers, Office No 2,
  38–40 Queen Street, Penzance,
  Cornwall TR18 4BH.
  01736 369 440.
  www.abrs-info.org

GOLF

Great Britain is very well supplied with golf courses which range from the links courses on the coast to the inland park courses. Most are privately owned but are happy to accept visitors. Municipal courses are usually very heavily used, with long queues at the first tee at weekends. In Scotland green fees are less expensive and queues are rare.

Michelin Maps 501 to 504 and the annual red-cover Michelin Guide Great Britain & Ireland give information about golf courses. For more choices visit www.uk-golfguide.com

GAME SHOOTING

Game shooting takes place all over Great Britain but the famous grouse moors are in Scotland and the shooting season opens on 12 August.

* **British Association of Shooting and Conservation**
  Marferd Mill, Rossett, Wrexham, Wales LL12 0HL.
  01244 573 000.
  www.basc.org.uk

SKIING

Only Scotland has ski resorts – at Lochaber, Glenshee, Lecht and Aviemore in the Cairngorms and the Nevis Range near Fort William. All have ski schools and Aviemore is the most fully developed resort. Forest trails have been opened up for cross-country skiing. The best snow conditions are usually found in March and April but up-to-the minute snow reports are essential. Information available from **Ski Scotland;** http//ski.visitscotland.com. There are several dry ski slopes all over Great Britain.

HIKING AND CLIMBING

Throughout the country there are many miles of bridleways and official footpaths, including way-marked **Long Distance Footpaths** which give access to some of the best hill and coastal scenery. Some of the best walking and hiking is provided by the National Parks. For fell-walkers and mountaineers, the Lake District, Wales and Scotland provide the most challenging ascents. All hikers and climbers should be aware of potential dangers and be properly equipped. Climbers are also advised to inform the police or someone responsible of their plans before hazardous climbs.

Narrow boat on the River Avon

©Ann Taylor-Hughes/iStockphoto.com

- ◆ **Ramblers' Association**
  2nd Floor, Camelford House, 87-90 Albert Embankment, London, SE1 7TW. ☎020 7339 8500. www.ramblers.org.uk

- ◆ **British Mountaineering Council**
  177-179 Burton Road, West Didsbury, Manchester, M20 2BB. ☎0161 445 611. www.thebmc.co.uk

WATER SPORTS

Britain has many miles of coastline, estuaries, rivers, lakes and canals, all of which offer a world of different facilities for water sports of all kinds.

Boating, Sailing and Cruising

Great Britain provides various opportunities for amateur and professional sailors – a cabin cruiser on the Norfolk Broads, a narrow boat on the canal network, a punt or a rowing boat on the river.

On the rivers, lakes and reservoirs there are marinas and moorings for cruisers, yachts and sailing boats; along the coast there are facilities for ocean-going yachts.

Most of the **canal network** has been rescued from dereliction, to offer angling, pleasant towpath walks and cruises and holidays on narrow boats.

- ◆ **Association of Pleasure Craft Operators**
  British Marine Authority, Marine House, Thorpe Lea Road, Egham, Surrey TW20 8BF. ☎01784 473 377. www.britishmarine.co.uk

- ◆ **Norfolk Broads Authority**
  Dragonfly House, 2 Gilders Way Norwich, NR3 1UB. ☎01603 610 734. www.broads-authority.gov.uk

- ◆ **British Waterways**
  64 Clarendon Road, Watford Hertfordshire WD17 1DA. ☎0845 671 5530 . www.waterscape.com

- ◆ **British Canoe Union**
  18 Market Place, Bingham, Nottingham NG13 8AP. ☎0845 370 9500 or 0300 0119 500 www.bcu.org.uk

- ◆ **British Water Ski Federation**
  The Tower Thorpe Road, Chertsey, Surrey, KT16 8PH. ☎01932 570 885. www.bwsf.co.uk

Windsurfing

Schools and changing facilities for windsurfers are available on many inland waters and at popular places along the coast. Newquay is the UK's surfing capital.

- ◆ **British Surfing Association**
  The International Surfing Centre, Fistral Bay, Newquay, Cornwall TR7 1HY. ☎01637 876 474. www.britsurf.co.uk

FISHING

There are over 3.7 million fishermen in Britain. The coarse fishing season runs from 16 March to 16 June; permits and advice on local waters can be obtained from any tackle shop.
The waters around Britain provide ample opportunity for anglers to test their skills. Salmon and trout fishing, for which licences are required, is found in Scotland, England and Wales. Sea angling is popular, particularly along the southwestern and Northumbrian coastlines. Sea angling festivals are regular features in some resorts.

◆ **Angling Trust**
Eastwood House, 6 Rainbow Street, Leominster, Herefordshire, HR6 8DQ. ✆0844 7700616. www.anglingtrust.net

◆ **National Federation of Sea Anglers**
Hamlyn House, Mardle Way, Buckfastleigh, TQ11 0NS. ✆01364 644643. www.nfsa.org.uk

◆ **Salmon and Trout Association**
Fishmongers Hall, London Bridge, London EC4R 9EL. ✆020 7283 5838. www.salmon-trout.org

NATURAL SETTINGS

The 12 National Parks of England and Wales and four forest parks in Scotland are areas of protected natural beauty set aside for conservation and recreation. In addition to marked trails there are picnic sites, visitor centres and facilities for outdoors activities.
Campaign for National Parks – 6/7 Barnard Mews, London SW11 1QU. ✆020 7924 4077. www.cnp.org.uk
Conservation is the main aim of the **National Nature Reserves** (NNRs). These include wildfowl sanctuaries, sand dunes, moorland and a variety of other ecological areas.

◆ **Natural England**
1 East Parade, Sheffield, S1 2ET ✆0845 600 3078. www.naturalengland.org.uk

◆ **Scottish Natural Heritage**
Great Glen House, Leachkin Road, Inverness, IV3 8NW. ✆01463 725000. www.nnr-scotland.org.uk, www.snh.org.uk

The following are Britain's leading animal conservation organisations:

◆ **Royal Society for the Protection of Birds**
The Lodge, Sandy, Bedfordshire SG19 2DL. ✆(see website). www.rspb.org.uk

◆ **Wildfowl and Wetlands Trust**
Slimbridge, Gloucestershire GL2 7BT. ✆01453 891 900. www.wwt.org.uk

◆ **Scottish Wildlife Trust**
Cramond House, Kirk Cramond, Cramond Glebe Road, Edinburgh EH4 6NS. ✆0131 312 7765. www.swt.org.uk

ACTIVITIES FOR CHILDREN

In this guide, sights of particular interest to children are indicated with a KIDS symbol (👥). All attractions offer discount fees for children.

SHOPPING
OPENING HOURS

Traditional British shopping hours are Mondays to Saturdays from 9am/9.30am to 5.30pm/6pm. Many larger shops, particularly in out-of-town locations, also open Sundays from 10am or 11am to 4pm. There is late-night shopping (until 7pm/8pm) in most large cities on Wednesdays or Thursdays; supermarkets usually close later than other shops. Smaller individual shops may close during the lunch hour; on the other hand some stay open until very late. Many towns have an early closing day when shops are closed during the afternoon. Traditionally the winter sales before and after Christmas and New Year, and the summer sales in June and July have always been a popular time for

Fishing on tranquil Loch Voil, Perthshire

© Louise McGilvray/Fotolia.com

shopping, as prices are reduced on a great range of goods. However sales now appear on the High Street at other times of year too.

WHAT TO BUY

Great Britain is a good place to buy clothes. There is a wide choice of woollen articles in cashmere or lambswool, particularly in Scotland; classic styles are sold by well-known names such as Jaeger, Burberry, Marks and Spencer, John Lewis, Debenhams and House of Fraser. The very best made-to-measure (bespoke) clothing for men is traditionally available in London in Savile Row (tailors) and Jermyn Street (shirt-makers). The best makes of porcelain – Wedgwood, Royal Worcester, Royal Doulton – are available in London and elsewhere; seconds can be bought at the factory or in "reject shops". Great Britain is equally well known for modern fashion. Those interested in history, antiquities will find plenty to divert them. Popular foody souvenirs include Scotch whisky, smoked salmon, tea and marmalade.

BOOKS

Reference/Biography

A Brief History of British Kings & Queens.
 Mike Ashley (2002).
 A useful and interesting biography of all the country's rulers.

Travel

Notes from a Small Island.
 Bill Bryson (1995: 2001).
 Amusing account of Bryson's first trip to Britain and its many foibles.

Fiction

Brighton Rock. Graham Greene (1938).
 Violence and gang war are the themes of this murder thriller set in the 1930s in the famous seaside resort of Brighton

The Buddha of Suburbia.
 Hanif Kureishi. (1990).
 A darkly comic romp through the lives, hopes and fears of young Asians in the London of the 1980s.

England England. Julian Barnes. (2000).
 A satire on the country's obsession with heritage featuring a 'theme park England' on the Isle of Wight.

Fever Pitch. Nick Hornby. (1992).
 Hornby specialises in the modern British male, in this case, an autobiographical obsession with football and specifically Arsenal Football Club. Also read: *High Fidelity* by Nick Hrnby.

Oliver Twist. Charles Dickens. (1838).
 Dickens' most famous work is a strident social commentary on a grim and unforgiving London, albeit with a happy ending for Oliver, if not for all. Also see: *Great Expectations, David Copperfield, Our Mutual Friend*.

Tess of the D'Urbervilles.
Thomas Hardy. (1891)
This tragedy of class consciousness
and sexual double standards
paints an indelible picture of Eng-
land's fading rural West Country.
Also read: *Far from the Madding
Crowd* by Thomas Hardy.

FILMS

Billy Elliot (1999).
An inspiring and sometimes gritty
tale set in a northern England
mining town during the Miners
Strikes of 1984 where a young boy
discovers his talent for ballet.
Calendar Girls (2003).
Based on a true story, a group of
mature Women's Institute ladies
in North Yorkshire decide to raise
funds for charity by posing nude
for a calendar and in the process
become internationally famous.
*Four Weddings and a
Funeral* (1994).

A romantic comedy drama set in the
1990s following the lives and loves
of a group of friends set around
the title events.
The Full Monty (1997).
Six unemployed steel workers
from Sheffield form an unlikely
male striptease act in this comedy
drama set in the post-industrial
North of England.
The Queen (2006).
Concerning the intriguing interaction between Queen Elizabeth
II and Prime Minister Tony Blair
following the death of Diana,
Princess of Wales in 1997.
Pride and Prejudice (2005).
Beautiful costume drama adaptation of the Jane Austen novel, set
in an idyllic Georgian England.
Trainspotting (1996).
The mean (non-tourist) streets of
Edinburgh is the setting for this
disturbing story about disaffected
youths turning to heroin.

Calendar of Events

25 JANUARY
January 25 – Burns Night. A celebration of the Scottish poet, Robert
Burns, featuring a supper of haggis
and whisky. www.scotland.org.

LAST TUESDAY IN JANUARY
Lerwick, Shetland – Up Helly Aa:
torchlit procession, burning of
Viking longship, night-long celebrations. www.up-helly-aa.org.uk

APRIL
Putney – Oxford-Cambridge Boat
Race. www.theboatrace.org

EARLY MAY
Spalding – Flower Parade and Festival. www.spaldingnet.com
Helston – Flora Day Furry Dance:
spectacular processional dances
throughout the day.

LAST WEEKEND IN MAY
Blair Castle – Atholl Highlanders
Annual Parade, Highland Games.
www.blairatholl.org.uk

MAY
London – Chelsea Flower Show:
www.rhs.org.uk/chelsea

EARLY MAY–MID-SEPTEMBER
Peak District – Well Dressing: in such
Peak villages as Eyam, Monyash,
Warksworth and Youlgreave.
www.derbyshireuk.net

MAY–AUGUST
Glyndebourne – Festival of Music and
Opera. www.glyndebourne.com

MAY–OCTOBER
Pitlochry – Pitlochry Festival Theatre
Season. www.pitlochry.org.uk

LATE MAY–EARLY JUNE
Isle of Man TT – motor cycle races.
www.iomtt.com

Ladies' Day at Ascot

A. Taverner/MICHELIN

JUNE
Ascot – Royal Ascot (the highlight of the horseracing calendar). www.ascot.co.uk
Aldeburgh Festival: music festival. www.aldeburgh.co.uk

2ND OR 3RD SATURDAY IN JUNE
London – Trooping the Colour: the Queen's official birthday parade on Horse Guards Parade. www.army.mod.uk/events

LATE JUNE–EARLY JULY
Wimbledon – Lawn Tennis Championships. www.wimbledon.org
Ludlow – Shakespeare Festival. www.ludlowfestival.co.uk

FIRST WEEK IN JULY
Henley Royal Regatta: premier amateur regatta. www.hrr.co.uk

EARLY–MID-JULY
River Thames – Swan-Upping. Marking of swans on the Thames. www.thamesweb.co.uk

JULY
Llangollen – International Eisteddfod. International Musical Competitions. www.llangollen.com

JULY–SEPTEMBER
London – Henry Wood Promenade Concerts: Royal Albert Hall. www.royalalberthall.com

JULY
King's Lynn – Festival of Music and the Arts. www.kingslynnfestival.org.uk

AUGUST
Jersey – Battle of Flowers. www.battleofflowers.com
Aboyne – Highland Games. www.aboynegames.com
Edinburgh – Edinburgh International Festival, including the Military Tattoo and the Fringe. www.eif.co.uk
Oban – Argyllshire Highland Gathering. www.obangames.com
London – Notting Hill Carnival www.nottinghillcarnival.biz

FIRST SATURDAY IN SEPTEMBER
Braemar – Highland Gathering. www.braemargathering.org

Summer Music Festivals
Britain is well served with music festivals. The biggest is Glastonbury. Other festivals that attract big name acts are Reading Festival; Leeds Festival; O2 Wireless Festival, Hyde Park, London; Guilfest, Guildford; Isle of Wight Festival. Popular crossover music and world music festivals include Bestival, (Isle of Wight) and WOMAD (Charlton Park, Wiltshire). Visit www.efestivals.co.uk.

SEPTEMBER AND OCTOBER
Blackpool – Blackpool Illuminations.
www.blackpooltourism.com

1ST SUNDAY IN NOVEMBER
London to Brighton –
Veteran Car Run. www.lbvcr.com

5 NOVEMBER
Throughout the country – fireworks
and bonfires commemorate Guy
Fawkes and the Gunpowder Plot.

**LATE NOVEMBER –
EARLY DECEMBER**
London – State Opening of
Parliament. www.parliament.uk

2ND SATURDAY IN NOVEMBER
London – Lord Mayor's Show
and Procession.
www.lordmayorsshow.org

DECEMBER
London – Christmas highlights in
London include the Midnight Mass
at St Paul's Cathedral; lights and
dressed shop windows on Regent
Street (www.regentstreetonline.
com) and Oxford Street (www.
oxfordstreet.co.uk); and the enormous Trafalgar Sq. Christmas tree.
Edinburgh – On New Years Eve Scots
celebrate 'Hogmanay' in riotous
fashion throughout the country.

Know Before You Go

USEFUL WEBSITES
VISITBRITAIN
The website of **Visit Britain,** the country's official tourist authority, is *www.
visit.britain.com.* However, the official
national websites are more user-
friendly. All offer accommodation,
holidays, what to see and do, links to
all geographical areas and subsections
on sports and culture:
♦   **www.enjoyengland.com**
♦   **www.visitscotland.com**
♦   **www.visitwales.com**

The official website for **London**:
♦   **www.visitlondon.com**

The official website of **Edinburgh:**
♦   **www.edinburgh.org**

OTHER WEBSITES
London
♦   **www.thisislondon.co.uk**
♦   **www.londontown.com**

Travel Planning
♦   **www.viamichelin.com**
Plan your trip with Michelin's
online route planner via the

best places to see, dine and stay.
Explore further with Michelin's
online magazines for tourists
motorists and gastronomists. You
can even upload details of your
own journeys and discover other
users' favourite journeys to down-
load onto your Michelin GPS.

Travel
♦   **www.scotland-info.co.uk**
The 80,000 word Guide to Scotland is a personal labour of love
by a Scottish author, largely based
on her personal travels. A very
professional site with excellent
suggestions on accommodation.
♦   **www.aboutscotland.com**
Well designed good looking
site, with clickable maps, good
pictures, personally tested accommodation and lively features and
articles about visiting Scotland.
♦   **www.walesinfo.com**
Entertaining and attractive visitors' website with personal recom-
mendations.

News
♦   **www.bbc.co.uk/news**
The BBC front page with breaking
news, magazine stories and links
to the rest of the **BBC website**.

TOURIST OFFICES

Visit Britain, formerly known as the British Tourist Authority, provides assistance in planning a trip to Great Britain and an excellent range of brochures and maps. It works in cooperation with the three National Tourist Boards (for England, Wales and Scotland), the Regional Tourist Boards and other tourist organisations. .

The **British Travel Centre** is located at 1 Lower Regent Street, London SW1Y 4NS (personal callers and written enquiries only).

There are **Tourist Information Centres** in all parts of the country with information on sightseeing, accommodation, places to eat, transport, entertainment, sports and local events. They are usually well signposted, but some are open only during the summer season; the address and telephone number of the local tourist office can be found in sidebars throughout this guide.

The **British Tourist Authority** (BTA) has over 40 offices worldwide including Belgium, Brazil, Denmark, Germany, Hong Kong, Ireland, Italy, Japan, the Netherlands, Norway, Spain, Sweden and Switzerland as well as those listed on the opposite page.

INTERNATIONAL VISITORS
EMBASSIES AND CONSULATES

Australia
- **High Commission**:
  Australia House, The Strand,
  London WC2B 4LA.
  𝒫020 7379 4334.
  www.australia.org.uk
- **Honorary Consulate Scotland:**
  Mr Richard Jeffrey
  Chamber of Commerce
  Capital House, 2 Festival Square
  Edinburgh EH3 9SU .
  𝒫0131 228 4771.

Canada
- **High Commission**:
  Canada House, Trafalgar Square,
  London SW1Y 5BJ.
  𝒫020 7258 6600.
  www.canada.org.uk

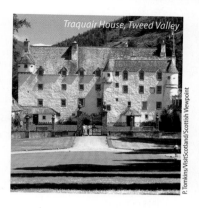

Traquair House, Tweed Valley

P. Tomkins/VisitScotland/Scottish Viewpoint

- **Consulate:**
  55 Colmore Row, 3rd Floor,
  Birmingham, B3 2AS.
  𝒫0121 236 6474.

Japan
- **Embassy and Consulate:**
  101 Piccadilly, London, W1J 7JT.
  𝒫020 7465 6500.
  www.uk.emb-japan.go.jp
- **Consulate Scotland:**
  2 Melville Crescent, Edinburgh
  EH3 7HW. 𝒫0131 225 4777.
  www.edinburgh.uk.emb-japan.
  go.jp

New Zealand
- **High Commission:**
  New Zealand House,
  80 Haymarket, London SW1Y 4TQ.
  𝒫020 7930 8422.
  www.nzembassy.com.
- **Honorary Consulate, Scotland:**
  Mr Eric Milligan. 𝒫0131 222 8109.

South Africa
- **High Commission:**
  South Africa House, Trafalgar
  Square, London WC2N 5DP.
  𝒫020 7451 7299.
  www.southafricahouse.com.

USA
- **Embassy:**
  24-31 Grosvenor Square, London
  W1A 1AE. 𝒫020 7499 9000.
  www.usembassy.org.uk.
  Note: the US Embassy will be relo-
  cating to Nine Elms, Wandsworth.

BRITISH TOURIST AUTHORITY OFFICES (ALL OFFICES: WWW.VISITBRITAIN.COM)	
United States	551 5th Avenue, Suite 701, New York, NY 1017. ✆212-986-1188
	625 N. Michigan Avenue, Suite 1001, IL 60611, Chicago. ✆312 787 0464
	10880 Wilshire Boulevard, Suite 570, CA 90024, Los Angeles. ✆310 470 2782
Canada	5915 Airport Road, Suite 120, Mississauga, L4V 1T1, Ontario. ✆905-405-1720
France	22, Avenue Franklin Roosevelt, 75008, Paris. ✆01 58 36 50 50
Australia	Level 2, 15 Blue Street, North Sydney, NSW 2060. ✆2 90 21 44 00
New Zealand	17th Floor, 151 Queen Street, Auckland 1. ✆09 309 1899

Call the Information Resource Center between 10am and noon, Mon–Fri. ✆020-7894-0925 for date of move.

◆ **Consulate Scotland:** 3 Regent Terrace, Edinburgh EH7 5BW. ✆0131 556 8315. www.usembassy.org.uk/scotland

◆ **Welsh Affairs Office:** ✆020 7984 0131 www.usembassy.org.uk/wales

ENTRY REQUIREMENTS

Despite the law, which came into force on 1 January 1993, authorising the free flow of goods and people within the European Union, it is nonetheless highly advisable for EU nationals to hold some means of identification, such as a **passport**. Non-EU nationals must be in possession of a valid national passport. Loss or theft should be reported to the appropriate embassy or consulate and to the local police. A visa to visit the United Kingdom is not required by nationals of the member states of the European Union and of the Commonwealth (including Australia, Canada, New Zealand, and South Africa) and the USA. Nationals of other countries should check with the British Embassy and apply for a visa if necessary in good time.

The US Department of State provides useful information for US nationals on obtaining a passport, visa requirements, customs regulations, medical care etc. for international travel online at http://travel.state.gov.

CUSTOMS

Tax-free allowances for various commodities are governed by EU legislation except in the Channel Islands and the Isle of Man, which have different regulations. Details of these allowances and restrictions are available at most ports of entry to Great Britain. It is prohibited to import into the United Kingdom any drugs, firearms and ammunition, obscene material featuring children, counterfeit merchandise, unlicensed livestock (birds or animals), anything related to endangered species (furs, ivory, horn, leather) and certain plants (potatoes, bulbs, seeds, trees).

British customs regulations and "duty free" allowances are outlined on their website; visit www.hmrc.gov.uk (insert Customs Allowances in 'Search'). US allowances can be found at http://travel.state.gov.

HEALTH

Visitors to Britain are entitled to treatment at the Accident and Emergency Departments of National Health Service hospitals. For an overnight or longer stay in hospital, payment will probably be required. It is therefore advisable to take out adequate insurance cover before leaving home. Visitors from EU countries should apply to their own National Social Security Offices for a **European Health Insurance Card (EHIC)** – the replacement for Form E111 – which entitles them to medical treatment under an EU Reciprocal Medical Treatment arrangement. Nationals of non-EU countries should take out comprehensive insurance. American Express offers a service, "Global Assist", for any medical, legal or personal emergency – visit www.americanexpress.com (from

outside the US you can call collect
☎ 715-343-7977).

ACCESSIBILITY
Many of the sights described in this
guide are accessible to disabled
people; they are designated by the
♿ symbol in the Admission Times and
Charges for the attractions.
The red-cover **Michelin Guide Great
Britain & Ireland** indicates hotels
with facilities suitable for disabled
people; it is advisable to book in
advance. The **Royal Association
for Disability and Rehabilitation
(RADAR)** publishes an annual guide
Holidays in Britain and Ireland as well
as *Accessible Scotland* with information
on hotels and holiday centres as well

as sections on transport, accommodation for children and activity holidays.
Apply to RADAR, 12 City Forum, 250
City Road, London EC1V 8AF. ☎020
7250 3222, www.radar.org.uk.
A useful government website is
www.direct.gov.uk/en/Disabled
People/TravelHolidaysAndBreaks,
which gives information on tailored
holidays and breaks for disabled
people, families and carers. Other
organisations such as Visit Britain, the
National Trust and the Department of
Transport publish info booklets.
* **Tourism For All**
  c/o Vitalise, Shap Road Industrial
  Estate, Shap Road, Kendal, Cumbria LA9 6NZ . ☎0845 124 9971.
  www.tourismforall.org.uk

Getting There Getting Around

BY AIR
Various national and other independ-
ent airlines operate services to the
capital's five airports. Heathrow and
Gatwick service the majority of flights:
* **Heathrow (LHR)**
* **Gatwick (LGW)**
* **Luton (LTN)**
* **Stansted (STN)**
* **City (LCY)**

Services also run to major regional
airports (Aberdeen, Birmingham, Cardiff, Edinburgh, Glasgow, Liverpool,
Manchester, Newcastle, Prestwick).

BY SEA
There are numerous cross-Channel
(passenger and car ferries, hovercraft)
and other ferry or shipping services
from the continent. For details apply
to travel agencies or to the ferry
companies.

* **Brittany Ferries**
  Millbay, Plymouth, Devon,
  England, PL1 3EW.

☎0871 244 0744 (*UK reservations*).
www.brittany-ferries.com

* **Irish Ferries**
  Corn Exchange Building,
  Ground Floor, Brunswick Street,
  Liverpool L2 7 TP.
  ☎08705 17 17 17.
  www.irishferries.com

* **P&O Ferries**
  Channel House, Channel View
  Road, Dover, Kent CT17 9TJ.
  ☎08716 645 645.
  www.poferries.com

* **Stena Line**
  Stena House, Station Approach,
  Holyhead, Anglesey, LL65 1DQ.
  ☎08705 70 70 70.
  www.stenaline.com

BY TRAIN
The **Channel Tunnel** provides a
direct Eurostar rail link from London
St Pancras International to France and
Belgium. Eurostar also runs from Ebbs-
fleet International and from Ashford
International station (both in Kent).
There is also a road/rail link between
Folkestone and Calais (France).

◆ **Eurostar**
Eurostar House, Waterloo station,
London SE1 8SE.
www.eurostar.com
℘08705 186 186
(ticket and bookings);
℘020 7928 0660
(lost property);
℘01777 77 78 79
(international customer relations).

BritRail Passes and **Eurail Passes**
are available to visitors from North
America and certain Asia-Pacific countries including Australia, New Zealand
and South Africa. BritRail Passes allow
travel on consecutive days for various
periods and Eurail Passes allow travel
on a number of days within a given
month. These concessions can be
obtained only outside Britain and
should be purchased from appointed
agents before the beginning of the
journey in question; they are worth
considering by those who intend to
travel extensively in Britain by rail.
For more details on BritRail Passes visit
www.britrail.com.
For Eurail Passes information before
you arrive from North America, visit
www.railpass.com.
An **InterRail Pass** can be bought
by European visitors; for details visit
www.raileurope.co.uk.
For information on rail services and on
other concessionary tickets, including
combined train and bus tickets once
you are in Great Britain ℘08457 48
49 50. www.nationalrail.co.uk.
To buy train tickets either go to
the station, or buy online in advance
for discounted fares at www.thetrain
line.com or from operators like Virgin
Trains (www.virgintrains.co.uk).

BY COACH/BUS
National Express, in association with
other bus operators, run express coach
services covering the whole country.
℘0875 808 080 (National call centre).
www.nationalexpress.com.
Cheap inter-city bus companies
include www.megabus.co.uk and
www.easybus.co.uk. These operators

also often offer cheap airport transfer
services.
For comprehensive public transport
information in the UK, call ℘0871 200
22 33 or visit www.traveline.org.uk.

BY CAR
DOCUMENTS
EU nationals require a valid **national
driving licence;** US driving licence
valid for 12 months; a permit is available from your local branch of the
American Automobile Association;
℘**www.csaa.com.**
Other nationals require an international driving licence. It is necessary
to have the **registration papers** (log-
book) for the vehicle and a nationality
plate of the approved size.

INSURANCE
Insurance cover is compulsory and
although an **International Insurance
Certificate** (Green Card) is no longer
a legal requirement in Britain, it is
the most effective proof of insurance
cover and is internationally recognised
by the police and other authorities.
Certain UK motoring organisations
offer accident insurance and breakdown service plans for members.
Europ-Assistance (www.europassist
ance.com) and the American Automobile Association (www.aaa.com)
have special plans for their respective
memberships.

MOTORING ORGANISATIONS
The major motoring organisations
in Great Britain are the Automobile
Association and the Royal Automobile
Club. Each provides services in varying
degrees for non-resident members of
affiliated clubs.
Automobile Association
Fanum House, Basingstoke, Hants,
RG21 2EA. ℘0800 085 2721
(breakdown cover sales).
www.theaa.com

Royal Automobile Club
Great Park Road, Bradley Stoke,
Bristol BS32 4QN. ℘08705 722
722 (general), 08000 966 999

Congestion Charging

At present London is the only city in the UK with a congestion charge. This is payable by drivers entering the central part of the city Mon-Fri 7am-6pm. Driving into London is not recommended for visitors at any time, but if you do have to bring in your vehicle at these times, then you must familiarise yourself with how to pay by visiting www.tfl.gov.uk/roadusers/congestioncharging

©Transport for London 2005

(breakdown cover) or 0800 82 82 82 (at the scene). **www.rac.co.uk**

ROAD REGULATIONS

The **minimum driving age** is 17 years old. Traffic drives **on the left** and overtakes on the right. Headlights must be used at night even in built-up areas and at other times when visibility is poor. There are severe penalties for driving after drinking more than the legal limit of alcohol.

Important traffic signs are shown at the end of the red-cover Michelin Guide Great Britain and Ireland. Signage in the UK corresponds in general to international norms.

Seat Belts

It is compulsory for all passengers to wear seatbelts in the UK.

Speed limits

Maximum speeds are:
- **70mph/112kph**, Motorways or dual carriageways
- **60mph/96kph**, other roads
- **30mph/48kph**, in towns and cities.

PARKING

Off-street parking is indicated by blue signs with white lettering (Parking or P); payment is made on leaving or in advance for a certain period. There are also parking meters, disc systems and paying parking zones; in the last case tickets must be obtained from ticket machines (small change necessary) and displayed inside the windscreen.

Illegal parking is liable to fines and also in certain cases to the vehicle being clamped or towed away.

The usual restrictions are as follows:
- **Double red line** = no stopping at any time (freeway)
- **Double yellow line** = no parking at any time
- **Single yellow line** = no parking for set periods as indicated on panel
- **Dotted yellow line** = parking limited to certain times only.

ROUTE PLANNING

The whole of Great Britain is covered by the **Michelin map series 501-504** (scale 1: 400 00) and the **Michelin Road Atlas of Great Britain and Ireland** (scale 1: 300 000). In addition to the usual detailed road information, they indicate tourist features such as beaches or bathing areas, swimming pools, golf courses, race courses, scenic routes, tourist sights, country parks etc. These publications are an essential complement to the annual **Michelin Guide Great Britain & Ireland,** which offers an up-to-date selection of hotels and restaurants organised alphabetically by town, all inspected and graded by Michelin and marked on maps throughout.

Traffic in and around towns is heavy during the rush-hour (morning and evening). It is also very heavy on major roads at the weekend in summer, particularly bank holiday weekends.

CAR RENTAL

There are car rental agencies at airports, railway stations and in all large towns throughout Great Britain. European cars usually have manual transmission but automatic cars are available on demand. An international driving licence is required for non-EU nationals. Most companies will not rent to drivers aged under 21 or 25. The following firms operate on a national basis:

- ◆ **Avis**
  ℘0844 581 0147.
  www.avis.co.uk
- ◆ **Budget**
  ℘0844 581 2231 (pre-rental enquiries), 0844 444 0002 (post-rental enquiries).
  www.budget.co.uk
- ◆ **National Car Rental**
  ℘0870 400 4581.
  www.nationalcar.co.uk
- ◆ **Europcar**
  ℘0870 607 5000.
  www.europcar.co.uk
- ◆ **Hertz**
  ℘0870 844 8844.
  www.hertz.co.uk
- ◆ **EasyCar**
  ℘08710 500 444

PETROL/GAS

In service stations dual-pumps are the rule. Unleaded pumps have green handles or a green stripe.

TOLLS

Tolls are rare; they are levied only on the most recent bridges (London QE II, Severn, Humber and Skye), the M6 toll road (bypasses Birmingham traffic), a few minor country bridges as well as road tunnels (Dartford, Tyne).

Where to Stay and Eat

✕*Hotel and restaurant listings can be found in the Address Books featured throughout the guide.*

WHERE TO STAY
USEFUL WEBSITES
www.visitbritain.co.uk/ accommodation
The official Visit Britain site includes Britain's largest accommodation listing with over 37,000 places to stay.

www.viamichelin.com
Plan your trip around some of Britain's finest places to see, dine and stay with Michelin's online route planner and magazine.

www.distinctlydifferent.co.uk
Visit this site If you would like to stay in a former windmill, a lighthouse, a church, a gypsy caravan, dovecote …

TYPES OF ACCOMMODATION

Accommodation in Britain runs the whole range, from a room in a characterful historic pub to an anonymous but comfortable night in a chain hotel, from cheap "digs" in a B&B (private house offering a room for the night plus breakfast) to being pampered in some of the world's finest and most sophisticated hotels. London is still the most expensive place to stay in the UK though top hotel rates in the big provincial cities are now on a par with London prices. If price is not a problem you can find top-quality designer hotels, many offering spa facilities and wellness treatments, in many large British cities and all over the countryside. At the other end of the price spectrum, there is also a proliferation of chain hotels offering very competitive deals.

Wherever you choose to stay, try to book in advance online for the best deals, but if you do simply turn up at the hotel desk, ask what is the best deal they can offer you (do not simply accept the published room rate) and be prepared to haggle - the later in the day it is, the better your chances of securing a cheaper room.

RESERVATION SERVICES

Most Tourist Information Centres will provide, free of charge, an information booklet listing all hotels, bed and breakfast and other accommodation. Many will arrange accommodation for a small fee. Room prices are normally just that—the price per room—however even for a double room, they may be quoted per person.

In London the **British Hotels Reservation Centre** can help. 13 Grosvenor Gardens, London SW1W 0BD. ✆020 7592 3055. www.bhrc.co.uk.

BUDGET ACCOMMODATION

Bed and Breakfast (B&B)

Many private individuals take in a limited number of guests. Prices include bed and breakfast, usually the cooked variety. A few offer an evening meal though the choice will of course be limited. Local Tourist Information Centres usually have a list of the bed and breakfast establishments in the area and book if necessary for a fee. Many houses advertise with a "B&B" sign.

◆ **Bed & Breakfast GB**
PO Box 47085, London SW18 9AB. ✆**www.bedbreak.com.**

Rural Accommodation

An interesting way of spending a holiday is to stay on one of the many different types of working farm – arable, livestock, hill or mixed – sometimes set in the heart of glorious countryside. For information apply for the booklet **Farm Stay UK** supplied by the company of the same name. Visit www.farmstayuk.co.uk for details.

Universities and Colleges

During student vacations many universities and colleges offer low-cost accommodation in the halls of residence for a typical rate of £20 a night. If interested, apply to:
The Workstation, Paternoster Row, Sheffield S1 2BX ✆0114 249 3090. www.venuemasters.co.uk

Youth Hostels

The 250 youth hostels in Great Britain are open to members of the **Youth Hostel Association,** or to those with an international membership card. Trevelyan House, Dimple Road, Matlock, Derbyshire DE34 3YH ✆01629 592700 (reservations). www.yha.org.uk.

◆ **Scottish Youth Hostels Association**
7 Glebe Crescent, Stirling FK8 2JA. ✆ 01786 891 400 (general enquiries), 0845 293 7373 (reservations). **www.syha.org.uk**

◆ **International Youth Hostel Federation**
2nd Floor, Gate House, Fretherne Road, Welwyn Garden City, Herts, AL8 6RD. ✆01707 324 170. **www.hihostels.com**

Camping

The British Tourist Authority publishes **Camping and Caravanning in Britain** and local Tourist Information Centres supply lists of camping and caravan sites.

The **Camping and Caravanning Club of Great Britain and Ireland,** Greenfields House, Westwood Way, Coventry CV4 8JH. ✆0845 130 7631. www.campingandcaravanningclub.co.uk.

WHERE TO EAT
USEFUL WEBSITES

www.viamichelin.com

A useful trip planner featuring some of Britain's finest places to stay and eat eat alongside a gastronomy, tourism and motoring magazine.

www.squaremeal.co.uk

Reviews of restaurants and bars in London and around the UK by food critics, alongside foodie event reviews

www.london-eating.co.uk

This site is based on reader reviews and also features money-saving offers.

RESTAURANTS

Dining out in the UK has undergone a revolution in the last two decades and now ranks among the very best in the world. Thanks to its colonial past and its cosmopolitan nature, the UK offers authentic tastes from all over the world, often cooked by native chefs, or collected, magpie-like, by celebrity chefs from culinary tours of the world. Restaurants are becoming less and less formal with only the top hotel dining rooms and traditional establishments still stipulating dress codes. Hours too have become more flexible though many places still serve lunch from around 12 noon to around 2.30pm and dinner from around 7pm to 10pm, and close in between. Only in London and the more buzzing metropolises will you find a good selection of late-dining restaurants. Prices tend to be high compared to many other parts of the world, though eating at lunchtime from set menus can save you a small fortune.

Making a reservation for weekend nights and Sunday lunchtime is recommended and if you want to eat in Britain's top restaurants you may need to book weeks in advance (though it's always worth checking at the last minute for cancellations). A selection of places to eat can be found in the Address Books through-out this guide. The Legend at the back of the book explains the symbols used in the Address Books.

BISTROS, BRASSERIES AND CAFÉS

These European-style establishments, usually serving a variety of relatively simple, pan-European dishes, are the places for snacks, informal meals and drinks in trendy upbeat surroundings right throughout the day and night. The UK now has a profusion of US-style cafés, (most notably Starbucks) on the high streets of most large towns. Less common these days is the traditional English cafe, sometimes called a 'caff' or "greasy spoon". This is traditionally the place for a good old-fashioned fry-up (bacon, eggs, sausages etc), washed down with a mug of strong tea.

PUBS (PUBLIC HOUSES)

Gastropubs

Eating out in public houses ("pubs") has changed enormously over the last decade or so, with more and more establishments putting the emphasis on serving food rather than merely serving drinks. This has led to the rise of the so-called "gastropub," originally only found in London and the Home Counties (the regions around the capital) but now spread to all parts of the country. The typical gastropub is a sort of British bistro; stylish, blending modern with traditional, and serving a relatively short menu of modern European/modern British food. Prices vary enormously and in many places you may spend as much as you would in a smart restaurant.

Beware that the pub-food revolution means that many pubs with no history of serving food have jumped onto the bandwagon, many with little expertise or knowledge, consequently serving poor quality overpriced food. Steer clear of pubs offering long menus and complicated dishes, unless they have an established name.

Pub Hours and Regulations

Pubs' statutory maximum licens-ing hours have until recently been: Mon–Sat 11am–11pm, and Sun 12.30pm–10.30pm, with many closing during the afternoon. In 2005, "24-hour drinking laws" came into opera-tion allowing the country's pubs, clubs and bars to open, in theory, around the clock. In practice relatively few premises have applied for a licence to extend their hours. Pubs that serve meals (now the majority) normally allow children on the premises as long as they remain within the eating area and even more traditionally inclined pubs may allow children in before a certain time (say 8pm or 9pm). The best policy is to ask someone behind the bar before marching in.

Michelin Guide (Red Cover)

The **Michelin Guide Great Britain & Ireland** is an annual publication which presents a selection of hotels and restaurants. All are classified according to the standard of their amenities and their selection is based on regular on-the-spot visits and enquiries. Pleasant settings, attractive décor, quiet or secluded locations and a warm welcome are identified by special symbols. The guide not only celebrates the very best chefs and cuisine that Great Britain has to offer but also reflects the trend towards informal eating with its Bib Gourmand award to restaurants and other establishments offering good food at moderate prices. Michelin's **Eating out in Pubs** guide selects the 500 best dining pubs.

You must be 18 to be served with alcohol (though not to consume it) and if you look younger you may be asked for some form of identification.

GLOBAL CUISINE

Every town in the UK has its share of Indian and Chinese establishments. Indeed chicken tikka masala, the nation's favourite dish, is an Anglo-Indian invention. In places where large Asian immigrant communities have settled (eg. Bradford or Birmingham) restaurants from the Indian sub-continent are ubiquitous. After years of simply being the cheap option after the pubs closed, many ethnic restaurants have moved upmarket to enjoy critical acclaim.

In the major cities of the United Kingdom you can expect to find the cuisines of almost every country in the world. Increasingly modern Britain, unlike many of her European neighbours, has learned to embrace global cuisine and cooking, even at home.

Basic Information

BUSINESS HOURS
LAST ADMISSION TIMES

In the Discovering section of the guide the times we generally give are opening hours, for example 10am–6pm means the site *closes* at 6pm. In practise many places have a last admission time of 30 mins to an hour before closing time. If the last admission time is more than an hour before closing time (normally only larger attractions stipulate this) or the attraction specifically states last admission time (as opposed to closing time) we also state this. In general however it is always best to arrive at least 90 minutes before an attraction closes for the day.

COMMUNICATIONS

Prepaid phonecards, of varying value, are available from post offices and many newsagents; they can be used

00 61	Australia
00 1	Canada
00 353	Republic of Ireland
00 64	New Zealand
00 44	United Kingdom
00 1	United States of America
155	International Operator

100	Operator
118 505	BT Directory Enquiries in the UK (£1.50/min, £2.25 minimum charge)
999	Emergency number (free nationwide); ask for Fire, Police, Ambulance, Coastguard, Mountain Rescue or Cave Rescue

in booths with phonecard facilities for national and international calls. Some public telephones accept credit cards. Since deregulation a number of telephone operators have set up in competition with the previous state-run British Telecommunications (BT). Rates vary enormously between operators. For calls made through BT, daytime rates are Mon-Fri, 6am-6pm; evening, Mon-Fri, before 6am and after 6pm; weekend midnight Friday to midnight Sunday.

International Calls
To make an international call dial ✆00 followed by the country code, followed by the area code (without the intitial 0), followed by the subscriber's number.

ELECTRICITY
The electric current is 230 volts AC (50 HZ); 3-pin flat wall sockets are standard. An adaptor or multiple point plug is required for non-British appliances.

EMERGENCIES
Dial **999** and an operator will ask you which service (Police, Fire or Ambulance) you require. These calls are free from any phone.

MAIL/POST
Post Offices are generally open Mondays to Fridays, 9.30am to 5.30pm and Saturday mornings, 9.30am to 12.30pm.

Somewhat confusingly Royal Mail pricing is now based on the *size* of a letter as well as the more traditional weight. **Postcard/standard** small letter secon-class rate: UK 27p, Europe 50p, rest of the world 56p. You will need to go in person to a Post Office if you are sending anything else, or visit www.royalmail.com.

Stamps are available from post offices newsagents and tobacconists, and some supermarkets. **Poste Restante** items are held for 14 days; proof of identity is required. **Airmail** delivery usually takes 3 to 4 days in Europe and 4 to 7 days elsewhere in the world.

MONEY
BANKS
Banks are generally open from Mondays to Fridays, 9.30am to 3.30pm; some banks offer a limited service on Saturday mornings; all banks are closed on Sundays and bank holidays. Most banks have cash dispensers (ATMs) that accept international credit cards; most do not charge a fee for cash withdrawals (be sure to look for a notice to that effect).

Exchange facilities outside these hours are available at airports, currency exchange companies, travel agencies and hotels.

Some form of identification is necessary when cashing travellers cheques or Eurocheques in banks. Commission charges vary; hotels usually charge more than banks.

CREDIT CARDS
The main credit cards (American Express; Access/Eurocard/Mastercard; Diners Club; Visa/Barclaycard) are widely accepted in shops, hotels, restaurants and petrol stations. Most banks have cash dispensers which accept international credit cards.

CURRENCY
The official currency in Great Britain is the pound sterling. The decimal system (100 pence =£1) is used throughout Great Britain; Scotland has different notes including £1 and £100 notes, which are legal tender outside Scotland, though you may well have difficulty getting English shopkeepers to accept them; the Channel Islands and Isle of Man have different notes and coins, which are not valid elsewhere. The common currency – in descending order of value – is £50, £20, £10 and £5 (notes); £2, £1, 50p, 20p, 10p, 5p (silver coins) and 2p and 1p (copper coins). The Euro may be accepted in some stores in London; check in advance if planning to make large purchases.

PUBLIC HOLIDAYS
The table opposite gives the public (**bank**) holidays in England and Wales, when most shops and municipal museums are closed.

In addition to the usual school holidays in the spring and summer and at Christmas, there are half-term breaks in February, May and October.

PUBLIC HOLIDAYS

1 January	New Years Day
Good Friday	Friday before Easter Day
Easter Monday	Monday after Easter Day
First Monday in May	May Day
Last Monday in May	Spring Bank Holiday
Last Monday in August	Bank Holiday
25 December	Christmas Day
26 December	Boxing Day

SMOKING

While no smoking had been the policy in many eating places for a long while, on 1 July 2007 new legislation came into place in England and Wales — Scotland and Northern Ireland had already implemented the ban — forbidding smoking in **all** public places, including (often traditionally smoky) public houses (pubs).

TAX

VAT

Many stores in London, Edinburgh and other tourist cities and towns partici-pate in the Retail Export Scheme (look for the sign "Tax Free Shopping"). This means that customers may be entitled to receive a refund of VAT paid on goods (currently 15%) exported to destinations outside the European Community. There is no statutory minimum sale value although retailers may set a minimum transaction value (for example, £50) below which they will not operate the scheme. Ask the sales assistant for the form for reclaim-ing the tax. Fill in the form, keep it safe and present it again at the point of exit from the UK for the refund to be passed onto you. Note that VAT refunds cannot be processed after you return home.

GIFT AID AND DONATIONS

Gift Aid is a government scheme of tax relief on money donated to UK chari-ties, which since 2007 may be applied at the entrance to visitor attractions with charitable status. The scheme is only for UK residents and you will be asked for your postcode and name, which will be verified instantly (electronically) by a machine at the site entrance in order to minimise any waiting time. You will then be given the choice of buying a ticket with or without gift aid. The former is ten per cent higher. Beware that in some cases you may be asked for the gift aid inclusive price straight away, thus putting the onus on you to ask for the cheaper ticket. If so remember there is absolutely no obligation for you to pay the higher amount (and if you are an overseas visitors the scheme does not apply to you anyway).

In a few instances if you do choose to pay the higher price you may be given an incentive to pay the higher price in the form of a voucher redeemable in the shop, or against refreshments. If you spend the full amount of this voucher (which in most cases will only amounts to the price of a coffee or less) then you will pay less overall but the charity/visitor attraction will still gain extra revenue.

Within this guidebook we have given admission prices without gift aid/charitable donation.

TIME

In winter, standard time throughout the British Isles is Greenwich Mean Time (GMT). In summer clocks are advanced by an hour to give British Summer Time (BST). The actual dates are announced annually but always occur at the weekend in March and October.

Edinburgh Military Tatoo, Edinburgh Castle

The Country Today

21ST CENTURY BRITAIN
POPULATION

2001 census; 58,789,194

Great Britain has long been a cosmopolitan place, shaped by the cultures and peoples that have arrived through invasion, migration, empire and trade, ever since rising sea levels separated the island from mainland Europe. Much of the white population is a hodge-podge of pre-Celtic, Celtic, Roman, Viking, Anglo-Saxon and Norman ancestry. More recent arrivals follow in the shadow of the dwindling memory of the British Empire and the United Kingdom's continuing high profile in international affairs. Alongside increasing movement of citizens within the European Union, all of this ensures that above all, Britain remains a place of change.

It is said that there are around 200 different languages spoken within these shores. Around 8–10 per cent of the population is from ethnic minorities, but the concentration of immigrants varies enormously by region and by area. In wealthy rural and semi-rural parts of the country the population is overwhelmingly white, whereas many inner city suburbs of London and provincial cities such as Birmingham and Bradford have substantial communities of other ethnicity.

The United Kingdom has a long history of immigration, with large-scale **European influxes** in the 19th century and early 20th century. After the Second World War many **West Indians** were invited to help with the shortage of labour and they were followed around a decade later by immigrants from **India** and **Pakistan**. There has also been a steady stream of **Chinese**, most notably from the former colony of Hong Kong. British society is far more integrated than it was 30 years ago, but it is still to some extent insular. Recent statistics indicate that social mobility is not as high as the government has previously hinted. However, the rigid class divisions of the past have relaxed considerably and equal opportunities continues to be a leading issue. This is perhaps best represented by the huge numbers of students of all classes and ethnicities that join the workforce each year from Britain's government subsidised universities.

21st Century trends

Since the relaxing of laws on labour movement and the expansion of the European Union, more Europeans (particularly from eastern Europe), have made Britain their home. **Poles** in particular have arrived in large numbers and have been among the most successful at assimilating into the community, largely as a result of their value in the skilled manual labour market.

The recent conflicts and degree of polarisation between the **Muslim** and Christian worlds has exacerbated tensions in some areas of Great Britain, and in some instances radical Muslim clerics have been arrested or expelled from the country. However, the moderate majority, who now account for over 3 per cent of the population, flourish in the UK.

Multiculturalism is an important political topic in modern Great Britain with an ongoing debate that focuses on balancing the rights and responsibilities of immigrants. On the whole, Britain continues to be a very tolerant society and it is usually only the minority on the far right of the political spectrum who dispute that most immigration over recent decades has been good for both the economy and overall quality of life in Great Britain. National polls regularly indicate that the favourite meal on the nation's tables is the British-Indian dish, chicken tikka masala.

Britain continues to be a safe haven for **political refugees** and asylum seekers from several trouble spots of the world. While many residents would like to wash their hands of such problems, others point to the legacy of empire and the leading role that Great Britain still plays in many parts of the world.

Being British

By the time the Millennium drew to a close the concept of being British had becoming increasingly nebulous. The country is now home to immigrants from over 100 different ethnic backgrounds, and many are now second generation, some retaining the garb and traditions of their country but speaking in a broad English regional accent. Sport is the most obvious melting pot where English-born players of Indian fathers play cricket for England against India, while many top British athletes and footballers are of Afro-Caribbean extraction. Meanwhile, "being British" abroad has taken something of a battering as a result of football hooliganism and the continuing popularity of cheap, boozy holidays by the sea.

With streamlined 21C communications, a growing interest in all things regional (from dialects to food, music and handicrafts), and with fashionable wealthy cities like Cardiff and Edinburgh to call their own, Scotland and Wales are no longer sleepy backwaters to be patronised by London. Of the three mainland British nations it is the English who have suffered the most with regard to their sense of identity. The regionalisation of power to Scotland and Wales (even if the really big decisions are still taken in Whitehall), large-scale immigration, and the demands and legislation of the European Union, have taken their toll on the English national psyche. Meanwhile the Scots and Welsh, with their gleaming new assemblies have grown in confidence.

LIFESTYLE

Over the last three decades British lifestyle has become increasingly Americanised with more time spent at work, less time spent on the family, a move from the city to the suburbs, shopping at out-of-town centres rather than in neighbourhood corner shops and an increasing reliance on the motor car over public transport. Materialism and conspicuous consumption reached its zenith in the late 1980s and early 1990s as typified by "yuppies" (young

upwardly-mobile professionals) flaunting expensive cars and massive salaries, at least until the recession of the early 90s. The new millennium boom in London's financial services industry brought enormous City bonuses, while exacerbating a spendthrift consumer culture. All of this came to an abrupt end in 2008 with the collapse of credit markets around the globe. Economic conditions have been cautious ever since.

British society has shifted from the relatively tight-knit community-structure of the 1950s and 1960s to a culture of the individual. While many people have benefited in material terms from the economic boom years, lifestyle changes have had serious implications on the country's physical infrastructure, behaviour and health. Topical debate is dominated by recurring issues of "binge (excessive) drinking", teenage pregnancies, poor child care, increasing obesity and lack of moral leadership.

RELIGION

Sunday has long ceased to be the "day of rest", when it was once *de rigeur* to attend church. The main Sunday pastimes are now shopping and sport. Church attendances in the UK have plummeted to half of what they were 50 years ago and the UK is third from bottom in this respect in the European Union. It is reckoned that only around 15 per cent of Britons attend church at least once a month, though it is also estimated that nearly 60 per cent still place their faith in Christianity. Of course, with the huge influx of immigration in the UK there are also many other religions now being practised here.

SPORT

The British have long been a sporting nation, popularising many international sports (football/soccer, golf, cricket, rugby, tennis). Football remains the most popular team game with the English Premier League acknowledged widely as the best (and certainly the richest) in the world. However its make up (over 55 per cent of players are foreign) is one of the principal reasons for the over-hyped

2012 Olympic Games

The celebrations following the award of the Games to London (made in July 2005) were cut short by terrorist bombings the very next day. Ever since, Britain has looked forward to the Games with a mixture of hope and apprehension. Will Britain be able to build on our athletes' excellent performance in the Beijing Games of 2008? Will it be able to get close to the spectacle and efficient running of the Beijing Games? Can building costs be kept down? What about the terrorist threat? And most importantly, what will the legacy of the Games be to local people once the circus has left town? Progress on actual construction is gathering apace and looks to be on schedule but the jury is still out on some of these big issues.

but under-performing English national team, which has failed to win an international tournament since 1966. The influx of foreign players (and coaches) is also now widely felt in other traditional English sports, such as rugby and cricket.

MEDIA

British media varies from the sublime to the ridiculous, as represented by the "tabloid" (small-format) newspapers, which specialise in deliberately outlandish features and celebrity gossip, garnished with soft porn. Despite claims of "dumbing down" to retain its audience in the face of increasing multi-channel satellite and cable TV competition, the BBC retains its unique licence fee subsidy and maintains a strong presence in global media, underpinned by informative programming and a welcome absence of advertising. The BBC dominates the airwaves with several national radio stations and many more local frequencies, while its controversial investment in the online iPlayer has paid dividends in the long-run, with many users choosing to watch key events, such as Wimbledon tennis, online instead of on TV.

Of the broadsheet newspapers, *The Daily Telegraph*, *The Times*, *The Guardian* and *The Independent* are all good quality serious daily reads peppered with informed opinion leaning towards the left (The Guardian) and the right (The Daily Telegraph) with varying shades of politics in between.

Red-top tabloid newspapers enjoy far wider circulation and run the gamut of entertainment from the ostentatious headlines of the *News of the World* to the best-selling pages of the *Sun*. The *Daily Mirror*, *Daily Mail* and *Daily Express* are other populist newspapers, each enjoying large readerships nationwide.

LANGUAGE

English

The English language owes its rich vocabulary to the many peoples who have settled in Great Britain or with whom the British have come into contact

Celebrity

The current British fixation with celebrity really kicked off in the 1980s. It was fuelled by tabloid newspapers, such as the *Sun*, and magazines such as *Hello* which quickly spawned a whole raft of cheap sensationalist "celeb"-spotting titles which now form a mind-boggling display on the racks in high street newsagents. The groundbreaking "reality televison" programme Big Brother came to the UK in 2000. It put members of the general public in a house and simply watched their behaviour and interactions – the more controversial the better – live over many weeks, with its 8 million-strong TV audience voting on who should stay and who should go on a regular basis. The reward for the final "survivor" was a large cash prize and all sorts of media offers to sell their story. Now anyone could be a celebrity, irrespective of talent or achievements.

through overseas exploration and conquest. Old English's origins are Anglo-Saxon and thus West-Germanic, with a peppering of Old Norse (Viking). Middle English was Norman influenced, while Modern English continues to develop and adopt from other languages. In 1600 there were about 2 million English speakers. The number is now nearer 400 million, including not only the population of countries such as Australia and New Zealand, Canada and the United States of America, but also of those where English is the only common and thus official second language.

Old English, Anglo-Saxon and Norman French – Old English, a Germanic dialect spoken in AD 400 from Jutland to northern France, was established in Britain by AD 800 and by the 16C had taken on the syntax and grammar of modern English. Although Norman French was made the official language after the Norman Conquest, Anglo-Saxon eventually gained precedence and Norman French survives principally in formal expressions used in law and royal protocol. It continued to be spoken in the Channel Islands long after it became obsolete in England.

Modern English – English is a very flexible language which has readily absorbed a considerable inheritance from Celtic, Roman, Anglo-Saxon, Viking and Norman-French origins. Although the spoken language owes most to Anglo-Saxon, the written language shows the influence of Latin, which for many centuries formed the major study of the educated classes.

Immigration over the past hundred years or so has brought many other languages into everyday use by sizeable communities in Britain. Yiddish-speaking Jews came from Russia in the 19C and early 20C and their German-speaking co-religionists fled from Nazi persecution in the 1930s.

The largest immigrant communities in Britain today are from Europe – mainly Germany, Italy, Poland and Spain – and from the Caribbean Islands, Africa, Hong Kong, India and Pakistan. Generations born here are often bilingual, speaking the mother tongue of their community and current English with the local accent.

Celtic

Celtic-speakers were pushed westward by the invading Anglo-Saxons and their language was relegated to "second class" status. Gaelic, as some of the various branches of the Celtic language are now known, is however still spoken to some extent in Scotland, Wales and Ireland. One major reason for the suppression and decline of the Gaelic tongue in both Scotland and Ireland was the support shown there for the losing side in England's quarrels with the Pope.

Cornish – This branch of the Celtic languages was the only language of the Cornish peninsula until towards the end of the reign of Henry VIII. Although Dolly Pentreath, who was born in Mousehole in 1686 and died in December 1777, is claimed to be the last speaker of Cornish, there were no doubt other Cornish speakers, none of whom would have outlived the 18C. Modern efforts to revive the language have had some success.

Welsh – In the Statute of Rhuddlan in 1284, Edward I recognised Welsh as an official and legal language. After the Battle of Bosworth in 1485 Welsh nobles hopefully followed the Tudors to London but Henry VIII decreed that "no person shall hold office within the Realme, except they exercise the English speech".

The tradition of poetry and literature in the Welsh language, guarded by the bards and *eisteddfodau*, dates from Taliesin in the 7C. In 1588 the Bible was published in Welsh by Bishop Morgan and it was largely the willingness of the Church in Wales to preach in Welsh which saved the language from extinction. Reading in Welsh was encouraged by the Sunday School Movement, begun in Bala in 1789.

The University of Wales was established in 1893. Teaching in Welsh was introduced in primary schools in 1939 and in secondary schools in 1956. Since 1982 Channel S4C has broadcast television in

Traditional Festivals and Festivities

Many rural traditions have declined owing to population mobility, the building over of land once dedicated to festivals and the adoption of new farming methods. On the other hand the popularity of outdoor activities, particularly those connected with sport and horses, has led to many of them evolving into fashionable events in the social calendar.

Morris Dancing

The origins of Morris dancing are uncertain. According to some the word Morris derives from Moorish. The dancers are traditionally men, dressed in white shirts and trousers, with bells tied below the knee and sometimes colourful hats. Their dances are energetic; for some they carry two handkerchiefs and for others a stout stick which they knock against their partner's stick.

The Maypole

Until the 17C many parishes had permanent maypoles, pagan fertility symbols belonging to a spring festival, tacitly accepted and tamed by the Christian church. In 1644, however, under the Puritans, the Maypole was banned throughout England but returned at the Restoration (1660), marking both May Day and Oak Apple Day, 29 May, anniversary of Charles II's entry into London. Permanent maypoles still stand at Barwick-in-Elmet, Yorkshire (80ft/24m) and at Welford-on-Avon (70ft/21m).

Pancake Day

Shrove Tuesday, the day preceding the first day of Lent, is the occasion for cooking, tossing and eating sweet pancakes, which are served with sugar and lemon juice. Pancake races are held in which the competitors have to run a certain distance tossing a pancake in a frying pan on the way.

Cheese rolling

Parish of Brockworth, Gloucestershire.
A Whit Monday/Spring Bank Holiday festival. A cheese is rolled down a steep slope, with the youth of the village and other nutters allowed to chase after it at the count of three. Injury frequently occurs, but the tradition somehow survives in this generally risk-averse culture. Cheese used to be paraded around the church in Randwick, Gloucestershire, on May Day.

The Furry Dance

Helston. The sole remaining example of a communal spring festival dance in Britain, this dance has taken place in Helston, Cornwall, for centuries, on 8 May, feast day of St Michael the Archangel, patron saint of the church. Despite the thousands of tourists who come to see the dance, it has not changed in character and would be recognisable to any pre-Christian inhabitant of the town.

Well dressing

Christianity forbade the worship of water spirits but many wells were simply "purged" and re-dedicated to the Blessed Virgin or one of the saints. In Derbyshire the custom of decking wells or springs with flowers still continues, under the auspices of the church. Large pictures are formed on boards covered with clay, the design being picked out in flowers, pebbles, shells or any natural object; manufactured materials are not used. It is said that the most famous well dressing, at Tissington, began in its present form either after a prolonged drought in 1615 when only the wells of Tissington continued to give water or in thanksgiving for deliverance from the Black Death (1348-49). St Anne's Well near Buxton, is another famous well.

Eisteddfodau

Wales is famous for its international cultural festivals offering song, music and dance (Builth Wells, Llangollen). Many contestants perform in their national costumes.

Highland Games

The games, which originated in 11C contests in the arts of war, are held in Scotland between June and September. The heavy events include putting the shot, throwing the hammer and tossing the caber as straight as possible. Other events are athletics, dancing, piping and massed pipe bands.

Welsh to speakers of an everyday living language.

Manx – The language spoken in the Isle of Man was similar to the Gaelic of the Western Isles of Scotland but there has been no viable Manx-speaking community since the 1940s. The present Manx dialect of English shows much influence from Lancashire owing to fishing and tourism in the 19C.

Scots Gaelic – In Scotland the Gaelic-speaking area, the *Gàidhealtachd*, is mostly confined to the Western Isles. The language, which was the mother tongue of 50per cent of the population in the 16C, is now spoken by less than two per cent. The "Normanised" kings of Scotland, particularly David I (1124-53) introduced the Anglo-Norman language and later contact with the English court led to English becoming the language of the aristocracy. After the Union of the two kingdoms in 1603, the Statute of Iona attempted to impose the teaching of English on the sons of the chiefs and in 1616 the Westminster Parliament decreed – "*that the Inglishe tongue be universallie plantit and the Scots language, one of cheif and principalle causis of the continewance of barbaritie and incivilitie amongst the inhabitantis of the Ilis and Heylandis, may be abolisheit and removeit*".

In 1777 a Gaelic Society was formed in London, the first of many all over the world, which maintain and encourage Gaelic language and literature. The percentage of Gaelic speakers in Scotland is increasing slowly, particularly in Lowland areas.

Norn

This Viking language, akin to Icelandic, survived in Orkney and Shetland, until the 18C. It was the dominant tongue in Orkney until the Scottish-speaking Sinclairs became Earls of Orkney in 1379 and it remained the language of Shetland until well after the pledging of the Northern Isles to James III of Scotland in 1468-69. Modern dialects of both Shetland and Orkney still contain a sizeable body of words of Norn origin – types of wind and weather, flowers, plants and animals, seasons and holidays. A high percentage of place names throughout the islands are Norn.

CUISINE

Great Britain provides a cosmopolitan choice of food but also has a rich tradition of regional dishes, all using local fish, game, fruit and dairy products to best advantage. Some of the treats listed below can be hard to find and do not appear in touristy restaurants. You may need to enlist the services of local specialists, such as independent butchers and food shops and farmers markets in order to track them down.

London and the South East

Steak and kidney pie is chief among the many varieties of pie found. The Kentish marshes nurture fine *lamb* while Whitstable is famous for its *oysters; Dover sole* and other fresh fish are available along the coast. *Chelsea Buns,* dough buns folded round dried fruit, have been enjoyed since Georgian days. *Maids of Honour* are small puff pastry tarts with ground almond, served almost exclusively at the eponymous tea rooms in Kew, next to the famous Royal Botanical Gardens.

The West Country

Devon and Cornwall are known for *clotted cream,* served on scones with strawberry jam. It is equally delicious on the *apple pies,* richly flavoured with cinnamon and cloves, for which the region is renowned. *Fresh and potted mackerel* are a coastal delicacy, as are *pilchards. Cheddar cheese* is named after the caves in which it is ripened. Cornwall has given its name to the *Cornish pasty,* a mixture of beef (skirt), turnip or swede, potatoes and onion baked in a pastry case, shaped like a half-moon, so that it could be carried down the mine to be eaten at midday.

Heart of England

The Vale of Evesham is England's fruit growing area – *plums* and *greengages* are a speciality, with *apples* and *pears.* Herefordshire raises fine beef; the local cider, a refreshing but deceptively potent drink, is used in local dishes, including a pigeon casserole, with cider and orange. Gloucestershire produces excellent cheeses. Worcestershire asparagus, in season, rivals any in flavour and Worcestershire sauce, a blend of anchovies, garlic, treacle and spices, has been enjoyed worldwide since 1839.

Thames and Chilterns
Brown Windsor soup made with beef, mutton, carrots and onions is delicious. Aylesbury duck and green peas might be followed by Bucks cherry bumpers, cherries in shortcrust pastry, or some Banbury apple pie. Breakfasts should always finish with chunky Oxford marmalade on toast.

East Midlands
Lincolnshire grows fine *potatoes* and these feature in many dishes particularly with delicate pink, green and white slices of *stuffed chine of pork,* a piece of back of fat pig, stuffed with green herbs. Three regional cheeses enjoyed countrywide are *Stilton, Red Leicester* and *Derby sage. Bakewell tarts* are made of shortcrust pastry with an almond and jam filling. *Melton Mowbray pies* comprise succulent lean pork in jelly, with a little anchovy flavouring in a pastry case.

East Anglia
Norfolk is famed for its *dumplings. mussels in cider and mustard.* During the summer *samphire*, "poor man's asparagus", grows wild along the salt marshes and is eaten with melted butter. In Suffolk they serve a *spicy shrimp pie,* cooked with wine, mace and cloves in a puff pastry case. *Cromer crabs* are full of flavour and Colchester *oysters,* introduced by the Romans, are excellent.

Yorkshire, Humberside and the Northeast
Roast beef and *Yorkshire pudding* – a succulent batter pudding on which the juices of the roasting meat have been allowed to drip – rivals *York ham* and *parkin* – a dark oatmeal cake made with cinnamon, ginger, nutmeg and treacle

– as Yorkshire's great contribution to British gastronomy. *Wensleydale cheese* goes well after any of the many *game pies* or *potted grouse* for which the area is renowned. Newcastle has *potted salmon* and along the Northumberland coast *baked herrings* are a delicacy.

Cumbria and the Northwest
Fish of all sorts from the Irish Sea, *cockles, scallops,* the smaller flavourful *"Queenies"* from the Isle of Man, *potted shrimps in butter,* from Morecambe Bay, and *Manx kippers* are the glory of this region. *Char,* a fish from the deepwater lakes of the Lake District, is eaten fresh-caught or potted. Cheshire produces two fine *cheeses,* one white and one a *blue vein. Cumberland sauce* goes perfectly with ham or game pies.

Wales
Lamb is traditionally eaten with mint sauce, mutton with redcurrant jelly. *Welsh honey lamb* is delicious, cooked in cider, with thyme and garlic, basted with honey. *Caerphilly* produces a light, crumbly cheese. *Leeks,* the emblem of Wales, appear in many dishes. A speciality of the Gower is the local sea trout – *sewin* – stuffed with herbs before being cooked. Welsh cakes and griddle scones with currants are best eaten hot with butter. *Bara brith* is a rich cake bread, full of dried fruits and citrus peel.

Scotland
Scottish beef and *lamb* are renowned, as is Scottish *venison, grouse* (in season) and *salmon. Partan Bree* is a tasty *crab soup* and there are *Arbroath smokies* and *kippers* to rival kedgeree, made with salmon, haddock or other fish, with rice, hard-boiled eggs and butter. *Haggis* served with swede (the Scots refer to this as turnip or *"neeps")* is a tasty meal traditionally accompanied by a wee dram of whisky. *Mutton pies* are made with hot water pastry and *oatmeal bannocks* may be spread with local honey. Dundee makes a rich, dark and chunky *orange marmalade. Raspberries* from this part of the world are a treat too.

BEER

Beers in Britain can be divided into two principal types: *ales* and *lagers* which differ principally in their respective warm and cool fermentations. Beer is served in kegs or casks.

Keg beer is filtered, pasteurised and chilled and then packed into pressurised containers from which it gets its name.

Cask beer or "Real Ale" is neither filtered, pasteurised nor chilled and is served from casks using simple pumps. It is considered to be a more flavoursome and natural beer.

Bitter is the traditional beer in England and Wales. Most are a ruddy brown colour with a slightly bitter taste imparted by hops. Some bitters are quite fruity in taste and the higher the alcoholic content the sweeter the brew.

Mild is normally only found in Wales, the West Midlands and the North West of England. The name refers to the hop character as it is a gentle, sweetish and full flavoured beer. It is generally lower in alcohol and darker in colour than Bitter, caused by the addition of caramel or by using dark malt.

Stout can be either dry, as brewed in Ireland (Guinness is the standard bearer) with a pronounced roast flavour with plenty of hop bitterness, or sweet. The latter sweetened with sugar before being bottled are now rare.

In addition there are **Pale Ales** (like Bitter), Brown Ales (Sweet, like Mild) and Old Ales (sweet and strong) and Barley Wine which in fact is a very sweet, very strong beer.

In **Scotland** the beers are often known as 60/- (shillings), 70/-, 80/- or even 90/-. This is a reference to the now defunct shilling which indicated the barrel tax in the late 1800s calculated on alcoholic strength. The 60/- and 90/- brews are now rare. Alternatively the beers may be referred to as Light, Heavy, or Export which refers to the body and strength.

WHISKY (WHISKEY)

The term whisky is derived from the Gaelic for "water of life". **Scotch Whisky** (spelt without an 'e') can only be produced in Scotland, by the distillation of malted and unmalted barley, maize, rye, and mixtures of two or more of these.

Malt whisky is produced only from malted barley traditionally dried over peat fires. A single malt whisky comes from one single distillery and has not been blended with whiskies from other distilleries.

The whisky is matured in oak, ideally sherry casks, for at least three years which affects both its colour and flavour. All malts have a more distinctive aroma and more intense flavour than grain whiskies and each distillery will produce a completely individual whisky. There are approximately 100 malt whisky distilleries in Scotland.

Grain whisky is made from a mixture of any malted or unmalted cereal such as maize or wheat and is distilled in the Coffey, or patent still, by a continuous process. It matures more quickly than malt whisky. Very little grain whisky is ever drunk unblended.

Blended whisky is a mix of more than one malt whisky or a mix of malt and grain whiskies to produce a soft, smooth and consistent drink. There are over 2000 such blends which form the vast majority of Scottish whisky production.

Deluxe whiskies are special because of the ages and qualities of the malts and grain whiskies used in them. They usually include a higher proportion of malts than in most blends.

Irish Whiskey is traditionally made from cereals, distilled three times and matured for at least seven years.

CIDER

Cider has been brewed from apples in Great Britain since Celtic times. Only bitter apples are used for "real" West Country cider which is dry in taste, flat (non-sparkling) and high in alcoholic content. A sparkling cider is produced by a secondary fermentation.

WINE

Britain's wine industry has improved by leaps and bounds and there are now several high quality small vineyards mostly in the south of the country. One of the most famous, Denby's, is in Surrey.

GOVERNMENT

Great Britain is composed of England, Wales, Scotland, the Channel Islands and the Isle of Man. The first three countries are part of the United Kingdom, which also includes Northern Ireland but not the Channel Islands and the Isle of Man, which have their own parliaments and are attached to the Crown.

MONARCHY

The United Kingdom is a **Constitutional Monarchy**, a form of government in which supreme power is nominally vested in the Sovereign (the King or Queen). The origins of monarchy lie in the seven English kingdoms of the 6C to 9C – Northumbria, East Anglia, Mercia, Essex, Wessex, Sussex and Kent. Alfred the Great (871-899) began to establish effective rule, but it was Canute (Cnut), a Danish king, who achieved unification. The **Coronation** ceremony gave a priestly role to the anointed monarch, especially from the Norman conquest (1066) onwards. The monarchy became hereditary only gradually. The Wars of the Roses, which dominated the 15C, were about dynastic rivalry and the Tudors gained much from their exploitation of the mystique of monarchy. Although the kingdoms of England and Scotland were united in 1603, the parliaments were not united until the Act of Union in 1709. The stubborn character of the Stuarts and the insistence of Charles I on the "Divine Right" of Kings was in part responsible for the Civil War and the King's execution, which was followed by the **Commonwealth** (1649-60) under Oliver Cromwell, the only period during which the country was not a monarchy.

At the **Restoration** (1660) the monarch's powers were placed under considerable restraints which were increased at the Glorious Revolution (1688) and the accession of William of Orange.

The last vain attempt made by the Stuarts to regain the crown was crushed in the Jacobite risings in 1715 and 1745.

During the reign of Queen Victoria (1837-1901) the monarch's right in relation to ministers was defined as "the right to be consulted, to encourage and to warn", although Victoria clung tenaciously to her supervision of the Empire.

PARLIAMENT

The United Kingdom has no written constitution. The present situation has been achieved by the enactment of new laws at key points in history. The document known as **Magna Carta** was sealed by a reluctant King John at Runnymede (near Windsor) on 15 June 1215. Clause 39 guarantees every free man security from illegal interference in his person or his property. Since the reign of Henry VII (or perhaps even earlier) "Habeas Corpus" has been used to protect people against arbitrary arrest by requiring the appearance in Court of the accused person within a specified period.

The supreme legislature in the United Kingdom is Parliament, which consists of the **House of Commons** and the **House of Lords**. Medieval parliaments were mainly meetings between the king and his lords. The Commons were rarely summoned and had no regular meeting place nor even the right of free speech

Monarchy in Modernity

1997 saw the death of **Diana, Princess of Wales** in a car accident in Paris. This was the culmination of a series of recent events (divorces, scandals, revelations) that had rocked the Royal Family and caused the British public to seriously question their validity. However, by the time the Queen celebrated her jubilee year in 2002 most of Britain had regained their sense of affection for her. However the question of succession remains. Prince Charles treads a fine line between traditionalist and moderniser with a common touch, but his marriage to long-term lover and divorcee Camilla Parker Bowles, makes many prefer his eldest son, Prince William.

until the 16C. Between 1430 and 1832 the right to vote was restricted to those possessing a freehold worth 40 shillings. The Reform Act of 1867 enfranchised all borough householders; county householders were included in 1884. In 1918 the franchise was granted to all men over 21 and women over 30; in 1928 the vote was extended to women over 21. Today all over the age of 18 are entitled to vote provided they have entered their names on the electoral roll. Since 1949 the parliamentary constituencies have been organised on the principle that each should contain about 65 000 voters, which produces 659 Members of the House of Commons.

The member elected to represent a constituency is the candidate who receives the largest number of votes. The government is formed by the party that wins the greatest number of seats. The **House of Lords**, at whose meetings the sovereign was always present until the reign of Henry VI, consists of the **Lords Spiritual** (the senior bishops of the Church of England) and the **Lords Temporal** (Dukes, Marquesses, Earls, Viscounts and Barons). Under the Crown, the country is governed by laws which are enacted by the **Legislature** – the two Houses of Parliament – and enforced by the **Judiciary** – the Courts of the land.

ECONOMY
AGRICULTURE AND FISHING

Until the 18C, the economy of Great Britain was largely agricultural. In the 18C a combination of social and economic conditions led to landowners devoting their wealth and attention to improving land and methods of cultivation, giving rise to the **Agricultural Revolution.** Rapid population growth made it necessary to increase domestic agricultural productivity, as this was before the days of extensive overseas trade of consumables. Land enclosure became increasingly widespread, with even common land being suppressed by acts of Parliament, landowners arguing that the system of enclosure was better for raising livestock, a more profitable form

of agriculture than arable farming. Landowners enlarged their estates by taking over land abandoned by people leaving the countryside for the town, or emigrating to the New World, and developed a system based on maximising profit by introducing many efficient new farming methods. Milestones in this evolution include the use of fertiliser, abandoning the practice of leaving land to lie fallow every three years, and the introduction of new crop varieties (root crops for fodder and cultivated pasture) which in turn fostered the development of stock raising and increasing selectivity.

Nowadays, the average size of a British farm is around 170 acres/68ha, one of the highest figures in Europe. Agriculture, mechanised as much as possible, employs only 2.3 per cent of the workforce. The practice of mixed farming, combining stock raising and crop farming, means that modern Britain meets its domestic needs in milk, eggs and potatoes, and almost totally in meat (with a national flock of about 29 million head, the United Kingdom is ninth in the world for farming sheep). The European Union's Common Agricultural Policy has hit British farmers hard, the imposition of quotas forcing them to cut production of milk and adopt less intensive farming methods.

The **fishing industry,** once a mainstay of the island's economy, has declined considerably mainly because of modifications to national fishing boundaries and their attendant fishing rights. Arrangements drawn up for the Anglo-Irish zone and the approved quotas have stabilised the annual catch for UK vessels at around 800,000 tons, but have not succeeded in arresting the decline of once-great fishing ports such as Kingston-upon-Hull or Grimsby after the departure of the canning factories.

ENERGY SOURCES

Coal was mined well before the 18C (Newcastle was exporting 33,000 tons of coal per year as early as the mid-16C), but became a large-scale industry only after the invention of the steam engine. Since the industry's heyday in the early

20C, production has been dropping steadily, despite a brief revival in the 1950s. Nowadays, in the wake of sweeping pit closures, in which deposits were exhausted or where it was felt extraction was no longer profitable, production has dropped significantly. In 2005, total UK production was 20 million tonnes, mainly concentrated in Yorkshire and Nottinghamshire. Production figures have not been helped by the fact that the high cost of exploiting most mines means that Britain can import coal more cheaply from countries such as Australia, nor by competition from oil and gas.

In the 1960s, prospecting in the **North Sea** gave rise to sufficiently promising results for the countries bordering the sea to reach an agreement, under the Continental Shelf Act of 1964, on zones for extracting **natural gas**. Thanks to deposits along the Norfolk and Lincolnshire coasts, Britain is the world's fifth largest producer, however domestic demand is so great that gas nonetheless has to be imported from Norway. Further north, off Scotland and the Shetland Islands, oil deposits give Great Britain further independence in the energy sector, with total crude oil production at 70 million tons in 2007, but still down from 124 million tons in 1998.

Like the majority of developed countries, the United Kingdom converts a large proportion of its primary energy sources into electricity. About 70 per cent of the electricity currently produced is thermal in origin (the Drax power station in Yorkshire is the most powerful in Europe). **Hydroelectricity** is negligible, as the relatively flat relief makes it impossible to build any sizeable hydroelectric power stations (only existing stations are in Scotland and Wales).

Nuclear energy, which has evolved since the construction of the experimental reactor at Calder Hall inaugurated in 1956, is produced by a dozen or so nuclear power stations, nearly all of which are to be found on the coast so that they can be cooled adequately. More recently, the wind has been harnessed to produce energy at Burgar Hill in the Orkneys, among other places.

INDUSTRY

In the second half of the 18C, hot on the heels of the Agricultural Revolution, capital began to flow from the land into industry, with new industrialists using the money from their family's success as cultivators of the land to set up factories, mills and businesses.

The presence of iron ore in Yorkshire, the Midlands and Scotland gave rise to the **iron and steel industry** (*see IRON-BRIDGE GORGE MUSEUM*) which at its peak in the 19C was one of the industries at the core of the country's economy. However, by the beginning of the 20C the mineral deposits were exhausted, and Great Britain found itself importing ore from abroad, effectively bringing about the decline of its own inland iron and steel regions (Durham, the Midlands) in favour of those located on the coast (Teesside) and in South Wales (Port Talbot, Newport). UK steel production is currently at 13–14 million tons per year. Metal processing industries have equally suffered gravely in the face of competition from abroad. There are few remaining large UK **shipyards** operating in the commercial sector, although a large naval shipbuilding programme for the Royal Navy, replacing old aircraft carriers, promises some continuity for the naval yards of Portsmouth, Plymouth, the Clyde, Barrow and Rosyth.

Britain's **car industry** once led Europe, with production levels of 2.3 million vehicles in the mid-1960s. It included some prestigious national companies, such as Triumph, Rover, Jaguar, Bentley and Rolls Royce. Industrial disputes gave rise to a management crisis, however, culminating in nationalisation (British Leyland in 1975) and privatisation. In 2004 the UK's automotive industry ranked ninth in the world by size. Japanese firms like Honda, Nissan and Toyota have assembly plants in the UK. VW owns Bentley, Ford owns Aston Martin, while BMW holds a corral of largely defunct British brands, but does produce the Mini (Oxfordshire) and Rolls Royce cars (Chichester). As of 2008, Tata, an Indian car manufacturer, owns Jaguar Land Rover.

Great Britain has contributed to the rapid evolution of the **electronics and computer industries**. Foreign companies such as Honeywell, Burroughs, IBM, Hewlett-Packard and Mitsubishi have set up business in Scotland, providing a much-needed economic impetus in place of the region's defunct traditional industries. In 2009, the government placed much emphasis on 'Digital Britain' as one of the pillars of the plan to beat the recession, with continuing investment in **communications** and bolstering of **creative industries**.

Great Britain developed a flourishing **textile industry**, thanks to its large numbers of resident sheep and the ground-breaking inventions of the Industrial Revolution, and maintained its position as world leader until the mid-20C. Yorkshire, with Bradford as capital, was home to 80 per cent of wool production. Lancashire, with Manchester as its centre, specialised in cotton. However, this national industry has declined, overtaken by artificial fibres, illustrating the preponderant role that the **chemical industry** now plays in Great Britain's economy. Some of Britain's largest industrial groups are chemical-based: Coats Viyella, synthetic fibres; Courtaulds, synthetic fibres, paint and varnish production; ICI, paint, varnish and fertilisers. The largest British chemicals firm is British Petroleum (BP), and two other giants in the field of petrochemicals are supported by an Anglo-Dutch financial association: Shell and Unilever.

TRADE

Great Britain imports more primary materials than it exports. Services, particularly insurance, banking and business services, account for the largest proportion of GDP, while industry, particularly heavy industry, continues to decline in importance. A reduction in trade with North America has been offset by an increase in volume of trade with European Union member-states, which counts for half of British exports.

Settlement markets, marine and air insurance brokers (Lloyd's, the world's

leading marine risk insurers), life insurance, bank loans, deposits and other financial services combine to make the City of London the world's foremost **financial centre**. The huge profits generated by this business sector and the interest from investments abroad guarantee the United Kingdom's income.

Great Britain was the first European country to emerge from the economic crisis of the late 1980s/early 1990s; and during the second half of the decade and the early part of the Millennium continued to outperform its European neighbours and most other world economies in terms of unemployment rate, inflation and other indicators of economic growth. The credit freeze resulting from the sub-prime mortgage market fallout and debt crisis placed the UK back in recession from 2008 onwards. This has been met by the government with enormous cash subsidies and controversial 'quantitative easing' (the creation, if not physical printing, of new money).

49

History

Great Britain is positioned at the western edge of Europe, from which it has received successive waves of immigrants who have merged their cultures, languages, beliefs and energies to create an island race which has explored, traded with, dominated and settled other lands all over the world.

ORIGINS

The ancient history of the British peoples is a melting pot of Celts, Romans, Germanic tribes and Scandinavians.

THE FIRST SETTLERS

Some 8 000 years ago, Britain, until then part of the greater European land mass, became detached from continental Europe by the rise in sea level caused by retreating glaciers.

Around 5 000 BC the first agricultural peoples arrived and began work transforming the British landscape into the pattern much as we see it even today. Having satisfied their survival needs, between 4 000 BC and 1 800 BC they began grander, more spiritually inclined projects such as the construction of Stonehenge and other stone alignments. Around 700 BC saw the arrival of the "**Beaker**" people who brought a knowledge of metal working and the Aryan roots of the English language – words such as father, mother, sister and brother.

THE CELTS

Also around 700 BC Celtic settlers arrived. The **Celts** brought their language, their chariots, the use of coinage and a love of finery, gold and ornaments. Iron swords gave them an ascendancy in battle over the native Britons, estimated at around a million, who were pushed westwards. By 100 BC their lifestyle and customs were well established in Britain. However the different groups of Celts had only a dialect in common and their lack of any idea of "nationhood" made them vulnerable to the might of Rome.

THE ROMANS

The **Romans** had no strategic interest in the offshore island of Britannia but the lure of corn, gold, iron, slaves and hunting dogs was enough to entice them to invade. By AD 70 much of the north and Wales had been subdued and 50 or more towns had been established, linked by a network of roads. Rome gave Britain its law and extended the use of coinage into a recognised system, essential to trade in an "urban" society. In 313 Christianity was established as the official religion.

Hadrian's Wall - Cuddy's Crags near Housesteads Roman Fort

©Martyn Unsworth/iStockphoto.com

55 BC – Julius Caesar lands in Britain
AD 42 – Roman invasion of Britain under the Emperor Claudius
61 – Revolt of the Iceni under Queen **Boadicea**
122 – Beginning of the construction of **Hadrian's Wall**
410 – Roman legions withdrawn from Britain following the sack of Rome by Alaric the Goth

ANGLO-SAXONS AND VIKINGS

Saxons in the form of Germanic mercenaries had manned many of the shore forts of Britain before the final withdrawal of regular Roman troops. As pay became scarce they seized tracts of good farming land and settled permanently.

When St Augustine arrived in Kent in 597, he found that Christianity was already established at the court of King Ethelbert of Kent, whose wife Queen Bertha was a Christian princess. Until the Synod of Whitby in AD 664 the practices of the Roman church existed side by side with those of the Celtic church, which had a different way of calculating the date of Easter and a strong and distinctive monastic tradition. The Saxon kingdoms of Britain, which traded as far afield as Russia and Constantinople, were constantly engaged in power struggles not only with one another but also with the Angles and Jutes.

Viking Invasions

Under the **Vikings**, who took to trading and barter instead of their former piracy, London again became a great trading port, as it had been during the Roman period. By AD 911 eight vassal kings paid homage to King Edgar for almost the whole country. During the disastrous reign of Ethelred, the "Redeless" (lacking wise counsel), England was attacked by Norsemen; in 1013 Swein, King of Denmark, invaded and briefly became king. Ethelred fled to Normandy. His son, Edmund "Ironside", was left to battle against the invaders. After his murder the parliament (Witenagemot), preferring strength to weakness, elected the Danish invader **Canute** (Cnut) as his successor. Seven years after Canute's death Edward, son of Ethelred and his Norman wife, Emma, was chosen to be King.

Edward the Confessor, who spent much of his childhood in exile in Normandy, gave land and positions to Normans who viewed the easy-going English with scarcely concealed contempt. Edward gained popular approval as a devout saintly character, but suffered from rebellious and powerful earls, in particular the Godwins of Wessex.

To guard the southeast shoreline against invasion and pillage Edward the Confessor established the enduring maritime federation known as the **Cinque Ports** (5 ports), in which Sandwich, Dover, Romney, Hythe and Hastings grouped together to supply ships and men for defence. As part of is claim to the English throne, his great-nephew, **Duke William of Normandy**, is said to have made Harold, son of Earl Godwin, swear an oath to help William succeed on Edward's death. On 5 January 1066, days after the consecration of his abbey church at Westminster, Edward died, Harold took the throne and the stage was set for a Norman invasion.

449 – First waves of Angles, Saxons and Jutes land in Britain; Hengist and Horsa land at Ebbsfleet in east Kent
597 – **Augustine**, sent by Pope Gregory to convert the British to Christianity, founded a Benedictine monastery in Canterbury
827 – King Egbert of Essex became first king of England
851 – Viking raiders wintered regularly in Britain and became settlers
871-99 – Reign of **Alfred the Great**, King of Wessex, who contained the Vikings in 871
911 – Kingdom of Normandy founded by Rollo, a Viking
1016-35 – Reign of **Canute** (Cnut), first Danish king of England
1042-66 – Reign of **Edward the Confessor**

FEUDAL PERIOD

The Norman Conquest solidified England's feudal system from the Battle of Hastings in 1066 onwards. In the following centuries, dynastic struggles were to plague both Britain and the continent.

NORMANS

The **Normans** were descendants of Norsemen, Vikings, who had settled in northern France in 876. Following the death of Edward the Confessor, Duke William of Normandy, accompanied by some 5 000 knights and followers, invaded England and defeated Harold at the **Battle of Hastings** on 14 October 1066, the last time the country was successfully invaded. Duke William, better known as William the Conqueror, overcame a nation of 1.5-2 million people – descendants of Celts, Romans, Vikings and Saxons – and imposed a strong central authority on a group of kingdoms which ranked among the richest in western Europe.

By the time of the **Domesday Survey** only a handful of English names feature amongst the list of "tenants in chief", revealing a massive shift in ownership of land, and only one of 16 bishops was an Englishman; by 1200 almost every Anglo-Saxon cathedral and abbey, reminders for the vanquished English of their great past, had been demolished and replaced by Norman works. Forty years after the conquest however, English soldiers fought for an English-born king, **Henry I**, in his French territories.

1066 – Harold Godwinson defeated at the **Battle of Hastings** by Duke William of Normandy, who was crowned William I in Westminster Abbey on Christmas Day
1086 – Domesday Survey made by William I to reassess the value of property throughout England for taxation purposes
1100-35 – Reign of **Henry I** whose marriage to Matilda of Scots united the Norman and Saxon royal houses
1135-54 – Reign of **Stephen**. Henry of Anjou acknowledged as heir to the throne by the Treaty of Winchester

PLANTAGENETS

Henry II, Count of Anjou, married Eleanor whose dowry brought Aquitaine and Poitou to the English crown. His dispute over the relative rights of Church and State with Thomas Becket, whom he himself had appointed as Archbishop of Canterbury, led to Becket's murder. Henry's reign deserves to be remembered for the restoration of order in a

Norman motte and bailey

In the immediate post-Conquest years the Normans built timber castles, using an artificial or natural earthen mound ("motte"). A stockaded outer enclosure combined stables, storehouses etc ("bailey"). From c 1150 rebuilding took place in stone.

Timber stockade
Tower
Motte
Drawbridge
Bailey
Ditch and rampart

R. Corbel/MICHELIN.

ravaged country, the institution of legal reforms, which included the establishment of the jury, the system of assize courts and coroners' courts, two reforms of the coinage and the granting of many town charters. He also encouraged the expansion of sheep farming as English wool was of high quality; the heavy duties levied on its export contributed to England's prosperity.

Welsh Marcher Castles

Between 1276 and 1296 17 castles were built or re-fortified by Edward I to consolidate English power in North Wales. The four best-preserved fortresses that once patrolled the North Welsh borders (or Marches) are Conwy, Caernarfon, Harlech and Beaumaris. They are among the most remarkable group of medieval monuments to be seen in Europe.

The four major castles were the work of the greatest military architect of the day, **Master James of St George**, brought by Edward from Savoy. Most were built to be supplied from the sea, as land travel in Snowdonia was impossible for Edward's forces. Square towers were replaced by round, which were less vulnerable to undermining; concentric defences, the inner overlooking outer, made their appearance. The garrisons of these massive stone fortifications were small – only some 30 men-at-arms plus a few cavalry and crossbowmen. Planned walled towns, similar to the "bastides" of southern France, housed the settlers who helped hold the territory. Documents detailing the conscription of labour from all over England, the costs of timber, stone, transport, a wall, a turret, even a latrine, can still be read.

CAERNARFON – A bastide town and castle of the late 13C, North Wales

English kings laid out numerous planned towns ("bastides") to attract settlers and control territory in areas like Gascony and Wales. Though the medieval houses of the English colonists have long since disappeared, Caernarfon retains its castle, its walls and its rectangular street layout.

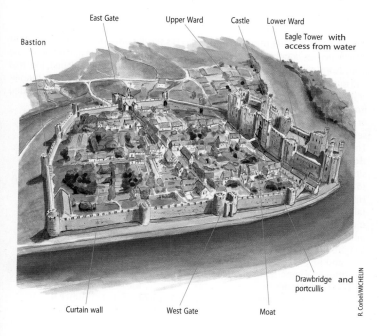

Bastion · East Gate · Upper Ward · Castle · Lower Ward · Eagle Tower with access from water · Curtain wall · West Gate · Moat · Drawbridge and portcullis

R. Corbel/MICHELIN

CAERPHILLY CASTLE, South Wales

A late 13C concentric castle which served as a model for Edward I's strongholds in North Wales

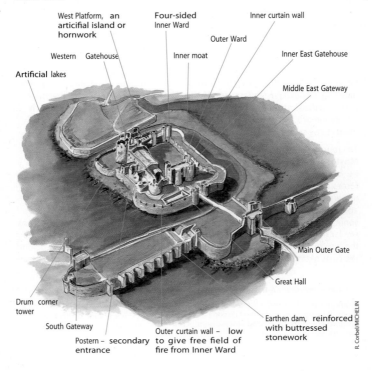

West Platform, an artificial island or hornwork

Four-sided Inner Ward

Inner curtain wall

Western Gatehouse

Inner Ward

Outer Ward

Inner moat

Inner East Gatehouse

Artificial lakes

Middle East Gateway

Main Outer Gate

Great Hall

Drum corner tower

South Gateway

Postern – secondary entrance

Outer curtain wall – low to give free field of fire from Inner Ward

Earthen dam, reinforced with buttressed stonework

R. Corbel/MICHELIN

The despotic manner of ruling and of raising revenue adopted by Henry's son, **King John**, caused the barons to unite and force the king to sign **Magna Carta** which guaranteed every man freedom from illegal interference with his person or property and the basis of much subsequent English legislation.

The ineffectual reign of John's son, **Henry III**, was marked by baronial opposition and internal strife. He was forced to call the first "parliament" in 1264.

His son, **Edward I**, a typical Plantagenet, fair-haired, tall and energetic, was for much of his reign at war with France and Wales and Scotland; on the last two he imposed English administration and justice. During his reign the constitutional importance of Parliament increased; his Model Parliament of 1295 included representatives from shire, city and borough.

His son, **Edward II**, cared for little other than his own pleasure and his reign saw the effective loss of all that his father had won. His wife, Isabel of France, humiliated by her husband's conduct, invaded and deposed Edward.

1154 – Accession of **Henry II**, Count of Anjou (Plantagenet)
1170 – Murder of Thomas Becket in Canterbury Cathedral
1189 – Henry II defeated in battle by his son Richard
1189-99 – Reign of **Richard I** (the **Lionheart**)
1199-1216 – Reign of **King John**. Most of Normandy, Maine, Anjou. and Brittany lost
1215 – John forced to sign **Magna Carta** by the Barons
1216-72 – Reign of **Henry III**,
1271-1307 – Reign of **Edward I**

BODIAM CASTLE, Sussex

Based on French and southern Italian strongholds of the previous century, Bodiam (late 14C) is a perfectly symmetrical square castle, surrounded by a moat and with an array of well-preserved defensive features.

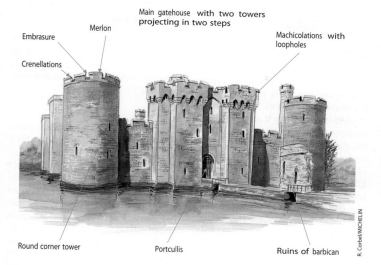

Main gatehouse with two towers projecting in two steps

Merlon

Embrasure

Machicolations with loopholes

Crenellations

R. Corbel/MICHELIN

Round corner tower

Portcullis

Ruins of barbican

1296-98 – North of England ravaged by Scots under **William Wallace**; defeated at Falkirk and executed in 1305

1307-27 – Reign of **Edward II**

1314 – Edward II defeated at Bannockburn by Robert I, King of Scotland

1327 – Edward II murdered at Berkeley Castle

1327-77 – Reign of **Edward III**

1328 – Robert I recognised as king of an independent Scotland

HUNDRED YEARS WAR (1337-1453)

The son of Edward II, **Edward III**, sought reconciliation with the barons and pursued an enlightened trade policy. He reorganised the navy and led England into the **Hundred Years War**, claiming not only Aquitaine but the throne of France in 1348 the Black Death plague reached England and the labour force was reduced by one-third.

The throne passed from Edward III to his grandson, **Richard II**, with his uncle, John of Gaunt, acting as Regent. In time Richard quarrelled with the barons. John

of Gaunt was exiled together with his son Henry Bolingbroke, who returned to recover his father's confiscated estates, deposed Richard and became king.

Henry IV was threatened with rebellion by the Welsh and the Percys, Earls of Northumberland, and with invasion from France.

Henry V resumed the Hundred Years War and English claims to the French throne. On his death his infant son was crowned **Henry VI** in 1429 in Westminster Abbey and in 1431 in Notre Dame in Paris.

1337 – Beginning of the **Hundred Years War** with France

1348 – The **Black Death**

1377-99 – Reign of **Richard II**

1381 – Peasants' Revolt, in part provoked by the government's attempt to control wages

1398 – Richard II deposed by Henry Bolingbroke

1399-1414 – Reign of **Henry IV**

1400 – Death of Richard II

1413-22 – Reign of **Henry V**

1415 – English defeat French at Battle of Agincourt

1420 – Treaty of Troyes making Henry V heir to the French throne
1422-61 – Reign of **Henry VI** with Duke of Gloucester and Duke of Lancaster as Regents
1453 – Hundred Years War ends

WARS OF THE ROSES

The regency created by the deposing of Edward II fostered the counter-claims of York and Lancaster to develop into the **Wars of the Roses**. The Lancastrians (**Henry IV, Henry V** and **Henry VI**), represented by the red rose of Lancaster, claimed the throne by direct male descent from John of Gaunt, fourth son of Edward III. The Yorkists (**Edward IV, Edward V** and **Richard III**), represented by the white rose of York, were descended from Lionel, Edward's third son, but in the female line. The dispute ended when Elizabeth of York married Henry Tudor, a Lancastrian.

Edward V and his younger brother, Richard, known as the **Little Princes in the Tower**, were imprisoned by their uncle Richard, Duke of Gloucester. Their claim to the throne was deemed illegitimate by Parliament. Gloucester was proclaimed **Richard III** and the princes were probably murdered at the Tower of London.

1455-87 – **Wars of the Roses**, over 30 years of sporadic fighting and periods of armed peace, between the houses of Lancaster and York, rival claimants to the throne
1461-83 – Reign of **Edward IV**
1465 – Henry VI captured and imprisoned in the Tower of London
1470 – Restoration of Henry VI by Warwick and flight of Edward
1471 – Murder of Henry VI and Prince Edward by Edward IV following his victory at Tewkesbury
1483 – Reign of **Edward V** ending in his and his brother's imprisonment in the Tower of London
1483-85 – Reign of **Richard III**
1485 – Battle of Bosworth Field: Richard defeated and killed by Henry Tudor

ABSOLUTE MONARCHY

The Renaissance period witnessed the growing conflicts between royalty and other institutions (notably the church and parliament). The Tudors in the 16th century and the Stuarts in the 17th century were the embodiment of absolute monarchy. This period was also all about the struggle between the Catholic, Protestant and Anglican churches and communities.

TUDORS

Henry VII ruled shrewdly and his control of finances restored order and a healthy Treasury after the Wars of the Roses.

His son, **Henry VIII**, was a "Renaissance Man", an accomplished musician, linguist, scholar and soldier. He was an autocratic monarch of capricious temper and elastic conscience, who achieved union with Ireland and Wales and greatly strengthened the Navy. Thomas Wolsey, appointed Chancellor in 1515, fell from favour for failing to obtain papal approval for Henry to divorce Catherine of Aragon; his palace at Hampton Court was confiscated by the King. The **Dissolution of the Monasteries** caused the greatest re-distribution of land in England since the Norman conquest. Wool, much of which had been exported raw in the previous century, was now nearly all made into cloth at home.

The popularity of **Mary**, daughter of Henry VIII and Catherine of Aragon, was undermined by her insistence on marrying Philip II of Spain, who was a Roman Catholic, the burning of 300 alleged heretics, and war with France, which resulted in the loss of Calais, England's last possession in continental Europe.

Elizabeth I, daughter of Henry VIII and Anne Boleyn, restored a moderate Anglicanism, though potential Roman Catholic conspiracies to supplant her were ruthlessly suppressed. She sought to avoid the needless expense of war by diplomacy and a network of informers controlled by her Secretaries, Cecil and Walsingham. Opposition to Elizabeth as Queen focused on **Mary Queen of Scots** and looked to Spain for assistance. The long struggle against Spain, mostly fought out at sea, culminated in the launch of the Spanish Armada, the final and unsuccessful attempt by Spain to conquer England and re-establish the Roman Catholic faith; its defeat was the greatest military victory of Elizabeth I's reign. Elizabeth I presided over a period of exploration and enterprise, a flowering of national culture and the arts; most of **William Shakespeare**'s greatest plays were produced between 1592 and 1616.

1485-1509 – Reign of **Henry VII**
1509-47 – Reign of **Henry VIII**
1513 – Defeat and death of James IV of Scotland at Flodden
1535 – Execution of Sir Thomas More, Chancellor, for refusing to sign the Act of Supremacy, acknowledging Henry VIII as head of the Church in place of the Pope
1536-39 – Dissolution of the Monasteries. Excommunication of Henry VIII
1547-53 – Reign of **Edward VI**,
1553-58 – Reign of **Mary I**; Roman Catholicism re-established
1558-1603 – Reign of **Elizabeth I**
1567-1625 – Reign of James VI, King of the Scots
1580 – Circumnavigation of the world by **Francis Drake**
1587 – Execution of Mary Queen of Scots.
1588 – Defeat of the Spanish Armada

STUARTS

Elizabeth I was succeeded by **James I** of England and VI of Scotland. The **Gunpowder Plot** was a conspiracy of Roman Catholics who attempted to assassinate James in Parliament, despite his willingness to extend to them a measure of toleration.

Charles I inherited his father's belief in an absolute monarchy – the "divine right of kings" – and attempted to rule without Parliament from 1626 to 1640. Moreover his marriage to a Roman Catholic, Henrietta Maria of France, was unpopular with the people. When he was finally forced to recall Parliament,

the Members of the House responded by condemning his adviser, the Earl of Strafford, to death for treason, refusing to grant the King money until he discussed their grievances and they passed a Bill preventing any future dissolution of Parliament without their consent. When in 1642 Charles I attempted to arrest five members of Parliament he sowed the final seeds for the coming conflict.

1603-25 – Reign of **James I** (also James VI of Scotland)
1605 – Gunpowder Plot intended to assassinate the King in Parliament
1620 – Pilgrim Fathers set sail for America
1625-49 – Reign of **Charles I**
1626 – Dissolution of Parliament by the King

THE ENGLISH CIVIL WAR

The **English Civil War** broke out in August 1642. Charles I established his headquarters in Oxford but the balance was tilted against him by Scots support for the Parliamentarians. The North was lost after the Battle of Marston Moor in 1644 and, following the formation of the **New Model Army** by **Cromwell** and **Fairfax** and its victory at Naseby in 1645, the Royalists surrendered at Oxford the following year. The King surrendered to the Scots who handed him over to Parliament in 1647. A compromise was attempted but Charles wavered. He played off one faction in Parliament against another and sought finance and troops from abroad. In 1648 the war resumed. The Scots, to whom Charles promised a Presbyterian England in return for their help, invaded England but were defeated in August at Preston and Charles I was captured. The army demanded his death.

Under the **Commonwealth and Protectorate** the monarchy and the House of Lords were abolished and replaced by a Council of State of 40 members. Attempts by the "Rump" Parliament to turn itself into a permanent non-elected body caused Cromwell to dissolve it and form the Protectorate in 1653, in which he, as Lord Protector, ruled by decree. He was accepted by the majority of a war-weary population but, on his death in 1653, the lack of a competent successor provoked negotiations which led to the Restoration of the Monarchy.

1649 – Trial and execution of the king
1649 – Beginning of the **Commonwealth.** England is ruled not by a monarch but by Oliver Cromwell, a commoner
1651 – Coronation at Scone of Charles II. He is defeated at the Battle of Worcester and flees to France.

THE RESTORATION

The **Restoration** in May 1660 ended ten years of Puritan restriction and opened a period of optimism and a flourishing of theatre, painting and the arts. In the Declaration of Breda Charles II appeared to promise something for almost every political faction. The **Navigation Acts,** specifying that English goods must be carried in English ships, did much to develop commerce.

In 1685, just after the death of Charles II, his illegitimate son, the Duke of Monmouth, whom he had refused to legitimise, led a rebellion against James II, which was brutally repressed. This and the introduction of pro-Catholic policies, two Declarations of Indulgence in 1687 and 1688, the trial and acquittal of the Seven Bishops and the birth of a son James, who became the "Old Pretender", all intensified fears of a Roman Catholic succession. Disaffected politicians approached William of Orange, married to Mary, James' daughter, and offered him the throne.

1660-85 –Reign of **Charles II**
1665 – **Great Plague** in which more than 68 000 Londoners died
1666 – **Great Fire of London** which destroyed 80per cent of the City of London
1672 – Declaration of Indulgence relaxing penal laws against Roman Catholics and other dissenters
1672-74 – War against the Dutch
1673 – Test Act excluding Roman Catholics and other non-conformists from civil office
1677 – Marriage of Charles II's sister, Mary, to William of Orange
1679 – Habeas Corpus Act reinforcing existing powers protecting individuals against arbitrary imprisonment
1685-88 –Reign of **James II**
1685 – Monmouth Rebellion – unsuccessful attempt to claim the throne by the Duke of Monmouth, illegitimate son of Charles II
1687 – Dissolution of Parliament by James II

THE GLORIOUS REVOLUTION

William III landed in England in 1688. In 1689 he was crowned with his wife Mary as his Queen. Jacobite supporters of the exiled James II were decisively defeated in both Ireland and Scotland and much of William's reign was devoted, with the Grand Alliance he formed with Austria, the Netherlands, Spain and the German states, to obstructing the territorial ambitions of Louis XIV of France.

Queen Anne, staunch Protestant and supporter of the Glorious Revolution (1688), which deposed her father, James II, also strove to reduce the power and influence of France in Europe and to ensure a Protestant succession to the throne. Marlborough's victory at Blenheim and his successes in the Low Countries achieved much of the first aim. After 18 pregnancies and the death of her last surviving child in 1701, Anne agreed to the **Act of Settlement** providing for the throne to pass to Sophia, Electress of Hanover, grand-daughter of James I, or to her heirs.

The **"Whigs"** were the members of the political party which had invited William to take the throne. They formed powerful juntas during the reigns of William and Anne and ensured the Hanoverian succession. In the 1860s they became the Liberal Party. The **"Tories"** accepted the Glorious Revolution but became associated with Jacobite feelings and were out of favour until the new Tory party, under Pitt the Younger, took office in 1783. They developed into the Conservative Party under Peel in 1834.

The **Jacobites**, supporters of the Stuart claim to the throne, made two attempts to dethrone the Hanoverian George I. James II's son, the "Old Pretender", led the first Jacobite rising in 1715 and his eldest son, Charles Edward Stuart, "Bonnie Prince Charlie", the "Young Pretender", led a similar rising in 1745, which ended in 1746 at Culloden, the last battle fought on British soil. He died in exile in 1788 and his younger brother died childless in 1807.

1688 – William of Orange invited to England. Exile of James II to France
1689-94 – Reign of **William III and Mary II**
1689 – Defeat of Scottish Jacobites at Killiecrankie. Londonderry besieged by James II; Grand Alliance between England, Austria, the Netherlands and German states in war against France
1690 – Battle of the Boyne and defeat of James II and the Irish Jacobites
1694-1702 – Reign of **William III** following the death of Mary II
1694 – Triennial Act providing for Parliament to meet at least once every three years and to sit for not more than three years
1694 – Foundation of the Bank of England
1695 – Foundation of the Bank of Scotland
1702-14 – Reign of **Queen Anne**

BRITISH EMPIRE

With the battles between parliament and the monarchy concluded, maritime supremacy established and industrial output exploding, Britain focused on international trade and colonisation.

HANOVERIANS

By the time **George I** ascended the throne in 1714, the United Kingdom was already a European economic and naval power which had played a major part in weakening the influence of France in Europe.

George II is notable for being the last monarch to command his forces personally in battle, at Dettingen in 1743 in the war of the Austrian Succession.

He was succeeded by his grandson, the unfortunate **George III**, prone to bouts of apparent madness (possibly due to porphyria or arsenic poisoning). He was unable to reverse the trend towards constitutional monarchy but he did try to exercise the right of a king to govern. This caused great unpopularity, and he was forced to acknowledge the reality of party politics. Foreign policy was dominated by the King's determination to suppress the American Revolution and the **Napoleonic Wars** which arose from the threat posed by the Revolution in France to established European powers.

George IV had supported the Whig cause as a symbol of opposition to his father's Tory advisers and was much influenced by the politician Charles James Fox.

William IV was 65 when he succeeded his unpopular brother. Dissatisfaction with parliamentary representation was near to causing revolutionary radicals to join forces with the mob.

1704 – Gibraltar captured by the English; English victory at Blenheim
1707 – Act of Union joining the parliaments of England and Scotland
1714-27 – Reign of **George I**
1715 – Jacobite rebellion, led by James Edward Stuart, the Old Pretender
1727-60 – Reign of **George II**
1745 – Jacobite rebellion led by Bonnie Prince Charlie, the Young Pretender, which ended at Culloden in 1746
1752 – Gregorian Calendar adopted

Queen Victoria

A. Taverner/MICHELIN

1756 – Beginning of the Seven Years War. Ministry formed by Pitt the Elder

1757 – Recapture of Calcutta. Battle of Plassey won by Clive

1759 – Defeat of the French army by General Wolfe on the Heights of Abraham, Quebec

1760-1820 – Reign of **George III**

1760 – Conquest of Canada

1763 – Seven Years War ended in the Treaty of Paris

1773 – **Boston Tea Party**, a protest against forced imports of cheap East India Company tea into the American colonies

1776 – American Declaration of Independence; *The Wealth of Nations* published by Adam Smith

1781 – British surrender at Yorktown

1793 – War against Revolutionary France

1799 – First levy of income tax to finance the war

1805 – Naval victory at Trafalgar and death of Nelson

1807 – Abolition of the slave trade within the British Empire

INDUSTRIAL REVOLUTION

Vast social changes occurred as the labour force moved from the land into town; overcrowding often bred unrest between worker and employer. The Napoleonic Wars both stimulated this industrialism and aggravated the unrest but by the mid 19C it was clear that in Britain industrial revolution would not be followed by political revolution.

1731 – Agriculture revolutionised by the invention of the horse hoe and seed drill by Jethro Tull

1733 – Invention of the flying shuttle by John Kay

1769 – Patents issued for Watt's steam engine and Arkwright's water frame

1781 – Patent issued for Watt's steam engine for rotary motion

1787 – Invention of the power loom by Cartwright

1825 – Opening of the Stockton and Darlington railway. Completion of the Menai Bridge by Telford

1833 – Factory Act abolishes child labour

1834 – Tolpuddle Martyrs transported to Australia for forming an agriculture Trade Union

1851 – Great Exhibition in the Crystal Palace in Hyde Park

1856 – Invention of the Bessemer process of steel making in industrial quantities.

THE VICTORIAN ERA

As William IV's two daughters had died as infants, he was succeeded on his death by his niece, Victoria.

Queen **Victoria**, the last monarch of the House of Hanover, was only 18 when she came to the throne. She went onto become Britain's longest-reigning Sovereign and to give her name to an illustrious age. Her husband, the **Prince Consort, Albert of Saxe-Coburg**, was her closest adviser until his premature death in 1861. He persuaded her that the Crown should not be aligned with any political party – a principle that has endured. He was the instigator of the **Great Exhibition** which took place between May and October in 1851. It contained exhibits from all nations and

Scientific Progress

Between 1760 and 1850 the **Industrial Revolution** turned Britain into the world's first industrial nation. Power-driven machines replaced human muscle and factory production replaced cottage industry medieval crafts. New methods supplied expanding markets – new machines were invented to satisfy growing demand.

Power

In 1712 **Thomas Newcomen** designed the first practical piston and steam engine and his idea was later much improved by **James Watt**. Such engines were needed to pump water and to raise men and ore from mines and soon replaced water wheels as the power source for the cotton factories which sprang up in Lancashire. Then **Richard Trevithick** (1771-1833), Cornish tin miner, designed a boiler with the fire box inside which he showed to **George Stephenson** (1781-1848) and his son, **Robert** (1803-59) . This became the basis of the early "locomotives".

Without abundant coal, however, sufficient iron could never have been produced for all the new machines. By 1880, 154 million tons of coal were being transported across Britain. Cast iron had been produced by Shropshire ironmaster **Abraham Darby** in Coalbrookdale in 1709 and was used for the cylinders of early steam engines and for bridges and aqueducts. Wrought iron with greater tensile strength was developed in the 1790s, allowing more accurate and stronger machine parts, railway lines and bridging materials. In 1856 **Sir Henry Bessemer** devised a system in which compressed air is blown through the molten metal, burning off impurities and producing a stronger steel.

Transport

Thomas Telford (1757-1834) built roads and bridges for the use of stage coaches and broad-wheeled wagons transporting people and goods. However these were often impassable in winter so cheap transport for bulk goods was also provided by over 4 000 miles of canals, pioneered by **James Brindley** (1716-72). Eventually heavy goods and long-distance passenger traffic passed to the railways.

Engineered by **George Stephenson** (of in 1825, the Stockton and Darlington Railway was the first passenger-carrying public steam railway in the world. By 1835 the railway had become the vital element of the Industrial Revolution – swift, efficient and cheap transport for raw materials and finished goods. The success of Stephenson's *Rocket* proved the feasibility of locomotives. **Isambard Kingdom Brunel** (1806-59), Chief Engineer to the Great Western Railway, designed the Clifton Suspension Bridge and also the first successful trans-Atlantic steamship, the *Great Western,* in 1837.

William Henry Morris – Lord Nuffield, the most influential of British car manufacturers, began with bicycles and made his first car in 1913. He is probably best remembered for his 1959 "Mini". **John Boyd Dunlop** started with bicycles too. In 1888 this Scottish veterinary surgeon invented the first pneumatic tyre. It was **John Loudon McAdam**, an Ayrshire engineer, who devised the "Tarmacadam" surfacing for roads.

More recently **Christopher Cockerell** patented a design for the first hovercraft in 1955.

Aviation

The names of **Charles Rolls** and **Henry Royce** will always be associated with the grand cars they pioneered although their contribution to aviation is arguably even greater. A Rolls-Royce engine powered Sir Frank Whittle's Gloster E28/29, the first jet aircraft, and the De Havilland Comet, the world's first commercial passenger-carrying jet airliner which made its maiden flight in 1949. British aerospace designers worked with their French counterparts in the development of Concorde, the world's first supersonic airliner.

Science

In 1660 Sir **Francis Bacon** (1561-1626) founded the Royal Society; it was granted a Charter by Charles II in 1662 "to promote discussion, particularly in the physical sciences". **Robert Boyle** and **Sir Christopher Wren** were founder members and Sir Isaac Newton was its President from 1703 to 1727. **Michael Faraday** was appointed assistant to Sir Humphrey Davy, inventor of the miners' Safety Lamp, in 1812. It was Faraday's work with electromagnetism which led to the development of the electric dynamo and motor. An early form of computer, the "difference engine" was invented by **Charles Babbage** in 1833 and can be seen in the library of King's College, Cambridge. **Edmond Halley,** friend of Newton, became Astronomer Royal in 1720. He is best remembered for the comet named after him, and for correctly predicting its 76-year cycle and return in 1758.

The radio telescope at Jodrell Bank, set up by **Sir Bernard Lovell** in 1955, is still one of the largest in the world and contributes to our widening knowledge of our Universe. In 1968 **Antony Hewish**, a British astronomer at Cambridge, first discovered pulsars, cosmic sources of light or radio energy. In 1988 **Professor Stephen Hawking** studied black holes and wrote his seminal treatise, *A Brief History of Time*.

Medicine

It was **William Harvey,** physician to James I and Charles I, who discovered the circulation of the blood. More recent British achievements in medicine have been those of Dr Jacob Bell who, with Dr Simpson from Edinburgh, introduced chloroform anaesthesia, which met with public approval after Queen Victoria used it during the birth of Prince Leopold in 1853. **Sir Alexander Fleming** discovered the effects of penicillin in killing bacteria in 1928, The "double-helix" structure of DNA (de-oxy-ribo-nucleic acid) – the major component of chromosomes which carry genetic information and control inheritance of characteristics – was proposed by Francis Crick working at the Cavendish Laboratory in Cambridge, with his American colleague, James Watson, in 1953. The cloning of Dolly the sheep, in 1996, by the Roslin Institute in Scotland marked a new era in genetic engineering.

Natural History

John Tradescant and son were gardeners to Charles I and planted the first physic (medicinal plant) garden in 1628, leading to the remarkable Chelsea Physic Garden, founded in 1673, open to the public today. James Hutton (1726-97) wrote a treatise entitled *A Theory of the Earth* (1785) which forms the basis of modern geology. **Sir Joseph Banks** (1743-1820), botanist and explorer, accompanied James Cook's expedition round the world in *Endeavour* (1768-71) and collected many previously unknown plants. Together with the biologist Thomas Huxley (1825-95), they supported the pioneering research of **Charles Darwin** (1809-1882), the father of the theory of evolution outlined in his famous work, *On the Origin of Species*, which had a great impact on the study of natural sciences.

The geologist and naturalist **John Muir** (1838-1914) is commemorated as the founder of the American National Parks. The British passion for gardening has led to the domestication of exotic species such as azaleas, rhododendrons, orchids among others. The role of Kew Gardens, which has accumulated a seed bank of some 5 000 species over the past 200 years, is vital in the conservation of endangered plant species. During the 1960s and 1970s the zoologist Desmond Morris propounded provocative theories on human behaviour based on animal studies. More recently the ornithologist Sir Peter Scott, and the naturalists Gerald Durrell, David Bellamy and Sir David Attenborough have increased public awareness of conservation and other environmental issues.

Exploration

Maritime exploration spurred on by the enquiring spirit of the 16C led to the discovery of new worlds. Following the voyages of Portuguese explorers, **John Cabot**, a Genoese settled in Bristol, discovered Nova Scotia and Newfoundland. Rivalry between England and Spain and other European nations in search of trade, as well as scientific advances in navigational aids and improvements in ship construction, led to an explosion of maritime exploration. English mariners included: John Hawkins (1532-95), who introduced tobacco and sweet potatoes to England; **Sir Francis Drake** (c 1540-96), the first Englishman to circumnavigate the world; **Sir Walter Raleigh** (1552-1618), who discovered Virginia; Martin Frobisher, who explored the North Atlantic and discovered Baffin Island (1574). Hudson Bay in Canada is named after the explorer Henry Hudson (1610). Captain **James Cook** (1728-79) explored the Pacific, and charted the coasts of Australia and New Zealand and surveyed the Newfoundland coast.

Other famous explorers include **Mungo Park** (1771-1806), who explored West Africa and attempted to trace the course of the Niger river; **David Livingstone** (1813-73), a doctor and missionary who campaigned against the slave trade and was the first to cross the African mainland from east to west and discovered the Victoria Falls and Lake Nyasa (now Lake Malawi); Alexander Mackenzie (1755-1820), the first man to cross the American continent by land (1783); and John McDouall Stuart (1815-66) who explored the Australian desert.

was a proud declaration of the high point of the Industrial Revolution, celebrating the inventiveness, technical achievement and prosperity which are the hallmarks of the Victorian Age. Her son, **Edward VII**, who was excluded from royal duties and responsibilities until 1892, greatly increased the prestige of the monarchy by his own charm and by reviving royal public ceremonial.

1812-14 – Anglo-American War ended by Treaty of Ghent
1815 – Battle of Waterloo; defeat of Napoleon; Congress of Vienna
1820-30 – Reign of **George IV**
1823 – Reform of criminal law and prisons by Peel
1829 – Catholic Emancipation Act. Formation of the Metropolitan Police
1830-37 – Reign of **William IV**
1832 – First parliamentary Reform Act
1837-1901 – Reign of **Victoria**
1840 – Marriage of Victoria to Prince Albert. Introduction of the penny post
1842 – Chartist movement campaigns for parliamentary reform
1846 – Repeal of the Corn Laws
1848 – Cholera epidemic. Public Health Act

1854-56 – **Crimean War**, ends with the Treaty of Paris
1857 – Indian Mutiny
1858 – Government of India transferred from the East India Company to the Crown
1861 – Death of Prince Albert
1863 – Opening of the first underground railway in London, the Metropolitan Railway
1871 – bank holidays introduced
1876 – Victoria made Empress of India. Elementary education made obligatory
1884 – Invention of the steam turbine by Parsons
1888 – Local Government Act establishing county councils and county boroughs
1895 – First Motor Show in London
1899-1902 – Boer War ends in the Peace of Vereeniging, leading to union of South Africa (1910)

20TH–21ST CENTURY

Following the two world wars Great Britain took its place at the top table of the free world. As the second decade of the 21st century approaches, Britain's military powers may have diminished, but it remains a key player in world politics.

WORLD AT WAR

The assassination of Archduke Ferdinand at Sarajevo in 1914 plunged Europe (and beyond) into a futile stalemate war in which a million British troops died and many millions more lost their lives. Meanwhile in Ireland a desire for independence had also reached crisis point and in Easter 1916 an uprising in Dublin was ruthlessly put down by British troops.

A significant after-effect of the First World War in Great Britain was a loosening of **class structure**. The "lions led by donkeys" were now much less likely to follow orders in peacetime and the Labour Party made great strides, coming to power for the first time (albeit in a Liberal coalition) in 1923.

Across the water in Ireland the independence movement was continuing and in 1921 an Irish Free State was created. It led to the Irish Civil War, which ended in 1923.

In Britain the **General Strike** of 1926 underlined the country's growing restlessness and this unrest worsened in the 1930s, as the worldwide economy slumped into the Great Depression.

World War II

A policy of appeasement was taken towards the growing ambitions of Adolf Hitler, characterised by Prime Minister Neville Chamberlain in 1938 who returned from a meeting with the Führer and delivered the now infamous words 'I believe it is peace in our time'. When it became clear however in 1939, with the invasion of Poland, that war was the only option for Britain, the country found itself seriously unprepared. By mid-1940 Britain was isolated and prepared to be invaded by Hitler's army from across the Channel. The evacuation of troops at Dunkirk was the nadir. The tide however was about to turn. In May **Winston Churchill** became Prime Minister and the **Battle of Britain** had halted the Luftwaffe's ambitions. This led to the **Blitz** over London and other major cities, in the autumn and winter of 1940/41. In 1941 the **United States** entered the war and the Germans became disastrously entrenched on the **Eastern Front** in Russia. By 1944 the German armies were in retreat and the **Normandy (D-Day) Landings** spearheaded the liberation of Europe.

1900 – Labour Party formed
1901-10 – Reign of **Edward VII**
1903 – Women's suffrage movement started by Mrs Pankhurst
1905 – First motor buses in London
1910-36 – Reign of **George V**
1914-18 – First World War
1914 – Formation of Kitchener's "Volunteer Army"
1916 – Easter Rising in Dublin
1917 – Name of the royal family changed to Windsor by George V
1918 – Women over-30 granted vote
1919 – Treaty of Versailles
1921 – Creation of the Irish Free State
1924 – British Empire Exhibition
1926 – General Strike
1928 – Women over-21 granted vote
1931 – **The Depression** – many people out of work
1936 – Accession and abdication of **Edward VIII**
1936-52 – Reign of **George VI**
1939-45 – **Second World War**
1940 – **Winston Churchill** becomes Prime Minister
1940 – Evacuation of Dunkirk; **Battle of Britain**
1944 – **Normandy landings**

King George VI and Prime Minister Winston Churchill on the balcony of Buckingham Palace on Victory in Europe Day, May 8, 1945

© Corbis

POST-WAR BRITAIN

The years following the Second World War marked the end of the British Empire. In most cases this was a peaceful transition. India achieved independence in 1947 and within the next ten years virtually all of Britain's overseas dependencies followed suit. These new self-governing Dominions, which had stood by Britain during two World Wars, changed into the **British Commonwealth,** an informal non-political union which fosters economic co-operation and best practices between member nations.

After 1945 key industries were nationalised and the **Welfare State** was born with the National Health Service, improved pensions and benefits.

Elizabeth II, who succeeded to the throne in 1952, has done much to strengthen the role of monarchy both at home and abroad and even following the royalty's recent troubled years the Queen remains enormously popular within and outside Great Britain.

The austere 1950s was succeeded by the "**Swinging Sixties**", a period of cultural upheaval and optimism which saw the rise of youth culture, London become the epicentre of the fashion universe, and, of course, the Beatles.

The decade ended badly in Northern Ireland where violent disputes, known as **The Troubles**, flared up between Protestant and Catholic organisations. Despite the efforts of the British Army and the Royal Ulster Constabulary, over the next 29 years some 3,700 people were to lose their lives, many in indiscriminate bombings.

THATCHERISM

By contrast with the upbeat 1960s the 1970s was a decade of industrial slump and strife. Against this background, in 1979, **Margaret Thatcher**, Britain's first ever female party leader (of the Conservatives) also became Britain's first ever female prime minister. She went on to become the most charismatic leader since Winston Churchill but her ideology, which came to be known as Thatcherism – deeply in favour of individualism over collectivism and capital-

ism over social responsibility – polarised the country. The bitter year-long miners' strikes of 1984-85 and subsequent pit closures and massive job losses were the most obvious sign of this. Yet while Britain's industrial base declined other sectors of the economy (mostly services) boomed. Thatcher went on to win three general elections and while she was reviled by many, some still look back fondly on her premiership.

NEW LABOUR

Although Britain had joined the **European (Economic) Union** in 1973, European policy issues had remained mostly on the back burner. In the post-Thatcher years however these, alongside other issues like the immensely unpopular poll tax, led to the unravelling of the Conservatives. John Major gave the Tories another term in government after Thatcher stepped down, but failed by 1997 to unite and modernise his party, making room for a revitalised, centrist Labour party, reborn as the media-savvy New Labour under **Tony Blair**. His dynamic, reformist and optimistic brand of politics earned him a massive majority in Parliament, with policies that moved away from traditional labour values in favour of the City, big business and closer links with Europe.

The creation of the Scottish Parliament and the Welsh Assembly, both ratified in 1997, marked a new stage in the relationships between the constituent parts of the United Kingdom though most of the real power has remained firmly rooted in Whitehall and Westminster. Devolution and national identity remain controversial topics in Great Britain.

The end of Tony Blair's reign in 2008 and the prime ministerial succession of Gordon Brown, without public election, occurred in the shadow of a host of problems, from unpopular wars in **Iraq** and **Afghanistan** to increasing crime, human rights and privacy issues, and the beginning of a serious recession.

1947 – Independence and partition of India. Nationalisation of railways and road transport

Coronation of Elizabeth II at Westminster Abbey, 2nd June 1953
©UPPA/Photoshot

Beginning of **"The Troubles"** in Northern Ireland

1973 – United Kingdom becomes a founding member of the EEC

1979 – **Margaret Thatcher** elected first woman Prime Minister (serves until 1991)

1982 – Falklands War

1990–1991 – Gulf War

1992–1995 – Bosnian War

1997 – Election of a **Labour Government.** Approval of Scottish and Welsh Assemblies

1998 – Good Friday Agreement, referendum and meeting of Northern Ireland Assembly

1999 – Opening of Scottish Parliament and Welsh Assembly

2001—present – Afghanistan War

2002 – Queen's Golden Jubilee.

2003 – Iraq War

2005 – Terrorist bombs explode in London killing 52 people

2007 – Gordon Brown becomes the new prime minister as Tony Blair steps down

2008 – UK economy enters recession. Troops withdrawn from Iraq.

1950–1953 – Korean War

1952 – Accession of **Elizabeth II**

1958 – Treaty of Rome creating the European Economic Community/EEC (now the European Union/EU)

1959 – Discovery of oil in the North Sea

1965 – Death of Sir Winston Churchill

1969 – Investiture of Prince Charles as Prince of Wales at Caernarfon Castle

Art and Culture

ARCHITECTURE
ROMAN

Pre-Roman, Iron Age architecture is best observed in impressive hillforts such as at Maidenhead and in Scottish *brochs*. The Roman invasion began in Kent; **Richborough Castle** was part of the Roman system of coastal defences, a series of forts in the southeast under the control of the "Count of the Saxon Shore". Their capital was St Albans, linked by military roads to other major settlements in Bath, Chester, Lincoln and York. London was a trading post near a river crossing on the Thames.

Examples of domestic Roman architecture in Britain are the theatre at St Albans and the ruined **villas** at Chedworth, Fishbourne, Bignor and Brading with their mosaics.

Their greatest military enterprise was **Hadrian's Wall**, a defensive wall reinforced by military camps stretching from Wallsend on the Tyne to Bowness on the Solway Firth (73mi/117 km) to guard the northern boundary of the Empire.

PRE-ROMANESQUE

Few buildings survive from this period, AD c 650 to the Norman Conquest. Much Saxon work, in timber, was destroyed in Viking raids. **All Saints, Brixworth** (c 680) in Northamptonshire makes use of Roman brick and the apse was surrounded by an external ring-crypt, a feature first found in St Peter's in Rome (c 590). **All Saints,** at **Earl's Barton** nearby, has a late Saxon tower. Saxon crypts survive at **Hexham, Repton** and **Ripon**.

ECCLESIASTICAL ARCHITECTURE

Saxon towers

EARL'S BARTON, Northamptonshire – Late 10C

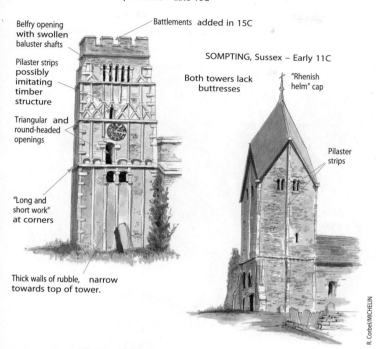

Belfry opening with swollen baluster shafts

Battlements added in 15C

SOMPTING, Sussex – Early 11C

Pilaster strips possibly imitating timber structure

Both towers lack buttresses

"Rhenish helm" cap

Triangular and round-headed openings

Pilaster strips

"Long and short work" at corners

Thick walls of rubble, narrow towards top of tower.

R. Corbel/MICHELIN

ROMANESQUE (NORMAN)

These bold, massive buildings continued to be erected until after the death of Henry II in 1189 and nowhere else in Europe is there such a richness or variation of Norman work, nor such an abundance of surviving examples. In English cathedrals, the naves tend to be much longer than on the Continent, for example **Ely** (13 bays) and **Norwich** (14); the eastern end was usually shorter. **Durham Cathedral**, begun in 1093, where the whole interior is one Romanesque scheme, is a fine example of Norman work in Britain, though externally only the lower parts of the tower and nave and the choir show true Romanesque work. Its stone vaulting, completed in 1133, survives in its original form. **Southwell Minster** has a west front c 1130, with later Perpendicular windows. The eastern end of **Norwich** cathedral

is tri-apsidal. Its spire and clerestory are later Gothic, but the remainder is Norman. **Rochester, Gloucester, Peterborough, Lincoln, Exeter, Hereford, St Albans,** and the abbey churches of **Tewkesbury** and **Waltham,** are all part of England's heritage of Norman work. Every county boasts many parish churches with a Norman nave or tower, west doorway, or south porch or chancel arch. **Iffley Church**, Oxfordshire, west front (c 1170), **St Mary and St David, Kilpeck**, Herefordshire (c 1140) with Scandinavian influence in the carving, and **St Nicholas, Barfreston**, Kent, are just some of the hundreds well worth visiting. Most secular buildings are fortifications. The **White Tower**, the keep of the Tower of London, was the first work (1080) of William the Conqueror; it had four storeys (over 90ft/30m high), massive walls (over 20ft/6m thick at the

Norman cathedral

Durham Cathedral was largely completed between 1095 and 1133. It exemplifies the grandeur and solidity of Norman architecture. The characteristic rounded arch prevails, but the pointed-rib vaults anticipate the structural achievements of Gothic architecture.

The side elevation of the nave is divided into: triforium/clerestory and arcade

Corbel

Rounded crossing arch

Diagonal ribs

Pointed-rib vault

Blind arcade

Round pier with incised chevrons

Compound pier

Pier with lozenge decoration

Nave

Choir

Cushion capital

18C rose window

19C rood screen

R. Corbel/MICHELIN

Norman doorway

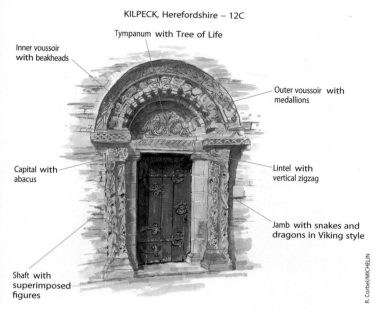

KILPECK, Herefordshire – 12C

Tympanum with Tree of Life

Inner voussoir
with beakheads

Outer voussoir with
medallions

Capital with
abacus

Lintel with
vertical zigzag

Jamb with snakes and
dragons in Viking style

Shaft with
superimposed
figures

R. Corbel/MICHELIN

base) and small well-protected openings. **Rochester Castle** c 1130, though ruined, gives an impression of living conditions, with passages, garderobes and bedchambers in the thickness (12ft/3.5m) of the walls. **Chepstow Castle** (1067) is one of the earliest secular stone buildings in Britain.

GOTHIC

The style evolved in northern France; the Abbey of St Denis outside Paris is the earliest example. Gothic designs resulted in larger and higher buildings, flooded with light. Heavy columns were replaced by slimmer clustered column shafts; towers became taller and more slender.

In England Gothic architecture remained in use much longer than elsewhere in Europe, as it evolved through four distinct phases and retained its distinctive English characteristics.

Transitional (1145-89)

Transitional buildings have both pointed and round arches, especially in windows and vaults. **Ripon Cathedral** (1181) is a good example but the most outstanding is the choir of **Canterbury Cathedral.**

Early English (c 1190-1307)

Distinctive features are the ribbed vaults, narrow pointed arches and lancet windows. **Salisbury Cathedral**, built, apart from tower and spire, between 1220 and 1258, is the only English cathedral to have been built virtually in one operation, hence in a single style. See also **Wells**, the façades of **Peterborough** and **Ripon**, much of **Lichfield**, and the Abbeys of **Tintern** and **Fountains**, and **Bolton Priory**.

Decorated (c 1280-1377)

Ely Cathedral, with its octagon and lantern (1323-30), was one of the early experiments in new spatial form and lighting. Other examples include the west façades of **Exeter** and **York**.

Perpendicular

The last – and longest – phase of Gothic architecture in Britain is uniquely English in style. There is an emphasis on vertical lines but the principal features are

Gothic

SALISBURY CATHEDRAL (1220-58)

Of great length and highly compartmentalised in layout like most English cathedrals, Salisbury is exceptional in having been completed in a single style – Early English – in a short space of time. The only major addition was the tall crossing tower and spire (404ft) built c 1334.

Close – A distinctive feature of many English cathedrals, a precinct with houses for cathedral officials. Grassed area formerly a graveyard.

Nave   Transept   Spire and crossing tower

Choir Transept

Chancel

Lady Chapel dedicated to the Virgin Mary

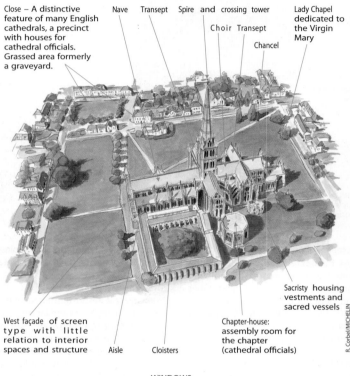

Sacristy housing vestments and sacred vessels

West façade of screen type with little relation to interior spaces and structure

Aisle

Cloisters

Chapter-house: assembly room for the chapter (cathedral officials)

R. Corbel/MICHELIN

WINDOWS

Simple 5-lancet Early English window c 1170, tall, narrow and with acutely-pointed arch

Space between lancets enlivened by addition of quatrefoil c 1270

Window in Decorated style with fully developed flowing tracery c 1350

Large window in Perpendicular style with 4-centred arch and horizontal emphasis through use of transoms

R. Corbel/MICHELIN

VAULTING

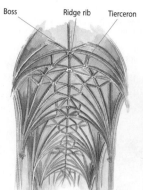

Boss   Ridge rib   Tierceron

Nave vault with liernes (linking ribs not joined to central boss or springer) Canterbury Cathedral c 1390 - 1405

Fan vault with pendants: the ultimate development of this highly ornamental, non-structural vault Henry VII's Chapel, Westminster 1503-12

R. Corbel/MICHELIN

panelled decoration all over the building, an increase in window area and the consequent development – very much later than in France – of the flying buttress. Fan-vault roofing, a peculiarly English design, can best be seen in **King's College Chapel,** Cambridge (1146-1515), **Eton College Chapel** (1441) and **St George's Chapel,** Windsor (1475-1509).

Contemporary with the fan-vault, and equally English, was the development of the **timber roof**. Tie and collar designs from the 13C and 14C developed into more complex 15C and 16C **hammerbeam** roofs over churches and guildhalls, of which **Westminster Hall** (Hugh Herland, c 1395) is an example. Others are the Great Hall at **Hampton Court** (1535) and **Rufford Old Hall,** near Ormskirk, Lancashire (1505). England also has a wealth of medieval timber-framed houses, built in areas where stone was scarce – **Rufford Old Hall**, the **Guildhall** at Lavenham and the **Feathers Hotel** in Ludlow.

TUDOR-JACOBEAN

This period began with the accession of Henry VII in 1485 and covers the transition from Gothic to Classicism. Tudor Gothic, both ecclesiastical and secular, can be seen in **Bath Abbey** and the brick-built **Hampton Court Palace.**

From 1550 to 1620 building was largely domestic, for a thriving middle class and a wealthy aristocracy. **Longleat House** (1550-80) in Wiltshire, **Montacute House** (1588-1601) in Somerset, and Bess of Hardwick's **Hardwick Hall** (1591-97) in Derbyshire are outstanding examples. The courtyard layout of medieval days was abandoned for the E or H shaped plan, a central rectangular block with projecting wings. The **Long Gallery** – used for exercise on winter days – became a feature of all the great houses of the Elizabethan period.

Half-timbered houses were built in areas where stone was scarce – **Little Moreton Hall** (1559) in Cheshire and **Speke Hall**, near Liverpool, begun in 1490 and still being added to in 1612. The staircase began to assume an importance in the design of Elizabethan houses and by Jacobean times had become, in many houses, the focus of the whole interior – Ham, Hatfield, Knole and Audley End.

The architectural ideas of the **Renaissance** were brought to England by **Inigo Jones** (1573-1652). His two most outstanding public buildings are the **Banqueting Hall** (1619-22) in London and the **Queen's House** (1616-35) in Greenwich.

He also rebuilt part of **Wilton House** (1647-53) in Wiltshire, where his adherence to Classical proportions is evident in the "double cube" room. Architects in

LITTLE MORETON HALL, Cheshire

A moated manor house built between the mid-15C and c 1580 with elaborate timber-framing and carved decoration characteristic of the Welsh Marches, Cheshire and Lancashire. Despite its date, this, and many other houses like it, is still medieval in character.

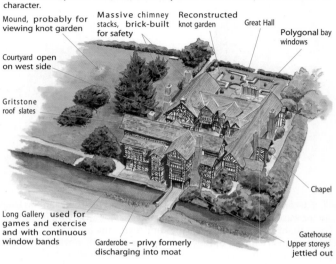

Mound, probably for viewing knot garden

Massive chimney stacks, brick-built for safety

Reconstructed knot garden

Great Hall

Polygonal bay windows

Courtyard open on west side

Gritstone roof slates

Long Gallery used for games and exercise and with continuous window bands

Garderobe – privy formerly discharging into moat

Chapel

Gatehouse Upper storeys jettied out

R. Corbel/MICHELIN

BLENHEIM PALACE AND PARK, Oxfordshire

Built 1705-22 by Sir John Vanbrugh, the Palace with its vast scale, heroic proportions and rich profusion of forms represents the culmination of the Baroque style in England. The park was transformed between 1764-74 by Lancelot "Capability" Brown, whose masterpiece it is.

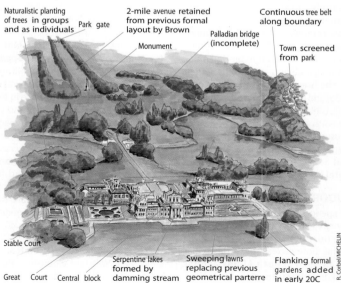

Naturalistic planting of trees in groups and as individuals

Park gate

2-mile avenue retained from previous formal layout by Brown

Monument

Palladian bridge (incomplete)

Continuous tree belt along boundary

Town screened from park

Stable Court

Great Court Central block

Serpentine lakes formed by damming stream

Sweeping lawns replacing previous geometrical parterre

Flanking formal gardens added in early 20C

R. Corbel/MICHELIN

English Baroque

ST PAUL'S CATHEDRAL, City of London, West façade

Built by Sir Christopher Wren between 1675 and 1710, the cathedral combines Renaissance and Baroque elements in a masterly way. The dome, inspired by St Peter's in Rome, is in three parts: the lightweight and beautifully shaped outer dome, an inner dome, and between them an (invisible) brick core carrying the heavy lantern which helps hold the outer dome in place.

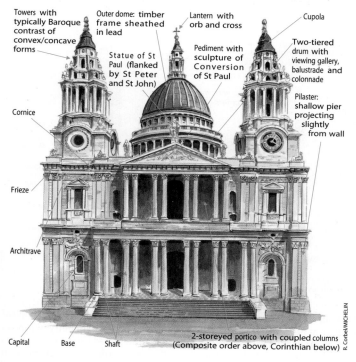

Towers with typically Baroque contrast of convex/concave forms

Outer dome: timber frame sheathed in lead

Lantern with orb and cross

Cupola

Statue of St Paul (flanked by St Peter and St John)

Pediment with sculpture of Conversion of St Paul

Two-tiered drum with viewing gallery, balustrade and colonnade

Cornice

Pilaster: shallow pier projecting slightly from wall

Frieze

Architrave

Capital   Base   Shaft

2-storeyed portico with coupled columns
(Composite order above, Corinthian below)

R. Corbel/MICHELIN

England who had never seen an ancient Classical building based their work on "Pattern Books" published by Renaissance designers.

Tudor Forts

In 1538, faced with the threat of invasion to re-establish the Pope's authority, Henry VIII began to construct a chain of forts and batteries to prevent an enemy invasion fleet from making use of the principal anchorages, landing places and ports.

The first forts built in 1539-40 – Deal, Walmer and Dover in Kent, Calshot and Hurst, overlooking Southampton Water and The Solent, and St Mawes and Pendennis in Cornwall – were squat with thick walls and rounded parapets. In

most a central circular keep was surrounded by lower round bastions or enclosed by a circular curtain wall. They were designed to be defended by cannon mounted on carriages and sited on several tiers of platforms to compensate for the limited vertical traverse of each cannon. Lateral traverse was limited only by the splay of the gun ports.

CLASSICISM

Though Classicism was introduced by Inigo Jones, it was in the reign of Charles I (1625-49) that the style really began to make its mark on the English scene. The dominant figure was Sir **Christopher Wren** (1632-1723). After the Great Fire of London, he was responsible for 53 churches and the new **St Paul's**

VICTORIAN ARCHITECTURE

ST PANCRAS STATION, London

The Midland Hotel, completed in the Gothic Revival style in 1876 by Sir George Gilbert Scott, conceals the great train shed whose iron and glass arch was the widest (249ft) in the world at the time. Marrying Venetian, French, Flemish and English Gothic in a triumphal synthesis, Scott's building was also a functional masterpiece, housing the myriad activities of a railway terminus on a restricted, triangular site.

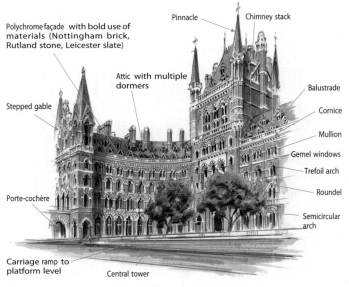

Polychrome façade with bold use of materials (Nottingham brick, Rutland stone, Leicester slate)

Pinnacle

Chimney stack

Attic with multiple dormers

Balustrade

Cornice

Stepped gable

Mullion

Gemel windows

Trefoil arch

Porte-cochère

Roundel

Semicircular arch

Carriage ramp to platform level

Central tower

R. Corbel/MICHELIN

Cathedral, as well as the **Royal Naval College** at Greenwich and a new wing for **Hampton Court Palace,** which harmonises well with the Tudor brickwork. The **Sheldonian Theatre** (1669) at Oxford, and the **Library** of **Trinity College**, Cambridge (1676-84) are two of his best-known works outside London. **Sir John Vanbrugh** (1664-1726), soldier and playwright, who turned architect in 1699, was one of the chief exponents of the **Baroque** in England; his masterpieces, produced in collaboration with **Nicholas Hawksmoor** (1661-1736), are **Castle Howard, Blenheim Palace** and **Seaton Delaval**. Hawksmoor, under a commission of 1711, designed six London churches. **St Mary Woolnoth** in the City of London survives to show his style.

Baroque architecture brought fantasy and movement to the classical order but found little favour in England. It was replaced in the 1720s with

Palladianism, also a foreign "implant" but one with a symmetry which was eagerly adapted by architects such as **Colen Campbell (Houghton Hall)** and **William Kent (Holkham Hall)**. Palladian houses were set carefully in landscaped parks – many by **Lancelot "Capability "Brown** – a far cry from the formality of French and Italian gardens of the period. He designed over 170 parks, remodeling the great estate parks of the English gentry to resemble an ordered version of nature.

Robert Adam (1728-92), son of a Scottish architect, returned from the Grand Tour, having absorbed the principles of ancient architecture and learnt much neoclassical theory. He and his brothers set up in practice in London in 1758, introducing a lighter, more decorative style than the Palladian work then in vogue. Most of Adam's buildings are domestic and he also had great flair as an interior designer.

GEORGIAN HOUSING AND PLANNING

In the 18C and early 19C, extensions to inland spas, and later to seaside towns saw a fusion of urban planning and landscape design. In Bath, John Wood the Elder and John Wood the Younger built the splendidly urbane sequence of Queen Square (1736), Gay Street (1734-60), The Circus (1754) and Royal Crescent, the latter a palace-like composition made up of relatively small terraced houses facing out to parkland.

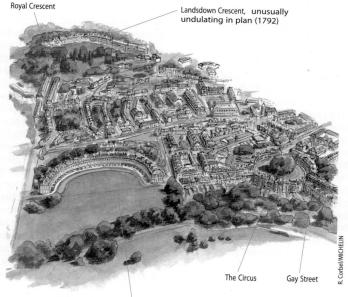

Royal Crescent

Landsdown Crescent, unusually undulating in plan (1792)

The Circus   Gay Street

Ha-ha sunken wall permitting uninterrupted view

R.Corbel/MICHELIN

In London, strict regulations governed the design of terraced houses which were rated 1-4 according to their size and value.

Sash-windows with thin wooden glazing bars help unify façades. Small or square windows of top floor act as visual stop. Classical appearance aided by low-pitched roofs (sometimes partly concealed by parapet) and lack of emphasis on chimneys. Tall windows emphasize importance of first floor reception rooms.

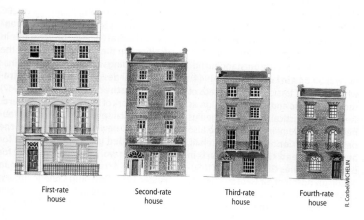

First-rate house

Second-rate house

Third-rate house

Fourth-rate house

R.Corbel/MICHELIN

19C AND 20C ARCHITECTURE

The 19C was predominantly an age of stylistic revivals. The Industrial Revolution and the movement of people into towns stimulated the construction of factories and mills and housing. Iron and glass played a part in the mass-production of these buildings. At first individual craftsmanship was evident in mouldings, decoration and furniture but by 1900 much of this had vanished.

John Nash (1752-1835), builder of many terraces round Regent's Park and down Regent Street in London, also designed the **Royal Pavilion** at Brighton. **Sir John Soane** (1753-1837), probably the last of the original designers, is represented by his house at Lincoln's Inn Fields, now the **Sir John Soane Museum.**

From 1840 the trend was towards the Gothic revival which reached its height between 1855 and 1885. **Sir Charles Barry** (1795-1860) rebuilt the **Palace of Westminster** after the 1834 fire. Alfred Waterhouse (1830-1905) designed the Natural History Museum and built Manchester Town Hall.

The 19C was also the Railway Age. **Isambard Kingdom Brunel** (1806-59), Chief Engineer to the Great Western Railway in 1833, also designed the Clifton Suspension Bridge. **Thomas Telford** (1757-1834) built roads, bridges and canals throughout the country. He was responsible for the London-Holyhead road and for the bridge (1826), which carries it over the Menai Strait. In the 20C Art Nouveau had little influence on architecture but there was passing interest in interior decoration, fabrics and stained glass in the new style. Reinforced concrete was the main structural development.

Between the Wars, the outstanding figure was **Sir Edwin Lutyens** (1869-1944), who adapted Classicism to the needs of the day, in civic and housing design as well as ecclesiastical. His was the genius behind New Delhi in India and he also designed the **Cenotaph** in Whitehall, and **Hampstead Garden Suburb** in London. **Sir Giles Gilbert Scott** (1880-1960), grandson of Sir George, the 19C architect, built the last great cathedral in the Gothic style, the red sandstone

Anglican Cathedral of Liverpool. He also set the pattern for power stations with his 1929 design for **Battersea Power Station**.

"Urban planning" was not a 20C idea. Haussmann re-designed much of Paris in the 1860s and the Italian Renaissance painter Martini has left us his picture, painted in 1475, of *The Ideal City*. In Britain, **Welwyn Garden City**, built near St Albans in 1920, was the first of the New Towns, an extension of the idea of the Garden Suburb. The planned layout of streets, cul-de-sacs and closes, romantically named and lined with semi-detached and detached houses, was copied all over the country after the 1939-45 war, in an attempt to check the "urban sprawl" in London, Lancashire, the Clyde Valley and South Wales. The 1946 New Towns Act provided for 28 such New Towns; **Harlow New Town** by Gibberd was built in 1947, **Cumbernauld**, near Glasgow, in the 1950s and **Milton Keynes** in rural Buckinghamshire in the 1970s. As costs escalated and concern grew over the decay of city centres the building of complete new towns was halted. Pedestrian zones and the banishing of traffic have helped to conserve both the fabric and spirit of established town and city centres. **Poundbury** village in Dorchester, Dorset (1993-94), which stresses the importance of architecture on a human scale and is sponsored by the Prince of Wales, represents the latest trend in urban planning.

Outstanding among examples of 20C architecture is Sir Basil Spence's **Coventry Cathedral** (1956-62), remarkable in itself and in the way it blends with the older buildings around it. The imaginative circular design of **Liverpool Metropolitan Cathedral** (consecrated 1967) was the work of **Sir Frederick Gibberd**. In the secular sphere, education – established and new universities – and the arts provided good opportunities for pioneering work: Sainsbury Centre for the Visual Arts, East Anglia, Norman Foster 1991; Downing College library, Cambridge, Quinlan Terry 1987; St John College Garden Quad, Oxford, 1993.

Custom-built galleries were designed for the Sainsbury Collection (1970s) at Norwich (Norman Foster), Burrell's donation in Glasgow (B Gasson) and the Tate Gallery at St Ives (1993, Evans and Shalev).

Other areas which have provided great scope for exciting modern architecture over the last few years are sports venues – the new Wembley Stadium and Lord's Cricket Ground stand (Michael Hopkins); opera houses – Glyndebourne and Covent Garden, Royal Opera House refurbishment and extension; London office developments – Lloyd's Building, Canary Wharf, Broadgate, The Ark, Swiss Re Tower ("The Gherkin") and City Hall. Major commissions (bridges, community and other projects) approved by the Millennium Commission heralded an explosion of original design for the turn of the century. Many of these are now popular visitor attractions: the Eden Project, Cornwall; Dynamic Earth, Edinburgh; the Great Glasshouse at the National Botanic Garden of Wales; in Manchester, The Lowry, The Imperial War Museum of the North and Urbis, ; in Glasgow the Glasgow Science Cen-

Lloyd's Building

© PhotoDisc, Inc.

tre and The Armadillo. All break new ground in structural and materials technology.

The most controversial projects have been the reviled Millennium Dome, London, and the Scottish Parliament building in Edinburgh.

The Parliament building was finally completed in 2004, three years late and ten times over-budget. The Dome was a commercial failure for many years and only recently (under its new guise

EARLY MODERN ARCHITECTURE

GLASGOW SCHOOL OF ART

In touch with continental Art Nouveau and looking forward to 20C functionalism, Charles Rennie Mackintosh was also inspired by the robust forms of Scottish baronial architecture. Rising castle-like from its steeply sloping site, his Glasgow School of Art (1897-1909) combines strict utility of purpose with innovative, near-abstract forms and decorative Art Nouveau elements.

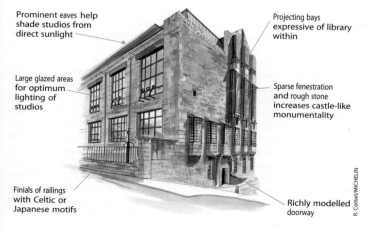

Prominent eaves help shade studios from direct sunlight

Projecting bays expressive of library within

Large glazed areas for optimum lighting of studios

Sparse fenestration and rough stone increases castle-like monumentality

Finials of railings with Celtic or Japanese motifs

Richly modelled doorway

R. Corbel/MICHELIN

as the O2 Arena) has found success as a concert venue.

The regeneration of derelict industrial sites and obsolete docks has met with considerable success in Liverpool, Cardiff and particularly the massive London Dockland scheme of the 1990s (still ongoing).

The conservation and re-use of existing industrial buildings is most apparent in two huge and stunning art galleries at opposite ends of the country: Tate Modern, in London (formerly a power station): the Baltic Centre for Contemporary Art, in Gateshead (formerly a flour mill).

PARKS AND GARDENS

A keen appreciation of country life and the pleasures of nature goes back to the Middle Ages when Royal Forests covered much of the land and every person of consequence had a deer park. It was in the 18C, however, that the face of lowland Britain was transformed in pursuit of the aesthetic ideals of the country's "greatest original contribution to the arts", the **English Landscape Movement**. Ruthlessly sweeping away the grand avenues, parterres and topiary of the previous century, the grandees and lesser gentry of the Georgian age, aided by professionals like **Lancelot "Capability" Brown** (1716-83) and **Humphry Repton** (1752-1818), swept away the boundaries separating house, garden and surrounding countryside to make ambitious compositions fusing buildings and statuary, lawns and woodland, lakes and rivers into a picturesque vision of idealised nature. The movement embraced the Ideal Theory of Art, where everyday objects were seen as imperfect copies of universal Ideas, for the artist to perfect. As well as their grander creations (Blenheim, Stourhead), there are many lesser achievements in the field of landscape beautification, which has bequeathed a national passion for landscaping and horticulture.

Britain has a wonderful heritage of gardens, many of which are open to visitors. Owing to the vagaries of the climate, particularly the closeness of the Gulf Stream, conditions have proved favourable to many of the plant collections brought back from all over the world, particularly in the 18C and 19C. The chief name in garden design in the late 19C and early 20C was Gertrude Jekyll (Knebworth and Broughton Castle), who often worked in collaboration with the architect Sir Edwin Lutyens.

Plant trials and serious **horticultural study** are conducted at Kew Gardens in London, at Wisley in Surrey, the gardens of the Royal Horticultural Society, at Harlow Carr and the Botanic Gardens in Edinburgh (17C) and Glasgow. A few of the earliest **medicinal gardens** are still in existence, such as the Botanic Gardens (1621) in Oxford and the Chelsea Physic Garden (1673) in London.

A Museum of **Garden History** occupies Lambeth parish church and graveyard, where John Tradescant, gardener to King Charles I, is buried. Examples of the early knot garden have been created here and at Hampton Court. Formal gardens with geometric layout can be seen at Hampton Court, Ham House and Pitmedden.

The most prevalent style is the famous English Landscape, promoted by Capability Brown and Humphry Repton – Stourhead and Castle Howard.

The art of **topiary** is practised at Levens Hall and Earlshall in Scotland. The vogue for follies, usually an artificial ruin at the end of a vista, produced Studley Royal which achieves its climax with a view of the ruins of Fountains Abbey.

Less contrived gardens incorporate the natural features of the site, such as **Glendurgan**, which occupies a deep combe on the Cornish coast.

Gardens range from the most southerly, Tresco **Abbey Gardens** in the Scilly Isles, created and maintained since 1834 by successive generations of the same family, to the most northerly, **Inverewe** in Wester Ross, where, despite the northern latitude, the gardens are frost-free, owing to the warm North Atlantic Drift. Sissinghurst and Crathes Castle are examples of themed gardens, where the different enclosures are distinguished by colour, season or plant species.

VERNACULAR ARCHITECTURE

CRUCK COTTAGE, HEREFORDSHIRE
Late medieval

The simplest form of timber construction, using the two halves of a massive, curving branch or tree-trunk

HOUSE AT CULROSS, SCOTLAND 16C

Crow-stepped gable

Rubble walls covered in rough cast ("harling") and colour-washed

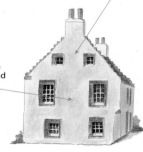

WEALDEN HOUSE, KENT c 1500

Upper floor jettied out

Hipped roof, originally thatched, now tiled

Close-studded vertical timbers

Smoke vent, later replaced by chimney stack

TIMBER-FRAMED HOUSE, Kent 17C

Timber frame clad in contrasting materials: upper floor with hung tiles, ground floor in weather-boarding

STONE COTTAGES, Gloucestershire

Built of oolithic limestone, possibly as a 14C monastic sheephouse and converted into cottages in 17C

Steep-pitched roof with graded stone slates

SEMI-DETACHED SUBURBAN HOUSES

Urban outskirts anywhere in Britain c 1930

Picturesque Arts and Crafts outline and detail. Contrasting treatment: pebble-dash on left, applied "half-timbering" on right

R. Corbel/MICHELIN

VERNACULAR ARCHITECTURE

From the end of the medieval period, relative peace meant that security was no longer paramount and the fortified castle gave way to the rural residence designed as a setting for artistic patronage, culture, the social round, field sports and farm management; each generation of the rich and powerful seeking to establish or consolidate its status by building or rebuilding in accord with architectural fashion.

It is however the everyday architecture of cottage, farmhouse and barn that expresses most strongly the individuality of particular places. The range of materials used is enormous, Every type of stone has been quarried and shaped, from the most intractable of Scottish and Cornish granites to the crumbling chalk of the south. Limestones are often exploited to wonderful effect, as in the **Cotswolds** or the **Yorkshire Wolds**. Where stone is lacking, timber is used as in the **cruck-built cottages** of Herefordshire and the elaborate half-timbered houses of much of the Midlands, or as **"weather-boarding"** cladding in the southeast. In the claylands, most villages once had their own brickfield, producing distinctive tiles as well as bricks, while reedbeds provided thatch for roofing.

Building forms vary too: from the solid **timber-frame** of a Kentish Tudor house to the humble one-roomed dwelling of a crofter in northwest Scotland.

Settlement patterns are also almost infinitely varied; a few cottages and farms may be loosely grouped to form a hamlet; elsewhere, true villages may predominate, street villages accompanying a road for part of its way, others cluster sociably around the green.

Architectural Terms

Aisle – lateral divisions running parallel with the nave in medieval churches and other buildings.

Ambulatory – passage between the choir and apse of a church.

Apse – rounded or polygonal end of a church.

Arcade – a series of arches, resting on piers or columns.

Architrave – the beam, or lowest portion of the entablature, extending from column to column. Also used as the moulded frame around the head and side of a window or door opening.

Baldachin – canopy supported by pillars set over an altar, throne or tomb.

Baptistery – building, separate from the church, containing the font.

Barbican – outwork of a medieval castle, often with a tower, defending a gate or bridge.

Barrel vaulting – continuous arched vault of semicircular section.

Battlements – parapet of medieval fortifications, with a walkway for archers or crossbowmen.

Broach spire – octagonal spire rising from a square tower without a parapets.

Buttress – vertical mass of masonry built against a wall, so strengthening it and resisting the outward pressure of a vaulted roof.

Capital – crowning feature of a column or pillar.

Chancel – part of the church set aside for clergy and choir, to the east of the nave.

Chantry chapel – chapel endowed for religious services for the soul of the founder.

Chapter-house – place of assembly for the governing body of a monastery or cathedral.

In medieval England, often multi-sided, with vaulting supported on a central pillar.

Chevron – Norman decoration of zig-zag mouldings used around windows and doorways.

Choir – western part of the chancel, used by the choir, immediately east of the screen separating nave and chancel.

Clerestory – upper storey of the nave of a church, generally pierced by a row of windows.

Corbel – stone bracket, often richly carved, projecting from a wall to support roof beams, the ribs of a vault, a statue or an oriel window.

Cornice – crowning projection, the upper part of the entablature in classical architecture. Also used for the projecting decoration around the ceiling of a room.

Crossing – central area of

a cruciform church, where the transepts cross the nave and choir. A tower is often set above this space.

Crypt – underground chamber beneath a church, used as place of burial or charnel-houses. They often also housed the bones or relics of a saint or martyr.

Cupola – hemispherical roof.

Drum – vertical walling supporting a dome, sometimes with windows.

Embrasure – the space between two merlons, on a battlement, through which archers could fire, whilst protected by the merlons.

Entablature – in classical architecture, the entire portion above the columns, comprising architrave, frieze and cornice.

Fan vaulting – system of vaulting peculiar to English Perpendicular architecture, all ribs having the same curve, resembling the framework of a fan.

Finial – top or finishing portion of a pinnacle, gable, bench end or other feature.

Fluting – narrow concave channelling cut vertically on a shaft or column.

Flying buttress – external arch springing over the roof of an aisle and supporting the clerestory wall, counteracting the thrust of the nave vault.

Frieze – central division of the entablature – horizontal decorative design at high level.

Gable – triangular end section of a wall of a building, enclosed by the line of the roof.

Hammerbeam roof – late Gothic form of roof construction with no tie-beam. Wooden arches rest on corbels and beams bracketed to the walls and eaves.

Harling – wall plastered with roughcast. Often painted or with colour incorporated.

Jamb – upright side of a window or door opening.

Keep – inner tower and strongest part of a medieval fortress.

Keystone – central, wedge-shaped stone which locks an arch together.

Lancet – Early English (13C) sharp-pointed arch.

Lantern – glazed construction, for ventilation and light, often surmounting a dome.

Lierne – short intermediate rib in Gothic vaulting.

Loggia – open-sided gallery or arcade.

Machicolation – in medieval military architecture, a row of openings below a projecting parapet through which missiles could be rained down on the enemy.

Misericord – tip-up seat in choir stalls, with a small projection on the underside, to support a person having to stand through a long service. Often fancifully and grotesquely carved.

Mullions – vertical ribs dividing a window into a number of lights.

Narthex – western portico at the entrance to early Christian churches.

Nave – central main body of a church, west of the choir, into which lay persons were admitted, chancel and choir being reserved for the priests.

Ogee – arch used in late Gothic period, combining convex and concave curve, ending in a point.

Oriel – window projecting from a wall on corbels.

Pediment – triangular termination above the entablature, in classical architecture sometimes "broken" in Renaissance designs.

Pilaster – rectangular pillar, projecting from the wall.

Rose window circular window with mullions converging like the spokes of a wheel.

Screen – partition, often richly carved, separating nave from choir and chancel.

Spandrel – triangular space between the curves of arches and the frame in which they are set.

Squinch – arch placed diagonally across the internal corner angles of a square tower, converting the square into an octagonal form.

Tierceron – secondary rib in Gothic vaulting.

Transept – arms of a cruciform church set at right angles to nave and choir.

Transom – horizontal cross-bar or division of a window.

Tympanum – space between the flat lintel and the arch of a doorway.

Undercroft – vaulted chamber partly or wholly below ground, in a medieval building.

Volute – spiral scroll used at the corners of Ionic, Corinthian and Composite capitals.

SCULPTURE

The idea of erecting statues, in stone and bronze, introduced largely by the Romans, fell into disuse in Britain in the Dark Ages. Gradually, however, pagan influences and Celtic scroll-work were put to Christian service, in standing crosses and in church decoration. Massive carving in Norman churches gave way to glorious tracery, windows, ribs and vaults in Early English and Perpendicular churches and cathedrals, complemented by carved wooden misericords, bench ends, altar screens and font covers. Impressive statuary such as that on the west front of Wells Cathedral has survived Reformation and Puritan depredations, to give an idea of the skills of early craftsmen.

Until the early 18C, statuary tended to be confined to tombs and memorials. The fashion for portrait busts was introduced by those who made the "Grand Tour" of Europe.

First Classical and then Baroque memorials began to grace both cathedrals and churches in the flowering of British sculpture which took place between 1720 and 1840. In the Victorian age in many towns and cities statues were erected to the memory of industrialists and benefactors, municipal worthies and military heroes. There are also some very fine sculpted memorials executed in commemoration of those who died in battle. In the 20C British sculpture has been enlivened by the sometimes controversial works of **Jacob Epstein** and also of **Henry Moore**, whose technique of "natural carving" allowed the grain and shape of the material to dictate the final form. **Barbara Hepworth**, who settled in St Ives in 1943, **Reg Butler** and **Kenneth Armitage** are among other famous modern sculptors.

Monumental sculptures by Jacob Epstein, Eric Gill, Frank Dobson, Henry Moore, Barbara Hepworth and Eduardo Paolozzi among others set the standard for public art in cities, by the sea and in the countryside. Spectacular modern schemes – Broadgate in London, Herne Bay Sculpture Park, Brighton seafront, sculpture at Goodwood near Chichester, Stour Valley Art Project, Yorkshire Sculpture Park, the Gateshead Riverside Sculpture Park, the Northern Arts Project, Glenrothes in Scotland – have inspired major artists to create large-scale outdoor sculptures and promote interest in art in a wider public.

On the contemporary scene the trend is a break with the past as many artists (Damien Hirst, Anish Kapoor, Richard Deacon, Cornelia Parker, Tracey Emin, Alison Wilding, Stephen Hughes, Tony Cragg, Rachel Whiteread among others) invent new idioms which are sometimes provocative. The Turner Prize awarded by the Tate Gallery is often controversial. Installations engaging the viewer's preconceptions are increasingly popular.

PAINTING
Early Art

The Celtic peoples loved rhythm and curvilinear scroll patterns, which they used in jewellery and later in manuscripts. The Romans brought their wall paintings and mosaics and both later inspired the didactic medieval church murals, which are some of Britain's earliest paintings. Surviving painting from the Saxon and medieval periods consists largely of exquisite work on illuminated manuscripts, such as the **Lindisfarne Gospels** from Holy Island, though the drawings of **Matthew Paris** are notable departures from this stylised work. One of the earliest surviving English paintings is the **Wilton Diptych** (c. 1400), now in the National Gallery.

16C-18C

British artists never enjoyed that scale of patronage given to European artists by absolute monarchs and the Papacy. Much early portraiture, other than the **Holbein** pictures of Henry VIII and his court, tend to be flat and stiff but the art of the miniature flourished at the court of Elizabeth, where **Nicholas Hilliard** and **Isaac Oliver** created their masterpieces, capturing both the likeness and something of the spirit of the sitters.

The Dutchman **Sir Anthony van Dyck**, knighted by Charles I, enjoyed his patronage and was the first to record

Detail of Marriage A-la-Mode: 1, The Marriage Settlement (c. 1743) by William Hogarth, The National Gallery

Photo Art Media/HIP/Scala, Florence

the atmosphere of the Stuart Court, in full size paintings, before the Civil War. Canaletto, a Venetian, enjoyed some aristocratic support in the 1740s, as did **Sir Peter Lely** and **Godfrey Kneller,** both of German origin, who worked in England for long enough to be considered founders of the English portrait painting school. **William Hogarth,** English-born and bred, famous for his vivid commentaries on the life of his day, started the idea of public exhibitions of painting, leading ultimately to the founding in 1768 of the **Royal Academy. Sir Joshua Reynolds,** its first President, and his contemporary, **Thomas Gainsborough,** raised the status of English painting, especially portraiture, though it was still much influenced by Dutch and Italian example. **Richard Wilson,** a founder of the Royal Academy, was much inspired by the French masters, Claude and Poussin, and founded the English school of **landscape painting,** a fashion which developed in England and spread to include marine scenes as well as country houses and estates.

19C TRENDS

The visionary, **William Blake,** heralded the dawn of English Romanticism. Portraiture by **Sir Thomas Lawrence** and the works of **Sir Henry Raeburn** in Scotland added **Romanticism** to the traditions of Reynolds.

John Crome founded the Norwich School in 1803, a regional treatment of landscape painting which was uniquely English. It was continued after his death by **John Sell Cotman. John Constable** and **Joseph MW Turner** carried this tradition and its studies of the effects of ever-changing light into the 19C. From 1840 to 1850 **Dante Gabriel Rossetti's** group, the **Pre-Raphaelites** and **Sir Edward Burne-Jones**, made a short-lived return to primitive values and religious and moral subjects. Their designs inspired Art Nouveau, best expressed in England by the work of **William Morris** and **Aubrey Beardsley.**

Alfred Sisley, born in Paris of English parents, was an Impressionist whose sense of colour and tone owed much to the founder of the movement, Claude Monet, with whom he painted *en plein air* in France. The **Camden Town Group,** around **Walter Sickert,** returned to the realism of the Post-Impressionists, whose work **Roger Fry** had exhibited in 1911 and the next 20 years saw many short-lived and loose "movements" such as the **Bloomsbury Group. Augustus John** was known for his fashionable portraits in an almost Impressionist style.

20C

Post-war artists include **Paul Nash** (landscapes infused with symbolism); **Graham Sutherland**, painter of religious themes, landscapes and portraits; **Sir Stanley Spencer** who painted Biblical scenes in familiar British settings.

In the 1950s **Ben Nicholson** was the major abstract artist. The optimistic 1960s brought Pop Art: **Peter Blake, David Hockney, Bridget Riley** ("op art"). The portraits and figures of **Francis Bacon** and **Lucian Freud** show a darker, more pessimistic outlook.

Contemporary artists who have won acclaim include Gilbert and George, Paula Rego, Beryl Cooke, Ken Currie, Adrian Wizniewski, Stephen Conroy, Peter Howson, Lisa Milroy, Richard Wentworth, Julian Opie, Damien Hirst among others.

The Goldsmith College of Art and the Glasgow School of Art are two of the well-known educational establishments which nurture young talent.

Hirst himself was partially responsible for founding The Young British Art group (Angela Bulloch, Michael Landy, Gary Hume etc), the country's most recent art phenomenon. Their work is still championed by the Saatchi Gallery, though many YBAs have now been assimilated into the mainstream.

MUSIC
FROM POLYPHONY TO INSTRUMENTAL COMPOSITION

As with painting and sculpture, early and medieval English music was largely inspired by religion. The **Chapel Royal** – an institution, not a building – has fostered English music since 1135. **Thomas Tallis** (c 1505-85), organist at Waltham Abbey near London (until it was dissolved) and later at Queen Elizabeth's Chapel Royal, can be credited with beginning the particularly rich tradition of **church music** for which England is famous. He arranged the harmony for the plainsong responses of Merbecke's English church service (Festal Responses in four and five parts) which are still widely in use and also arranged a setting of the Canticles in Dorian Mode, composed numerous anthems, Latin mass settings, lamentations and motets, of which his most famous is the magnificent *Spem in Alium* for forty voices, and of course his equally famous Canon (c 1567). Together with **William Byrd** (1542/3-1623), himself a prolific composer of high quality church music with whom Tallis was joint organist at the Chapel Royal, he was granted a monopoly on music printing in England (1575).

From the end of the 16C to c. 1630, **madrigals**, originally an Italian form, with amorous or satirical themes, were being produced in large numbers by English composers, such as Byrd and **John Dowland** (1562-1626), a talented lute player. Folk music dating back much further accompanied the country dance, which survives today as the **Morris Dance**. Composers such as Byrd and **Thomas Morley** (1557-1602), who wrote settings for several of Shakespeare's plays, spread music into the theatre. **John Bull** (1562-1628), a skilled performer and composer for the virginals, ranks for many as one of the founders of the English keyboard repertoire. He is also sometimes linked with the original tune for *God Save The Queen*. **Ben Jonson** (1573-1637) and **Henry Lawes** (1596-1662) among others were leading exponents of the **masque**, which became popular in the 17C, combining music, dance and pageantry.

Orlando Gibbons (1583-1625), organist of the Chapel Royal under James I and one of the finest keyboard players of his day, wrote quantities of superb church music, madrigals and music for viols and virginals. **Henry Purcell** (1659-95), considered the greatest British composer of his generation (and by some of all time), wrote much splendid church music, stage music (opera *Dido and Æneas*), music for State occasions and harpsichord and chamber music.

MUSIC APPLIED TO DRAMA

Chamber music (music not intended for church, theatre or public concert room) truly came into its own in the 18C, which also saw great strides taken in the development of English **opera** and the emergence of a new form, the **oratorio**, under the German-English composer **George Frideric Handel** (1685-1759), perhaps its greatest exponent. His vast output included more than 40 operas, 20 or so oratorios, cantatas, sacred music, and numerous orchestral, choral and instrumental works. In 1719-28 the **Royal Academy of Music** was founded as an operatic organisation linked with Handel. The following century (1822) it became an educational institution, later to be joined by the Royal College of Music (1883) and the Royal School of Church Music (1927).

POST-ROMANTICISM AND THE MODERN AGE

The composer Thomas Arne (1710-78) set to music the words of James Thomson, *Rule Britannia,* in a masque for Alfred, Prince of Wales in 1740. The late 18C to early 19C was rather a fallow period for Britain in terms of musical composition, although the Romantic movement that swept through Europe made itself felt in other arts such as literature (Wordsworth, Coleridge, Scott), and Romantic song cycles were fashionable with the British public in the 19C.

The next British composer of note was **Sir Edward Elgar** (1857-1934), the first to win international acclaim in almost 200 years. His love of the English countryside (he lived near the Malvern Hills) shaped his music, which is infused with an Englishness that captures the spirit of a nation in its heyday as a world power. Works such as *The Enigma Variations* and *The Dream of Gerontius* placed him on the world stage, and his many orchestral works exhibit the composer's masterly orchestration (Symphonies in A flat and E flat, Cello Concerto). **Frederick Delius** (1862-1934), championed by the conductor Sir Thomas Beecham, composed orchestral variations, rhapsodies, concerti and a variety of other orchestral and choral works stamped with his very individual, chromatic approach to harmony. The compositions of **Ralph Vaughan Williams** (1872-1958) were influenced by his study of English folk

songs and Tudor church music; throughout his life he took an active interest in popular movements in music. **Gustav Holst** (1874-1934), prevented from becoming a concert pianist by neuritis in his hand, studied music at the Royal College of Music under Sir Charles Villiers Stanford (1852-1924), an Irish composer of church music and choral works. Holst, an ardent socialist, influenced by his love of the works of Grieg and Wagner as well as a certain innate mysticism, produced his most famous work, the seven-movement orchestral suite *The Planets*, in 1914-16.

Sir William Walton (1902-83) rose to fame with his instrumental settings of poems by Edith Sitwell (*Façade*, 1923) and went on to compose symphonies, concerti, opera, the Biblical cantata *Belshazzar's Feast* and film music (Laurence Olivier's *Henry V, Hamlet* and *Richard III*).

Sir Michael Tippett (1905-98) won recognition with his oratorio *A Child of Our Time,* reflecting the unrest of the 1930s and 1940s, and went on to produce a rich and varied output, including operas *(The Midsummer Marriage, King Priam),* symphonies and other orchestral works in which he exhibits formidable powers of imagination and invention, combining inspiration from earlier sources such as Purcell with his interest in popular modern music such as blues and jazz.

Sir Benjamin Britten (1913-76) studied under John Ireland (1879-1962) at the Royal College of Music and after a couple of years in the USA returned to England where he produced mainly vocal or choral works (one exception being his *Variations and Fugue on a Theme of Purcell,* or *Young Person's Guide to the Orchestra)*, notably the operas *Peter Grimes, Billy Budd* and *A Midsummer Night's Dream, A Ceremony of Carols* and the immensely moving *War Requiem.*

John Tavener (b. 1944), whose haunting *Song for Athene* ended the funeral service of Diana, Princess of Wales, at Westminster Abbey in September 1997, draws the inspiration for his predominantly religious music from his Russian Orthodox faith.

Still popular since their inception by **Sir Henry Wood** (1869-1944) in 1895 are the **Promenade Concerts,** which are held at the Royal Albert Hall every summer *(mid-July to mid-September).* The chorus *Jerusalem* sung as an unofficial anthem at the end of each season of Promenade concerts is perhaps the best known work of Sir Hubert Parry (1848-1918). Conductors and composers such as Sir Peter Maxwell Davies, Sir Neville Mariner, Sir John Eliot Gardner, Sir Colin Davis, Sir Simon Rattle, Christopher Hogwood and Andrew Davies ensure the continuation of healthy and creative British music.

Eisteddfods in Wales and Mods in Scotland carry on a tradition of the Celtic bards. Festivals, such as the **Three Choirs** at Hereford, Worcester and Gloucester Cathedrals and – in completely different spheres – opera productions at **Glyndebourne** and the **English National Opera** contribute to the aim of maintaining public interest in live classical music. However, Glyndebourne remains the reserve of the rich, while opera is usually targeted at the wealthy middle and upper classes.

CODA

On a lighter note, the meeting in 1875 of **Sir William Gilbert** (1836-1911) and **Sir Arthur Sullivan** (1842-1900) produced an enduring and well-loved English musical tradition in the form of "Gilbert and Sullivan" operas, staged by Richard D'Oyly Carte. **Musical comedy,** an English development of the European operetta, was born in the 1890s at the Gaiety Theatre in London, with shows like *The Gaiety Girl.*

Another typically British institution, the **music hall**, also became popular – variety entertainment with the audience being able to eat and drink while watching the performance. Two names, **Ivor Novello** (1893-1951) and **Sir Noël Coward** (1899-1973), will always be associated with British musical comedy between the World Wars. The tradition of British musicals has since been continued most notably by **Sir Andrew Lloyd Webber** (b. 1948).

POP AND ROCK

British Pop Music began in the 1950s with early pioneers being **Lonnie Donegan** with his skiffle sound and a very youthful **Cliff Richard** doing his best to be the British Elvis Presley. It was the **Beatles** however who did more than any band to bring the new genre of "popular music" to the fore. Their first chart hit was in 1962 and they broke up in 1969. During that short but explosive period of incredible creativity, their influence on British and world pop and rock music was incalculable and reverberates around concert halls and in recording studios even today. They spawned a whole "Liverpool Sound" though the Beatles' most famous contemporaries are the equally iconic **Rolling Stones** (from London), still touring and recording today. The 1960s closed to the sound of **Black Sabbath**, **Deep Purple** and **Led Zeppelin** – heavyweights, who were to rule the burgeoning rock music scene for much of the decade until the advent of punk rock in 1977, led most (in)famously by the **Sex Pistols**. The 1980s saw the dance and club scene take off and the rise of Manchester bands such as **The Smiths**, **Stone Roses** and **Happy Mondays**. The decade is best remembered for its frothy pop and pop-soul sounds however, typified by **Wham** (featuring George Michael), **Culture Club** (Boy George) and **Simply Red**. The 1990s was the era of Britpop, most famously **Blur** and **Oasis**; both quintessentially English bands drawing heavily on 1960s influences. It was also the decade of "boy bands" (**Take That**, **Westlife**, **Blue**) and "girl bands" (**The Spice Girls**, **All Saints**) a vocals-only genre which continues to defy critical disdain and sells millions of albums well into the 21C. Since 2000 television talent shows such as *Pop Idol* and *The X Factor* have "manufactured" Britain's cheesiest pop stars such as **Will Young**, **Gareth Gates** and **Leona Lewis**. Bands such as **Coldplay** and **Radiohead** maintain mainstream British rock. **Dizzee Rascal** leads the local hip-hop and 'grime' scene, while **Amy Winehouse** and **Pete Doherty** are tabloid rehab favourites.

LITERATURE

MIDDLE AGES

Geoffrey Chaucer (c. 1340-1400), the first great English poet, was influential in the evolution of "standard" English from cruder medieval dialects. The language of the *Canterbury Tales* is consequently as recognisable to us today as are Chaucer's vividly etched characters. **William Langland** (c 1330-1400) in the *Vision of Piers Plowman*, and **Sir Thomas Malory** (d. 1471) in *Le Morte D'Arthur* also brought a new depth and expressiveness to literature.

THE ENGLISH RENAISSANCE AND THE ELIZABETHAN AGE

The sonnet was introduced and blank verse became the regular measure of English dramatic and epic poetry. The supreme achievement of this dynamic, expansive period was in the theatre. Ambitious dramatic forms developed by the fiery **Christopher Marlowe** (1564-94) were perfected by the genius of **William Shakespeare** (1564-1616), the greatest dramatist and poet of this or any age. His monumental 37 plays appealed to all classes. **Ben Jonson** (1572-1637) created the English comedy of humours.

SEVENTEENTH CENTURY

John Donne (1572-1631), courtier, soldier and latterly Dean of St Paul's, was the most important of the Metaphysical poets whose "witty conceits" were concerned with the interaction between soul and body, sensuality and spirit. **John Milton** (1608-74), after Shakespeare arguably England's greatest poet, was also a powerful pamphleteer for the Puritan cause. He overcame blindness and political disappointment to write his epic masterpiece *Paradise Lost*, concerning the Judeo-Christian story of the Fall of Man, in 1667.

Puritan control was responsible for closing the theatres for nearly 20 years until the Restoration of Charles II in 1660. Restoration drama primarily reflected the licentiousness of the Court by the use of broad satire, farce, wit and bawdy comedy.

In prose, the language of the Bible exerted a strong influence, most notably in the work of **John Bunyan** (1628-88) whose *Pilgrim's Progress* was more widely read than any book in English except the Bible itself. The diaries of **John Evelyn** (1620-1706) and **Samuel Pepys** (1633-1703) detailed the minutiae of everyday life at the time.

EIGHTEENTH CENTURY

The early development of the novel is probably best exemplified in the work of Daniel Defoe (1660-1731). While his *Journal of the Plague Year* is a lively but primarily factual piece of journalism, *Robinson Crusoe*, though it utilises similar reporting techniques, is entirely fiction. Defoe's style was imitated and developed by **Samuel Richardson** (1689-1761), **Henry Fielding** (1707-54) and **Laurence Sterne** (1713-68) .

The rise of the novel, the newspaper) and the expansion of a newly literate middle class were part of the Age of Reason. **Alexander Pope** (1688-1744), the finest satirical poet of the time, was matched in both poetry and prose by **Jonathan Swift** (1667-1745), famous for the incisive political and social satire of *Gulliver's Travels*. The era was dominated, however, by the influence of **Samuel Johnson** (1709-84), the subject of Boswell's famous biography and author of the first *English Dictionary* in 1755.

NINETEENTH CENTURY

The French Revolution was a primary inspiration for the Romantic movement, which stressed intensity of emotion and freedom of expression. This rebellious spirit was epitomised in the life of **Lord Byron** (1788-1824) though perhaps a better representative of Romantic poetry is **William Wordsworth** (1770-1850), whose best poems reflect his belief that intense joy could arise from deep harmony with Nature. **Percy Bysshe Shelley** (1792-1822) wrote more directly of the power of joy as a reforming influence, while the intense, lyrical verse of **John Keats** (1795-1821) stressed the power of beauty. Though

Charles Dickens

© UPPA/Photoshot

lyricism, nature and the exotic continued to attract Victorian poets such as **Robert Browning** (1812-89), faith in joy and the senses waned and the verse of **Alfred, Lord Tennyson** (1809-1902) is noble but sombre.

The novel, meanwhile, had continued to develop in range and appeal from the carefully structured domestic comedies of **Jane Austen** (1775-1817) to the more popular, if less deep, historical novels of her contemporary, **Sir Walter Scott** (1771-1832). Popular too were Scott's Victorian successors, **William Makepeace Thackeray** (1811-63), **Anthony Trollope** (1815-82) and, above all, **Charles Dickens** (1812-70), whose sentimental but funny and sometimes despairing vision of city life in the Industrial Revolution struck a sharp chord with the reading public. Mary Ann Evans (1819-80), under the pseudonym **George Eliot,** wrote realistic works about the problems of the provincial middle class. The **Brontë** sisters, **Charlotte** (1816-55) and **Emily** (1818-48), took inspiration from their upbringing on the wild moors of Yorkshire to write their respective masterpieces, *Jane Eyre* (1846) and *Wuthering Heights* (1847). Most important of the writers of the century is **Thomas Hardy** (1840-1928), whose novels express a passion for man's tragic involvement in Nature and estrangement from it.

Influenced by the new drama in Europe, **George Bernard Shaw** (1856-1950) brought a new purpose and seriousness to the English theatre which had, for nearly two centuries, failed to find a clear direction. The witty comedies of **Oscar Wilde** (1854-1900) were less profound but equally well crafted. They reflected the aims of the Decadent movement which stressed flagrantly amoral beauty – a direct reaction against Victorian moral earnestness.

Twentieth Century

The early modern masters of the **novel – Henry James** (1843-1916), **Joseph Conrad** (1857-1924) and **EM Forster** (1879-1970) – were still working in a recognisably Victorian tradition. The Dubliner **James Joyce** (1882-1941) used the stream-of-consciousness technique in the highly experimental *Ulysses* (1922) and *Finnegans Wake* (1939). This insistent excavation of personal experience is also found in the very different novels of **Virginia Woolf** (1882-1941) and of **DH Lawrence** (1885-1930) who challenged the taboos of class and sex, particularly in his novel *Lady Chatterley's Lover.* Concurrent with the serious "literary" novel, there developed a growing market for lighter fiction – entertainments – to serve the needs of an increasingly literate public; from the adventure novels of **Robert Louis Stevenson** (1850-94) and the *Sherlock Holmes* stories of **Arthur Conan Doyle** (1859-1930) to the spy thrillers of John Le Carré and Len Deighton in our own time. **George Orwell's** (1903-59) dark political novels *(Animal Farm, 1984)* condemned the evils of communism.

Throughout the century there have been a number of important and stylish writers – less iconoclastic than their more innovative peers – who have continued to work with more traditional subjects and themes. The novelists **Aldous Huxley** (1894-1963), **Evelyn Waugh** (1903-66), and **Graham Greene** (1904-91) achieved considerable critical as well as commercial success, while **Somerset Maugham** (1874-1965) and **JB Priestley** (1894-1984) triumphed equally as playwrights and novelists.

The novel has, in all its forms, become the dominant vehicle of literary expression in the modern age. Eminent contemporary writers range from Anthony Powell (A Dance to the Music of Time); Paul Scott (1920-78, The Raj Quartet, Staying On); **Anthony Burgess** (A Clockwork Orange and Earthly Powers); Lawrence Durrell (Alexandria Quartet (1957); William Golding, Lord of the Flies (1954) and Rites of Passage (1980), studies of human behaviour; Iris Murdoch (1919-99; Under the Net; The Sea, The Sea) which deal with complex psychological issues; John Fowles' haunting stories (The French Lieutenant's Woman, The Magus). Doris Lessing (The Golden Notebook), Muriel Spark (The Prime of Miss Jean Brodie), **Daphne du Maurier** (Rebecca, Jamaica Inn) and Olivia Manning (The Balkan Trilogy) are also distinguished authors.

Among the new generation of writers who have won acclaim are **Martin Amis** (London Fields, The Information), Julian Barnes (The History of the World in 10 1/2 chapters), JG Ballard (The Empire of the Sun, Crash, Cocaine Nights), Angela Carter (Wise Children, The Magic Toyshop), AS Byatt (Possession), Anita Brookner (Hotel du Lac), Beryl Bainbridge (Every Man for Himself), Jeanette Winterson (Oranges Are Not the Only Fruit), Graham Swift (Last Orders), Pat Barker (Regeneration Trilogy), Irvine Welsh (Trainspotting).

J K Rowling almost single-handedly revived the children's adventure story (in the process becoming richer than the Queen) and introduced a new generation of children to reading with her record-breaking Harry Potter series.

The English language tradition is enriched by writers from the Commonwealth and other countries who bring different perceptions: VS Naipaul, Caryl Phillips from the Carribean, Nadine Gordimer, André Brink, JM Coetzee, Ben Okri from Africa; Peter Carey, Thomas Keneally, JG Ballard from Australia, Keri Hume from New Zealand, **Salman Rushdie**, Vikram Seth, Arundhati Roy from the Indian sub-continent and Kazuo Ishiguro from Japan.

Poetry, comparatively speaking, is less widely read than in previous times. The Romantic decadence of the early 20C was swept aside by the modernist poets **Ezra Pound** (1885-1972) and **TS Eliot** (1888-1965) whose The Waste Land (1922) is a dense and highly literary meditation on the situation of modern man. Less dramatically modern but equally influential was the slightly earlier poetry of **Thomas Hardy** and **WB Yeats** (1865-1939). The poets of the First World War, particularly **Wilfred Owen** (1893-1918) and **Siegfried Sassoon** (1886-1967), voiced their horror of mass warfare. **WH Auden** (1907-73) led a prominent group of intellectual left-wing poets in the 1920s and the exuberant imagery and lyrical rhetoric of **Dylan Thomas** (1914-53) caught the public's imagination. Only **John Betjeman** (1906-84), has achieved comparable popularity in recent times. Philip Larkin (1922-91) was the leading figure of the group known as the Movement; the cool tone and tight form of his poetry expressing his melancholy sensibilities was in reaction to the romantic excesses of the 1940s. Poet Laureate Ted Hughes (1930-98), known for his violent and symbolic nature poems, is one of the most influential contemporary poets alongside Tom Paulin, Andrew Motion, Roger McGough, Benjamin Zephaniah, Carol Ann Duffy, Wendy Cope, and Helen Dunmore.

The **theatre** of the first half of the century was dominated by well-crafted "traditional" plays and the sophisticated comedies of Noël Coward. In the 1950s The Theatre of the Absurd, which saw man as a helpless creature in a meaningless universe, was explored by the Irish writer **Samuel Beckett** (1906-89). Later in the decade, disillusionment with contemporary Britain was vented by **John Osborne** (1929-94) in his play Look Back In Anger. The pithy "comedies of menace" by **Harold Pinter** (1930-2008) and the socialist plays of writers such as **Arnold Wesker** (b. 1932) subsequently led to the development of a diverse and challenging contemporary theatre. Trenchant plays by Edward Bond, Peter Shaffer, Alan Ayckbourn, David Hare and Tom Stoppard are still stalwarts in the British theatre season with strong attendance.

Nature

The exceptionally diverse geological foundation of Britain has given rise to landscapes of great variety, a natural heritage enhanced by a continuous human presence over several millennia which has shaped and reshaped the material to form the present uniquely rich pattern of fields and fells, woods and parks, villages and farmsteads. Celebrated in literature and art, this densely textured landscape, usually domesticated but with its wilder beauties too, has become a kind of national emblem, lived in lovingly and vigorously defended against change by its inhabitants.

LANDSCAPE

The country can be broadly divided into **Upland** and **Lowland** Britain. The former, generally of older, harder material, comprises much of the north and southwest of England and virtually the whole of Wales and Scotland. As well as rolling, open moorlands, where the eye ranges freely over vast expanses of coarse grass, bracken or heather, there are mountain chains, modest in elevation but exhibiting most of the features of much higher and more extensive systems, attracting serious climbers as well as walkers.

To the south and east the gentler relief of Lowland Britain is mostly composed of less resistant material. Much is "scarp and vale" country where undulating chalk and limestone hills terminate in steep escarpments commanding grand panoramas over broad clay vales.

Most of the course of the Earth's history can be traced in these landscapes. From the unimaginably distant Pre-Cambrian, more than 600 million years ago, came the Torridonian sandstone and Lewisian gneiss of northwest Scotland as well as the compact, isolated uplands of Charnwood Forest in Leicestershire and the Malvern Hills in Worcestershire. The violent volcanic activity of Ordovician times left the shales and slates of **Snowdonia** and the **Lake District.** Extreme pressure

from the southeast in the Caledonian mountain-building period produced the northeast/southwest "grain" of ridges and valleys so evident in much of Wales and Scotland. Most of the abundant reserves of coal originated in the tropical vegetation of Carboniferous times. Except for the extreme south, the whole country was affected by the action of the often immensely thick ice sheets of the series of Ice Ages. The characteristically sculpted forms of the high mountains testify to the great power of the glaciers as they advanced and retreated, eroding and transporting vast quantities of material, much of which was spread over the lowlands by the mighty ancestors of today's rivers. As the last of the ice melted, the sea level rose, the land bridge joining Britain to the continent of Europe was flooded, and a truncated **Thames**, hitherto a tributary of the Rhine, acquired its own outlet to the sea.

DOMESTICATION

The taming and settling of the landscape can be traced back to the fifth millennium BC when Neolithic farmers began to clear the wildwood, the dense forests which had spread northwards in the wake of the retreating ice. The imprint of each succeeding age may be traced, not only in the obvious features of prehistoric stone circles, burial mounds and hill-forts, the planned network of Roman roads or the countless medieval churches, but also in the everyday fabric of the working countryside, where a track may first have been trodden in the Bronze Age or a hedge planted by Saxon settlers.

The many-layered landscape is now characterised by **enclosure**, a web of fields bounded by hedges in the lowlands, by drystone walls in the uplands and by dykes in areas reclaimed from the sea. Small fields with irregular boundaries are likely to be ancient in origin; a regular chequer-board of hawthorn hedges is the result of agricultural "Improvement" in the 18C and 19C.

In spite of conditions which are ideal for tree growth, only eight per cent of

National Parks

👆 *See the Discovering section.*
Britain's 15 National Parks comprise the Brecon Beacons, the Broads (Norfolk and Suffolk), Cairngorms, Dartmoor, Exmoor, Lake District, Loch Lomond, New Forest, North York Moors, Northumberland, Peak District, Pembrokeshire Coast, Snowdonia, South Downs, Yorkshire Dales. These comprise the finest upland scenery in England and Wales, much of it farmed and in private ownership, controlled and managed by each National Park authority to conserve the characteristic landscape and make it accessible to the public.

The first National Park was established in 1951 to preserve the distinctive characteristics of certain rural areas of England and Wales. The scheme was not extended to Scotland where the law of trespass was different, enabling people to walk where they wished provided they did no damage.

For more information visit www.nationalparks.gov.uk.

the land surface is wooded. About half of this consists of recent coniferous plantations, mostly in the uplands. In many parts of the lowlands, the lack of great forests is compensated for by an abundance of small woods and by the countless individual trees growing in parks and gardens, and above all, in the hedgerows.

Standing out from this orderly pattern are the "commons", rough open tracts of grass and scrub. Once the villager's source of fodder, food and game, they now provide fresh air and exercise for both town and country people.

The country is well-watered. The abundant rainfall, carried off the hills by a multitude of streams, feeds the rivers which, though of no great length, often end in splendid estuaries which bring salt water and the feel of the sea far inland.

The irregular outline of the country and the complex geology combine to form a long and varied coastline. Where the mountains meet the sea there is exceptionally fine coastal scenery, such as the spectacular chalk-white cliffs near Dover, symbol of English insularity. Many of the better stretches of sand and shingle have been appropriated by seaside resorts but there are some quieter beaches as well as remote marshlands and lonely sand dunes.

Seven Sisters, East Sussex
©Edmund Nägele/Pictures Colour Library

London is the commercial, political and artistic capital of the United Kingdom, and one of the great financial centres of the world. One city plays several roles, and has twin centres; the City of London, known as The City, for trade and commerce; and the City of Westminster, incorporating the West End, for royal palaces and parliament, theatres, entertainment, art and fashion.

A Bit of History

The City of London began to take shape under the Romans, who made it the hub of their road system. They enclosed it with walls and built the first London Bridge. Remains of the Roman walls, together with medieval additions, are still visible on the street called London Wall and near the Tower of London.

It was Edward the Confessor (1042–66) who established the rival centre at Westminster, when he built a royal palace and founded an abbey, its minster in the west, as opposed to St Paul's Cathedral, its minster in the east.

In fact London did not become the official capital of England until the mid-12C, taking over from Winchester. The City and its busy port gained considerable freedom and independence from the crown, which was often dependent on City merchants for raising money for military expeditions. The great houses of the nobility lined the Strand along the north bank of the Thames, while merchants built elegant mansions in the less crowded West End, or nearby villages like Islington, Holborn and Chelsea.

Overcrowding was somewhat reduced by the ravages of the Great Plague (1665), in which 75,000 out of 460,000 people died, and of the Great Fire (1666), which destroyed 80 per cent of the buildings. Within six days of the end of the fire, Christopher Wren, then 33 years old, submitted a plan to rebuild the city with broad straight streets. It was rejected, though Wren was commissioned to build the new St Paul's Cathedral and the majority of the city's churches.

As the population continued to expand, poor-quality housing proliferated, accompanied by limited investment in sanitation. The appalling conditions of the 18C are strikingly illustrated in the work of William Hogarth. Charles Dickens continued to document the poverty and dreadful living conditions well into the 19C. Eventually in 1855 the Government established the Metropolitan Board of Works, a central body with special responsibility for mains sewerage and the tide of filth began to turn.

Destruction was to again play a role in the modernisation of the city when the piles of rubble left by German bombers during the The Blitz of 1944 provided opportunities for modern and imaginative re-development such as the arts centres at the South Bank Arts Centre, and the Barbican.

Population: 6,679,699.

Michelin Map: Michelin Atlas p19-21 and map 504 T 29.

Info: For tourist information, see the Address Book.

Location: Most sightseeing and tourist activities are confined to Westminster, the West End and Kensington. The Underground is the most effective way of getting around town, though buses will allow you to see more. Taxis are expensive. Always catch a licensed taxi cab. Short distances are best covered on foot. There are various bus sightseeing tours, of which The Big Bus Company (℘020 7233 9533; www.bigbustours. com) is among the best. Buses run throughout the UK from Victoria coach station, a short walk from Victoria underground station and Buckingham Palace. Trains run from:

London Today

The City remains a financial powerhouse, thronged with pin-striped suits by day but deserted by night and on weekends. Its itinerant citizens almost all commute to the suburbs or much farther afield. The rest of London, and particularly the West End, is lively at all hours – by day with shoppers and office workers and by night with people going to the theatres, pubs, restaurants and nightclubs .

London has grown organically over the centuries absorbing other towns and villages as it sprawls ever outwards. Most Londoners live in the old belt of "villages" (such as Hampstead, Chiswick, Kensington or Chelsea) which have retained their own character.

The cosmopolitan atmosphere of London has been greatly reinforced in the latter half of the 20C by easier foreign travel, higher standards of living, immigration from the former Empire and Britain's membership of the European Union; as reflected in the large number of foreign restaurants and food stores. Modern multi-cultural London has many of its own traditions from Hindu Diwali to the **Notting Hill Carnival** (last weekend of Aug), London's biggest festival and the second largest street festival after Rio. Between one and two million visitors turn this area of London into a giant free party each year.

The most recent large-scale redevelopment project is the regeneration of the **Docklands**, eight square miles of derelict warehouses and dock basins east of the City, which have been converted into office accommodation of sometimes epic proportions; at 774ft/235m, Canary Wharf Tower is the tallest building in the UK. Around the Docklands modern flats, low-rise housing and even water sports facilities have been laid out.

A massive building programme is now underway in preparation for the **2012 Olympics**. The Olympic Park in the Lea Valley, just east of the Docklands, is one of the largest construction and engineering projects in Europe. It will feature the Aquatics Centre, Hockey Stadium, Multi-sport arenas, 80,000-seat Olympic Stadium and Velopark, as well as the Olympic Village and Media Centre.

Traditional London

Tradition still plays an important role in London life. The ceremonial **Changing of the Guard** at Buckingham Palace (daily at 11.30am in summer; otherwise every other day) and **Horse Guards** (daily at 11am; Sun at 10am) draw the crowds. There is more pageantry and military precision when the Queen attends **Trooping the Colour** on Horse Guards Parade (2nd or 3rd Saturday in Jun) and the **State Opening of Parliament** (Nov). In the **Lord Mayor's Show** (second Sat in Nov) the newly elected Lord Mayor of London proceeds through the City in the Golden State Coach before taking his oath at the Royal Courts of Justice in the Strand.

Euston, Kings Cross/St Pancras (northern destinations and Eurostar); Paddington and Marylebone (western destinations); Waterloo, Victoria and London Bridge (the south); and Liverpool Street and Fenchurch Street (the east).

Don't Miss: The London Eye, British Museum, National Gallery, Covent Garden, Westminster Abbey, St Paul's Cathedral, Natural History Museum, Science Museum, Tower of London, Kew Gardens, Hampton Court Palace, Greenwich by river boat, London Zoo.

Kids: Most major London attractions are good for families and kids; look for the Kids symbol in the following pages.

Walking Tours: There are many walking tour operators, the best is the Original London Walks (*020 7624 3978; www.walks.com*).

TOURIST INFORMATION

The main tourist information point is the Britain and London Visitor Centre (*1 Lower Regent Street, SW1Y 4NS; ☎0870 156 6366 (infoline); www.visitlondon.com*).

For what is happening specifically in the City (London's ancient Square Mile), go to the City of London Information Centre *(St Paul's Churchyard; www.cityoflondon.gov.uk)*. There are also information centres at Richmond (*☎020 8940 9125; www.visitrichmond.co.uk*) and Greenwich (*☎0870 608 2000; www.greenwich.gov.uk*).

PUBLIC TRANSPORT

London's five **airports** are each connected to the city by some form of public transport. Express trains to central London run from Gatwick, Heathrow, Stanstead and Luton (shuttle first). City Airport is quite central, with shuttles to Docklands TFL stations. The most enjoyable way of travelling to France or Brussels is by **Eurostar** (www.eurostar.com), a high-speed train service from St Pancras sation to the Continent via the Eurotunnel.

Transport for London (*☎020 7222 1234. www.tfl.gov.uk)* runs the tube (Underground), buses, Docklands Light Railway and Thames riverboats, while regional train companies service the majority of the suburbs, particularly in south London**.** The **journey planner** on www.tfl.gov.uk should be your first point of call when planning daytrips.

Oyster Card

©Transport for London

Individual and combined **tickets** are available by the journey, day, multiple days or longer, suitable for every kind of travel. The **Oyster card** (*https://oyster.tfl.gov.uk*) is the cheapest and easiest way to travel, valid on all public transport (except taxis). This credit card ticket can be used repeatedly and loaded with virtually any fare They are available at any Underground station. The simplest option for most visitors is to top-up credit; the card then automatically calculates the cheapest overall ticket for journeys made that day.

SIGHTSEEING

The Underground obscures the true layout and character of London, but is often the fastest way of getting around. If possible you should avoid using the Underground in central London at rush hours. If you are touring Westminster you are often better off walking and using buses for longer hops.

Certain TFL **bus routes**, such as the 11, give a fantastic tour of the city for very little money. Be warned though, in Westminster buses may require you to buy a ticket before you board. Bus drivers generally do accept cash, but usually only coins; use an Oyster instead.

Tours on **open-topped buses** start from Victoria, Green Park, Piccadilly, Coventry Street, Trafalgar Square, Haymarket, Lower Regent Street, Marble Arch, Baker Street, Tower Hill. Some tours are non-stop; some allow passengers to hop on or off and continue on a later bus. For guided walking tours consult the Britain and London Visitor Centre or press listings, particularly *Time Out.*

Thames cruises start from Westminster Pier, Charing Cross Pier, Tower Pier, Greenwich Pier. Evening cruises with music and/or a meal are also available. River transport is still the most expensive branch of London Transport, but is becoming more popular.

The **London Waterbus Company** operates a regular service along the Regent's Canal (*☎020 7482 2550. www.londonwaterbus.com*). Other operators are Jason's Trip. (www.jasons.co.uk) and Jenny Wren *☎020 7485 4433.*

City of London★★★

SIGHTS

St Paul's Cathedral★★★ (F2)

⊖*St Paul's.* ⏰ *Open Mon–Sat 8.30am–4pm (last admission). Galleries 9.30am–4.15pm. Sun services only (admission free).* ◎*£11.* ☞*Guided tours £3.* ♿✕. ✆*020 7246 8348 (recorded info). www.stpauls.co.uk.*

St Paul's Cathedral

J. Malburet/MICHELIN

The present cathedral, the fourth or fifth on a site dating back to AD 604, is considered to be the masterpiece of **Sir Christopher Wren** (1632–1723). After the Great Fire of 1666, old St Paul's was a sad ruin. The foundation stone was laid on 21 June 1675. 33 years later Wren saw his son set the final stone in place – the topmost in the lantern. When Wren died 15 years later he was buried within the walls; beneath the dome his own epitaph reads in Latin: "Reader, if you seek his monument, look around you."

Exterior – The most striking feature is the **dome**, even today a dominant feature of the City skyline. Unlike the dome of St Peter's, which fascinated and influenced Wren, it is not a true hemisphere. The drum below it is in two tiers, the lower encircled by columns and crowned by a balustrade, the upper recessed behind the balustrade so as to afford a circular viewing gallery, the **Stone Gallery**. On top of the dome, the lantern is restrained English Baroque with columns on all four sides and a small cupola serving as a plinth to the 6.5ft-/2m-diameter golden ball.

The **west end**, approached by two wide flights of steps, is composed of a two-tier portico of Corinthian and composite columns below a decorated pediment surmounted by St Paul. On either side rise Wren's Baroque spires. A notable feature of the exterior is the profuse carving by **Grinling Gibbons** and others.

Interior – The immediate impression is one of space, of almost luminescent stone and, in the distance, gold and mosaic. In the **nave** the entire space between two piers in the north aisle is occupied by the Wellington monument; in the south aisle hangs Holman Hunt's *The Light of the World.* From the **Whispering Gallery** in the dome (259 steps) there are impressive views of the concourse below, and close views of the interior of the dome, painted by Thornhill. A whisper spoken close to the wall can be clearly heard on the diametrically opposite side. The **views★★★** from the **Golden Gallery** at the top of the dome are better than from the Stone Gallery (543 steps). In the **choir** the dark oak stalls are the exquisite work of Grinling Gibbons. The iron railing, the gates to the choir aisles and the great gilded screens enclosing the sanctuary are the work of Jean Tijou. The graceful sculpture of the Virgin and Child in the north aisle is by Henry Moore (1984). In the south aisle is a rare pre-Fire relic, a statue of **John Donne**, the great poet and Dean of St Paul's 1621–31. The **Crypt** contains tombs of many illustrious individuals and memorials, too numerous to list.

Barbican★ (FG2)

The project (1962–82) combines residential accommodation with schools, shops, open spaces, a conference and arts centre, a medieval church and the Museum of London.

Museum of London★★ (FG2)

⊖*Barbican, Moorgate. London Wall.* ⏰ *Open year-round daily 10am–5.50pm (last admission 5.30pm) and until 9pm on first Thu of each month.*

White Tower

Ph. Gajic/MICHELIN

⏱ Closed Dec 24–26, Jan 1. ♿✕.
☎020 7001 9844. www.museumof
london.org.uk.
The biggest city history museum in
the world presents the story of London
from prehistory to the present day, with
exhibits as various as the sculptures from
the Roman temple of Mithras, medieval
pilgrim badges, the Cheapside Hoard
of Jacobean jewellery, a diorama of the
Great Fire, the doors from Newgate Gaol,
19C shops and interiors, the Lord May-
or's Coach, souvenirs of the women's
suffrage movement... right through
the swinging 60s and 21C issues.

🚻 Tower of London★★★ (GH2)

🚇Tower Hill. ⏱ Open Mar–Oct
Tue–Sat 9am–5.30pm, Sun–Mon
10am–5.30pm. Nov–Feb closes 4.30pm.
⏱Closed 24–26 Dec, 1 Jan. 🎟£17, child
£9.50. Buy tickets online (at a discount)
or by phone to save waiting time.
🗣 Guided tour (1hr) by Yeoman
Warders from the Middle Tower (exteri-
ors plus Chapel of St Peter-ad-Vincula).
Last tour: summer 3.30pm, winter
2.30pm. ♿✕. ☎0844 482 7777.
www.hrp.org.uk.
William I constructed a wooden fortress
in 1067, replacing it with one in stone (c.
1077–97) in order to deter Londoners
from revolt; its vantage point beside the
river also gave immediate sighting of
any hostile force coming up the Thames.

Norman, Plantagenet and Tudor successors recognised its value and extended
it until it occupied 18acre/7ha.
From 1300–1810 the Tower housed the
Royal Mint; because of its defences it
became the Royal Jewel House and also
served as a feared prison. Monarchs have
been associated with the Tower from
William the Conqueror to Elizabeth i.
The **Jewel House** (😊queues tend to
be shorter early in the day) displays the
Crown Jewels★★★ which date from the
Restoration to the present day, almost
all of the earlier regalia having been sold
or melted down by Oliver Cromwell. The
Chapel of St Peter ad Vincula, consecrated in the 12C, rebuilt in the 13C
and 16C, is the burial place of several
dukes and two of Henry VIII's queens,
beheaded in the Tower.
Traitors' Gate was the main entrance
to the Tower when the Thames was
still London's principal thoroughfare;
later, when the river served only as a
secret means of access, the entrance
acquired its chilling name. The Bloody
Tower gained its name in the 16C and
was perhaps the place where the little
Princes in the Tower were murdered in
1483. Sir Walter Raleigh was imprisoned
in it from 1603–15.
The **White Tower**★★★ keep is one of the
earliest fortifications on such a scale in
western Europe, begun by William I in
1078 and completed 20 years later by
William Rufus. The 100ft/31m- high
stone walls form an uneven quadrilat-
eral, its corners marked by one circular
and three square towers. The **Armour
Collection**, one of the world's greatest,
was started by Henry VIII and increased
under Charles II. On the second floor,
St John's Chapel★★ remains much as
it was when completed in 1080, a 55ft-
/17m- long stone chapel rising through
two floors. An inner line of great round
columns with simply carved capitals
bear circular Norman arches and is
echoed above in a second tier.
Beauchamp Tower★, built in the 13C,
has served as a place of confinement
since the 14C. The walls of the main
chamber are inscribed with dozens of
carved graffiti.

Tower Bridge★★ (H3)
⊖*Tower Hill, London Bridge. River boat to Tower Pier. Tower Bridge Road.*
🕐 *Open daily, Apr–Sept 10am–6.30pm. Oct–Mar 9.30am–6pm.* 🕐 *Closed 24–26 Dec.* ⬛£6. ♿. 📞020 7403 3761. www.towerbridge.org.uk.*

The familiar Gothic towers, high-level walkways and the original engine rooms form part of the tour which traces the design of the bridge by Sir John Wolfe-Barry and Horace Jones, its construction (1886–94) and explains the functioning of the hydraulic mechanism which, until 1976, raised the 1100t drawbridge-like-bascules (now operated by electricity).

St Katharine Docks★ (H2)
In 1828 **Thomas Telford** developed this series of basins and warehouses next to the City and they prospered for over a hundred years. After wartime bombing however the dock was abandoned until 1968, when moorings were organised for private yachts. Telford's main Italianate-style building was restored as **Ivory House** with apartments above a shopping arcade.

Westminster ★★★

SIGHTS
Westminster Abbey★★★ (E3)
⊖*Westminster. Abbey:* 🕐 *Open year-round Mon–Sat 10am–4.30pm (1.45pm Sat). Wed until 7pm (winter 6pm). Sun for services only.* ⬛£10. •— *Guided tours £5.* ♿. 📞020 7222 7110.
Cloister: 🕐 *Open daily 8am–6pm.*
Chapter House, Pyx Chamber *and* ***Abbey Museum:*** *Open daily 10.30am–4pm.* 🕐*Closed Dec 24–26 and Jan 1 except services.* ⬛£1 *(free with abbey ticket).* ***College Garden:*** 🕐 *Open Tue–Thu, 10am–6pm (4pm Oct–Mar). Brass band concerts in garden (⬛free) Jul–Aug 12.30pm–2pm (📞020 7654 4900). www.westminster-abbey.org.*

The abbey, in which William the Conqueror was crowned as **William I** on Christmas Day 1066, was built by **Edward the Confessor** in the Norman style; only after the rebuilding by the Plantagenet Henry III in 1220 did it acquire its Gothic appearance. Henry III began with the Lady Chapel, to provide a noble shrine for the Confessor, who had been canonised in 1163. Gradually the existing building was demolished as new replaced the old; progress halted after the construction of the first bay of the nave and it was another two centuries before the nave was finished. When Henry VII constructed his **chapel** at the east end (1503–19) he produced the jewel of the age. The west towers

©Galen Goyer/iStockphoto.com

by Wren and Nicholas Hawksmoor (1722–45) and repairs by George Gilbert Scott kept to the Gothic spirit. The abbey escaped destruction at the Dissolution in 1540 and in 1560 Queen Elizabeth I granted a charter establishing the Collegiate Church of St Peter.

Inside, the vaulting is glorious, the carving on screens and arches delicate, often beautiful, sometimes humorous; the ancient tombs in **Henry VII's**, **St Edward's** and the ambulatory chapels are dignified. The transepts and aisles abound with sculpted monuments, particularly in the famous **Poets' Corner**★

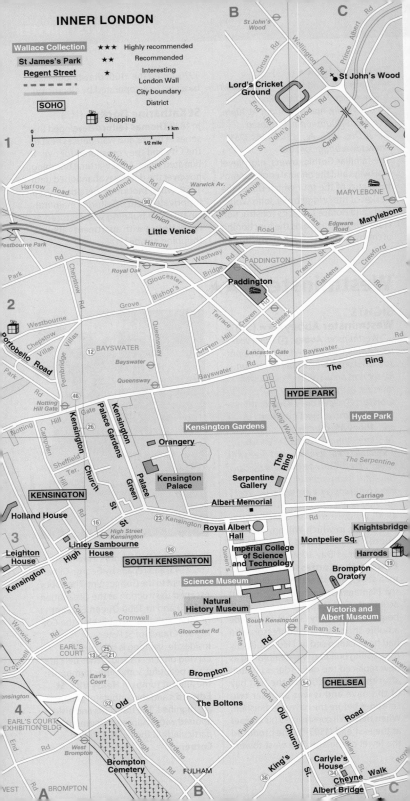

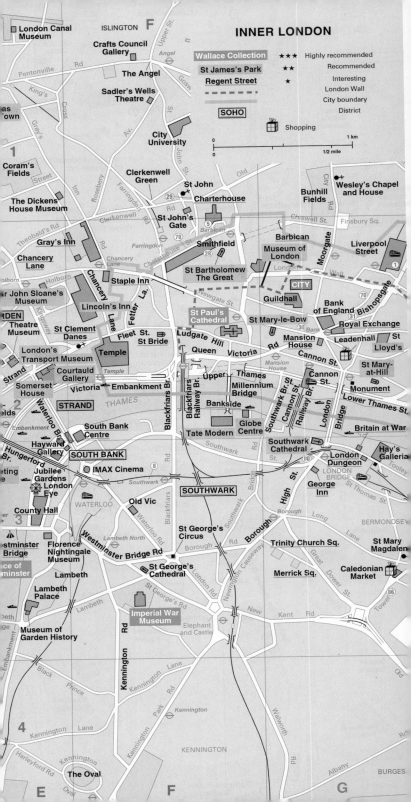

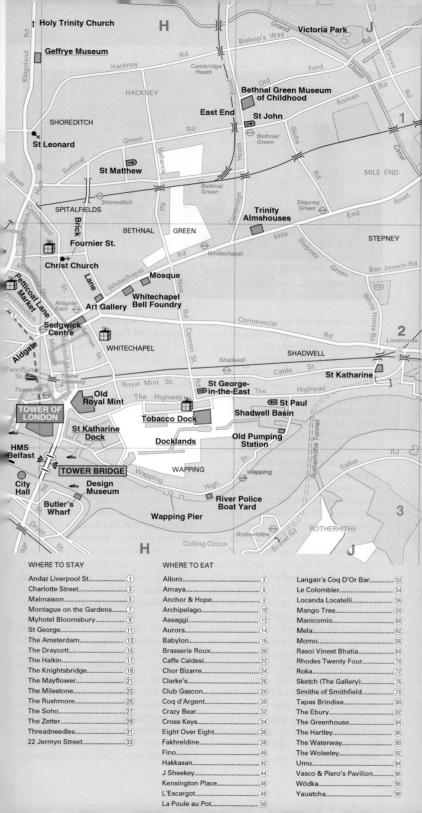

Houses of Parliament

©David Joyner/iStockphoto.com

(south transept) where there are monuments to many great poets though few are actually buried here; the tomb of Geoffrey Chaucer was the first in this corner, others interred here include Alfred Lord Tennyson and Robert Browning.

The **sanctuary** beyond the **choir** is where the **Coronation ceremony** is performed. To the right hangs a 16C tapestry behind a large 15C altarpiece of rare beauty. Beyond is an ancient 13C sedilia painted with full-length royal figures (Henry III, Edward I). The **Henry VII Chapel**★★★ with its superb fan-vaulted roof is the most glorious of the abbey's many treasures. The banners of the Knights Grand Cross of the **Order of the Bath** hang still and brilliant above the stalls with inventive 16–18C misericords. The **Chapel of Edward the Confessor**★★ is rich in history, with the Confessor's shrine ringed with the tombs of five kings and three queens. In the centre against a carved stone **screen** (1441) stands the Coronation Chair which until recently contained the Stone of Scone beneath the seat (*see EDINBURGH and PERTH*).

The **Chapter House**★★ (1248–53) is an octagonal chamber (60ft/18m in diameter) with vaulting springing from a slim central pier of attached Purbeck marble columns. Its walls are partially decorated with medieval paintings.

Palace of Westminster (Houses of Parliament)★★★

(E3). ⊖Westminster. ⏰Open Aug–Sept (summer recess) by guided tour (75min) starting from the Victoria Tower. £13. 0870 906 3773. www. keithprowse.com. www.parliament. uk. Advance booking strongly advised, available from March onwards.

When Parliament is in session the general public are allowed into the Visitors' Gallery free of charge to watch the proceedings in the House of Commons. Be prepared to queue for popular sessions such as Prime Minister's Question Time if you do not have advance tickets.

The palace built by Edward the Confessor was enlarged and embellished by the medieval English kings but most of the surviving buildings, by then occupied by Parliament, were destroyed in a disastrous fire in 1834. The oldest part is **Westminster Hall**★★ which William Rufus added to his father's palace between 1097 and 1099. This scene of royal banquets and jousts in the Middle Ages was altered and re-roofed by command of Richard II between 1394 and 1399. For this the upper parts were rebuilt and what is perhaps the finest timber roof of all time was built, a superb **hammerbeam**★★★ designed by the king's master carpenter, Hugh Herland, carved with flying angels. After the 1834 fire which, fortunately, did not damage

Westminster Hall, **Charles Barry** and **Augustus Pugin** won a competition for a new design for the palace, which became known as the Houses of Parliament. These ardent Gothicists created a masterpiece of Victorian Gothic architecture. It was completed in 1860, with over 1,000 rooms, 100 staircases and 2mi/3km of corridors over 8 acres/3ha. The Clock Tower (316ft/96m) – the most famous feature of this distinctive building, was completed by 1859.

The name **Big Ben**★ applied originally to the great bell, probably so called after Sir Benjamin Hall, the Commissioner of Works and a man of considerable girth. The clock, which has an electrically wound mechanism, proved reliable for 117 years, except for minor stoppages, until it succumbed to metal fatigue in 1976 when it required major repairs. Big Ben was first broadcast on New Year's Eve 1923 and its chimes have subsequently become the most famous in the world.

The **House of Commons**★, re-built after being bombed in 1941, seats 437 of the 659 elected Members of Parliament; at the end of this simply decorated chamber is the canopied Speaker's Chair. Red stripes on both sides of the green carpet mark the limit to which a Member may advance to address the House – the distance between the stripes is reputedly that of two drawn swords.

The **House of Lords**★★ is a masterpiece of design and workmanship. The throne and steps, beneath a Gothic canopy mounted on a wide screen, all in gold, occupies one end of the chamber. The ceiling is divided by ribs and gold patterning above the leather benches and the Woolsack, seat of the Lord Chancellor since the reign of Edward III, adopted as a symbol of the importance to England of the wool trade.

Whitehall★★ (E3)

The wide street, which leads north from Parliament Square and Parliament Street, is lined by government offices. In the middle stands the Cenotaph, the austere war memorial designed by Sir Edwin Lutyens. On the left is

Downing Street (no public access) where a relatively modest Georgian house (no 10) has been the residence of the Prime Minister since 1732. **Banqueting House**★★ (⊖*Westminster. Whitehall;* 🕐 *open (government functions permitting) Mon–Sat 10am–5pm;* 🕐*closed Good Fri, Dec 24–26, 1 Jan and bank hols;* ✆ £4.80; ♿ ; ✆ 08707 515 178; www.hrp.org.uk), the only part of the great Whitehall Palace to survive destruction by fire, was designed by Inigo Jones in 1619. The north entrance and staircase were added in 1809 and the exterior refaced in 1829. The hall is a double cube with a delicate balcony on gilded corbels; the ceiling is divided by richly decorated beams into compartments filled with magnificent paintings (1634–35) by Rubens. It was on a platform erected in front of this building that Charles I was executed in January 1649.

Opposite stands **Horse Guards**★ **(EY)**, famous for the presence of the **Household Cavalry sentries**. The famous ceremonial mounting of the **Queen's Life Guard**★★★ occurs daily at 11am (10am Sun) in summer on Horse Guards Parade. The dismount ceremony is daily at 4pm in the Front Yard of Horse Guards. The cavalry rides along the Mall between Horse Guards and their barracks in Hyde Park (✆*020 7414 2353. www.army.mod.uk*). At the rear is the parade ground, where Trooping the Colour takes place in June

St James's Park★★ (DE3)

⊖*St James's Park.*

The oldest and most beautiful royal park in London dates from 1532 when Henry VIII had **St James's Palace (DY)** built. The park was landscaped in the 19C by John Nash who was also responsible for the majestic **Carlton House Terrace**★ **(EY)** in the northeast corner.

From the bridge over the water there is a fine **view** of Whitehall and Buckingham Palace. Look out for the park's famous pelicans; the first was a gift to Charles I from a Russian Ambassador – it promptly flew off and was shot while over Norfolk.

Buckingham Palace★★ (D3)

⊖ St James's Park, Victoria. 🕐 Open late Jul– late Sept daily 9.45am–6pm (3.45 pm last admission) by timed ticket only. ⊗£16.50. Joint ticket with Royal Mews and Queen's Gallery £29.50. ♿. ✆020 776 7300. www.royalcollection.org.uk.

Buckingham House was built by the Duke of Buckingham in 1703 and purchased in 1762 by George III. Under George IV it was converted into a palace (1825–37) by John Nash and Edward Blore; the east front containing the famous balcony was added in 1847. The tour includes Throne Room, Drawing Rooms, Dining Room and the Picture Gallery, hung with royal portraits and old masters (Charles I, Van Dyck; portraits by Rembrandt and Frans Hals; seascapes by Van de Velde; A Lady at the Virginals, Vermeer; pastoral and religious scenes by Rubens…) and furnished with many pieces collected by George IV.

When the sovereign is in residence, the Royal Standard flies over the palace.

The **Changing of the Guard**★★ (🕐 takes place usually May–end Jul/ early-Aug, daily at 11.30am except in very poor weather; rest of year alternate days at 11.30am. www.changing-the-guard.com) takes place in the palace forecourt. Arrive early for a good view.

The **Queen's Gallery**★★ (separate entrance; 🕐 open daily 9.30am/10am– 5.30pm by timed ticket (last admission 4.30pm), ⊗£8.50; ♿; ✆020 7766 7301; www.royalcollection.org.uk) exhibits portraits, paintings, drawings and furniture in the priceless Royal Collection.

Southwark★ (FG3)

"The Borough" (of Southwark), was infamous in the 16C for its brothels and theatres, on account of its location outside the jurisdiction of the City of London. Near the site of the original Globe Theatre, where Shakespeare's plays were performed, now stands the landmark **Shakespeare's Globe**★ (⊖ Mansion House, London Bridge; 21 New Globe Walk; 🕐 open daily winter 10am–5pm winter, in summer when matinees play, no access to Globe Theatre, tour of Exhibition and Rose Theatre 9am–12.30pm (11.30am Sun) or 1am–5pm (Sun noon–5pm); 🕐 closed 24–25 Dec; ⊗£10.50; ♿✕; ✆020 7902 1400; www.shakespeares-globe. org), which replicates the original 16C structure. The Elizabethan playhouse's stage thrusts into a large circular yard surrounded by three tiers of roofed seating in the round. **Stage productions**★★ are held in this authentic outdoor setting each summer (late Apr– early Oct, see website for schedule) but the site also has an excellent permanent **exhibition**★.

The most spectacular local medieval building is the **George Inn**★(GY), still a functioning pub, built round three sides of a courtyard, although only one of the galleried ranges has survived.

Along the river old warehouses have been converted to new uses – **Hays Galleria** with its shops, pubs and modern sculpture, and the acclaimed **Design Museum (HY)** (⊖ Tower Hill; Shad Thames; 🕐 open year-round daily 10am–5.45pm; 🕐 closed Dec 25; ⊗£8.50; ♿✕; ✆0870 833 9955; www.design museum.org), are two examples. The latter illustrates the evolution of contemporary design.

Globe Theatre

©John Tramper/Shakespeare's Globe

LONDON BRIDGE

London Bridge has two horror-themed attractions. The long-established **London Dungeon**★ *(G3;* 👤👤*;*⊖*London Bridge. Tooley Street.* 🕐 *open year-round daily; summer and holidays 9.30am–6.30pm; other times of year 10am/10.30am–5pm/5.30pm;* 🕐*closed Dec 25;* 🌐 *see website for prices; buy timed tickets in advance to make significant savings and to avoid waiting time;* ♿✕*;* ☎*020 7403 7221.www.the dungeons.com)* under the station arches is a gruesome all-too-lifelike exhibition of death, disease, disaster and torture in past centuries, which is hugely popular with teenagers but unsuitable for young children and anyone who is squeamish or prone to nightmares.

Nearby, under London Bridge itself is the new **London Bridge Experience** *(G3;* 👤👤*;*⊖ *London Bridge. Tooley Street;* 🕐*open year-round Mon–Fri 11am–5pm (last entry), Sat–Sun 10am–6pm (last entry); Dec 24–1 Jan 11am–4pm (last entry);* 🕐 *closed Dec 25;* 🌐*see website; buy timed tickets in advance to make significant savings and to avoid waiting time;* ♿✕*;* ☎*0800 0434 666; www.thelondon bridgeexperience.com),* a newcomer that weaves ghostly happenings and special effects into the colourful history of London Bridge. It is less gory and intense than the London Dungeon (though still not suitable for little ones) and its actors amuse the whole family.

On Tooley Street (64–66) is the **Winston Churchill's Britain at War Experience**★ *(G3;* 👤👤*;* ⊖ *London Bridge;* 🕐*open year-round daily 10am– 5pm (4.30pm Nov–Mar);* 🕐*closed 24–26 Dec;* 🌐*£10.45;* ♿*;* ☎*020 7403 3171; www. britainatwar.co.uk),* a re-creation of the London Blitz of the 1940s in all its fury with special effects of sights and sounds, artefacts, and even the dust and smoke of an air raid.

Head to the river from here and you will find **HMS Belfast** *(G3;* ⊖*London Bridge, Morgan's Lane, Tooley Street;* 🕐*open daily 10am–6pm (5pm Nov–Feb);* 🕐*closed Dec 24–26:* 🌐*£10.70;* ✕*;* ☎*020 7940 6300; www.iwm.org.uk).* This great grey cruiser (1938) moored against the south bank of the Thames saw service with the North Atlantic Convoys and on D-Day in 1944.

Follow the riverbank west and you will come to **Southwark Cathedral**★★ *(G3;* ⊖*London Bridge;* 🕐*open year-round daily 8am–6pm (Sat–Sun and bank hols 9am–6pm);* 🌐*£4 contribution requested;* ♿✕*;* ☎*020 7367 700; www. southwark.anglican.org)* on the other side of London bridge. The cathedral began life in 1106 and its earliest work is the fragment of a Norman arch in the north wall. The massive piers supporting the central tower and the Early English **chancel** date from the 13C. The **altar screen** (1520) appears in sumptuous Gothic glory; it remained empty until 1905 when statues were carved to fill the niches. The nave was rebuilt in 1890–97 to harmonise with the chancel. Notable features are the **Harvard Chapel**, the 1616 **monument** to Alderman Humble and his wives, and the 12 **bosses** rescued from the 15C wooden roof which collapsed in 1830.

The cathedral bounds **Borough Market**★ *(G3;* ⊖*London Bridge; Borough High Street;* 🕐*open year-round Thu 11am–5pm, Fri noon–6pm, Sat 9am–4pm;* ♿*;* ☎*020 7407 1002; www.boroughmarket. org.uk),* not only London's oldest food market but also the country's most important retail market for fine foods. Food lovers of every kind, from curious tourists and hungry students, to celebrity London chefs, come here to shop or merely drool over the mouthwatering range of delights. There are several stalls offering ready-to-eat food either to take away or to eat in, at small tables next to the market stall.

Continuing west from here along the river you come to the **Golden Hinde** *(G3;* 👤👤*;*⊖*London Bridge, Monument. St Mary Overie Dock;* 🕐 *open Mon–Sat 10am–5pm, Sun call for times and availability;* 🎧 *guided tour Sat 1pm, 3pm (call to check);* ☎*020 7403 0123; www. goldenhinde.org).* "Hands-on" learning with costumed interpreters is the order of the day on board this seaworthy replica of Sir Francis Drake's 16C flagship, in which he circumnavigated the world.

Blue Plaques

All over the capital you will find blue plaques affixed to buildings where famous people have lived. In total there are over 760 in London including actors, authors, politicians, painters, scientists, sportsmen, campaigners and reformers – people from different countries, cultures and backgrounds – have all been commemorated in this way. In order to be eligible for a plaque there are a number of criteria to be met: the person must have been dead for 20 years, or have passed the centenary of their birth, whichever is the earlier; be considered eminent by a majority of members of their own profession or calling; have made an important positive contribution to human welfare or happiness; be recognisable to the well-informed passer-by; deserve national recognition; have resided in a locality for a significant period, in time or importance, within their life and work. To illustrate their diversity, in Mayfair there is a plaque to George Frederick Handel at 25 Brook Street and next door at no. 23 a plaque to Jimi Hendrix.

SOUTH BANK AND LAMBETH

Head west along the river fro London Bridge and you will come to the **Tate Modern**★★ (⊖Southwark, Blackfriars. Bankside; ⏱open year-round daily 10am (galleries 10.15am)–6pm (10pm Fri–Sat); ⏱closed Dec 24–26; ⬚Charge only for temporary exhibitions; ♿▯ (disabled visitors only) ✗; ✆020 7887 8888 (recorded information), 020 7887 8008; www.tate.org.uk). The former Bankside Power Station, with its single chimney (325ft/99m) and giant internal dimensions makes a striking home for London's newest major gallery, devoted to international 20C and 21C art. The wealth of the collection is largely due to the bequests of Sir Roland Penrose, one-time friend of Picasso and Ernst, and that of Edward James, a former patron to Dalí and Magritte. Gigantic sculptures by contemporary artists are set off by the vast spaces of the Turbine Hall (500ft/155m long and 115ft/35m high) where overhead cranes recall the building's working life. Themed displays mean that you can never quite be sure what will be here at any one time. World-class special exhibitions are regularly staged.

Further on you come to the **South Bank Centre**★★ (E3/F3, E2/F2; ⊖Waterloo; www.southbankcentre.co.uk, www.nationaltheatre.org.uk, www.bfi.org.uk). This is the UK's most important arts and theatre complex. The Brutalist-style grey concrete buildings house: the **National Theatre**, which stages the finest theatre productions in the country outside London's West End; the **BFI (British Film Institute) Southbank**, formerly known as the National Film Theatre, which screens both classic and cult movies; the **Royal Festival Hall** specialises in orchestral concerts; the **Queen Elizabeth Hall** hosts chamber orchestras, quartets, choirs, dance performances and opera (and also contains the Purcell Room); The **Hayward** (formerly known as the Hayward Gallery) has a rotating exhibition of contemporary art.

Bookshops, cafés, restaurants and live foyer events ensure that the South Bank is lively for much of the day as well as during evening performances.

Carrying on west along the riverbank you wil find the **London Eye**★★ (E3; ⊖Westminster; South Bank; ticket office in County Hall. ⏱ Open daily. Oct–Apr 10am–8pm (closes earlier 24, 31 Dec). May–Sept 10am–9pm (Jul–Aug 9.30pm); due to popularity, visitors should book a time slot in advance; limited number of tickets sold on-site; ⏱closed Dec 25 and second week Jan for annual maintenance; ⬚£17 (fast-track ticket £27); ♿✗; ✆0870 990 8883 (enquiries); 0870 5000 600 (bookings); www.londoneye.com). On the opposite side of the river to Parliament this giant observation wheel is a spectacular Millennium landmark on the Thames. Sightseers are accommodated in glass pods to enjoy unparalleled **views**★★★of London 443ft/135m high during their 30-minute ride.

Next to the Eye, inside County Hall are two attractions. The **London Aquarium**★ (E3; 👥; ⊖*Westminster. County Hall;* 🕒*open year-round daily 10am–6pm (Sat–Sun 7pm);* £8.25, child £6.75, save by booking online; ♿✕; 020 7967 8000; www.londonaquarium.co.uk) is one of Europe's largest aquariums with sharks in spectacular large-scale tanks, piranhas at feeding time and stingrays in a touch-tank. There are also exhibits on London and British marine life. The **Movieum** (E3; ⊖*Westminster; County Hall;* 🕒*Open year-round daily 10am–5pm (Sat, Sun and bank hols 6pm;* £12 (save online); ♿; 020 7202 7040; www.the movieum.com) opened in 2008. This "movie-museum" is a little raw around the edges but has enough in the way of film memorabilia to interest most regular cinema fans.

A short walk away from Westminster, , is the **Imperial War Museum**★★★(F3; ⊖*Lambeth North, Elephant and Castle; Lambeth Road;* 🕒*open year-round daily 10am–6pm;* charge for temporary exhibitions; ♿✕; 020 7416 5000; www. iwm.org.uk). This sensitive and thought-provoking exhibition honours those who served but also remembers those who stayed at home or were caught up as civilians in the conflicts of the 20C. A wide range of weapons and equipment is on display: armoured fighting vehicles, field guns and small arms, together with models, decorations, uniforms, posters and photographs, masses of archive material, including moving first-hand oral accounts of warfare as well as a selection from the museum's outstanding collection based on the work of two generations of official war artists.

West End★★

TRAFALGAR SQUARE★★
(EX)⊖Charing Cross.
Begun in 1829, the square was completed in the 1840s, when Charles Barry levelled it and built the north terrace for the National Gallery (🕒*see below*). In 1842 **Nelson's Column** was erected; the monument is 185ft/56m tall, with the pedestal, fluted granite column, bronze capital and a 17ft/4.5m statue of the great admiral who lost his life in victory at the Battle of Trafalgar.

Note the equestrian statue (south) of **Charles I** cast by Le Sueur in 1633. A plaque in the road next to it marks the spot from where all road distances to/from London are measured. Ironically the square is now pedestrianised. Note the four plinths at each corner of the square. While three of these are occupied by conventional historical statues, the fourth ("Artists' Plinth") is now the location for specially commissioned artworks.

The church of **St Martin-in-the-Fields**★ (*Trafalgar Square;* 🕒 *open daily 8am–6pm;* guided tour Thu 11.30am; ♿✕; 020 7839 8362; www.stmartin-in-the-

fields.org) was built by James Gibbs in 1722–26, with a Corinthian portico and elegant spire. Today it is one of London's most active churches, staging free **lunchtime recitals** (*Mon–Tue and Fri at 1.05pm*), **classical concerts** (*Thu–Sat 7.30pm;* 020 7766 1100), home to the **London Brass Rubbing Centre** (*Mon–Wed 10am–7pm, Thu–Sat 10am–10pm, Sun noon–7pm*), the award-winning Café in the Crypt restaurant and a daily market held at the rear of the church.

National Gallery★★★ (E2)
⊖*Leicester Square, Charing Cross. Trafalgar Square.* 🕒 *Open year-round daily 10am–6pm (9pm Fri).* 🕒 *Closed Dec 24–26, Jan 1. Charge only for temporary exhibitions.* Guided tour (1hr) daily at 11.30am, 2.30pm. ♿✕. 020 7747 2885. www.nationalgallery.org.uk. This landmark building was completed in 1838, its pedimented portico of Corinthian columns forming a climax to Trafalgar Square. The sixth and latest extension to the original building is the Sainsbury Wing (1991) by Robert Venturi.

There are now more than 2,000 paintings in the collection; they represent the jewels in the public domain from early to

High Renaissance Italian painting, early Netherlandish, German, Flemish, Dutch, French and Spanish pictures and masterpieces of the English 18C. The fuller representation of British art, particularly the more modern and 20C work of all schools is in Tate Britain).

The galleries are arranged chronologically starting with the period 1260–1510 in the **Sainsbury Wing**. Leonardo's fragile preparatory "cartoon" of *Virgin and Child with St Anne and John the Baptist* is spectacular while his *Virgin on the Rocks* is similarly enigmatic and engaging. Ucello exploits strong lines and colour in his epic *Battle of San Romano*. Haunting realism and solemn stillness are the keywords in the works of Van Eyck and Van der Weyden particularly in the former's legendary *Arnolfini Portrait*. Botticelli is represented by *Venus and Mars* and *Portrait of a Young Man* while other Italian masters in this gallery are Raphael, Mantegna and Bellini whose perfect use of oils is encapsulated in his *Madonna and Child*. Earlier German and Netherlandish work is also represented by Dürer, Cranach, Bosch and Memlinc. Paintings in the **West Wing** range from 1510 to 1600. *The Ambassadors* by Holbein is a wonderful large scale historical portrait and its famous *trompe l'oeil* skull is a great favourite with gallery visitors. Tintoretto, El Greco, Michelangelo and Veronese are also here.

In the North Wing are paintings by the French School, the Spanish School and from the Low Countries. Works by Claude and the great British landscape artist JMW Turner are exhibited together and should not be missed. Rembrandt and Rubens, Caravaggio, Velazquez and Van Dyck (his huge *Equestrian Picture of Charles I* is unmissable) also star here. Paintings from 1700 to 1900 are exhibited in the **East Wing**. The British School is exemplified by classics such as *The Haywain* by Constable, *The Fighting Temeraire* and *Rain, Steam and Speed*, by JMW Turner. There are works by Canaletto, Goya, Tiepolo and Delacroix but many visitor's favourites are the Impressionist collection starring Pisarro, Renoir, Monet, Manet, Degas and Cézanne. Van

River cruises

There's no better way to spend a sunny day in London than an excursion to **Greenwich**★★★, by river cruiser from Westminster, Charing Cross or Tower Pier. Make sure you pick one with a live (rather than a pre-recorded) commentary. You can return a different route, by the foot tunnel under the Thames to Island Gardens. There is a fine **view**★★ of Greenwich Palace from Island Gardens on the north bank, which can be reached via the foot tunnel. From here return west on the Docklands Light Railway (DLR), enjoying the scenic ride on its elevated track (℘020 7222 1234; www.tfl.gov.uk).

Gogh's *Chair* and *Sunflowers* (once the world's most expensive painting) stand out as crowd pleasers. Seurat's *Bathers at Asnière* is another favourite. Another distinctive and popular artist is Henri Rousseau whose *Tiger in a Tropical Storm* is a classic.

National Portrait Gallery★★ (E2)

◯*Leicester Square, Charing Cross. St. Martin's Lane.* ◐ *Open year-round daily 10am–6pm (9pm Thu–Fri).* ◐*Closed Dec 24–26.* ▱*Charge for temporary exhibitions only.* ♿✖. ℘020 7306 0055. www.npg.org.uk.

Here you will find portraits of almost every British person of significant public or historical interest from the Middle Ages to the present day, some painted, sculpted or photographed by the famous artists of the day. They range from the raffish picture of **William Shakespeare** (his only known contemporary portrait) through Sir Winston Churchill and Margaret Thatcher to modern icons such as Diana, Princess of Wales and David Beckham.

MAYFAIR★ (D2)

The most luxurious district of London takes its name from a cattle and general fair held annually in May until it was closed in 1706 for unruly behaviour. It contains the most elegant hotels and the smartest shops in all of London: **Burlington Arcade**★ **(DX)** (1819) where the bow-fronted boutiques sell fashion, jewellery, leather goods; **Bond Street**★ famous for art auctioneers and dealers (Sotheby's, Phillips, Agnew's, Colnaghi), jewellery (Asprey, Cartier) and fashion (Fenwick, Yves St Laurent); **Regent Street** well known for elegant stores (Austin Reed, Aquascutum, Burberry, Jaeger and **Liberty**★★); **Oxford Street** lined with the more popular department stores (John Lewis, Debenhams, DH Evans, Selfridges and Marks & Spencer). Less well known is **Shepherd Market**, a charming maze of lanes, alleyways and paved courts linked by archways with a village atmosphere. Victorian and Edwardian pubs and houses, antique shops and small inserted shop fronts which serve in summer as pavement cafés line its streets.

You will find it hard to hear a nightingale singing in **Berkeley Square** (created 1737) these days but it is still a very impressive plane-tree lined ensemble – the trees are not much younger, many dating from the late 1780s. Look for the late 18C houses on the west side with ironwork balconies, lamp holders at the steps and torch snuffers.

Piccadilly Circus★ (E2)

This famous road junction (circus), once considered the hub of the British Empire, is still dominated by **Eros**, the Angel of Christian Charity, surmounting the fountain erected in memory of the philanthropist, Lord Shaftesbury, in 1892. It is famous for its garish neon advertising hoardings and as a meeting place. Appropriately, London's gaudiest attraction, a branch of ⛪**Ripley's Believe It or Not! Museum**★ (⊖*Piccadilly Circus;* ⏰*open year-round daily 10am–midnight, last admission 10.30pm;* 🎫 *£17.95, child £13.95;* ♿✕; ✆*020 3238 0022; www.ripleys.com)* has recently located here and wows the crowds with its inimitable mixture of amazing facts and jaw-dropping artefacts.

Off the Circus, **Shaftesbury Avenue**, created as a slum-clearance measure, is at the heart of theatreland.

MARYLEBONE
Wallace Collection★★★ (D2)
⊖*Bond Street. Manchester Square.* ⏰ *Open daily 10am–5pm.* ⏰ *Closed Dec 24–26, Jan 1.* ♿✕. ✆*020 7563 9500. www.wallacecollection.org.*

This gathering of one of the world's finer collections of 18C French art was the life's work of the fourth Marquess of Hertford (1800–70). These sit along Italian masters, 17C Dutch painting, 18C French furniture (note the magnificent cabinets by A C Boulle), and Sèvres porcelain. Don't miss the formidable display of European weapons and arms, nor **Gallery 22** hung with the larger 17C pictures and Old Master paintings including works by Rubens, Murillo, Velazquez, Rembrandt, Van Dyck, Gainsborough and the most popular work in the museum, *The Laughing Cavalier* by Frans Hals.

⛪ COVENT GARDEN★★ (E2)

Covent Garden Piazza, the first London square, was designed by Inigo Jones in 1631. It was originally surrounded by colonnades, long demolished.

St Paul's Church is an original survivor, its elegant portico dominating the west side of the square.

At the centre are the **Central Market Buildings**★★, designed in 1832 by Charles Fowler, to house the fruit and vegetable market which moved out in 1974. The tiny shops and market stalls which now occupy it sell a great variety of goods – books, cooking pots, fashion, jewellery, crafts and refreshment – and licensed musicians and street artists perform on the open cobblestones.

Covent Garden has long been synonymous with opera, and its **Royal Opera House**★ has been magnificently refurbished. Its design incorporates the original iron framework of the old Floral Hall. Recently revamped with great success ⛪ **London's Transport Museum**★ (⏰*open Sat–Thu 10am–6pm, Fri 11am–9pm;* 🎫*£10, child free;* ♿✕; ✆*020 7565*

7299; www.ltmuseum.co.uk) tells the fascinating story of the capital's public transport history with a large collection of historic vehicles, interactive displays and archive materials that really bring its subject to life.

It is well worth exploring the narrow side streets in and around Covent Garden, particularly **Neal's Yard** (off Shorts Gardens, a two-minute walk from Covent Garden underground station) complete with period hoists, dovecotes, trees in tubs, geranium-filled window boxes and a whole raft of eco-friendly shopkeepers, vegetarian and wholefood restaurants and food outlets. It's a particularly attractive spot in summer.

The Courtauld Gallery★★ (E2)

Temple, Embankment, Covent Garden. Somerset House, The Strand. Open year-round daily 10am–6pm. Closed Dec 25–26. £5. Free Mon 10am–2pm (except Bank Hols). 020 7872 0220. 020 7848 2526. www.courtauld.ac.uk.

The gallery is housed in one of central London's finest riverside buildings, **Somerset House**, designed by **Sir William Chambers** and built 1776–86. Samuel Courtauld's splendid private collection of **Impressionists** is the heart of the gallery, including canvases by Manet (Bar at the Folies-Bergère), Degas, Bonnard, Gauguin (Tahitian scenes), Van Gogh (Peach Trees in Blossom, Self-Portrait with Bandaged Ear), Cézanne (Lake at Annécy) and Seurat. Other outstanding pieces include 30 oils by **Rubens** and six drawings by **Michelangelo** as well as works by Breugel, Da Vinci, Tiepolo, Dürer, Rembrandt, Bellini, Tintoretto and Kokoschka; paintings of the Italian Primitive school and of the Renaissance; paintings by the **Bloomsbury Group**. In the summertime Somerset House stages open-air film screenings; in winter there is an ice-rink.

SOHO★ (DE2)

This very cosmopolitan district (Leicester Square, Piccadilly Circus), where immigrants once tended to congregate, is the home of the music and film trades, evening entertainment (theatres and restaurants) and night-life of every kind. In the latter decades of the 20C it became synonymous with sex-clubs, prostitution and low-life.

Today, although sex clubs and sex shops can still be found, the night scene is more reputable (and much safer), including some of London's best places to eat and drink. Soho is particularly popular with the gay community. There are dozens of excellent restaurants, including many French, Italian, Greek and Chinese. Many of the latter can be found in and around Gerrard Street, London's small **Chinatown**★ district. This colourful area is marked by oriental gates and other exotic street furniture and abounds in eating places, supermarkets selling eastern foodstuffs and oriental goods. At **Chinese New Year** this is the scene of one of London's most colourful street festivals.

Gerrard Street leads onto **Old Compton Street**, the spiritual heart of this bohemian area lined with pubs, wine merchants, pastry shops and Italian food stores. In summer grab a sandwich or snack and retreat to bucolic **Soho Square** (created 1680), between Greek Street and Frith Street.

At **Leicester Square**★ the bohemian character of Soho dissipates with the huge crowds that traverse this tree-shaded pedestrian precinct, made garish by the lights of cinemas and cheap food outlets.

At the **TKTS Leicester Square** building, (formerly known as the Half-Price Ticket Booth), and regulated by the **Society of London Theatres** (open Mon–Sat 10am–7pm for matinée and evening shows; Sun noon–3pm, matinées only. Cash only; service charge £3 per ticket, maximum four tickets per person; www.officiallondontheatre.co.uk/tkts) you can buy tickets for leading West End shows at a significant discount, though tickets for the most popular shows are rarely if ever available. Beware; there are other non-official reduced-price theatre ticket booths around the square who may not offer the best service.

HOLBORN★ (EF2)

The medieval manors at this former crossroads have been transformed into Lincoln's Inn and Gray's Inn, two of the four Inns of Court (⊙ *see below*). The fields where beasts once grazed are less in extent but still open; on the north side stands the remarkable time capsule of **Sir John Soane's Museum**★★ **(E2**; ⊖*Holborn; 13 Lincoln's Inn Fields;* ⊙*open Tue–Sat 10am–5pm, candle-lit evening first Tue of each month 6pm–9pm; arrive early, particularly on Sat and Tue evening, to avoid waiting in line;* ⊙*closed bank hols, Good Fri and Dec 24–26;* ⊸*free admission, £5 Tue evening;* ⊶*guided tour Sat 11am (*⊸*£5; no booking; 22 tickets on sale from 10.30am);* ✆*020 7405 2107; www.soane.org).* This remarkable little museum presents the highly individual collection of Classical sculpture, architectural fragments, drawings, prints and paintings, assembled by Soane, the architect, in his own house and left virtually untouched as stipulated in his will in 1833. The highlight is the **collection of pictures** mostly assembled on folding and sliding planes which make the most of the very limited available space. There are drawings by Piranesi, paintings by Canaletto, Reynolds and Turner and 12 of Hogarth's minutely observed paintings of London's unpleasant 18C underbelly including *The Election* and *The Rake's Progress*.

Lincoln's Inn★★ **(F2**; ⊖*Holborn; Entrances on Chancery Lane, Carey Street and Serle Street;* **Grounds:** ⊙*open year-round Mon–Fri excl bank hols;* **Chapel:** ⊙*open Mon–Fri (excl bank hols), noon–2.30pm; call to confirm;* ✆*020 7405 1393; www. lincolnsinn.org.uk)* is the grandest of the four Inns of Court, dating back to the late 15C. The Old Hall dates from 1490; the Old Buildings are Tudor, refaced in 1609, while the Chapel was rebuilt 1620–23. The **Temple**★ (⊖*Temple; entrances on Fleet Street and Embankment;* ⊙*see website for church opening times;* ✆*020 7353 3470; www.templechurch.com, www. innertemple.org.uk),* another remarkable ancient complex, comprises two of the four Inns of Court, **Inner Temple** and **Middle Temple**. The gabled, half-

---

The Inns of Court

The area around High Holborn and Fleet Street has been the centre of legal London since the 14C, housing some of the world's oldest surviving legal training establishments, Lincoln's Inn, Gray's Inn, Inner Temple and Middle Temple, known collectively as the Four Inns of Court. Each inn (which meant "house" in Old English) resembles a small university campus, comprising rooms for practising barristers, a dining hall, a library and a chapel. They are oases of calm, little known to most Londoners, and the grounds and some buildings are open to the public from Monday to Friday.

---

timbered three-storey Tudor **Inner Temple Gateway** leads off Fleet Stret into the Temple, past 19C buildings and the houses (right) where Dr Johnson (of Dictionary fame) lived in the 1760s. It leads to **Temple Church**, made famous recently by *The Da Vinci Code* film. This was built in the 12C in the round style of the Church of the Holy Sepulchre in Jerusalem. On the stone floor lie 10 effigies of knights in armour dating from the 10C to the 13C. The highlight of Middle Temple is the magnificent **Middle Temple Hall** (⊙*open Mon–Fri 10am–11.30am, 3pm–4pm (functions permitting, call ahead);* ✆*020 7427 4800; www.middle temple.org.uk).* The Elizabethan Great Hall has ancient oak timbers, panelling and fine carving, heraldic glass, helmets and armour and a remarkable double hammerbeam construction roof (1574). The splendid dining table is reputedly made from the hatch of Sir Francis Drake's flagship *Golden Hinde*, and the suits of armour standing guard around the hall are of similar vintage.

On High Holborn **Gray's Inn**★ **(F2**; ⊖*Holborn;* **Gardens:** ⊙ *open Mon–Fri, noon–2.30pm;* **Squares:** ⊙ *open Mon–Fri 9am–5pm; both closed bank hols;* ✆*020 7458 7800; www.graysinn.org.uk)* was founded in the 14C. Its buildings date from the 16C though many have had to be renewed since the war. On the opposite side of the road, a contemporary survivor, from the late 16C, is the row of **half-timbered houses** (1586–96), forming the front of **Staple Inn★ (F2)** which was also once a legal training establishment, albeit never an Inn of Court.

Just around the corner is another remarkable little half-timbered house, known as the **Old Curiosity Shop (E2)** (*Portsmouth Street, southwest corner of Lincoln's Inn Fields*) immortalised by Dickens in his eponymous novel (1841). It is a rare example of an Elizabethan building (c. 1567) to survive intact in London. It has had many recent guises and currently sells shoes (🕐 *open Mon–Sat 11am–7pm*).

BLOOMSBURY★ (E1/2)

This former residential area with its many squares is dominated by two learned institutions, the British Museum (👤*see below*) and the University of London. The development of Bloomsbury Square in 1661 brought a new concept in social planning; the fourth Earl of Southampton erected houses for the well-to-do around three sides of a square, a mansion for himself on the fourth, northern side and a network of service streets all around with a market nearby. A century later, in 1775, the elegant **Bedford Square★★ (E2)** was developed. It is still complete, with its three-storey brick terrace houses with rounded doorways and first-floor balconies. Other squares, now partly incorporated into the university precinct, followed in the 19C. The most famous residents were the 1920s **Bloomsbury Group** of writers, artists and philosophers, including Virginia Woolf, Vanessa Bell and Roger Fry.

British Museum★★★ (E2)

🚇*Russell Square. Great Russell Street.* 🕐 *Open year-round daily 10am–5.30pm (8.30pm Thu–Fri).* 🕐 *Closed Good Fri, Dec 24–26, Jan 1.* 💷*Charge for temporary exhibitions only.* 🚶*Various guided tours (charge).* ♿✕. ✆*020 7323 8299. 020 7323 8181 (bookings). www.thebritishmuseum.ac.uk.*

Since the millennium the British Museum has undergone the biggest revolution in its centuries-old existence. **The Great Court**, designed by Sir Norman Foster, is now the hub of the museum – Its glass and steel roof spans the space to the Reading Room – and makes for a stunning entrance foyer.

It all began back in 1753 when Sir Hans Sloane's collection was bequeathed to the nation. This augmented the old Royal Library of 12,000 volumes assembled by monarchs since Tudor times. Acquisitions, increased dramatically in the 19C and 20C with finds by archeologists attached to the museum, bringing the museum its reputation as one of the greatest centres of world antiquities.

Notable among the Egyptian antiquities are the **mummies**, and the **Rosetta Stone** which provided a key for deciphering heiroglyphics. No less fascinating is **"Ginger"** (so-named after the colour of his hair) a 5,000-year old corpse buried in hot sands c. 3300 BC and naturally preserved intact.

The collection of Western Asiatic antiquities is particularly wide-ranging, including the world-famous **Elgin Marbles** (👤*see below*). Look carefully at the exquisite Roman **Portland Vase** and you can see that it has been carefully pieced back together again after it was smashed it into 200 pieces in 1845.

Lindow Man (1C AD), garroted and preserved in a peat bog, is evidence of human sacrifice. Reminders of Roman Britain include the 4C silver set of tableware known as the **Mildenhall Treasure**, found in Suffolk, and considered to be the finest pieces of their kind anywhere in the Roman Empire. This was eclipsed in 1994 by the **Hoxne Hoard** – thousands of coins, jewellery and silver plate, also found in Suffolk.

In the Medieval, Renaissance and Modern Collections is the **Sutton Hoo Ship Burial** which shows the rich variety of artefacts retrieved from a royal tomb including fabulous gold jewellery, weapons and armour. Note too the beautifully carved mid-12C walrus ivory **Lewis Chessmen** found on the Isle of Lewis in the Outer Hebrides.

The Western Asiatic section, covering Mesopotamia and Asia Minor includes breathtaking **Assyrian sculptures** from the cities of Nimrud, Khorsabad and Nineveh. From ancient Iran the rich artistic tradition of the Persian Empire shines through in the **Luristan Bronzes** c. 1200 BC, and the fabulous **Oxus Treasure** (5–4C BC).

The circular, domed **Reading Room** (40ft/12m wide) dates from 1857, and was designed to ensure that the "poorest student" as well as men of letters should be able to have access to the library. It accommodates 400 readers and 25mi/40km of shelving (1,300,000 books). The restored blue and gold decoration of the dome recreates the original setting, where Karl Marx, Lenin and George Bernard Shaw, among many others have sat and studied

British Library★★ (E1)

⊖Euston Square. 96 Euston Road. **Galleries:** Open Mon–Sat, 9.30am–6pm (Tue 8pm, Sat 5pm), Sun and bank hols 11am–5pm. ♿✕. ℘020 7412 7332 (visitor services). www.bl.uk.

The new British Library houses the world's second largest collection of written works after the Library of Congress in the US. Opened in 1997, it is a monumental free-form, asymmetric building of red brick, Welsh slate and metal and granite. The entrance piazza is dominated by a huge bronze statue of Newton by Sir Eduardo Paolozzi.

The library's most famous treasures include a copy of **Magna Carta**, the **Lindisfarne Gospel**, **Codex Sinaiticus** the Gutenberg Bible, Diamond Sutra, Essex's death warrant, Nelson's last letter, Shakespeare's signature and **First Folio** (1623) and Beatles' manuscripts. Advanced technology makes it possible to turn the pages of rare books (if only virtually) at the touch of a button. The **Pearson Gallery of Living Words** reflects the diversity of the library's collection through interactive displays. The **Workshop of Words**, **Sound and Images** is a hands-on gallery tracing the story of book production from the earliest written documents to the 21C.

REGENT'S PARK★★ (CD1)

This beautiful park (⊖Regent's Park), bounded to the north by the Regent's Canal and surrounded by dazzling white Regency terraces and splendid villas was laid out in the early 19C by John Nash. The park has long been famous for its zoo, and is much loved for its rose garden and boating lake. Bordering it to the south is the busy Marylebone Road with the ever-popular Madame Tussaud's.

👥 London Zoo★★ (C1)

⊖Regent's Park, Camden Town. Outer Circle, Regent's Park. Open daily 10am–5.30pm (4pm Oct–Feb); last admission 1hr before closing. £13.90, child £10.90. ♿✕. ℘020 7722 3333. www.londonzoo.co.uk.

The London Zoological Society opened on a 5 acre/2ha site in Regent's Park in 1828. Today it covers 36 acres/14ha with around 8,000 animals from 900 species. The emphasis nowadays is placed on breeding endangered animals and on foreign conservation projects.

The zoo's once-famous elephants have been transferred to an outreach (Whipsnade Park, where they have more space) but there are still family favourites such as lions, tigers, rhinos and giraffes to see. As you enter the zoo pick up a programme of activities (talks, feeding times, grooming/bathing the animals...

Madame Tussaud's★ (C1)

⊖Baker Street. Open daily year-round 9.30am (9am–6pm Sat–Sun, bank and school hols) to 5.30pm (last admission); Aug 9am–7pm. Closed 25 Dec. £25. £12.50 after 5pm Aug. Book online to avoid queues and for a discount. ♿. ℘0870 400 3000. www.madame-tussauds.com.

The famous waxworks include Louis XV's mistress, portrayed as Sleeping Beauty, made by Madame Tussaud herself, plus statesmen of several ages and countries, modern celebrities in the worlds of sport and entertainment, murderers at the scene of their crimes in the Chamber of Horrors (complete with live actors) as well as a ride through the history of London.

Inner Suburbs★★

CAMDEN

Set immediately north of Regent's Park, gritty **Camden** (⊖Camden Town) provides a stark contrast to the park's grand Palladian villas. This is one of London's more bohemian areas and is famous for its **markets** ★★(Camden Market, Camden Lock Market and Canal Market), which sell antiques, fashion and bric-a-brac, catering to a young and alternative lifestyle. The area is also lively by night with good **live music** venues, down-to-earth pubs and cheap eats.

KNIGHTSBRIDGE

One of London's most exclusive suburbs, Knightsbridge (⊖Knightsbridge) is synonymous with **Harrods**★★ (est. 1849), the world's most famous department store, and its neighbour, **Harvey Nichols**★, where "ladies who lunch" come for the very best in fashion, beauty and home accessories. Both stores are renowned for their displays; "Harvey Nicks" for its window dressing and Harrods for its cornucopian turn-of-the-century **Food Halls**. At night, Harrods' famous terracotta façade, added in 1901, is illuminated by around 11,000 lightbulbs and is a fine sight.

KENSINGTON★★

Kensington is one of London's wealthiest suburbs. South Kensington is home to three world-famous national museums (&see below). **Kensington High Street** (⊖) offers local as well as brand-name shops and just off here, **Holland Park** (⊖) is a pretty, bucolic retreat from the crowds. Immediately north is **Notting Hill** (⊖), famous for its huge Rio-style **carnival** (last weekend Aug), and weekly (Sat) **Portobello Road Market**.

The antiques market here is claimed to be the world's largest; many of the shops are also open in the week.

Kensington Palace★★ (BY)

⊖Queensway, High Street Kensington. ○ Open daily 10am–6pm (Nov–Feb 5pm. ○ Closed 24–26 Dec. ☞£12.50. ♿ ✆0844 482 7777. www.hrp.org.uk.

This early 17C Jacobean house has passed through three principal phases: under the House of Orange it was William III 's private residence, with **Sir Christopher Wren** as principal architect; under the early Hanoverians it became a royal palace, with William Kent in charge of decorative schemes; since 1760 it has been a residence for members of the royal family, most notably the late **Diana**, **Princess of Wales**. The **State Apartments** are approached by the Queen's Staircase, designed by Wren. The **Queen's Gallery** has carving by Grinling Gibbons and portraits by Kneller and Lely. The **Privy** and lofty **Presence Chamber**, **Cupola** and **Drawing Rooms**, added for George I in 1718–20, were decorated by William Kent during 1722–27, covering the walls and ceiling with trompe l'œil paintings. For many visitors the highlight is the **Royal Ceremonial Dress Collection** showing the dresses and uniforms which have been worn at court occasions spanning 12 reigns from 1750, including the new **Diana**, **Fashion and Style Exhibition** which explores the princess' iconic style including dresses belonging to Diana, Princess of Wales.

Kensington Gardens★★ (B2/3)

⊖Queensway, High Street Kensington. At weekends the gardens are a favourite walk with Kensington locals, most famously nannies with their small charges. The **Round Pond** is the focal point for avenues radiating northeast, east and southeast to the **Serpentine**, where rowing boats may be hired, and **Long Water**. The early 18C **Orangery**★, Hawksmoor's splendid Baroque centrepiece (1705) now houses a restaurant. Beyond the Flower Walk on the south side of the gardens stands the **Albert Memorial**★ (1876), designed by George Gilbert Scott. Beneath a highly ornamented neo-Gothic spire surrounded by statues and a frieze of 169 named figures of poets, artists, architects and composers, sits a bronze statue (14ft/4.25m) of the Prince Consort who did so much to further the arts and learning, until his premature death in 1861.

Opposite stands the **Royal Albert Hall**★ (1867–71), a popular venue for meetings, conferences and concerts, notably the eight-week summer season of **Promenade Concerts**.

Hyde Park★★ (C2/3)

Adjoining Kensington Gardens to the east, Hyde Park (⊖*Marble Arch, High St. Ken., Hyde Park Corner*) is less formally laid out and very popular with office-workers and tourists alike, who come to enjoy the fresh air.

Speakers' Corner (CX) is a relatively modern feature of the park; not until 1872 did the government recognise the need for a place of public assembly and free discussion. Anyone can stand up and speak here as they frequently do on a Sunday morning, as long as they are not blasphemous, nor must they incite a breach of the peace. To its north stands **Marble Arch (CX)**, the triumphal arch designed by John Nash in 1827 as a grand entrance to Buckingham Palace in commemoration of the battles of Trafalgar and Waterloo. Embarrassingly it was never used, as it was too narrow to accommodate the royal Gold Stage Coach, and eventually ended up here.

Natural History Museum★★ (B3)

⊖*South Kensington. Cromwell Road.* ⏱ *Open year-round daily 10am–5.50pm.* ⏱ *Closed Dec 24–26.* ✉*Free admission to main galleries, charge for special exhibitions.* ♿✖. ☛*Tours.* ℘*020 7942 5000. www.nhm.ac.uk.*

Alfred Waterhouse's vast palace, inspired by medieval Rhineland architecture, was opened in 1881 to house the British Museum's ever-growing natural history collection, which today illustrates all forms of life, from the smallest bacteria to the largest creatures. This is now one of the country's favourite family museums, superbly combining education and entertainment with spectacular exhibits such as the famous **blue whale** model and huge **dinosaur skeletons**. Dinosaurs and fossils are still most visitors' favourite area and the diplodocus skeleton in the foyer has

become a museumm icon. Elsewhere you can learn about human biology, creepy crawlies, the origin of the species, take a behind-the-scenes tour, visit the Earth Galleries and get caught in a real earthquake simulation. The latest big development is the **Darwin Centre** dedicated to evolution.

Science Museum★★★

(B3) ⊖*South Kensington. Exhibition Road.* ⏱ *Open daily 10am–6pm.* ⏱ *Closed Dec 24–26. Free admission to main galleries, charge for IMAX cinema, motion-ride simulators and special exhibitions.* ♿✖. ℘*0870 870 4868. www.sciencemuseum.org.uk.*

This factory-laboratory of Man's continuing invention extends over 7 acres/3ha. Large-scale exhibits range from early beam engines to actual spacecraft, the first biplanes to jet aircraft, historic railway engines, road vehicles, and it is quite easy to spend a whole day here simply marvelling at the hardware without the need for any technical knowledge.

For more enquiring minds there are innumerable working models, handles to pull, buttons to push, huge floor areas devoted completely to **hands-on** experiments and cutting-edge technology. Children also love the **IMAX** theatre with its 3-D films. Try not to miss the often overlooked **Wellcome Galleries** or the **History of Medicine**, on the upper floors.

Victoria and Albert Museum★★★ (C3)

⊖*South Kensington. Entrances in Cromwell Road and Exhibition Road.* ⏱ *Open year-round daily 10am–5.45pm (selected galleries 10pm Fri).* ⏱ *Closed Dec 24–26. Admission to main galleries free.* ☛*Guided tours hourly 10.30am–3.30pm.* ♿✖. ℘*020 7942 2000. 0870 442 0809 (infoline). www.vam.ac.uk.*

This fabulously rich and varied collection was started, in part, with the purchase of contemporary works manufactured for the Great Exhibition of 1851. It includes the national collection of furniture, British sculpture, textiles, ceramics, silver and watercolours, as well as world-famous displays of fashionable dress, jewellery, Italian Renaissance sculpture, and art from India and the Far East. Even by London museum standards this is a huge rambling collection and for newcomers its size is overwhelming.

Renaissance Sculptures – The most highly prized work is Michelangelo's *Slave*, a wax model for a figure intended for the tomb of Pope Julius II.

Cast Courts – Plaster casts made 1860–1880 for art students who could not go abroad to see the real thing, include Trajan's Column, *St George* (Donatello) and *Dying Slave* (Michelangelo).

Prints, **Drawings and Paintings** – The most valuable collection here is the **Raphael Cartoons**, seven huge tapestry patterns, commissioned in 1515 by Pope Leo X for the Sistine Chapel.

Furniture and Woodwork – The collection ranges from the Middle Ages to the present day and encompasses just about every culture. **The Great Bed of Ware**, mentioned by Shakespeare, is the most remarkable piece of ancient British furniture. It is said to have once slept 52 people (26 butchers and their wives).

Textiles and Dress. One of the world's most extensive collections of textiles.

Metalworks and Jewellery – This is perhaps the most diverse and eclectic national collection, ranging from the 2C BC to the 21C AD, and encompasses a very broad spectrum and some magnificent pieces. The **Gilbert Collection** of gold, silver, micro-mosaics and gold boxes is a beautiful recent addition.

Eastern works of art – Some 60,000 artefacts from China, Korea and Japan. The most famous exhibit is **Tipu's Tiger**, a near-lifesize painted wooden tiger mauling its white victim. Within the tiger is an organ that simulates both the tiger's roars and its victim's groans.

CHELSEA★★

Riverside Chelsea (⊖ *Sloane Square, Pimlico*) has always attracted artists, architects, writers and actors. Chelsea once had a reputation for fashionable Bohemian living, but it is currently better known as a well-heeled suburb. In 1955 the opening of Bazaar clothes boutique by Mary Quant led to a radical change in dress with the launch of the mini skirt. During the 1960s, the **King's Road**★ became "the navel of swinging London", then in 1971, Chelsea fashion was re-invigorated by Vivienne Westwood, who opened her clothes shop at 430 Kings Road. The road became the launching point for the Punk movement. Punk fashions are rarely seen here today, but you may spot the occasional celebrity.

Royal Hospital★★ (CD4)

Royal Hospital Road. **Hospital:** ⏱ *Open daily, 10am–noon and 2pm–4pm, closed Sun during Oct–Mar and bank hols.* **Grounds:** ⏱ *Open daily 10am (Sun 2pm)–dusk.* ☎*020 7881 5204. www.chelsea-pensioners.co.uk.* The Royal Hospital was founded by King Charles II in 1682 as a retreat for veterans of the regular army who had been retired from duty after 20 years' service, or had become unfit for duty, as a result of wounds or disease. Wren produced a quadrangular plan and today the hospital still fulfils its original purpose; the **Chapel**, **Great Hall** and museum, are open to visitors. Every summer, the **Chelsea Flower Show** is held in the hospital grounds, attracting thousands of visitors.

PIMLICO
Tate Britain★★★ (E4)

⊖*Pimlico, then 5min walk (signed). Millbank.* ⏱ *Open year-round daily, 10am–5.50pm (first Fri of month 10pm).* ⏱ *Closed 24–26 Dec.* ✎*Charge for temporary exhibitions only.* ↝ *Guided tours 11am, noon, 1pm, 3pm.* ♿✕. ☎*020 7887 8888 (recorded information), 020 7887 8008. www.tate.org.uk.* In 1897 Henry Tate, sugar broker and British art collector, offered his collection to the nation and £80,000 for a building, if the government would provide a site. The museum is devoted exclusively to British art from 1500 to the present day. The Clore Gallery Turner Collection is a highlight and is one of the relatively few permanent exhibits.

Outer London★★

GREENWICH★★★
A Maritime Centre

The Tudors preferred Greenwich to their other residences and Henry VIII, who was born here, built a vast palace with a royal armoury; he also founded naval dockyards at Deptford and at Woolwich. During the Commonwealth the palace became derelict and only the Queen's House survived (🕯 see below).

After the Restoration, Charles II commissioned John Webb, a student of Inigo Jones, to build a King's House. William and Mary, who preferred Hampton Court (🕯 see below), granted a charter for the foundation of a Royal Hospital for Seamen at Greenwich, with **Wren** as surveyor. In 1873 the Webb and Wren buildings were transformed into the Royal Naval College, and eventually the Queen's House became part of the National Maritime Museum.

National Maritime Museum★★

Romney Road. 🕐 *Open year-round daily 10am–5pm (6pm summer). Timed ticket to Planetarium shows.* 🕐 *Closed Dec 24–26.* ✆£6 planetarium, all other areas free. ♿✗ Play area. ☏020 8858 4422, 020 8312 6565 (24hr recorded information). www.nmm.ac.uk.

As part of its £20 million Millennium make-over this museum of Britain's naval past – the largest maritime collection in the world with over two million seafaring-related objects – boasts an impressive single-span glazed roof, the largest in Europe, above a neo-Classical courtyard. The museum's fine collections of art is on display in the **Art and the Sea** gallery. For children, the **Bridge** links with the **All Hands** interactive gallery. Within the complex is the **Queen's House**★★. This elegant white Palladian villa was commissioned by James I from Inigo Jones, who designed it in 1615 as the very first Classical mansion.

Greenwich Park and Royal Observatory★

– The park, the oldest enclosed royal domain, extends for 180 acres/72ha, rising to a point 155ft/47m above the river, crowned by the Old Royal

Millennium Dome to O2

Built to celebrate the millennium and sited right on the Meridian Line, the Millennium Dome is the largest single-roofed structure in the world. Its external appearance is that of a huge (1,197ft/365m diameter) white marquee held up by twelve 312ft-/95m-high towers. Its circumference exceeds 0.62mi/1km and the floor space is large enough to park 18,000 London buses. The Dome has been re-christened the O2 and currently stage major concerts and other events; visit www.theo2.co.uk for details.

Observatory, built by Wren in 1675 "for finding out the longitude of places for perfect navigation and astronomy" (🕐 *admission free, included with National Maritime Museum ticket;* ♿), and the **General Wolfe** Monument.

Inside Wren's brick **Flamsteed House** is the lofty Octagon Room, beautifully proportioned, equipped with what John Evelyn called "the choicest instrument". The **Meridian Building** was added in the mid 18C to house the growing **telescope collection**★★. Note Airey's Transit Circle, through which the meridian passes, and outside a brass rail marking the meridian of 0°. Adjacent is the **Astronomy Centre** including three galleries and the state-of-the-art **Peter Harrison Planetarium**.

Old Royal Naval College★★

Painted Hall and Chapel and Greenwich Gateway Visitor Centre. 🕐 *Open daily, 10am (Sun 11am service) to 5pm. Free admission.* 🗪 *Guided tours* ✆£5. ☏020 8269 4791. www.oldroyal navalcollege.org.

After demolishing the Tudor Palace (🕯 *see above*), Wren retained the King Charles Block to which he added three symmetrical blocks named after King William, Queen Mary and Queen Anne. For the Queen's House (🕯*see above*) he provided a river vista (150ft/46m) flanked by twin cupolas over the Chapel

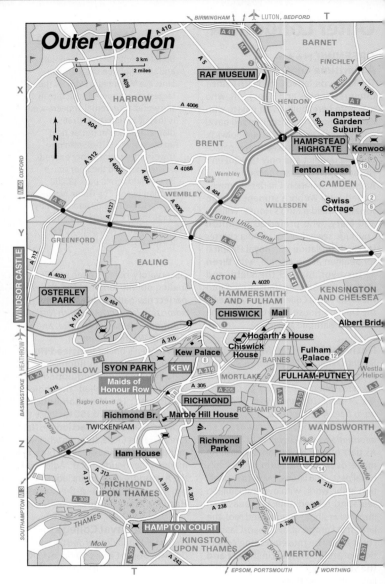

Outer London

BIRMINGHAM — LUTON, BEDFORD — T

A 410 — A 41 — A 5 — A 1 — A 1000

RAF MUSEUM

BARNET — FINCHLEY

A 4006 — HENDON — Hampstead Garden Suburb

HARROW — BRENT

A 404 — A 312 — A 4005 — A 404 — A 4088

Wembley — **HAMPSTEAD HIGHGATE** — Kenwood

Fenton House

CAMDEN

A 40 — A 4127 — WEMBLEY — A 4005 — A 404 — A 406

WILLESDEN — Swiss Cottage

Grand Union Canal

GREENFORD — A 40

EALING

A 4020 — ACTON — A 4020

KENSINGTON AND CHELSEA

OSTERLEY PARK — B 454 — A 4127 — HAMMERSMITH AND FULHAM

M4 — **CHISWICK** — Mall — Albert Bridge

A 315 — **Hogarth's House** — Fulham Palace

Chiswick House

FULHAM-PUTNEY

HOUNSLOW — **SYON PARK** — Kew Palace — **KEW**

BARNES — Westla... Helip...

Maids of Honour Row — MORTLAKE

A 4 — A 305 — A 205

Rugby Ground — **RICHMOND**

Richmond Br. — **Marble Hill House**

ROEHAMPTON — A 3

Crane — TWICKENHAM

WANDSWORTH

Ham House — **Richmond Park** — A 308

WIMBLEDON

A 316 — A 313 — A 311 — A 310 — A 307

RICHMOND UPON THAMES

A 308 — A 238

Wandle — A 219 — A 24...

THAMES — Mole — **HAMPTON COURT**

KINGSTON UPON THAMES — A 3 — MERTON

A 243 — A 298 — Beverley Brook

T — EPSOM, PORTSMOUTH — WORTHING

and the Painted Hall down to a new river embankment. The college is a Baroque masterpiece of English architecture set in landscaped grounds.

The **Painted Hall** ★ in the domed refectory is the work of **Sir James Thornhill**. The ceiling is covered by the **largest painting** (106ft/32m by 51ft/15m) in Great Britain, the *Triumph of Peace and Liberty*, by Sir James Thornhill.

WEST AND SOUTHWEST
Osterley Park★★ (T3)

NT. ⊖Osterley then 20min walk. *Jersey Road, Isleworth.* **House:** ⏱ Open Mar–Oct Wed–Sun and Bank Hol Mon 1pm–4.30pm; early to mid-Dec Sat–Sun 12.30pm–3.30pm. **Park:** ⏱ Open year-round daily 8am–dusk. ⬤£8.40. Gardens only, £3.70. 🅿 (£3.50)♿✕. ☎020 8232 5050 (Enquiries), 01494 755 566 (Infoline);

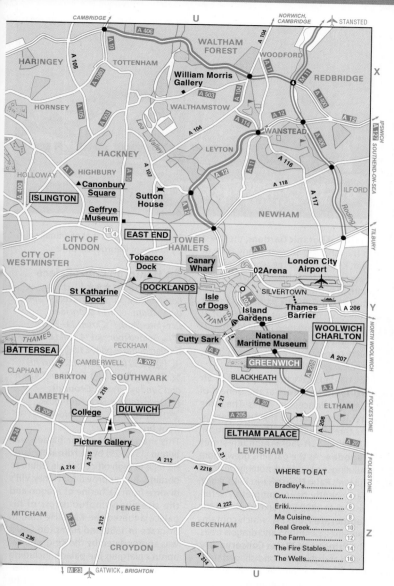

WHERE TO EAT

Bradley's.................... ②
Cru............................ ④
Eriki.......................... ⑥
Ma Cuisine................. ⑧
Real Greek................. ⑩
The Farm................... ⑫
The Fire Stables......... ⑭
The Wells.................. ⑯

www.nationaltrust.org.uk.
www.osterleypark.org.uk.
Osterley is the place to see **Robert Adam** rich interior decoration at its most complete – room after room just as he designed them between 1761 and 1780, in every detail from ceilings and walls to the furniture. This magnificent neo-classical house also has a landscape park and 18th-century gardens.

Royal Botanic Gardens, Kew ★★★ (T3)

Gardens: ⏰ Open daily from 9.30am. Closes late Oct–early Feb 4.15pm; Feb–Mar 5.30pm; Apr–Oct 6.30pm (7.30pm Sat–Sun and bank hols). **Palace:** ⏰ Open late Mar–Sept times as above. ⌖£5. ⌖£13. 🚶 Guided tour from Victoria Gate 11am, 2pm (1 hour). ♿✗. 📞 020 8332 5655. www.kew.org.

Royal Botanic Gardens, Kew

A. Williams/MICHELIN

The **Royal Botanic Gardens**, the finest in the land, are superb at any time of year. Kew is one of the world's leading botanic gardens, holding over one in eight of known plant species.

This 300acre/1200ha garden is not just a pleasure garden but the offshoot of laboratories engaged in the identification and conservation of plants from every corner of the earth, for economic, medical and other purposes.

The gardens were begun in 1756 by **Sir William Chambers** at the behest of Augusta, Princess of Wales. The same architect designed the **Orangery★**, the three small classical temples and in 1761 the 163ft-/50m- high ten-storey **Pagoda★**. As the gardens grew, more buildings were added, notably Decimus Burton's **Palm House★★** in 1848, which has recently been completely refurbished. In 1899 Burton completed the **Temperate House★**, which contains camellias, rainforest and dragon trees. The **Princess of Wales Conservatory**, a steel and glass diamond-shaped structure, boasts ten different tropical habitats ranging from mangrove swamp to sand desert.

Kew Gardens' latest treat is the **Rhizotron** and **Xstrata Treetop Walkway**, which takes visitors under the ground and then 59ft/18m up in the air.

Within the grounds, close to the river stands **Kew Palace★★** built for a London merchant in 1631. It was leased by George II for Queen Caroline in about 1730 and purchased by George III in 1781. The interior is that of a small country house of George III's time.

👥 Hampton Court Palace and Gardens★★★ (T4)

East Molesey, Surrey. **Palace:** 🕐 *Open daily, 10am–6pm (4.30pm late-Oct–late-Mar).* 🕐 *Closed 24–26 Dec.* 🔹 *Guided tour.* £14, child £7. Privy Garden or maze only, £3.50, child £2.50. ♿ 🅿 *(£3.50 for 3hrs then 55p per hr)* 🍴. **Chapel Royal:** 🕐 *12.45pm–1.45pm and Sunday services.* **Grounds:** 🕐 *Open daily.* *Free, 7am–dusk.* ☎ *0 844 482 7777 (24-hr infoline). www.hrp.org.*

This magnificent Tudor palace was begun (1514–29) by **Cardinal Wolsey**. He rose to high office but his failure to obtain papal approval for Henry VIII's divorce from Catherine of Aragon and the size and sumptuousness of his palace angered the King. He died in disgrace in 1530 and Hampton Court was appropriated by the King who set about enlarging the palace, including the splendid Great Hall with its hammer-beam roof, and lavishly transformed the chapel. The remarkable Astronomical Clock in Clock Court, though made for him in 1540, was brought here from St James's Palace in the 19C.

In 1688 Wren re-built the east and south fronts, the **State Apartments** and the smaller royal apartments. These rooms were decorated with carvings by **Grinling Gibbons** and painted ceilings by **Verrio**. The apartments and rooms contain a superb collection of **paintings** and **furniture**, while the **kitchens** and the **King's Beer Cellars** and the **wine cellars** offer a glimpse of life in Tudor times, all enhanced by costumed actors who interact with visitors. The **gardens**★★★ as seen today are the results of various schemes. The famous triangular **maze** was planted in 1690. In 1768 under George III, Lancelot Capability Brown planted the **Great Vine**★, now a plant of remarkable girth which produces an annual crop of around 500–600 bunches of grapes.

Syon Park★★ (T4)

⊖ *Gunnersbury then bus 237 or 267. Brentford.* **Gardens:** ⊙ *Open daily 10.30am–5pm/dusk.* **House:** ⊙ *Open mid-Mar–Oct Wed–Thu, Sun and bank hols 11am–5pm.* ⊜ *£9; Gardens and conservatory only £4.50.* ⭐⬜✕. ✆*020 8560 0881. www.syonpark.co.uk.*
The first Earl of Northumberland remodelled this ancient house in 1762, commissioning **Robert Adam** who richly ornamented and furnished it. A number of notable Stuart portraits by Van Dyck, Lely and others further embellish the interior. **Lancelot Capability Brown** re-designed the gardens and extended them to the river; two of his mulberry trees still survive and a vast rose garden is in bloom from May to August. The **Great Conservatory**, a beautiful semi-circular building with a central cupola and end pavilions, dates from 1827.

Ham House★★ (T4)

NT. ⊖*Richmond then bus. Ham Street.* **House:** ⊙ *Open third week Feb, mid-Mar–Oct Sat–Wed and Good Fri noon–4pm.* **Garden:** ⊙ *Open Sat–Wed 11am–5pm/dusk (late Dec–mid-Feb 4pm).* ⊙*Closed Dec 25–26 Dec, Jan 1.* ⊜*£9. Gardens only, £3.* ⭐⬜✕. ✆*020 8940 1950. www.nationaltrust.org.uk.*
This is an exquisite three-storey 17C brick house. Much of the original furnishing has survived and is lavish even by the standards of the age. The house is rich in ornate plasterwork on the ceilings and splendid carved wood panelling on the walls. The Great Staircase of 1637, built

of oak around a square well and gilded, has a beautiful balustrade of boldly carved trophies of arms. Notable among the many fine paintings are portraits by Lely, Kneller and Reynolds.

Richmond★★ (T3)

 Possessing what has been called the most beautiful "urban village" green in England, Richmond grew to importance between the 12C and 17C as a royal seat. Today private houses stand on the site of Henry VII's Royal Palace which he had sumptuously rebuilt and in which he died in 1509 (as did his granddaughter, Elizabeth I, in 1603). Among other fine Georgian houses in the "village" note the **Maids of Honour Row**★★ on the Green, built in 1724.
Climb **Richmond Hill's** steep road, lined by 18C houses with balconied terraces, to enjoy the excellent views immortalised by artists such as Turner and Reynolds. At the top **Richmond Park**★★ (TYZ) is the largest of the Royal Parks and is known for its herds of red and fallow deer. From the top of Henry VIII's Mound, near Pembroke Lodge and the Richmond Gate, on a clear day the **panorama**★★★ extends from Windsor Castle to St Paul's Cathedral in the City.

NORTH
Kenwood House★★ (The Iveagh Bequest) (T2)

EH. ⊖*Archway or Golders Green, then 210 bus. Hampstead Lane.* **House:** ⊙ *Open daily 11am–5pm (4pm Nov–Mar).* ⊙ *Closed Dec 24–26, Jan 1.* ⊜*Charge for temporary exhibitions only.* **Grounds:** ⊙ *Open daily 8am–dusk.* ⭐⬜✕, *picnic area.* ✆*020 8348 1286. www.english-heritage.org.uk.*
Set in leafy grounds beside Hampstead Heath, this is one of London's outstanding country houses, remodelled by Robert Adam 1764–79. The richly decorated library, ★★ is one of Adam's great masterpieces. Kenwood also possesses superb paintings including a Rembrandt (*Self Portrait in Old Age*). Its lakeside summer concerts, in a magnificent natural setting, are a highlight of the northwest London social scene.

STAY

CITY

🛏🍽🖥🖥 **Andaz Liverpool St**, *EC2M 7QN.* ⊖*Liverpool Street.* ℰ*020 7618 5000. www.andaz.com.* Behind the classic Victorian railway-hotel façade is one of London's best post-Millennium hotels, with bright spacious bedrooms, highly fashionable bars and restaurants.

🛏🍽🖥🖥 **Threadneedles**, *5 Threadneedle St, EC2R 8AY.* ⊖*Bank.* ℰ*020 7657 88080. www.theetoncollection.com.* "The City's boutique hotel", occupies a magnificent classic 1856 banking hall with stained glass cupola; rooms are stylish with CD players and Egyptian cotton sheets.

COVENT GARDEN, SOHO

🛏🍽🖥🖥 **The Soho**, *4 Richmond Mews, W1D 3DH.* ⊖*Tottenham Court Road.* ℰ*020 7559 3000. www.firmdale. com.* This very stylish small–medium luxury hotel has two large drawing rooms, up-to-the-minute bedrooms, all boasting hi-tech extras plus a contemporary bar and restaurant.

PICCADILLY

🛏🍽🖥🖥 **22 Jermyn Street**, *22 Jermyn Street, SW1Y 6HL.* ⊖*Piccadilly Circus.* ℰ*020 7734 2353. www.22jermyn.com.* A discreet entrance on this famous street leads to this exclusive boutique hotel with stylishly decorated bedrooms.

BLOOMSBURY

🛏🍽🖥🖥 **Montague on the Gardens**, *15 Montague St, WC1 5B.* ⊖*Holborn.* ℰ*020 7637 1001; www.montague-hotel.com.* Located near the British Museum, this charming hotel features a host of amenities and friendly staff. Rooms, each individually decorated, are elegantly comfortable.

🛏🍽🖥🖥 **Myhotel Bloomsbury**, *11–13 Bayley St, Bedford Square.* ⊖*Tottenham Court Road.* ℰ*020 7667 6000. www.myhotels.co.uk.* This very trendy minimalist mix of East meets West features Mybar, a library and Yo Sushi! conveyor belt dining.

KNIGHTSBRIDGE, BELGRAVIA

🛏🍽🖥🖥 **The Halkin**, *Halkin St, SW1X 7DJ.* ⊖*Hyde Park Corner.* ℰ*020 7333 1000. www.halkin.co.uk.* A London favourite, the Halkin was one of the first minimalist hotels in town. Its cool marbled reception has an understated charm and the spacious bedrooms have every facility.

🛏🍽🖥🖥 **The Knightsbridge**, *10 Beaufort Gardens, SW3 1PT.* ⊖*Knightsbridge.* ℰ*020 7584 6300. www.firmdale.com.* A very artfully renovated town house drawing on many influences from the UK and abroad, including two drawing rooms with an African feel, a romantic library, and bedrooms in fresh modern English style.

🛏🍽🖥🖥 **The Milestone**, *1 Kensington Court, W8 5DL.* ⊖*High Street Kensington.* ℰ*020 7917 1000. www. milestonehotel.com.* Behind a glorious Victorian façade this luxury boutique hotel and apartments has a charming oak-panelled lounge and snug bar, and meticulously decorated English country-style bedrooms.

CHELSEA, EARLS' COURT

🛏🍽 **The Amsterdam**, *7–9 Trebovir Road, SW5 9LS.* ⊖*Earl's Court.* ℰ*020 7370 2814. www.amsterdam-hotel.com.* A former "Best B&B in London", this privately run individually styled boutique hotel boasts light and airy bedrooms, some with their own balcony.

🛏🍽 **The Rushmore**, *11 Trebovir Road, SW5 9LS.* ⊖*Earl's Court.* ℰ*020 7370 3839. www.rushmore-hotel.co.uk* Small, elegant townhouse hotel with a welcoming reception, an attractive piazza-style conservatory and 22 individually designed rooms.

🛏🍽 **The Mayflower**, *26–28 Trebovir Road, SW5 9LS.* ⊖*Earl's Court.* ℰ*020 7370 0991. www.mayflower-group. co.uk.* Each of the 48 good-sized rooms of this handsome town house hotel are decorated in a distinctive style with an Asian influence.

🛏🍽🖥🖥 **The Draycott**, *26 Cadogan Gardens, SW3 2RP.* ⊖*Sloane Square.* ℰ*020 7730 6466. www.draycotthotel. com.* Charming 5-star Victorian country-house style hotel in a residential area with an elegant sitting room which overlooks tranquil gardens.

CLERKENWELL, ISLINGTON

🍽🍽🛏🛏 **Malmaison**, *Charterhouse Square, EC1M 6AH.* ⊖*Barbican.* ✆*020 7012 3700. www.malmaison. com.* Hidden behind a Victorian-brick façade in the cobbled courtyard of leafy Charterhouse Square are stylish comfy public areas, bold bedrooms with lots of cutting-edge extras and luxury touches.

🍽🍽🛏🛏 **The Zetter**, *St John's Square, 86–88 Clerkenwell Road, EC1M 5RJ.* ⊖*Farringdon.* ✆*020 7324 4444; www.thezetter.com.* An old five-storey warehouse in fashionable Clerkenwell has been converted into a small luxury hotel and restaurant, featuring discreetly trendy modern design with extras ranging from old paperbacks to plasma-screen TVs.

MARYLEBONE

🍽🛏 **St George**, *49 Gloucester Place, W1U 8JE.* ⊖*Marble Arch.* ✆*020 7486 8586. www.stgeorge-hotel.net.* A charming grade-II listed town house, a short walk from Oxford Street and Baker Street offering a warm welcome and 19 attractive bedrooms.

🍽🍽🛏🛏 **Charlotte Street**, *15–17 Charlotte Street, W1T 1RJ.* ⊖*Goodge Street.* ✆*020 7806 2002. www.firmdale. com.* Another very artistic townhouse conversion by the same company behind the Knightsbridge Hotel and the Soho Hotel (🕯*both, see above*) with a charming understated English feel.

🍽 EAT

Pubs and Restaurants – London has a huge choice. See the Michelin Red Guide to London and Michelin's Eating Out in Pubs for detailed information and prices. Afternoon tea at some of the large hotels or at Fortnum and Mason is a treat, albeit often very expensive.

CITY

🍽🍽 **Almeida**, *30 Almeida Street, N1 1AD.* ⊖*Angel.* ✆*020 7354 4777. www. danddlondon.com.* This spacious open-plan restaurant serves high quality classic French dishes in a contemporary setting next to Islington's Almeida Theatre.

🍽🍽 **Coq d'Argent**, *1 Poultry, EC2R 8EJ.* ⊖*Bank.* ✆*020 7395 5000. www. conran-restaurants.co.uk.* Regional French food, highlighted by popular shellfish dishes, is served in a spectacular dining room which, like its spacious, lawned, al fresco roof terrace offers unique City views.

🍽🍽 **Metrogusto**, *13 Theberton St, N1 0QY.* ⊖*Highbury and Islington.* ✆*020 7226 9400. www.metrogusto. co.uk.* Progressive Italian cooking is the theme at this stylish, smart contemporary Islington restaurant adorned with striking modern art.

🍽🍽 **Smiths of Smithfield**, *Top Floor, 67–77 Charterhouse St, EC1M 6HJ.* ⊖*Barbican.* ✆*020 7251 7950. www.smithsofsmithfield.co.uk.* The higher you go the more formal it gets at this ever-popular bustling three-storey shrine to modern British cooking with good views of Smithfield Market from the top terrace.

🍽🍽🍽 **Club Gascon**, *57 West Smithfield, EC1A 9DS.* ⊖*Barbican.* ✆*020 7796 0600. www.clubgascon.com.* The rich flavours of southwest France, with foie gras specialities, are the forte of this acclaimed intimate rustic restaurant on the edge of Smithfield Market.

🍽🍽🍽 **Rhodes Twenty Four**, *Tower 42, 25 Old Broad St, EC2N 1HQ.* ⊖*Liverpool Street.* ✆*020 7877 7703. www. rhodes24.co.uk.* On the 24th floor of the City's tallest tower block, the quality of the modern Classic British cuisine (try braised oxtail cottage pie) served by one of the country's best known chefs, is as elevated as the views.

INNER LONDON

🍽🍽 **Archipelago**, *110 Whitfield Street. W1T 5ED,* ⊖*Great Portland Street,* ✆*020 7383 3346. www. archipelago-restaurant.co.uk.* Eccentric in both menu (reindeer carpaccio, cricket and locust salad, blackened kangaroo etc.) and décor, this is not for the faint hearted!

🍽🍽 **Crazy Bear**, *26–28 Whitfield Street, WT1 2RG,* ⊖*Goodge Street* ✆*020 7631 0088. www.crazybear group.co.uk.* Sleek and savvy, this new hyper-chic restautant is a mixture of Orient Express and New York style with art-deco inspired fittings and an Asian menu with strong Thai leanings.

Fakhreldine, *85 Piccadilly, W1J 7NB.* Green Park. *020 7493 3424. wwwfakhreldine.co.uk.* Long-established Lebanese restaurant with fine views of Green Park serving a long list of mezes, plus a modern European styled menu of original Lebanese dishes.

Mela, *152–156 Shaftesbury Avenue, WC2H 8HL.* Piccadilly Circus. *020 7836 8635. www.melarestaurant.co.uk.* Tasty Indian "country-style" food in a bright, modern, buzzing setting.

Momo, *25 Heddon Street, W1B 4BH.* Oxford Circus. *020 7434 4040. www.momoresto.com.* Long-established ever-popular Moroccan restaurant which is a treat for the palate, eyes and ears (check out their CDs). Popular basement bar too.

Sketch (The Gallery), *9 Conduit Street, W12 2XG.* *0870 777 4488. www.sketch.uk.com* Oxford Circus. Conceived by French master chef Pierre Gagnaire (holder of three Michelin stars) and Algerian restaurateur "Momo" Mazouz, this is London's most arresting "destination" where the highest quality food, art and music collide in ultra-trendy surroundings.

Fino, *33 Charlotte Street (entrance on Rathbone Street), W1T 1RR.* Goodge Street. *020 7813 8010. www.finorestaurant. com.* This new-wave Spanish tapas bar in a trendy basement offers a wide range of authentic dishes and is acclaimed as one of the best Iberian restaurants in London.

Hakkasan, *8 Hanway Place, WT1 IHD.* Tottenham Court Road. *020 7927 7000.* Beautifully lit and styled, this is London's most distinctive modern interpretation of Cantonese cooking (specials include Peking Duck with Beluga caviar).

COVENT GARDEN, SOHO AND CHINATOWN

Aurora, *49 Lexington Street, W1F 9AJ.* Piccadilly Circus. *020 7494 0514.* An informal Bohemian bistro with a languid atmosphere, a small but pretty walled garden terrace and a short but balanced menu of simple fresh food.

L'Escargot, *48 Greek Street, W1D 4EF.* Tottenham Court Road, *020 7437 6828. www.whitestarline.org.uk.* This old favourite, now under Marco Pierre White, features a chic vibrant brasserie while upstairs the Picasso Room is famed for its artworks and provides an intimate and discreet ambience for fine French dining.

Vasco & Piero's Pavilion, *15 Poland Street, W1F 8QE.* Tottenham Court Road. *020 7437 8774. www. vascosfood.com.* A long-standing family-run Italian restaurant with a loyal local following, offering a warm welcome and traditional cooking.

J Sheekey, *28–32 St Martin's Court WC2N 4AL.* Leicester Square. *020 7240 2565. www.j-sheekey.co.uk.* One of London's oldest traditional fish restaurants, festooned with photos of thespians, its wood panels and alcove tables create a famed intimate atmosphere.

Yauatcha, *15 Broadwick Street W1F 0DL.* Tottenham Court Road. *020 7494 8888.* This upmarket Chinese restaurant is a conversion of a Soho post office; below is a smart cool tea room, above a spacious dining room serving unusual authentic dishes.

MAYFAIR

Chor Bizarre, *16 Albemarle Street, W1S 4HW.* Green Park. *020 7629 9802. www.chorbizarrerestaurant.com.* The London branch of one of New Delhi's most innovative and popular restaurants has a vibrant kaleidoscopic interior and romantic atmosphere. North Indian and Kashmiri cuisine.

Umu, *14–16 Bruton Place, W1J 6LX.* Bond Street. *020 7499 8881. www.umurestaurant.com.* The only Kyoto-style restaurant in the UK, this exclusive Michelin-starred restaurant has a central sushi bar and uses the highest quality ingredients.

The Greenhouse, *27a Hays Mew, W1X 7RJ.* Hyde Park Corner. *020 7499 331. www.greenhouse-restaurant.co.uk.* A pleasant courtyard off a quiet mews leads to this Michelin-starred British restaurant.

PICCADILLY, ST JAMES'S

Brasserie Roux, 8 Pall Mall, SW1Y 5NG. ⊖Piccadilly Circus, ☏020 7968 2900. www.sofitelstjames.com. Informal smart classic brasserie with large windows, serving classic French dishes.

Alloro, 19–20 Dover Street, W1S 4LU. ⊖Green Park. ☏020 7495 4768. www.alloro-restaurant.co.uk. One of the new breed of stylish modern Italian restaurants with contemporary art and leather seating plus a separate bustling bar.

The Wolseley, 160 Piccadilly, W1J 9EB. ⊖Green Park. ☏020 7499 6996. www.thewolseley.com. One of London's most popular meeting places, open all day, the Wolseley has the feel of a grand Europeancafe, with pillars, high vaulted ceiling and mezzanine tables.

KENSINGTON

Wódka, 12 St Alban's Grove, W8 5PN. ⊖High Street Kensington. ☏020 7937 6513. www.wodka.co.uk. Some of London's best Polish and eastern European food (plus vodkas) served in a simple mellow setting in a former dairy retaining its old tiles and panelled walls. Good-value lunch.

Assaggi, 39 Chepstow Place (above Chepstow Pub), W2 4TS. ⊖Bayswater. ☏020 7792 9033. Polished wood floorings, tall windows and modern artwork provides the bright surroundings for this perennially popular establishment serving a concise menu of robust Italian dishes.

Babylon, (at the Roof Gardens) 7th Floor, 99 Kensington High Street W8 5SA (entrance on Derry Street). ⊖High Street Kensington. ☏020 7368 3993. www.roofgardens.com. In a stunning rooftop garden setting with an al fresco option in warm weather, this stylish modern dining room offers contemporary British cooking. Very good-value lunch.

Belvedere, off Abbotsbury Rd, Holland Park, W8 6LU. ⊖Holland Park, ☏020 7602 1238. www.whitestarline. org.uk. Dating back to the 17C this was once the summer ballroom to the Jacobean mansion that was Holland House, then the orangery, set in the middle of one of London's most beautiful parks. Modern take on classic dishes.

Clarke's, 122–4 Kensington Church Street, W8 4BH. ⊖Notting Hill Gate, ☏020 7221 9225. www. sallyclarke.com. One of London's top restaurauteurs, Sally Clarke, personally oversees the kitchen providing modern British cooking in comfortable bright neighbourhood surroundings.

Kensington Place, 201 Kensington Church Street, W8 7LX. ⊖Notting Hill, ☏020 7727 3184. www.danddlondon. com. This long-established restaurant set the trend for large bustling informal eating and still attracts the crowds with its modern cooking.

KNIGHTSBRIDGE, CHELSEA

Cross Keys, 1 Lawrence Street, SW3 5NB. ⊖Sloane Square. ☏020 7349 9111. www.thexkeys.co.uk. Behind a 200-year old pub façade lies a spacious bar with tall windows that goes up to a gallery with large mirrors, a huge curly chandelier and rustic tools. Flavoursome generous modern British food.

The Ebury, 11 Pimlico Road, SW1W 8NA. ⊖Sloane Square. ☏020 7730 6784. www.theebury.co.uk. Typical attractive new-wave London brasserie with walnut bar, simple tables, a large seafood bar and a very high standard of modern cooking with a wide-ranging menu from snacks to full meals.

Amaya, Halkin Arcade, 19 Motcomb St, SW1X 8JT. ⊖Knightsbridge. ☏020 7823 1166. www. realindianfood.com. This acclaimed top-end Indian restaurant specializes in different Indian grilling methods in a specially designed open-show kitchen.

Mango Tree, 46 Grosvenor Place, SW1X 7EQ. ⊖Hyde Park Corner. ☏020 7823 1888. www.mangotree. org.uk. Authentic traditional Thai dishes become works of art in this minimalist Belgravia dining room.

La Poule au Pot, 231 Ebury St, SW1W 8UT. ⊖Sloane Square. ☏020 7730 7763. Subdued lighting and friendly informality make this one of London's more romantic restaurants serving a classic French menu with extensive *plats du jour*.

CHELSEA AND EARL'S COURT

Eight Over Eight, *392 Kings Rd, SW3 5UZ.* ⊖*Sloane Square,* ✆*020 7349 9934. www.ricker-restaurants.com.* Enjoy inventive unusual Pan-Asian combinations in chic, comfortable Chelsea surroundings with bargain lunchtime deals and dim sum available all day.

Langan's Coq D'Or Bar and Grill, *254–260 Old Brompton Rd, SW5 9HR.* ⊖*Earl's Court.* ✆*020 7259 2599. www.langansrestaurants.co.uk.* This classic buzzy brasserie bar and grill with outdoor terrace offers excellent value classic and modern British cooking.

Le Colombier, *145 Dovehouse St, SW3 6LB,* ⊖*South Kensington.* ✆*020 7351 1155.* A fiercely Gallic restaurant with bright and cheerful surroundings including an attractive enclosed terrace, serving traditional French cooking.

Manicomio, *85 Duke of York Square, SW3 4LY,* ⊖*Sloane Square.* ✆*020 7730 3366. www.manicomio. co.uk.* Choose from the main restaurant or the café next door, both serving rustic Italian food; a perfect venue for outdoor dining on a delightful terrace overlooking the square.

Rasoi Vineet Bhatia, *10 Lincoln St, SW3 2TS.* ⊖*Sloane Square.* ✆*020 7225 1881. www.vineetbhatia. com.* Owned and run by the first Indian chef to be awarded a Michelin star, this is one of London's top Indian restaurants, set in an elegant mid-19C Chelsea townhouse.

LITTLE VENICE

The Waterway, *54 Formosa Street, W9 2JU.* ⊖*Warwick Avenue.* ✆*020 7266 3557. www.thewaterway.co.uk.* Pub (though hardly recognizable as such) with a thoroughly modern metropolitan ambience right on the waterfront in leafy Maida Vale; the young and trendy tuck into modern British favourites on a large decked terrace.

MARYLEBONE AND NORTH

The Salt House, *63 Abbey Road. NW8 0AE.* ⊖*St John's Wood.* ✆*020 7328 6626.* Grand gastropub with a summer patir, a snazzy duck-egg blue dining room with French posters, high ceilings and ornate mirror. Modern Mediterranean style menus.

Sardo Canale, *42 Gloucester Avenue, NW1 8JD.* ⊖*Chalk Farm.* ✆*020 7722 2800. www.sardocanale. com.* Next to the Regent's Canal, sit indoors in one of five snug modern dining rooms or out on the terrace by the 200-year old olive tree while enjoying authentic Sardinian cuisine.

Caffe Caldesi, *118 Marylebone Lane, W1U 2QF.* ⊖*Bond Street.* ✆*020 7935 1144. www.caldesi.com.* Drop in to this attractive converted pub for a cappuccino, pizzas and pastas or full meals featuring robust and authentic dishes with Tuscan specialities.

Roka, *37 Charlotte Street, W1T 1RR.* ⊖*Tottenham Court Road.* ✆*020 7580 6464.* Behind the striking glass and steel frontage lies an airy interior of teak, oak and paper wall screens where authentic flavoursome Japanese cuisine with a variety of grill dishes is served.

Locanda Locatelli, *8 Seymour Street, W1H 7JZ.* ⊖*Marble Arch. www. locandalocatelli.com.* Giorgio Locatelli is probably the best Italian chef in town and the quality of food at this stylishly appointed restaurant (banquettes and cherry wood with glass dividers) attracts the rich and famous.

SOUTHWARK

The Hartley, *64 Tower Bridge Road, SE1 4TR.* ⊖*Borough.* ✆*020 7394 7023. www.thehartley.com.* This small classic 19C red-brick pub has had a gastropub makeover.

Anchor & Hope, *36 The Cut, SE1 8LP.* ⊖*Southwark.* ✆*020 7928 9898 (no bookings).* One of London's best gastropubs, plain from without, offering cooking with a French regional rustic base.

Tapas Brindisa, *18–20 South-wark Street, Borough Market, SE1 1TJ.* ⊖*London Bridge.* ☏*020 7357 8880 (no bookings).* Top-quality produce is sold in the owner's shop while the bustling tapas bar is an authentic taste of Spain.

OUTER LONDON

NORTHWEST

Eriki, *4–6 Northways Parade, Finchley Rd, NW3 5EN.* ⊖*Swiss Cottage.* ☏*020 7722 0606.* This is a relaxing venue with good service of carefully presented flavoursome contemporary dishes from southern India.

The Wells, *30 Well Walk, NW3 1BX.* ⊖*Hampstead.* ☏*020 7794 3785. www.thewellshampstead.co.uk.* This attractive 18C pub-restuarant comprises a smart modern Hampstead bar downstairs and linen-covered formal tables upstairs where the menu is from a classical French repertoire.

Bradley's, *25 Winchester Road, NW3 3NR.* ⊖*Swiss Cottage.* ☏*020 7722 3457.* Warm pastel colours and modern artwork give a Mediterranean ambience to this neighbourhood restaurant, which is complemented by the cooking.

NORTH EAST

Cru, *2–4 Rufus St, Hoxton, N1 6PE.* ⊖*Old Street.* ☏*020 7729 5252. www.cru.uk.com.* This bar-deli-restaurant complex in a trendily converted 19C warehouse caters for all tastes and pockets with bar food as well as full meals from all over Europe.

Real Greek, *14–15 Hoxton Market, N1 6HG.* ⊖*Old Street.* ☏*020 7739 8212. www.therealgreek.co.uk.* Set in the heart of super-trendy Hoxton in an old Victorian pub, the food here is regional Greek home-style cooking.

SOUTH–SOUTHWEST

The Farm, *18 Farm Lane, SW6 1PP.* ⊖*Fulham Broadway.* ☏*020 7381 333. www.thefarmfulham.co.uk.* This converted pub with leather sofas and contemporary open fireplaces is ultra stylish and the menus are Modern British with a French accent.

The Fire Stables, *27–29 Church Rd, Wimbledon, SW19 5DQ.* ⊖*Wimbledon.* ☏*020 894 6101. www.firestableswimbledon.co.uk.* There's a high vaulted ceiling in this very popular old pub diner, a startling abstract painting on the wall, modern and retro furniture and an unfussy Modern British menu.

SOUTHWEST

Ma Cuisine, *The Old Post Office, Station Approach, TW9 3QB.* ⊖*Kew Gardens.* ☏*020 8332 1923. www.macuisinekew.co.uk.* This "petit bistrot" complete with red gingham table-cloths and pavement tables used to be the Kew Post Office – it now delivers good-value classic French food.

🛒SHOPPING

Shops in central London vary from the vast new Westfield Centre mall in Shepherd's Bush to upmarket Knightsbridge *(Harrods, Harvey Nichols)* and Bond Street *(fashion, antiques)*, Oxford and Regent Streets *(department stores)*, King's Road *(boutiques, antiques)*, Kensington High Street *(large stores and boutiques)*, Covent Garden *(boutiques and crafts)* and Piccadilly *(gentlemen's outfitters, sportswear)*. The main markets worth visiting are Portobello Rd *(antiques/nick nacks)*, Borough Market *(food)* and Camden Market *(clothing/alternative)*.

🎭 ENTERTAINMENT

The heart of London's nightlife is found in the streets around Leicester Square, Piccadilly and Covent Garden. Brixton, Camden, Hackney, Islington and Shoreditch offer more alternative music and entertainment, while every central London suburb has its own nightlife scene, from artsy Notting Hill to posh Chelsea. The vast dome of the O2 *(www.o2.co.uk)* in the Docklands is now the host of London's biggest concerts. Consult the daily press *(Evening Standard)* or *Time Out* (published Wednesdays) for London listings.

THE SOUTH EAST

"London's Countryside", also known as the Home Counties, is a densely populated affluent region which, given its busy infrastructure, is also surprisingly green. The rim of the basin containing Greater London is formed by sculpted chalk hills; the Chilterns to the northwest, the great estuary of the Thames to the east, the peaceful meandering picturesque Thames Valley to the west and the North Downs to the south. Further south, the coastal fringe faces continental Europe with which it has many links. Its towns range from major ports to holiday resorts, though in general this is a low-key tourist region.

Highlights

1. Marvel at the unique Oriental-Gothic **Brighton** Pavilion (p134)
2. Discover naval sea power at **Portsmouth** Historic Dockyard (p156)
3. Visit a house and grounds fit for a king at **Blenheim Palace** (p132)
4. Make your own pilgrimage to Chaucer's **Canterbury** Cathedral (p137)
5. Experience **Oxford** University at historic Christ Church College (p151)

North of London

The Chiltern Hills have offered travellers a route across southern England since the Iron Age and long before. Today you will find stately homes, beautiful gardens and excellent walking along these ancient routes. St Albans traces its history back to the Romans and ancient Verulamium, one of Rome's principal settlements in the province of Britannia Superior. Scattered around it are three of England's most interesting estates; Hatfield House, Knebworth and Woburn Abbey. Even these pale in comparison to majestic Blenheim Palace, some 50mi/80km north. Oxford, 10mi/16km to the south, is home to the oldest university in the English-speaking world, tracing its history of learning as far back as 1096.

◔ **Blenheim Palace** ◔ **Chilterns**
◔ **Oxford** ◔ **St Albans**

By the Thames

There really is no better way of absorbing the spirit of the Thames than a lazy summer boat trip between Windsor and Cookham, watching the bucolic countryside and splendid houses passing by along the river banks. Its gently winding course between Kew and its source in the Cotswolds, passes through typically English countryside of low hills, woods, meadows, country houses, pretty villages and small towns. Often there is no other road than the towpath. Dominating both riverside and town, 900-year-old Windsor Castle is the principal seat of the British Royal Family, though by no means the only attraction here. In Windsor Park, the castle's "back garden", young families will enjoy Legoland, while all enjoy strolling through the stretching gardens, particularly in spring.

◔ **Thames Valley** ◔ **Windsor**

Surrey and Hampshire

Surrey has become the capital's south west commuter belt, yet, despite its busy infrastructure, it is England's most wooded county, followed closely by Hampshire, famous for its ancient New Forest (◔ *see box, opposite*). Winchester retains echos of King Alfred's rule when it was capital of all England and is one of Southern England's finest county towns, surrounded by beautiful countryside.

◔ **New Forest** ◔ **Winchester**

Kent

The former cradle of British sea power, but better known since Victorian times as home of the greatest British writer since Shakespeare, Rochester is as synonymous with Charles Dickens as the Royal Naval Dockyard. An equally famous writer, Geoffrey Chaucer, is indelibly linked to Canterbury, said to be the ecclesiastical capital of England with a cathedral to match, and a rich legacy of religious buildings. Leeds Castle, near Maidstone, has a justifiable claim to

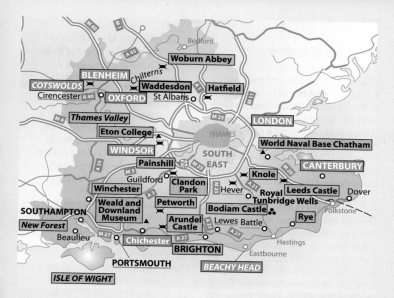

being the "loveliest castle in the world", while Tunbridge Wells is a delightful spa town developed by the Georgians and Victorians. And as the "Garden of England", so-named for its abundance of orchards and hop gardens, it is no surprise that Kent also boasts many fine gardens, as well as stately homes and castles to explore.

- 🏛 **Rochester**
- 🏛 **Royal Tunbridge Wells**
- 🏛 **Canterbury**

The Channel Coast

The White Cliffs of Dover are an iconic reference-point for travellers arriving at, or returning to, England. Despite the Channel Tunnel, Dover is still an important gateway to Europe. Moving east to west, the little port of Rye is a preserved gem, long abandoned by the retreat of the sea. Brighton has been known as "London-by-the-Sea" since the Regency period. The Great British Seaside was invented here and the town has a bohemian character not found anywhere else in Britain. The vista of Chichester Cathedral and water meadows is quintessential England, while its shoreline is a yachtsman's paradise. Portsmouth is home to the Royal Navy past and present, from *HMS Victory* to nuclear submarines; its Historic Dockyard is an essential lesson in understanding how Britannia once ruled the waves. A short ferry ride away is the Isle of Wight, a favourite resort since Queen Victoria built her splendid holiday home, Osborne House, here. Neighbouring Southampton has a proud shipping history. Every great British ocean liner sailed from here, including *Titanic*.

- 🏛 **Brighton**
- 🏛 **Dover**
- 🏛 **Portsmouth**
- 🏛 **Southampton**
- 🏛 **Isle of Wight**
- 🏛 **Chichester**
- 🏛 **Lewes**
- 🏛 **Rye**

New Forest

The New Forest was originally the royal forest of William I (the Conqueror), created in 1079 for private royal hunting. Two of William's sons later died in the forest in suspicious hunting accidents; Prince Richard and William Rufus. Today the forest comprises woodland, marshland and heath where ponies, donkeys, deer and cattle wander, often perilously close to the roadside. The forest is an excellent place for walking, cycling and even canoeing.

Blenheim Palace★★★

This greatest building of the English Baroque, residence of the Dukes of Marlborough, is matched in splendour by the sublime landscape of its vast park. At the park gates is the elegant town of **Woodstock**, built of mellow Cotswold stone, where old coaching inns and antique shops cluster round the Classical town hall.

A BIT OF HISTORY

"Royall and National Monument" – The Royal Manor of Woodstock (8mi/ 13km northwest of Oxford) once the hunting ground of Saxon kings, was the birthplace of Edward the Black Prince (b. 1330), also known as Edward of Woodstock. In the 18C the royal manor was given by Queen Anne to **John Churchill, Duke of Marlborough** (1650–1722), to mark his victory in 1704 over the armies of Louis XIV at Blenheim in Bavaria. Seemingly limitless funds from the national purse were made available for a *"Royall and National Monument"* to be erected in celebration of this decisive check to France's pan-European ambitions. Leading architects and craftsmen were employed, foremost among them **Sir John Vanbrugh**, one of England's most original architects, whose inventiveness and sense of drama found full expression here. Alas, court intrigues led

Michelin Map: Michelin Atlas p 18 or Map 504 P 28

Location: The palace is set in Woodstock, eight miles north of Oxford. On the first floor "Blenheim Palace: The Untold Story" is a good introduction to the 300-year history of house and estate. Take the guided tour of the house; a train will take you around the pleasure garden.

Don't miss: Grounds; the view from Woodstock Gate.

Opening: Allow at least three hours. *Park:* Open daily (except Dec 25) 9am–4.45pm (last admission). *Grounds:* Open mid-Feb–mid-Dec daily 10.30am–5.30pm during summer, see website for other times. *Entry:* Palace and park £17.50 (winter £14.50); Park only, £10 (winter £7.80); child £5 (winter £2.70). Park only £4 (child £3). Guided tour (1hr) except Sun, bank hols and busy periods. 01993 810 570. www. blenheimpalace.com.

Kids*:* The maze and butterfly house.

Blenheim Palace

By kind permission of 11th Duke of Marlborough and © Skyscan

to Marlborough's fall from the Queen's favour; the flow of money was cut off and building stopped. When it resumed it was at the Duke's own expense. His disputatious Duchess, Sarah, her sense of value for money now sharpened, quarrelled constantly over supposed extravagance, provoking Vanbrugh's resignation. The grandiose project, truly a monument rather than a home, was completed only after the first Duke's death in 1722. A century and a half later, on 30 November 1874, his direct descendant, **Winston Churchill**, grandson of the 7th duke, was born here. This most illustrious of Englishmen is now buried in the churchyard in Bladon *(3mi/4.8km south)*.

PALACE★★★

The palace's huge scale and fortress-like character are relieved by dynamic, almost theatrical composition and exuberant detail. Its silhouette has a romantic, even medieval air, with an array of turrets, pinnacles and disguised chimney-pots, and the Great Court (450ft/137m long) is like a stage set, a succession of colonnades, towers and arcades leading the eye inexorably to the main façade with its imposing portico. Symbols of military prowess and patriotism abound, from heaped-up trophies to centurions standing proudly on the parapet; over the courtyard gateway the unfortunate cockerel of France is mauled by the haughty English lion.

Interior

A series of splendidly decorated rooms continues the monumental theme. In the **Great Hall** (67ft/20m high) the ceiling is painted with an allegory of Marlborough's victory. Sir Winston Churchill's life is celebrated in a suite of rooms, including the one in which he was born. State apartments are furnished with original pieces, many of the highest quality. There are portraits by Reynolds, Romney, Van Dyck and one, by Sargent, of the ninth Duke with his family and American-born wife Consuelo. The vast **Saloon** has a great painted colonnade, apparently open to the sky, thronged with figures representing the four continents. The main axis of the park runs through this room, terminating in the spire of Bladon Church. The **Long Library**, with a magnificent stucco ceiling, runs the entire length (180ft/55m) of the west front. In the Chapel is the overwhelming marble **tomb** of the first Duke.

GROUNDS★★★

The ancient hunting park, with its venerable trees and deer-proof wall (9mi/15km long), was worked upon in the early 18C by the royal gardeners. The **Italian Garden** to the east of the palace and the spectacular Water Garden to the west are modern, as is the symbolic maze of trophies, cannon and trumpets in the walled garden, but they capture something of the spirit of the formal avenues and geometrical parterres which were mostly swept away by **Lancelot "Capability" Brown**, the greatest of English landscape architects. The redesigned park is his masterpiece, offering from the Woodstock Gate what has been described as "the finest view in England". Sweeping grassy slopes, noble groves of trees and the curving outline of the great lake, crossed by Vanbrugh's **Grand Bridge**, combine to "improve upon Dame Nature" and provide a more than worthy setting for the palace.

A huge **Doric column** (134ft/41m high), topped by a statue of the first Duke with Victory in his grasp, forms one focal point of the recently replanted axis which on the north side of the palace runs 2mi/3km to the Ditchley Gate. By the lake is the site of old Woodstock Manor, long demolished, and Fair Rosamund's Well, a reminder of this favourite of Henry II. Downstream, Brown's water engineering terminates in his **Grand Cascade**, over which the little River Glyme foams to rejoin its former bed.

In the Pleasure Grounds (the area nearest the house) are various attractions including Blenheim Bygones, a lavender garden, a maze, a butterfly house (closed winter) and an adventure play area. You are also free to wander the 2100 acres of stunning parkland.

Brighton★★

East Sussex

Brighton is where the English seaside tradition was invented and brought to a pitch of perfection. Within easy reach of the capital, the town has long been a weekend retreat for Londoners. Its south-facing beach is punctuated by piers and backed by a wide promenade and elegant Georgian, Regency and Victorian architecture. The labyrinthine lanes of the old fishing town, with their jewellers and trendy shops, contrast with lavishly planted open spaces and parkways.

A BIT OF HISTORY

Modern Brighton began in the mid-18C with the promotion by Dr Richard Russell of the healthy effect of drinking and bathing in seawater. The town received a royal seal of approval from the Prince of Wales, following his first visit in 1783. From the 1840s the London, Brighton and South Coast Railway brought ever-increasing numbers of holidaymakers of all social classes to what had truly become "London-by-the-Sea". Today's mature town has remained young, stage-managing its raffish appeal to attract successive generations of visitors, while acquiring all the ingredients of a miniature metropolis: specialist shops, trendy restaurants, entertainments of all kinds, and on its outskirts, the modern University of Sussex.

ROYAL PAVILION★★★

🕐 Open daily. Apr–Sept 9.30am–5.45pm (last tickets 5pm). Oct–Mar 10am–5.15pm (last tickets 4.30pm). 🕐Closed from 2.30pm on Dec 24 and all day Dec 25–26. ♿ (Ground floor only). 👛£8.30. ☎0300 0290 900. www.royalpavilion.org.uk.
This fantastic oriental confection in stucco and stone reflects the brilliant personality of George Augustus Frederick, Prince of Wales 1762–1811, Regent 1811–20, finally **King George IV**.
Its exotic gateways and extraordinary silhouette, all bulbous domes, pinnacles,

▶ **Population:** 200,168.
🜪 **Michelin Map:** Michelin Atlas p 11 or Map 504 T 31
🛈 **Info:** Royal Pavilion Shop, Royal Pavilion. ☎0906 711 2255 (50p/min, UK only); www.visitbrighton.com.
▷ **Location:** 55mi/88km due south of London. Trains and buses run here frequently from London; the train station (Queen's Road) is a 5–10-min walk from the centre, while the bus station (Old Steine) is centrally located just back from the seafront. The town is compact and easily explored on foot. To get an overview, jump aboard the City Sightseeing open-top bus (☎01273 886 200; www.city-sightseeing.com), or take the Volks Railway for a 1.25 mi/2km ride along the beachfront (☎01273 292 718; www.volks electricrailway.co.uk).
🖝 **Don't miss:** The Royal Pavilion; The Lanes and the North Laine.
🕐 **Timing:** In summer you'll want to spend at least one night here to catch the evening buzz. The Brighton Festival runs for three weeks every May, and is the biggest mixed arts festival in England. www.brightonfestival.org.
👪 **Kids**: Pier; Sea Life Centre.

turrets and spikes pricking the skyline, are a free interpretation of "Hindoo" architecture. Within, throughout a series of gorgeously furnished and decorated interiors, Chinoiserie prevails, taken to astonishing lengths in the **Music Room**, lit by lotus-shaped gaseliers, where painted serpents and dragons writhe beneath the gilded scales of a great dome. Equally sumptuous is the great **Banqueting Room**; from its dome (45ft/14m high) hangs a one-ton crystal lighting device, at its apex a huge winged dragon in silver outlined against enormous trompe l'oeil plantain leaves. The deliciously refurbished **royal apartments** on the first floor are reached by a staircase whose cast-iron bannister is cunningly disguised as bamboo.

All this exuberance is set in restored **gardens**, which have been remodelled and replanted to correspond as closely as possible to their Regency state.

Just northwest of the Royal Pavilion is its former stables on Church Street, home to the **Brighton Museum and Art Gallery** (🕐 *open Tue–Sun and bank hols, 10am (2pm Sun)–5pm (7pm Tue);* 🕐 *closed Jan 1, Good Fri, Dec 25–26;* ♿; *℘01273 292 882;www.brighton. virtualmuseum.info*). In addition to its local history collection, Dutch and English paintings, porcelain and pottery, and its fashion and ethnographical gallery, the intimate interior also houses a well-presented display of 20C decorative arts.

SEAFRONT★★

The meeting of Victorian Brighton and the sea is marked by a broad **promenade**, carried on massive brick vaults and with generous ramps and stairs leading to a roadway at beach level. A wealth of light-hearted detail, from splendid decorative ironwork to jaunty little kiosks and shelters, sets the holiday mood, and is extended into the sea on the **West Pier** of 1866 and Palace Pier, now **Brighton Pier** (👥👤🕐 *open year-round daily from 10am, 9am school sum-mer holidays, until late;* 🕐 *closed Dec 25;* ♿; *℘01273 609 361; www.brightonpier. co.uk*), a lively place of funfair-style rides and amusements, and refreshments. Close by is the **Sea Life Centre** (👥👤 🕐 *Marine Parade open year-round daily, 10am–5pm; 4pm winter;* 🕐 *closed Dec 25;* 👛*£9.95 if booked online, child £6.95;* ♿; *℘0871 423 2110; www.sealife europe.com*) offering a variety of ways to view marine life at close quarters in the original Victorian vaulted aquarium – the largest in the world when it opened in 1872. The pioneering electric **Volks Railway** of 1883 runs eastward along the foot of the cliff to the **Marina**.

Within the continuous wall of seafront building is a succession of architectural set-pieces: the most distinguished is **Brunswick Square** (1825–27), with stucco, bow windows, Classical details and elegant ironwork; the earliest is **Royal Crescent** (1798–1807), in black mathematical tiles; the grandest, to the east, is the Victorian panache and elegance of **Lewes Crescent/Sussex Square**, (1823 onwards) exemplified in the many-storeyed and richly decorated Grand and Metropole hotels.

TOWN CENTRE

A maze of animated **lanes**★ (alleyways) in the old town, lined with countless boutiques and antique shops, focuses on **Brighton Square**. West of here in the Lanes are Brighton's famous jewellers, while to the east lie the quirky boutique shops of the North Laine. Tucked away behind the train station to the northeast, **St Bartholomew's**★ (Ann

Royal Pavilion, Brighton

©diwat26/SXC

Street; ◷ *opening hours vary;* ✆*01273 419 409; www.brighton.world-guides. com/brighton_churches.html)* is the most outstanding of Brighton's many Victorian churches. The sublime simplicity of patterned brick walls carrying the nave to the awesome height of 135ft/41m contrasts with rich **furnishings** (Lady Altar, main altarpiece, giant candlesticks), masterworks of the Arts and Crafts Movement.

ADDRESSES

🛏 STAY

🍴🍴 **Hotel du Vin**, *Ship Street. t01273 718 588. www.hotelduvin. com.* Style is the keyword in this 19C neo-Gothic building, with 37 striking minimalist rooms plus a first-class bistro (🍴🍴 booking essential).

🍴🍴 **Adelaide**, *51 Regency Square. t01273 205 286. www.adelaidehotel.co.uk.* This fine Regency house is on Brighton's premier seafront square.
12 rooms in a range of prices.

🍴🍴🍴 **Brighton Pavilions**, *7 Charlotte Street.* ✆*01273 621 750. www.brightonpavillions.com*

EXCURSION
Beachy Head★★★
22 mi/35km east. Few prospects are more exhilarating on a sunny day than that of the blue sea washing against the toy-like lighthouse at the foot of the dazzling white 500ft/150m cliffs. West of this viewpoint extends a "Heritage Coast" of sweeping downland ending in chalk headlands, of which the most famous is the **Seven Sisters** formation.

The town's original boutique-style B&B hotel with high quality architect-designed interiors offering themed (Royal Pavilion, Pompeii, Greta Garbo, Titanic etc.) bedrooms.

🍽 EAT

🍴🍴 **Havana**, *32 Duke Street.* ✆*01273 773 388.* Formerly the late-18C Theatre Royal, buzzing Havana is still a theatrical experience with mock Colonial styling and a Cuban theme which carries through to the food and drinks.

🍴🍴 **Terre à Terre**, *71 East Street.* ✆*01273 729 051. www.terreaterre.co.uk.*

Hearty portions of bold vegetarian cuisine are served at this long-established smart little centrally located restaurant.

Canterbury★★★
Kent

The ecclesiastical capital of England, rich in medieval atmosphere, is dominated by its renowned cathedral. The city lies on Watling Street, the great Roman thoroughfare linking London with the port of Dover. It is the terminus of the **Pilgrims' Way**, a trackway of prehistoric origin used by many of the worshippers at the shrine of St Thomas, England's best-known martyr.

A BIT OF HISTORY
Early settlement – Canterbury's recorded history begins with Emperor Claudius' invasion of AD 43 and the foundation of the walled town of Durovernum. After the Roman withdrawal early

▶ **Population:** 36,464
◔ **Michelin Map:** Michelin Atlas p 13 or Map 404 X 30
🛈 **Info:** 12/13 Sun Street. ✆01227 378 100. www.canterbury.co.uk.
⊘ **Don't Miss:** The Cathedral and the Black Prince's tomb.
▶ **Location:** 56mi/90km east of London. The town has two train stations. Canterbury East, just outside the old walls, receives trains from London Victoria and Dover; Canterbury West is 5-mins or so walking time from the western section of wall, with services from London Charing Cross. The

in the 5C, the city was settled by Jutish invaders and renamed *Cantwarabyrig*, or "stronghold of the Men of Kent".

A Christian See – In AD 597 **St Augustine** arrived in Kent to convert the pagan population to Christianity. The city became the centre of the English Church and Augustine was consecrated as first archbishop.

In 1170 a later archbishop, **Becket**, was assassinated in the cathedral by four of Henry II's knights who had taken all too literally their ruler's desire to be "rid of this turbulent priest". Thomas was canonised two years later and his shrine immediately attracted countless pilgrims, many of whose stories are recounted in **Chaucer's** *Canterbury Tales*. The cathedral's monastery was the largest in the country and by the 13C Grey Friars and Black Friars were established here as well. This thriving monastic life came to an end with the Dissolution of the Monasteries; the cathedral's treasures were appropriated by Henry VIII, the saint's shrine was destroyed and the pilgrimages ended.

A prosperous city – The post-Reformation saw the arrival of French Huguenot refugees, at the invitation of Elizabeth

Bell Harry Tower, Canterbury
© Marek Bernat/stock.xchng

l. These skilled craftsmen contributed to Canterbury's prosperity and in spite of the depredations of the Puritans in the Civil War, the city continued to flourish.

Greater damage was suffered in the "Baedeker" bombing raids of 1942, when part of the historic centre was reduced to rubble though fortunately the cathedral remained untouched.

Today Canterbury is the thriving centre of eastern Kent and the seat of a new university. The city exerts nearly as strong a pull on the modern tourist as in medieval times and remains a religious centre. The See of Canterbury remains the focal point of the worldwide Anglican Communion.

CANTERBURY CATHEDRAL★★★

🕐 *Open (services permitting) summer Mon–Sat 9am–6pm (winter 5pm). Crypt opens 10am; Sun year-round 12.30pm–2.30pm. Check website for additional hours and closures before visiting.* £7.50. *Guided tour (75min), Mon–Sat £4.50.* &. 01227 762 862. *www.canterbury-cathedral.org.*

The original cathedral built by St Augustine was destroyed in 1067 and replaced by the first Norman Arch-

bus station is on St George's Lane inside the walls.

🕐 **Timing:** A day minimum.

Walking Tours: Canterbury Walks tours start from the Visitor Information Centre (daily Apr–Oct; £5; 01227 459 779; www.canterbury-walks. co.uk. A 'Ghostly Tour of Old Canterbury' departs from opposite Alberry's Wine Bar (8pm Fri, Sat; 07779 575 831; www.greenbard.8m.com).

Kids: The Canterbury Tales; Museum of Canterbury with Rupert Bear Museum; Howlett's Wild Animal Park.

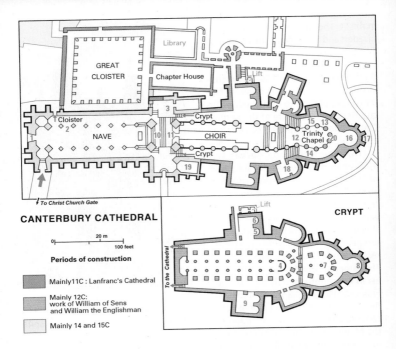

CANTERBURY CATHEDRAL

0 — 20 m / 100 feet

Periods of construction

Mainly11C : Lanfranc's Cathedral

Mainly 12C:
work of William of Sens
and William the Englishman

Mainly 14 and 15C

CRYPT

bishop, **Lanfranc**. Archbishop **Anselm** replaced his predecessor's choir with an ambitious structure. It too was gutted by fire in 1174, four years after Becket's murder, though the crypt and nave were spared. As the cathedral had become the most important centre of pilgrimage in Northern Europe, the opportunity was seized to rebuild in a manner worthy of the martyr, in an early Gothic style which was to be of great subsequent influence in the development of English architecture. The work was started by the French architect **William of Sens** and completed by another William – "the Englishman".

The nave and cloisters were rebuilt in Perpendicular style in the 14C; the transepts and towers, including **Bell Harry Tower**, crowning the entire building, were completed in the 15C. The north-west tower was demolished in 1832 and replaced by a copy of the southwest tower.

Christ Church Gate★ (D), built in the early 16C and decorated with coats of arms, is the main entrance to the cathedral. **Mercery Lane★** (AB 21), a bustling street which has kept its medieval charm, offers an impressive view of Christ Church Gate and the western towers of the cathedral.

Interior

Enter through the southwest porch.

In the **nave** built (1392–1404) by Henry Yevele, the slender columns soar majestically to the lofty vault and aisles. The

Black Prince's effigy

A. F. Kersting/MICHELIN

great west window (**1**) contains 12C glass (note Adam delving). Near the north door stands a 17C classical marble **font** (**2**) depicting the Four Evangelists and the Twelve Apostles. In the north transept the "Altar of the Sword's Point" and a modern cruciform sculpture commemorate the **site of Becket's martyrdom** (**3**). Steps lead down to the 12C vaulted **crypt**. The delicate screens of the **Chapel of Our Lady Undercroft** (**4**) and the capitals are masterpieces of Romanesque carving. The transept houses the altars of St Nicholas (**5**) and St Mary Magdalene (**6**). In the eastern extension (post-1174) with its massive columns and pointed vaults is the site (**7**) where the body of St Thomas Becket was entombed until 1220. Beyond is located the admirable Jesus Chapel (**8**). The south transept was the Black Prince's Chantry (**9**), subsequently the Huguenots' Church; it is still used for services in French today.

Leave the crypt on the south side to return to the upper level.

Turn right into the crossing to admire the lace-like **fan vaulting underneath the Bell Harry Tower** (**10**); the bosses are decorated with coats of arms of those responsible for building the tower.

Pass through the iron gates into the choir which contains a mid-15C **screen** (**11**) with figures of six kings, the High Altar and the 13C marble **St Augustine's Chair** (**12**) traditionally used for the enthronement of the Archbishop, Primate of All England. From either of the choir aisles the long vistas back to the nave reveal the evolution of Gothic style over three centuries.

The wonderful medieval **stained glass** windows includes one depicting the Miracles (**13**) wrought by St Thomas in the Trinity Chapel. His shrine, placed here in 1220, has long gone, though the fine Roman mosaic pavement in front of it remains. Among the remarkable tombs is that of the **Black Prince** (**14**) (d 1376); above hang replicas of his helm, crest, shield, gauntlets and sword; the fragile originals are displayed nearby. Opposite is the alabaster **tomb of Henry IV** (**15**) (d. 1413) and Queen Joan of Navarre. In the **Corona** (**16**), a circular chapel said to have housed the top of St Thomas' skull, there is an early 13C **Redemption window** (**17**) behind the altar.

The **Chapel of St Anselm** (**18**) – *(southwest corner of Trinity Chapel)* is mostly Norman and contains a rare 12C wall painting (high up in the apse).

Off the south transept *(main exit)* is the **Chapel of St Michael** (**19**) with Renaissance and Baroque memorials.

Exterior

The great cathedral with its soaring buttresses, pinnacles and towers above which Bell Harry rises to a height of almost 250ft/76m, is an impressive sight. The elaborate vaulting of the galleried **Great Cloister** (rebuilt c. 1400) is ornamented with grotesque faces, religious symbols and scenes of everyday life. Off the east walk is the **Chapter House** with its intricately ribbed oak roof and Perpendicular windows with glass depicting characters in the cathedral's history.

On the eastern side of the cathedral precincts is the **King's School★(B)**, an ancient foundation remodelled by Henry VIII in 1541. It occupies buildings of the former cathedral monastery grouped in the main around Green Court. The immense length of the cathedral is best appreciated from this point. Note the splendid **Norman staircase** (12C).

CITY CENTRE WALK

Arriving from Canterbury West train station, take a right on St Dunstan's Street and then left on London Road to see **St Dunstan's Church** (○ *open year-round daily, Mon–Sat 8/9am–4/5pm, Sun 8am–7.30pm;* ○ *closed Good Fri and Christmas week;* ℘*01227 463 654*). The church was founded in the late 11C and used by Henry II in 1174 when he changed into penitential garments for his involvement in the murder of St Thomas Becket. The head of Sir Thomas More is thought to be buried in the Roper family vault.

Start your tour of the city centre at the **West Gate Towers★** *(St Peter's Street;* ○ *open year-round Mon–Sat 11am–12.30pm, 1.30pm–3.30pm;* ○*closed Good*

Fri, Christmas week; £1.25, combined ticket with Museum of Canterbury and Roman Museum £6.20; 01227 789 576; www.canterbury-museums.co.uk. This city landmark is the last of the gatehouses that once formed part of the city walls. It later served as a prison and now houses a museum with an interesting arms collection. From the battlements there are fine **views** of the city and cathedral.

Head southeast from here along St Peter's Street and make a detour up St Peter's Lane to **Blackfriars Monastery**. All that remains of this 13C Dominican Friary are the Great Hall and the Refectory, now the Blackfriars Arts Centre.

Back on St Peter's Street, as you approach the bridge, you will find the **Canterbury Weavers** on your left. This group of picturesque Tudor houses overlooking the River Stour takes its name from the refugee Huguenot weavers who settled in the area.

You may now choose to take the scenic route marked on the map walking up to King's School, or simply continue on the High Street, where, over the bridge, you will find the **Eastbridge Hospital, Greyfriars Chapel and Franciscan Gardens** (*closed Dec 25–26;* 01227 471 688; www.east bridgehospital.org.uk). On the High Street is the Hospital of St Thomas the Martyr (*open year-round Mon–Sat*

St Augustine's Abbey

Y. Duhamel/MICHELIN

10am–5pm), founded in 1180, which served as lodgings for poor pilgrims to the shrine of St Thomas. After the Dissolution in the 16C, the hospital was refounded as a boys' school and then as an almshouse, a role it still fulfils today. The building presents a black flint exterior. The 14C door leads into a vaulted hall (11C). South of here on Stour Street are the **Chapel and Garden** (*6 Stour St;* open Easter–Sept Mon–Sat 2pm–4pm), part of the same complex and the first English Franciscan Friary, built in 1267. The undercroft was originally a pilgrims' dormitory. Upstairs are the refectory and the Chapel. The chapel has a fine timber roof. **Greyfriar's House** is the only building now remaining of the first English Franciscan Friary, built in 1267 in the life time of St Fancis of Assisi, 43 years after the first Friars settled in Canterbury. A new exhibition explores the history of this important settlement.

Back on the High Street, you continue past **Canterbury Royal Museum**, now closed for refurbishment, and take a left up to the **Canterbury Roman Museum** (*Longmarket;* open year-round Mon–Sat 10am–5pm (last admission 4pm). Jun–Oct, also Sun 1.30pm–5pm (last admission 4pm); closed Good Fri and Christmas week; £3, combined ticket with West Gate Towers and Museum of Canterbury £6.20; ; 01227 785 575; www.canterbury-museums.co.uk). Deep below the Longmarket shopping centre, part of Canterbury's excavated Roman levels have been transformed into this modern museum, which uses contemporary techniques to bring the Roman city of Durnovernum Cantiacorum to life. Reconstructions include a Roman market place with stalls and a house with its kitchen set out in authentic detail.

Return to the High Street and continue on, past the Whitefriars Shopping Centre until you come to a roundabout and the **city walls**. A walk follows the top of the well-preserved medieval walls, stoutly built on Roman foundations.

Follow the wall south and you will come to the **Dane John Mound**, which overlooks a charming park and a **memorial** to Christopher Marlow, born in Can-

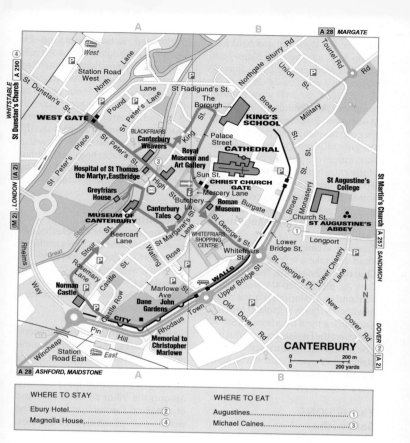

terbury. At the end of this stretch of the wall you will find the 11C **Norman castle** built of flint with bands of stone, of which only the keep remains.

Head north from here along Stour Street and you will come to the **Museum of Canterbury with Rupert Bear Museum★** (♿👤🕐 *open year-round Mon–Sat 10.30am–5pm, also Jun–Sept Sun 1.30pm–5pm (4pm last admission);* 🕐*closed Good Fri and Christmas week;* ✎*admission charge only to Rupert Bear Museum £2.25, child £1.20; combined ticket with West Gate Towers and Roman Museum £6.20;* ✆*01227 475 202; www. canterbury-museums.co.uk).* This modern museum is housed in the Poor Priests' Hospital, founded in the 13C as an almshouse. It presents the history of Canterbury from prehistoric to modern times including lively interactive displays, plus

a museum within the larger museum devoted to the long-standing British children's favourite character, Rupert Bear. Returning to the High Street via St Margaret's Street for **The Canterbury Tales** (♿👤🕐 *open year-round daily, Jul–Aug 9.30am–5pm, Mar–Jun and Sept–Oct 10am–5pm, Nov–Feb 10am–4.30pm;* 🕐*closed Dec 2, Jan 1;* ✎*£7.75, child £5.75;* ♿; ✆*01227 479 227; www.canterbury tales.org.uk).* The converted interior of St Margaret's Church is the setting for this entertaining multi-media attraction, which popularises and brings to life the vivid characters created by Chaucer as they make their pilgrimage from the Tabard Inn in Southwark, London to the shrine of St Thomas at Canterbury.

If you leave the old walled city to the east on Church Street you come to **St Augustine's Abbey★★** *(EH;* 🕐*open* *late Mar–Jun Wed–Sun and bank hols 10am–5pm, Jul–Aug daily 10am–6pm, Sept–late Mar Sat, Sun 11am–5pm;* ⓒ *closed Jan 1 and Dec 24–26;* ◌ *£4.10;* ♿ *;* 🕿 *01227 767 345; www.english-heritage.org.uk),* founded in AD 597 by St Augustine. Extensive ruins remain of the great Norman abbey church, such as the early 14C Great Gateway. There are also vestiges of Saxon burial places and of the church of St Pancras (7C), once a pagan temple; the walls are built of Roman brick (a museum interprets the site). The medieval abbey buildings are today occupied by **St Augustine's College**.

Continue on Longport to North Holmes Road and take a left for **St Martin's Church★** (ⓒ *open Tue, Thu, Sat 11am–3pm;* ♿*;* 🕿*01233 720 410; www.martinpaul.org)* on St Martin's Hill, the oldest functioning church in England. When St. Augustine arrived from Rome in 597 AD to convert the English, he set up his mission here. It has Roman brickwork in its walls and a Perpendicular tower. Inside there is a Norman font, a Norman *piscina* and a "Leper Window".

EXCURSIONS
Sandwich★
13mi/21km east by A 257.
The road from Canterbury runs through the pretty village of **Wingham**. The fascinating medieval borough of Sandwich was one of the original Cinque Ports, is still largely contained within its earthen ramparts and seems to have changed little since the River Stour began to silt up in the 15C. Its pretty houses of all periods cluster around its three **churches**: St Clement's with a sturdy, arcaded Norman tower; St Peter's with a bulbous cupola reflecting Flemish influence; and St Mary's, much reduced by the collapse of its tower in 1668.

👥 Howletts Wild Animal Park
3 mi/5km south off the A2. Bekesbourne Road, Bekesbourne ⓒ *Open summer 10am–6pm (4.30pm last admission). Winter 10am–5pm (3.30 pm last admission).* ⓒ*Closed Dec 25.* ◌ *£14.95, child £11.95 (book online for discount).* ♿🅿✕*.* 🕿*0870 750 4647. www.howletts.net.*
Set in 90 acres of beautiful ancient parkland, Howlett's is famous as the home of not only the world's largest family group of gorillas in captivity but also the UK's largest group of African Elephants. Among the 90 or so other rare and endangered species from around the world are tigers and clouded leopards, black rhinos, tapirs and giant anteaters. Visitors can even stay overnight in a safari lodge.

ADDRESSES

🏠 STAY
◌◌◌ **Magnolia House**, *36 St Dunstan's Terrace.* 🕿*01227 765 121. www.magnoliahousecanterbury. co.uk.* Characterful late Georgian guest house, with calm sunny interiors, set in a quiet residential street just ten minutes' stroll from Canterbury city centre. The guest house's secluded walled garden is a pleasant place to unwind after a day's exploration.

◌◌◌ **Ebury**, *65–67 New Dover Road.* 🕿*01227 768 433. www.ebury-hotel.co.uk.* This centrally located elegant Victorian house has 15 spacious rooms plus a small indoor pool and spa. It also boasts a good restaurant with a French chef, serving fine Anglo-French cuisine (◌◌)and self-catering flats and cottages.

🍴 EAT
◌◌ **Augustines**, *1–2 Longport.* 🕿*01227 453 063. www.augustinesrestuarant.co.uk.* This family-run restaurant is set in a charming Georgian town house close to the heart of town. Home-cooked favourites using fresh local produce.

◌◌ **Michael Caines**, *Abode Hotel, High Street.* 🕿*01227 826 684. www. michaelcaines.com.* Good value accomplished Modern British cuisine from the protégé of one of Britain's star chefs, plus a champagne and cocktail bar.

Chichester★★
West Sussex

On the flatlands between the South Downs and the sea, Chichester and its picturebook cathedral spire present a quintessential English scene.

A BIT OF HISTORY

Many English towns grew up around their cathedral, but Chichester was already a thousand years old before the cathedral was thought about; its North, South, East and West Streets running off the 1501 ornamental **Market Cross** still conform to their Roman plan.

Chichester enjoyed a golden age in the 18C; the harmonious Georgian town-scape is best seen in **The Pallants**.

CITY CENTRE

In the heart of Chichester, close to the market cross (the centrepoint of the city's main pedestrianised shopping streets), is the **Cathedral★★** *(West Street;* ⏰ *open daily 7.15am–7pm (6pm Nov–Mar);* ✉£5 *contribution requested;* ➡ *guided tour Mon–Sat 11.15am, 2.30pm (45 min);* ✉£4.50 *contribution requested;* ♿✗; ℘01243 782 595; www. chichestercathedral.org.uk).

The cathedral took almost 100 years to build, from 1091–1184. The interior is Romanesque in style and spirit and its austere nave is Norman, though every architectural movement of the Middle Ages has left its mark. The nave is best viewed looking west, when it appears small, almost intimate. Its splendid screen is Perpendicular Gothic.

The Lady Chapel ceiling paintings are notable but the cathedral's greatest treasures are the 12C **stone panels★★** in the south choir aisle; they depict scenes from the Raising of Lazarus and are among the finest examples of Norman sculpture in England.

In the south transept, lit by a Decorated window, are early 16C paintings of the cathedral. In the north transept is the grave of the composer Gustav Holst (1874–1934); east of this is a stained-glass window by the French painter Marc

- ▶ **Population:** 26 050
- ⚲ **Michelin Map:** Michelin Atlas p 10 or Map 503 R 31
- ▤ **Info:** 29a South Street. ℘01243 775 888. www. chichester.gov.uk.
- ▷ **Location:** 81mi/130km southwest of London on the River Lavant, very close to the South coast. Trains and buses run regularly here from London. The train station is on Stockbridge Road, the bus station close by at South Street; both are a 10-min walk from the centre.
- ▣ **Parking:** Park by the river for the classic view.
- ☺ **Don't Miss:** the cathedral, and its Norman stone panels.
- ⏰ **Timing:** Allow a couple of hours for the city centre and a couple of days to visit the surrounding area.

Chagall (1887–1985). Head due east from the cathedral for one block and you will come to North Pallant Street, home to the **Pallant House Gallery★** *(9 North Pallant;* ⏰ *open Tue–Sat 10am–5pm, Thu 10am–8pm, Sun and bank hols 12.30pm– 5pm;* ✉£7.50. *Thu 5pm–8pm, Tue £3.75;* ♿; ℘01243 774 557; www.pallant.org. uk). This Queen Anne town house was built in 1712. Today its tastefully furnished period rooms are home to one of the best collections of 20C British art in the world.

EXCURSIONS
Petworth House★★

14mi/22km northeast on the A 27 and A 285. NT. House: ⏰ *Open mid-Mar–early Nov Sat–Wed and Good Fri, 11am–5pm (Mar 4pm). Grounds:* ⏰ *open Feb–Dec.* ✉£9.40 *(Park and grounds only, £3.60).* ♿▣*(£2)*✗. ℘01798 342 207, 01798 343 929 (info-line). www.nationaltrust.org.uk.

This grand 17C mansion (1688) is the nearest there is to a French château in

Arundel Castle

B. Kaufmann/MICHELIN

England. The **grounds**★★, by Lancelot "Capability" Brown, enjoy fine views of the South Downs.

Interior – The rooms contain exquisite carvings, antique statuary and a fine collection of paintings. The most spectacular feature is the **Grand Staircase** with its painted walls and ceiling by Laguerre. The **Turner Room** contains the largest collection of his works outside the Tate Gallery. Other famous artists represented are Reynolds, Van Dyck and Kneller. Lely's *Children of Charles I* hangs in the Oak Hall, Bosch's *Adoration of the Magi* in the Dining Room. **Grinling Gibbons'** carvings adorn the **Carved Room**.

Arundel Castle★★

11mi/18km east on the A 27. ⏲ *Open bank hols and early Apr–Oct Tue–Sun 10am–5pm (4pm last admission); keep opens 11am, rooms open noon.* ⬭£15 *Full visit; keep, chapel and grounds only, £7.* ♿🅿✕. ✆01903 882 173. *www.arundelcastle.org.*

The castle is the home of the Duke of Norfolk, the premier duke of England. The original Norman **gatehouse and keep** (1138) survive after 750 years of assaults and sieges. Climb up its 131 steps to enjoy panoramic views.

In the castle's Victorian rooms are the **Chapel** and **Barons' Hall** (paintings by Mytens, Kneller, Van Loo and Van Dyck); in the **Drawing Room** hang portraits by Van Dyck, Gainsborough and Reynolds. The Gothic-Revival style **Library**

(122ft/70m long) dates from c. 1800. On the boundary of the castle grounds stands the Decorated private **Fitzalan Chapel**, crowded with tombs and monuments to the Norfolk dynasty.

Weald and Downland Open Air Museum★★

6mi/10km north on the A 286. ⏲ *Open Apr–Oct daily 10.30am– 6pm. Mid-Feb–Mar, Nov–late Dec and Jan 1, daily 10.30am–4pm. Jan 3–mid-Feb Wed, Sat, Sun 10.30am– 4pm. Last admission 1hr before closing.* ⬭£8.95. ♿🅿✕. ✆01243 811 363. *www.wealddown.co.uk.*

Over 40 historic buildings have been re-erected on the beautiful Downland slopes. They include a cottage, shop, farmhouse, Tudor market hall, working watermill, toll cottage and school. Many of the interiors have also been re-created and there are demonstrations of typical bygone rural activities.

Fishbourne Roman Palace★★

1.5mi/2.4km west on the A 259. ⏲ *Open Mar–Oct daily 10am–5pm, Aug daily 10am–6pm, Feb and Nov–mid-Dec 10am–4pm). Mid-Dec–Jan, Sat–Sun 10am–4pm.* ⬕ *Guided tour (1–2hr) Sat–Sun and bank hols 11am, 2.30pm.* ⬭£7.30. ♿🅿✕. ✆01243 785 859. *www.sussexpast.co.uk.*

This splendid Roman palace, built c. AD 75, was probably the home of Cogidubnus, an ally of Imperial Rome. The lavish complex, which included guest lodgings and grand colonnades, burned down in the 3C. The tableaux tracing its history palace and its rich **mosaics**★ are highlights.

Bignor Roman Villa

Pulborough, 13mi/21km northeast on the A 27 and A 29. ⏲ *Open Mar–Apr Tue–Sun and bank hols, May and Oct daily 10am–5pm. Jun–Sept daily 10am–6pm.* ⬭£4.60. ♿🅿✕. ✆01798 869 259. *www.bignorromanvilla.co.uk.*

Some of the finest Roman **mosaics**★ in England are preserved here at this Roman farm uncovered in 1811 by a farmer's plough..

Chiltern Hills★

Buckinghamshire

The chalk downs known as the Chiltern Hills run some 60mi/96km on a southwest to northeast axis bordered by the River Thames and Luton respectively. They rise gently to their highest point at Coombe Hill (852ft/260m). Two of Britain's ancient roads, the **Icknield Way** and the **Ridgeway**, follow the line of the hills.

🐾 WALKING

The gentle rolling Chilterns are ideal for walkers. The Ridgeway National Trail was one of Iron Age Britain's main highways; today it is a waymarked long-distance footpath. Another easy route is the Thames Path which follows the river and crosses the Ridgeway. Tourist offices will be able to provide detailed walking maps, but you can also visit the *www.chilternsaonb.org* website when planning your trip.

AYLESBURY AREA

Aylesbury, Buckinghamshire's county town, was a major market town in Anglo-Saxon times and played a large part in the English Civil War. The **Buckinghamshire County Museum** on Church Street (🕐 *open mid-Feb–Oct Mon–Sat 10am–5pm, Nov–Feb Mon–Sat 10am–4pm; Dahl Gallery open year-round Mon–Sat, times vary, call or see website;* 👛*museum free;* 👫 *Roald Dahl Gallery £4. 50, child £4; admission by timed ticket; visits last an hour and entry is on the hour, booking (£1 fee) is advised;* ✕; ✆*01296 331 441; www.bucksccc.gov.uk)* traces local history but many visitors head straight for the **Roald Dahl Children's Gallery** – a delight for fans of the great author.

South of Aylesbury in the village of Hartwell is **Hartwell House**, now a hotel, first mentioned in the Domesday book and once the home of an illegitimate son of William the Conqueror.

5mi/8km northwest of Aylesbury via the A 41 is **Waddesdon Manor★★** (NT; 🕐*open Apr–Oct Wed–Sun and bank hol Mons noon–4pm, Sat–Sun 11am–4pm;*

- 🕿 **Michelin Map:** Michelin Atlas pp 18, 19 and 28 or Map 503 Q R 27 and 28
- 🅸 **Info:** Kings Head, Market Square, Aylesbury. ✆01296 330 559. The Old Gaol, Market Hill, Buckingham. ✆01280 823 020. www.visitbuckinghamshire.org.
- 🔘 **Location:** Main tourist centres are Buckingham, Aylesbury, Marlow and Henley-on-Thames.
- 👁 **Don't Miss:** Waddesdon Manor; Stowe Gardens.
- 🕐 **Timing:** Two days minimum.
- 👫 **Kids:** Roald Dahl Gallery and Roald Dahl Museum.

House also open between Christmas and New Year Wed–Sun, see website for details. 👛£12–£13.70 (gardens only, £5–£6.30); in peak periods booking for house tickets recommended (free online); ♿🅿✕; ✆01296 653 226; www.waddesdon.org.uk), built in 1874–89 in French Renaissance style, for Baron Ferdinand de Rothschild, is set in 150 acres of landscaped grounds. It contains the acclaimed **Rothschild collection** of Dutch, French and English paintings, French furniture, porcelain, carpets and many other works of art. Twenty rooms are furnished with French 18C royal furniture, Sèvres porcelain and Savonnerie carpets. Works by Gainsborough, Reynolds and Romney, plus pictures by Rubens, Cuyp, Van der Heyden and Dutch masters grace the walls.

Roald Dahl

Roald Dahl lived and wrote for 36 years in the village of Great Missenden; it is now home to **The Roald Dahl Museum and Story Centre**, the home of the author's archive (👫🕐 *open year-round Tue–Sun 10am–5pm, also occasional Mon, see website;* 👛£5.50, child £3.95; ✆01494 892192; *www.roalddahl.com*

10mi/16km northwest of Aylesbury, off the A 41 to Waddesdon is **Claydon House★** (Middle Claydon. NT; ⏱ open early Mar–Oct Sat–Wed, 1pm–5pm; ✆£6; ♿🅿✗; ✆01296 730 349, 01494 755 561 (infoline); www.nationaltrust.org. uk), famous for its extravagant Rococo eccentricities by Hugh Lightfoot, the parquetry staircase and the "gothic chinoiserie" woodwork of the Chinese Room. More conventionally beautiful are the Mytens and Van Dyck oils. There are mementoes of Florence Nightingale, who was a frequent visitor.

BUCKINGHAM AREA

Buckingham was Buckinghamshire's county town until Aylesbury took over in the 16C. Today it is best used as a base for walks in the surrounding area and for visiting **Stowe Landscape Gardens★★** (NT; 3mi/5km northwest, off the A 422; **Gardens:** ⏱ open Mar–Oct, Nov–Feb Wed–Sun and bank hol Mons 10.30am–5.30pm, Nov–Feb Sat–Sun 10.30am–4pm, last admission 1hr 30mins before closing; **House:** ⏱ times vary, visit www.shpt.org for information; ⏱ closed Christmas hols, last Sat May; ✆gardens £6.50, house £4 (NT members £3.40); 🅿✗; ✆01280 822 850, 01494 755 568 (info); www.nationaltrust.org.uk). These magnificent landscaped gardens, some of the finest in Europe, were created over a period of 200 years starting in 1700. In 1733 **William Kent** began work and in 1741 **Lancelot "Capability" Brown** was appointed head gardener. The long, straight approach up the **Grand Avenue** (1.5mi/2.5km) gives glimpses through the trees of the temples, columns and arches and also a full view of the north front of the house (property of Stowe School). A full tour of the gardens would take several hours but a shorter walk close to the house provides a visit or a view of the major features. Nearby, the **parish church** is the sole survivor of the medieval village of Stowe.

Dover

Kent

Flanked by the famous white cliffs, Dover has been the southeast gateway to England since Roman times, receiving sailing ships, steam ships and hovercraft. Despite the opening of the Channel Tunnel the port's cross-Channel ferry traffic remains intense. The town was badly damaged during the Second World War but retains many historic properties giving Dover islands of elegance rarely seen in a working port.

TOWN CENTRE

German bombs and shells from batteries on the French coast devastated Dover but, together with postwar redevelopment, helped reveal the archeology of this ancient port.

Head east from Dover Priory train station and you come to York Street, then New Street, home to the **Roman Painted House** (⏱ open Apr–Sept, Tue–Sat (also

▶ **Population:** 34,179

● **Michelin Map:** Michelin Atlas p 13 or Map 504 X, Y 30

ℹ **Info:** Old Town Gaol, Biggin Street. ✆01304 205 108. www.whitecliffscountry. org.uk. For an introduction to the iconic cliffs, including spectacular views, visit the Gateway to the White Cliffs Visitor Centre (Langdon; ✆01304 202 756; www. nationaltrust.org.uk).

◐ **Location:** 75mi/121km SE of London; Dover Priory train station (Approach Road), has a frequent service and shuttle buses to the docks. The bus station is on Pencester Road. Both are a 5-min walk from the centre.

👫 **Kids:** Dover Castle Secret Wartime Tunnels.

Mon and bank hols Jul–Aug) 10am–5pm; Sun 1pm–5pm; ♿£2; ℘01304 203 279), which has the finest Roman wall-decorations to be seen in situ north of the Alps. Just around the block is the **Dover Museum**, *(Market Square;* ◷ *open year-round Mon–Sat 10am–5.30pm, Sun Apr–Aug noon–5pm;* ◷ *closed Jan 1, Dec 25–26;* ♿£2.50; ♿; ℘01304 201 066; www.dovermuseum.co.uk)* whose artefacts include a 50ft/9.5m section of the world's oldest known seagoing boat, the 3,000-year-old **Dover Bronze Age boat**.

CASTLE★★

EH. ◷ *Open late Mar–Sept daily 10am–6pm, (Aug open 9.30am), Oct daily 10am–5pm. Nov–Jan Thu–Mon 10am–5pm. Feb–Mar daily 10am–4pm.* ◷*Closed Dec 24–26, Jan 1.* ♿£10. 🅿✕. ℘01304 211 067. www.english-heritage. org.uk.*

The high land to the east, commanding town and port, has been fortified since the Iron Age. The Romans built a lighthouse (Pharos) which still stands within the castle walls, and the Saxons church (St-Mary-in-Castro). The defences were strengthened by William the Conqueror, then by Henry II, who in the 1180s added the splendid **keep**. The spectacular **Constable's Tower** dates from the early 13C. The warren of tunnels and secret chambers beneath the castle dates from early times but was greatly added to in the Napoleonic period and during the Second World War. Operation Dynamo, the evacuation from Dunkirk in 1940, was planned and directed from here.

A guided tour (timed ticket system) of the **Secret Wartime Tunnels**★ takes visitors through the dimly-lit chambers and passageways of the underground hospital and communications centre for the Combined Headquarters, known as Hellfire Corner. Realistic sound effects and sometimes gruesome props evoke all the atmosphere of this Orwellian world which, in the event of nuclear war, would have been a Regional Seat of Government.

EXCURSIONS

Nearby sights of interest include the 16C artillery fortress of **Deal Castle** *(EH. 8.5mi/14km east on the A 258)* and the harbour town of **Folkestone** *(8mi/13km west on the A20)* with ferry links to the Continent.

Guildford

Surrey

Guildford was a prosperous 18C town, when it was crowded with coaching inns and travellers breaking their journey between Portsmouth and London. Today it is the quintessential wealthy middle-class southern town, complete with university.

TOWN CENTRE

The elegant cobbled High Street descends towards the River Wey, with the green slopes of the Mount beyond. The High Street is dominated by the **Guildhall**, *(*◷*open Mon–Sat 9am–5pm, tours Tue, Thu, 2pm, 3pm; ℘01483 444 035)* with its ornate projecting clock. Nearby, the **Guildford House Gallery**

▸ **Population:** 65,998
⚭ **Michelin Map:** Michelin Atlas p 19 or Map 504 S30.
🛈 **Info:** 14 Tunsgate. ℘01483 444 333. www.guildford.gov.uk.
▷ **Location:** Guildford lies 31mi/50km southwest of London. Both the train station and the bus station (behind the Friary Centre) are centrally located with regular services to London, Portsmouth and Winchester. A commuter town, Guidlford has a fast London rail service
👪 **Kids:** Thorpe Park, Chessington World of Adventures.

Surrey Theme Parks

Close to Guildford lie two of the UK's leading theme parks. **Thorpe Park** (*℘0870 444 4466; www.thorpepark.com*) and  **Chessington World of Adventures** (*℘0870 999 0045. www.chessington.com*). Both are open all summer long (Thorpe Park is famous for its cooling water rides) and at other times of year; call or see the websites for details. Thorpe Park is a rollercoaster theme park aimed at teens and adults, while Chessington focuses on younger children. However there are thrills aplenty at both parks, which get very busy at holiday times. Try to arrive early and book ahead online for discounts.

(*155 High Street;* ⊕ *open Tue–Sat, 10am–4.45pm;* ✕; ℘ *01483 444 740. www.guildford.gov.uk*) is an elegant late 17C townhouse displaying paintings from the Borough's art collection.

Opposite the landmark **Angel Hotel**, is the fine vaulted stone **Undercroft**, (⊕*open May–Sept Wed 2.15pm–4pm, Sat noon–4pm;* ℘*01483 444 750; www.guildford.gov.uk*) built by a 13C wool merchant beneath a shop. It may also be visited on the free guided city tour (*May–Sept Mon 11am, Wed 2.30pm, Thu 7pm, Sun 2.30pm, meet at Tunsgate;* ℘*01483 444*

333, booking not necessary), which also includes the Tudor-style **Abbot's Hospital**, founded by Archbishop Abbot in 1619, and still in use as a home for the elderly.

Guildford Castle

Grounds: ⊕*Open daily dawn–dusk. Keep:* ⊕*Open Apr–Sept daily 10am–5pm. Oct and Mar Sat–Sun 11am–5pm (daily during half-term).* ⚲*Keep £2.50.* ℘*01483 444 750.*

A 12C sandstone keep is virtually all that remains of the castle first built by William the Conqueror shortly after the Battle of Hastings in 1066. Inside the grounds is Jeanne Argent's 1990 sculpture *Alice Through the Looking Glass* commemorating Lewis Carroll, a frequent visitor to Guildford who rented a nearby house for his sisters. He died while visiting them and is buried in the Mount Cemetery.

WISLEY GARDEN

6mi/9km northeast of Guildford on the A3. ⊕ *Open Mar–Oct daily 10am–6pm/dusk, Nov–Feb daily 10am–4.30pm (Sat–Sun 9am).* ⊕*Closed Dec 25.* ⚲*£8.50.* ♿🅿✕. ℘*0845 260 9000. www.rhs.org.uk.*

The gardens of the Royal Horticultural Society are a beautiful experience at all seasons. In the setting of an old site, with many fine trees, there is a great range of different sorts of gardens – pinetum, alpine house, rock garden and more.

Lewes★

East Sussex

Lewes is renowned as much for its architectural heritage as for the rolling of burning tar barrels on Bonfire Night (5 November) amid other celebrations. Celebrations in Lewes were once like riots and were briefly banned by Oliver Cromwell. The site was originally a strategic Saxon stronghold on account of its commanding coastal views. Today it is a charming, characterful little county town with much visible history. The

▶ **Population:** 15,376

⚲ **Michelin Map:** Atlas p 11 or Map 504 T, U 31

🛈 **Info:** Corn Exchange Building, 187 High Street. ℘01273 483 448. www.lewes.gov.uk/leisure.

▶ **Location:** 9 mi/14km northeast of Brighton.

◉ **Don't Miss:** The Bluebell Railway, running on the East/West Sussex border.

A BIT OF HISTORY

The strategic value of the site was appreciated by William de Warenne who built his castle here soon after the Conquest. In 1264 Simon de Montfort's rebellion against Henry III led to the defeat of the royal forces at the **Battle of Lewes**, fought on nearby Mount Harry.

The religious conflicts of the 16C were marked by the burning at the stake of 17 Protestant martyrs, commemorated (along with Guy Fawkes and the Gunpowder Plot) on 5 November with torchlit processions, tar-barrel rolling, fireworks and giant bonfires.

TOWN AND CASTLE

The well-preserved **High Street**★ in town has a delightful variety of traditional building materials: flint, stone, brick, timber, stucco, hung tiles, and the local speciality, "mathematical tiles", which in the 18C were used on older timber buildings to simulate a fashionable brick façade. Cobbled **Keere Street**★ is very pretty, dropping steeply downhill to a fragment of the old town walls and to **Southover Grange**, built of stone taken from the priory.

In Southover High Street is the beautiful Tudor timber-framed **Anne of Cleves' House**, now a local history museum (🕐open year-round Tue–Thu 10am–5pm; Sun–Mon 11am–5pm; 𝄢01273 474 610; ⊜£3.90; www.sussexpast.co.uk). Entry to **Lewes Castle** is via **Barbican House**, a fine 16C timber-framed building with a late-Georgian façade. It too is now home to a local museum (🕐 for details of opening times and joint ticket with Anne of Cleves' House visit www.sussexpast.co.uk). A perfect flint-built 14C **barbican** also guards the castle precinct. From one of its towers there are fine **views**★ of the town and the gracefully-sculpted outlines of the chalk hills all around.

EXCURSIONS

Sheffield Park Garden★

RHS. 9.5mi/15km north by A 275.
🕐 Open Mar–mid-Jan Tue–Sun 10.30am–5.30pm (also Mon in May and Oct). Mid-Jan–Mar Sat–Sun only 10.30am–4pm. ⊜£7. ⚭🅿✗. 𝄢01825 790 231. www.nationaltrust.org.uk.
This large 18C and 19C landscaped park with its four **lakes** linked by cascades was enriched early this century with thousands of trees and shrubs from around the world.

Bluebell Railway

🕐 Operates year-round, see website or call for schedule and fares. ⚭🅿✗. 𝄢01825 720 825 (24hr infoline); 𝄢01825 720 800 (general enquiries). www.bluebell-railway.co.uk.
5mi/8km of former London Brighton and South Coast Railway track now carry the nostalgically preserved **steam trains** of Britain's first preserved standard gauge passenger railway.

New Forest★★

Hampshire

This ancient landscape near the coast just west of Southampton has remained more or less unchanged since William the Conqueror named the area his "new hunting forest" in 1079. The ancient system to protect and manage the woodlands and wilderness heaths is still in place today, maintained through the efforts of Verderers, Agisters and Commoners – literally the judges, stockmen and land users of the forest. Today it is

- 🜨 **Michelin Map:** Michelin Atlas p 9 or Map 503 O, P 31
- ℹ **Info:** Lyndhurst. 𝄢023 8028 3444. www.thenewforest.co.uk.
- ▷ **Location:** The New Forest is in southern Hampshire, covering around 220sq mi/570sq km.
- ☺ **Don't Miss:** Beaulieu National Motor Museum; Buckler's Hard.

a National Park where New Forest ponies, donkeys, deer and cattle roam in England's largest remaining tract of un-enclosed pasture.

BEAULIEU★★

This pretty village at the head of the Beaulieu River is famous for the National Motor Museum, one of the world's most comprehensive collections of motor vehicles, set in the grounds of a Cistercian monastery founded in 1204 by King John. After the Dissolution of the Monasteries, the **abbey** fell into ruin, its stone being in demand for Henry VIII's coastal forts; only the footings remain. The cloister has partly survived, notably the lay brothers' quarters, now housing the **Monastic Life Exhibition** (*same ticket as National Motor Museum, ♿ below*) and the 13C refectory, converted into the parish church. **Palace House**, the home of the first Lord Montagu, is a strange mixture of medieval monastic architecture and Victorian home comforts.

The **National Motor Museum★★** (♿♿🕐*open year-round daily 10am–6pm (5pm Oct–late May);* 🕐*closed Dec 25;* ✺*£15.50, child £8.25 (includes Monastic Life Exhibition and Palace House);* ♿📷❌; ✆*01590 612 345; www.beaulieu.co.uk*) has a collection of over 250 vehicles and celebrates the story of motoring from 1895 to the present day. The Classic Car Hall of Fame presents the great motoring pioneers and veteran and vintage cars while racing and record-breaking heroes are commemorated in another section You can take a ride through 100 years of motoring with "Wheels" and browse a re-created 1930s country garage. Hands-on stations encourage children to explore how vehicles work.

BUCKLER'S HARD★

2mi/3km SE of Beaulieu. 🕐*Open daily 10am–5pm (Jul–Aug 5.30pm, Nov–Feb 4.30pm).* 🕐*Closed Dec 25.* ✺*£5.25 (includes museum).* 📷❌. ✆*01590 616 645. www.bucklershard.co.uk.*
This charming hamlet comprises one very wide street lined with 18C cottages running down to the Beaulieu River. In the 1740s the village became a shipbuilding centre for the Navy. As iron replaced wood in shipbuilding the industry declined. The **Maritime Museum and Buckler's Hard Story★** illustrates many aspects of life and work in the 18C with the reconstructed interiors of two cottages and the New Inn, furnished in the style of the 1790s. Boat trips from the wharf (✺*£4*).

LYNDHURST

Capital of the New Forest, this attractive town was where the forest rulers held court in the 17C **Queen's House**. The **New Forest Centre**, (*High Street;* 🕐*open daily 10am–5pm;* 🕐*closed Dec 25–26;* ✺*£3;* ✆*023 8028 3444; www.newforest museum.org.uk*) gives an excellent introduction to the area.

Minstead

This attractive unspoilt village just north of Lyndhurst is home to the 13C **All Saints Church**. North of the church is **Furzey Gardens**, (*Garden:* 🕐*open daily 10am–5pm/dusk; Gallery:* 🕐*open Mar–Oct daily 10am–5pm;* ✺*garden £7, gallery free;* ♿❌; ✆*023 8081 2464; www. furzey-gardens.org*), with a 16C thatched cottage showing how New Forest workers lived over 400 years ago.

FOREST DRIVES
Bolderwood Ornamental Drive★★

2mi/3.2km from Lyndhurst on the A35 towards Christchurch, take a right turn for this lovely drive through enclosures created in the 19C with many fine, mature trees. **Walks** enable visitors to see forest deer up close from observation platforms. At the end of the drive is the venerable Knightwood Oak, said to be over 375 years old.

Rhinefield Ornamental Drive★★

2m/3.2km from Lyndhurst on the A35 towards Christchurch, take a left turn for this magnificent drive along an avenue of trees planted in 1859. Today they are Britain's finest collection of mature conifers. Some stand 150ft/46m high.

Oxford★★★

Oxfordshire

The city of Oxford is famous as the home of England's oldest University. Its romantic townscape of "dream-ing spires", mellow golden stone walls and students in black gowns on bicycles has been the setting for any number of works of fiction, from Harry Potter to Inspector Morse and Jude the Obscure.

A BIT OF HISTORY

Oxford developed in Saxon times around the 8C nunnery of St Frideswide, now Christ Church, and still maintains its original street plan and parts of its city walls. Religious foundations sprang up and in about 1200 the uni-versity emerged; it was essentially a federation of monastic halls and is still a federation of autonomous colleges. It was the headquarters of the Royalists during the Civil War (Charles I staying at Christ Church and Henrietta Maria at Merton College). Reform came in the 19C, with the Anglo-Catholic Oxford Movement, which revived the Catholic tradition within the Anglican Church, and the growth of scientific research. In the 20C women were admitted and most of the colleges are now co-educa-tional. The essence of Oxford however remains unchanged – "a city where too many bells are always ringing in the rain" (Elmer Davis).

The bicycle shop opened in Longwall Street by **William Morris** in 1902, where he began to make motor cycles, has since developed into a vast motor manufactur-ing enterprise in the suburb of Cowley where BMW now produces Minis.

MUSEUMS WALK

From the bus station head northeast towards the **Ashmolean Museum★★** (**M**[1]; *Beaumont Street;* closed during 2009 for major redevelopment, see web-site or call for opening details; 01865 278 000; www.ashmolean.org). Built in 1845, this museum houses the Universi-ty's archeology and art collections. Greek and Roman sculptures, Egyptian antiq-

▶ **Population:** 118,795

Michelin Map: Michelin Atlas p 18 or Map 504 Q 28.

Info: 15–16 Broad Street. 01865 252 200. www.visitoxford.org.

Location: 58 mi/93km northwest of London. The train station is west of the bus station, a 10-min walk from the centre. The bus station is in the centre at Gloucester Green. Oxford is compact and can be covered on foot, or from an open-top bus (01865 790 522. www.citysightseeing oxford.com).

Don't Miss: Punting on the river; Christ Church; Bodleian Library; Ash-molean Museum; University Museum of Natural History/ Pitt Rivers Museum.

Timing: Three days minimum. Many of the col-leges are open only in the afternoon; visiting times are usually displayed at the porter's lodge. Confirm college opening times by visiting www.ox.ac.uk.

Walking Tours: Contact the tourist office.

Kids: Oxford Castle Unlocked.

uities, and the decorative and fine arts of China, Japan, Tibet, India and Persia are well represented. The outstanding object here is the exquisite late 9C Alfred Jewel, probably made for Alfred the Great. The principal art collections are: Italian paintings, with masterpieces by Uccello and Piero di Cosimo; Renaissance works by Bellini, Veronese, Tintoretto and Giorgione; outstanding Pre-Rapha-elite paintings including works by Hunt and Charles Collins; a good selection of French Impressionists ; and 20C British works from the Camden Town School. From the Ashmolean, head east on Beaumont Street, past the **Martyr's**

Radcliffe Camera

A. Williams/MICHELIN

Memorial (**D¹**) and enter **Balliol College** (note the scorch marks on the inner and outer quad doors from the 16C burning of two Protestant bishops in Broad Street) to access **Trinity College** (*Broad Street;* ◷ *open year-round daily 10.30am (noon/12.30pm some weekends)–noon and 2pm–4pm;* ◷ *closed Christmas hols.* ✆*£1.50;* ✆*01865 279 900; www.trinity. ox.ac.uk).*

Trinity was founded 1555. Standing well back from Broad Street behind gardens in the Front Quad is the **chapel**★, with Grinling Gibbons' exquisite carvings. Note in the Durham Quad the 17C Library and in the Garden Quad, facing **Trinity Gardens**★, the north range by Sir Christopher Wren.

Head north from Trinity up Parks Road to visit the **University Museum of Natural History**★ (*Parks Road off Broad Street;* ◷ *open year-round daily 10am–5pm;* ◷ *closed Easter and over Christmas;* ⅗*;* ✆*01865 272 950; www. oum.ox.ac.uk).* Founded in 1860, the museum's natural history contents (including the famous Oxford Dodo) arguably tell us more about the Victorians than the natural world, though both sink into insignificance beside the extraordinary building: a cast-iron neo-Gothic cathedral designed like a railway station, with 19C decorated stone carvings of animals and plants by the Irish sculptor-mason family, the O'Sheas. A doorway at the end leads to the **Pitt Rivers Museum**★, Oxford's splendidly bizarre anthropological collection of masks, musical instruments, jewellery, skulls, totem poles and armour.

RADCLIFFE AND CENTRE

The sights listed below are grouped according to their position relative to the **Radcliffe Camera**★ (**P**; ☛*closed to the public).* The landmark Baroque rotunda and its quadrangle designed by James Gibbs, is a useful reference point when exploring the many colleges that branch off it. The route marked on the map offers a tour of all of the colleges, but you may prefer simply to wander and admire the architecture.

North of the Quadrangle

On the north side of the quadrangle you will find one of the world's great libraries, the **Bodleian Library**★★ (**A**; *Broad Street;* ◷ *Divinity School, Old Schools Quadrangle and Exhibition Room open year-round Mon–Sat 9am–5pm (Sat 4.30pm);* ☞ *tours Mon–Sat 10.30am, 11.30am, 2pm, 3pm;* ◷ *closed Good Fri, Easter Sat, Christmas hols.* ✆*£1–2 Divinity School; £6 library tour;* ⅗*;* ✆*01865 277 224; www.bodley.ox.ac.uk),* which contains a copy of every book printed in Britain. Established in the 14C and rebuilt in the 17C, the Bodleian contains more than 6 million books, manuscripts and maps. The main entrance leads to Old Schools Quadrangle, built in 1439 in the Jacobean-Gothic style. On the right is the Tower of the Five Orders, richly decorated with the five classical orders of architecture. Opposite is the 15C Divinity School, famous for the bosses and pendants of its **lierne vaulting**★. Above is Duke Humphrey's Library (1610–12), with its decorated **ceiling**★★.

Just north of the Bodleian you will find the **Clarendon Building** and nextdoor lies the **Sheldonian Theatre**★ (*Broad Street;* ◷ *open (university functions permitting) Mon–Sat 10am–12.30pm, 2pm–4.30pm (3.30pm Nov–Feb);* ◷ *closed Easter and Christmas;* ✆*£2;* ⅗*;* ✆*01865 277 295; www.sheldon.ox.ac.uk).* Built 1664–69, Oxford's first Classical building and Sir Christoper Wren's first work of architecture was designed to accommodate formal University ceremonies, a function it fulfils today, alongside its role as a recital room for small music concerts.

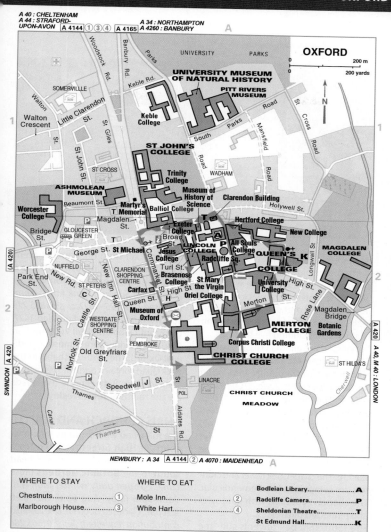

A 40 : CHELTENHAM
A 44 : STRAFORD-
UPON-AVON A 4144 ① ③ ④ A 4165 A 34 : NORTHAMPTON
A 4260 : BANBURY A

OXFORD

0 ────── 200 m
0 ────── 200 yards

N

NEWBURY : A 34 A 4144 ② A 4070 : MAIDENHEAD A

WHERE TO STAY	WHERE TO EAT	
Chestnuts............................①	Mole Inn.............................②	Bodleian Library.........................**A**
Marlborough House.............③	White Hart.........................④	Radcliffe Camera........................**P**
		Sheldonian Theatre...................**T**
		St Edmund Hall..........................**K**

Next door is Hawksmoor's 1713 Palladian **Clarendon Building (BZ),** now part of the Bodleian Library.

East of the Quadrangle

On the east side of the quadrangle you first come to **All Souls College** (*High Street;* ⏰ *open year-round Mon–Fri 2pm–4pm;* ⏰ *closed Easter, Aug and Dec 25–Jan 1;* ✆ *01865 279 379; www.all-souls.ox.ac.uk).* Founded in 1438 as a memorial to those killed in the Hundred Years War, the Front Quadrangle is mid-15C and the larger North Quad, by Nicholas Hawks-

moor, is 18C. Between them is the 1442 Perpendicular **chapel**★, with 15C glass in the antechapel, and a magnificent medieval reredos.

Leaving All Souls, you pass **Hertford College** on your left as you head towards **New College** (*New College Lane Gate summer, Holywell Gate winter;* ⏰ *open daily Easter–early Oct 11am–5pm (early Oct–Easter 2pm–4pm);* 👓 *£2 (winter, free);* ✆ *01865 279 555; www.new.ox.ac.uk).* Founded by William of Wykeham in 1379, New College still maintains some of its original buildings. The Great Quad

153

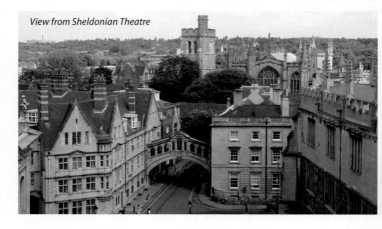

View from Sheldonian Theatre

is quintessential English Perpendicular; the hall is the oldest in Oxford. The 15C **chapel**★ is vast, complete with 14C glass. The cloister is a place of calm, offering a view of the 1400 Bell Tower. In the gardens is Oxford's finest section of city walls, including five bastions.

Leaving New College, cross Longwall Street to access **Magdalen College**★★ (🕐 *open year-round daily 1pm (noon Jul–Sept)–dusk/6pm;* 🕐 *closed Christmas;* ⊙*£4;* ✕ *(Summer only);* 📞*01865 276 000; www.magd.ox.ac.uk).* Founded in 1458 Magdalen (pronounced "maudlin") was originally the Hospital of St John the Baptist; the wall running along the High Street is even earlier, dating from the 13C. The chapel, bell tower and cloisters are sumptuous late Perpendicular. The chapel is adorned with gargoyles and pinnacled buttresses.

The 150ft/46m bell tower is still "the most absolute building in Oxford" (James I). The gargoyles on the cloister buttresses are a familiar feature of the Great Quadrangle.

West of the Quadrangle

Just west of the quadrangle is **Brasenose College** (*Radcliffe Square;* 🕐*open year-round daily, usually 2pm–4.30pm;* 🕐*closed Dec 25–26;* ⊙*£1;* 📞*01865 277 830; www.bnc.ox.ac.uk).* Founded 1509, the Gatehouse, Front Quad and Hall are early 16C, the Library and Chapel mid-17C and the old kitchen a 14C relic of Brasenose Hall (the name refers to a

doorknocker from the hall). Adjacent to Brasenose is **Lincoln College**★ (*Turl Street;* 🕐*open year-round daily 2pm (11am Sun and bank hols) –5pm;* 🕐*closed 1 Jan, 25–26 Dec;* 📞*01865 279 800; www.linc.ox.ac.uk).* Founded 1427, the Front Quad and Hall were built in 1436 and provide a rare glimpse of medieval Oxford. The 1610–31 chapel in the Back Quad contains original 17C Flemish stained glass. Between the two quads are the rooms of **John Wesley**.

CHRIST CHURCH AND SOUTH

The following walk explores the sights south of High Street. Starting from Magdalen College (👉*see above),* head south to the **Botanic Gardens** (*Rose Lane;* 🕐*open daily (winter Mon–Fri) 9am–5pm (May–Aug 6pm, Nov–Feb 4.30pm);* 🕐*closed Good Fri, Dec 25;* ⊙*£3 contribution requested;* ♿*;* 📞*01865 286 690; www.botanic-garden.ox.ac.uk).* Established in 1621, these are the oldest botanic gardens in England. They provide a view of both the college towers and spires and the River Cherwell, crowded with punts in the summer (Magdalen Bridge Boathouse is a good place to hire one).

Heading west from here you first come to **Merton College**★★ (🕐*open year-round Sat–Sun 10am–4pm;* 🕐*closed Easter week and Christmas;* 📞*01865 276 310; www.merton.ox.ac.uk).* Founded in 1264, Merton has the oldest and most picturesque college buildings in

Oxford. The oldest square is **Mob Quad**, a complete 14C quadrangle with the **Library** (1371–78) – the first medieval library to put books on shelves – on two sides. Adjacent is the **Decorated Chapel** (1294–97) with 14C transepts, and stained glass.

Leaving the chapel you immediately see **Corpus Christi College** (⊙*open daily 1.30pm–4.30pm;* ⊙*closed Easter and Christmas;* ☎*01865 276 700; www.ccc.ox.ac.uk).* Founded in 1517, the gateway and Front Quad are early Tudor. The Pelican Sundial in the centre of the quad was designed in 1581, the 16C Hall has a splendid hammerbeam roof and the 16C chapel contains an altarpiece attributed to the studio of Rubens.

Just beyond Corpus Christi is **Christ Church★★** *(College, Cathedral and hall:* ⊙ *open year-round Mon–Sat 9am–5pm, Sun 2pm–5pm; Picture gallery:* ⊙ *open May–Sept Mon–Sat 10.30am–5pm (Oct–Apr 1pm), Sun 2pm–5pm (Oct–Apr 4.30pm);*▨*Cathedral and hall £6 (less if Cathedral and/or hall are closed); picture gallery £3;* &*; www.chch.ox.ac.uk).* Founded in 1525 by Cardinal Wolsey "The House" is Oxford's biggest and grandest Renaissance college. Oxford's largest quadrangle is **Tom Quad★**. Above the gatehouse is Wren's synthesis of Baroque and Gothic, **Tom Tower★**, a fine domed gateway. The **Tudor Hall★★**, by James Wyatt, boasts a magnificent fan-vaulted entrance stairway, hammerbeam roof and portraits by Kneller, Romney, Gainsborough, Lawrence and Millais. The internationally renowned drawings collection in the **Picture Gallery** at Christ Church is regarded as one of the most important private collections of Old Master drawings in the country and includes work by Leonardo, Michelangelo, Dürer, Raphael and Rubens. Picturesque Christ Church Meadow stretches from St Aldate's to the River Thames. **The cathedral★**, originally the church of St Frideswide's Priory, is late Norman with a 16C roof, and the smallest cathedral in England. Its glory is its 15C stellar vaulted **choir roof★**.

If you head north towards the centre from Christ Church on St Aldate's Road, you pass the **Museum of Oxford** (⊙*open year-round Tue–Fri 10am–5pm; Sat–Sun noon–5pm;* &*;* ☎*01865 252 761; www.museumofoxford.org.uk).* Here you will discover the story of the city including its earliest residents' medieval crafts, Civil War, famous literary connections and the growth of the modern city.

A little further up St Aldate's Road is **Carfax** (⊙*open daily Apr–Sept 10am–5pm, rest of year 10am–4pm;* ☎*01865 790 522;*▨*£2.10;* ⊙*No children under five admitted),* the centre of the Saxon and medieval city. This 14C tower is all that remains of St Martin's Church. There are good views of the High Street, known as "the High", from the top of the tower.

Head west from here on Queen Street to visit **Oxford Castle Unlocked** (⊙*open year-round daily 10am–5.30pm (last tour 4.20pm);* ⊙*closed Dec 25;*▨*£7.50,child £5.35;* & ✗*;* ☎*01865 260 666; www.oxfordcastleunlocked.co.uk).* St George's Tower is a striking survival from Oxford Castle, built 1071. It has always been used as a place of incarceration right up until its closure as HM Prison Oxford in 1996. The more colourful events – violence, executions, escapes, betrayal, even romance – which shaped its grim history, are explored here with some relish.

ADDRESSES

STAY

⊜⊜ **Chestnuts**, *45 Davenant Road.* ☎*01865 553 375. www.chestnutsguesthouse.co.uk.* This small 7-room guest house is under friendly personal management with touches such as bathrobes and mineral water in bedrooms, and is just a short walk to the town's water meadows and centre.

⊜⊜⊜ **Marlborough House**, *321 Woodstock Road, Summertown.* ☎*01865 311 321. www.marlbhouse.co.uk.* This modern three-storey houses offers 16 simple yet spacious rooms, each with its own kitchenette, a short bus ride from the town centre.

♈/ EAT

😑😑 **White Hart**, Wytham, 3 mi/5km north west of city centre. ℘01865 244 372. www.thewhitehartoxford.co.uk. Pretty 18C village pub, serving modern British food on a delightful courtyard terrace or in a flag-stoned dining room with scrubbed tables and roaring fires.

😑😑 **Mole Inn**, Toot Baldon, 5.5mi/9km south east on the B 480. ℘01865 340 001. www.themoleinn.com. The standard of cuisine at this immaculately refurbished inn is several notches higher than standard Oxfordshire pub fare, running from earthy classics to modern.

SIGHTSEEING

After taking a walking tour enjoy a relaxing boat trip on the Cherwell or the Thames; self-hire and chauffered punts are available by the hour. For longer trips there are electric boats, a steam boat and river cruisers. Boat houses and punting stations are at Magdalen Bridge, Folly Bridge and Bardwell Road.

➢ SHOPPING

Oxford's main shopping streets are **Queen Street**, **Magdalen Street** and **Cornmarket Street**. Shoppers browsing for books, souvenirs, gifts and antiques should visit **Broad Street**, **High Street** and **Turl Street**. An open-air market is held in **Gloucester Green** every Wednesday, and an antiques market every Thursday. Also of interest, either for shopping or just browsing, is the delightful **Victorian Covered Market**, open Monday to Saturday.

Portsmouth★

Hampshire

Britain's premier naval base is set between two almost landlocked harbours. The early 15C saw the development of the naval base and in 1495 the first dry dock in the world was built. By the end of the 17C Portsmouth had become the principal naval base in the country. In the 18C when France was Britain's major enemy, the fortifications were strengthened. After heavy bombing in the Second World War the city was rebuilt and expanded onto the mainland.

HISTORIC DOCKYARD

Victory Gate, Queen Street and the Hard; ⏱ *Open daily Apr–Oct 10am–6pm, Nov–Mar 10am–5pm Oct–Mar; last admission 90 mins before closing.* ⏱*Closed Dec 24–26.* 😑*Passport ticket £18.50 (includes harbour boat tour), child £14. Single/double attraction £12, child £8; Royal Naval Museum only, £4.50.* 👅 *Guided tour HMS Victory (45min) subject to availability, usually only at off-peak visiting times (😑 arrive early).* ♿🅿(£5)✗. ℘023 9272 8060. www.historicdockyard.co.uk.

- ▶ **Population:** 174,690
- 👆 **Michelin Map:** Michelin Atlas p 10 or Map 504 Q 31
- 🔲 **Info:** ℘023 9282 6722. www.visitportsmouth. co.uk.
- 🕐 **Location:** 81 mi/130km south of London. Portsmouth Station is a 10–15 min walk from the centre. More convenient is Harbour Station, on The Hard, which includes the bus station, and is adjacent to the main sights. The Southsea Land Train is a useful way of getting around, or take a tour (www.localhaunts.com).
- 😑 **Don't Miss:** The Historic Dockyard; the view from the Spinnaker Tower.
- 🕐 **Timing:** Two days minimum.
- 👥 **Kids:** Historic Dockyard (HMS Victory and Action Stations); the beach, seaside amusements and Blue Reef Aquarium at Southsea; Explosion!

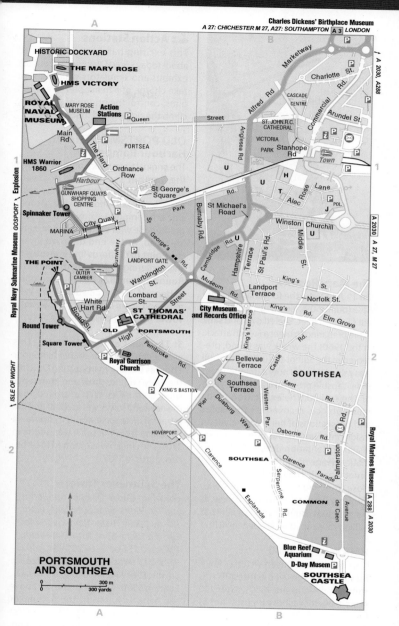

Charles Dickens' Birthplace Museum
A 27: CHICHESTER M 27, A27: SOUTHAMPTON A 3 LONDON

PORTSMOUTH
AND SOUTHSEA

0   300 m
0   300 yards

HMS Victory★★★

On 21 October 1805, Admiral Horatio Nelson's splendid three-masted flagship (built Chatham 1759) led the victorious attack on a combined French and Spanish fleet off Cape Trafalgar in Spain – at the cost of her admiral's life. In the 1920s the *Victory* was brought into dry dock after 150 years at sea.

Today she continues to serve as the flagship of the Commander in Chief Naval Home Command, still manned by serving Royal Naval and Royal Marines personnel.

HMS Victory

Y. Duhamel/MICHELIN

The Mary Rose★★

On 19 July 1545, the four-masted *Mary Rose* (built 1509), vice-flagship of Henry VIII's English fleet, keeled over and sank while preparing to meet a French attack. In the 1960s the wreck was found, preserved in the Solent silt; in 1982 the hull was raised and it is now a unique Tudor time-capsule preserved after 437 years on the seabed. The **exhibition** of the many objects recovered – treasures and possessions of her crew – gives an insight into Tudor nautical life. An audio-visual presentation describes the dramatic salvage operation.

Unfortunately the ship hall is likely to close from mid-September 2009, with the *Mary Rose* withdrawn from view, as construction commences on a new £35 million museum due to open in 2012.

HMS Warrior 1860

Once the pride of Queen Victoria's Navy, Britain's first iron-clad battleship was commissioned in the 1860s. After 100 years of use for various purposes she has been restored and now displays a living exhibition of life in the Victorian Navy.

Royal Naval Museum★★

The museum stands alongside HMS *Victory* and the *Mary Rose*. The galleries are packed with mementoes of those who have served their country at sea through a thousand years of peace and war.

🏃 Action Stations

This exciting hands-on centre is all about today's Royal Navy with high-tech exhibits and simulators which let you take charge of a helicopter, fire ship's guns, control the bridge of a warship, climb the rigging and much more.

OLD PORTSMOUTH★
Harbour Ramparts

The original town which grew up around the **Camber** south of the dockyard was once entirely enclosed by ramparts; today only those on the harbour side are complete, forming a pleasant promenade with **views** of Gosport and Spithead. At the end of Broad Street the **Point (BY)** affords fine **views**★★ of ships entering and leaving the port. The **Round Tower (BZ)**, built on the orders of Henry V, was modified in Henry VIII's reign and again in the 19C. The **Square Tower (BZ)** was built in 1494.

St Thomas Cathedral★ **(BZ)** – This was built c. 1180 as a chapel to honour **Thomas Becket**, martyred in 1170. Only the Early English **choir** and **transepts** survived the Civil War; in around 1690 the nave and tower were rebuilt and the attractive octagonal wooden **cupola** – a landmark from the sea – was added in 1703. The church was elevated to cathedral status in 1927.

The Spinnaker Tower★

Gunwharf Quays. 🕐 *Open Apr–Jun Sun–Fri 10am–6pm, Sat 10am–10pm. Jul–Aug daily 10am–10pm. Sept–Mar Sun–Fri 10am–5pm, Sat 10am–10pm.* 🕐*Closed 25 Dec.* ✦*£6.20.* ♿✗. ✆*023 9285 7520 (Wheelchair users must call in advance). www.spinnakertower.co.uk.* Soaring 558ft/170m into the sky above the historic harbour, the Spinnaker Tower, completed in 2005, is the tallest public viewing tower in Great Britain, with wonderful panoramic views which stretch as far as the Isle of Wight.

SOUTHSEA

The strip of land at the south of Portsea Island was rough marshland until the 19C when a coastal resort began to grow and the Common became a pleasure area. At the southernmost tip of the island stands the **Castle**★ *(Clarence Esplanade;* 🕐 *open Apr–Sept daily 10am–5.30pm;* 🕐 *closed 24–26 Dec;* ∞*£3.50;* ♿*;* ✆*023 9282 7261; www.portsmouthmuseums. co.uk),* built by Henry VIII in 1544 as part of the chain of forts protecting the ports along the south and east coast. The central **keep**, surrounded by a dry moat, is still mainly Tudor; inside are displays of the growth of Portsmouth's fortifications.

The **D-Day Museum and Overlord Embroidery (CZ)** (♿ *Clarence Esplanade;* 🕐 *open daily 10am–5.30pm (Nov–Mar 5pm);* 🕐 *closed 24–26 Dec;* ∞*£6;* ♿ (disabled visitors only)✕*;* ✆*023 9282 7261; www.portsmouthmuseums. co.uk)* illustrates the major events of the Second World War. The centrepiece is the Overlord Embroidery with 34 panels telling the story of D-Day.

Blue Reef Aquarium *(Clarence Esplanade;* ♿ 🕐 *open daily 10am–5pm, Nov–Feb 10am–4pm;* 🕐*closed 25 Dec;* ∞*£9, child £7;* ♿✕*;* ✆*023 92 875 222; www.bluereefaquarium.co.uk)* is one of the country's new-wave aquaria with large high-visibility tanks and special viewing features.

The **Royal Marines Museum**★ *(Eastney Esplanade, along Clarence Parade, A 288* **(CZ)**; 🕐*open daily 10am–5pm;* 🕐*closed Dec 23–26;* ∞*£5.95;* ♿✕*;* ✆*023 9281 9385; www.royalmarinesmuseum.co.uk)* set in the original 19C officers' mess, describes the past and present of the Royal Marine Corps. Of note are the presentations on the Marines' work in Arctic and jungle conditions, the D-Day landings, the Marines' service in the UN and the "talking head" of Hannah Snell, who joined disguised as a man.

ADDITIONAL SIGHTS
Charles Dickens' Birthplace Museum
393 Old Commercial Road. 🕐 *Open Feb 7 and mid-Apr–Sept daily 10am– 5.30pm.* ∞*£3.50.* ✆*023 9282 7261. www.charlesdickensbirthplace.co.uk.*
The small, neat city-centre terrace house where Dickens was born in 1812, and

spent the first four months of his life, has been restored and furnished in the style of the period. A small exhibition includes the green velvet couch on which he died at Gad's Hill Place in Kent.

Royal Navy Submarine Museum
Gosport (cross harbour by shuttle ferry). Haslar Jetty Road. 🕐*Open daily, 10am–5.30pm (Nov–Mar 4.30pm).* 🕐*Closed Dec 24–25.* ∞*£8.* ♿🅿✕. ✆*023 9252 9217. www.rnsubmus.co.uk.*
Five actual submarines, torpedoes, a Polaris missile and hands-on exhibits of periscopes and diving equipment all help tell the story of submariners and their role in peace and war.

♿ Explosion! Naval Fire Power Museum
Gosport (cross harbour by shuttle ferry **(CY)**. *Priddy's Hard.* 🕐 *Open Sat–Sun 10am–4pm.* 🕐*Closed Jan 1, Dec 25–26.* ∞*£4.* ♿🅿✕. ✆*012 9250 5600, 023 9250 5678 (infoline). www.explosion.org.uk.*
The story of naval firepower is traced through audio-visual presentations-workers' testimonies and exhibits on mines, torpedoes, missiles and more.

EXCURSIONS
Royal Armouries Fort Nelson
Fort Nelson, Portsdown Hill Road; 9mi/14km northwest on M 27 **(CY)**. 🕐 *Open daily Apr–Oct 10am–5pm (Wed open 11am). Nov–Mar daily 10.30am–4pm (Wed open 11.30am).* 🕐 *Closed Dec 25–26.* ♿🅿✕. ✆*01329 233 734. www.armouries.org.uk.*
This superbly restored Victorian fort is one of a chain built high across Portsdown Hill to defend Portsmouth from French invasion. There are sweeping **views** from the fort walls.
Alongside re-created barracks, the collection of artillery includes ornate medieval bronze cannons from India, China and Turkey, anti-aircraft guns and three sections of the immense "Supergun" impounded in 1990, en route for Iraq in the guise of petro-chemical piping.

Rochester

Kent

The Romans built Durobrivae to dominate the point where Watling Street crossed the River Medway. A 12C Norman castle now stands tall, while the walled town is cut in two by "the silent High Street, full of gables with old beams and timbers" (Charles Dickens). In fact Rochester and the Medway area are the scene of several of Dickens' novels, notably Pickwick Papers and Great Expectations.

▶ **Population:** 23,971.
🚗 **Michelin Map:** Michelin Atlas p 12 or Map 504 V 29.
ℹ **Info:** 95 High Street. ☎01634 843 666. www.medway.gov.uk.
⊙ **Location:** 35 mi/53 km east of London. The train station is on the High Street with a frequent London service.
👪 **Kids:** World Naval Base, Chatham; Dickens World.

CITY

The river Medway cuts Rochester in tow. In the centre of town, on the south side of the river near the High Street bridge is the **Castle★** (E.H; ⊙open daily, 10am–6pm (4pm Oct–late-Mar); ⊙closed 24–26 Dec, 1 Jan; ☜£5; ☎01634 402 276, 0870 333 1181; www.english-heritage.org.uk), whose early **curtain walls** were built by Gundulf, Bishop of Rochester and architect of Rochester Cathedral and the Tower of London. The present massive **keep** was built in 1127; its ruins are an outstanding example of Norman military architecture.

South of here is the **Cathedral★** (⊙open daily year-round 7.30am–6pm (5pm Sat); ☞ guided tours £4; ♿✗; ☎01634 810 073; www.rochestercathe dral.org), where Bishop Gundulf (1024–1108) held England's second episcopal see, from 1077. The cathedral was extended at least twice and is mostly 12C and 13C. Of particular interest is the Norman west front, and its centrepiece, the exuberantly sculptured **west doorway** (1160). Beyond the six Norman **nave bays** the cathedral is essentially Early English. The painting on the choir wall is the Wheel of Fortune and dates from the 13C when the whole of the cathedral walls were similarly painted. Note the carvings on the chapter room doorway (c. 1350). On the north side between the two transepts is Gundulf's **tower** (c. 1100).

Back on the High Street, the **Guildhall** (⊙ open year-round Tue–Sun 10am–4.30pm; ⊙closed Christmas; ♿; ☎01634 848 717; www.medway.gov.uk) is a handsome Renaissance building containing a museum with an actual-size section of a piece of an infamous Medway hulk (prison ships) alongside displays on more genteel Victorian life.

EXCURSIONS

👪 World Naval Base, Chatham★★

2mi/3km northeast. Open mid-Feb–late Mar daily 10am–4pm. Late Mar–late Oct daily, 10am–6pm. Last week Oct daily and Nov Sat–Sun 10am–4pm.

The Roman Conquest

The Medway area is rich in prehistoric and Roman sites. During Emperor Claudius's invasion of Britain, Roman legions landed near Richborough in Kent and moved westwards. An unhewn stone (15ft/5m high), erected near a ford on the Medway at Snodland, south of Rochester, in 1998, is a belated memorial to a decisive Roman victory in AD 43 over the army of the Celtic king Cunobelinus – Shakespeare's Cymbeline. This event sealed the fate of Britain coming under the Roman Empire. The battle probably took place near a fordable point on the Medway – near Snodland according to modern historians.

£14, Child £9.50. &♿️ 🅿️✕. *☎01634 823 800, 01634 823 807. www.chdt.org.uk.*
Established in the reign of Henry VIII, this cradle of British sea power built nearly 500 ships, including HMS *Victory*, before the Royal Navy finally left in 1984. The large complex (80 acres/32ha) of historic maritime buildings and docks now reinterprets the life of the dockyard through exhibits and demonstrations, from the **Sail and Colour Loft** (flags and sails) to the **Ropery**, the award-winning **Wooden Walls** (construction of large wooden ships) **Lifeboat!** and **3 Slip** – when built in 1838, this immense covered slipway was Europe's largest wide-span timber structure.

👥 Dickens World

Leviathan Way, Chatham.
🕐*Open year-round daily 10am–5.30pm, last admission 4pm.* 🕐*Closed Dec 25.* *£12.20 (£9.75 after 3.30pm) child £7.30 (£6 after 3.30pm).*
&♿️🅿️✕. *www.dickensworld.co.uk.*
This theme park dedicated to the life, works and times of one of Britain's greatest novelists is set on the site where Dickens' father worked as a clerk in the Naval Dockyard. Young Charles lived most of his childhood in Chatham, drawing on it for inspiration in his novels.
The attraction includes a dark boat ride, the Haunted House of Ebenezer Scrooge, a state-of-the art animatronic show, a Victorian School Room, a 3-D film show and re-creations of city streets, complete with sounds and smells.

Leeds Castle★★

Maidstone, 11mi/18km southeast on the A 229 and M 20. **Castle:** 🕐 *Open daily 10.30am–6pm (Oct–Mar 4pm).* **Park:** 🕐 *Open daily 10am–5pm, last entry (Oct–Mar last entry 3pm).* 🕐*Closed Dec 25.* *£15.* &♿️🅿️✕. *☎01622 765 400. www.leeds-castle.com.*
Originally Norman, built on two islands in a lake, it was described by Lord Conway as "the loveliest castle in the world", and is certainly one of the most picturesque in Great Britain. A romantic stone **bridge** links the keep, which rises sheer from the lake, with the turreted and battlemented main building. The interior is graced by splendid **works of art** (14C–19C): statues, carvings and tapestries. The glorious **park** and **gardens** include an aviary, grotto and maze.

Royal Tunbridge Wells
Kent

A graceful combination of Georgiana and Victoriana amid parks, vistas and a vast semi-wild common, Tunbridge Wells owes its good fortune to the accidental discovery of its mineral springs in 1606 by Lord North; it soon became a magnet for the fashionable. Queen Henrietta Maria spent six weeks there, in a tent, after the birth of her son, Charles II. Queen Anne provided the tiled paving after which the Pantiles are named and Queen Victoria, who spent holidays here, commented "Dear Tunbridge Wells, I am so fond of it."

> ▶ **Population:** 60,272.
> 🧭 **Michelin Map:** Michelin Atlas p 12 or Map 504 U 30.
> 🛈 **Info:** Old Fish Market, The Pantiles. ☎01892 515 675. visittunbridgewells.com.
> 🧭 **Location:** 42mi/67km SE of London. The train station is at the south end of the High Street.
> 👥 **Kids:** Hever Castle (jousting tournaments.

THE PANTILES★

This perfect pedestrian precinct is on two levels, with an Upper Walk and a Lower Walk. The **Bath House** (1804) still shows off its spring; the **Corn Exchange** (1802), once a theatre, displays Doric columns and Ceres, Goddess of the Harvest, on the roof; and the **Music Gallery** remains a reminder of the town's past elegance. **Union House** (1969, by Michael Levell) at one end of the Pantiles is an object lesson on how old and new can stand together in dignity. The 17C **Church of King Charles the Martyr** at the other end is also worth a visit.

Calverley Park★ – Not so much a park as a neo-Classical new town by Decimus Burton. Inspired by Bath, it is best seen around Calverley Park Crescent.

EXCURSIONS
Knole★★

NT. Sevenoaks. 15mi/24km north on the A 26, A 21 and A 225. **House:** ⊕ *Open last three weeks Mar Sat–Sun noon– 4pm; Apr–third week Jul and Sept–Oct, Wed–Sun noon–4pm; third week Jul– Aug Tue–Sun 11am–4.30pm.* **Garden:** ⊕ *Open Easter–Oct Wed 11am–4pm.* **Park:** ⊕ *Open daily to pedestrians.* ⊜*House £9, garden only £2.* ♿🅿✕. ✆*01732 462 100,* ✆*01732 450 608 (infoline). www.nationaltrust.org.uk.*

This great late-medieval, Tudor and Jacobean mansion – the childhood home of **Vita Sackville-West**, English poet, novelist and gardener (1892–1962) – is one of the finest buildings of its kind in England. The present building and its collection reflects the efforts of the Earls of Dorset in the 17C–18C. The **Great Hall** with its exquisite Jacobean screen is impressive. The elaborate grisaille decor of the **Great Staircase** sets off a life-size nude of the beauty Gianetta Baccelli in the lobby; the second-oldest harpsichord case made in England in 1622 is displayed in the **Spangle Dressing Room**. The rooms are ornamented with splendid friezes, ceilings, panelling and chimney-pieces, in particular the **Ballroom**, **Crimson Drawing Room** and **Cartoon Gallery** where are displayed ornate furnishings and fine paintings (17C–18C family portraits, works by Lely, Reynolds and copies of Raphael's Cartoons). The highlight of Knole is the **King's Room**, with its gaudy grisailles, ostrich feathers, expensive embroidery and silver ornamentation.

Ightham Mote★★

NT. 10mi/16km north on the A 26 and A 227. Ivy Hatch. **House:** ⊕*Open mid-Mar–Oct Thu–Mon 11am–5pm; Nov–late Dec Thu–Sun 11am–3pm.* **Garden:** ⊕*Open 10am–5.30pm.* ⊜*£9.40, winter weekends £5.* ♿🅿✕. ✆*01732 810 378, 01732 811 145 (infoline). www.nationaltrust.org.uk.*

Ightham (pronounced "item"), built of stone and timber in 1340, is the best preserved moated manor house in England; its survival is probably largely due to its secluded site.

The crenellated gatehouse leads into the courtyard, where the atmosphere is one of calm and privacy. Opposite is the **Great Hall**, built in the 1340s. The carved **frieze** above the fireplace and the **panelling** were designed by Norman Shaw in the 1870s. In the stairwell beyond, the **Jacobean staircase** has a Saracen's head, the Selby family crest, carved on the newel post.

The **New Chapel** has a unique **barrel-vaulted roof**, dating from 1470–80 and with early 16C painted panels.

Sissinghurst Castle Garden★

NT. Near Cranbrook, 13mi/21km east via the A 264, A 21 and A 262. ⊕ *Open mid-Mar–Oct Fri–Tue 11am (10am weekends)–6.30pm/dusk.* ⊜*£8.80.* ♿🅿✕. ✆*01580 710 700. 01580 710 701 (infoline). www.nationaltrust.org.uk.*

In 1930 **Vita Sackville-West** (⊘*see Knole)* and her husband Harold Nicolson discovered the Sissinghurst estate. "I fell in love… I saw what could be made of it… a castle running away into sordidness and squalor, a garden crying out for rescue." The **tower** became her study and the **garden** their monument.

Penshurst Place★

8mi/12km west via the A 26 and B 2176. **House:** ⊕*Open late Feb–late Mar Sat–Sun and late Mar–Oct daily, noon– 4pm.* **Grounds:** ⊕*Open year-round daily 10.30am–6pm (Nov–Feb 4.30pm).* ⊜*£8.50; garden only £7.* ⤷*Guided tours house and garden £12, just house or garden £8.50.* ♿🅿✕. ✆*01892 870 307. www.penshurstplace.com.*

Hever Castle

A. F. Kersting/MICHELIN

This mansion, formerly the home of the Elizabethan poet **Sir Philip Sidney** (1554–86), is set in a pretty neo-Tudor village, clustering around the 13C church of St John the Baptist, with its Sidney Chapel. The original Great Hall (1346), built of coarse sandstone, has been added to with early Tudor, Jacobean and neo-Gothic wings.

Inside the Hall, the chestnut **timber roof** is held up by unusual life-size carvings of humble peasants. The open hearth is a rare feature and the screens are decorated with tracery. The elegant **furnishings** of the formal rooms include rare furniture, tapestries and portraits.

The great terrace is the focus of the formal **gardens** with their clipped hedges. There is a nature trail, a farm museum and an enchanting **Toy Museum** with puppets, rocking horses and 19C dolls.

Chiddingstone

16mi/24km northwest on the A 26, B 2176, B 2027 and local roads.

The delightful 16C–17C dwellings, timber-framed, tile-hung, pargeted and gabled, clustered around St Mary's Church, present a rare combination of 14C Gothic and Jacobean styles. The village is owned by the National Trust.

To the west, near Edenbridge, stands **Chiddingstone Castle** (🕐 openGood Fri–last Sun Sept, Sun–Wed 11am–5pm (check website for other days); ⬛£6; ♿🅿✕; 📞01892 870 347; www.chiddingstonecastle.org.uk) a 19C setting for Buddhist, Egyptian, Japanese and English Stuart period works of art amassed by the eccentric Denys Eyre Bower, a bank clerk with a remarkable eye and great enthusiasm.

👪 Hever Castle★

13mi/21km west on the A 264 and B 2026. **House:** 🕐 Open Apr–Oct daily noon–6pm, Mar–Easter Wed–Sun noon–5pm, Nov–Dec Thu–Sun noon–4pm (Dec 3pm last admission). **Gardens:** 🕐 open daily 10.30am, close as house. Mazes open Easter–Oct weather permitting. ⬛£12; Gardens only, £9.50. ♿🅿✕. 📞01732 865 224. www.hever-castle.co.uk.

This fortified manor house protected by a moat and the drawbridge and portcullis of the massive gatehouse stands in an idyllic countryside setting. Formerly the childhood home of **Anne Boleyn**, the neglected castle was bought In 1903 by William Waldorf Astor who lavishly restored both castle and grounds.

Much of the **woodwork** is a re-creation of the finest Renaissance craftsmanship. There are portraits of Anne, and one, by Holbein, of Henry; in her little room is the Book of Hours the young queen took to her execution on 19 May 1536. A costumed figure exhibition and tableaux represent the life and times of Anne Boleyn.

Gardens

The lake (38 acre/15ha), is approached via an elaborate loggia and an **Italian garden** with **antique statuary and sculpture**. Two mazes, an adventure playground and a lively programme of activities, including jousting, make this a good place for children too.

Chartwell

NT. 15mi/24km northwest via the A 264 and B 206. Mappleton Road.
House, gardens and studio: ○ *Open mid-Mar–Oct Wed–Sun and bank hols 11am–5pm (Jul–Aug also Tue). Gardens close 4pm winter. Admission to house by timed ticket.* ∞£10.60 (garden and studio only, £5.90). ♿ 🅿 ✕. ✆01732 868 381, ✆01732 866 368 (Infoline). www.nationaltrust.org.uk.*

This restored Tudor house was the home of **Sir Winston Churchill** (1874–1965). It is packed with Churchilliana, including many of his paintings, and reflects comfortable domestic life. The **walls** of the fine gardens were partly built by Churchill himself; there is a splendid southward prospect over rolling countryside.

Rye★★

East Sussex

This exquisite little hill town standing at the confluence of three rivers is visible far across the vast expanse of eastward-stretching levels – a multitude of red-roofed houses building up to a massive squat-towered church. Tranquil centuries of decline and its former remoteness have preserved Rye's charming townscape, though much of its medieval fabric wears a Georgian exterior. Many artists and writers, among them Henry James, have lived here.

A BIT OF HISTORY

Rye's early history was one of struggle both on and with the sea. It lies just 40mi/64km northwest of Boulogne and from 1191 was one of the **Cinque Ports**, the maritime league of Kent and Sussex towns established by Edward the Confessor to supply ships and men for the defence of the realm; despite this it suffered repeated sackings by the French. It was also battered by storms that changed the course of the River Rother in the 13C and later destroyed many of its buildings. The town is still a minor port, though the sea's retreat has left it two miles inland.

> ▶ **Population:** 3,708.
> ⚲ **Michelin Map:** Michelin Atlas p 12 or Map 504 W 31.
> 🛈 **Info:** Heritage Centre, Strand Quay, Rye. ✆01797 226 696. www.ryeheritage.co.uk. Queens Square, Priory Meadow, Hastings. ✆0845 274 1001. www.1066country.com.
> ◑ **Location:** 66mi/106km southeast of London.

OLD TOWN★★

With its steep narrow streets, a wealth of different building materials and sudden glimpses of the countryside, the whole of Rye repays exploration on foot.

Cobbled **Mermaid Street**★ rises sharply. Its varied buildings include the 15C **Mermaid Inn**, once the haunt of ruthless smuggler gangs. Looking towards Church Square is the handsome Georgian façade of Lamb House, home of Henry James from 1897 and later of the satirical novelist EF Benson.

South of Cinque Ports Street is **St Mary's Church** *(Church:* ○ *open daily (except during services) 9am–5.30pm (4.30pm winter); Tower: £2.50 contribu-*

tion requested. &; ☎01797 224 935), a
large impressive building, begun in the
12C. Note the 16C clock, its pendulum
(18ft/5.5m) swinging inside, its elaborate face on the outside of the north
transept, flanked by jolly painted quarter boys who strike the quarters (but not
the hours). From the tower there is an
incomparable **view**★ of Rye's rooftops
and its countryside.

EXCURSIONS
Bodiam Castle★★
*13mi/21km northwest on the A 268.
After 11mi/18km turn left at Sandhurst
and follow minor roads.* ⊙ *Open mid-
Feb–Oct daily 10.30am–6pm. Nov–Dec
Wed–Sun 10.30am–4pm. Jan–mid-
Feb Sat–Sun 10.30am–4pm.* ⊜£5.20.
&▣(£2)✕. ☎01580 830 196.
www.nationaltrust.org.uk.
In a pretty landscaped setting among
low hills, overlooking the levels of the
River Rother, this perfect example of
a late-medieval castle sits four-square
within its protecting moat. It was built
in 1385–88 to block movement inland
by marauding Frenchmen up the (then
navigable) river, and it retains its great
gatehouse, curtain walls and drum towers (60ft/18m high) at each corner.

Hastings Castle
and The 1066 Story
*NT. 12mi/19km southwest on the A 259.
Castle Hill Road.* ⊙ *Open year-round
daily 11am–5pm (Oct–Easter 4pm).*
⊜£3.75. ☎01424 781 111.
www.discoverhastings.co.uk.
The ruins of William the Conqueror's
first English castle (originally a wooden
structure) stand high above the Old
Town and seaside resort below. The
history of castle and the famous battle
of 1066 are told in an informative audio-
visual presentation.

Battle★
*18mi/29km southwest on the A 259,
B 2093 and A 2100.*
The momentous victory, on 14 October
1066, of the Normans over King Harold's
English army is marked by the remains of
the great commemorative **Abbey**★ *(EH;*

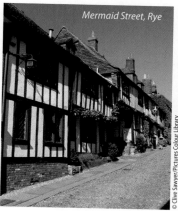
Mermaid Street, Rye
© Clive Sawyer/Pictures Colour Library

⊙ *open year-round daily 10am–6pm,
Oct–Mar 4pm;* ⊙*closed Jan 1 and Dec
24–26;* ⊜£6.40; &▣*(charge)*✕; ☎01424
775 705; www.english-heritage.org.uk)
built on its hilltop site by William the
Conqueror, and also in the name of the
little town which grew up to serve it.
The **Abbey Visitor Centre** uses the latest technology and interactive displays
to draw a vivid picture of the social and
political events, both for Saxons and
Normans, and allows visitors to follow
the individual stories of ordinary characters around the battlefield.
Over the humble buildings of the town's
marketplace rises the imposing 14C
gatehouse, battlemented and richly
decorated. Most of the great Benedictine abbey beyond was dismantled at
the Dissolution, though its outlines may
be traced. The church altar, erected at
William's command over the spot where
Harold fell, is marked by a plaque.
A **museum** in the gatehouse presents
an exhibition on monastic life and the
history of the abbey.

Battlefield★
From the **terrace walk** there is a view of
the tranquil scene over which this most
decisive of English battles was fought. It
was on this ridge that Harold deployed
his men after their exhausting forced
march from York. The day-long battle
was fierce and bloody; a pathway with
topographical models at intervals follows its course along the fateful slopes.

Southampton
Hampshire

This great south coast port, naturally favoured with a double tide, began as a Roman coastal garrison, Clausentum, on the east bank of the Itchen. By the 8C the Saxon port of **Hamwic** was already serving the royal city of Winchester and it has continued to grow, becoming one of Britain's major container ports. After severe bombing in the Second World War, the town began a successful recovery in the fifties and, alongside medieval remains, a modern city has grown up, with a lively university and renewed industry.

▶ **Population:** 210,138.

Michelin Map: Michelin Atlas p 9 or Map 504 P 31.

Info: 9 Civic Centre Road. ℘023 8083 3333. www. visit-southampton.co.uk.

Location: On the south coast, 78mi/125km SW of London; the central train station has a regular direct connection. The bus station is also centrally located, on the other side of the civic centre. Take a tour around the harbour from Ocean Village (℘02380 223 278; www.bluefunnel.co.uk).

Kids: Birds at the Hawk Conservancy Trust.

OLD TOWN WALK

A good deal of the medieval defences and town buildings can still be seen today. The impressive northern gate to the town, the **Bargate**★, built c. 1180, was given its large towers c. 1285 and its forbidding north face in the 15C. The **west wall** of the early defences rises spectacularly above the **Western Esplanade**, where Southampton Bay once lapped the shore. Note the 15C **Catchcold Tower** and the **Arcade** running from the site of **Biddlesgate** to the **Blue Anchor Postern**. At the top of Blue Anchor Lane the large early 16C **Tudor House**★ incorporates an earlier banqueting hall which houses a museum (closed for refurbishment); outside, a 16C **garden** of flowers and herbs and a "knot garden" have been re-created. At the far end steps lead down to the shell of the **Norman House**, a fine example of a 12C merchant's house, which was incorporated into the town wall defences in the 14C. **St Michael's Church** is the oldest building in the medieval town, built soon after the Norman conquest and enlarged throughout the Middle Ages and in the 19C.

Back on the Western Esplanade is **Wool House Maritime Museum** (open year-round Tue–Sat 10am–4pm, Sun 1pm–4pm; £1.95; ℘023 8063 5904; www.southampton.gov.uk/leisure), set in a beautifully restored 14C stone warehouse. It displays models of ships and exhibits from the history of this great port, including a *Titanic* exhibition. **God's House** was founded c. 1185 as an almshouse and hostel for travellers. To its east stand the early 14C **God's House Gate**, and the early 15C **God's House Tower** (details as Wool House, see above), containing the local archeological museum.

East of the rail station on Commercial road is the **City Art Gallery**★ (open year-round Tue–Sat 10am–5pm, Sun 1pm–4pm; (Charge); ℘023 8083 2277; www.southampton.gov.uk), which has an excellent collection of modern art, including works by Spencer, Sutherland and Lowry.

EXCURSIONS

See NEW FOREST.

Broadlands★

8mi/13km NW on the A 3057 (off X), or 1mi/2km short of Romsey. Closed for renovations to 2010. ℘01794 505 010. www.broadlands.net.

In 1736 the first Viscount Palmerston bought a small Tudor manor near Romsey and set about transforming its grounds. His son commissioned **Lancelot "Capability" Brown** to con-

Romsey Abbey

©Ian Whatmore/Fotolia.com

tinue this work and rebuilt the house in the Palladian style to produce a noble **west front**, overlooking the beautiful River Test. **Henry Holland** created the east entrance front and the elegant dining room – the setting for three splendid **Van Dyck** paintings. The house is notable for the **Wedgwood Room** with its friezes and mouldings, a fine collection of 18C Wedgwood pieces and four portraits by Sir Peter Lely. The white and gold plasterwork of the **saloon** and the medallions in the drawing room ceiling are exquisite. In the 20C the house was Lord Mountbatten of Burma's (1900–79) residence.

Romsey Abbey★

9mi/15km NW on the A 3057 (off X).
⊙*Open daily 7.30am–6pm.*
✆*01794 513 125.*
www.romseyabbey.org.uk.
The town of Romsey grew up around a nunnery founded by Edward the Elder, son of Alfred the Great, in 907 and rebuilt c. 1120–1230. At the Dissolution the buildings were destroyed but the abbey church survived to serve as the parish church. The purity and simplicity of the **interior**★★ make this an excellent example of late

Norman architecture. In the east chapel of the south choir aisle is a **Saxon crucifix** of c. 1100, depicting Christ crucified, with two angels, the Virgin and St John. A second Saxon sculpture, the 11C **rood**, is outside on the south side, next to the finely decorated Abbess's Doorway. Opposite the Abbey on Church Street. **King John's House** is a 13C merchant's house with original roof timbers. It now serves as the **King John's House and Heritage Centre** incorporating Tudor and Victorian museum sections (⊙*open*

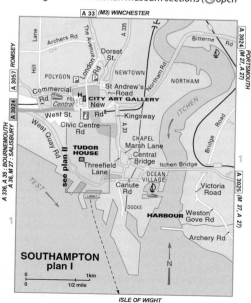

SOUTHAMPTON plan I

167

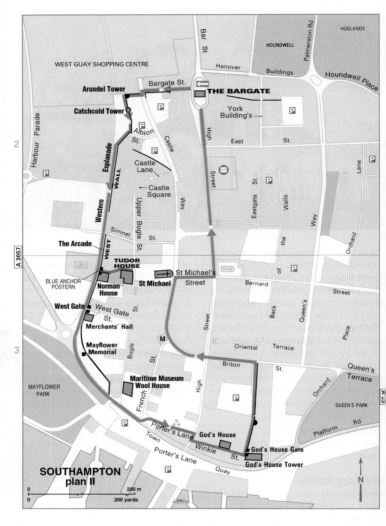

SOUTHAMPTON
plan II

Mon–Sat 10am–4pm; £2.50 (Oct–Mar £1.50) ; ✕; ℰ01794 512200; www.king-johnshouse.org.uk).

👥 Hawk Conservancy Trust

Andover. ◷ Open mid-Feb–Oct daily 10.30am–5.30pm; Nov–mid-Feb Sat–Sun 10.30am–4.30pm. £9.10, child £5.95 (after 4pm, £6.09, child £3.77). 🅿✕. ℰ01264 773 850. www.hawk-conservancy.org.
Majestic birds of prey are kept in large enclosures on the wooded grounds, with free-flying demonstrations.

Mottisfont Abbey

NT. **House:** ◷ Open mid-Mar–Oct daily 11am–5pm. **Garden:** Open mid-Feb–Oct daily 11am–5pm (winter 4pm). ◷House and garden closed Fri Jul–Nov (and other Fridays, see website). £7.20. 🔵. ℰ01794 340 757. www.nationaltrust.org.uk.
Formerly a 12C Augustinian priory, the charming house boasts a drawing room decorated by Rex Whistler and a collection of 19C–20C paintings. The original building was a priory, founded by William Briwere in 1201.

St Albans★
Hertfordshire

The Romans built Verulamium on the south bank of the River Ver. Following their departure the town's building blocks were transferred to the other bank of the river to build an abbey, beside which a new town developed. After the Dissolution (16C) the abbey church became the parish church and in 1877 it was raised to the status of a cathedral.

VERULAMIUM★

Verulamium, the third-largest city in Roman Britain, was established in AD 49 on Watling Street and rebuilt at least twice – once after being sacked by Boadicea in AD 61 then again c. 155 after a major fire. When the Romans withdrew, Verulamium fell into ruins, was lost and not uncovered until the 20C. Verulamium Park, beside the river, includes town wall remains and the hypocaust of a large villa in situ. At nearby Bluehouse Hill is the remains of a **Roman Theatre** (*open daily 10am–5pm; 4pm Nov–Mar; £2; 01727 835 035; www. romantheatre.co.uk*).

Verulamium Museum★

St Michael's Street. Open year-round daily 10am (2pm Sun)–5.30pm. £3.30. (Charge). 01727 751 810. www.stalbansmuseums.org.uk.
The museum displays some of the most impressive Roman works to be unearthed in Britain – ironwork, jewellery, coins, glass, pottery and **exceptional mosaics**.

CATHEDRAL★

Open daily 8am–5.45pm. £2.50 contribution requested. Guided tours Mon–Fri 11.30am, 2pm, Sat 2pm only, Sun 2.30pm only. 01727 860 780. www.stalbanscathedral.org.uk.
The original abbey was a Saxon shrine to St Alban, England's first Christian martyr. The present building, dominated by its Norman tower, was started in 1077. A hundred years later the impressive Norman nave was lengthened in the

Early English style. The very Victorian west front dates from 1879 and the chapter house from 1982.
The beauty of the interior lies not in the structure but in the furnishings – the exquisite medieval wall paintings and ceiling panels, the nave screen (1350), the reredos (1484), the Lady Chapel (1320) and the **shrine** of St Alban.

EXCURSIONS
Hatfield House★★

6mi/10km east of St Albans on the A 414. House: Open Easter Sat–Sept Wed–Sun and bank hols noon–5pm (admission by guided tour only Wed–Fri, except in Aug). Park and Gardens: Open Easter Sat–Sept Wed–Sun and bank hols (Jul–Aug daily) 11am–5.30pm. East Garden only open Thu (additional £3.50 charge). House, park and gardens £10.50. Park and west gardens only, £6. Park only, £3. 01707 287 010. www.hatfield-house.co.uk.
This is one of the finest and largest Jacobean houses in England, the home of the Cecil family since the time of Henry VIII. The **interior** of the house has several characteristic features of the period, notably the hall, staircase

> **Population:** 80,376.
> **Michelin Map:** Michelin Atlas p 19 or Map 504 T 28.
> **Info:** Town Hall, Market Pl. 01727 864 511. www.stalbans.gov.uk.
> **Location:** St Albans is 27mi/43km northwest of London. The train station, with a direct link to London, is a 10-min walk from the centre. Most buses stop at the central clock tower.
> **Don't Miss:** Verulamium Museum; Cathedral; Woburn Abbey; Hatfield House.
> **Timing:** Allow half a day.
> **Kids:** Woburn Safari Park; Whipsnade Wild Animal Park.

Elizabeth I at Hatfield

It was at Hatfield under an oak tree that Elizabeth I heard of her succession – "It is the Lord's doing and it is marvellous in our eyes." All that remains of her childhood home, a palace built by Cardinal Morton, is the Hall – "one of the foremost monuments to medieval brickwork in the country" according to Pevsner. The Cecils have played an important role in national politics – William Cecil, Lord Burghley, was chief minister to Elizabeth I; he was succeeded by Robert Cecil who also served James I (VI of Scotland). In the 19C Robert Cecil, Lord Salisbury (1830–1903) was three-times Prime Minister, serving Queen Victoria.

and long gallery. In the **Marble Hall** the magnificently carved screen, minstrels' gallery and panels are Jacobean, the gigantic 17C allegorical tapestry is from Brussels. The **Ermine Portrait** of Elizabeth I is attributed to Nicholas Hilliard while the one of her cousin Mary Queen of Scots is said to be by Rowland Lockey. The **grand oak staircase** is Jacobean carving at its best. Note the relief of the horticulturist John Tradescant, gardener to Charles I, on one of the newels at the top of the stairs, and the *Rainbow Portrait* of Elizabeth I. The **long gallery** holds Queen Elizabeth's silk stockings, hat and gloves. In the library is displayed a letter from Mary Queen of Scots and her execution warrant. An Elizabethan **knot garden** and a traditional **herb garden** are recent additions.

Knebworth House★

5mi/8km north by A 1 junction 7.
Open late Mar–Sept Sat–Sun noon–5pm. Jul–Aug daily noon–5pm. Also open school holidays, see website for details. All tours are guided, except on busy weekends. £9.50; Park, playground and gardens only, £7. 50. 01438 812 661. www.knebworthhouse.com.
The great hall with its richly carved screen and minstrels' gallery has hardly changed since the house was built in the 15C. The Gothic style was introduced by **Bulwer-Lytton**, the writer of historical fantasies; it is best seen in the **State Drawing Room** with its turreted fireplace, painted panels and stained-glass windows. Knebworth is famous for its huge rock concerts, from Pink Floyd in 1975 to Linkin Park in 2009.

Whipsnade Wild Animal Park★

Dunstable. 13mi/21km north west via the A 5183. Open daily late Mar–Sept 10am–6pm (Sun and bank hols 7pm); Oct 10am–5pm; Nov–late Mar 10am–4pm. Closed 25 Dec. £13.90, £10.90 (child). 01582 872 171. www.zsl.org.
This park, managed jointly with London Zoo, has played a major role in animal conservation and welfare. Species include elephants, rhinos, lions and giraffes, birds, and aquatic mammals.

Woburn Abbey★★

22mi/35km north via the M 10, then M 1 to junction 12 and minor road west. **Abbey:** Open Mar weekends only, first weekend Apr–first weekend Oct daily 11am–4pm (5pm Sun and bank hols). **Deer Park:** Open 10am–5pm (4.30pm Oct–Mar). £13. Grounds and Deer Park only £2.50 per person in car. Combined tickets with safari park (see below) £18.50, £20. Guided tours. 01525 292 148. www.woburnabbey.co.uk.
Woburn was a Cistercian abbey for 400 years before becoming a private mansion. The north range was refurbished in 1630 but the more significant changes date from the 18C. The **interior** contains sumptuously furnished apartments including the **Mortlake Tapestries**, based on Raphael's *Acts of the Apostles*. The State Rooms include **Queen Victoria's Bedroom** with etchings by Victoria and Albert; **Queen Victoria's Dressing Room** with walls adorned by superb 17C Dutch and Flemish paintings including *Nijmegen on the Vaal* and *Fishermen on*

Ice by Aelbert Cuyp, and *Jan Snellinck* by Van Dyck; the **Blue Drawing Room** with its ceiling (1756) and its fireplace by Duval and Rysbrack; the **State Saloon** with its ornamental ceiling and Rysbrack chimneypiece; the **State Dining Room** graced by a Meissen dinner service and a portrait by Van Dyck; the **Reynolds Room** displaying 10 of his portraits; and the **Canaletto Room** hung with 21 Venetian views. The **Library**, the finest room in the Holland range, is divided into three parts by Corinthian columns; on the walls hang *Self-Portrait* and *Old Rabbi* by **Rembrandt**. The **Long Gallery**, also divided by columns, by Flitcroft, is hung with 16C paintings including the *Armada Portrait* of Elizabeth I.

The park (3,000 acres/1,200ha) was landscaped by Humphry Repton and contains nine different species of deer (1,000 head), including Milu, originally the Imperial herd of China, which is preserved here.

Woburn Safari Park

Entrance 1mi/1.5km from the house.
🕐 *Open early Mar–late Oct daily 10am–5pm/dusk. Late Oct–early Mar (weather permitting) Sat–Sun 11am–3pm/dusk.* ✏️*£10.50–£17.50, child £8.50–£13.50. Passport ticket to abbey and safari park £18.50, £20.* ♿🅿️✕. ✆*01525 290 407. www.woburnsafari.co.uk.*

This is the largest safari park in Great Britain and includes white rhino, elephant, tiger, lion, giraffe, bear, wolves, monkeys, eland, oryx, gemsbok, zebra, camel, bison and many more animals. You can **drive your own vehicle** through the reserves as often as you wish before parking in the Wild World Leisure Area. From here you can make another trip on the off-road **Safari Lorry** and come back to spend the rest of the day at Elephant Encounter, watching the sea lion or birds of prey displays, listening to keeper talks and letting the children loose in the excellent play areas.

Thames Valley★★

🕭 *for the lower Thames, see London*

The Thames gently winds between Kew and its source in the Cotswolds, offering many varied pleasures as it passes through typically English countryside of low hills, woods, meadows, country houses, pretty villages and small towns.

WINDSOR TO OXFORD
71mi/114km

Windsor★★★
🕭*See WINDSOR .*

Cookham
This pretty village has been immortalised by the artist **Sir Stanley Spencer** (1891–1959). The Chapel which Spencer attended as a boy is now the **Stanley Spencer Gallery**★ (🕐 *open Apr–Oct*

🕭 **Michelin Map:** Michelin Atlas p 18 or Map 504 Q, R 28 and 29.

🛈 **Info:** King's Arms Barn, Kings Road, Henley-on-Thames. ✆0149 578 034. www.visithenley-on-thames.co.uk. Old Abbey House, Abingdon. ✆01235 522 711.

daily 10.30am–5.30pm. Nov–Easter Thu–Sun (Christmas hols daily) 11am–4.30pm; ✏️*£3;* ♿*;* ✆*01628 471 885; http://stanley-spencer.org.uk).* Cookham features in many of his paintings.

Henley-on-Thames
In the first week of July some of the world's best oarsmen visit this charming town for the **Henley Royal Regatta**, England's premier rowing event.
The **River and Rowing Museum** (*Mill Meadows;* 🕐 *open daily 10am–5.30pm,*

Henley Royal Regatta

A. Williams/MICHELIN

*Sept–Apr 5pm; €7 ; & P ✗; ℘01491
415 600; www.rrm.co.uk)* illustrates the
evolution of rowing; the River Thames
as a habitat for wildlife, a means of
trade and source of pleasure; the history of Henley-on-Thames and the Royal
Regatta. The **Wind in the Willows** gallery celebrates Kenneth Grahame's
famous story set on the Thames.

Mapledurham★

🕐 *Open Easter–Sept Sat–Sun and bank
hols 2pm–5.30pm. €House £4.25,
water mill £3.25, combined ticket
£6.75. & P ✗. ℘0118 972 3350.
www.mapledurham.co.uk.*
An Elizabethan **manor house** beside
a 14C church and a fully operational
watermill dating back to the 15C form
an almost perfect riverside picture.

Pangbourne

Kenneth Grahame lived here 1922–32,
and wrote *The Wind in the Willows.*

Basildon Park★

NT. 🕐 *Open mid-Mar–Oct Wed–Sun
and bank hols noon–5pm (grounds
open 11am). €House £7, grounds only,
£3.60. & P ✗. ℘0118 984 3040.
www.nationaltrust.org.uk.*
The splendid Palladian villa overlooking a lush part of the Thames valley, was
built by John Carr in 1776. It is rich in

exquisite **plasterwork** and boasts a fine
collection of 18C paintings.

Goring and Streatley

These two villages, with the weir and
Goring Lock, are set in one of the most
beautiful parts of the Thames, offering
enjoyable riverside walks.

Dorchester★

This historic village dates back to the
Bronze Age and boasts a fine Norman
abbey church, (🕐 *open daily 8am–
6pm/dusk, abbey museum early Apr–Sept
daily 2pm–5pm; P ✗; ℘01865 340 007;
www.dorchester-abbey.org.uk).*

Abingdon★

The town grew up around an abbey
founded in the 7C, though the only
remaining abbey buildings are the
13C **Chequer** with its tall chimney, the
c. 1500 **Long Gallery** with an oak-
beamed roof and the 15C **gateway**
beside the medieval church of St Nicholas. Abingdon's skyline is characterised
by the 15C spire of the wide five-aisled
St Helen's Church, (🕐 *open summer
Mon–Sat 9.30am–4pm, Sun 8am–3pm;
℘ 01235 520 144).* Delightful 15C
almshouses★ border the churchyard.

Oxford★★★

👣 *See OXFORD.*

Isle of Wight★★

The Isle of Wight has been a holiday destination ever since Queen Victoria chose Osborne House for her country retreat. Visitors are attracted mainly by the quiet pace of life, the sandy beaches and the yachting. **Cowes** is the premier yachting centre in Britain, staging the Cowes Week regattas in August.

ISLE
Alum Bay
The western-most bay of the island, where alum was mined, is a remarkable geological phenomenon, its sandstone cliffs richly coloured with more than 20 mineral hues. In the afternoon sun, a boat trip to the **Needles**, sea stacks 100ft/30m offshore, gives fine views of the colourful slopes and chalk cliffs.

Brading★
St Mary's Church★, built c. 1200, boasts impressive 17C family tombs.
Southwest of the village the remains of the 3C **Brading Roman Villa**★ (◷open year-round daily 9am–5pm;. ◷ closed Christmas hols; ⬚£5; ♿ P ✗; ℘01983 406 223; www.bradingromanvilla.org.uk), comprise the ground plan of the west wing, with some fine 4C **mosaics** and a display of artefacts in the exhibition and visitor centre.
Just north of the village, ♟ **Brading The Experience** began life as a simple wax museum illustrating the history of the island but has extended to an eclectic collection including stuffed animals, steam engines, veteran and vintage cars, bygones and shops (◷open daily Easter–Oct 10am–5pm, last admission 90 mins before closing; call for winter times; ⬚£7.25, child £5.25; ♿P✗; ℘ 01983 407 286; www.bradingthe experience.co.uk). **Nunwell House**★ (1mi/2km west; Coach Lane). ◷ open Jul–early Sept Mon–Wed 1pm–5pm, also late Spring Bank Hol Sun and Mon 1pm–5pm; ⬚£5, garden only, £2.50; ✦ guided tour of house 2pm, 3.30pm; P✗; ℘01983 407 240; www.islandbreaks.co.uk) has been a family home since 1522. The owner, Sir

▶ **Population:** 124,577.
◉ **Michelin Map:** Atlas p 9 or Map 504 P, Q 31 and 32.
▯ **Info:** Fountain Quay, Cowes. Guildhall, High St, Newport. 81–83 Union Street, Ryde. High St Sandown, 67 High St, Shanklin. The Quay, Yarmouth. ℘01983 813 818. www.islandbreaks.co.uk.
◐ **Location:** An island in the English Channel, immediately south of Portsmouth, between 2mi/3.2km and 5mi/8km from mainland.
⊚ **Don't Miss:** Osborne House.
♟ **Kids**: Dinosaur Isle; Brading The Experience.

John Oglander, was host to Charles I on his last night of freedom in 1648.

Carisbrooke Castle★★
EH. 1.25 mi/2km south Newport.
◷ Open daily 10am–5pm (Oct–Mar 4pm). ◷ Closed 24–26 Dec, 1–2 Jan. ⬚£6.40. ♿ P ✗(Summer only). ℘01983 522 107. www.english-heritage.org.uk.
In 1100 Richard de Redvers built the keep and curtain walls on the site of a Roman stronghold. The castle was further fortified against the Spanish in the late 16C. During the imprisonment of King Charles I in 1647–48, prior to his trial in London, the **bowling green** was created for his entertainment. He is said to have walked daily around the **battlements**. He also made two attempts to escape from here. The last resident governor, Queen Victoria's daughter, Princess Beatrice, died here in 1944.
The Norman curtain wall encloses the high motte and 12C **keep** (with **views**★ for miles around). The late-12C **Great Hall** houses a museum of island history. An interactive exhibit in the Old Coach House explores life in the castle and the donkey centre houses the famous Carisbrooke donkeys who give regular demonstrations in the **well-house** of

173

Fossils and Dinosaurs

Many important dinosaur discoveries have been made on the Isle of Wight including the carnivoric **Neovenator**, a relative of the Allosaurus from the American land mass, which was much closer to Britain 115 million years ago. The crumbling chalk cliffs have revealed fossilized skeletons of unknown species. **Dinosaur Isle** (⌚ *see below*) is the island's main centre for all things palaeontological but afficionados will also wish to visit **Dinosaur Farm Museum** *(on the coast road, A 3055, near Brighstone ⌚ open mid-Feb–Oct 10am–5pm, visit website for details; ∞ £3.50. guided fossil hunt book in advance, £4; ✆01983 740 844; www.dinosaur-farm.co.uk) where many other finds are displayed.*

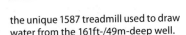

the unique 1587 treadmill used to draw water from the 161ft-/49m-deep well.

Osborne House★★

EH. 1mi/1.6km southeast of East Cowes. (EH). ⌚ Open late Mar–Sept daily 10am–6pm (house closes 5pm). Oct–Mar 10am–4pm (Nov–Mar closed Mon–Tue and admission by pre-booked guided tour only). ∞£9.80, grounds only, £6. ♿▣☒. ✆01983 200 022. www.english-heritage.org.uk.

In a delightful position with views of the sea which reminded him of Naples, Prince Albert worked with Thomas Cubitt to create this enormous Italianate villa with terraced gardens, completed in 1851. For Queen Victoria, Osborne was a favourite home for family vacations with her children, grandchildren and great-grandchildren. After Albert's death in 1861 she spent much of her widowhood at Osborne, dying there in 1901. Her insistence that everything should be kept exactly as it had been during Albert's life gives a remarkable picture of royal family life, from richly furnished state rooms to the intimacy of the **Queen's Sitting Room** where she worked beside her husband at twin desks. The only major addition to the house after Albert's death was the **Durbar Wing** ★★built in 1890; its amazing principal room celebrating Victoria's role as Empress of India was created by Bhai Ram Singh and John Lockwood Kipling, Rudyard's father.

A carriage ride through the **grounds** takes visitors to the **Swiss Cottage**, imported from Switzerland and erected in 1853, where the royal children learned to cook on small ranges and entertained their parents. Their natural history collections are displayed in a smaller chalet **museum**, near their miniature **fort** with cannon, the Queen's bathing hut and a collection of tiny wheelbarrows, each bearing the initials of its royal owner.

👥 Sandown Dinosaur Isle

Culver Parade, Sandown Bay. ⌚Open daily 10am–4pm/5pm/6pm. ∞£4.95, child £2.95. ♿▣☒. ✆01983 404 344. www.dinosaurisle.com.

Housed in a striking building in the shape of a giant pterodactyl this newcomer brings to life prehistoric times with moving models and intelligent interpretations of the days when dinosuars ruled the Isle of Wight. An impressive Brachiosaurid skeleton has pride of place.

GETTING AROUND

Three operators service the island. The fastest route takes about 15 minutes, the slowest 40 minutes. **Red Funnel** runs a vehicle ferry and a high-speed passenger-only ferry, both between Southampton and Cowes, (✆0844 844 99 88. www.redfunnel.co.uk). **Hover-travel** operate a hovercraft service (passenger only) between Southsea and Ryde, (✆01983 811 000 www.hovertravel.co.uk). **Wight Link** operate vehicle ferries between Portsmouth and Fishbourne, and Lymington and Yarmouth, and a passenger-only catamaran between Portsmouth and Ryde. (✆0871 376 4342; www.wightlink.co.uk).

Winchester★★

Hampshire

This ancient cathedral city was the capital of King Alfred's **Wessex** and then of England, from the early 9C to about 100 years after the Norman conquest. Today it is a lively regional shopping, historical and cultural centre.

A BIT OF HISTORY

It was only after the Roman invasion of AD 43 that the city known as **Venta Bulgarum** was founded. After the Romans withdrew, the city declined until the Saxons rebuilt a church and created a bishopric in 662. After 878 **Alfred the Great** consolidated his defence of Wessex against Danish attacks by setting up a series of fortified **burghs**, of which Winchester was the largest.

At the time of the Norman conquest the city was already of such importance that **William I** was crowned there as well as in London. He built a castle in the southwest angle of the city walls and established a new cathedral in 1070. After the 12C Winchester yielded to London as the preferred royal residence. During the Civil War the Norman castle was largely destroyed, the cathedral damaged and the city looted by Parliamentary troops. After the Restoration the city recovered and in 1682 Charles II commissioned Sir Christopher Wren to design a great palace, though work stopped on the monarch's death in 1685.

CATHEDRAL★★★

○ *Open year-round. Cathedral 8.30am–6pm (Sun 5.30pm). Visitor centre 9.30am–5.30pm. ₤5 (£8 including tower tour). Guided tours available. 𝒞01962 857 200. www.winchester-cathedral.org.uk.*

The cathedral stands surrounded by lawns on the same site as the 7C Saxon minster, the foundations of which were located in the 1960s. An early bishop of Winchester, **St Swithin**, was buried outside the west end of the minster in 862. There was torrential rain on the day in 1093 when his grave was transferred

▶ **Population:** 36,121.
◔ **Michelin Map:** Michelin Atlas p 9 or Map 504 P, Q 30.
🛈 **Info:** Guildhall, High Street. 𝒞01962 840 500. www.visitwinchester.co.uk.
◑ **Location:** Winchester is 66mi/106km southwest of London. The train station, with direct London service, is 1mi/1.6km from the centre, on Stockbridge Road. The bus station is right in the centre, on Broadway. Winchester is a small city and can easily be covered on foot.
☻ **Don't Miss**: The Cathedral; St Cross Hospital; Winchester College.
○ **Timing**: Allow a full day in Winchester.
👥 **Kids**: Mid-Hants Watercress Line specials, Marwell Zoo.

inside the new church, though he had expressly asked to be buried in the open air; this gave rise to the legend that if it rains on St Swithin's Day (July 15) it will rain for forty days.

William Walkelyn, appointed bishop by William I, began building the new cathedral in 1079. In 1202 the east end was reconstructed and in the early 14C the Norman choir was rebuilt in the Perpendicular style and the nave and west front were rebuilt between 1346 and 1404. After further remodellings of the nave, Lady Chapel and chancel from 1486–1528, the longest Gothic church in Europe (556ft/169m) was complete.

When, in 1652, Parliament ordered the cathedral (ransacked in the Civil War) to be destroyed, it was saved only by a petition of the citizens. Early in the 20C the east end, built on marshland and supported on a 13C beech tree raft, began to sink, causing the walls to crack and the roof to fall; the cathedral was saved by a diver, William Walker, who worked alone from 1906–12 replacing the rotting rafts with cement.

Exterior

Built largely of stone from the Isle of Wight, the cathedral's exterior, with its squat Norman **tower** is impressive, though less exciting than the interior.

Interior

Bishop William of Wykeham (1324–1404) rebuilt the Norman pillars in the lofty twelve-bay nave, with its bosses and **stone lierne vault**, to support the graceful Perpendicular arches surmounted by balconies with clerestory windows. Of special note are the **west window**, the ornate William of Wykeham's Chantry, Jane Austen's tomb, window and brass, the 12C black Tournai marble **font** and the Jacobean pulpit. In the Norman transept the rounded arches are surmounted by twin-arched galleries below irregular clerestory windows.

The **Holy Sepulchre Chapel** has exquisite 13C wall paintings. In the chancel the **choir stalls** (1308) are ornamented with remarkable **misericords**; the marble tomb of the "ungodly" King William Rufus (d. 1100) stands under the tower. The **stone reredos** with statues above the altar is early 16C; the early Tudor **vault** has outstanding **bosses**.

In the Early English retro-choir (13C) the chapels and chantries are dedicated to 15C–16C bishops. The early 13C Lady Chapel lit by seven-light windows is adorned with fine Tudor woodwork and **wall paintings**.

The 12C **Winchester Bible** is the jewel of the rich collection of manuscripts and books in the 12C Library (access from south transept).

In the north aisle of the nave is the grave of the great author **Jane Austen** (1775–1817), who moved to Winchester for treatment in her last illness.

The **Crypt** (only open by tour) houses the very beautiful and critically acclaimed **Sound II** sculpture by Anthony Gormley, creator of Angel of the North (&see NEWCASTLE).

Cathedral Close

The few remaining monastic buildings south of the cathedral include the **Deanery**, formerly the Prior's Lodging, with a three-arched porch and a 15C hall. The 14C **Pilgrims' Hall**, (3 The Close; ⏱open daily, call for opening times; ℘01962 854 189) now part of the choir school, has possibly the oldest **hammerbeam roof** in existence. Beside the sturdy **St Swithin's Gate** stands the 15C timber-framed **Cheyney Court** and early 16C stables, also timber-framed and now part of the Pilgrims' School.

CITY

Winchester College★

⏱ Open by guided tours year-round Mon, Wed, Fri, Sat 10.45am, noon, 2.15pm, 3.30 pm; Tue, Thu, 10.45am, noon. Sun 2.15pm, 3.30pm. The college is sometimes closed for functions (especially Sat afternoon). See website for details. ⏱Closed Christmas and New Year. ⌧£4. ℘01962 621 209. www.winchestercollege.org.

The college was founded in 1382 by **Bishop William of Wykeham** (pronounced wick-um), to provide an education for poor scholars, as well as "commoners" from wealthy families, to be continued at New College, Oxford, which Wykeham had already founded in 1379. Pupils are still known as "Wykehamists". The school has the longest unbroken history of any in the country.

The school is entered by the 14C **Outer Gate** in College Street. Through the Middle Gate is **Chamber Court**, the centre of college life, surrounded by Wykeham's original late 14C buildings. The **Hall** on its south side (1st floor) has fine 16C wooden panelling on which hang portraits of former pupils and a 16C portrait of the founder. The **chapel**, with its prominent 15C pinnacled tower was heavily restored in the 19C, but retains its medieval **wooden vault**, one of the first attempts at fan vaulting in England and the original 14C **choir stalls** with fine misericords. In the centre of Wykeham's 14C cloister stands the early 15C **Fromond's Chantry**, the only example in England of a chapel so placed. The red-brick and stone **school** (west of cloister), was built in 1683–87 for the increasing number of "commoners". Sir Herbert Baker's simple peaceful **War**

Cloister, built in 1924, commemorates Wykehamists who fell in World Wars.

Castle Great Hall★

🕐*Open daily mid Feb–Oct 10am–5pm (4pm rest of year).* 🕐*Closed 25–26 Dec.* 🚶*50p–£1 contribution requested.* 📞*01962 846 476. www.hants.gov.uk/ greathall.*

The Hall is the only surviving part of the castle, built in Norman times and slighted by order of Parliament in the Civil War. The room (110 x 55 x 55ft/34 x 17 x 17m) dating from 1222–36, is a splendid example of a medieval hall, with its timber roof supported on columns of Purbeck marble.

On the west wall hangs the oak **Round Table** (18ft/5m diameter) which dates from the 14C; it is decorated with paintings of the Tudor Rose in its centre, King Arthur and a list of his knights around the edge. It was once thought to date from Arthur's time but carbon-dating has since disproved this.

High Street

At the east end (The Broadway) stands a bronze statue to Alfred the Great, erected in 1901. Among the buildings in the pedestrian street are the former **Guildhall** (now a bank), built in 1713, opposite the timber-framed **God Begot House**★ dating from 1558 (now a restaurant). Note also the 15C stone carved **Butter Cross**, around which markets were held.

St Cross Hospital★★

1mi/2km south. 🕐 *Open Apr–Oct, Mon–Sat 9.30am–5pm, Sun 1pm–5pm. Nov–Mar Mon–Sat 10.30am–3.30pm.* 🕐*Closed Good Fri, 25 Dec.* 🚶*£3.* ♿📶✕*. (Apr–Oct Mon–Sat).* 📞*01962 851 375. www.stcross.f2s.com.*

A lovely walk from the city centre across the water meadows leads to the oldest charitable institution in England. Founded by Bishop Henry de Blois in 1136, its almshouses are still in use today. The **chapel** (late 12C– late 13C) is a fine example of Norman architecture, rich in zig-zag stone carving on the arches and chancel vaulting. In the **Lady Chapel** is a

Flemish triptych of c. 1530. The **Brethren's Hall** has a minstrels' gallery and an impressive late-15C timbered roof.

EXCURSIONS

👥 Mid-Hants Watercress Line

Alresford. 8mi/13km northeast on the A 31 and B 3046. 🕐 *Station and rolling stock open year-round daily. For train times and fares visit website.* 🅿*(charge).* ♿✕*.* 📞*01962 733 810. www.watercressline.co.uk.*

Named for the watercress beds which can still be seen in and around the handsome small Georgian town of Alresford (pronounced Arlsford), the old-fashioned steam engines run for 10 miles/16km over the hills to the market town of Alton with special themed services, for adults and children, throughout the year.

Jane Austen's House

Chawton. 18mi/29km northeast via the A 31 and B 3006. 🕐 *Open Jun–Aug daily 10am–5pm. Mar–May and Sept–Dec daily 10.30am–4.30pm. Jan–Feb Sat– Sun 10.30am–4.30pm.* 🕐*Closed 25–26 Dec.* 🚶*£7.* ♿*.* 📞*01420 83262. www. jane-austens-house-museum.org.uk.*

The eight years Jane spent sharing this peaceful red-brick house with her mother and sister Cassandra were some of her happiest and most productive. The tiny table at which she wrote and revised her novels stands in the dining parlour. Early editions are displayed alongside letters, family portraits and pieces of needlework.

👥 Marwell Zoo

Colden Common. 6 mi/10km southeast on the B 2177. 🕐*Open year-round daily 10am–4pm/5pm/6pm. Last entry is 90 mins before closing time* 🕐*Closed 25 Dec.* 🚶*£10.90–£16.35, child £8.17– £12.72.* ♿🅿✕*.* 📞*01962 777 407. www.marwell.org.uk.*

The grounds of 16C Marwell Hall are home to over 200 species of animals and birds, including large cats, primates, giraffes and rhinos, with an emphasis on conservation.

Windsor★★

Berkshire

Windsor is synonymous with its castle, but there is more to the town than just one building. Windsor Great Park stretches out for miles beyond the castle and is a wonderful place for summer walks and picnics. Windsor town has been a royal borough since being granted the status by Edward I in 1277.

TOWN

The network of old **cobbled streets** bordered by High Street, Castle Hill, Church Lane and Street and Albans Street contains a number of fine 16C–18C timber-framed houses with oversailing upper floors rising to pointed gables.

The short High Street is distinguished by St John's parish **church**, re-built in 1822, and the **Guildhall**, begun by Sir Thomas Fitch c.1637 and completed by Sir Christopher Wren in 1690.

WINDSOR CASTLE★★★

⏲ *Open daily 9.45am–5.15pm (4.15pm Nov–Feb); subject to change at short notice, check before visiting; last admission 1hr 15min before closing. St George's Chapel closed Sun. Changing of the Guard on alternate days 11am (exc. Sun), weather permitting.* ⏲*Closed 25–26 Dec and various days throughout year (see website).* ◉*£15.50, £8.50 during closure of state apartments.* ☞☜ *Guided tours daily at regular intervals (free).* ♿. ℘*020 7766 7300. 01753 831 118 (24hr*

St George's Chapel, Windsor

A. F. Kersting/MICHELIN

- ▶ **Population:** 30,136 (including Eton).
- ♿ **Michelin Map:** Michelin Atlas p 20 or Map 504 S 29.
- 📖 **Info:** The Old Booking Hall, Windsor Royal Station, Thames Street. ℘01753 743 900. www.windsor.gov.uk.
- ▶ **Location:** Windsor lies 23mi/37km due west of London. There are two stations, Riverside and Central, both centrally located, both with direct London services. The old town, comprises one main street, **Thames Street**, intersected by the road leading down from the castle gate, and then continues as High Street and Sheet Street.
- 👪 **Kids**: Legoland.

info line) www.royalresidences.com. England's biggest castle is also the largest inhabited stronghold in the world and has been a favourite royal residence, frequently extended and rebuilt, since William the Conqueror first built a motte and bailey on the site c.1080.

A Bit of History

By 1110, the Castle had become a royal lodge where Henry I held his first court. Henry II erected the first stone buildings between 1165 and 1179, constructing one range of royal apartments in the Upper Ward (to the east of the Round Tower) and one in the Lower Ward. Faced with rebellion by his sons he modernised the defences, rebuilding the earthen walls and wooden Round Tower in stone. Under Henry III (1216–72) this work was virtually completed. Edward III (1327–77) reconstructed the royal apartments for his newly-founded Order of the Garter. Under Charles II the State Apartments were rebuilt in an ambitious renovation project which included the reconstruction of St George's Hall and the King's Chapel, in which the architect Hugh May concentrated on fitting out the interior in a manner fit for a king, insulating the rooms with oak panelling festooned with Grinling Gibbons carvings. However, the principal changes were made in the early 19C when George IV commissioned Sir Jeffry Wyatville as his architect; he built the machicolated walls and several towers, raised the massive Round Tower, giving the castle its famous outline, and remodelled the State Apartments, adding the Waterloo Chamber. This section was badly damaged by fire in 1992. The principal change under Queen Victoria was the addition of a private chapel in memory of Prince Albert, who died here on 14 December 1861. Queen Mary, wife of George V, carried out careful restoration work on the castle at the turn of the century, and it became the childhood home of HRH the Princesses Elizabeth and Margaret during the Second World War, since which it has remained the royal family's principal home. The Court is in official residence throughout April and for Ascot Week in June when the annual Garter Day ceremonies are held.

The impressive **Round Tower** stands on the site of William I's original fortress and houses the Royal Archives (o⊶ *not open to the public*). Adjacent, the **North Terrace** (c.1570) affords **views**★★ of Eton College and London *(east)*.

Chapels
St George's Chapel★★★
This great Perpendicular chapel was begun by Edward IV to replace Henry III's chapel to the east which Edward III had enlarged and dedicated to his **Most Noble Order of the Garter**.

The slender clustered piers lead the eye to the crowning glory of the chapel, the **lierne vault**, rich with coloured bosses – completed in 1528. The blank panelling between the tall arcades and the clerestory windows is topped with smiling angels. The aisles are notable for their **fan vaulting**. The impressive Perpendicular **west window** depicts 75 figures mainly in early 16C glass. The ornate **stalls**★★★, abounding in misericords and other carvings,

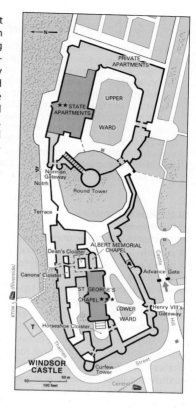

were built in 1478–85; the top tier, surmounted by a richly carved canopy, is for the Knights of the Garter. Edward III's **battle sword** (6ft 8in/2m) is in the south chancel aisle. The glorious **east window** (30ft/9m high and 29ft/8.8m wide; 52 lights) commemorates Prince Albert (incidents from his life illustrated in the lower tier, below the Resurrection and the *Adoration of the Kings*).

Albert Memorial Chapel
The original chapel (1240) was given its magnificent Victorian embellishment by Sir George Gilbert Scott after the death of Albert and is a supreme example of the 19C revivalist age with Venetian mosaics, inlaid marble panels and statuary. Prince Albert's tomb was later removed to Frogmore Mausoleum (⌖*see Box, FROGMORE HOUSE*).

The Order of the Garter

The highest order of chivalry in the land is also the oldest to survive in the world. It was established by Edward III in 1348 when England was engaged in the Hundred Years War with France and may have been modelled on the legendary story of 5C King Arthur and his Knights of the Round Table. It was to reward men who had shown valour on the battlefield, and also to honour those who manifested the idealistic and romantic concept of Christian chivalry. Tradition relates how at a ball celebrating the conquest of Calais in 1347, the king retrieved a fallen garter and returned it to its rightful owner, the young and beautiful Joan of Kent, Countess of Salisbury, with the words, *"Honi soit qui mal y pense"* (Shame on him who thinks evil of it) – the emblem and motto of the Order. A more likely derivation is a strap or sword-belt from a suit of armour to denote the bond of loyalty and concord.

State Apartments★★
Public Rooms

In the **Waterloo Chamber** hangs a series of portraits by Sir Thomas Lawrence, of the monarchs and leaders involved in Napoleon's final defeat. The **Grand Reception Room** features Gobelins tapestries and is decorated with gilt plasterwork, massive chandeliers and bronze busts. **St George's Hall** hall was built by Edward III for the Knights of the Garter and the Baroque chapel was built for Charles II. The 700 past Garter Knights' escutcheons are set in the panelling of the plaster ceiling. The new octagonal **Lantern Lobby**, created after the fire in 1992, was joint winner of the Building of the Year award.

The Queen's Rooms

The **Queen's Guard Chamber**, leads into the panelled Queen's Presence Chamber which, with the adjoining **Queen's Audience Chamber**, is essentially unchanged since the time of Charles II. The **Queen's Drawing Room** contains some of the earliest plate glass in England. Eight Van Dyck portraits hang in the ballroom while the drawing room including paintings by Holbein.

The King's Rooms

The **King's Drawing Room** contains paintings by Rubens and his followers and Chinese porcelain. The **King's Bedchamber** has a grandiose "polonaise" bed made for the visit by Emperor Napoleon III and his wife Eugénie in 1855. On the walls of the **King's Dressing Room** are a number of **masterpieces**★★ by Dürer, Memling, Clouet, Holbein, Rembrandt, Rubens and Van Dyck. The **King's Dining Room** retains much of the character it had under Charles II: Verrio ceiling depicting a banquet of the gods and panelling decorated with carvings by Gibbons and Henry Philips.

Queen Mary's Dolls' House

The Dolls' House, designed by Sir Edwin Lutyens, was presented to Queen Mary in 1924. The fascination of this piece is that everything is exactly on a 1:12 scale – not only the furniture, but even the printed leather-bound books in the library, paintings and the cars in the garage.

WINDSOR PARK★

In the mid 18C George II charged his son, William Duke of Cumberland, with the task of organising the vast Windsor Forest, hunting ground of Saxon leaders and medieval knights. 4,800 acres/1,942ha of overgrown woodland were cleared and streams were diverted to drain the marshes into newly dug ponds, which eventually flowed into the especially created 130 acres/53ha of Virginia Water. George III continued this land reclamation work and established two farms.

The park is now divided into **Home Park**, which is private, and **Great Park**, most of which is public. A significant feature of the park is the **Long Walk**, a 3mi/5km avenue running south as far as the **Copper Horse**, an equestrian statue of George III in Great Park. Under Charles II the avenue was planted with elm trees, in 1685, the year in which he died, but in 1945 the trees, which had fallen victim to Dutch Elm disease, had to be replaced by chestnuts and planes. Two former royal residences are tucked away in the park: Royal Lodge, used as a retreat by George IV and by the late Queen Elizabeth the Queen Mother, and Cumberland Lodge, where William Duke of Cumberland resided while redesigning the park. Smith's Lawn is an area reserved for polo matches, and beyond it stretch the **Valley Gardens** as far as Virginia Water.

The **Royal Mausoleum**, Frogmore Garden, in Home Park was begun in 1862, the year after Prince Albert's death, specifically so that Queen Victoria and Albert could be buried side by side. The rich interior reflects the Consort's passion for the Italian Renaissance. **Frogmore House** (1684) is furnished largely with possessions accumulated by Queen Mary (black *papier maché* furniture, wax and silk flowers).

ETON COLLEGE★★

10 min on foot across Windsor Bridge. Visit by guided tour only 2pm, 3.15pm on some Wed, Fri, Sat and Sun during term time, and daily during college hols. Call ahead to check. £5. 01753 671 177. www.etoncollege.com.
The most prestigious of all British schools, Eton was founded in 1440 by Henry VI to give free education to 70 poor scholars and choristers.
Henry then founded King's College, Cambridge, so the boys could continue their education and it soon became fashionable for the nobility to send their sons to Eton.
The paved **School Yard**, centre of college life, is dominated by the 16C red-brick **Lupton's Tower** on the east side. To the north is **Lower School**, the 15C brick building originally constructed by Henry VI to house the Scholars. **Upper School** on the west side was built in the 17C to accommodate the increasing number of boys. In the centre of the

yard stands a 1719 bronze statue of the founder.
The **College Chapel**★★, built from 1449–82, is one of the best examples of Perpendicular architecture in England. The 15C **wall paintings**★ are also the finest in the country. The modern stained glass (Evie Holme, John Piper), and the tapestry reredos and panelling by William Morris from designs by Burne-Jones are notable. The brick **Cloister Court** dates back to Henry VI's time. It contains the 15C College Hall where the "collegers" eat; in the undercroft is the **Museum of Eton Life**.

LEGOLAND WINDSOR

2mi/3km southwest of Windsor on B 3022. Bus from Windsor town centre, by both railway stations. Open daily from 10am mid-Mar–late Oct; closing times vary, 6pm weekends, 7pm school hols, 5pm other times. See website for details. £35.24 ticket at the gate, £28 online; book in advance. Child £26.43/£22. 08705 04 04 04. www.legoland.co.uk.
Millions of Lego building blocks are used to impressive effect in this beautifully landscaped park. Moving models and miniature European towns show the skills of professional Lego-builders; children can have a go at building in the Imagination Centre. An array of theme park rides, attractions and live shows are geared for children up to the age of 12, with an emphasis on hands-on fun.

Frogmore House

The last resting place of both Victoria and Albert is in the Frogmore Mausoluem. It is attached to Frogmore House, renowned for its beautiful landscaped garden and 18C lake set in Home Park, the private part of Windsor Park. The house and mausoleum are only open on Spring and late August bank holiday weekends each year (open 10am–4pm; £7; 020 7766 7305; www.royalcollection.org.uk).

THE SOUTH WEST

The English mainland's southwest promontory is one of Britain's best loved and most distinct areas. Most Brits have travelled this way at least once on family holidays, leaving with cherished memories of golden beaches, quaint West Country foods and folklore, and occasional sheltering from the rain. There is however a world of difference between cultured Georgian Bath and youth-oriented Newquay, the levels of Somerset and the wild rocky Lizard Peninsula. To the north of this region is the Bristol Channel and Wales, to the south is the English Channel and France, and to the west is the Atlantic Ocean and, ultimately, the USA. The region is almost an island within England, leading some locals to think of it as its own country.

Highlights

1 Take tea in the Cotswolds at **Chipping Campden** (p215).

2 Visit the stately home and safari park of **Longleat** (p242)

3 Chill out among the art at pretty seaside **St Ives** (p211)

4 Puzzle over enigmatic **Stonehenge** (p251)

5 Celebrate biodiversity at the pioneering **Eden Project** (p207)

Devon and Cornwall

With two very distinct coastlines, historic towns and cities (Plymouth, Exeter, Penzance…) picture-postcard villages and fishing harbours (Mevagissey, Mousehole, Polperro…), unspoiled moors and National Parks (*see Box*), stately homes and even statelier gardens (from the Lost Gardens of Heligan to The Eden Project), and a fascinating and unexpected industrial heritage, Devon and Cornwall pack a lot of interest into a small geographical area. Whatever the weather it is not simply a cliché to say that there is always plenty to see and do. The north coast is generally rugged and windblown (Newquay, for example, is a world-class surfing centre) while the south is characterised by sheltered coves and creeks reaching far inland, though both coasts have sheltered resorts enjoying beautiful golden beaches. While the coast is commercialised in parts and farming is still strong inland, much of the region and many of its inhabitants, locals and particularly newcomers, have a bohemian and arty character; from the hippy culture of Totnes to the modern art of St Ives.If you have more time you can leave the English mainland altogether, to explore the quiet unspoiled Scilly Isles or French-influenced Channel Islands.

- Channel Isl.
- Dartmoor
- Exeter
- Plymouth
- St Ives
- Cornish Coast
- Dartmouth
- Ilfracombe
- Scilly, Isles of
- Totnes

Safari Park, Longleat

© Ochterbeck/Michelin

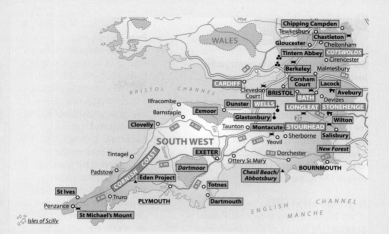

Wessex

Originally the ancient kingdom of the West Saxons, Wessex is most easily defined as that chunk of the West Country that is not Devon or Cornwall, and is a gentle and cultured introduction to the holiday playground beyond. Rural Wessex enjoys a particularly luxuriant version of the rolling English patchwork field pattern while its towns and cities include several elegant Georgian and Victorian survivors. Bath, with its eponymous Roman springs and its glorious 18C architecture, is the epitome of provincial high culture. Neighbouring Bristol was built upon its maritime trade and is a more robust city with plenty of modern attractions and a life independent of visitors. Thomas Hardy's late-19C literary Wessex comes to life around Dorchester, while 21C alternative culture can be found aplenty in Glastonbury.

In the Cotswolds picture-postcard villages, cream teas on manicured lawns beside thatched cottages and golden limestone buildings are clichés that come to life with surprising regularity.

Bath	Bournemouth
Bristol	Cheltenham
Cotswolds	Devizes
Dorchester	Exmoor
Glastonbury	Gloucester
Lacock	Longleat
Stonehenge	Stourhead
Salisbury	Sherborne
Taunton	Truro
Wells	Yeovil

National Parks

Exmoor – Rising to 1,500ft/460m, from Chapman Barrows to Dunkery Beacon, the park heartland is still the windswept haunt of falcon and hawk. Cliffs, broken by deep valleys with waterfalls, make protected breeding sites for seabirds. With the Quantocks, Exmoor is the last secure habitat in the south of England for the red deer. A small breeding herd of Exmoor ponies has been established to maintain declining numbers.

Dartmoor – This is the largest and wildest stretch of open country in southern Britain. Two plateaux, rising to over 2,000ft/610m and covered with blanket bog and heather moorland, are divided by the River Dart. Ponies – descendants of those turned out in the Middle Ages – still graze much of the lower-lying heather moorland and there are hundreds of ancient sites – chambered tombs, hillforts, stone circles, medieval crosses and waymarks.

Bath★★★
Bath and Northeast Somerset

Set in rolling Somerset countryside, just over 100 miles west of London, Bath's hot springs, Roman Baths, splendid abbey and Georgian stone crescents have attracted visitors for centuries. The city combines the grace and elegance of the 18C with a long and varied past, in addition to housing springs used since long before the Romans.

A BIT OF HISTORY

In 500 BC, according to legend, **Prince Bladud** (the father of King Lear), was cured of his leprosy by wallowing in the mud here. The **Romans**, in the 1C AD, made Bath England's first spa resort with baths and a temple.

In the 11C the Bishop of Wells bought Bath for £500. He began a vast Benedictine cathedral priory, and built a palace, new baths and a school. Bath became a prosperous wool town, but at the Dissolution the monks were forced to sell off parts of the abbey. In 1574 Queen Elizabeth I set up a fund to restore the abbey and enhance the town, and by the early 18C it had become very popular.

In 1704 **Beau Nash** (1673–1762) came to Bath, opened the first Pump Room for taking the waters and organised concerts, balls and gambling. Bath prospered – as did Nash – and became England's most fashionable city.

While Nash structured Bath society, **Ralph Allen** (1694–1764) and John Wood (1700–54) transformed its architecture and urban plan. Inspired by Bath's Roman past they built in the Palladian style with the local honey-coloured stone, now known as **Bath Stone**.

CITY
Roman Baths★

Pump Room, Stall Street. ⏱ *Open Jan–Feb & Nov–Dec 9.30am–5.30pm. Mar–Jun and Sept–Oct 9am–5 pm. Jul–Aug 9am–9pm. Last entry 1hr before closing.* ⏱*Closed Dec 25–26.* 🎫*£11 (Jul–Aug £11.50), combined ticket*

▶ **Population:** 85,202.
♿ **Michelin Map:** Michelin Atlas p 17 or Map 503 M 29.
ℹ **Info:** Abbey Church Yard. 📞0906 7112 000/ 📞0906 711 2000 (50p/min). From overseas 📞0870 847 5257. www.visitbath.co.uk.
▷ **Location:** Bath lies 107mi/173km southwest of London. Bath Spa train station and Bath bus station are on Manvers Street in the centre of town. The city centre is compact and most of the major sights are within walking distance of each other. Bath Bus Company/City Sightseeing operate a hop-on hop-off bus tour (⏱daily £11; 📞01225 330 444; www.bathbuscompany.com).
☺ **Don't Miss:** The Baths, Royal Crescent, American Museum.
⏱ **Timing:** Allow at least two full days.
🐾**Walking Tours:** The Mayor's Guides free walking tours depart (⏱daily in summer Sun–Fri 10.30am and 2pm, Sat 10.30am, May–Sept also Tue and Fri 7pm) from outside the Roman Baths entrance, There are many other different themed walking tours; for details visit www.visitbath.co.uk.
🅿 **Parking:** A park and ride system is in operation (follow the signs).

with Museum of Costume £14.50. 🍴♿. 📞*01225 477 785. www.roman baths.co.uk.*

One of the best-preserved Roman spas in the world, the baths are fed by a spring which pours out 250,000 gallons/1,136,500 litres of water per day at a temperature of 116°F/46.5°C.

Roman Baths

Roman Baths/Bath Tourism Plus/visitbath.co.uk

The Roman complex consisted of the Great Bath, a large warm swimming pool, now open to the sky, and two baths of decreasing heat; later a *frigidarium* was built on the west side with openings at the north, overlooking the sacred spring, and two more heated chambers (*tepidarium and caldarium*). The east end was enlarged, the baths were elaborated and the *frigidarium* transformed into a cold-plunge circular bath.

After the Romans had left, the drains soon clogged through lack of attention and mud covered the site. In the early Middle Ages the Normans constructed the King's Bath around the tank which the Romans had lined with Mendip lead. Modern excavations have revealed the temple and baths complex and a wide variety of artefacts.

Bath Abbey★

13 Kingston Buildings.
Abbey: ⏱ *Open Apr–Oct Mon–Sat 9am–6pm, Sun 1pm–2.30pm, 4.30pm–5.30pm. Nov–Mar Mon–Sat 9am–4.30pm, Sun 1pm–2.30pm.* ⏱*£2.50 contribution requested.*
Tower: ↗⏱*Mon–Fri 11am, noon and 2pm, Sat each hour 10am–3pm.* ⏱*£5.* ♿. ✆*01225 422462.*
www.bathabbey.org.

The present sanctuary, on the site of an abbey founded early in the reign of King Offa (757–96), was begun in 1499 by Bishop Oliver King. From the pillars of the Norman church arose the pure late Perpendicular abbey. At the Dissolution, the incomplete building fell into disrepair, but restoration was begun in the late 16C. Inside, the nave, chancel and narrow transepts soar to **fan vaulting** by Robert and William Vertue (of Westminster Abbey fame).

Pump Room★

⏱ *Open daily for lunch and light refreshments.* ⏱*Closed Dec 25–26.* ♿. ✆*01225 444 477 (table reservations). www.romanbaths.co.uk.*

The present Pump Room was built in 1789–99. The interiors are elegantly fur-

Royal Crescent

nished with ornamental pilasters, gilded capitals, a coffered ceiling, antiques and a glass chandelier. The bay overlooking the King's Bath contains the drinking fountain, from which people can still take the waters.

Thermae Bath Spa
The Hetling Pump Room, Hot Bath Street. ⏲ *Open year-round daily–* ***New Royal Bath:*** *9am–10pm (last entry 7.30pm).* ***Cross Bath:*** *10am–8pm (last entry 6.30pm).* ***Visitor Centre:*** *10am–5pm (Sun 4pm).* ⏲*Closed Dec 25–26 and 31.* 👓*Spa session from £12 for 1hr 30min. Visitor centre free.* 📞*01225 331 234.*

Opened in 2006 Britain's much-awaited only natural thermal spa is a combina-

tion of the best of the original Georgian spa (housed partly in an 18C building and partly in a glass-sided ultra-modern building, offering 21C comforts and facilities, including four thermal baths and the latest therapies.

Royal Crescent★★★
The great arc of thirty terrace houses, in which the horizontal lines are counterbalanced by 114 giant Ionic columns rising from the first floor to the pierced parapet, was the great achievement of John Wood II, built 1767–74. **No.1 Royal Crescent**★★ (⏲*open mid-Feb–Nov Tue–Sun, bank hols and Mon during Bath Festival, 10.30am–5pm (4pm Nov);* ⏲*closed Good Fri;* 👓*£5;* 📞*01225 428 126; www.bath-preservation-trust.org.uk)* has been authentically restored, providing a perfect setting for Chippendale, Sheraton and Hepplewhite furniture and for porcelain and 18C glassware.

The Circus★★★
The King's Circus, although one of John Wood the Elder's earliest concepts, was built in 1754. It is a tight circle of identical houses, pierced by three equidistant access roads. The houses of pale Bath stone, decorated with coupled columns, rise three floors to a frieze and acorn–topped balustrade.

Assembly Rooms★
NT. Bennett Street. ⏲*Open to view free of charge when not in use for booked*

Jane Austen (1775–1817)
Jane visited Bath when staying with her aunt and uncle, the Leigh Perrots, at No.1 The Paragon, and it was in Bath that she set much of *Northanger Abbey*.

In May 1799, the Austen family took lodgings at 13 Queen Square; later, they resided at 4 Sydney Place; it was during their time at 27 Green Park Buildings, that Jane's father died in January 1805; on two further occasions, the remaining ladies of the family lived both at 25 Gay Street and in Trim Street.

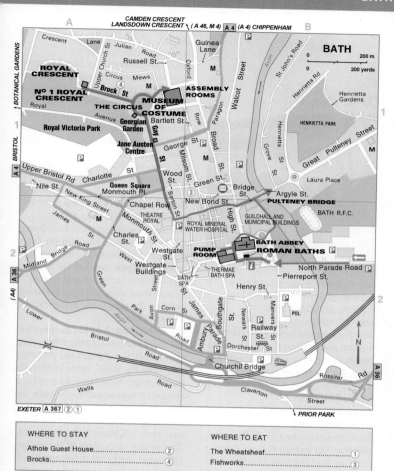

BATH

WHERE TO STAY		WHERE TO EAT	
Athole Guest House	②	The Wheatsheaf	①
Brocks	④	Fishworks	③

functions (check ahead) daily Mar–Oct
10.30am–6pm; Nov–Feb 5pm. Closed
Dec 25–26. ℰ 01225 477 173.
www.nationaltrust.org.uk.

These elegant rooms were built in 1769–
71 for the evening assemblies – at which
people met to dance, play cards, drink
tea and to gossip. The **Octagon** was
intended as a small card room. The **Tea
Room** has a rich interior with a splendid
two-tiered screen of columns at its west
end. Within the Assembly Rooms the
fascinating **Museum of Costume**★★★
(open daily Mar–Oct 10.30am–5pm,
Nov–Feb 4pm; closed Dec 25–26; £7,
combined ticket with Roman Baths £14.50;
ℰ 01225 477 173; www.museumof
costume.co.uk) presents a colourful and

elegant display of every sort of garment
from the Stuart period to the present
day. Note the museum's oldest complete
attire, the **Silver Tissue Dress** (1660s),
and its selection of superb gloves.

Pulteney Bridge★

This magnificent bridge, built in 1769–
74 to Robert Adam's design, has small
shops on both sides, domed end pavilions and a central Venetian window. It
is best viewed from Parade Gardens by
the crescent weir.

Jane Austen Centre

40 Gay Street, Queen Square. Open
mid-Mar–Oct daily 9.45am–5.30pm.
(Jul–Aug Thu–Sat 7pm). Nov–mid-Mar

Bradford–on–Avon

©Bath Tourism Plus/visitbath.co.uk

Sun–Fri 11am–4.30pm, Sat 9.45am–5.30pm. ○Closed Dec 24–6, 1 Jan. ⊛£6.50. ℘01225 443 000. www.janeausten.co.uk.
Jane Austen knew Bath (🕯 *see above*), as a visitor and a resident, and this exhibition is devoted to every place in Bath associated with Jane or her novels.

EXCURSIONS
American Museum in Britain, Claverton★★
3mi/5km east on the A 36. ○ Open mid–Mar–Oct and late Nov–mid–Dec Tue–Sun, Bank Hol Mon, Mon in Aug noon–5pm. ⊛Museum £8, grounds and temporary exhibition only, £5.50.

ADDRESSES

🛏STAY
⊜⊜ **Athole Guest House**, *33 Upper Oldfield Park. ℘01225 32 0000. www.atholehouse.co.uk.* This large Victorian home has been restored to give four quiet and spacious bedrooms with contemporary styling and sleek furnishings. Quiet location away from main streets.

⊜⊜ **Brocks**, *32 Brock Street. ℘01225 338 374. www.brocksguesthouse.co.uk.* This elegant Georgian house built by John Wood the younger in 1765 is

&⊡🅿✕. *℘01225 460 503. www.americanmuseum.org.*
Housed in Claverton Manor, this remarkable collection of folk and decorative arts shows the diverse and complex nature of American culture and is the only museum of Americana outside the United States. The nucleus of its collection is a series of furnished rooms dating from the late 17C to the middle of the 19C presenting 200 years of American life and styles.

Bradford–on–Avon★★
8mi/13km via the A 4 and A 363.
The houses rising up the hillside from the River Avon give Bradford-on-Avon its charm and character. The nine-arched **bridge★**, built in 1610 with a small square, domed chapel topped by a weather-vane, is the best starting point for the walk to the top of this attractive town.
The Saxon **Church of St Laurence★★**, (○ *open year-round daily 10am–7pm, 4pm winter; &; ℘01225 865 797*) may date from the 7C–8C when St Aldhelm built a church here. Having served as a school, cottage and charnel house, the church was re–discovered in 1856. A short walk along thr River Avon lies a vast early 14C stone **tithe barn★** (& ○ *open year–round daily 10.30am–4pm; 🅿(charge). www.english-heritage.org.uk*) with gabled doorways and a superbly constructed wooden cruck roof.

ideally situated in the loveliest part of Bath between the Circus and Royal Crescent.

🍽 EAT
⊜⊜ **The Wheatsheaf**, *Combe Hay ℘01225 833 504. www.wheatsheaf-combehay.com.* This revamped pub 4mi/6.4km south of Bath offers starkly modern dining rooms and contemporary rustic chic.

⊜⊜ **Fishworks**, *6 Green Street. ℘01225 448707. www.fishworks.co.uk.* A bustling place set above its own fish shop, serving an extensive range of un-fussy fish and seafood dishes.

Bournemouth

Dorset

The Grand Old Lady of England's south central coast, Bournemouth has been a popular summer and winter resort since the late 19C. It is famous for its two piers and the ever-colourful public gardens, which have recently revived its fortunes and image. A lively student population ensures a good number of busy pubs and nightclubs.

▶ **Population:** 155,488.

Michelin Map: Michelin Atlas p 9 or Map 503 O 31.

Info: Visitor Information Bureau, Westover Road. ☎0845 051 1701. www.bournemouth.co.uk.

Location: Bournemouth is located 105mi/168km southwest of London. The bus station and train station are together, 1mi/1.6km east of the centre. To navigate the seafront jump aboard the land-train which runs for 6mi/10km along the promenade (Mar–Oct only).

Don't Miss: Russell-Cotes Art Gallery and Museum; Compton Acres; the view of Old Harry Rocks from the Southwest Coast Path.

Timing: In summer allow at least two days.

Kids: The beaches and Europe's first artificial surf reef (www.bournemouthsurfreef.com) due to open late summer 2009.

SIGHTS

Russell-Cotes Art Gallery and Museum★★

East Cliff, Russell-Cotes Road. ◷ *Open year-round Tue–Sun 10am–5pm, banks hols.* ◷ *Closed Good Fri, Dec 26.* ⚅✕. ☎01202 451 858. http://russell-cotes.bournemouth.gov.uk.

Housed in **East Cliff Hall**, decorated in archetypal ornate High Victorian taste, with inlaid furniture, painted ceilings, decorative windows and coloured wallpaper, the collections include numerous paintings (William Frith, Landseer, Leighton, Birket-Foster, Rossetti, Alma-Tadema, Edwin Long), fine English china, gold and silver plate, and souvenirs from abroad (the Orient, Germany, Egypt).

Christchurch★

At the heart of this pretty and prosperous little coastal town is a Norman **priory**★ (◷ *open Mon–Sat 9.30am–5.00pm)* and Norman castle grouped around a harbour filled with fishing and pleasure craft.

EXCURSIONS

Compton Acres★★

164 Canford Cliffs Road, 2mi/3km west by A 338. ◷ *Open daily, Apr–Oct 9am–6pm, Nov–Mar 10am–4pm.* ◷ *Closed Dec 25–26.* ≤£7.95. ⚅🄿✕. ☎01202 700 778. www.comptonacres.co.uk.

This series of nine distinct **gardens** (Italian, rock, water and Japanese) spreads over 15 acres/6ha in a rift in the sandstone cliffs; it is famous for having flowers in bloom throughout the year. The **English Garden** lies open to sunsets and a westerly **view**★★★ of Poole Harbour, Brownsea Island and the Purbeck Hills.

Poole★

4mi/6km west on the A 338.

With its fine sandy beach at Sandbanks and its situation on one of the largest harbours in the world, Poole is a holiday resort, yachting haven and a major roll-on, roll-off port. By the quay is the recently refurbished **Poole Museum** (*High Street;* ◷ *open late Mar–Oct daily, Mon–Sat 10am–5pm, Sun noon–5pm; Nov–Mar Tue–Sat 10am–4pm, Sun noon–4pm;* ⚅; ☎01202 262 600; www.poole.gov.uk) telling the history of the port and town. Adjacent is **Scaplen's Court** (◷ *open same hours and contact details as Poole Museum),* a domestic

Poole Harbour from Studland Heath

A. Taverner/MICHELIN

building from the late medieval period. Poole was the busiest lifeboat station in the southwest in 2008 when the volunteer crews launched 156 times, rescuing 213 people. You can visit their **RNLI Lifeboat Museum** (*West Quay Road;* 🕐 *open year-round daily 10am–4.30pm;* &; ℘*01202 665 607; www.poolelifeboat. co.uk),* weather permitting and volunteers available. The attractive 18C **Old Town** and the 18C Guildhall building are also of note.

Brownsea Island★

NT. Access by boat from Poole, Sand-banks and Bournemouth. & 🕐 *Open mid-Mar–third week Jul and Sept 10am–5pm. Third week Jul–Aug/early Sept 10am–6pm. Oct 10am–4pm. Check time of last boat.* 🕾*Landing fee £4.90.* 🐾 *Guided tour of nature reserve* ℘*01202 709 445.* ✕. ℘*01202 707 744. www.nationaltrust.org.uk.*
This 500-acre island, covered in heath and woodland and fringed by inviting beaches along its south shore, consists of two nature reserves, either side of **Middle Street** along the central spine of the island. The north reserve is a sanctuary for waterfowl and other birds, and the south reserve, where visitors can wander at will, is likewise home to numerous birds, including peacocks.
There is an excellent **view**★★ across Poole Bay to the Purbeck Hills from **Baden-Powell Stone**, which commemorates the first Boy Scout camp held here in 1907.

Corfe Castle★

18mi/29km southwest by the A 35 and A 351. 🕐 *Open daily 10am–6pm (5pm Mar and Oct, 4pm Nov–Feb).* 🕐 *Closed Dec 25–26.* 🕾*£5.36.* & 🄿 ✕. ℘*01929 481 294. www.nationaltrust.org.uk.*
Corfe Castle has dominated the landscape since the 11C, first as a towering stronghold and since 1646 as a dramatic ruin. From the high mound on which it stands, the **views**★★ are spectacular. In 987 the 17 year-old King Edward, son of Edgar, visiting his half-brother at the castle, was murdered by his stepmother, Queen Aethelfrith; in 1001 he was canonised as **St Edward**, **King and Martyr**. It was the home of Sir John Bankes, Chief Justice to King Charles I. His wife resolutely defended it from 1643–45 and when it fell, owing to the treachery of one of the garrison, it was looted and blown up by the Parliamentarians.

Lulworth Cove★

8mi/14km west of Corfe Castle via the B 3070.
The road passes **Blue Pool**★, a beautiful blue-green lake (3 acres/1.2ha) fringed by silver birch and pine woods, gorse and heather, through which sandy paths meander, giving views of the Purbeck Hills. The circular sweep of Lulworth Cove is almost enclosed by the downland cliffs. From here, the Dorset Coast Path leads to the striking cliff archway of **Durdle Door** to the west, a dramatic climax to the whole of this spectacular area of headlands and bays.

Swanage★

5mi/8km east of Corfe Castle via A 351.
A scenic stretch of road leads to this quarry town and harbour, from which stone and marble were shipped to build Westminster Abbey and the cathedrals of Exeter, Lincoln and Salisbury. Swanage also boasts a good beach and a range of seaside leisure facilities. Take the Southwest Coast Path east of Swanage to discover **Old Harry Rocks**★★, two stacks of gleaming chalk once part of an unbroken shoreline from The Needles but now separated from the mainland and each other (Old Harry is the larger stack, his "wife" is the slimmer!).

ADDRESSES

🛏 STAY

🍴🍴 **Druid House**, *26 Sopers Lane, Christchurch.* ☎*01202 485615. www.druidhouse.co.uk.* Overlooking a quiet park in the centre of Christchurch, this 1930s house is bright and airy with a cottagey ambience and eight spacious bedrooms (two with balconies).

🍴🍴🛏 **The Orchid**, *34 Gervis Road.* ☎*01202 551 600. www.orchid-hotel.co.uk.* This personally run, modern, minimalist, Asian-inspired boutique hotel offers particularly good value out of season. Designer-chic.

🍷 EAT

🍴🍴 **Noble House**, *3–5 Lansdowne Road.* ☎*01202 291 277. www.noble-house.co.uk.* This friendly operation in the city centre offers a comprehensive choice of Chinese dishes.

🍴🍴 **West Beach**, *Pier Approach.* ☎*01202 587 785. www.west-beach.co.uk* A perfect location right on the beach, plus excellent fish and seafood.

🍴🍴🛏🛏 **Oscars**, *De Vere Hotel, Bath Road.* ☎*01202 555 555. www.devere-hotels.com.* French country cooking in the elegant setting of arguably Bournemouth's finest hotel with freshly landed fish and shellfish,

Bristol★★

Bristol

In the 10C Bristol was a settlement at the western limit of Saxon influence, trading with Ireland. Its port flourished and by the Middle Ages Bristol was England's second city. By the 17C its trade had expanded to the Canaries, South and North America, Africa and the West Indies. In the 18C and 19C new industries developed locally: iron, brass, copper, porcelain, glass, chocolate and tobacco. To overcome the problems caused in the port by the exceptionally high tidal range (the second highest in the world), an elaborate system of locks was constructed in 1804–09 to maintain a constant water level along the city's extensive quaysides, so creating the **Floating Harbour★★**. The Industrial Revolution drew interests north however, and the city declined. Modern docks on the estuary of the Severn now enable commercial shipping to avoid the difficult passage through the Avon Gorge.

BRISTOL TODAY

Bristol's present affluence and regeneration is underpinned by the electronic age: high-technology research and assembly continues to maintain Bris-

▶ **Population:** 407 992.
🕐 **Michelin Map:** Michelin Atlas p 17 or Map 503 M 29.
ℹ **Info:** Harbourside: Explore-At-Bristol. City Centre: Travel Bristol Centre, Colston Avenue. Broadmead: The Mall Galleries. ☎0906 711 219.
▶ **Location:** 118mi/190km W of London and 13mi/20.5km NW of Bath. Bristol has two mainline stations, Parkway (out of town) and Temple Meads, a 20min walk from the centre. The bus station is in Marlborough Street a 5–10min walk from the centre. Try the open-top hop-on hop-off bus (☎0870 4440654; www.bristolvisitor.co.uk).
🚹 **Don't Miss:** The Georgian House; Clifton.
🕐 **Timing:** Two days minimum.
👫 **Kids:** Bristol Zoo; Explore-At-Bristol; SS Great Britain.
🚤 **Boat Trips:** The Bristol Packet Ltd operate a city docks tour and river trips including a day-trip to Bath (☎0117 926 8157; www.bristolpacket.co.uk).

Bristol Harbour and the spire of St Mary Redcliffe in the background

©Asher Welstead/iStockphoto.com

tol's strong engineering tradition. The quaysides have become thriving leisure and recreation areas and the setting for two arts centres, the **Arnolfini** and the **Watershed Media Centre** (**CZ**).
Bristol is strongly linked with the visionary engineer **Isambard Kingdom Brunel** (1806–59), designer of the Clifton Suspension Bridge, the *SS Great Britain* and architect of the impeccably planned, broad-gauge Great Western Railway, which reached its terminus here, at the Station Building (**DZ**), in 1841. In 1940–42 the city was heavily bombed and much of today's centre is the result of post-war rebuilding.

CITY

👥 Explore-At-Bristol★

Harbourside. ⏱ *Open year-round Mon–Fri during school term 10am–5pm; all weekends and all weekdays during school hols 10am–6pm.* ⏱*Closed Dec 24–26.* ⮾*£9, child £6.50.* ♿🅿✕. ✆*0845 345 1235.* *www.at-bristol.org.uk.*
This 21C science centre combines hands-on activities with the very latest multimedia techniques. Science is brought alive through some stunning visuals and over 170 interactive experiences. There is also a planetarium and an IMAX cinema. A registered charity, Explore aims to make science accessible to all.

St Mary Redcliffe★★

Redcliffe Hill. ⏱ *Open Easter–Oct Mon–Fri 8.30am–5pm. Nov–Easter Mon–Fri 9am–4pm. Year-round Sun 8am–7.30pm.* ✕. ✆*0117 929 1487.* *www.stmaryredcliffe.co.uk*
"The fairest, goodliest, and most famous parish church in England" according to Queen Elizabeth I, represents the most perfect expression of the Gothic style. The Parish Church has stood for over 800 years. The **spire** (1872) rises 292ft/90m above the city. The Decorated hexagonal **north porch** (1290) is the antechamber to the shrine of Our Lady, in an inner, more modest Early English porch (1185). The church contains a number of interesting furnishings (late 16C wooden statue of Queen Elizabeth I and armour of Admiral Sir William Penn, in the **American chapel**.

Museum of Bristol

Princes Wharf. ⏱ *Scheduled to open 2011.* ♿. ✆*0117 922 2000. www.bristolcity.gov.uk/museums.*
The new Museum of Bristol will be housed in historic dockside sheds and explore the city's history and culture through the experiences of Bristol people and communities past and present, by use of state-of-the-art displays and items from the city's historic collections.

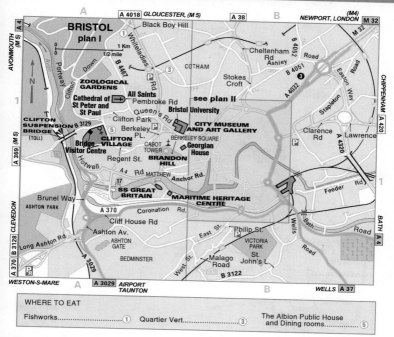

WHERE TO EAT

Fishworks..............................①   Quartier Vert.........................③   The Albion Public House
and Dining rooms................⑤

Georgian House★★

🕐 *Open year-round daily Sat–Wed, 10am–5pm.* 🕐 *Closed Good Fri, Dec 24–28.* 📞*0117 921 1362. www.bristol-city.gov.uk/museums.*

This handsome, typical Bath-stone house was built c. 1790 for the merchant and sugar planter John Pinney. Among the fine furniture note the mid-18C **bureau-bookcase**, the **desk** and the **long-case clock** (c. 1740) in the hall; the elaborate gilded **girandoles** in the first-floor drawing room; the **double secretaire bookcase** (c. 1800) and the collector's cabinet in the rich green library. The service rooms include a well-equipped **kitchen**, laundry room, the housekeeper's room, and the **cold-water plunge bath** which Pinney used daily.

Bristol Cathedral★

College Green 🕐 *Open Mon–Fri 8am–6pm. Sat 8am–5.30pm, Sun 7.30am–5pm.* 👥 *Guided tours most Sat 11.30am, 1.30pm (see website).* 💷*£2 contribution requested.* 📞*0117 926 4879. www.bristol-cathedral.co.uk.*

A church has stood here for over a thousand years. The cathedral is a 14–15C Perpendicular Gothic church; the nave and twin west towers are 19C. Note the screen, the choir stalls (lively **15C misericords**), the 19C reredos and, over the nave, the highly original early-14C vault which is unique in English cathedrals. The east end is a **hall church** with chancel and aisles rising to an equal height. The **East Lady Chapel** (added

Library, Georgian House

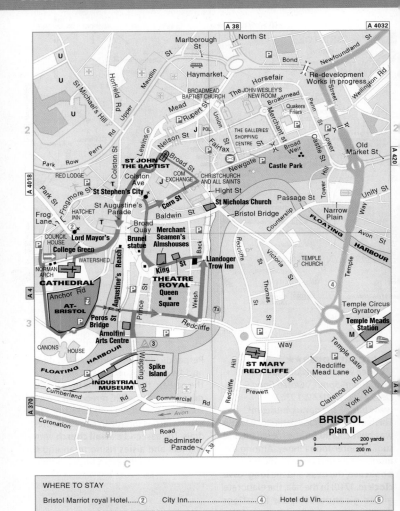

BRISTOL
plan II

1298–1330) has a riot of medieval colour highlighting the elaborately carved stone. The **Harrowing of Hell**, a remarkable 1,000 year-old Saxon carved stone coffin-lid, stands in the south transept. The late Norman rib-vaulted **chapter house** and columned vestibule were built 1150–70.

👥🏛 SS Great Britain★

🕐 Open Apr–late Oct 10am–5.30pm last week Oct and Feb–Mar 10am–4.30pm. Nov–Jan 10am–4pm. 💷£10.95, child £5.95. ♿ 🅿✕. ☎0117 926 0680. www.ssgreatbritain.org.

The *SS Great Britain* was launched in 1843 and was the first iron-built, propeller-driven Atlantic liner. Her vast hulk, 322ft/98m long and 51ft/16m across, has been painstakingly restored here in her original dry dock. The innovations of Brunel's design, and the saga of the great vessel's history and of Bristol shipbuilding since the 18C are described in the insightful **Dockyard Museum** exhibition.

The SS Great Britain continued sailing until 1886, travelling 32 times around the world and nearly one million miles at sea. She was finally abandoned in the

SS Great Britain

©Nick Hawkes/iStockphoto.com

Falkland Islands, in 1937, after more than 40 years use as a floating warehouse. In 1970 a salvage project brought her home to Bristol, where she is conserved in the dry dock in which she was originally built.

Lord Mayor's Chapel★

🕐 *Open Wed–Sun 10am–noon and 1pm–4pm. Sun, for services only.* 👓*Donation requested.* ✆*0117 929 4350. www.bristol.gov.uk.*
St Mark's Chapel was once part of a medieval hospital. The impressive Perpendicular chapel beside the narrow nave contains 15–17C **tombs**. Note the 16C continental **glass**, the mayors' hatchments, the gilded sword rest (1702) and the fine wrought-iron gates.

St John the Baptist★

Tower Lane. 🕐 *Open Thu 10am–1pm; call for other times.* ✆*07972 767 010. www.visitchurches.org.uk.*
This 14C church with its battlemented tower and spire stands over a triple arch, one of the six medieval gateways in the city walls. It contains some interesting 17C woodwork (lectern, communion table, hour-glass) and an earlier brass (chancel).

St Stephen's City★

St Stephen's Street. 🕐 *Open year-round Mon–Fri 10am–4pm.* ✕. ✆*0117 927 7977. www.ststephensbristol.co.uk.*
The 15C tower of the city parish church rises 130ft/40m by stages of ogee arched openings to a distinctive crown and two-tier pierced balustrade linking corner turrets adorned with fountains of pinnacles. The interior houses memori-

"Shipshape and Bristol fashion"

This expression was coined to describe the many and varied preparations required before a ship sailed up the river. Given the dramatic rise and fall of the tide, ships were often left askew when stranded on the mudflats; if cargo was not properly stowed it was liable to fall or spill. Appropriately enough, it was a Bristol-born man, **Samuel Plimsoll**, who came up with the idea of limiting cargo weight and checking whether it was correctly loaded by means of the elementary concept known as the Plimsoll line.

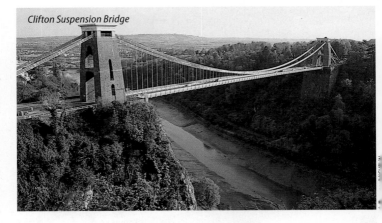

Clifton Suspension Bridge

als to local merchants, 17C wrought-iron gates and a medieval eagle lectern. The church offers free lunchtime recitals (call or see website for details).

City Museum and Art Gallery★

Queen's Road ⏱ *Open year-round daily 10am–5pm.* ⏱ *Closed Dec 25–26.* ♿✕. ☎*0117 922 3571. www.bristol.gov.uk.*
Contained in an Edwardian Baroque building on Queen's Road, next to the Wills University building, is a substantial collection of artefacts including antique, oriental and locally-produced glassware, pottery, porcelain and silverware, local archaeology and geology, fine art (works from the Italian, 19C French and 19–20C British schools), selections from the Hull-Grundy costume jewellery bequest, Assyrian and Ancient Egyptian antiquities, scale models of locomotives, and maritime history.

King Street

This cobbled street contains 18C and 19C warehouses at the harbour end, 17C almshouses and pubs and the **Theatre Royal★★ (T)**, which opened in 1766 but was granted a royal licence by George III in 1778 and is the oldest playhouse in the country still in use. At the northwest end are the **Merchant Seamen's Almshouses★**, built in 1544 and enlarged in 1696, with the coloured arms of the Merchant Venturers on the outside wall.

CLIFTON★★

The elegant suburb of Clifton began to take shape on the heights above the Avon Gorge in the early 1790s, with a frantic rush of building abruptly halted by a wave of bankruptcies.
When building picked up again in about 1810 a more assured Grecian style was applied, giving birth to distinguished crescents, squares and terraces generously interspersed with greenery. Streets such as The Mall, Caledonia Place, Princess Victoria Street and Royal York Crescent make up the delightful **Clifton Village★ (AX)** with terraced houses, small shops and G E Street's 1868 **All Saints Church (AX)** with John Piper windows.

Clifton Suspension Bridge★★

🚶 *Guided tours (free) every Sun afternoon Easter Sun–mid-Sept 3pm from toll booth at the Clifton end of the Bridge. To arrange tours at other times (⌖£2.50) call ☎0117 974 4664. www. clifton-suspension-bridge.org.uk.*
Designed by Brunel in 1829, this is arguably the most beautiful of early English suspension bridges. Unfortunately funds ran out and Brunel never saw his 702ft-/214m-long bridge completed; he died five years too soon, in 1859.
Among countless bridge stories, Sarah Ann Henley's is the happiest: in 1885, a lovers' quarrel induced a lover's leap, but Sarah Ann's petticoats opened and

she parachuted gently down to the mud below – she subsequently married and lived to be 85. Close to the suspension bridge on the cliff stands the 1729 Observatory Tower at the top of which is an 18C camera obscura, affording views for miles around.

Cathedral of St Peter and St Paul★

Clifton Park. ☎*0117 973 8411. www.cliftoncathedral.org.uk.*
This Roman Catholic cathedral is an impressive hexagonal edifice in white concrete, pink granite, black fibreglass, lead and glass; it was consecrated in 1973. Note the windows and the stations of the cross carved in stone.

Bristol Zoo Gardens★★

🕐 *Open year-round daily 9am–5.30pm (5pm Sept–May).* 🕐*Closed Dec 25.* ☞*£11.36, child £7.04.* & ✗. ☎*0117 973 8951. www.bristolzoo.org.uk.*
This famous venerable zoo opened in 1836, making it the fifth-oldest in the world. Today it features over 400 species of animals – from gorillas in their landscaped compound to Bug World – accommodated in various architect-designed houses; see the Reptile and Ape Houses in particular.

A popular new attraction is **Explorers' Creek** including a wet play area, a tropical bird house and a walk-through parrot feeding area.

EXCURSION
Clevedon Court★

NT. 11mi/16km west on the A 370, the B 3128 and the B 3130. 🕐*Open Apr–Sept Sun, Wed, Thu and bank hols 2pm–5pm.* ☞*£6.30.* ✗. ☎*01275 872 257. www.nationaltrust.org.uk.*
William Makepeace Thackery often stayed at Clevedon, sketching and writing. This well-preserved early 14C house features a 12C tower and 13C Great Hall. The exterior dates to 1570, but inside you will find evidence of earlier centuries. The **Great Hall** has Tudor windows and fireplaces; the remarkable Hanging Chapel, with its unusual reticulated window tracery, contains 17C prayer desks and 15C and 16C Biblical carvings. The contents of the 14C State Bedroom reflect ten generations of family taste, while the Justice Room displays local Nailsea glass made between 1788 and 1873. Georgian terraced gardens.

ADDRESSES

🏨 STAY

☞☞☞☞ **Hotel du Vin**, *The Sugar House, Lewins Mead.* ☎*0117 925 5577. www.hotelduvin.com.* Beneath the massive chimney of this former sugar refinery are very stylish loft rooms in minimalist decor with dark leather and wood, low-slung beds and subtle wine theming and curiosities.

☞☞☞☞ **Bristol Marriot Royal Hotel**, *College Green.* ☎*0117 925 5100.* Striking central Victorian edifice with classic individual bedrooms combining period styling with all mod cons.

☞☞☞☞ **City Inn**, *Temple Way.* ☎*0117 925 1001. www.cityinn.com.* Intelligent contemporary design, all mod cons and central location are the City Inn hallmarks; smart brasserie (☞☞☞☞).

🍽/ EAT

☞☞ **The Albion Public House and Dining Rooms**, Clifton Village. ☎*0117 973 3522. www.thealbionclifton.co.uk.* Tasty typical West Country dishes are served in this characterful and countrified 17C pub tucked away in Clifton.

☞☞ **Quartier Vert**, *85 Whiteladies Road, Clifton.* ☎*0117 973 4482. www.quartiervert.co.uk.* Simple modern European cooking in a bustling attractive restaurant using local, organic ingredients. There is also a café area serving snacks and tapas.

☞☞☞ **Fishworks**, *128 Whiteladies Road, Clifton.* ☎*0117 974 4433. www.fishworks.co.uk.* Only the freshest seasonal fish and shellfish is served, invariably in a simple classic style, in the setting of a former fishmonger's shop.

Channel Islands★★

The Channel Islands lie west of the Cherbourg peninsula of the Normandy coast. Blessed by better weather than mainland Britain and unspoilt rural countryside, the islands have developed tourist facilities to attract sailors, surfers and swimmers, bird-watchers, walkers and cyclists. Life in general is lived in the slow lane and a characteristic feature of the islands is the "honesty boxes" along the road, advertising fresh, home-grown produce.

A BIT OF HISTORY

The islands are rich in prehistoric tombs and monuments indicating human habitation from 7500–2500 BC. They were annexed by the Normans in 933 and later attached to the English crown by William the Conqueror. Some customs and traditions and the Norman–French dialect heard on these islands, which have only been universally English-speaking since the early 20C, date back to this period. In 1204 King John was forced to cede Normandy to the French, but the Channel Islanders chose to remain loyal to the English Crown in return for certain privileges, one of which was an independent parliament. Despite this, the French tried repeatedly to capture the island. Threats of invasion by Napoleon account for the many Martello defence towers built along the coasts. The islands were occupied by the Germans from 1940–45, the only British territory to fall to the enemy during the Second World War, and the islanders suffered considerable hardship during this period.

The Channel Islands are divided into the **Bailiwick of Jersey** and the **Bailiwick of Guernsey**. The original Norman laws and systems have been renewed and modified by subsequent monarchs, though in matters of defence and international relations the islands are subject to decisions made by the Home Office in London. The Channel Islanders benefit from a **VAT-exempt** economy

- ▶ **Population:** 146 314.
- **Michelin Map:** Michelin Atlas p 5 or Map 503 P, Q 33.
- **Info:** Jersey: Liberation Place, St Helier. ✆01534 44 88 00. www.jersey.com. Guernsey: North Esplanade, White Rock, St Peter Port. ✆01481 713 888. www.visitguernsey.com.
- **Location:** Stay on either Jersey or Guernsey and use it as a base from which to visit the other main island and the smaller islands.
- **Don't Miss:** Durrell (Jersey Zoo); Jersey War Tunnels; St Peter Port, Guernsey; if you seek peace and quiet, Sark and Herm.
- **Timing:** Allow a few days to relax here.
- **Kids:** Durrell (Jersey Zoo). Both Guernsey and Jersey have good sandy beaches.

and lower rates of income tax. Coins, bank-notes and postage stamps are issued locally and are not legal tender elsewhere. The islands have therefore become a tax haven for British citizens and developed a buoyant industry in **financial services**. **Farming** still plays an important part in the local economy and maintains a supply to mainland Britain of early vegetables (potatoes, tomatoes, grapes), cut flowers and rich Channel Island milk, produced by the famously pretty local cattle.

JERSEY★★

The largest and southern-most of the group, only 12mi/19km from the coast of France, Jersey possesses a charming combination of English and Norman–French traditions and local features echo both Normandy and Cornwall. Being so close to the Gulf Stream, it is thick with flowers in spring and summer. The sandy bays which characterise the coastline occur even among the steep pink granite cliffs of the sparsely populated north.

GETTING THERE

By Air – Direct to Jersey, Guernsey and Alderney from UK by: Aurigny Air Services Ltd (℘0871 871 0717. www.aurigny.com); British Airways (℘0870 850 9850. www.britishairways.com); bmi baby (℘09111 54 54 54, www.bmibaby.com); Thomsonfly (℘0871 231 4787. www.thomsonfly.com); VLM (℘0871 666 5050. www.flyvlm.com); Blue Islands (℘08456 20 21 22. www.blueislands.com).

Aurigny also operate flights from Cherbourg and Dinard.

Jersey Airport ℘01534 446 247. www.jerseyairport.com.

Guernsey Airport ℘01481 237766. www.guernsey-airport.gov.gg

Alderney Airport ℘01481 822 551. www.alderney.gov.gg

By Sea – Condor Ferries from Weymouth, Poole and Portsmouth. ℘01202 207 216. www.condorferries.com.

St Helier

The capital is named after the 6C hermit saint who brought Christianity to the island. On an islet (access on foot via causeway at low tide, at other times DUKW vehicle) stands **Elizabeth Castle**, (🕐open early Apr–early Nov daily 10am–6pm; ∞£8 (inc ferry £10); ℘01534 723 971; www.jerseyheritagetrust.org) begun in the mid 16C. In the Civil War it was adapted to resist attacks by the Parliamentarians and during the Second World War the occupying German forces made their own additions. West of the **Militia Museum** (mementoes of the Royal Jersey Regiment) the Upper Ward encloses the Mount (keep) affording **views**★ across St Aubin's Bay. Today a breakwater leads south to the 12C hermitage chapel on the rock on which St Helier lived (procession on or about 16 July, St Helier's Day). The centre of the town is marked by the charming **Royal Square** with a statue of George II dressed as a Roman emperor. St Helier's two main collections are the **Jersey Museum**★ (The Weighbridge; 🕐 open daily year-round 10am–4pm; 🕐 closed Jan 1 and 29, Feb 2, Dec 24–26; ∞£7; ❤; ℘01534 633 300; www.jerseyheritagetrust.org) containing award-winning displays of maritime exhibits and the story of Jersey; and the **Maritime Museum** (🕐open daily Apr–Oct 9.30am–5pm. Nov–Mar 10am–4pm; 🕐 closed Jan 1 and Dec 24–26; ∞£7.50; ❤; ℘01534 811 043. www.jerseyheritagetrust.org), installed in converted 19C warehouses, celebrating the importance to Jersey of the sea and

displaying a twelve-panel tapestry (6ft x 3ft/2m x 1m) illustrating the Occupation of Jersey during World War II, each scene based on archive photos.

👪 Durrell (Jersey Zoo)★★

4 mi/6.4km north of St Helier. Trinity. 🕐 Open year-round daily 9.30am–6pm (winter 5pm); 🕐 closed Dec 25. ∞£12.90, child £9.40. ❤ 🅿 ✕. ℘01534 860 000. www.jerseyzoo.co.uk.
The remit of this famous zoo, named after its founder, the naturalist **Gerald Durrell**, is to preserve and breed rare and endangered species that live in an environment as similar as possible to their natural habitat. Its success has led to exchanges with other leading UK zoos and the re-introduction of a number of threatened species to the wild.

Eric Young Orchid Foundation★

Victoria Village, Trinity. 🕐 Open Wed–Sat 10am–4pm. 🕐Closed Jan 1 and Dec 25–26. ∞£3.50. ❤. ℘01534 861 963. www.ericyoungorchidfoundation.co.uk.
A fabulous show of prize plants appealing to amateurs and professionals.

La Hougue Bie★

2.5mi/4km northeast of St Helier. Grouville. 🕐 Open early Apr–Oct daily 10am–5pm. ∞£6.50. ❤ 🅿. ℘01534 853 823. www.jerseyheritagetrust.org.
La Hougue Bie, is a cruciform **Neolithic tomb**★ dating from 3000 BC, a 33ft/10m passage grave, roofed with granite slabs

leading to a 10ft/3m x 30ft/9m funeral chamber and three side chambers. On top of the mound stand the 12C **Chapel of Our Lady of the Dawn** and the 1520 **Jerusalem Chapel** containing early 16C frescoes of archangels.

Hamptonne Country Life Museum★

3mi/5km from St Helier. La Rue de la Patente, St Lawrence.
🕐 *Open early Apr–Oct daily 10am–5pm.* ☕£6.50. ♿. ✆01534 863 955. *www.jerseyheritagetrust.org.*
Part-thatched and with bags of atmosphere, Hamptonne House is thought to have been completed in 1637. It provides an insight into family life-style during the 17C and early 18C with staff dressed in period costume.

Jersey War Tunnels★

Meadowbank, Les Charrieres Malorey.
🕐 *Open mid-Feb–Nov daily 10am–6pm (last admission 4.30pm).*
🕐 *Closed May 9, Aug 9, 14, Sept 11.*
☕£9.85. ♿ 🅿 ✕. ✆01534 860 808. *www.jerseywartunnels.com.*
This large complex of tunnels is kept as a memorial to the forced labourers who worked on its construction for three and a half years under the harshest conditions. Wartime films, archive photographs, newspaper cuttings, letters and memorabilia document the personal suffering and trauma of those caught up in the events.

Mont Orgueil Castle
©AJ/Fotolia.com

Mont Orgueil Castle★

The charming old port of **Gorey** is dominated by Mont Orgueil Castle (🕐 *open Apr–Oct daily 10am–6pm, Nov–Mar Fri–Mon 10am–dusk;* ☕£9.30; ✆01534 853 292; *www.jerseyheritagetrust.org*) which dates back to the 13C. Set on a rocky promontory, its position and defensive strength account for the name (Mount Pride). A spiral network of steps and passages between separate defence systems leads up to excellent **views**★★ at the top. Other sights include the **Jersey Pottery**★, (♿🕐 *Gorey Village; open daily 9am, 10am Sun, to 5.30pm;* 🕐*closed Dec 25–Jan 1;* 🅿✕; ✆01534 850 850; *www.jerseypottery.com*) set in a magnificent garden, and the 49ft/15m **Faldouet Dolmen**, dating from 2500 BC, with a 20ft/6m wide funeral chamber.

St Matthew's Church

Millbrook. 🕐*Open year-round Mon–Fri 9am–6pm (Oct–Mar 4.30pm). Sat–Sun for services only.* ♿🅿✕ (Thu only). ✆01534 502 864. *www.glasschurch.org.* The "Glass Church", built in 1840, is remarkable for **René Lalique's** rich **glasswork**★ interior executed in 1934.

Fishermen's Chapel

St Brelade. 🕐*Open year-round daily 7am–7pm. www.stbreladeschurch.com.* Built in the 11–12C the chapel is decorated with delicate medieval **frescoes**★.

GUERNSEY★

The second principal Channel Island features wild, dramatic **southern cliffs**, while the sandy beaches and rocky promontories of the west and north coasts are excellent for bathing, surfing and rock pool exploring.

St Peter Port★★

The island capital, attractively situated on a hillside on the east coast, overlooks a sheltered harbour. A late-18C building boom produced a delightful Regency town built in local granite. **Castle Cornet**★ (🕐 *open Apr–Oct daily 10am–5pm;* ☕£7.25; 🅿✕; ✆01481 706

961; www.museums.gov.gg), dating back to c. 1206 and reinforced under Elizabeth I, remained loyal to the king in the Civil War, being the last of the royal strongholds to surrender, after eight years of siege. In 1672 the gunpowder store was struck by lightning and the resulting explosion decapitated the castle, destroying the tower and medieval banqueting hall. The castle had to be rebuilt. It now houses the Royal Guernsey Militia Museum and the Guernsey Maritime History Museum. The Ceremony of the **Noonday Gun** is performed by two Guernsey Militia men daily. St Peter Port **Town Church**★ dates back as far as 1048, when it also served as a fort, and was completed around 1475. It now contains several memorials to famous Guernseymen. **Victor Hugo** lived on Guernsey in political exile at **Hauteville House**★ (🕓 open Apr–Sept (except bank hols) Mon–Sat 10am–4pm. ✆£5; 📞01481 721 911; www.victorhugo. gg) which he decorated in a highly individual way. Set in Candie Gardens the **Guernsey Museum and Art Gallery** (🕓open year-round daily 10am–5pm, 4pm winter; 🕓closed Dec 25–Jan 1; ✆£4.50 ; ♿✗; 📞01481 726 51; www. museums.gov.gg) contains art and archeological collections.

Rest of the Island

At **St Martins** is the elegant Queen-Anne period **Sausmarez Manor** (Sausmarez Road; 🕓house by guided tour only, Apr–Oct 10.30 am, 11.30 am, Jun–Sept 10.30 am, 11.30 am, 2pm; subtropical gardens and art park open daily 10am–5pm; ; ✆subtropical garden £5, Art park £5, House £6.90. ♿📦✗; 📞 01481 235 571. www.sausmarez manor.co.uk), also home to a subtropical garden and an "art park" with 150–250 pieces of sculpture. Copper, tin and silversmiths may be seen at work; other attractions include golf and train rides. Not to be confused with the Manor, **Saumarez Park**★ is the venue for the annual **Battle of Flowers**, a famous parade held on the fourth Thursday in August, originally started in 1902 to celebrate the coronation of Edward VII.

Sons and daughters

The most famous name connected with Jersey is **Lillie Langtry** (1853–1929), the "Jersey Lily" who became an actress and captivated British high society with her beauty and who was also a close friend of Edward VII – she is buried in St Saviour's churchyard.
The fashionable 19C painter, **Sir John Everett Millais** (1829–96), who won acclaim with his painting entitled *Bubbles*, grew up in Jersey and belonged to an old island family. So too did **Elinor Glyn** (1864–1943), who became a novelist and Hollywood scriptwriter.
The well-known French firm which makes Martell brandy was founded by **Jean Martell** from St Brelade.

Afterwards the floats are broken up and the crowd pelt each other with flowers. The **Guernsey Folk Museum**★ (NT; 🕓 open late Mar–mid-Oct daily 10am–5pm; ✆£4; 📦; 📞01481 255 384; www. nationaltrust-gsy.org.gg) is housed in the outbuildings of the manor.
Halfway between St Peter Port and Guernsey Airport is the **German Military Underground Museum** (Les Eperons, La Vassalerie; 🕓 open daily Apr–Oct 10am–noon, 2pm–4pm Nov and Mar limited opening, call for times; ✆£3.50; 📞01481 239100). The largest construction in the Channel Islands, yet almost invisible from the surface, this tunnel complex covers 1.7acres/0.7ha. It was hewn out of solid rock by slave workers of many nationalities.
The island's most notable **prehistoric remains** are the burial chambers **Déhus Dolmen** (north), **le Trépied Dolmen** (west) and **La Gran'mère du Chimquière**, a Stone Age figure at the gate to St Martin's churchyard. A similar female figure stands outside the 12C church of **Ste Marie du Câtel** which also contains 13C frescoes. Guernsey's satellite islands, **Alderney**, **Herm** and **Sark**★★are well worth a visit. Sark has stayed remarkably remote from modern society, to the extent of being totally free of cars.

ADDRESSES

🛏 STAY

JERSEY

Au Caprice, *Route de la Haule, St Brelade*. ☎01534 722 083. www.aucapricejersey.com. Light and airy white guesthouse close to a large sandy beach; good value, homely rooms.

GUERNSEY

La Michele, *Les Hubits, St Martin*. ☎01481 238 065. www.lamichelehotel.com.
This 16-room hotel enjoys a quiet country location, a short walk from picturesque Fermain Bay. Conservatory lounge, secluded garden and small pool. Tariff includes breakfast and evening meal.

🍽 EAT

JERSEY

Borsalino Rocque, *La Rocque*. ☎01534 852 111. This long-established family business, 8mi/12km from St Helier specialises in seafood and offers a wide choice of menus.

Old Court House Inn, *St Aubin's Harbour*. ☎01534 746 433. www.old-courthousejersey.com. This atmospheric 15C inn offers a cosmopolitan menu with a seafood emphasis.

GUERNSEY

Fleur du Jardin, *Kings Mills, Castel*. ☎01481 257 996. www.fleurdujardin.com. Set in the heart of the island, the beamed restaurant of this 15C hotel inn offers daily seafood menus.

Cheltenham ★
Gloucestershire

The benefits of the waters of this most elegant of English spas were discovered early in the 18C but it was at its most fashionable in the Regency period, when it developed the Classical architecture, squares, terraces and crescents in a delightful setting of trees and gardens which are still its pride today. Despite its older residents and retirement-home status it has an animated cultural life, with internationally important musical and literary festivals. The Cotswolds rear up northwest of the town and Cheltenham is also an excellent centre for exploring the Severn Vale, the Wye Valley, the Forest of Dean and the Malvern Hills.

TOWN CENTRE★
Of pre-spa Cheltenham there remains the secluded Church of St Mary and the line of the much re-built High Street. At right angles is the **Promenade**; its spacious lower part is lined on one side by the **Municipal Offices**, an imposing terrace of 1823; its upper part, twice as

▶ **Population:** 91 301.
▣ **Michelin Map:** Michelin Atlas p 17 or Map 503 N 28.
▣ **Info:** 77 Promenade. ☎01242 522 878. www.visitcheltenham.gov.uk.
▶ **Location:** Cheltenham is 55mi/88km north of Bath and 96mi/155km west of London. The train station is on Queen's Road, around 1mi/1.6km east of the centre, the bus station is central on Royal Well Road. Most points of interest are on The Promenade or the High Street. Walking tours depart from the tourist office (late-Jun–mid-Sept Mon–Fri 11am, Sat 11.30am. £4.)
▣ **Don't Miss:** The Promenade, one of the country's prettiest main streets, or a glass of Cheltenham mineral water at the Pump Room.
▣ **Timing:** Allow half a day for town, extra for excursions.

broad, rises gently to the stately stuccoed façade of the **Queen's Hotel** of 1838. To the east are the **Imperial Gardens**, a floral cocktail in summer; to the west, behind an avenue of trees, are some of the refined **Regency houses** with classical details and exquisite balcony ironwork which characterise the town. Farther south is **Montpellier Walk**, whose mid-19C shop-fronts are divided up by Grecian caryatids; it terminates in the colonnade and dome of **Montpellier Spa** (now a bank).

Cheltenham Art Gallery and Museum

🕐 *Open year-round Mon–Sat 10am (11am first Thu in month)–5pm (8pm third Thu in month).* 🕐*Closed bank hols, Easter and Dec 25–6.* ♿✕. *🖉01242 237 431. www.cheltenhammuseum.org.uk.* Among the paintings, porcelain and pottery and local exhibits is a good **collection of applied art** illustrating the importance of the Cotswolds in the Arts and Crafts movement.

PITTVILLE

This distinguished district of Classical terraces and villas (*1mi/1.6 km north of the High Street*) was laid out in the early 19C by Joseph Pitt. In romantic **Pittville Park** great trees and sweeping lawns surround a picturesque lake.

Pittville Pump Room★

🕐 *Open year-round Wed–Mon 10am–4pm.* 🕐 *Closed bank hol Mons, Dec 25–26.* 🅿. *🖉01242 523 852. www.pittvillepumproom.org.uk.* During the Regency this was the most magnificent of several buildings where the spa waters were taken. This outstanding Grecian building (1825–30), with its Ionic colonnade and domed interior, was designed by Joseph Pitt. You may enter as long as there is not a function on, and sample a glass of water.

Holst Birthplace Museum

4 Clarence Road, Pittville. 🕐 *Open mid-Jan–mid-Dec Tue–Sat (and some bank hols) 10am–4pm.* ⊛*£3.50.* *🖉01242 524 846. www.holstmuseum.org.uk.*

Near the park entrance is the Regency house where Gustav Holst, composer of *The Planets*, was born in 1874.

EXCURSIONS
Deerhurst

7mi/12km north of Cheltenham via the A 4019, the A 38 and a minor road west. Deerhurst (village population 100) possesses two important **Anglo-Saxon** buildings.

Once part of a flourishing monastery, parts of **St Mary's Church**★ (🕐*open daily 8.30am–dusk;* ♿; *🖉01684 292 562;)* date from the 8C, and it is strongly Saxon in character.

Odda's Chapel *(EH;* 🕐*open year-round daily Apr–Sept 10am–6pm, Nov–Mar 4pm;* 🕐*closed Jan 1, Dec 25–26;* 🅿*; www. english-heritage.org.uk)* was dedicated by Earl Odda in 1056 and consists of a nave and chancel, both of touching simplicity. It was re-discovered in the 19C, having served as the kitchen of the adjoining farmhouse.

Tewkesbury★

8mi/13km north of Cheltenham on the A 4019 and A 38.

This little Saxon town is dominated by the great Norman abbey church. Tewkesbury grew little in the 19C and has conserved its historic character almost intact.

Tewkesbury Abbey★★

Church Street.🕐*Open year-round daily 7.30am–6pm (Sunday 7pm, winter 5.30pm).* ⟐ *Guided tour Easter–Oct (£3).* ♿✕. *🖉01684 850 959. www.tewkesburyabbey.org.uk.* The church, once part of a wealthy and important Benedictine abbey, combines a noble simplicity of structure with great richness of detail, and many of the abbey's noble benefactors are buried here. At the Dissolution it was saved from demolition by the townsfolk, who bought it for £453.

The most impressive elements are the huge 12C **tower** and the grandeur of the **west front**, with its recessed arch (65ft/20m high).

The Norman **nave**★★, is covered by a beautiful 14C vault which replaced an earlier timber roof. The church's many monuments are grouped around the choir. Bishop Wakeman is grotesquely commemorated by a **memento mori**, a decomposing cadaver crawling with vermin.

The 14C **stained-glass windows** of the choir depict local notables. The choir **vault**★ is a gloriously intricate web of ribs and bosses.

There are two survivals from monastic days – the **Abbey House** and the **Gatehouse**, just outside the precinct.

Sudeley Castle★

7mi/11km northeast of Cheltenham via the B 4632. Castle Street Winchcombe. ◷*Open Apr–Oct 10.30am–5pm.* ⊷*£7.20.* ♿🅿✕. ℘*01242 602 308.* *www.sudeleycastle.co.uk.*

The house is surrounded by the dramatic scenery of the Cotswold escarpment. Once a medieval stronghold, it was also the home of **Katherine Parr**, widow of Henry VIII, besieged and largely destroyed in the Civil War. In the 19C the house was restored, although some parts were left ruined. The collection includes Turner, Van Dyck and Rubens.

Cornish Coast★★★

Cornwall

Remoteness and wildness are the charms of the Cornwall peninsula with its long rugged coastline. The Cornwall Coast Path – part of the larger Southwest Coast Path – winds a sinuous course (268mi/430km) above the sheer cliffs and indented coves and is the ideal way to discover the scenic splendours of the peninsula. The footpath is clearly waymarked and there is a wide choice of inland paths as shortcuts.

DRIVING TOUR

1 SOUTH COAST

Immediately west of the bustling historic city of Plymouth the picture-postcard villages and beaches of holiday-makers' Cornwall begin. The relatively sheltered conditions here make this a yachtsman's paradise. Inland the climate is also benevolent, encouraging some of England's finest gardens.

TRURO TO PLYMOUTH
Truro

54mi/86km southwest of Plymouth. Population 16,522. Info: Municipal Buildings, Boscawen Street.

- ♿ **Michelin Map:** Michelin Atlas pp 2, 3 or Map 503 D to H 32, 33.
- ✺ **Don't Miss:** *Southwest Tip:* Tate St Ives, Land's End cliff scenery, Minack Open-Air Theatre, St Michael's Mount. *South Coast:* The Eden Project, Trewithen Garden, Fowey.
- ◷ **Timing:** *Southwest Tip:* Allow a day in St Ives, at least two days for excursions. *South Coast:* Allow four days.
- 👪 **Kids:** *North Coast:* Newquay Zoo. *Southwest Tip:* Wonderful beaches, Land's End, Geevor Tin Mine. *South Coast:* National Seal Sanctuary, Kynance Cove, Mullion Cove.
- 🅿 **Parking:** Park on the edge of towns and villages as the streets can be narrow.

℘*01872 274555. www.truro.gov.uk. 11 Market Strand, Prince of Wales Pier, Falmouth.* ℘*01326 312 300. www.acornishriver.co.uk.*
Truro, once a river port and mining centre, is the most notable Georgian town west of Bath, with a host of 18C houses and and a more recent cathedral.

Trewithen Garden

©Charles Francis/Trewithen Gardens

Just south of St Clement Street is **Truro Cathedral** (⏰*open year-round Mon–Sat 7.30am–6pm, Sun 9am–7pm.Bank hols 9.30am–6pm;* 🚶*Guided tours Apr–Oct Mon–Thu and Sat 11am, Fri 11.30am, school hols Mon–Fri 2pm;* ♿✕; ☎*01872 276 782; www.trurocathedral.org.uk*). Completed 1910, the building is has a mixture of Normandy Gothic with upswept vaulting, vistas through tall arcades and, outside, three steeple towers which give the building its characteristic outline.

Four minutes walk west (via Boscawen Street) of the cathedral is the **Royal Cornwall Museum**★★ *(River Street;* ⏰*open year-round Mon–Sat 10am–4.45pm:* ⏰*closed bank hols;* ♿✕; ☎*01872 272 205; www.royalcornwallmuseum.org.uk*).Cornwall's oldest and most prestigious museum is the repository for a variety of artefacts relating to the geology, archeology and social history of Cornwall as well as a collection of fine and decorative arts.

▷ *Head south via the A 39 and B 3289.*

Trelissick Garden★★

NT. Feock, nr Truro. ⏰ *Open mid-Feb–late Oct daily 10.30am–5.30pm. Rest of year daily 11am–4pm.* ✎*£7.* ♿✕. ☎*01872 862 090. www.nationaltrust.org.uk.*

From the gardens beyond the Classical, porticoed house (built 1750, remodelled 1825), there are superb **views**★★ over the park, Falmouth and out to sea. The woodland dropping down to the river has a variety of trees, shrubs, exotics and perennials. Spacious areas of lawn feature hydrangeas (over 130 varieties), azaleas and rhododendrons. The Cornish Apple Orchard has been created to preserve as many traditional varieties of apple as possible.

▷ *B 3289 and the **King Harry Ferry** across the Carrick Roads (Fal Estuary).*

St Just-in-Roseland★★

The **church** here, built on a 6C Celtic site in the 13C and restored in the 19C, has a remarkable setting in an enchanting, steep churchyard garden. The church stands so close to the creek and little harbour that at high tide it is reflected in the water.

St Mawes★

In 1539–43 Henry VIII constructed this cloverleaf-shaped **castle**★ *(EH.* ⏰*open Jul–Aug Sun–Fri 10am–6pm, Apr–Jun and Sept Sun–Fri 10am–5pm, Nov–late Mar Fri–Mon 10am–1pm, 2pm–4pm;* ⏰*closed 1 Jan and 24–26 Dec;* ✎*£3.90; ☎01326 270 52; www.english-heritage.org.uk*), with motte and bailey, as a pair with Pendennis Castle on the opposite bank of the Fal to safeguard the mile-wide entrance to the estuary. Situated in pleasant gardens, it affords excellent

views★ right out to Manacle Point 10mi/16km south.

Veryan★
This village's unique charm comes from four curious little white-walled **round houses** with Gothic windows and conical thatched roofs, surmounted by a cross.

Trewithen★★★
Grampground Road.
Garden: *Open Mar–Sept Mon–Sat (also Sun Mar–May), 10am–4.30pm. ⊚£5.* **House:** *Visit by guided tour Apr–Jul Mon–Tue and Aug bank hols 2pm–4pm (last entry). ⊚£5.75. 01726 883 647, 01726 882764. www.trewithengardens.co.uk.*
The estate is famous for its 28 acres/11ha of beautiful landscape and woodland **gardens** which include, in season, magnificent banks of rhododendrons, camellias and magnolias. The gardens provide an elegant setting for a fine Georgian **country house** (1715–55) containing period furniture, paintings and porcelain.

Mevagissey★★
This picturesque old fishing village, with its old quayside boathouses and sail lofts, maze of twisting backstreets and nets of all shapes and colours drying on walls, attracts crowds of visitors all summer. It boasts an unusual double harbour with a 1770s pier.

Lost Gardens of Heligan★
Pentewan. ◷ *Open year-round daily 10am–6pm (5pm Oct–Mar). Last entry 90 mins before closing.* ◷ *Closed 24–25 Dec. ⊚£8.50. 01726 845 100. www.heligan.com.*
These 57 acre/23ha gardens, originally laid out in the 18C by Thomas Gray but left to grow wild by the 20C, have been painstakingly recovered from dereliction since 1991. They include Flora's Garden (rhododendrons), a walled vegetable garden, fruit orchards, "The Jungle"

(exotic trees planted in the 19C) and "The Lost Valley" (indigenous species and a water-meadow).

▷ *The road follows St Austell Bay.*

Fowey★★
🛈 *5 South Street. 01726 833 616.*
First settlement around Fowey date to the 11C. This small town (pronounced "foy"), on the hillside above an excellent natural harbour at the mouth of the river Fowey, was once one of England's busiest ports. It is well worth walking out

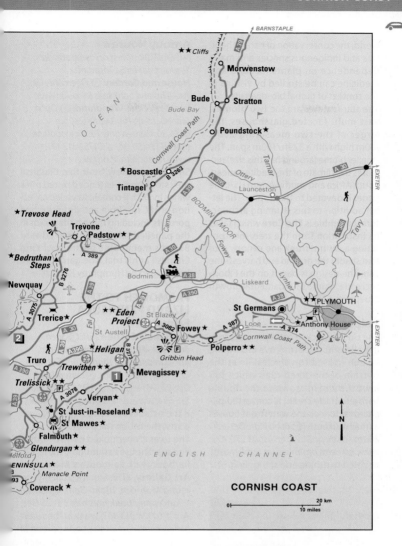

BARNSTAPLE

★★ *Cliffs*

Morwenstow

Bude • **Stratton**
Bude Bay

Poundstock ★

★ **Boscastle** B 3263

Tintagel Ottery

Launceston

OCEAN

Tamar

EXETER

A 30

BODMIN MOOR

★ *Trevose Head*

Trevone

Padstow ★

Camel

Fowey

★ *Bedruthan Steps* A 389

B 3276

Bodmin A 38

Newquay Liskeard

A 390

Lynher

Tavy

EXETER

A 3075

Trerice ★

★★ *Eden Project*

St Blazey

A 3082 **Fowey** ★

St Austell

St Germans

★★ **PLYMOUTH**

Anthony House

Truro

A 390

★ *Heligan*

Gribbin Head

Polperro ★★

Cornwall Coast Path

Looe

A 374

Trewithen ★★

Mevagissey ★

Trelissick ★★

Veryan ★

St Just-in-Roseland ★★

St Mawes ★

N

Falmouth ★

Glendurgan ★★

Helford

ENGLISH CHANNEL

ENINSULA ★

Manacle Point

Coverack ★

CORNISH COAST

20 km

10 miles

to **Gribbin Head**, from where there are **views**★★ for miles around, and also taking a **boat trip** round the harbour and coast where the cliffs rise dark and sheer from the water, or up-river between wooded hillsides.

In town, walk along **Fore Street**, lined with picturesque old houses, and visit the 14–15C **church of St Nicholas** (on the site of a Norman church dedicated to St Fimbarrus), with its tall, pinnacled tower, two-storey porch in Decorated style, fine wagon roof and Norman font of Catacleuse stone.

Eden Project★★

5mi/8km northwest of Fowey via the A3082 to St Blazey. Bodelva. ○ *Open daily late Mar–late Oct 10am–6pm. Late Oct–late Mar daily 10am–4.30pm. Last admission 90 mins before closing.* ○*Closed Dec 24–25.* ○£15. ♿️🅿️✕. ✆01726 811911. www.edenproject.com. An abandoned china-clay pit (197ft/60m deep) has been converted into an extraordinary gigantic botanical "green theme park" project, which has been both critically acclaimed and a huge commercial success. Here the plant world, the conservation of natural habitats and indigenous species and man's dependence on plants for food and medicine can be studied by visitors in the context of global bio-diversity.

The star features are the two **biomes**, vast multi-faceted glasshouses, the larger of the two measuring 200ft /60m high with a 329ft/100m span. The smaller biome (around half this size) recreates the climate of the Mediterranean, South Africa and southwestern USA; the larger is devoted to the tropics. The latest addition to this stunning architectural ensemble is **The Core** which takes its inspiration from the tree, incorporating a central trunk and canopy roof that shades the ground and harvests the sun. The design is based on the Fibonacci code, nature's fundamental growth blueprint.

Polperro★

The closely-packed cottages and winding alleys of this attractive old fishing village (closed to vehicles) lie at the bottom of the steep road which follows the stream down to the double harbour in the creek. A converted pilchard factory on the waterfront houses a small **museum** (⟳ open Mar–Oct daily 10am–6pm; ⟷£1.75; ✆01503 272 423; www.polperro.org/museum.html) mostly devoted to fishing and smuggling.

Lizard coastline
R. Besse/MICHELIN

Antony House★

NT. 6mi/10km west of Plymouth via Torpoint car ferry. Torpoint.
House and Garden: ⟳ Open Apr–Oct Tue–Thu and bank hols (also Jun–Aug Sun) 1pm–5pm. **Woodland:** ⟳ Open Mar–Oct Sat–Thu 11am–5.30pm. ⟷£6.30; Garden only £3.25; woodland (not NT) £4.50. ✗. ✆01752 812 191. www.nationaltrust.org.uk.

Sir William Carew built this Classical grey stone house extended by red brick wings in 1721. It contains a varied collection of 18C furniture and distinguished portraits, including three by Reynolds in the panelled salon and one of Edward Bower's memorable portraits of King Charles I at his trial. The gardens were landscaped by Humphrey Repton.

FALMOUTH TO THE LIZARD PENINSULA
Falmouth★

Pendennis Castle★ (EH. ⟳open daily: Jul–Aug 10am–6pm/Sat 4pm, Apr–Jun and Sept 10am–5pm/Sat 4pm, Oct–Mar 10am–4pm; ⟳closed Jan 1, Dec 24–26; ⟷£5.40; ♿❑✗; ✆01326 316 594; www.english-heritage.org.uk), is the sister to **St Mawes** (⟳see above) across the Fal, on the point.

The river is overlooked by 18C houses and warehouses standing on the 17C harbour wall. Falmouth's **Municipal Art Gallery**, (The Moor; ⟳open year-round Mon–Sat 10am–5pm; ⟳closed 1 Jan, winter bank hols and 25–26 Dec; ♿; ✆01326 313 863; www.falmouthartgallery.com), contains a good selection of maritime, Victorian and early 20C paintings. Housed in an award-winning new building on the waterfront, the **National Maritime Museum Cornwall** (⟳ open year-round daily 10am–5pm; ⟳Closed 25–26 Dec; ⟷£8.75; ♿❑✗; ✆01326 313 388; www.nmmc.co.uk), documents local maritime history including smuggling, myths and superstition and the small ship-building industry.

Glendurgan Garden★★

NT. Mawnan Smith, nr Falmouth.
⟳ Open mid-Feb–Oct Tue–Sat; Aug, Mon, 10.30am–5.30pm. ⟳ Closed Good

Fri. £5.76. *P* 01326 250 906.
www.nationaltrust.org.uk.
This beautiful garden, richly planted
with subtropical trees and shrubs, drops
down to Durgan hamlet on the Helford
River. It is home to an interesting laurel
maze and a maypole.

Lizard Peninsula★
This southern-most part of England is
famous for its rocky coves and its glossy
green and black-velvet serpentine stone.
The National Seal Sanctuary★(;
Gweek. Open summer daily from 10am,
call for winter opening times; closed 25
Dec; £12.95, child £9.95 (book online for
significant discounts); *P* 01326
221 361; www.sealsanctuary.co.uk), set
on the picturesque **Helford Estuary**
has been rescuing seals for 50 years and
always has a number of cute residents.
On the south side of the estuary is the
Manacles (an underwater reef responsible for many a shipwreck); the famous
old fishing and smuggling village of
Coverack★; **Landewednack**★ with its
thatched roofs and **church**★ decorated
with serpentine stone; the Lizard and
its 1751 lighthouse (altered in 1903) on
the southernmost tip of England; and
the popular picture-postcard **beaches**
of **Kynance Cove**★★ and **Mul-
lion Cove**★★. **Helston** is the peninsula's
market town.

2a. NORTH COAST
This is arguably the most dramatic
stretch of the Cornish peninsula, in
places harsh and forbidding, formerly
feared by mariners for its wrecking
potential. Yet it is also home to beautiful
golden sand beaches, the most popular
of which are at **Newquay**, Britain's premier surf resort.

MORWENSTOW TO ST AGNES BEACON
North–south on A39 and coastal B roads.

Morwenstow
Cornwall's northernmost parish boasts
a fine **church**★ with a Norman door and
spectacular **cliffs**★★ (450ft/133m high)
reaching out to offshore rocks.

Dancing Furries
On 8 May (or the previous Saturday if this falls on a Sunday or
Monday), Helston town is closed
to traffic for the famous **Flora Day
Furry Dance**★★. Five processional
dances are performed along a
1.8–2.4mi/3–4km route (beginning and ending at the Guildhall),
including the children's procession
at 10am and the Invitation Dance
for couples at noon.

Bude
This cliffside harbour town is a popular
resort with golden sandy beaches and
breakers ideal for surfing. The **breakwater**★★ has a good sea view.

Poundstock★
The 13–15C **church**★, with its square
unbuttressed tower and square 14C
font, the lychgate and the unique,
sturdily-built 14C **guildhouse**★ form a
secluded group in a wooded dell.

Boscastle★
Off the B 3263. The pretty village strag-
gles downhill to a picturesque natural
harbour inlet between 300ft/91m
headlands.

Tintagel
17mi/27km SW of Bude.
Population 1,721. P 01840 779 084.
www.visitboscastleandtintagel.com.
Tintagel in particular and the West
Country in general are associated with
the elusive legend of **Arthur**, "the once
and future king". The story lives on, per-
petuated by tourism and the New Age
movement.
Tintagel Castle *(EH; open daily late
Mar–Sept 10am–6pm, Oct 10am–5pm,
Nov–Mar 10am–4pm; closed 1 Jan and
24–26 Dec; £4.60; P 01840 770 328;
www.english-heritage.org.uk)* occupies
a dramatic **site**★★★, which overlooks
the sea from precipitous rocks. The site
is more impressive than the fragmentary
castle ruin, which includes walls from
the 1145 chapel and great hall, built on
the site of a 6C Celtic monastery, and

Old Post Office, Tintagel

N. Benavides/MICHELIN

other walls dating from the 13C – all centuries after Arthur's time.

On Fore Street, which leads from the B3263 to the castle, is the **Old Post Office**★ (NT; ○open daily mid-Mar–Sept 11am–5.30pm, mid-Feb–Mar and Oct 11am–4pm; ≈£3; ℘0840 770 024; www.nationaltrust.org.uk), a small manor house with thick walls and undulating slate roofs dating from the 14C. The atmospheric, compact house has simple country furniture and a delightful cottage garden.

Padstow★

The harbour is enclosed by quays lined with attractive old houses, while a network of narrow streets behind the quay ends at **St Petroc's Church** and **Prideaux Place**★ (○open Easter week and mid May–early Oct, Sun–Thu 1.30pm–4pm (last tour); grounds open Sun–Thu 12.30pm–5pm; ≈£7. 50, grounds only £2; ℘01841 532 411; www.prideauxplace. co.uk), an Elizabethan house with 18C battlements, set in gardens and landscaped parkland.

Trevone

The **Cornwall Coast Path**★★ (5mi/8km on foot) is a spectacular way of reaching Trevone from Padstow, circling the 242ft/74m Stepper Point and passing the natural rock arches of Porthmissen Bridge. The village and chapel (with a slate spire) stand in a small, sandy cove guarded by fierce offshore rocks. A large

blowhole leading directly down to the sea can be found in one of the cliffs.

Trevose Head★

6mi/9km west on the B 3276 and by-roads; last half-mile on foot.
From the lighthouse on the 243ft/74m head, it is possible to see that of Hartland Point, 40mi/64km northeast, and that of Pendeen on West Penwith. The **views**★★ take in bay after sandy cove after rocky island.

Bedruthan Steps★

NT. **Cliff staircase:** ○Open Mar–Oct. ✕.
The arc of sand (1mi/1.5km) spectacularly scattered with giant rocks worn to the same angle by waves and wind is visible over the cliff edge. Legend has it that the rocks were the stepping stones of the giant Bedruthan.

Newquay

This popular resort, with its sandy beaches, lies at the foot of cliffs in a sheltered, north-facing bay.
By the 18C Newquay was a pilchard port, exporting salted fish to Italy and Spain. The **Huar's House** on the headland, from which the huar summoned the fishermen when he saw shoals of fish enter the bay, dates from this period. Newquay has recently enjoyed a surfing-led revival and hosts world-class competitions.
In Trenance Gardens in the centre of Newquay, east of Edgcumbe Avenue,

is **Newquay Zoo**★ (👥👤; ⏱ *open daily Apr–Sept 9.30am–6pm, Oct 10am–5pm;* 👓*£6.27 summer, child £4.27;* ♿🅿; 📞*01637 873342; www.newquayzoo. co.uk),* which specialises in breeding many endangered species. Newquay Zoo is One of the UK's best wildlife parks, at the forefront of conservation and education, and in innovative enclosure design.

Trerice★

NT. Kestle Mill. ⏱ *Open mid-Mar–early Nov 11am (garden 10.30am)–5pm Sun–Fri.* 👓*£6.40. Garden only, £2.20.* ♿🅿✕*, picnic area.* 📞*01637 875 404. www.nationaltrust.org.uk.*
This small, silver-grey stone Elizabethan **manor house** was rebuilt 1572–73. The east front has a highly ornate exterior and interior notable for the quality of its 16C **plasterwork** and fine furniture.

St Agnes Beacon★★

The beacon, at 628ft/191m, affords a **panorama**★★ from Trevose Head to St Michael's Mount, with the typical north Cornish landscape, windswept and speared by old mine stacks.

2 b. ST IVES TO PENWITH

St Ives–St Michael's Mount.
Britain's southwestern extremity is most famous for Land's End with its spectacular cliffs and coastal scenery staring out to America. On the northern coast arty, crafty **St Ives** is one of the West Country's favourite resorts while immediately south, Penzance and Newlyn continue the age-old Cornish fishing tradition. **The Lizard** is another intriguing peninsula, both in name and character; like the North Cornish coast, it is rocky and rugged but dotted with perfect little beaches.

ST IVES★★

17mi/28km northeast of Land's End. Population 10,092. Info: The Guildhall, Street-an-Pol. 📞*01736 796 297. www.visit-westcornwall.com.*
This picturesque fishing harbour on the north Cornish coast is a much-visited summer resort and has been a favourite

Window for St Ives (1992) by Patrick Heron, Tate St Ives
©Tate St Ives

with artists since the 1880s when Whistler and Sickert followed in the footsteps of Turner.
Today its network of stepped winding alleys and hillside terraces, all lined by colour-washed, slate-roofed fishermen's houses, crowded shoulder to shoulder is still home to a working artists' community.

Tate St Ives★★

Porthmeor Beach. ⏱*Open Mar–Oct daily 10am–5.20pm. Nov–Feb Tue–Sun 10am–4.20pm.* ⏱*Closed Dec 24–26.* 👓*£5.75, joint admission to Barbara Hepworth Museum £8.75.* ♿✕. 📞*01736 796 226. www.tate.org.uk/stives.*
This splendid building (1973) enjoys a **view**★★ over the sands of Porthmeor Beach. The asymmetrical gallery consists of swirling forms spiralling upwards while inside, stairways climb through airy space for access to the changing exhibitions of post-war modern works from the London Tate collection. These concentrate particularly on artists associated with St Ives including Alfred Wallis, Ben Nicholson, Barbara Hepworth, John Wells, Terry Frost and Patrick Heron (who designed the stained glass window on the ground floor). A number of ceramics works by Bernard Leach are also on display.

Barbara Hepworth Museum★★

Barnoon Hill. ⏱*Admission details as Tate St Ives (👆see above). Restricted admission during high season.*

Penwith coastline

R Reese/MICHELIN

Barbara Hepworth (1903–75) came to St Ives with Ben Nicholson in 1943, decided to settle, and stayed here until her death. The house she lived in, filled with sleek, polished wood and stone abstract **sculptures** spanning a life's work, and workshops with unfinished blocks of stone, left pretty much as they were at the artist's death, contrast with the small white-walled garden which provides a serene setting for some twenty abstract compositions in bronze and stone.

Parish Church★

The church dates mostly from the 15C and is dedicated to the fishermen-Apostles St Peter and St Andrew, and St Ia, the early missionary who arrived in the area from across the sea on a leaf and after whom the town is named. It stands by the harbour, distinguished by its pinnacled 85ft/26m tower of Zennor granite. Note the **wagon roof**, carved **bench ends** and stone **font**. The **Lady Chapel** contains the tender *Mother and Child* (1953) by Barbara Hepworth.

Smeaton Pier

The pier and its octagonal domed lookout were constructed in 1767–70 by the builder of the third Eddystone lighthouse, John Smeaton. At its shore end is the small St Leonard's sailors' chapel.

St Nicholas Chapel – The chapel on the "island" is the traditional seamen's chapel built as a beacon. It commands a wide **view★★** across the bay.

PENWITH★★
35mi/58km.

Penwith is the most westerly headland in England. Much of the area is a semi-bare plateau standing around 130m above sea level. This sparsely populated region has its own bleak beauty deriving from its granite foundation, the wind, the blue of the ocean and its small granite churches and Celtic wayside crosses. Leave the coast road for clifftop views. Penwith has many fine beaches. The principal towns of this largely rural district are Penzance and St Ives.

Zennor

The outdoor **Wayside Folk Museum** (◯ *open Apr–Oct Sun–Fri 11am–5pm also Sat during summer school and bank hols.* ◎*£3.25;* 🅿; ✆*01736 796 945*), set in an old miller's house, shows the evolution of implements from stone to iron. The 12C–13C granite **church★**, on a 6C site, was enlarged in the 15C and restored in the 19C. Inside are a tithe measure, now serving as a holy water stoup, two fonts of Hayle limestone and, on a bench-end, the 16C carving of the pretty **Mermaid of Zennor**.

Chysauster Ancient Village★

EH. ○*Open Apr–Oct daily 10am–5pm (6pm Jul–Aug, 4pm Oct).* ☞*£2.50.* ▣*.* ✆*07831 757 934. www.english-heritage.org.uk.*

This well-preserved prehistoric Cornish village was inhabited c. 100 BC–AD 250. It consists of at least eight circular stone houses, which would originally have been roofed with turf or thatch, in two lines of four just below the crest of the hill.

Geevor Tin Mine

Near Pendeen lighthouse. Pendeen. ○*Open Easter–Oct daily from 9am (tours 10am–4pm); last admission 3pm. Nov–Easter reduced hours (3 tours per day, 11am, 1pm, 3pm). Call or visit website for details.* ○*Closed Christmas week, 1 Jan.* ☞*£8.50, child £4.50.* ▣✗*. ✆01736 788 662. www.geevor.com.*

Until its closure in 1990 Geevor was a working tin mine, with almost 300 years of history. The miners not only searched for tin deep underground but also in shafts which went far below the sea. Today it is the largest preserved mining site in the UK with many surface buildings open to the public and a guided underground tour through 18C and 19C century workings, often with former employees who worked the mine. It also features a museum, which explains how tin was extracted and processed, as well as a mineral gallery.

St Just-in-Penwith

The prosperity enjoyed by this 19C mining town is reflected in the substantial buildings lining the triangular square, the fine terraces of cottages and the large Methodist chapel. The **church**★ features a 15C pinnacled tower, dressed granite walls, an elaborate 16C porch, wall paintings and a 5C tomb in the north aisle.

A mile to the west (partly on foot), the hillock of **Cape Cornwall**★ rises 230ft/70m, giving **views**★★ of Brisons Rocks, Land's End and the Longships Lighthouse. Just before reaching Land's End, the road passes through the little village of Sennen, home to the most westerly church in England (walk down to **Sennen Cove**★, 20min there and back, for a good **view**★ of Whitesand Bay, Brisons Rocks and Cape Cornwall).

Land's End★

The attraction of Land's End is less its physical beauty (and much less its visitor attractions) than its position at the western-most point of England, overlooking some of the finest local cliff **scenery**★★★ perpetually assailed by the surging swell of the Atlantic. For a peaceful view, come early and walk along the coastal path, or come at sunset and wait for the beams from the lighthouses to add a magical touch. Ramblers and walkers can approach along the Cornwall Coastal Path.

Part of Land's End has been commandeered by a mini theme park, also known as **Land's End** (*Site:* ○*open daily 10am–dusk;* **Attractions:** ○ *open Easter–Oct 10am–4pm/5pm, later at peak times, Nov–Easter 11am–4pm;* ○*closed 24–25 Dec and 2 Jan–1 Feb;* ☞*inclusive ticket £10.95, child £6.95, or pay per attraction £3–£4, child £2–£3;* ♿▣*(£4)* ✗*; ✆0870 4580 099; www.landsend-landmark.co.uk).* This comprises two **multi-media experiences** (*Last Labyrinth* and *Air Sea Rescue*); exhibitions on the **End to End Story** (devoted to the select band who have completed the length of Britain from Land's End to John O'Groats) and *Coast*, based on the popular TV series plus a **Doctor Who** exhibition and a farm.

Carry on along the B 3315, leaving the road to view the idyllic sheltered cove of **Porthcurno**★. Overlooking it is the famous **Minack Open-Air Theatre**★, (○*performances May–late-Sep, Mon–Fri at 8pm; also Wed and Fri at 2pm.* ☞*£7.50. ✆01736 810 181. www.minack.com)* founded in 1929 with its stunning ocean back-drop and views over Lamornae. The theatre's fascinating history is recounted in the **Visitor Centre** (○ *Open Apr–Oct most days 9.30/10am–5/5.30pm; Nov–mid-Mar, 10am–4pm;* ☞*£3.50.* ▣✗*; ✆01736 810 181; www.minack.com)* which gives access to the theatre (☞*performances £8.50).*

Mousehole★

Mousehole ("Mowzel") is an attractive village. Its **harbour** is protected by a quay of Lamorna granite and a **breakwater** dating from 1393. Set back from the low granite fishermen's cottages at the water's edge is the half-timbered Keigwin Arms, the only house left standing after a Spanish raid in 1595.

Newlyn★

Newlyn is the major fishing village in the southwest with a large fleet that brings in mackerel, whitefish, lobster, crab and – its signature fish – pilchards (adult sardines). The beautiful light and the charm of the cottages clustered round the harbour and on the hillside attracted a group of painters who founded the famous **Newlyn School** in the 1880s. Their works are on display in the recently refurbished **Newlyn Art Gallery** (open Easter–Oct Mon–Sat 10am–5pm, bank hols 11am–4pm, Nov–Easter Tue–Sat 10am–5pm; closed 25–26 Dec, 1 Jan; 01736 363 715; www.newlyn artgallery.co.uk).

Penzance★

This busy market town, built largely post-1800, has been a popular holiday resort for over 150 years (since the arrival of the Great Western Railway). The half-mile long **Western Promenade** reflects 19C Penzance's importance as a resort. The harbour area has a wonderful **outlook**★★★ over Mount's Bay and St Michael's Mount. It is from here that the MV **Scillonian III** sails to the **Isles of Scilly** (also served by Penzance Heliport, weather permitting). The town centre, particularly **Market Jew Street** and **Chapel Street**★, boasts some attractive 17C, 18C and 19C buildings including Market House, the surprising Egyptian House (1835), Abbey House and The Admiral Benbow. Close by, the **Penlee House Gallery and Museum**★ (Morrab Road; open Good Fri–Oct Mon–Sat 10am–5pm, Oct–Good Fri 10.30am–4.30pm; £3, Sat free; 01736 363 625; www.penleehouse.org. uk) is a centre of art and heritage for West Cornwall including a fine collection of art from 1750 to the present with works by the Newlyn School. Modern and contemporary works of art can be found in the **Exchange Gallery** (Princes Street; open, as Newlyn Art Gallery, above; 01736 363715).

Trengwainton Garden★★

NT. 2mi/3km northwest of Penzance. Open early Feb–Oct Sun–Thu and Good Friday, 10.30am–5pm. £5.20. 01736 363 148. www.nationaltrust.org.uk.
The garden's splendid rhododendron and azalea collection stems from the late 1920s when specimens were brought back from Burma, Assam and China. From here is a **view**★★ of Mount's Bay. A series of walled gardens contains magnolias and other flowering trees.

St Michael's Mount★★

NT. Causeway from Marazion. Access at high tide by ferry; at low water on foot across the sands and causeway. **Castle:** Open late Mar–Oct Mon–Fri and Sun 10.30am–5.30pm. Winter (subject to weather conditions) Tue and Fri, admission by guided tour only, 11am, 2pm. **Garden:** Open May–Jun Mon–Fri 10am–5.30pm. Jul–Oct open Thu–Fri only. £6.60. 01736 710 507, or 01736 710 265. www.stmichaels mount.co.uk. www.nationaltrust.org.uk.
According to Cornish legend, in AD 495 fishermen saw the archangel Michael on the granite rock rising out of the sea. The island became a place of pilgrimage and a Celtic monastery is said to have stood on the rock from the 8C to 11C. In c. 1150 Abbot Bernard of Mont-St-Michel, off the coast of Normandy, built a Benedictine monastery here. It was appropriated by the Crown in 1425 and dissolved in 1539. The rock frequently served as a strongpoint from the Middle Ages to 1647, when its last military commander, Colonel John St Aubyn, bought the castle as a family residence. It is now a hybrid of 14C–19C styles, with a Tudor doorway bearing the St Aubyn arms, a 14C entrance hall, a restored 14C church with 15C windows, and an 18C Rococo-Gothic drawing room.

Cotswolds ★★★
Cirencester to Chipping Campden

Rising gently from the Upper Thames valley in the southeast to a dramatic escarpment overlooking the Severn Vale in the west, the Cotswolds cover around 770sq mi/2,000sq km), encapsulating rural England in concentrated form. Airy open uplands, sheltered in places by stately belts of beech trees, alternate with deep valleys enfolding venerable golden limestone villages and small county towns.

A BIT OF HISTORY

The region has long been favoured for settlement. The commanding heights in the west are crowned more often than not by the hill-forts of prehistoric man, whose burial places also abound, from the chambered tombs of the Neolithic to the round barrows of the Bronze Age. Great estates were farmed from the Roman villas lying just off Ermin Street and the Fosse Way. In the Middle Ages it was the wool from countless sheep grazing on the fine pasture of the wolds which gave rise to a trade of European importance and to a class of prosperous merchants, whose monuments are the great "wool" churches which they built from the underlying oolitic limestone. Ranging in colour from silver or cream to deepest gold, this loveliest of building stone is synonymous with "Cotswold character". Yielding the sophisticated masonry of manor houses, the "tiles" of cottage roofs, rough-dressed walls of

- **Michelin Map:** Michelin Atlas pp 17 and 27 or Map 503 O 27 and 28.
- **Info:** 1 Cotswold Court, Broadway. ℘01386 852 937 (summer only). The Old Police Station, High Street, Chipping Campden. ℘01386 841 206. Corn Hall, Market Place, Cirencester. ℘01285 654 180. Victoria Street, Bourton-on-the-Water. ℘01451 820 211. www.visitcotswolds.co.uk.
- **Locarion:** Most of the centrally-located villages make a good base to explore from. Or you could stay in one of the surrounding towns of Oxford, Stratford, Cheltenham and Bath. Regular Cotswolds bus tours depart from all of these in summer.
- **Don't Miss:** The villages of Bibury and Chipping Campden; Chastleton House; Snowshill Manor; Hidcote Manor Garden; the view from Broadway Tower.
- **Warning:** Busy roads, crowded attractions and village centres in the summer holidays.
- **Timing:** Allow three days minimum.
- **Kids:** Cotswold Wildlife Park and Bourton-on-the-Water's many child-friendly attractions.

Chipping Campden

Y. Kanazawa/Michelin

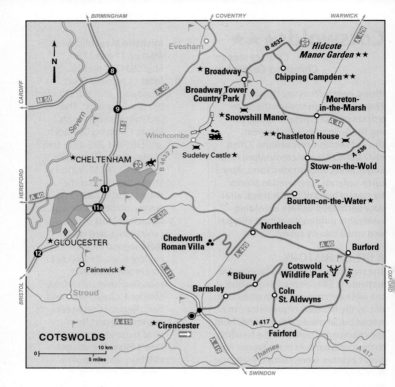

barns and even the drystone boundaries of fields, it creates a rare harmony of building and landscape.

Far removed from coalfields and big cities, the area escaped the effects of industrialisation; its rural pattern is intact, an idyllic setting for quiet exploration of the past.

DRIVING TOUR

CIRENCESTER TO CHIPPING CAMPDEN

40mi/64km; 1 day.

Starting in the Cotswolds' heart, this tour runs north through some of the region's most delightful small towns and villages towards the spectacular view from the escarpment above Broadway.

Cirencester★

The "Capital of the Cotswolds", which is still the market town for a prosperous rural region, was founded as a Roman fort, Corinium, established early in the Roman occupation at the junction of three major roads – Ermin Street, Akeman Street and the Fosse Way; by the 2C AD it had become a walled city, second only to London in size, the centre of a flourishing countryside of great villa estates. The old town is compact and has kept a traditional townscape, little marred by incongruous intrusions. It is hemmed in by the green spaces of two ancient estates: the gardens of the abbey sloping down to the pretty River Churn (the abbey buildings were demolished at the Dissolution) and the grandiose formal landscape of **Cirencester Park**, which contains the magnificent length of the **Broad Avenue** (5mi/8km) and the great house concealed from the town by a high wall and even higher yew hedge.

On Coxwell Street, the **Church of St John the Baptist (Cirencester Parish Church)**★ (🕐 *open year-round daily 9.30am–5pm (except during services);*

🕐 *closed Dec 25–26 except for services;*
📞 01285 659 317; www.acinc.org.uk) is
an important example of a Cotswold
"wool church" is of great interest and
beauty. The lofty tower of 1400–20,
supported by powerful spur buttresses,
rises grandly above the town. The unusual three-storey porch opening into the
market place once served as the town
hall. The nave is exceptionally high and
spacious; its immensely tall piers carry
angels bearing the coats of arms of
those pious townsfolk responsible for
the ambitious re-building of 1516–30.
Throughout the interior there is a wealth
of detail: an unusual pre-Reformation
pulpit; the **Boleyn Cup**, a gilt cup made
for Anne Boleyn; memorial brasses
grouped in the Chapel of the Holy Trinity; and, in the Lady Chapel, the charming effigies of Humfry Bridges (d. 1598),
his wife and their numerous children.
On Park Street, the **Corinium Museum**★
(🕐 *open year-round daily 10am (2pm
Sun)–5pm;* 🕐 *closed Dec 24–26;* ⊛*£3.95;*
♿✕; 📞 *01285 655 611; www.cotswold.
gov.uk)* is a modern well-arranged
museum explaining Cotswold history
from geological to recent times. The
Roman heritage is emphasised with
many local finds, including a series of
superb **mosaic pavements**★.

▶ *From Cirencester take the A 429
and the B 4425 east.*

Bibury★

William Morris' epithet of "the most
beautiful village in England" is justi-
fied by the combined prospect of the
friendly River Coln, stone bridges, weavers' cottages and the gables of Bibury
Court against a wooded background.
Dating from the 17C, **Arlington Mill** is
a particularly attractive property.

▶ *From Bibury return southwest by
the B 4425; at the crossroads turn left; in
Poulton turn left onto the A 417.*

Fairford

This old coaching village is famous for
the **Church of St Mary**★, harmoniously
re-built in the late 15C. Sculptures, some

Village of Bibury
Y. Kanazawa/MICHELIN

humorously grotesque, enrich the exterior. Inside, the screens, stalls and misericords of the choir are of exceptional
quality. But the church's glory is its wonderful set of **stained glass windows**★★
(c. 1500), tracing in colour the Bible's
story from Adam and Eve to the Last
Judgement.

▶ *From Fairford take the A 417 east
and the A 361 north.*

Cotswold Wildlife Park

🕐 *Open year-round daily 10am–6pm
(winter 5pm). Last admission 90 mins
before closing.* ⊛*£10, child £7.50 (additional charge for narrow-gauge railway
⊛£1, child £0.50).* ♿📷✕. 📞 *01993 823
006. www.cotswoldwildlifepark.co.uk.*
The peaceful and natural habitat of the
park and gardens (160 acres), set around
a listed Victorian Manor House, is home
to a wide variety of wildlife – rhinos,
zebras and ostriches protected by unob-
trusive moats, tigers and leopards in
grassed enclosures; monkeys and otters
in the old walled garden and tropical
birds and plants in the tropical house;
there is also a reptile house, aquarium
and insect house. Additional attractions
include an adventure playground, brass
rubbing centre, children's farmyard and
narrow-gauge railway.

▶ *Continue north on the A 361.*

Burford

One of the focal points of the wool trade, later an important coaching town, Burford's growth stopped when the turnpike road (A 40) bypassed it in 1812. With its wealth of beautifully preserved buildings, nearly all of Cotswold limestone, it is one of the region's "show villages". The single main street descends to cross the pretty River Windrush. About halfway down is the 16C Tolsey, once the courthouse, now the local museum. Slightly apart from the town is the large **Church of St John the Baptist**★, its tall spire rising gracefully above the watermeadows. Norman in origin, the church exhibits a rich variety of work from many periods; the pinnacled three-storey 15C porch is outstanding. Note the exuberant monument to Edward Harman (d. 1569), decorated with Red Indians and rows of kneeling children.

▷ *From Burford take A 40 west to Northleach. Then take A 429 south and turn right to Chedworth.*

Chedworth Roman Villa

NT. Yanworth, nr Cheltenham.
🕐 *Open Mar–mid-Nov, Tue–Sun and bank hols 10am–4pm (Apr–late Oct 5pm).* ⊜*£6.* 🅿. *℘01242 890 256. www.nationaltrust.org.uk.*
This large and rich villa stood at the head of a small valley beside its own spring. It was undoubtedly one of the grandest buildings of the Roman Cotswolds. The remains, including good mosaic floors, have been carefully excavated and are well presented. The museum displays items found on the site.

▷ *Return to Northleach and continue north on the A 429.*

👥 Bourton-on-the-Water★

The village owes its special charm to the clear waters of the Windrush which run between well-tended grass banks beside the main street and under elegant stone bridges. It is the most commercialised of the Cotswolds settlements with three popular family attractions: the Model Village *(Rissing-ton Road, behind Old New Inn;* 🕐*open year-round daily 10am–6pm/winter 4pm;* ⊜*£3.25, child £2.75;* ♿; *℘01451 820 467),* **The Cotswold Motoring Museum and Toy Collection** *(The Old Mill;* 🕐*open 10am–6pm late Feb–first Sun Dec;* ⊜*£3.80, child £2.60;* ♿; *℘01451 821255; www.cotswold-motor-museum. co.uk)* and **Birdland Park and Gardens** *(Rissington Road;* 🕐 *open year-round daily 10am–6pm/Nov–Mar 4pm;* ⊜*£5.50, child £3.30;* ♿✖; *℘01451 820 480).*

▷ *Make a detour west of the A 429 by a minor road to the Slaughters.*

Both **Lower** and **Upper Slaughter** are picturesquely sited by the River Eye.

▷ *Take the minor road northeast into Stow-on-the-Wold.*

Stow-on-the-Wold

This is the highest settlement in Gloucestershire and probably originated as a Roman lookout post on the Fosse Way. It is a regular stop for visitors on the traditional Cotswold circuit, to browse in the antique shops, admire the 14C cross in the market place or the Crucifixion by Caspar de Crayer (1610) in the church.

▷ *Take the A 436 northeast; at the crossroads turn left onto the A 44.*

Chastleton House★★

NT. Chastleton, nr Moreton-in-Marsh.
🕐*Open late-Mar/Apr–Sept Wed–Sat 1pm–5pm. Oct 1pm–4pm. Number of daily visitors limited; pre-book. ℘01608 674 981 between 9.30am–2.30pm Tue–Fri. No same-day bookings.* ⊜*£7.50.* 🅿*250m. ℘01494 755 560 (infoline). www.nationaltrust.org.uk.*
This perfect example of a Jacobean country house was built in the early 17C by a rich wool merchant and is a near-perfect time capsule.
The **Great Hall**, one of the last of its kind to be built, the richly decorated **Great Chamber** and the tunnel-vaulted Long Gallery, running the whole length of the top floor, evoke the atmosphere of domestic life in the 17C.

On the forecourt are the 17C stables and the little **Church of St Mary**. To the east of the house is a great rarity, a small formal **garden** surviving from about 1700.

▶ *Continue west on the A 44.*

The route passes through **Moreton-in-Marsh**, an attractive little market town, where the Fosse Way broadens out to form the main street.

▶ *After 6mi/10km turn left onto the B 4081.*

Snowshill Manor★

*NT. Snowshill, nr Broadway. **House:** Open mid-Mar–Oct Wed–Sun and bank hols noon–5pm. **Grounds and Priest's House:** Open 11am–5.30pm. Closed Good Fri. House and garden £7.70; garden only, £4.20. Admission to house by timed ticket only, issued at reception on first-come, first-served basis. On busy days (particularly bank hols and Sun) tickets may run out so arrive early to avoid disappointment. Last admission 40mins before house closes. ⏱️📱❌ Childrens play area. ☎01386 852 410. www.nationaltrust.org.uk.*
This typical Cotswold manor house (c. 1500) is snugly sited below the rim of the escarpment. The house is crammed with a jackdaw's nest of objects, most striking of which is the **Samurai armour** collection acquired by the eccentric Charles Wade, who also laid out the enchanting **terraced garden**★.

▶ *Return northeast on B 4081; turn left onto a minor road.*

Broadway Tower Country Park

Open Apr–Oct Mon–Fri 10.30am–5pm, Sat–Sun 11am–3pm. £3.80. ⏱️📱❌. ☎01386 852 390. www.broadway-cotswolds.co.uk/tower.html.
Broadway Tower, a battlemented folly (1800), marks one of the highest points (1,024ft/312m) in the Cotswolds. On a clear day the **panorama**★★★ extends to the Welsh borders. The Country Park

Snowshill cottage

includes a red deer enclosure and beautiful nature walks.

▶ *Continue on the minor road; turn left into the A 44, down a long hill.*

Broadway★

This handsome village, somewhat more formal than its neighbours, is famous for its variety of genteel upmarket antique and craft shops, cafés and restaurants, hotels and guest houses. The long, partly tree-lined "broad way" rises gently from the village green at the western end to the foot of the escarpment, flanked by mellow stone buildings which range from picturesque thatched cottages to the stately Lygon Arms hotel.

▶ *Take the B 4632 and B 4035 north and east to Chipping Campden.*

Chipping Campden★★

The long curving High Street, lined with buildings of all periods in the mellowest of limestone, makes Chipping Campden the embodiment of the Cotswold townscape. The town has been quietly prosperous since the great days of the medieval wool trade and something of its present state of preservation is due to the care and skill of the artists and craftspeople who were attracted to Chipping Campden in the early 20C.

Many of the houses in the **High Street** are substantial but, more than individual distinction, it is the overall harmony of the street scene which impresses. The centre of the town is marked by the arched and gabled **Market Hall** of 1627. Further north, distinguished by its two-storeyed bay window, is the **house of William Grevel**, "the flower of the wool merchants of all England", who died in 1401 and is commemorated by a fine brass in the parish church. In Church Street stand the Almshouses built in 1617 by Sir Baptist Hicks. His whose own mansion (opposite) was destroyed but two pavilions survive, together with pepperpot lodges and the gateway, near the entrance to the splendid "wool church" of **St James's Church**, (◷ open daily; ⊜£1 donation requested; ℘01386 841 927; www.stjames churchcampden.co.uk).

▶ Take minor roads north.

Hidcote Manor Garden★★

NT. Hidcote Bartrim. ◷*Open Jul– Aug daily 10am–6pm. Mid-Mar– Oct Sat–Wed 10am–6pm (Oct 5pm). Nov–Dec Sat–Sun noon–4pm.* ⊜*£8.10.* 🅿✕. ℘*01386 438 333. www.nationaltrust.org.uk.*

The horticulturalist Lawrence Johnstone has managed an enchanting variety of effects in such a small space (10 acres/ 4ha) and created one of the greatest English gardens of the 20C, an Arts & Crafts masterpiece. Calm expanses of lawns, vistas down avenues or into the countryside contrast with luxuriant but carefully controlled wildness. A labyrinth of "garden rooms" encloses an arrange- ment of herbs, plants entirely in white and a mysterious pool.

In 2009 Lawrence Johnston's all-weather court was restored and opeedn to play- ers. The Theatre Lawn is open for cro- quet, while the orchard was transformed into a working kitchen garden.

ADDRESSES

🛏 STAY

⊜⊜ **Alderley**, *Rissington Road, Bourton- on-the-Water.* ℘*01451 822 788. www.alderleyguesthouse.com.* Simple guesthouse offering THREE bright homely floral bedrooms and a summer terrace for good-quality breakfasts.

⊜⊜ **Cotteswold House**, *Arlington, Bibury.* ℘*01285 740 609. www.cottes woldhouse.org.uk.* This Victorian house has been thoroughly converted into a simple spotless guesthouse with three bedrooms and a manicured garden, just outside the picturesque village.

⊜⊜ **Windrush House**, *Station Road, Broadway.* ℘*01386 853 577. www. broadway-windrush.co.uk.* This Edward- ian house, a few minutes' walk from the village, offers five very attractive bedrooms decorated in mellow sooth- ing colours and a landscaped garden with countryside views.

⊜⊜⊜ **Nineveh Farm**, *Mickleton, Chipping Campden.* ℘*01386 438 923. www.ninevehfarm.co.uk.* This Georgian

farmhouse extends a warm welcome with five comfortable rooms, some with garden views.

🍽 EAT

⊜⊜ **The Carpenter's Arms**, *Fulbrook Hill, 0.5mi/0.8km northeast of Burford on A 361.* ℘*01993 8223 275. www. thecarpentersarmsfulbrook.co.uk.* Characterful pub with flagged floors, beamed ceilings, wood burners and contemporary art, serving carefully-pre- sented modern dishes.

⊜⊜ **Goblets**, *Lygon Arms, High Street, Broadway.* ℘*01386 854418. www.bar celo-hotels.co.uk/LygonArms.* A concise menu of light seasonal dishes is offered in this characterful firelit dining room in rustic dark oak. Booking advisable.

⊜⊜ **The Bell**, *Sapperton, nr Cirencester.* ℘*01285 760 298. www.foodatthebell. co.uk.* Charming pub 5mi/8km west of Cirencester made up of three beamed cottages with log fires inside and a terrace outside. Traditional English and classic European dishes.

Dartmoor★★

Devon

The largest of the five granite masses that form the core of south-west England. Dartmoor National Park welcomes eight million visitors each year. Many are curious holiday-makers taking a day out from the coastal Torbay resorts visiting the pretty villages on the edges of the moor. Others are serious walkers, delving deep into the heart of the Park and into the bleak unpopulated western areas.

THE MOOR

Dartmoor offers two very contrasting faces. The centre is open moorland, often bleak and windswept rising 1,000ft/300m high, while the **tors** (rocky outcrops), mainly to the north and west, are as much as 2,000ft/600m. To the east and southeast however are **wooded valleys**, cascading streams and small villages. Ponies, sheep and cattle graze freely on the moor, while a myriad of birds flock above. The whole area is a walker's paradise with hundreds of routes and trails mapped out to accommodate every level of walker. You can join one of the many Dartmoor National Park Authority walks led by a guide with a wealth of local knowledge or simply blaze your own trail, using one of the eight walks compiled on their website, but do take the usual precautions.

Ashburton

This former stannary, or coinage, town stands on a tributary of the River Dart at the beginning of the old road (B 3357) across the moor to Tavistock. The church with its tall Perpendicular granite tower was built in the 15C when the town was a wool centre. Slate-hung houses indicate its importance as a slate mining centre from the 16–18C.

Signposted from the town is the
River Dart Country Park (◷ *River Dart Adventures operate Easter/Apr–Sept weekends and school holidays;* ∞*£6.75, under-fives free;* ℘*01364 652 511; www. riverdart.co.uk*), a popular country park

- ⚙ **Michelin Map:** Michelin Atlas p 4 or Map 503 H, I 32.
- 🛈 **Info:** Town Hall, North Street Ashburton. ℘01364 653426. 3 West Street, Okehampton. ℘01837 53020. www. discoverdartmoor.co.uk.
- 🛈 **National Park Info:** Postbridge, Princetown. ℘01822 88 272. High Moorland Visitor Centre, Princetown. ℘01822 890414. Parke, Bovey Tracey, near Newton Abbot. ℘01626 832093. www.dartmoor-npa.gov.uk.
- ▶ **Location:** 365sq mi/945sq km of moorland in the centre of Devon.
- ⚠ **Warning:** The public does not have a universal right of access – on enclosed land, access is by public footpaths and bridleways only and it is an offence to drive or park more than 15yds/15m off a road.
- ◉ **Don't Miss:** South Devon Railway; Castle Drogo; Lydford; view from Brent Tor.
- ◷ **Timing:** Two days minimum.
- 👥 **Kids:** Miniature Pony Centre (Moretonhampstead); the adventure centres at Becky Falls and River Dart Country Park.

with a range of outdoor facilities for all the family plus good birdwatching.

👥 Becky Falls Woodland Park

Manaton, Newton Abbot. ◷ *Open mid-Feb–early Nov daily, 10am–5pm/dusk.* ∞*£6.50, child £5.50.* 🅿✕. ℘*01647 221 259. www.beckyfalls-dartmoor.com.*
The Becka Brook tumbles some 70ft/20m from the moor into a beautiful wooded glade. Children's activities include Animal Encounter Shows, Animal Feeding sessions and an Indoor Animal Theatre. The estate is criss-

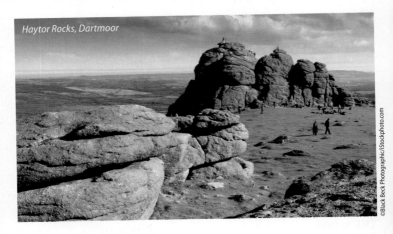

Haytor Rocks, Dartmoor

©Black Beck Photographic/iStockphoto.com

crossed by nature trails, making it a good departure point for moors walks.

Bovey Tracey

This small town is a gateway to Dartmoor. Many of its cottages are built of moor granite, mellowed by thatch in Devon fashion. The **church of St Peter, St Paul and St Thomas of Canterbury**★ was founded in 1170 by Sir William de Tracey, in atonement for his part in St Thomas Becket's murder, it is said. The church is largely 15C, although considerably restored, and contains some interesting Jacobean tombs, a 15C lectern and a carved pulpit and rood screen.

The **Riverside Mill** is home to the **Devon Guild of Craftsmen** (◷ *open daily 10am–5.30pm, Jun–early Sept Fri until 9pm;* &🅿✕; *℘01626 832 223; www.crafts.org.uk*), founded in 1954. This is now the largest contemporary crafts centre in southwest England, and exhibits a variety of top quality local work.

Brent Tor

The 1,130ft/344m hill of volcanic stone is crowned by St Michael's, a small 13C stone church with a low stalwart tower affording excellent **views**★★ for miles around.

Buckfast Abbey

Abbey and Grounds: ◷ *Open: Church Mon–Sat 9am (Fri 10am)–6pm. Sun noon–6pm.* *Visitor Centre:* ◷ *Open*

daily 9am–5.30pm (10am–4pm winter). &🅿✕. *℘01364 645 550. www.buckfast.org.uk.*

The present abbey church was consecrated in 1932, some 900 years after the original foundation under King Canute. The new church is Norman in style, following the plan of the Cistercian house dissolved under Henry VIII, and is built of grey limestone relieved by yellow Ham Hill stone. The interior of white Bath stone rises to a plainly vaulted roof, 49ft/15m above the nave floor. Note the ornate **high altar** and the modern **Blessed Sacrament Chapel** (1966) with walls of stained glass. An exhibition in the **crypt** retraces the history of the abbey.

Buckfastleigh

This market town on the southeast edge of the moor, which inspired the Sherlock Holmes mystery *The Hound of the Baskervilles,* is best known as the terminus of the steam-driven **South Devon Railway,** (◷ *operates Apr–late Oct daily, rest of year see website;* ⊜*Buckfastleigh–Totnes £9.90;* &🅿✕; *℘0845 345 1466; www.southdevonrailway.co.uk/what-to-see-and-do*), one of the most picturesque railway lines in England.

Buckland-in-the-Moor

Thatched stone cottages set in a wooded dell and the late medieval moorstone church form a particularly characteristic Devon village.

Castle Drogo★

NT. Drewsteignton. 🕐 *Open mid-Mar–Oct daily 11am–5pm.* ≈*£7.45; garden only, £4.77.* ♿🅿✕. ✆*01647 433 306. www.nationaltrust.org.uk.*
On discovering his descent from the 12C Norman nobleman Dru or Drogo, the successful grocer, Julius Drewe, commissioned **Edwin Lutyens** (1869–1944) to create an extravagant castle to the glory of his name. The castle was built in 1911–30 of granite partly from Drewe's own quarry; the exterior shows Norman and Tudor influences while the interior is very much Lutyens at his best (fine oak fittings).

Dartmeet

The West and East Dart Rivers converge from the uplands to flow on through a gorge-like valley between wooded hillsides lively with bird and animal life.

Haytor Rocks

The by-road from Bovey Tracey to Widecombe runs close by these rocks (1,490ft/454m), from which there is a good **view**★ as far as the coast at Widecombe.

Lydford★★

The village descends from the main road towards the River Lyd and the gorge, the buildings increasing in age to the 16C oak-timbered cottages and the inn. The castle testifies to Lydford's military importance as a Saxon outpost from the 7C to the 13C; the two-storey **keep**, now in ruins, was built in 1195 to hold prisoners. Alongside is the 16C oak-timbered Tudor **Castle Inn** which at one time served as the rector's house. **St Petroc's Church**, founded in the 6C, was re-built and enlarged on Norman foundations in the 13C, the south aisle and tower in

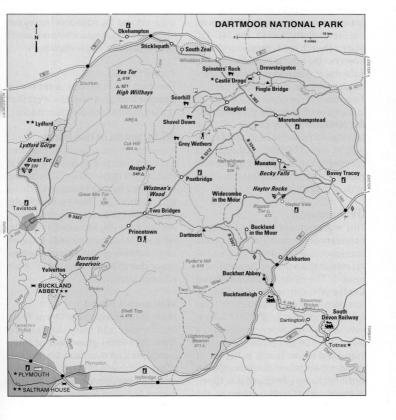

the 15C, and further changes were made in the 19C.

Lydford Gorge

NT. The Stables. ⏰ *Open mid-Mar–Oct daily 10am–5pm (4pm Oct). Late Dec–mid-Feb daily 11am–3.30pm (entrance to waterfall only). For other times see website.* £5.27. ♿ 🅿 ✕. ☎ *01822 820 320. www.nationaltrust.org.uk.*

The wooded gorge is about 1.5mi/2km long with rock walls in places about 60ft/18m high. The **Upper Path** gives excellent views of the river below and glimpses of Dartmoor. The **Lower Path** skirts the northwest bank at the water's edge. The **Third Path** leads from the Pixie Glen to the Bell Cavern via the thundering whirlpool known as the **Devil's Cauldron**. At the south end is the 90ft/30m **White Lady Waterfall**.

Moretonhampstead

Known locally simply as Moreton this old market town was a coaching stage on the Exeter–Bodmin road. The 14C–15C granite **church** has a commanding west tower but the most remarkable building is the row of thatched, colonnaded granite **almshouses**, dating from 1637.

Two miles/*three kilometres* west, set in 20 acres of beautiful parkland, the 👥 **Miniature Pony Centre** (⏰ *open late Mar–Oct daily;* £6.95, child £5.95; ♿🅿✕; ☎*01647 432400; www.miniatureponycentre.com*) is a great favourite with young children and also features a daily birds of prey display.

Okehampton

This market town on the northern boundary of Dartmoor was a Norman strongpoint. It prospered as a medieval market town during the great wool period. The ruins of **Okehampton Castle** (*EH; Castle Lane;* ♿ ⏰ *open late-Mar–Sept daily 10am–5pm (6pm Jul–Aug);* £3; 🅿 ; ☎ *01837 52844; www.english-heritage.org.uk*), enjoy a picturesque setting. Initially a Norman motte and bailey, rebuilt in the 13C, it includes the gatehouses, barbican, outer and inner baileys, keep and stair turret. In town, an 18C mill is home to the

Museum of Dartmoor Life. (*3 West Street;* ⏰ *open Easter Mon–Oct Mon–Sat 10.15am–4.30pm, for Sun and winter times call;* £2.75; ♿ 🅿 (disabled visitors only) ✕; ☎ *01837 52295; www.museumofdartmoorlife.eclipse.co.uk*), with exhibits reminiscing on rural Dartmoor life a century ago.

Postbridge

Clapper bridges – simple ancient structures of large flat granite slabs –are a feature of the moor. The famous Postbridge example has three openings spanned by slabs weighing up to 8t, each about 15ft/5m long, and is believed to date from the 13C when tin-mining and farming were being developed.

Sticklepath

This attractive rural village is home to the **Finch Foundry** (⏰*open late-Mar–Oct Wed–Mon 11am–5pm;* £4.20; 🅿✕. ☎*01837 840 046; www.nationaltrust.org.uk*), a restored 19C edge-tool factory and forge, offering regular demonstrations of tools and working waterwheels.

Two Bridges

The Two Bridges, one a medieval **clapper bridge**, across the West Dart at the junction of two ancient tracks.

Widecombe in the Moor

A cluster of white-walled, thatched cottages, grouped around the church, stands in the shallow valley (wide combe) surrounded by granite ridges which rise to 1,500ft/460m. The Perpendicular **Church of St Pancras**, a vast building with an imposing pinnacled 135ft/40m tall tower of red ashlar granite, is known as the **Cathedral of the Moor**. The two-storey **church house** dates to 1537, when it was an alehouse.

Wistman's Wood

North of Two Bridges. 3mi/5km on foot. On the steep and rocky slopes of the West Dart River grow eerie stunted mossy oaks, survivors and descendants of the primeval woodland which once clothed these uplands. Nearby are large groups of Bronze Age remains.

Dartmouth★★

Devon

Dartmouth enjoys one of the most beautiful and unspoiled settings in south west England. It occupies a deepwater haven in a tidal inlet encircled by verdant hills and the waterfront has changed little since the days of the nautical press gang.

A BIT OF HISTORY

Dartmouth grew wealthy on maritime trade and the quay was constructed in 1548, when it served as the centre of the town's activities. It is lined with elegant merchants' houses, built in the early–mid 17C.

The **Butterwalk**★ *(Duke Street)* is a terrace of four shops with oversailing upper floors supported on 11 granite pillars (built 1635–40). In the late 17C, however, when trade moved to Bristol and London, Dartmouth became purely a naval port, as the presence of the Britannia Royal Naval College, built at the turn of the century, now testifies.

TOWN
St Saviour's Church
Anzac Street.
The tall square pinnacled tower has been a landmark for those sailing upriver since it was constructed in 1372. Note especially the south door with its two iron-work lions and rooted Tree of Life, and the medieval altar with legs carved like ships' figureheads.

Higher Street
The Shambles, the main street of the medieval town, is still lined with houses of that period – the early 17C four-storey **Tudor House** and the **Carved Angel**, a late 14C half-timbered merchant's house, now an inn.

Britannia Royal Naval College
Guided tour Easter–Oct Wed and Sun 2pm. ☎01803 834 224 to book/confirm times and charges. www.britannia.ac.uk. On the hill above town, this huge majestic building (completed 1905), is a naval school where many members of the

Michelin Map: Michelin Atlas p 4 or Map 503 J 32.

Info: The Engine House, Mayor's Avenue. ☎01803 834 224. www.discover dartmouth.com. Torbay/English Riviera resorts: ☎01803 211 211. www.theenglishriviera.co.uk.

Location: 200mi/320km SW of London and 32mi/51km east of Plymouth. Dartmouth is easily covered on foot; a car is the easiest way to get around the Riviera towns. The River Link offers a combined bus, boat, ferry and train service between Paignton Seafront and Totnes Steamer Quay and Totnes Plains (☎01803 834 488; www.riverlink.co.uk).

Parking: Use the park and ride scheme in Dartmouth. Riviera roads and parking are extremely busy in the summer.

Timing: Allow two hours in Dartmouth excluding river and rail trips. Visit the Pannier Market on a Friday when it is busiest.

Sailing: The English Riviera offers some of the UK's best sailing waters. There is a large marina at Torquay and a smaller one at Brixham.

Kids: Paignton Zoo; Kent's Cavern.

Don't Miss: Paignton and Dartmouth Steam Railway. River Dart cruise.

Royal Family received their training, most recently Princes Charles and Andrew.

Dartmouth Castle
EH. 1mi/2km southeast by Newcomen Road, South Town and Castle Road.
Open daily 10am–5pm (6 pm Jul–Aug, 4pm Oct–Mar). Nov–Mar Sat

Britannia Royal Naval College

A Taverner/MICHELIN

and Sun only. 🕐 *Closed Dec 24–26, Jan 1.* ⊛£3.90. 🅿 *(charge).* 📞*01803 833 588. www.english-heritage.org.uk.*

The fort was begun in 1481 by the merchants of Dartmouth to protect their homes and deepwater anchorage, and modified in the 16C and 18C. It commands excellent **views**★★★ out to sea and across and up the estuary.

EXCURSIONS
Torbay★

This area, which markets itself as **"The English Riviera"**, encompasses **Torquay**, **Paignton** and **Brixham**, all originally fishing villages. These towns have capitalised on natural advantages which include a mild climate, exotic palm-tree vegetation, sea views and wide sandy beaches by adding hotels, promenades, piers, pavilions and public gardens to become fully-fledged holiday resorts.

Torquay

10mi/16km northeast of Dartmouth. Ferry across the Dart estuary, then the A 379 and A 3022.

This is the busiest summer resort in Devon. Houses extend up the hill behind the shore; large pale Victorian and Edwardian hotels and villas set in lush gardens are being replaced by modern apartment blocks and high-rise hotels. Excavations in the group of limestone caves known as 👥 **Kents Cavern**★

Dame Agatha Christie (1890–1976)

Agatha Miller was born and brought up in Torquay. At the outbreak of the First World War she worked in the Town Hall while it doubled as a Red Cross Hospital. This inspired Agatha to create Hercule Poirot, who was distilled from the many Belgian refugees stranded in Torquay at that time. After nursing she trained in a pharmacy – a perfect source of inside information for the poisons which feature in her crime novels. In 1938 she bought **Greenway House** on the River Dart as a holiday home and this was donated by her family to the National Trust in 2000. The beautiful 30-acre gardens and house have recently open to the public for the first time (*NT;* 🕐*open late Feb–late-Oct Wed–Sun 10.30am–5pm, also Tue late Jul–Aug; house visit by timed ticket;* ⊛£8.20; 📞*01803 842 382; www.nationaltrust.org*).

(Wellswood, Ilsham Road; ⏰*admission by guided tour daily 10.30am–4pm most of year, see website for details; ghost tours summer Wed–Fri 6.30pm, call to book;* ⏰*closed Dec 25–26 and 2 weeks mid-Jan;* ✆*£8.50, child £6.50;* ♿ 🅿 ✕*;* ✆*01803 215 136; www.kents-cavern.co.uk)* have shown that they were inhabited by prehistoric animals and by men for long periods from the Paleolithic era, 100,000 years ago, until Roman times. The tour *(0.5mi/0.8km)* leads through contrasting chambers with petrified "waterfalls"– beautiful white, red-brown and green crystals and many **stalactites** and **stalagmites**.

Torre Abbey

Torbay Road. ⏰*Open 10am–6pm (Nov–Feb 5pm).* ✆*£5.75.* ✆*01803 293 593. www.torre-abbey.org.uk.*
Set in luxuriant gardens, Torre Abbey consists of an 18C house, the so-called Spanish Barn and the ruins of the medieval abbey. The house is home to Torbay's art collection including about 600 oils and watercolours from the 18C to the mid-20C. They include Pre-Raphaelite works, with paintings by artists such as Holman Hunt and Burne-Jones.

Rail and River

Paignton and Dartmouth Steam Railway – *Queen's Park Station, Torbay Road.* ⏰ *Operates Jun–Sept, daily; Apr–May Oct and Christmas on selected dates. See website for timetable and prices.* ✆*01803 553 760. www.paignton-steamrailway.co.uk.*

Dart River Boat Trips and Coastal Cruises – ⏰ *Operate daily in summer, see website for out-of-season times and prices.* ✆*01803 834 488. www.riverlink.co.uk.*

👥 Paignton Zoo★★

A 3022 Totnes Road, 1mi/1.5km from Paignton town centre. ⏰*Open daily 10am–6pm (5pm Nov–Feb).* ⏰ *Closed Dec 25.* ✆*£8.95, child £6.* ♿ 🅿 ✕*.* ✆*01803 697 500. www.paigntonzoo.org.uk.*
This is one of Britain's largest and most popular zoos, covering over 80 acres. It features a large collection of animals, kept as part of a far-reaching conservation programme, and a luxuriant botanical garden.

Devizes

Wiltshire

Devizes flourished as a cloth market from medieval times to the 19C; from the 17C it profited from tobacco grown widely in the area and it is now probably best known for its brewery. All this accounts for the number of handsome 18C town houses, pubs and not one but two town halls.

▶ **Population:** 13,205.
⏱ **Michelin Map:** Michelin Atlas p 17 or Map 503 O 29.
📋 **Info:** Cromwell House, Market Place. ✆01380 729 408.
◗ **Location:** Devizes is 24mi/38km east of Bath and 90mi/145km west of London.

TOWN
St John's★★

39 Long Street. ⏰ *Open year-round daily, daylight hours.* ✆*01380 723 705. www.sjbnet.org.uk.*
This major Norman parish church has a mighty oblong **crossing tower** with, on the inside, round arches towards the nave and chancel and an early example of pointed arches towards the transepts. Inside, the vaulted east end is typically Norman, decorated with interlaced arches articulated with chevron and zig-zag mouldings. The side chapels (1483) are separated from the chancel and sanctuary by decorative stone screens

Stones, Avebury

A. Taverner/MICHELIN

and have fine lacunar roofs resting on carved corbels.

Wiltshire Heritage Museum★
41 Long Street. ○*Open year-round Mon–Sat 10am–5pm, Sun noon–4pm.* ⊚*£4 (free on Sun).* ⌖. ☏*01380 727 369. www.wiltshireheritage.org.uk.*
In addition to geology and natural history collections and an art gallery, the museum has a renowned archeological department where models of nearby Stonehenge and Avebury are displayed among a collection of local finds.

EXCURSIONS
Avebury★★
7mi/11km northeast on the A 361. NT, EH. *Gallery and Museum: Open year-round daily 10am–6pm (4pm Nov–Mar).* ○*Closed Dec 24–26.*

⊚*£4.20.* *Stones:* ○*Open access.* ⊚*Free.* ⌖⃣☓. ☏*01672 539 250. www.nationaltrust.org.uk.*
Though less famous than Stonehenge, for many visitors Avebury is more rewarding. The surrounding district is extremely rich in prehistoric monuments and earthworks, the earliest dating from c. 3700–3500 BC. The site is all the more fascinating as the village lies inside the circle of 30–40t sarsen stones within the earth "ramparts".

The Stones★
It is difficult to make out the plan of the stones, since the only vantage points are on the earth banks, reinforced by an inner ditch, around the 28 acre/11ha site. These are broken at the cardinal points of the compass to allow access to the centre (now used by modern roads) and

White Horses
Within a 30 mi/50km radius of Marlborough are no less than seven white horse figures carved into the chalky landscape. The oldest, largest and most famous is the **Uffington White Horse**, 20mi/33km northeast of Marlborough on White Horse Hill, Berkshire Downs. It is visible from the A 420 or B 4508 or B 4507 east of Swindon. This is one of England's oldest chalk hill figures. It is 365ft/111m long, though it can only be seen fully from the air, so leading to the theory that perhaps it was a sign to ancient gods. It was once thought that it might be from the Iron Age, as its shape is similar to those found on coins from the period; or perhaps Anglo-Saxon, constructed to celebrate King Alfred's victories over the Danes in AD 871. However, new testing methods on soil samples have revealed that the horse is in fact about 3,000 years old (late Bronze Age). But who carved it and why remains a mystery.

Kennet and Avon Canal

In 1794 a scheme to build a canal between navigable sections of the River Avon and River Kennet, thereby linking Bristol and Bath with Newbury and Reading began. In 1810 it was completed with its most spectacular section being the flight of locks up Caen Hill. However just three decades later the advent of the Great Western Railway meant canal traffic had declined to the point where the waterway was abandoned.

Recently restored, southern England's most picturesque canal is once more open to navigation, threading its way through the Avon Valley, the Vale of Pewsey and on into Berkshire. To see how the canal was built and to obtain details of boat trips visit the **Kennet and Avon Canal Trust Museum** (Canal Centre, Couch Lane, Devizes; ⏰open Mar–Christmas daily 10am–4pm; ✆£2; ☎01380 729 489; www.katrust.org).

enclose a circle of 100 sarsens from the Marlborough Downs and two inner rings. From the south exit, an avenue of about 100 pairs of stones (only some of which can still be seen), once led to the burial site known as the Sanctuary on Overton Hill (excavated in 1930). The **Barn Gallery and Alexander Keiller Museum** gives a valuable insight into this and neighbouring sites.

Neighbouring sites

Silbury Hill★ (2mi/3km south) is a 130ft/40m high man-made chalk mound, one of the largest of its kind in Europe. The reasons for its construction remain a mystery.

The **West Kennet Long Barrow**★ (3mi/5km south) is England's finest burial barrow (340ft/104m long x 75ft/23m wide), dating from 3500–3000 BC. The entrance at the east end is flanked by giant sarsens, and the passage, lateral vaults and chamber at the far end are roofed with massive capstones supported on upright sarsens and drystone walling. Some 50 skeletons from the early Neolithic period were discovered in the vaults.

The Ridgeway Path★★

This ancient trade route was already in use by the nomadic peoples of the Paleolithic and Mesolithic ages, who followed the line of the chalk ridge, as it was easier going than the lower slopes covered in forest or scrub. The modern path, opened in 1973, runs from Overton Hill near Avebury via the Uffington White Horse to the Ivinghoe Beacon near Tring in Hertfordshire (85mi/140km).

Marlborough★

This former market town strategically placed on the London–Bath road (A 4) has been home to the famous public school of **Marlborough College** since the 19C. To the north of the town stretch the **Marlborough Downs**, crossed by the Ridgeway Path and home to flocks of sheep (every town in Wiltshire was originally a wool town). The **High Street** leads from The Green at the east end of town to Marlborough College at the west end. It is lined by attractive houses, no two quite alike and, at the east end, pent houses supported on pillars. **St Mary's Church**, also at the east end, was re-built after a fire during the Commonwealth, hence its Puritan austerity. The High Street boasts a couple of interesting 17C **coaching inns** (Castle and Ball, Sun Inn). At the west end, the **Church of St Peter and St Paul** (now an arts and crafts centre) is Norman in origin, but was re-built in the 15C and extensively restored in the mid 19C.

A couple of miles southeast of Marlborough lies **Savernake Forest**★★, a privately-owned but publicly accessible forest. Its 4,000 acres/1,619ha is a wonderful place to explore on foot or by bicycle. Cutting through the forest northwest to southeast is the **Grand Avenue**★★★, lined with superb beeches laid by Lancelot 'Capability' Brown.

Dorchester★

Dorset

The Romans built the south west settlement of Durnovaria in the 1C AD on the London–Exeter highway, but Dorchester today is famous for being "Hardy Country", home to the great British novelist, Thomas Hardy and the setting for many of his 19C tales.

VISIT
Dorset County Museum★
High West Street. ○ *Open Mon–Sat 10am–5pm.* ◎*£6.50.* &. ℘*01305 262 735. www.dorsetcountymuseum.org.*
A splendid **Victorian gallery**, with painted cast-iron columns and arches supporting a glass roof, houses **Thomas Hardy** memorabilia: furniture and paintings and papers from **Max Gate**, the house Hardy built for himself in 1885, as well as a reconstruction of his study.

EXCURSIONS
Cerne Abbas★
8mi/13km north on the A 352.
The spectacular 180ft/55m long chalk outline of a naked giant, cut out of the turf, has been connected, for obvious reasons, with local fertility rituals, although his origin and date remain unclear. The **village**★ is notable for the beautiful range of timber-fronted 16C houses in Abbey Street, and for **St Mary's Church**, a mix of Early English and Perpendicular, with a spectacular **tower**.

Bere Regis Church★
11mi/18km east on the A 35.
The fine Perpendicular church of **St John the Baptist** is the only building in the village to have survived the last of a series of fires in 1788. Its **roof**★★ is a particular joy.

Maiden Castle★★
EH. 2mi/3km southwest on the A 354.
○*Open daily dawn–dusk.* ▣.
Britain's finest **earthwork ramparts** were begun c. 350 BC on the site of a Neolithic settlement. There were four

▶ **Population:** 15,037.
◉ **Michelin Map:** Michelin Atlas p 8 or Map 503 M 31.
▣ **Info:** Antelope Walk. ℘01305 267 992. www.visit-dorchester.co.uk.
◐ **Location:** Dorchester is 126mi/203km southwest of London. London trains arrive at Dorchester South, Bath and Bristol trains at Dorchester West; each a 5-min walk from the centre.
☺ **Don't Miss:** Abbotsbury Village and its Swannery, near Chesil Beach.
▲▲ **Kids:** Abbotsbury Children's Farm and Swannery.

main building phases before this massive 47 acre/19ha complex was fully equipped with defences c. 60 BC.

Chesil Beach/Abbotsbury ★★
10mi/16km southwest via Martinstown, and Portesham.
Chesil Beach, celebrated in the recent Ian Rankin novel, is a remarkable 8mi/13km shingle bank which forms a lagoon; at one end is the village of **Abbotsbury**. The unique ▲▲**Swannery**★ *(New Barn Road;* ○ *open late Mar–Oct daily 10am–5pm/6pm;* ◎*£9, child £6,* & ▣✕; ℘*01305 871 858; www.abbotsbury-tourism.co.uk),* was founded by the monks c. 1390 and now accommodates more than 400 birds. Close by, the ▲▲ **Children's Farm** *(Church Street;* ○*open as Swannery, Sat–Sun only Sept–Oct;* ◎*£7.50, child £6;* &; ℘*01305 871 817; www.abbotsbury-tourism.co.uk)* is housed in and around a splendid **Tithe Barn**. The neighbouring **Subtropical Gardens**★ *(Bullers Way;* ○ *open year-round daily 10am–dusk;* ◎*£9, child £6, combination ticket available;* ▣✕; ℘*01305 871 387; www.abbotsbury-tourism.co.uk),* contrast with the rugged setting of the wind-blown 14C **St Catherine's Chapel**★ *(EH.* ○ *open any reasonable time)* on its 250ft/76m downland crest.

Exeter★★

Devon

A visit to Exeter, the regional centre of this part of the south west, is rewarding for the charm of its crescents and terraces and in particular for its cathedral, standing out in elephant grey against the red sandstone of the city churches and city wall, and redbrick Georgian houses.

A BIT OF HISTORY

The Saxon town which succeeded the ancient Roman stronghold was devastated by the Danes in the 9C and 10C, but was re-built for the bishop's see to be transferred from Crediton to Exeter in 1050. Medieval trade prospered thanks to the city's position at the head of the navigable waters of the River Exe and it became one of the chief markets of country woollens. With steam power and machinery, however, Exeter's woollen trade declined and the city settled down to the calm life of a county town. Heavy bombing in 1942 destroyed much of the city's medieval fabric.

CATHEDRAL★★

Open year–round Mon–Sat 9.30am–5pm. £5. Guided tours (free). 01392 285 983. www.exeter-cathedral.org.uk.

▶ **Population:** 94,717.

Michelin Map: Michelin Atlas p 4 or Map 503 J 31.

Info: Dix's Field. 01392 265 260. www.exeter.gov.uk. 10a Broad Street, Ottery St Mary. 01404 813964. www.otterytourism.org.uk.

Location: 84mi/135km SW of Bath and 171mi/275km SW of London. There are two train stations, Central (in the heart of town) and St David's, around 0.5mi/0.8km northwest of the centre. Both are serviced by London trains. The bus station is on Paris Street in the centre. The city is compact and its attractions can be covered on foot.

Don't Miss: The cathedral nave vaulting and misericords; the Devon Gallery and ethnography collection in the Royal Albert Memorial Museum.

Timing: Allow a day.

Kids: Have fun at the play areas at Bicton Gardens.

Walking Tours: Free "Redcoat" walking tours operate daily. 01392 265 203.

Detail of the west front, Exeter Cathedral

B. Kaufmann/MICHELIN

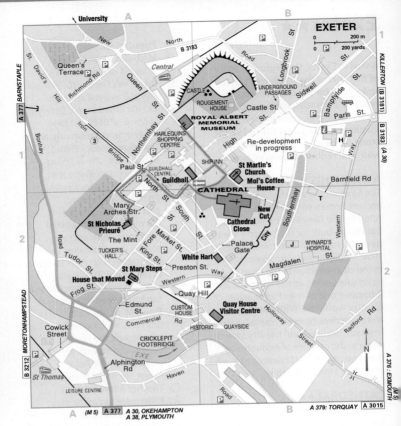

EXETER

Set in its **Close**, an island of calm amid the city's traffic, and surrounded by buildings from many periods, the west front of the cathedral rises through tier upon tier of carved angels, bishops and monarchs, through Decorated tracery to castellated parapets The **Norman transept towers** are the earliest part of the cathedral, since the majority of the building was remodelled and improved in the 13C.

Inside the cathedral, the most striking feature is the **nave vaulting**, extending 300ft/91m from west to east. Also impressive are the 14C **corbels** between the pointed arches of the arcade. Note the 14C **minstrels' gallery** (north side) with 14 angels playing instruments and the west rose window with reticulated tracery (20C glass).

Behind the high altar stands the **Exeter Pillar**, the prototype of all the others in the cathedral. Sir Gilbert Scott's canopied choir stalls (1870–77) incorporate the oldest complete set of **misericords** in the country, carved in 1260–80. The exquisite bishop's throne was carved in oak in 1312. Above the high altar the late 14C east window contains much original glass. In the north transept note the 15C clock with the Sun and Moon revolving around the Earth.

TOWN
Royal Albert Memorial Museum★

Queen Street. Closed for redevelopment until Summer 2010. 01392 665 858. www.exeter.gov.uk/ramm.
This dynamic, purpose-built museum contains four superb principal collections – natural history, archeology, ethnography and fine and decorative arts. The Devon Gallery presents local

geology and ecology and one of the most comprehensive collections of animal, vegetable and mineral specimens, from all five continents, to be found outside London. The **ethnography** display reflects the number of Exeter families with far-flung trade contacts. The specimens of tribal art include artefacts collected by Captain Cook. The museum's **art** collection spans the 17C–20C, concentrating on Devon–associated artists.

Quayside

Access via the Butts Ferry or the Cricklepit Footbridge. Quay House Visitor Centre, 46 The Quay. Open Apr–Oct daily 10am 5pm. Nov–Mar weekends 11am–4pm. 01392 271 611.

The quay dates from the days when Exeter was a tidal river port, during a period of prosperity which was brought to an abrupt end in the 13C, when Isabella, Countess of Devon, built a weir across the river and successfully diverted all trade from Exeter to Topsham. The visitor centre presents models, paintings and artefacts and an audio-visual history of Exeter. There is a regular programme of music and events throughout the summer months. Cruises (*07984 368442. www.exetercruises.com*) operate from the quayside.

EXCURSIONS

Bicton Gardens★

8mi/13km southeast on the B 3182 and B 3179, then a minor road. Open year-round daily 10am–6pm (5pm winter). Closed Dec 25–26. £6.95, child £5.95. Woodland railway £1.30. 01395 568 465. www.bictongardens.co.uk.

The grounds of Bicton house have been designed in formal Italian style and planted with specimen trees over the last 200 years. There are four glasshouses, the most notable being the beautiful **Palm House**, built in the 1820s to a daring curvilinear design, using 18,000 small glass panes in thin iron glazing bars. Among other features are an **American Garden** (started in the 1830s), a secluded **Hermitage Garden**,

Exeter city centre
Y. Duhamel/MICHELIN

a **museum** of bygone agricultural tools, a woodland railway, an adventure playground, an indoor play area and an 18-hole mini golf.

Queen Victoria, George VI and the late Queen Mother are among the monarchs who have worshipped at **St Mary's Church**, which adjoins the gardens.

Ottery St Mary★

12mi/19km east.

This attractive little town of winding streets and small squares with 17C and Georgian houses is attractively situated on the River Otter, surrounded by green hills. Its pride and joy is the twin–towered parish church of **St Mary's★**, consecrated in 1260 and converted into a collegiate foundation in 1336: the chancel, nave, aisle and Lady Chapel were remodelled in the Decorated style and many of the furnishings belong to this period, including **Grandisson's clock** in the south transept and the gilded wooden **eagle lectern**, one of the oldest and grandest in England. A special feature of the church is its varied **vaulting**, superb coloured **bosses** and **corbels**.

Ottery St Mary is famous for its flaming **Tar Barrels** and Tar Barrel rolling on November 5, and its **Carnival**, held on the Saturday before, with its parade of spectacular floats and marchers from many towns and villages in the area.

Exmoor★★
Somerset and Devon

This great southwest moor (267sq mi/692sq km) on the boundary between North Devon and Somerset is one of Britain's National Parks. Red deer, wild Exmoor ponies, sheep and cattle still roam the moor which is vividly described in R D Blackmore's famous novel *Lorna Doone* (1869). Exmoor's coastline is in places rugged and wild but also home to popular seaside resorts, such as Minehead.

SIGHTS
Dulverton★
The "capital" village of the area is sited 450ft/137m above sea level amid beautiful scenery and boasts a solid church (rebuilt in the 19C) with a 13C west tower and pretty cottages.

Dunkery Beacon★★★
At 1,705ft/519m the Beacon is the highest point on the Moor, visible for miles around with commanding **views**★★★.

Dunster★★
The beautiful old town of Dunster on the northeast edge of Exmoor enjoyed a flourishing coastal and continental trade until the sea retreated in the 15C–16C, whereupon it became a wool market and weaving centre. It is now a popular tourist destination in season. The red sandstone **castle**★★ (*NT; Castle: ○open mid-Mar–Oct Fri–Wed 11am–5pm, Garden and Park: ○open daily 10am–5pm, winter 11am–4pm; ◌£7.80 (garden and park only £4.30); ℘01643 821 314, ℘01643 823 004; www.nationaltrust.org.uk*), dominates the town from the tor on which a fortification has stood since Saxon times. The castle was begun by the Norman baron William de Mohun and in 1867 transformed to its present fortified Jacobean mansion.

The **water mill**★, (*NT; Mill Lane; ○open Apr–Oct daily 11am–4.45pm; ◌£3.25 inc. NT members; ✕; ℘01643 821 759; www.nationaltrust.org.uk*) on the River Avill, re-built and improved since Domesday, ground corn until the late 19C, came back into use during the Second World War and was rebuilt and restored to working order in 1979–80. The long, wide **High Street** lined by 17C–19C houses is graced by the unique 17C octago-

Literary associations
The 14C thatched pub, the **Rising Sun Inn** on Mars Hill, is said to have sheltered **RD Blackmore** while he wrote *Lorna Doone*. In 1797, the poets **Wordsworth** and **Coleridge** arrived here, having walked 30 miles from Nether Stowey. While staying at Culbone nearby (now called Ash Farm), Coleridge began his poem *Kubla Khan*. In 1812, the disowned young poet **Shelley** came to Lynmouth with his 16-year-old "bride" Harriet Westbrook and attendants. During his stay, Shelley distributed his revolutionary pamphlet, the *Declaration of Rights*: some he sealed inside bottles wrapped in oiled cloth and packed into crates fitted with a sail before being launched from the beach; others he despatched in miniature balloons.

nal, dormered **Yarn Market**. Many of the buildings along **Church Street** are related to the priory founded in 1090 including the 14C nunnery and Priest's House (restored 19C); the 20ft/6m high early medieval **dovecote**★ (beyond the gate in the end wall of the Priory Garden). **St George's Church**★ was originally built by the Normans in the 12C then re-built by the monks in the 14C. Its 110ft/34m **tower**, dating from 1443, houses a carillon. Inside are **wagon roofs**, a splendid 54ft/16m carved **screen**, a 16C Perpendicular **font** and the **Luttrell tombs**.

Lynton and Lynmouth★

These complementary towns in a hollow at the top and at the foot of 500ft/152m North Devon cliffs enjoy glorious **views**★ across the Bristol Channel to the distant Welsh coast. Lynton is predominantly Victorian–Edwardian while Lynmouth remains a traditional fishing village with small stone cottages and houses. The **Valley of the Rocks**★ (1mi/2km west) is a group of rocks rising from the wide grass-covered valley to crests of bare sandstone and shale spectacularly carved by the wind.

Oare

This tiny village owes its fame entirely to **Lorna Doone.** The Doone family is said to have lived here and it was in the restored 14C–15C church that Lorna was married to John Ridd. A path leads to **Doone Valley**★ *(6mi/9km)*, made

famous by Blackmore's novel, based on tales of a group of outlaws and cut-throats in the 1620s.

Porlock★

This is an attractive, though much visited, village – made infamous by "the man from Porlock", who interrupted Coleridge as he was writing *Kubla Khan*. The 13C **St Dubricius Church**★ with its truncated shingle-covered spire, is a reminder of Dubricius, a legendary figure who died aged 120 and is said to have been a friend of King Arthur. Inside is a remarkable canopied tomb with alabaster effigies.

Tarr Steps★★

The finest **clapper bridge**★★ (see *DARTMOOR*) in the country, dating back to the Middle Ages or earlier, crosses the River Barle at this point.

Watersmeet★

This beauty spot is where the Rivers East Lyn and Hoaroak meet in a deep wooded valley, the riverbed strewn with boulders around which the water swirls endlessly. It is worth a visit alone for its charming National-Trust administered **Edwardian tearoom and gardens**.

Winsford★

On this stretch of the River Exe you will find seven bridges within yards of each other, the oldest being the **packhorse bridge**.

Glastonbury★★
Somerset

Glastonbury Abbey, a ruin for centuries, was once one of the richest in the land and famous as a centre of learning. The town, which grew up around the abbey, has become an important centre of spiritualism and is now synonymous with an alternative lifestyle which finds its most public expression in the hugely successful annual open-air Glastonbury music festival.

▶ **Population:** 7,747.
Michelin Map: Michelin Atlas p 8 or Map 503 L 30.
Info: High Street. ✆01458 832 954. www.glastonburytic.co.uk.
Location: 29mi/47km southwest of Bath.
Timing: Allow half a day minimum to see the abbey and explore the town.

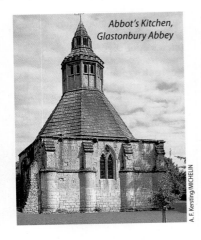
Abbot's Kitchen, Glastonbury Abbey

A. F. Kersting/MICHELIN

The ruins extend far across the lawns, standing tall amidst majestic trees. The Lady Chapel in Doulting stone has a corner turret, decorated walls, and rounded doorways, the one to the north enriched by carved figures. On the impressive Gothic transept piers remain the chancel walls and beyond them the site of the Edgar Chapel, a mausoleum for the Saxon Kings. The 14C **Abbot's Kitchen**★, the sole building to survive intact, features an eight-sided roof with lanterns, which served to draw the smoke from the corner fires in the kitchen up the flues in the roof. North of the abbey stands the **Glastonbury Thorn Tree**.

A BIT OF HISTORY

According to the Holy Grail legends an abbey was founded by Joseph of Arimathea, who caught the blood of the crucified Christ in the cup of the Last Supper. When he planted his staff in the ground it sprouted and became the famous **Glastonbury Thorn**, a tree whose ancestor still flowers here at Christmas and in May. The dual flowering was once considered miraculous. Another legend links **King Arthur** with Glastonbury: mortally wounded by his stepson Mordred, Arthur sailed to the the Isle of Avalon, held to be near Glastonbury. He and Guinevere were supposedly buried in Glastonbury, and their bodies "discovered" in the abbey cemetery in 1191.

The historian William of Malmesbury relates that in 688, Ine, King of the West Saxons, drove the Celts from Somerset, and built a second church here. **Dunstan**, Abbot of Glastonbury from 943–59, enlarged and re-built the abbey. After fire destroyed the church in 1184, rebuilding continued over the next two centuries. However, having acquired vast manorial holdings, it was dissolved in 1539.

SIGHTS
Abbey Ruins★★

🕐 *Open year-round daily. 9am/10am– 4.30pm/6pm, see website for details).* 🕐 *Closed 25 Dec.* ⊙£5. ♿. ✆*01458 832 267. www.glastonburyabbey.com.*

Town

Glastonbury's two main streets are **Magdalene Street**, lined with attractive little 17C–19C houses, and **High Street**, overlooked by the 15C **George and Pilgrims Hotel** and the 14C **Tribunal**. The latter houses the tourist information centre and **Lake Village Museum** *(EH; High Street; 🕐open daily Apr–Sept 10am–5pm, Oct–Mar 4pm. Fri–Sat all year 30min later; ⊙£2; ✆01458 832 954; www.english-heritage.org.uk)*, featuring excavated artefacts from an **Iron Age Lake Village** northwest of town.

The 134.5ft/41m tower of the 15C **church of St John the Baptist**★★ is one of the finest in Somerset. Inside St Katherine's chapel survives from the 12C building. The **Somerset Rural Life Museum**★ *(Abbey Farm, Chilkwell Street; 🕐 open Apr–Oct Tue–Fri and Bank Hol Mon 10am–5pm, Sat–Sun, 2pm– 6pm; Nov–Mar Tue–Sat, 10am–5pm; ♿📄✗(summer only); ✆01458 831 1197; www.somerset.gov.uk/museums)*, illustrates daily life on a Somerset farm in the 19C. The outstanding exhibit is the 14C barn of Glastonbury Abbey.

Glastonbury Tor★

The tor, 521ft/159m high, is a landmark for miles around. The tower at its summit is the last remnant of a Church to St Michael, built in the 14C. On a fine day, the **view**★★★ embraces the Quantocks, Bristol Channel and the Mendips.

Gloucester★
Gloucestershire

Gloucester (pronouced "*Gloster*") is a busy centre of administration, manufacturing and commerce, dominated by its glorious cathedral.

CATHEDRAL★★

Cathedral: 🕐 *Open daily year-round 7.30am–6pm.* 💷*£3 minimum contribution requested.* **Exhibition, Whispering Gallery, Treasury:** 🕐 *Open Mon–Fri 10.30am–4pm, Sat 10.30am–3.30pm.* 💷*£2 (Treasury free).* *Guided tours Mon–Sat 10.45 am–3.15pm, Sun noon–2.30pm. Tower tours most days summer 2.30pm (see website for details).* 💷*£3.* ♿✕. *℘01452 508210. www.gloucestercathedral.org.uk.*

The present structure is essentially the creation of the Norman Benedictine abbot, Serlo, and of his 14C successors, who pioneered the Perpendicular style and adorned the transepts and choir using funds provided by royal patronage or by pilgrims visiting the tomb of Edward II, who was murdered in 1327 in Berkeley Castle. The building was extended in the 15C by the addition of the Lady Chapel.

Massive Norman columns, reddened at the base by a fire in 1122, give an impression of enormous strength while Perpendicular elegance prevails in the exquisite tracery of the high **vault** (92ft/28m); the **east window** – the largest of its kind in medieval glass, commemorating the Battle of Crécy – and in the wonderfully light **Lady Chapel** of about 1500.

Edward's effigy, north of the choir, is protected by a 14C stonework canopy of rare delicacy. The **cloisters** contain the **lavatorium** where the monks washed their hands at the entrance to the refectory; the 14C fan vaulting, the earliest of its kind, is of exceptional richness.

The mid-15C **tower** (225ft/69m), with its unmistakable crown of parapet and pinnacles, rises gracefully above **College Green**, a pleasant combination of mainly 18C houses, replacements of earlier monastic buildings. **St Mary's Gate** is an impressive medieval survival.

▶ **Population:** 114,003.

🕐 **Michelin Map:** Michelin Atlas p 17 or Map 503 N 28.

🛈 **Info:** 28 Southgate Street. ℘01452 396 572. www.visitglouster.info.

▶ **Location:** 104mi/167km W of London and 47mi/75km N of Bath. The train and bus stations face each other on Way, a five min walk from the compact city centre. The docks are a short walk further on.

🅐 **Don't Miss:** Gloucester Cathedral; excursions to Berkeley Castle, Painswick and the Wildfowl and Wetlands Trust.

🕐 **Timing:** Allow 3–4 hours for the centre and docks.

👥 **Kids:** The House of the Tailor of Gloucester.

CITY
Gloucester Docks★

The fine 19C inland port and warehouses have been conserved. The **National Waterways Museum** *(Llanthony Warehouse;* 🕐 *open year-round daily 10am–5pm (Nov–Mar 11am–4pm);* 🕐 *closed Dec 25–26, Jan 1;* 💷*£7.50; £8.50 inc. boat trip (Easter–Oct. only); private boat hire all year;* ♿🅿*(charge)* ✕*; ℘01452 318 200; www.nwm.org.uk)* explores the long history of river and canal navigation in Britain through models, displays, text panels, video simulations and a variety of historic vessels moored by the quay.

Severn Bore

The village of Minsterworth *(4mi/ 6.5km west of Gloucester by A 40 and A 48)* is a good place from which to observe the phenomenon known as the Severn Bore, a roaring wall of water (up to 6ft/2m high) advancing up the Severn estuary, which occurs most vigorously at the time of the equinoxes.

City Centre

The point where the Roman streets intersect is marked by **St Michael's Tower**. The late-medieval timber **Bishop Hooper's Lodging**★ in Westgate Street, houses **Gloucester Folk Museum** (⊙open year-round Tue–Sat 10am–5pm; ℘01452 396 868; www.gloucester.gov.uk) where the lively exhibits include fishing on the Severn, toys, games and agricultural bygones.

♣♣ House of The Tailor of Gloucester (Beatrix Potter Museum)

⊙ Open daily 10am–4pm, Sun open noon. ℘01452 422856. www.tailor-of-gloucester.org.uk.
The Tailor of Gloucester, published 1903, was Beatrix Potter's personal favourite among her Peter Rabbit Books. In 1897, when on holiday here she became fascinated by a local folk tale about John Pritchard, a tailor who had been commissioned to make a fine suit of clothes for the Mayor of Gloucester, and so the story was born. The shop still exists today, selling a full range of Beatrix Potter merchandise alongside a museum.

EXCURSIONS
Painswick★

The streets of this hilltop village contain many old buildings of golden Cotswold stone. The elaborate Baroque tombstones in the parish churchyard are accompanied by 99 clipped yew trees.

Westonbirt Arboretum★

Tetbury, 20mi/32km south of Gloucester. ⊙ Open daily year-round 9am–8pm/dusk; Nov–Mar until 5pm/dusk; weekends open 8am. ⊙Visitor centre closed Christmas week. ⊙ £5–£8. ♿🅿(£5). ✗. ℘01666 880 220. www.forestry.gov.uk/westonbirt.
The road passes through **Tetbury**, an elegant town built of silver-grey stone round a quaint Market House (1655) and St Mary's Church, a refined 18C interpretation of medieval motifs.
The arboretum was first planted in 1829. Since then this important plant collection has grown steadily to comprise some 14 000 trees and shrubs from all over the world. There are many miles of signed walks and an attractive visitor centre. Some trees here are the largest of their kind in Britain. The many types of maple guarantee a spectacular autumn.

The Wildfowl and Wetlands Trust, Slimbridge★

15mi/24km southwest of Gloucester. ⊙ Open daily 9.30am–5.30pm (5pm in winter). ⊙£7.95. ⛵Canoe Safari Nov–Mar Sat–Sun and daily school hols 11am–3pm; Apr–Nov daily 10.30am–4.30pm (⊙£5 per canoe). ♿🅿✗. ℘01453 891 900. www.wwt.org.uk.
Bordering the extensive wetlands of the tidal Severn, this water-bird sanctuary, created by the late Sir Peter Scott, has acquired an international reputation for research and conservation and as a place where the public can observe a great variety of native and exotic wildfowl at close quarters. The hides and observatories permit experienced and amateur birdwatchers alike to enjoy the spectacular winter arrival of thousands of wild ducks, geese and swans.

Berkeley Castle★★

20mi/32km southwest of Gloucester. ⊙Open Jun–Aug Sun–Thu Apr–May, Sept–Oct Sun and bank hols, 11am–5.30pm. ⊙£7.50. Gardens only, £4. Butterfly house £2. 🅿✗. ℘01453 810 332. www.berkeley-castle.com.
This archetypal medieval stronghold commanded the narrow strip of lowland between the Cotswolds and the Severn; its defences could be strengthened by flooding the surrounding water meadows. The inner courtyard is dominated by the great drum of the **keep** of 1153. The **interior** is a confusion of twisting passages and stairways, vaulted cellars, ancient kitchens and deep dungeons. In the King's Gallery can be seen the chamber where the deposed **Edward I** was kept prisoner and then horribly murdered, possibly by agents of his former queen. Other rooms are richly furnished with reminders of the castle's continuous occupation since the 12C.

Ilfracombe

Devon

The most popular resort on the North Devon coast, the town's fine coves and cliff scenery are set against a backdrop of attractive wooded hills and valleys. The hills around the town provide good vantage points for surveying the area: **Capstone Hill** (156ft/47m) offers a good **view**★ of the town, the harbour mouth, the rock-enclosed bays and beaches; **Hillsborough**, at the centre of the pleasure ground, rises to 447ft/136m and affords an extensive **view**★★ along the coast.

- **Population:** 10,941.
- **Michelin Map:** Michelin Atlas p 6 or Map 503 H 30.
- **Info:** Landmark Theatre, Seafront. ℘01271 863 001. www.ilfracombe-tourism. co.uk. The Square, Barnstaple. ℘01271 375 000. www.staynorth devon.co.uk.
- **Location:** Ilfracombe lies on the coast, just west of Exmoor National Park.
- **Don't Miss:** Arlington Court; Clovelly; Lundy Island.
- **Kids:** Tunnels Beaches, Watermouth Castle.

TOWN
Holy Trinity
The parish church dates from the Norman period (enlarged in the 14C) and has an ancient, elaborately carved **wagon roof**★★.

St Nicholas' Chapel
Lantern Hill. ⏱*Open late May–mid Oct daily 10am–1pm, 2.30pm–5pm (May–Aug until dusk).*
In the early 14C the beacon set as a marker on Lantern Hill was replaced by this mariners' chapel, which still shines a red light to guide shipping. From the rock platform on which the chapel stands there is a good **view**★ over the almost land-locked harbour and out to sea.

Tunnels Beaches
Granville Road. ⏱*Open (subject to tide) Easter–Oct daily 10am–6pm (Jul–Aug 9.30am–7pm, Oct 5pm).* ◉£1.95. ♿✕. www.tunnelsbeaches.co.uk.
In the 19C the hill between the road and the sea was tunnelled and the rock cove, on the far side, made accessible. The cove was then equipped with a sea wall to prevent the tide running out and so provide all-day bathing.

EXCURSIONS
Watermouth Castle
1mi/1.6km southeast on the A 399.
⏱*Open late Mar/Easter–Oct*
Sun–Fri, peak 10am–5pm (last ride), off-peak 10.30am–4.30pm (last ride). ◉£10/£12, children under 36in/92cm free. ▣✕. ℘01271 867 474. www.watermouthcastle.com.
Overlooking picturesque Watermouth Cove, this Victorian folly castle is a handsome sight. Its landscaped gardens hosts a theme park for young children.

Barnstaple★
13mi/21km south.
Barnstaple is the regional centre and its 19C cast-iron-and-glass **Pannier Market** (⏱*open Apr–Dec Mon–Sat 8am/9am–3pm/4pm; www.barnstaple panniermarket.co.uk*), adjoining **Butchers' Row**, is busy selling local produce and arts and crafts.
Long Bridge★ *(520ft/158m)* was first built c. 1273; three of its 16 stone arches were replaced around 1539. The 13C **Parish Church**, (⏱ *open Mon–Fri 9am–3pm, Sunday services;* ℘*01271 344 589*) is notable for its memorial monuments and its 17C lead-covered spire. The 17C **Horwood Almshouses** and **Alice Horwood School** *(Church Lane)* have attractive wooden mullioned windows. The 19C **Guildhall** *(High Street;* ⏱*open Apr–Oct Sat 10am–2pm; to visit at other times call* ℘*01237 373 003)*, contains the Dodderidge Parlour, panelled

in 17C oak, in which the town's collection of corporation plate is displayed. The **Museum of North Devon**, *(The Square;* 🕐 *open year-round Mon–Sat 9.30am–5pm;* 🕐 *closed bank hols and Christmas week;* &; 𝒫 *01271 346 747; www.devonmuseums.net/barnsta ple)* traces regional history. Downriver from the bridge is the colonnaded **Queen Anne's Walk** (1609), built as a merchants' exchange and crowned by a statue of Queen Anne.

Arlington Court★★

NT. 8mi/13km north east of Barnstaple on the A 39. **House, carriages, Victorian garden:** 🕐 *Open late-Mar–Oct Sun–Fri 11am (10.30am garden)–5pm.* **Park/Cave:** 🕐 *Open Nov–Mar daylight hours.* ⌾*£7.40 (Gardens and carriage collection only, £5.20). 𝒫01271 850 296. www.nationaltrust.org.uk.*
This Classically-styled house (1820–23, altered 1865) contains the varied collections of *objets d'art* accumulated by its former owner, Miss Rosalie Chichester (1865–1949), the most remarkable of which is her collection of **model ships** including 36 made by Napoleonic prisoners of war.

Clovelly★★

30mi/50km southwest of Ilfracombe. 🕐 *Admission only via visitor centre Jul–Sept daily, 9am (9.30am Oct–Jun) to 6pm/dusk.* 🕐 *Closed Dec 25.* ⌾*£5.75. Landrover shuttle £1–£2.* & 🄿 ✕. 𝒫*01237 431 781. www.clovelly.co.uk.*
This charming picture-postcard village, mentioned in the Domesday Book, is now privately owned. The **Visitor Centre** outlines its history as a fishermen's community and its preservation. The steep, stepped and cobbled **High Street**, known as **Down-a-long** or **Up-a-long (**depending on the direction being faced), is lined with small, whitewashed 18C and 19C houses decked with bright flowers. Donkeys and mules are still the only form of transport up and down the High Street. At the bottom of the High Street lies **Quay Pool**, the small, restored 14C harbour protected from the open sea by a curving breakwa-

ter which offers a **view** extending from Lundy to Baggy Point. The pebble beach is backed by stone-built cottages and balconied houses, the old harbour lime-kiln, the inn and the lifeboat store.

Lundy Island★★

🕐 *2hr crossing by MS Oldenburg (267 passengers) operates (according to tide) from Bideford Quay all year, also from Ilfracombe Pier summer only.* ⌾*£32.50 day return. Also private launches from Clovelly (90min) and helicopter (£92). 𝒫01271 863 636 (sailing), 01237 470 422 (Lundy Island Manager). www.lundyisland.co.uk.*
Lundy Island derives its name from the Icelandic word for puffin, *Lunde.* The attraction of the island is its fascinating bird and marine life, in a peaceful setting free of many of the trappings of modern life (no cars, no telephones, no newspapers). Despite the island's name, there are reportedly only 30 breeding pairs of puffins on it *(May–Jul).* Other resident bird life includes razorbills, guillemots, fulmars, Manx shearwaters, shags, kittiwakes and various species of gull. Lundy has been designated a **Marine Nature Reserve** since 1986, with grey seals, basking sharks and porpoises. The clear waters and numerous wrecks offer excellent diving.
A complete circuit of the island is 11mi/18km and takes about four hours on foot. From Landing Beach, overlooked by 12–13C **Marisco Castle**, the track leads uphill to Lundy village, past the Classical-style granite **Millcombe House** (1830s). The strangely urban-looking village church, **St Helena's**, dates from 1896. Take the footpath west to the **Old Light** (1819), replaced in 1896 by the **North Light**, now automated. The path along the west coast leads past a **battery** which was used as a fog warning station, the site of a landslip, named after an earthquake in the 19C, past **Jenny's Cove** (good viewing point for gulls, auks and puffins) and **Devil's Slide** (rock-climbing). From North Light, take the path back along the east coast (past the quarries), or the more popular route along the spine of the island.

Lacock★★

Wiltshire

This peaceful picturesque stone-and-brick village is owned by the National Trust. It comprises little more than four streets laid out in a square but has provided the film set for numerous period television and movie dramas.

> **Population:** 1,068.
>
> **Michelin Map:** Michelin Atlas p 17 or Map 503 – N 29.
>
> **Info:** Town Hall, Market Lane, Malmesbury. ℘01666 823 748. www.visitwiltshire.co.uk, www.nationaltrust.org.uk.
>
> **Location:** 13mi/21km east of Bath.

VILLAGE

Village streets

The wide **High Street**★ leading to the abbey is lined with cottage-shops and houses of various heights, sizes and designs, some of which date from as long ago as the 14C and 16C. **West Street** and **East Street** are enclosed by interesting old houses and inns (the **George Inn**), is the oldest inn in the village, built 1361). **Church Street** (note the 14C Cruck House and 15C Sign of the Angel Inn) runs parallel to the High Street, leading into the village's original Market Place on the right.

St Cyriac★

🕐Open year-round daily 10am–5pm. ℘01249 730 272.

This Perpendicular church is a superb example of a "wool church" from the village's prosperity of the 14–17C.

Lacock Abbey and Fox Talbot Museum of Photography★

(NT). **Museum:** 🕐 Open late Feb–Oct daily 11am–5.30pm; Nov–late Feb Sat–Sun 11am–4pm. **Abbey:** 🕐 Open late-Mar–Oct, Wed–Mon 1pm–5.30pm. **Cloisters and garden:** 🕐 Open Mar–Oct daily 11am–5.30pm. ⊜£9.50 (abbey, cloisters and garden, £7.60; museum, cloisters and garden £5.70). 🕐Closed Good Fri. ♿. ℘01249 730 459. www.nationaltrust.org.uk.

To the east of the village lies the abbey, founded in the 13C and converted into a stately home following the Dissolution (the cloisters, sacristy and chapter house survive) in 1539. Successive generations of the **Talbot family** added decorative features following the tastes of their day. The pioneer photographer,

William Henry Fox Talbot (1800–77), the photography processing inventor, added three oriels to the south front in 1827–30, the central one of which was the subject of his first successful photograph (1835).

The Fox Talbot museum is housed in a 16C barn at the abbey gate. It is devoted to William Henry Fox Talbot and also the work of contemporary photographers.

CORSHAM COURT★★

5mi/8km north. 🕐 Open late-Mar–Sept Tue–Thu, Sat–Sun and bank hols 2pm–5.30pm. Oct–late-Mar (closed Dec) Sat–Sun 2pm–4.30pm. ⊜£7 (Gardens only, £2.50). ♿🅿. ℘01249 701 610. www.corsham-court.co.uk.

This Elizabethan mansion built in 1582 was bought by Paul Methuen in the mid 18C. Corsham was altered and enlarged on several occasions, by architects such as Lancelot "Capability" Brown in the 1760s, John Nash in 1800 and Thomas Bellamy in 1845–49, to house the extensive Methuen collection of Master **paintings** (16C and 17C Italian and 17C Flemish), **statuary**, **bronzes** and **furniture**.

The collection includes works by Caravaggio, Reni, Tintoretto, Veronese, Rubens and Van Dyck, as well as pieces by the Adam brothers and Chippendale and a splendid white marble fireplace. The **Cabinet Room** contains Fra Filippo Lippi's Annunciation (1463), while the highlight of the **Octagon Room**, designed by Nash, is Michelangelo's *Sleeping Cupid* (1496). Note also the fine family portraits by Reynolds.

MALMESBURY★

12mi/20km north.

The centre of this small south Cotswold market town is graced by a **market cross★★**, one of England's finest, built of local stone in 1490, when the town was known for its tanning, wool weaving and other textile industries. Malmebury is a hilltop town shaped by the course of two rivers, the Bristol and Tetbury Avons.

Abbey★

Abbey: ◷*Open daily 10am–5pm (winter 4pm).* ⊙*£2 contribution requested.*
Gardens: Open late-Mar–Oct 11am–5.30pm. ⊙*£6.50.* ⬙. ℘*01666 826 666. www.malmesburyabbey.com.*

Famous figures connected with the abbey, founded in the 7C, include St Aldhelm (639–709), one of the first abbots, the great historian William of Malmesbury (1095–1143) and Elmer the "Flying Monk" who launched himself from the top of the tower in 1010 and "flew" 250yds/230m before crashing but remained convinced it was only the lack of a tail which had brought him down.

The present church was begun in the 12C and by the 14C extended 320ft/97.5m from east to west. In 1479, the spire and central crossing tower were brought down by a fierce storm, destroying the east end transepts and crossing. A century later, the west tower collapsed, bringing down the three adjacent bays of the nave.

The masterpiece of the abbey is the **south porch**, an outstanding example of Norman sculpture and decoration featuring geometrical patterning and magnificent carved figures in a style reminiscent of that found in the churches of southwest France. The massive Norman pillars inside have scalloped capitals. On the south side is the watching loft from where the abbot or a monk could follow the service beyond the chancel screen. The medieval stone screen at the end of the south aisle marks the chapel of St Aldhelm, who was buried in an earlier abbey destroyed by fire in 1050.

The **Abbey House Gardens** are a delight all year round and feature the county's largest private collection of roses.

Longleat★★★

Wiltshire

Set within 900 acres of Capability Brown landscaped parkland, Longleat House is as one of the best examples of high Elizabethan architecture in Britain. In 1949 it became the first stately home to open to the public on a commercial basis but if that caused public debate then it was nothing compared to the furore in 1966 when it opened the very first safari park outside of Africa.

VISIT

Warminster. **House:** ◷ *Open Apr–Oct daily 10am–5pm (weekends, Bank Hols and school hols 5.30pm); off-season reduced hours (see website for details) and by guided tour only.* **Safari Park:** ◷ *Open Apr–Oct daily 10am–4pm (5pm Sat–Sun, bank hols, school hols). Off-season reduced hours, see website.*

⬙ **Michelin Map:** Michelin Atlas p 8 or Map 503 N 30.
▶ **Location:** Longleat is 19mi/30km south of Bath and well signed from the main roads.

Other attractions: ◷ *Open mid-Mar–early Nov daily 11am–5pm/dusk (10.30am–5.30pm weekends and hols).* ◷*Closed Dec 25.* 🖝 *"Private Chattels" Tours (rooms not normally open to the public) on certain days, see website for details (*⊙*£10).* 🖝 *Lord Bath's Murals tours (free with a valid Longleat House and Grounds Ticket or Passport Ticket).* **Entry:** ⊙*£23, Child £15 (Passport including all 11 attractions). House only £12, Safari Park only £12, Grounds only £4, for other attractions see website.* ⬙🅿✕. ℘*01985 844 400. www.longleat.co.uk.*

House

On the ground floor, the late 16C Great Hall with its fine hammerbeam roof contains a splendid pillared fireplace. The Ante-Library is graced by Italian furniture. The Red Library boasts *trompe-l'oeil* ceiling panels echoing those in Renaissance palazzi, while the gilded coffered ceiling of the Lower Dining Room is modelled on one in the Doge's Palace. In the Breakfast Room family portraits look down on Chippendale-style chairs and japanned gaming tables, while the walls are hung with modern works of art.

Upstairs, highlights include: the State Dining Room with its tooled Cordoba leather walls and a Meissen porcelain table centrepiece (c. 1760); the 90ft/27m 17C Long Gallery with a massive marble fireplace copied from one in the Doge's Palace; the State Drawing Room paintings and various pieces of 18C French furniture; the Apartments, dress collection and cabinets of porcelain. The Royal Bedrooms comprise an elegant dressing room hung with hand-painted Chinese wallpaper. The outbuildings comprise a butchery and stable block (with an eclectic collection of ephemera entitled Lord Bath's Bygones).

Safari Park and other attractions

The "drive-in zoo" is most famous for its lions; it also has enclosures for wallabies, giraffes, zebras, llamas, dromedaries, camels, white rhinos, fallow deer, rhesus monkeys (which may climb over the car), wolves and tigers. Once out of your car a **safari boat** takes you on a lake among seals and hippos. Longleat's other claim to fame is its **mazes**. Its conventional hedge maze is made up of more than 16,000 English Yews, and takes on average 90mins to complete! Within its **Adventure Castle** is the Blue Peter (wooden) Maze. There's also a Pets Corner, a steam railway and various other family activities.

Plymouth★

Devon

Plymouth is the principal town of the southwest. It is arranged in three distinct areas: the Hoe and its environs, adorned with the splendour of Victorian and Edwardian buildings; the older, bustling Barbican district by the harbour with its narrow streets; and the commercial centre, re-built after the war, with its wide shop-lined avenues.

A BIT OF HISTORY

The Plantagenet period brought trade with France and by the Elizabethan period trade had spread worldwide, so that for a time Plymouth was the fourth largest town in England after London, Bristol and York. From the 13C Plymouth also played a prime role as a naval and military port, from which warriors and explorers such as Drake, Raleigh, Hawkins and Grenville (all Devonians), Cook and the Pilgrim Fathers set sail.

▶ **Population:** 245,295.
Michelin Map: Michelin Atlas p 3 or Map 503 H 32 – local map; see cornish coast.
Info: Plymouth Mayflower, 3–5 The Barbican. ✆01752 306 330. www.visitplymouth.co.uk.
Location: Plymouth is on the border between Devon and Cornwall, delineated by the River Tamar. The station is 0.6mi/1km north of the centre, the bus station is next to Royal Parade in the heart of town. The Hoe and the Barbican areas are easily covered on foot.
Kids: National Marine Aquarium; Dockyards and Warships trip.

The Royal Naval Dockyard was founded by William III in 1691 at Devonport and today employs some 4,800 workers. In the Second World War the city suffered terrible bomb damage.

PLYMOUTH HOE
The Hoe
On *"that loftie place at Plimmouth call'd the Hoe"*, **Sir Francis Drake** (1540–96) is said to have seen the "invincible" Spanish Armada arriving one day in 1588 and decided to finish his game of bowls (perhaps waiting for the tide to turn) before going to battle. It remains an ideal point to **view** maritime traffic on the Sound, the natural harbour at the mouth of the Tamar and Plym rivers.

Smeaton's Tower, (*open year-round, Tue–Sat and bank hols 10am–noon, 1pm–3pm;* £2; *01752 304 775; www.visitplymouth.co.uk*) a red- and- white painted lighthouse, was erected on the Hoe in 1884 after 123 storm-battered years on Eddystone Rocks, some 14mi/23km southwest of Plymouth. The present **Eddystone Lighthouse**, built in 1878–82, can be seen from the Hoe and even better from the top of Smeaton's Tower, from where there is a splendid **view**★★. Other monuments testifying to Plymouth's role in history include Boehm's 1884 **Drake Statue**, the **Armada Memorial** and the **Naval War Memorial**.

Royal Citadel
EH. Open by guided tour May–Sept Tue, Thu 2.30pm. £4. *01752 304 849. www.english-heritage.org.uk.*
In 1590–91 Drake began a fort intended to protect the Sound against marauding Spaniards and it was in this place that Charles II had the present castle built in 1666–71. The **ramparts** command **views**★★ of the Sound, the Barbican and the Tamar.

BARBICAN, CITY CENTRE
Barbican
Old Plymouth survives in the Barbican, an area extending a quarter of a mile inland from Sutton Harbour, combining modern amenities with medieval houses, Jacobean doorways, cobbled alleys and the **Mayflower Stone** on the pier commemorating the voyage of the **Pilgrim Fathers**, who set sail in 1620 in their 90ft/27m ship, the *Mayflower*. Many other famous voyages are commemorated in the numerous stones and plaques on the pier.

National Marine Aquarium
Rope Walk, Coxside. Open year-round daily 10am–6pm (5pm Nov–Mar); last admission 1hr before closing. Closed 25 Dec. £11, child £6.50. *01752 600 301. www.national-aquarium.co.uk.*
Opened in 2001 this was the first aquarium in the UK to be set up solely for the purpose of education, conservation and research, and it remains Britain's foremost aquarium. The tanks represent different environments, such as a fresh stream, shallow sea and coral reef; with an array of fish, from delicate sea horses to mighty sharks.

Plymouth Mayflower Centre
3–5 The Barbican. Open Apr–Oct Mon–Sat 9am–5pm, Sun 10am–4pm. Nov–Mar Mon–Fri 9am–5pm, Sat 10am–4pm. £2. *01752 306 330. www.visitplymouth.co.uk.*
An exhibition above the tourist office traces the voyage of the Mayflower carrying the Pilgrim Fathers to America in the 1620s, and other contemporary events.

The Elizabethan House
32 New Street. Open Apr–Sept Tue–Sat and bank hols 10am–5pm. £2. *01752 304 774. www.plymouth.gov.uk.*
This house and its neighbour were built in the late 16C as part of a development for wealthy merchants and sea-captains.

Plymouth Gin Distillery
60 South Side Street. Visit by guided tour only (50min) Mon–Sat 10.30am–4.30pm, Sun 11.30am–3.30pm. £6. *01752 665 292. http://plymouthgin.com.*

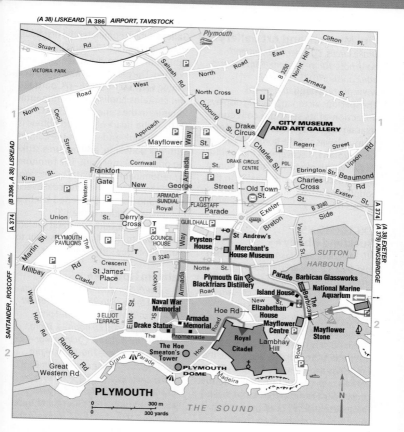

PLYMOUTH

The distillery is housed in what was once a Dominican Friary founded in 1425. You can take a guided tour to see how gin is made and enjoy a cocktail in a designer bar in the converted 15C refectory.

St Andrew's

🕐 Open daily 9am–4pm. &. 🖉 01752 661 414. www.standrewschurch.org.uk.
The church, founded in 1050 and re-built in the 15C, was firebombed in 1941; this left only the walls, granite piers, chancel arches and the 136ft/41m tower standing. The re-built church, re-consecrated in 1957, has six vividly coloured **windows** by John Piper (1904–92). On a window ledge is the so-called **Drake crest scratching** showing the Golden Hinde. It is thought to have been carved by a mason working in the church at the time of Drake's return from circumnavigating the world (3 November 1580). Among the **memorials** are a 12C–13C Purbeck marble effigy and tablets to Frobisher and Drake.

Just south of the church stands **Prysten House** (Finewell Street; 🕐 open Apr–Oct Mon–Sat 10am–3.30pm; ⬭£1; 🖉 01752 661 414), dating from 1490 and thought to be the oldest house in Plymouth. It is a fine three-storeyed building around an inner courtyard with open timber galleries.

Merchant's House Museum

33 St Andrew's Street. 🕐 Open Apr–Sept Tue–Sat and bank hols 10am–5pm. ⬭£2. 🖉 01752 304 774. www.plymouth.gov.uk.
This mid-16C timbered house, its upper floors supported on stone corbels houses the **Museum of Old Plymouth** including a reconstruction of an old city pharmacy★.

DISCOVERING THE SOUTH WEST

City Museum and Art Gallery★

Drake Circus. ⊙ *Open Tue–Sat and bank hols, 10am–5.30pm (5pm Sat and bank hols).* ☎*01752 304 774. www.plymouthmuseum.gov.uk.*

The spacious Victorian building displays a fraction of its splendid collections relating to the city's **maritime history**. Plymouth was also the home of **William Cookworthy**, discoverer of the Cornish kaolin which made the production of **hard paste porcelain** a reality in this country from 1768; an excellent display relates this story.

EXCURSIONS
Buckland Abbey★★

NT. Yelverton, 9mi/15km north. ⊙ *Open mid-Mar–early Nov Fri–Wed (daily Jul–Aug) 10.30am–5.30pm. Nov–mid-Dec and mid-Feb–early Mar, Fri–Sun 11am–4pm.* ☞*£7.40. Grounds only, £3.80.* ♿🅿✕. ☎*01822 853 607. www.nationaltrust.org.uk.*

Buckland was founded in 1278. At the Dissolution, the property was sold to the Grenvilles and converted into an Elizabethan mansion before their famous cousin, **Sir Francis Drake**, purchased the estate in 1581. The property has since been transformed from Tudor mansion to Georgian family home. The garden is largely 20C.

The house accommodates elements of the original church in its domestic context in a fascinating way, outlined in The **Four Lives Gallery**. The **Drake Gallery**, which dominates the first floor, was added in the 1570s and houses an exhibition on the great seaman and explorer. The panelled **Drake Chamber** is hung with a series of 16–17C portraits and contains English and continental furniture of the same period. The **Great Hall**, at the heart of the old abbey, is paved in pink-and -white tiles, lined with oak panelling. and features striking original plasterwork. The furniture is predominantly 16–17C. The kitchen, with French-style brick charcoal ovens and a range of old-fashioned kitchen utensils, was added in the 17C.

The **Great Barn**, buttressed and gabled, dates back to the 14C and was built to store the abbey's tithes and dues.

Saltram House★★

NT. 3.5mi/5.5km east on the A 374 then south on the A 38 to Plympton. **House:** ⊙*Open mid-Mar–Oct 11am–5pm Sat–Thu and Good Fri noon–4.30pm.* **Garden and gallery:** ⊙*Open Mar–Oct 11am–4.30pm (Sat–Thu 11am–4 pm rest of year).* ☞*House and garden £8.25. Garden only, £4.10.* ♿🅿✕. ☎*01752 333 500. www.nationaltrust.org.uk.*

This is a magnificent Georgian house with some of the finest 18C rooms in the country, with opulent Robert Adam interiors, gardens, follies and landscaped parkland. To complete Adams' interior design, Chippendale contributed furniture, Reynolds portraits and Angelica Kauffmann, paintings.

Saltram House

Salisbury★★

Wiltshire

Salisbury (pronounced "Sauls-bur-ee") is the quintessential English cathedral town. The view, as you approach it, is much as John Constable painted it some two centuries ago, unencumbered by high-rise modernity or sprawling suburbs. The spire, the tallest in England, is the classic city centre's focal point.

▶ **Population:** 39,268.

Michelin Map: Michelin Atlas p 9 or Map 503 O 30.

Info: Fish Row. ℰ01722 334956. www.visitwiltshire. co.uk/salisbury.

◖ **Location:** Near Southampton and just north of the New Forest, Salisbury is a transport hub with frequent services. The station is on South Western Road 0.5mi/0.8km from the centre. The bus station is central, on Endless Street.

A BIT OF HISTORY

The earlier city of **Old Sarum**★ (*2mi/3km north*), originally an Iron Age hill-top fort (28 acres/11ha), had been modified by the Romans and Saxons and became a Norman strongpoint where two successive cathedrals were built. By the beginning of the 13C the citizens and clergy of Old Sarum began to build their third cathedral on the banks of the River Avon. The hill-top buildings fell into ruin and New Sarum, or Salisbury, was born.

MEDIEVAL STREETS

Between the cathedral and the 19C **Market Square** extend medieval streets, lined by gabled half-timbered houses dating from the 14C–17C. At the centre in a small square stands the 15C hexagonal **Poultry Cross**.

At the northeast end of the high street is **Sarum St Thomas Church**★, a Perpendicular church dating from 1220 with a low square tower of 1390. It features a **doom painting** (c. 1475), with Christ in Majesty and the New Jerusalem.

CATHEDRAL★★★

🕐 *Open year-round daily 7.15am–6.15pm (early Jun–late Aug 7.15pm). £5 contribution requested. Joint ticket with Old Sarum available, £7.*

Guided tours (free). Tower tour £6.50 (book ahead on ℰ01722 555 156. &✗. ℰ01722 555 120. www.salisburycathedral.org.uk.

For many people, Salisbury Cathedral epitomises the Early English style at its best; medieval Gothic in its purest, most ascetic form. It is unique among England's older cathedrals, having been built in a single style, with the tallest spire in England (404ft/123m). Outside, the ornate **west screen** extends from the gabled portals up through lines of statue-filled niches, lancet windows and arcading to the pointed gable and corner towers with their miniature angel pinnacles and ribbed spires. The most spectacular feature of the cathedral, the **spire** over the heightened tower, was added almost a century later but harmonizes perfectly.

Inside, the **nave** (229.5ft/70m) extends over half the length of the whole building (449ft/137m), its vault towering to a height of 84ft/25m. On the south side the tomb chests of **Bishops Roger** (d. 1139) and **Joscelin** (d. 1184), the shrine of **St Osmund** (d. 1099) and the chain-mailed **William Longespée** (d. 1226), half-brother of King John. Giant piers of clustered black marble columns mark the **crossing**, intended to support the original tower, but since the 14C required to bear the additional 6,500 tons of the heightened tower and spire. The piers have in fact buckled a noticeable 3.5in/9cm, despite reinforcing.

A brass plate in the crossing marks the spot where a plumb-line let down from the spire point by Sir Christopher Wren in 1668 reached the floor; 29.5in/75.5cm off-centre to the southwest. In the north aisle is the oldest working clock in England (c. 1386). A **roof tour**, restoration work permitting, leads up the tower through the clock and bell chambers to the external gallery at the base of the spire.

Construction of the Decorated Gothic style **chapter-house** and **cloisters** was begun c. 1263, making the latter the earliest in any English cathedral; they are also the longest (181ft/55m). The vault of the octagonal chapter-house (58ft/18m across) is supported on a central column, surrounded by eight ringed Purbeck marble shafts which continue to rise from their foliated capitals as ribs to ceiling bosses, before dropping to clusters of slim columns framing the windows. An Old Testament frieze (restored in the 19C) fills the spandrels between the niches on either side of the canons' seats. The main floor display is dedicated to one of the four original copies of the **Magna Carta**.

Cathedral Close★

The Close is spacious and mellow with its 16–18C houses composed of ancient stone and terracotta bricks. The Close walls are of stone from the abandoned cathedral and castle of Old Sarum.

The medieval flint-and-brick house **Salisbury and South Wiltshire Museum**★ (◷open year-round Mon–Sat 10am–5pm, Jul–Aug also Sun noon–5pm; ◷closed Dec 24–1 Jan; ⏣£6; ⚘; ☏01722 332 151; www.salisburymuseum.org.uk)

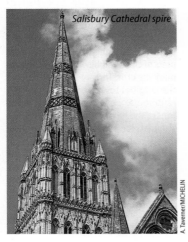
Salisbury Cathedral spire

A. Taverner/MICHELIN

contains the regimental museum and a **Stonehenge** collection, relics from Old Sarum, porcelain and pottery.

The museum of the Royal Gloucestershire, Berkshire and Wiltshire Regiment is housed in **The Wardrobe**★ (◷ open 10am–5pm, Apr–Oct daily, Nov and Feb–Mar Tue–Sun; ⏣£3.50; ⚘✕; ☏01722 419 419; www.thewardrobe.org.uk), one of the first houses to be built in the Close (1254) as the Bishop's document storehouse and wardrobe.

In Chorsiter's Close, **Mompesson House**★ (NT; ◷ open mid-Mar–Oct Sat–Wed and Good Friday 11am–5pm; ⏣£4.70; ⚘✕; ☏01722 335 659; 01722 420 980 (infoline); www.nationaltrust. org.uk) was built in 1701 by Charles Mompesson. It is notable for its ornate Baroque plasterwork and huge collection of some 370 types of English drinking glasses dating from 1700.

EXCURSIONS
Old Sarum★

EH. ◷ Open daily late Mar–Jun and Sept 10am–5pm; Jul–Aug 9am–6pm; Oct and Mar 10am–4pm; rest of year 11am–3pm. ⏣£2.90. ◷ Closed 24–26 Dec, 1 Jan. ▱. ☏01722 335 398. www.english-heritage.org.uk.

The mighty ramparts of this great earthwork were raised c. 500 BC by Iron Age peoples, then occupied by the Romans, the Saxons and, eventually the Normans. Here, William the Conqueror paid off his troops in 1070, and in 1086 summoned the great landowners of England to swear an oath of loyalty. A castle was built, then a royal palace. By the mid-12C a town had arisen complete with a new Norman cathedral, but the lack of water on the scorched hilltop made life almost unbearable. The answer was a move downhill to the burgeoning New Sarum (Salisbury), where a new cathedral was founded in 1220. Old Sarum went into rapid decline. Its cathedral was demolished and used for building materials and its castle was abandoned.

Today, Old Sarum remains an atmospheric place, the remains of its fortress palace, castle and cathedral still clear, and well interpreted in-situ.

Wilton House★★

House: ⏰ *Open May–Aug Sun–Thu and bank hols noon–5.30pm. Gardens:* ⏰ *Open May–Aug daily, Sept Sat–Sun only, 11am–5.30pm.* ⏰*Closed late Aug bank hol Sat.* ☛£12; *grounds only, £5.* ♿🅿✕.℘01722 746 714, 01722 746 729 *(info line).www.wiltonhouse.com.*

In 1544 the first Earl of Pembroke was given the land of the dissolved Benedictine convent at Wilton by Henry VIII and built a house here. The 4th Earl commissioned **Inigo Jones** to design the house anew in 1630 and the 11th Earl called in **James Wyatt** in 1801, who greatly altered the house.

The suite of **State Apartments** by Inigo Jones has a wealth of Classical detail. The furniture includes pieces by William Kent and the younger Chippendale.

The ceiling of the **Colonnade Room** boasts fantastical 17C monkey motifs. In the **Great Ante Room** are portraits by Rembrandt, Van Dyck and Clouet.

The white and gold **Double Cube Room**, measuring 60ft/18m x 30ft/9m x 30ft/9m), was specially designed by Inigo Jones to house the 4th Earl's unique collection of splendid **Van Dyck portraits**. It was here that strategic plans were laid by Eisenhower and Churchill (a frequent visitor) during the Second World War, when Wilton House was the Southern Command headquarters.

The house sits square on a flat lawn which stretches south to the river, marked by the **Palladian bridge** (1737) and a few trees, before becoming pasture beyond. The grounds also include an excellent adventure playground.

Shaftesbury

The town is perched on the crest of a 700ft/213m spur, an excellent **vantage point**★, used by King Alfred as a strongpoint in his wars against the Danes. The **Abbey** (*Abbey Museum:* ⏰*open Good Fri/ Apr–Oct, daily 10am–5pm;* ☛*£2.50;* ℘*01747 852 910; www.shaftesburyabbey.org.uk)*, founded in 888 by King Alfred, became the wealthiest nunnery in England. In the 15C–16C the saying went that if the Abbess of Shaston (Shaftesbury) were to marry the Abbot of Glaston (Glastonbury) their heirs would own more land than the king.

In 1539 Henry VIII dissolved both abbeys and now only the ground plan of Shaston remains visible. Shaftesbury's joy is the steep cobbled picture-book **Gold Hill**★, lined on one side with small 16C–18C houses and on the other by a massive buttressed 13C ochre-coloured wall.

Isles of Scilly★
Cornwall

This wind-battered archipelago off England's southwesterly tip is designated an Area of Outstanding Natural Beauty, a Heritage Coast, and its waters a Marine Park. The approach by sea or air gives a partial **view**★★★ of the five inhabited islands, 40 uninhabited islands, and 150 or so named rocks in a close group in the clear blue-green ocean.

VISIT
St Mary's

3mi/5km across at its widest, with a coastline of 9mi/15km, St Mary's is the largest and principal island on which all

▶ **Population:** 2,048.

⊙ **Michelin Map:** Michelin Atlas p 2 or Map 503 A, B 34 – 28mi/45km southwest of Land's End

ℹ **Info:** Hugh Street, St Mary's. ℘01720 424 031. www.simplyscilly.co.uk.

but a few hundred Scillonians live. The main settlement is **Hugh Town**, formerly home to the **Garrison**. The mid-18C **Guard Gate** gives access to **Star Castle**★ *(now a hotel, freely accessible to the public)* built in 1594 at the time of Elizabeth I's feud with Spain. From the rampart walls are excellent **views**★★.

GETTING THERE

The *Scillonian III* operates a summer boat service from Penzance to St Mary's. Fixed-wing aircraft services operate from Southampton, Bristol, Exeter, Newquay and Land's End. (*℘0845 710 555. www.islesofscilly -travel.co.uk*).
Helicopter flights take 20 minutes from Penzance to St Mary's and operate six days a week with regular flights throughout the day (*℘01736 363 871. www.islesofscilly helicopter.com*).

Tresco★

On being appointed Lord Proprietor in 1834, Augustus Smith built a Victorian medieval castle mansion near the ruins of a priory. Around these ruins he created the subtropical **Abbey Gardens**★★ (◷ *open daily 10am–4pm;* ⊜*£10;* ♿🅿✕; ℘*01720 424 108; www.tresco. co.uk*), from seeds and plants brought back by Scillonian sailors and plant collectors. From the terraces, there are fine **views**★★ over the gardens. On the edge of the gardens is **Valhalla**, an extraordinary collection of figureheads.

Sherborne★

Dorset

With its imposing abbey church, public school and fine warm **Ham Hill stone** buildings, Sherborne has the charm of a small cathedral city.

▶ **Population:** 7,606.
◔ **Michelin Map:** Michelin Atlas p 8 or Map 503 M 31.
🮲 **Info:** www.westdorset.com.
◗ **Location:** Sherborne is 47mi/75km south of Bath.

CITY

Abbey★★

◷ *Open daily 8am–6pm (winter 4pm).* 🚶 *Guided tours Apr–Sept Tue 10.30am, Fri 2.30pm (call to confirm).* ♿. ℘*01935 812 452. www.sherborne abbey.com.*
The abbey church, re-built during the 15C, contains elements which date back to Saxon times when Sherborne was made the See of the Bishop of Wessex, **St Aldhelm**, in 705. The Norman church extended as far west as the Saxon church, as the late Norman **south porch** proves.
The 15C **crossing tower** on massive Saxon-Norman piers and walls, has paired bell openings and twelve pinnacles. Inside, the **chancel** shafts rise directly from the floor up to the earliest large-scale **fan vault** in the country, and the effect is breathtaking. Even more impressive is the late-15C **nave vault**. A splendid, unadorned Norman **tower arch** divides the nave from the chancel. One of the original **Saxon doorways** can be seen at the end of the north aisle.

Sherborne Castle★

◷ *Open Apr–Oct Tue–Thu, Sat–Sun and bank hols 11am (castle 2pm Sat)–4.30pm (last admission).* ⊜*£9; grounds only £4. 50.* ✕. ℘*01935 813 182. www.sherbornecastle.com.*
The old castle, now a ruin, was built in 1107–35. In 1592 it was acquired by **Sir Walter Raleigh**, who the decided to build a new house, commonly known as Sherborne Lodge, which forms the nucleus of the present house, commonly known as Sherborne Castle, on the far bank of the River Yeo.
He created a four-storey house beneath a Dutch gable and balustrade, built of Ham Hill stone. Sir John Digby, who acquired the property following Raleigh's imprisonment, enlarged the castle in 1620–30, keeping to Raleigh's style. The house, set in parkland modelled by Lancelot "Capability" Brown in 1776–79, contains fine collections of paintings, furniture and porcelain. Take a look at the painting (1600) of Queen Elizabeth I in procession, and the 17C plaster ceiling in the Red Drawing Room.

Stonehenge★★★

Wiltshire

Stonehenge, Britain's most celebrated prehistoric monument, is between 4 000 and 5 000 years old; radiocarbon dating indicates that its construction was begun in c. 2950 BC and completed in three phases by c. 1550 BC. For centuries it has sent writers, painters and every sort of visitor into flights of fancy, for its purpose remains an enigma. Although many of the stones have fallen or disappeared it is still possible, from the centre of the circle, to see the sun rise over the Heel Stone *(at the entrance)* on midsummer's day; there are suggestions that it was constructed as an astronomical observatory or a sanctuary for a sun-worshipping cult, or even a combination of the two. The main axis has always been aligned with the midsummer sunrise and Stonehenge must have been a ceremonial centre celebrating the sun and marking the seasons.

- **Michelin Map:** Michelin Atlas p 9 or Map 503 O 30.
- **Info:** ℘0870 333 1181. www.english-heritage.org.uk.
- **Location:** Just north of Salisbury, 84mi/134km southwest of London.
- **Opeing:** *EH.* ⏱ *Open daily year-round. Mid-Mar–May and Sept–Oct 9.30am–6pm. Jun–Aug 9am–7pm. Mid-Oct–mid-Mar 9.30am–4pm (Dec 26 and Jan 1 10am–4pm).* ⏱*Closed 24–25 Dec.* ⬤£6.40. ♿🅿✖.

A BIT OF HISTORY

The Period – When work began the area was inhabited by nomadic hunters and early farming settlers who had crossed the Channel and North Sea in skin boats. By 2000 BC the Beaker Folk spread into Wessex along the chalk upland tracks, growing into a community of 12–15,000, ruled by the cattle-barons of Salisbury Plain, who also controlled the metal industry. There was a growing priesthood who, at peak periods in the construction of Stonehenge, could call on the population to provide the 600 men needed to haul a sarsen stone up the Vale of Pewsey, or 200 to erect it on-site.

The Building Design – Like many a medieval cathedral, Stonehenge was much remodelled after its foundation. In the **first phase**, 2950–2900 BC, a ditch with an inner bank of chalk rubble (6ft/nearly 2m high) was dug. This, with a ring of 56 holes, known as the Aubrey Holes, after the 17C pioneer of field archeology

Stonehenge

©René Mansi/iStockphoto.com

John Aubrey (1626–97), encloses an area 300ft/91m in diameter. To the northeast the bank and ditch were cut to make an entrance marked inside by two upright stones and outside by the **Heel Stone** (near the road). Inside the enclosure four **Station Sarsens** were set up at the cardinal points of the compass.

In the **second phase**, c. 2100 BC, a double ring of undressed **bluestones** was set up towards the centre; these stones, weighing up to 4t each, were transported 240mi/386km from the Presely Hills in southwest Wales, mainly by water, and finally along the wide **Avenue**, which was built from the River Avon to the entrance of the henge.

In the **third phase**, c. 2000 BC, the structure was transformed. The bluestone rings were replaced by a circle of tall trilithons. These standing stones were tapered at one end and tenoned at the top to secure the curving mortised lintels, which were linked to each other by tongues and grooves, having been levered gradually into position. Inside the circle five separate giant trilithons rose in a horseshoe, opening towards the Heel Stone. The entrance was marked by new uprights, one of which, the Slaughter Stone, now fallen, remains. By the end of this **final phase**, c. 1550 BC, the dressed bluestones were reintroduced in their present horseshoe formation, within the sarsen horseshoe.

Stourhead★★★
Wiltshire

One of the most celebrated gardens in the country, Stourhead is a supreme example of English landscape style including a Palladian mansion, delightful garden architecture and rare planting around a tranquil lake.

GARDEN

This idyllic scenery was created by the banker Henry Hoare II (1705–85), influenced by the landscapes he saw on his travels. Perhaps an even greater influence were the paintings of Claude Lorraine and Nicholas Poussin, in which nature is presented in luminous shades and focal points are provided by statuary or Classical buildings. He first had the great triangular lake formed, then began the planting of deciduous trees and conifers, "ranged in large masses as the shades in a painting". In collaboration with his architect, Henry Flitcroft, he began to build his garden architecture : the Temple of Flora, the Grotto, the Gothic Cottage, the Pantheon, the Temple of Apollo, and most famously, the **Palladian Bridge**.

He also created a quintessential English vista of lake, Turf Bridge, Cross, and, in

Michelin Map: Michelin Atlas p 8 or Map 403 N 30.
Info: ℘01747 841 152. www.nationaltrust.org.uk.
Location: Just outside Warminster, 18mi/30km south of Bath.
Times and Charges: NT. Stourton. *Garden:* Open year-round daily 9am–6pm/dusk. *House:* Open mid-Mar–Oct 11am–5pm Fri–Tue. *Tower:* Open daily mid-Mar–Oct 11am–5 pm. Garden and house £11.10, garden or house £6.60. Tower £2.50.

the background, Stourton church and village. His planting, now wonderfully mature, has been added to by his successors to give a wealth of exotic specimens and of ever-changing seasonal effects. At the far end of the "outer circuit" stands **Alfred's Tower**, a triangular brick folly built on the spot where Alfred allegedly raised his standard resisting the Danes, but more probably commemorating the succession of George III and peace with France (1762). At the top of the narrow tower is a viewing balcony (206 steps).

House

Colen Campbell's house of 1721 was built for the father of Henry Hoare II. In 1902 a fire destroyed the early 18C interiors, although the contents of the ground floor staterooms were largely saved.

The **hall**, a perfect 30ft/9m cube, is hung with family portraits. The long barrel-vaulted **library**, a particularly fine Regency interior, contains some splendid pieces of **Chippendale** furniture and **Canaletto** drawings of Venice. Further treasures are to be found in the South Wing (furniture) and **Picture Gallery**: landscapes by **Claude** and **Poussin**.

Palladian Bridge and the Pantheon in the background
©CanvinPhoto/iStockphoto.com

Taunton ★

Somerset

The county town of Taunton, gateway to the West Country, is an agricultural and commercial centre at the heart of the fertile Vale of Taunton (Taunton Deane), famous for its cider apples.

- ▶ **Population:** 55,855.
- 🕭 **Michelin Map:** Michelin Atlas p 7 or Map 504 K 30.
- 🛈 **Info:** Library, Paul Street. ℘01823 336 344. www.heartofsomerset.com.
- ◖ **Location:** Taunton is 53mi (85km) south west of Bath.

SIGHTS

Castle

The castle, dating from the 11C–12C, is especially known for its ownership by successive bishops of Winchester. The Civil War put Taunton, and the castle in particular, under siege three times. Part of it now houses the **Somerset County Museum★** (🕓 *closed until summer 2010 re-opening as the Museum of Somerset; ℘01823 320 201; www.somerset.gov. uk/museums*). Following his defeat at Sedgemoor in 1685 Charles II's natural son, the **Duke of Monmouth**, and many of his followers were tried by **Judge Jeffreys** in the great hall; 508 of them were condemned to death in the notorious **Bloody Assizes** and another thousand or so were transported to the West Indies. Monmouth was executed on Tower Hill a month later.

St Mary Magdalene★

🕓 *Open Mon–Fri 8.30am–5.15pm, Sat 9am–4pm.*

In the true Somerset tradition, this splendid medieval church culminates in a soaring tower (1488–1514) built of lovely red and tawny-gold Ham Hill stone. Inside, the roof carvings are typical of Somerset craftsmanship.

St James's★

This 14C–15C (except the north arcade and aisle) church features a 120ft/37m tower of Quantock red sandstone with Ham Hill stone decoration.

EXCURSIONS

Ilminster★

9.5mi/16km southeast.

This Ham stone market town, which flourished from the wool trade in the 15C–16C, was listed as having a **Minster★★** in Domesday. St Mary's most impressive feature is its 90ft/27m crossing tower, modelled on that of Wells Cathedral. It has two levels of bell openings up to a crest of gargoyles, pinnacles and a spirelet on the stair turret. The 15C Perpendicular building with nave, transepts, chancel and tower was extended with aisles in the 16C. Galleries were added above the nave and aisles in 1824–25 to accommodate larger congregations. Note the fan vaults inserted at the crossing and **Wadham Chapel** (north transept), built in 1452 to house the tomb chests of Sir William Wadham, and Nicholas, founder of Wadham College, Oxford.

Totnes★

Devon, England

Ancient Totnes is one of the most rewarding small towns in England, standing at the highest navigable and lowest bridging point on the River Dart on the south Devon coast. The narrow main street runs steeply between 16–17C wealthy merchants' houses built of brick and stone or colour-washed. Totnes is unusual for a town of its size, as it eschews chain stores and is devoted almost entirely to small individual shops and cafés, many catering for the bohemian-chic lifestyle for which Totnes is famous.

▶ **Population:** 7,018.
Michelin Map:
Michelin Atlas p 4 or Map 503 – I, J 32.
Info: Town Mill, The Plains. ℘01803 863 168. www. totnesinformation.co.uk.

TOWN
Fore Street
The half-timbered **Elizabethan Museum**★ *(70 Fore Street; ◔open mid-Mar–Oct and two weeks Dec Mon–Fri 10.30am–5pm; ☞£2; ☎01803 863 821. www.devonmuseums.net/totnes)*, the dark red-brick **mansion** (now a community education centre), a late 18C Gothic house (in Bank Lane), and other attractive buildings (nos 48 and 52) testify to Totnes' former prosperity.

High Street
Interesting features include; the mid-16C **Guildhall** (◔open Apr–Oct, Mon–Fri, some bank hols,10.30am–4.30pm; ☞£1.50; ℘01803 862 147; www.totnes information.co.uk), which occupies the site of an earlier Benedictine priory; the house at no. 16, now a bank built in 1585 by a local pilchard merchant; and the granite pillared **Butterwalk**★, which has protected shoppers from the rain since the 17C.

St Mary's★
The 15C parish and priory church with its red sandstone tower adorned with gruesome gargoyles contains a beautiful late 15C rood screen.

Castle
EH. ◔ *Open Easter/late Mar Oct–daily, 10am–5pm (6pm Jul–Aug, 4pm Oct). ☞£2.50.* 🅿 *℘01803 864 406. www. english-heritage.org.uk/totnes.*
High on a mound sits the castle, encircled by 14C ramparts built to strengthen the late 11C motte and bailey earthworks. The castle walls command excellent **views**★★★ of the Dart River valley.

View over Totnes town
©Ann Taylor-Hughes/iStockphoto.com

Wells★★

Somerset

The calm of the cathedral within its precinct contrasts with the bustle of the Market Square in England's smallest cathedral city. In the Middle Ages Wells prospered as a centre of the wool trade.

▶ **Population:** 9,763.

Michelin Map: Michelin Atlas p 16 or Map 503 M 30.

Info: Town Hall, Market Pl. *℘*01749 672 552. www.wellstourism.com.

Location: 23mi/38km southwest of Bath. Well's bus station is off Market Street and has an hourly service to Bath and Bristol.

Kids: Wookey Hole, Cheddar Gorge and Caves.

CATHEDRAL★★★

Open daily 7am–7pm (6pm Oct–Mar). £5.50 contribution requested. *Guided Tours (free) Mon–Sat.* *℘*01749 674 483. www.wells cathedral.org.uk.

Wells was the first cathedral church in the Early English style; it took more than three centuries to plan and build, from c. 1175 to 1508.

Despite weathering and much destruction by the Puritans, the **west front** is one of England's richest displays of 13C sculpture – with its figures coloured and gilded, it would have once resembled an illuminated manuscript or sumptuous tapestry. Although now monochrome, it is tinted at sunset and gilded by floodlights at night. The screen front is nearly 150ft/46m across, twice as wide as it is tall, with some 300 statues rising to a climax in the centre gable.

Inside the cathedral, set into the west wall of the north transept is a **quarterjack** – 15C knights who strike the bells with their pikes at the quarters. The most striking feature of the **nave** is the **scissor arch**, constructed in 1338–48, when the west piers of the crossing tower began to subside. The nave was completed in 1239. There are interesting carvings in the **south transept**: men's heads, animal masks and everyday scenes such as a man with toothache and two men caught in the act of stealing apples from an orchard. The medieval **misericords** show a man killing a wyvern and Alexander the Great being lifted to heaven by two griffins. In the north transept is an **astronomical clock** of 1390, with the sun and a star revolving round the 24hr dial and, above, a **knights' tournament** in which one knight is struck down at every quarter hour.

A wide curving flight of steps, laid c. 1290, leads to the splendid octagonal **chapterhouse**, completed 1306.

Cathedral Precinct

Three 15C **gates** lead from the city streets to the calm of the Green and the spectacular view of the cathedral exterior. The **Chain Gate** gives access to **Vicars' Close**, a street of identical cottages built c. 1348.

On the south side of the cathedral stands the 800-year-old **Bishop's Palace**★ (*open Apr–Oct daily 10.30am–6pm/ Sat 2pm, Nov– late-Dec Wed–Sun 10.30am–4.30pm;* £5. *℘*01749 678 691; www.bishopspalacewells.co.uk), stoutly walled and encircled by a moat. Inside are walled gardens and the well springs from which the city gets its name – 3,400,000 gallons a day, or 40 gallons a second (c. 15 million litres a

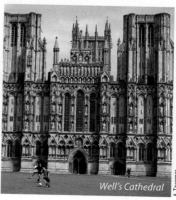

Well's Cathedral

A. Taverner

Cheddar Gorge

A. Taverner/MICHELIN

caves were inhabited by Iron Age man in 300 BC and later by Romano-British and Celtic peoples. The caves mix history and legends liberally and there are lots of family attractions besides, including a Fairy Garden, 20 life-size dinosaur replicas, a mirror maze, Victorian games arcade and adventure golf. Do make time to visit the **papermill**★ – paper was first made at Wookey Hole c. 1600.

♟♟ Cheddar Gorge and Caves★★

9mi/14km northwest. ⏱*Open daily 10.30am–5pm (10am–5.30pm Jul–Aug).* ⏱*Closed 24–25 Dec.* ☞*Caves and Gorge Explorer, inc bus tour, £16, child £10. Gorge Outdoors ticket £4.50, child £3.* ◻✕. ✆*01934 742 343. www.cheddarcaves.co.uk*

Evidence of human settlement at Cheddar Gorge dates back to the Upper Late Palaeolithic era. The gorge is 2mi/3km long with a one in six gradient, twisting and turning in its descent from the Mendips, and the cliffs rise vertically 350–400ft/107–122m.

The caves are near the gorge bottom on the south side *(left, going down).* **Cox's Cave** was discovered in 1837 and **Gough's Cave** in 1890. The series of chambers follows the course of underground streams through the porous limestone, past stalagmites stalactites and petrified falls. Also included in the ticket price is the **Crystal Quest** dark-walk fantasy adventure, **Jacob's Ladder**, a staircase of 274 steps leads up to a panoramic **view**★ and an open-top bus tour *(Mar–Oct only).* **Cheddar** village lies at the foot of the gorge.

day, or 180 litres a second). There are also the ruins of the old banqueting hall, the present palace and a **view**★★ of the cathedral.

EXCURSIONS
♟♟ Wookey Hole★

2mi/3km northwest. ⏱*Open daily 10am–5pm (Nov–Mar 4pm).* ⏱*Closed Dec 25.* ☞*£15, child £10 (book online for savings).* ◻✕. ✆*01749 672 243. www.wookey.co.uk.*

A hole in a 200ft/61m cliff-side from which the River Axe gushes in a torrent leads to **caves** containing six chambers through which the river flows, always present, in echoing cascades and deep blue-green pools. The tour leads through some 350yds/320m of caverns containing **stalactites**, **stalagmites**, "frozen" waterfalls and translucent pools. The

---

West Country Cheese

According to one fanciful legend, the history of West Country cheese began when monks on a pilgrimage to Glastonbury took shelter from a terrible storm in the Cheddar caves and found that the milk they were carrying in leather pouches had turned into a delicious cheese: Cheddar has since become synonymous with English cheese, notably abroad. In fact Cheddar Caves was inaccessible to all but climbers until the 19C. The truth is that itinerant holy men, especially early Celtic monks from Ireland, developed the art of cheese-making not only as a means of saving what otherwise might be wasted milk, but also for eating on days of fasting when meat was forbidden.

Yeovil

Somerset

Yeovil was an important leather and glove centre from the 14C onwards, and was later known for its flax. The opening of the railway link with Taunton in 1853 broadened the town's horizons. The population increased and the buildings we now see are mainly 19C–20C, albeit with a few scattered 18C–19C Georgian houses and older inns on the likes of Princess Street, High Street and Silver Street.

▶ **Population:** 28,317.
Michelin Map: Michelin Atlas p 8 or Map 403 M 31.
Info: Hendford. ℘01935 845 946. www.visit southsomerset.com.
`Location: Yeovil lies 41mi/66km south of Bristol.
Kids: Fleet Air Arm Museum.

EXCURSIONS

Fleet Air Arm Museum★★

Yeovilton. 6mi/10km north. Open Apr–Oct daily 10am–5.30pm. Nov–Mar Wed–Sun 10am–4.30. Last admission 1hr 30min before closing. Closed 24–26 Dec. £10.50, child £7.50. ℘01935 840 565. www.fleetairarm.com.
This entertaining museum set within aircraft hangers next to the Royal Naval Air Station where helicopters are daily put through their paces, is dedicated to Royal Navy aviation.
The display includes over 40 aircraft including the second prototype of **Concorde**, the famous Anglo-French jet airliner. A highlight is the **Aircraft Carrier Experience** where visitors feel the noise and rush of jets around them.

Montacute House★★

NT. 5m/8km west. Montacute. **House:** Open mid-Mar–Oct Wed–Mon 11am–5pm. **Garden:** Open Mar–Christmas Wed–Mon 11am–4pm (mid-Mar–Oct until 5.30pm, also open Mon). £8.90; garden and park only, £5.40 (£2 Nov–mid-Jan). ℘01935 823 289. www.nationaltrust.org.uk.
This handsome Elizabethan three-storey mansion was built 1597–1601 for Sir Edward Phelips, a successful lawyer, Speaker of the House of Commons (1604) and Master of the Rolls (1611). Entrance to the house is through the original east doorway into the screens passage. At the far end of the **Great Hall**, the charming **Skimmington Frieze** is a 17C plaster relief depicting the ordeals of a hen-pecked husband. The **Parlour**, with its original Ham Hill stone fireplace, Elizabethan panelling and frieze of nursery animals, contains some fine 18C furniture (beautiful centre table by Thomas Chippendale the Younger), as does the **Drawing Room**.
Lord Curzon's Room (first floor) contains his lordship's bath stowed in a "Jacobean" cupboard, a 17C overmantel of King David at Prayer, an 18C bed, a Dutch oak drop-leaf table and an 18C japanned skeleton mirror. The **Crimson Room**, so-called since the 19C when red flock wallpaper replaced the tapestries below the plaster frieze, contains a sumptuous oak four-poster bed carved with the arms of James I. The **Library**, once the formal dining room and destination of the dishes brought from the distant kitchens, features some remarkable heraldic glass – a tourney of 42 shields displaying the Phelips arms, those of the sovereign and of some of Phelips' neighbours and friends. Other interesting features in this former state room are the Portland stone mantelpiece, plaster frieze, Jacobean inner porch, 19C moulded plaster ceiling and bookcases.
The Long Gallery (172ft/52m), lit with oriels at either end, occupies the entire top floor; it is the longest in existence. It now provides the perfect setting for a panoply of Tudor and early Jacobean England through 90 portraits (on loan from the National Portrait Gallery). The formal layout of the gardens is designed to enhance that of the house, with lawns and yews providing a fine foreground to the warm hues of Ham Hill stone.

EAST ANGLIA

In the popular imagination East Anglia is a flat land devoid of interest, fringed by a handful of old-fashioned seaside resorts chilled even in summer by the winds from Eastern Europe. In fact England's largest area of low relief is a region of surprising individuality; densely populated in medieval times, it is unequalled in its wealth of ancient villages and small towns. In the early 19C Constable painted it as a rural idyll and pockets of such countryside still remain intact. Its dry climate and generally good soils mean that much of its gently undulating farmland is in arable cultivation supplying much of England's food crop; as a result however fields are large and many trees and hedges have been removed.

Highlights

1 Putting yourself in the picture in **Constable Country** (p268).

2 Taking a Tour of St John's College, **Cambridge** (p261).

3 The magnificent medieval cathedral at **Ely** (p267).

4 Palatial Palladian **Holkham Hall** with its paintings (p270).

5 Boating on the **Norfolk Broads** (p274).

Cambridgeshire

The county of Cambridgeshire is dominated by the Fens to the north. This monotonous landscape, similar to the *polders* of the Netherlands, was largely created by Dutch engineers who carried out much of the work which transformed the wetlands around the Wash – that great chunk bitten out of the northwest tip of East Anglia – into Britain's richest tract of arable land, providing cereals, root crops, vegetables, flowers and fruit. From these flatlands rise several fine churches and two outstanding cathedrals, once the two great monasteries of the Fens, Peterborough and Ely. Cambridge is the second-oldest university city in the English-speaking world with outstanding architecture, both old and new, while its elite student population brings a vitality, wealth and culture to the town.

- Cambridge
- Peterborough
- Ely

Medieval town of Lavenham near Bury St. Edmunds

Norfolk

Norfolk is best-known for its Broads, extensive shallow stretches of reedy water (see box), rich in wildlife. Since its commercial development in the 1960s it has been thronged with pleasure craft, exploring its 125mi/200km of navigable waterways. Away from the main centres is a land of peace and quiet and empty skies, excellent for nature-watching. The coast is known for its typically English seaside resorts, such as Great Yarmouth and Cromer; these fell out of vogue many years ago but still have a loyal following.

Set amid the Fenlands (see CAMBRIDGESHIRE opposite) Kings Lynn is rich in medieval merchant's houses while northern Norfolk is home to outstanding country houses including Sandringham, the Royal Family's country retreat. Norwich is the regional capital. It grew wealthy on the wool trade of medieval England and is famous for its Norman cathedral, castle and Sainsbury Centre for Visual Arts (part of the University of East Anglia) which was in the vanguard of modern architecture when it was built in the 1970s. Its preserved medieval, sometimes cobbled streets, lined with half-timbered houses, and a lively daily market, make it one of the most attractive and likeable cities in England.

- Norwich
- King's Lynn

Suffolk

This is the most picturesque and varied part of East Anglia. Bury St Edmunds and Lavenham are charming country towns, both with important religious buildings. The former is mainly Georgian and Victorian while Lavenham's ancient half-timbered houses are zealously preserved and the town is renowned for its pargeting, a form of exterior decorative stucco work which is a speciality of Suffolk. Ipswich is the bustling county town, a mix of Victorian and modern. South of here is Constable Country with Dedham and Flatford Mill, not so very different from the quintessentially English village scenes that were painted around 200 years ago. Slipping briefly into Essex, Colchester, once the capital of all England, is well worth a visit for its castle and collection of Roman antiquities. North of Ipswich is a delightful stretch of unspoiled coastline, which includes Aldeburgh, home of a famous classical music and arts festival, and fashionable Southwold, a fine, old, unspoiled and uncommercialised genteel resort.

- Ipswich
- Bury St Edmunds

National Parks

Norfolk and Suffolk Broads – Established as a National Park in 1989, the Broads are peat-diggings from the 9C, which flooded and became part of the river system in the 14C. Strenuous efforts by the Broads Authority in the 1980s partly halted environmental degradation, due to nutrients from effluents and fertilisers. The water is recovering its life but care is still needed from all who use and enjoy this park.

Bury St Edmunds★

Suffolk

The historic market town of Bury St Edmunds boasts the ruins of what was once one of the richest abbeys in Christendom, as well as a perfect late Perpendicular cathedral and a wide range of English architectural styles, from secular medieval (**The Guidhall**) through Georgian (**Athenaeum**), and Regency (**Theatre Royal**) to grand Victorian.

▶ **Population:** 31,237.

Michelin Map: Michelin Atlas p 22 or Map 504 W 27.

Info: Angel Hill. ☎01284 764 667. www.visit-burystedmunds.co.uk.

Location: 28mi/45km E of Cambridge. The train station is a 10-min walk north of the centre, the bus station is central, on St Andrew Street North. Bury's medieval grid layout makes orientation easy. Take a guided walking tour from the tourist office.

Don't Miss: The cathedral or an excursion to Lavenham.

Timing: Allow a day including Lavenham. Market days are Wednesday and Saturday.

TOWN

On Angel Hill in eastern Bury St Edmunds is the parish church, **St Edmundsbury Cathedral**★ (*open year-round daily 8.30am–6pm;* *£3 per adult, 50p per child contribution requested;* *guided tours Mar–Sept Mon–Sat 11.30am;* *; ☎01284 754 933; www.stedscathedral. co.uk*), which dates from 1530 and was dedicated to St James. It changed its name when it was granted cathedral status in 1914. A composition of nine bays leads the eye to the chancel and transepts (1960) by Stephen Dykes Bower. Note the Flemish stained-glass Susanna window (c. 1480) and hammerbeam roof (19C) with angels.

In the grounds behind the cathedral lie the **Abbey Ruins**★ (*open year-round Mon–Sat, 7.30am–30 min before dusk, Sun and bank hols 9am–30 min before dusk; ☎01284 757 490; www.stedmunds bury.gov.uk*). Founded in 633 and later renamed in honour of the Saxon king and martyr Edmund (d. 870). It was rebuilt by Benedictine monks in the 11C. Today only two of its monumental crossing towers still stand upright. Remnants of nave, chancel and transepts, together with the **Abbey Gate**, give some idea of its vastness (505ft/154m long).

The **Norman Tower's** richly decorated gateway frames a bronze of St Edmund by Elisabeth Frink and the cathedral precinct houses, built into the abbey's west end. The **Abbey Visitor Centre** (*open Easter–Oct daily 10am–5pm;*) provides an interpretation of the ruins.

EXCURSION
Lavenham★

11mi/18km southeast.

This is a superbly preserved medieval wool town crowded with timber–framed houses. The late 15C **Church of St Peter and St Paul**★ (*open year-round 8.30am–5.30pm/3.30pm;*), is one of the great "wool" churches with a noble tower and porch and enchanting misericords. The **Guildhall of Corpus Christi** facing the Market Place dates from c. 1520. It stages exhibitions and houses a **museum** (NT; *open Mar–Oct daily;* *£3.80;* *; ☎01787 247 646; www. nationaltrust.org.uk*) on the East Anglian wool trade and local history.

Manor House Museum

Honey Hill. *Open Wed–Sun, 11am–4pm.* *Closed Mon (except bank hols), Good Friday, 25–26 Dec.* *£2.50.* . ☎01284 757 072.

Under ornate plasterwork ceilings the collection concentrates on clocks but also includes costumes, textiles, portraits and *objets d'art* bequeathed by local families.

Cambridge★★★
Cambridgeshire

England's second-oldest university city (after Oxford), Cambridge established its academic reputation in the early 13C (c. 1209), attracting groups of scholars from Oxford and Paris interested in studying theology, church and civil law, and logic. The oldest Cambridge college, Peterhouse, was founded in 1284 and by 1352 seven more colleges had been built, all with their characteristic four–sided enclosed monastic courtyard.

CITY AND COLLEGES

Today the 31 colleges are totally independent self-governing bodies while the university undertakes all public teaching and confers the degrees. Cambridge is also a showpiece for new architecture, some controversial, both on college sites and on the west side of the city.

Some colleges charge admission March to September; most are closed during the examination period May–June. See the University website *www.cam.ac.uk* for all visiting details.

St John's College★★★

◷ Open Mar–Oct 10am–5.30pm; weekends only rest of the year. ⊛£2.80. ♿. ℘01223 338 600. www.joh.cam.ac.uk. St John's (founded 1511) is the second–largest college and its turreted gate–house is one of the most beautiful. **First**, **Second** and **Third Courts** are predominantly Tudor; Ruskin called the Second the most perfect in Cambridge. Behind Third Court is the 18C Kitchen Bridge, with its view of Hutchinson's exquisite **Bridge of Sighs**. The 13C **School of Pythagoras** is the oldest medieval stone house in Cambridge.

Trinity College★★

◷Open year-round most days 10am–5pm, see website or call ahead for details. Wren Library open Mon–Fri noon–2pm Sat in term time 10.30am–2.30 pm. ⊛£2.50 Mar–Oct. ℘01223 338 400. www.trin.cam.ac.uk.

▷ **Population:** 95, 682.
⚙ **Michelin Map:** Michelin Atlas p 29 or Map 504 U 27.
ℹ **Info:** Cambridge Tourist Information Centre, The Old Library, Wheeler Street, Cambridge CB2 3QB. ℘0871 226 8006; (from overseas) 0044 1223 464 732; (accommodation) 01223 457 581. www.visitcambridge.org.
◖ **Location:** 58 mi/93km N of London on the western edge of the East Anglian fenlands situated on the River Cam. The train station is 1mi/1.6km southeast of the centre, off Hills Road. The bus station is on Drummer Street, in town. The main colleges and the Fitzwilliam Museum are tightly clustered in the centre.
🅿 **Parking:** Park and ride system in operation. City centre closed to motor vehicles during the week 10am–4pm.
⊛ **Don't Miss:** St John's College; King's College Chapel, particularly listening to the Choir; punting on the river Cam.
◷ **Timing:** Two days minimum.
👪 **Kids:** Imperial War Museum, Duxford.
🚶 **Walking Tours:** Guided walking tours and ghost tours daily (℘01223 457 574).

The largest Cambridge college, Trinity, was founded in 1546 by Henry VIII; its oldest buildings surround the **Great Court** – the 1432 **King Edward's Tower** (clock tower) and the **Great Gate**, completed in 1535.

In cloistered **Nevile's Court** (1612) stands the **Wren Library**, completed in

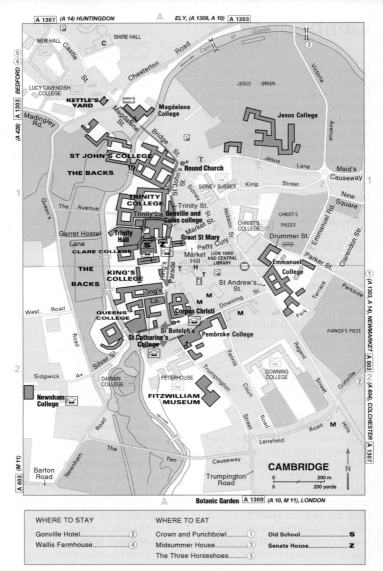

1695 and named after its designer. The bookcases are decorated with limewood carvings by Grinling Gibbons. Among the manuscripts are the 8C Epistles of St Paul, Shakespeare's First Folio and illuminated 15C French Books of Hours.

Trinity Hall
Down Senate House Passage.
🕐 *Open daily, dawn–dusk.* 🕐 *Closed mid-Apr–late June and Dec 24–Jan 2.*

College may be closed at other times without prior notice. 🖉 *01223 332 500. www.trinhall.cam.ac.uk.*

Trinity Hall was founded by Bishop Bateman of Norwich in 1350. Behind the 18C ashlar of **Principal Court** are three ranges (best viewed from North Court) which date from 1350, and beyond the delightful Elizabethan Library is the garden Henry James called "the prettiest corner of the world".

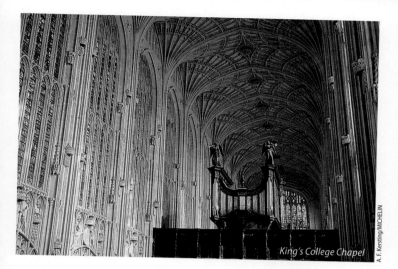

King's College Chapel

A. F. Kersting/MICHELIN

Clare College★

Old Court, Hall, Chapel and Gardens.
🕐 *Open usually all year daily 10.30am–5pm.* ✆*Easter–Sept £2.50.* 📞*01223 333 200. www.clare.cam.ac.uk.*

The college was founded in 1326. The 17C ranges are the work of father and son **Thomas** and **Robert Grumbold** and are among the most serene in Cambridge.
Clare Bridge was built by Thomas Grumbold, before the 17C ranges. Note the missing segment of one of the stone balls on the bridge's parapet. He had vowed never to complete the bridge unless he was paid. He never was.

King's College★★

Entrance: Gatehouse at front (Oct–Mar); north gate of chapel (Mar–Sept); temporary walkway at front of college (Jul–Aug). College: 🕐*Open (functions permitting), term-time, Mon–Fri 9.30am–3.30pm, Sat 9.30am–3.15pm, Sun 1.15–2.15. Out of term–time, Mon–Fri 9.30am–4.30pm, Sun, 10am–5pm. Choral Services: Sun 10.30am, 3.30pm. Mon–Sat 5.30pm.* 🕐*Closed late-April–mid-Jun (except chapel)* ✆*£5.* 📞*01223 331 212. www.kings.cam.ac.uk/visitors.*

Founded in 1441 and set back behind **William Wilkins'** Gothic revival **screen** and **gatehouse**, King's is dominated by

Gibb's Building in the Classical style and the soaring late Perpendicular buttresses of King's College Chapel.

King's College Chapel★★★

Built between 1446 and 1515 mainly by three Kings (Henry VI, Henry VII and Henry VIII), King's College Chapel is the final and most glorious flowering of Perpendicular. Turner painted its exterior, Wordsworth wrote three sonnets about it, and Wren, marvelling at the largest single-span vaulted roof in existence, offered to make one himself, if only someone would tell him where to lay the first stone.

The dimensions (289ft/88m long, 94ft/29m high, 40ft/12m wide) suggest a cathedral choir rather than a college chapel; the 18 side chapels and door emphasise the height of the 22 buttresses which take the weight of the roof. The 12-bay nave rises upwards on stonework so slender that it forms a mere frame to the 25 stained-glass windows (16C) illustrating episodes from the Old Testament (above) and from the New Testament (below). The vaulting (nearly 2,000 tons), appears weightless. The architect was **John Wastell**.

Note the splendid early Renaissance **screen** and **stalls** by foreign craftsmen and **Rubens'** *Adoration of the Magi*. Above the screen is the organ in its 17C

Coffin of the chief priest of Karnak, Nekht-ef-Mut (924 B.C. - 889 B.C.), Fitzwilliam Museum

©The Fitzwilliam Museum

case used for services broadcast live on Christmas Eve across the world featuring the famous King's College Choir.

Queens' College★

Visitors' Gate Queens' Lane. ◷ *Open year-round, most days 10am–4.30pm or 2pm–4pm, see website for details.* ◷*Closed third week May–third week Jun (exams).* ✆*£2.50 (Nov–Mar free).* ℘*01223 335 511. www.quns.cam.ac.uk.* Named after the patronage bestowed by two successive queens, Margaret of Anjou, wife of Henry VI, and Elizabeth Woodville, wife of Edward IV, the college was granted its first charter in 1446. **Old Court**, completed in 1449, shows late medieval brickwork; in charming **Cloister Court** the half-timbered building is the **President's Lodge**. The Dutch philosopher **Desiderius Erasmus** taught Greek at Queens' but his rooms (Erasmus' Tower) cannot be definitely identified; his name, however, lives on in the brick Erasmus Building (1960) by Basil Spence. Another recent addition is the glass and concrete Cripps' Court

(1981) by Powell, Moya and Partners. The famous wooden **Mathematical Bridge** over the river is a 20C copy (1904), the second, of the original one (1749) designed by James Essex.

The Backs★★

The "Backs" (of the colleges) along the River Cam are as fine as the fronts; they form a wonderful combination of buildings and lawns in a riverside setting and are best viewed from a punt (on hire at Silver Street Bridge).

Fitzwilliam Museum★★

Trumpington Street. ◷ *Open year-round Tue–Sat 10am–5pm. Sun and bank hols noon–5pm.* ◷*Closed Dec 24–26 and 31, Jan 1.* ☞ *Guided tour Sat 2.30pm (*✆*£3.50).* ♿✗. ℘*01223 332 900.* *www.fitzmuseum.cam.ac.uk.* Founded in 1816, the Fitzwilliam Museum houses world-class collections of art and antiquities from Egypt, Sudan, the Ancient Near East, Greece, Rome (look for the marble **Pashley sarcophagus**, AD 130–150), English and European pottery and glass, sculpture, furniture, armour, illuminated manuscripts, oriental art, Korean ceramics, coins and medals.
The art collection includes 25 watercolours by JMW Turner, (donated by John Ruskin) and a selection of some of William Blake's best works in addition to works by Gainsborough, Reynolds, Stubbs and Constable and an outstanding collection of prints by Rembrandt.
The paintings include **Old Masters** of exceptional quality with works by Domenico Veneziano, Leonardo da Vinci, Titian, Rubens and Van Dyck. The collection of French Impressionists includes landscapes by Monet, Seurat and Cézanne as well as studies by Renoir and Degas. Representing the 20C are pieces by Picasso, Nicholson and Sutherland.

Kettle's Yard★

Castle Street. **House:** ◷ *Open Apr–Sept Tue–Sun and bank hols 1.30pm–4.30pm; Oct–Mar Tue–Sun and bank*

hols 2pm–4pm. Gallery: ⏲ *Open Tue–Sun and bank hols 11.30am–5pm.* ⏲*Closed Good Fri, 24–26 and 29 Dec, 1 Jan.* ☎*01223 352 124. www.kettlesyard.co.uk.*

In complete contrast to the academic atmosphere of the Fitzwilliam is Kettle's Yard, which, according to its creator Jim Ede is "a living place where works of art can be enjoyed inherent in the domestic setting". This excellent collection of 20C art includes works by Ben Nicholson, Henry Moore, Barbara Hepworth, Eric Gill, Henri Gaudier-Brzeska and Miró, most of whom were friends of Ede; the pieces are set about the house among the furniture so that visitors may sit to admire the exhibits or read the books.

EXCURSIONS

👥 Imperial War Museum, Duxford★

9mi/14km south on the M 11. ⏲ *Open daily 10am–6pm (4pm late-Oct–mid-Mar).* ⏲*Closed Dec 24–26.* 🎫*£16, child free.* ♿🅿✖. ☎*01223 835 000. www.iwm.org.uk.*

Duxford is Europe's premier aviation museum as well as having one of the finest collections of tanks, military vehicles and naval exhibits in the country. It began as an airfield in the First World War and also played a vital role in the Second World War. Today its vast hangars (and notably **AirSpace**, its stunning new exhibition space) house dozens of civil and fighter aircraft, several of which, including Concorde, you can climb aboard. To celebrate the Second World War associations of this former Battle of Britain base with the USAAF it is also home to the **American Air Museum in Britain**.

Audley End★★

EH. 13mi/21km S. ⏲*Open Wed–Sun.* **House:** *late–Mar–Sept 11am–5pm, (Sat 3pm). Oct 11am–4pm.* **Gardens and Service Wing:** *late–Mar–Sept 10am–6pm. Oct 10am–5pm. Nov–late Dec 10am–4pm.* 🎫*£7.30.* ♿🅿✖. ☎*01799 522 399. www.english–heritage.org.uk.*

When this estate came into the possession of Thomas Howard, Earl of Suffolk and Lord High Treasurer in the early 17C, it was one of the greatest Jacobean houses in England. "Too large for a king, but might do for a Lord Treasurer" said James I who unintentionally helped to finance it at a cost of £200 000, and later imprisoned the Earl for embezzlement. It was partially demolished in 1721 when the interior was redesigned by **Robert Adam** and the grounds by **Lancelot "Capability" Brown**. The present house, vast enough, is but a shadow of its former glory. The interior is laden with the possessions of the third Baron Braybrooke, who inherited Audley End in 1825, filling it with paintings by Masters such as Holbein and Canaletto.

ADDRESSES

🛏 STAY

🛏 **Wallis Farmhouse**, *98 Main Street, Hardwick.* ☎*01954 210 347. www.wallis farmhouse.co.uk.* Set in a picturesque village 5mi/8km west of Cambridge, this late Georgian farmhouse offers B&B in spacious timbered bedrooms in a converted barn. The friendly owners serve hearty breakfasts. There are also four individual self-catering units.

🛏 **Gonville Hotel**, *Gonville Place.* ☎*01223 366 611. www.gonvillehotel. co.uk.* Popular family-owned personally run Best Western hotel with spacious and traditional interiors, located on the east side of the city centre and overlooking 25acres/10ha of open park land.

🍴 EAT

There is a list of places for eating out available from the Cambridge Tourist Information Centre.

🍽 **Midsummer House**, *Midsummer Common.* ☎*01223 369 299. Dinner only except lunch Fri and Sat.* Cambridge's finest restaurant enjoys an idyllic location beside the Cam, with conservatory dining. The

French-Mediterranean cuisine offers inventive and detailed cooking.

⊜⊜ **Crown and Punchbowl**, *Horningsea. 5mi/8km west of the city centre.* ℘*01223 860 643. www.thecrownand punchbowl.co.uk.* Formerly the 17C village inn this is now a tastefully converted full-blown restaurant serving Modern British cuisine. Spacious, relaxing attractive bedrooms (⊜⊜).

⊜⊜ **The Three Horseshoes**, *High Street, Madingley.* ℘*01954 210 221. www.huntsbridge.com.* A picture–perfect thatched pub 5 miles/8km west of Cambridge, with a stylish airy interior. The bar does a short well-priced grill menu; the lounge offers innovative seasonal Italian cuisine made with best local produce.

SIGHTSEEING

For daily guided walking tours (⊜*£8/£9*), ghost tours *(Fri 6pm. ⊜£5)* or punting and walking ghost tours *(Sat 7pm. ⊜£15)* contact the Visitor Information Centre (℘*01223 457 574).* City Sightseeing Tours operate hop-on hop-off open-top bus tours of the city, with buses running every 10–20 mins. Tickets (⊜*£10)* can be purchased directly from the driver, or in advance from the Cambridge Tourist Information Centre.

Riverboat cruises: contact Cambridge Passenger Cruises (℘*01223 307 694. www.georgina.co.uk).*

⊨ SHOPPING

Most high street and department stores can be found in **Petty Cury**, **Market Square**, **Lion Yard**, **St Andrew's Street** and the **Grafton Centre**. Shoppers looking for something slightly different or quirky should try the shops in **King's Parade**, **Rose Crescent**, **Trinity Street**, **Bridge Street**, **Magdalene Street**, **St John's Street** and **Green Street**. In **Market Square** there is a general market, open daily except Sundays.

⊇ ENTERTAINMENT

Lists of entertainment venues are compiled by the Cambridge Tourist Information Centre (⟲ *see above).*

The Cambridge Folk Festival, late Jul/early Aug, is Britain's best music festival of its kind (℘*01223 357 851. www.cambridgefolkfestival.co.uk).*

Punting – No trip to Cambridge would be complete without a punt trip.

Trinity Punts – Self-punting from Trinity College (℘*01223 338 400. www.trin.cam.ac.uk).*

The Granta Boat & Punt Company – Chauffeur and self-punting available (℘*01223 301 845. www.puntingincambridge.com).*

Scudamores – Chauffeur and self–punting available (℘*01223 359 750; www.scudamores.com).* Motorcycle tours and ghost tours also available.

Ely

Cambridgeshire

Once called Elig or Eel Island because of the abundance of eels, Ely lies on the River Ouse. It has been a place of worship since St Etheldreda, a Saxon queen, founded a religious community and built an abbey here in the 7C. The small town is still dominated by the cathedral and monastic buildings and retains many medieval houses. In 1066 Hereward the Wake made his last stand against the Normans in Ely. In the 17C Oliver Cromwell lived in the town.

▸ **Population:** 10,329.
⟲ **Michelin Map:** Michelin Atlas p 29 or Map 504 U 26.
▯ **Info:** Oliver Cromwell's House, 29 St Mary's Street. ℘01353 662 062. http://visitely.eastcambs.gov.uk.
◗ **Location:** 16mi/26km N of Cambridge. Its railway station is a 10min walk from the centre, on The Gallery. Regional buses stop right outside the cathedral.

CATHEDRAL★★

🕐 *Open Apr–Oct daily 7am–7pm. Nov–Mar daily 7.30am–6pm (5pm Sun). For opening times of specific attractions in the cathedral see the website.*
£5.50. Additional charges: Octagon and West Tower (£5 each). Stained Glass Museum £3.50. Reduction on all with combined cathedral ticket; Guided tours (free) daily. ♿️✕. ☎01353 660 344. www.cathedral.ely.anglican.org; www.stainedglassmuseum.com.

The superb Norman nave and transepts contrast with the surprises beyond: the wonderful Decorated east end and Lady Chapel, and that 14C masterpiece, the Octagon. After the sacking of Etheldreda's abbey by the Danes in 870, a second religious community was founded by the Benedictines in 970. The present church was begun in 1083; in 1250 the east end of the original Norman building was reconstructed. In 1321 work started on the Lady Chapel. The following year the great Norman crossing tower fell down. The solution, cutting off the four Norman corners of the crossing and building an octagonal space (three times the size of the Norman tower) on the eight points, was a triumph of medieval engineering.

The cathedral is best viewed from the northwest to appreciate its length (537ft/164m), castellated west tower (215ft/66m), Early English Galilee Porch, the Decorated **Octagon** (170ft/52m) and the wooden lantern above it.

Interior

The visitor is instantly overwhelmed by rich colours emanating from ceilings, stained glass windows and stone pillars. The **southwest transept** (c. 1200) is an outstanding example of the Romanesque period. The eye is led to the **Octagon**; its eight pillars support 200t of glass, lead and timber; below its high windows are panels decorated with angels. The Octagon is separated by a 19C **screen** by George Gilbert Scott from the beautifully vaulted Early English choir, with its splendid 14C **choir stalls**. In front of the High Altar lies the shrine of St Etheldreda. The light and spacious

Ely Cathedral

A. Williams/MICHELIN

Lady Chapel was the largest single span of vaulting in its time; most of its statues and windows were destroyed in 1541 during the Dissolution.

The **Stained Glass Museum** in the triforium, reached by a steep winding staircase, shows stained glass and lead-cutting processes by means of diorama models.

The group of medieval domestic buildings, together with the ruined cloisters, is the largest of its kind in England; some form part of the King's School or are in private hands.

OLIVER CROMWELL'S HOUSE★

29 St Mary's Street. 🕐Open Apr–Oct daily 10am–5.30pm. Nov–Mar Sun–Fri 11am–4pm, Sat 10am–5pm. ♿️. £4. ☎01353 662 062. www.olivercromwells house.co.uk.

For ten years Cromwell, Lord Protector of England, lived in Ely. His former house is the only surviving former Cromwell residence other than Hampton Court. The furnished rooms of this ancient house (13C) are few – kitchen, bedroom, study – but the flavour of the age and the history of its most illustrious resident is superbly evoked. The house is also home to the tourist information office.

Ipswich

Suffolk

This bustling country town is mostly Victorian and modern in character. All that remains of the distant past is its Anglo-Saxon street layout and about a dozen medieval churches, some just towers, built when the town was a rich port and trading centre. The Victorian Wet Dock, once the largest in the world, with its warehouses, merchants' houses and maltings, makes an interesting walk.

TOWN

In the centre of town, within Christchurch Park is **Christchurch Mansion** (☾*open daily 10am–5pm;* ☾*closed Good Fri, Jan 1, Dec 24–26;* 🅿 ✕; 🎧 *01473 433 554; www.ipswich.gov.uk)*, a much-restored Tudor manor house, set in pleasant parkland and full of treasures from Ipswich and the surrounding countryside. It holds a good collection of paintings by 17C Suffolk-born artists, including several by John Constable and Thomas Gainsborough.

Head due south on Northgate Street and take a right onto Buttermarket to see the **Ancient House** (☾*open Mon–Sat 9am–5.30pm)*. The exterior of this 15C house abounds in Restoration plasterwork, pargeting (ornamental plastering) and stucco reliefs of nymphs, pelicans and the four (then-known) continents. The coat of arms is that of Charles II who visited the building in 1668. Now a shop, visitors can view several panelled rooms (c. 1603) with wall pargeting, ornamental ceilings and 18C ceramic tilework.

🚗 DRIVING TOUR

STOUR VALLEY★

The lower Stour is **Constable Country**; the upper Stour is **Gainsborough Country**; in between is Sudbury, where Gainsborough was born and where Constable went to school.

◯ *Take the A 12 south for 8mi/13km, turn left on the B 1070 and follow signs.*

▶ **Population:** 130,157.
☾ **Michelin Map:** Michelin Atlas p 23 or Map 504 X 27.
🔲 **Info:** St Stephen's Church. 🎧 01473 258 070. www.visit-ipswich.com.
◯ **Location:** Ipswich is at the head of the Orwell estuary on the southeast Anglian coast. The train station is 10min from the centre; the bus station is in town.

Flatford Mill★

The mill (1773) was the home of John Constable, whose father was a miller and inspired some of his best-loved landscapes – *The Haywain, Boatbuilding* and *Flatford Mill*. It is now home to a field studies centre and there is no admission for individuals though group tours may be arranged (🎧*01206 298 283)*. **Bridge Cottage**, formerly known as **Willy Lott's Cottage** *(NT.* ☾ *open May–Sept daily 10.30am–5.30pm, Oct daily 11am–4pm, Mar–Apr Wed–Sun 11am–5pm, Nov–Dec Wed–Sun 11am–3.30pm, Jan–Feb Sat–Sun 11am–3.30pm;* ☾*closed Jan 1 and Dec 25;* 🅿 *(charge);* ✕; 🎧*01206 298 260; www.nationaltrust.org.uk)* has an exhibition on Constable and the valley.

◯ *Road west or the riverbank path.*

Dedham

This quintessential English village was painted many times by Constable.

◯ *Pass under the A 12 and take the B 1068 and the B 1087 for 6mi/10km.*

Nayland

St James' Church (15C) contains *The Last Supper* by Constable.

◯ *Continue on the B 1087; in Bures take the B 1508 to Sudbury.*

Gainsborough's House★

46 Gainsborough Street. ☾ *Open Mon–Sat 10am–5pm.* ⊚*£4.50.* 🎧*01787 372 958. www.gainsborough.org.*

The late medieval building behind an elegant 18C façade was the birthplace of Thomas Gainsborough (1727–88). On display are memorabilia and paintings.

▷ *Take the A 134 north for 3mi/5km.*

Long Melford
The long main street *(2mi/3km)* is lined with 16C, 17C and 18C timbered and pink-plastered houses. It terminates in a green and spacious triangle, overlooked by **Trinity Hospital** (1573) and **Holy Trinity Church** (late 15C), one of the great "wool churches" of East Anglia.

Melford Hall★
NT. ◷ *Open 1.30pm–5pm; May–Sept Wed–Sun and bank hols, Oct–Easter Sat–Sun and bank hols.* ◒£6. ♿🅿✕. ✆01787 376 395. *www.nationaltrust.org.uk.*
Although the house is early Elizabethan, built around three sides of a courtyard, only the **Main Hall** has preserved its Elizabethan features. The Drawing Room is splendidly Rococo. The West Bedroom contains the original Jemima Puddle-Duck watercolours by **Beatrix Potter** who was a frequent visitor.

Colchester Castle and Museum★
17mi/27km southwest. Castle Park. ◷ *Open Mon–Sat 10am–5pm, Sun 11am–5pm.* ◷ *Closed Jan 1, Dec 25.* ◒£5.50. 🐾 *Guided tour of castle vaults, roof and chapel daily (£2 extra).* ♿✕. ✆01206 282 939. *www.colchestermuseums.org.uk.*
Built with 12ft/4m-thick walls on the vaults of the Roman Temple of Claudius, its massive dimensions (151ft/46m by 110ft/34m) make it half as big again as the White Tower at the Tower of London. it is now a museum housing one of the largest collections in Britain of **Roman antiquities** gathered from one site.

King's Lynn
Norfolk

This town dates from the Norman Conquest (1066). In the Middle Ages it was a bustling port and member of the Hanseatic League, exporting cloth and wool. Today's fine townscape is especially rich in medieval merchants' houses; many with their own well-constructed warehouses line the River Ouse.

🐾 TOWN CENTRE WALK
In **Queen Street**, which is mainly Georgian in character, stands Thorseby College, founded in 1502 for training priests but later converted into a merchant's house with a 17C courtyard. The Dutch-inspired Custom House (17C) is home to the Tourist Information Centre.
King's Staithe Lane, which leads to the quayside on the River Ouse, contains 16C and 17C warehouses; in cobbled King's Staithe Square stands a grand double-fronted red brick house, crowned with a statue of King Charles I.

▶ **Population:** 41,281.
⚅ **Michelin Map:** Michelin Atlas p 30 or Map 504 V 25.
🯄 **Info:** The Custom House, Purfleet Quay. ✆01553 763 044. www. west-norfolk.gov.uk.
▷ **Location:** On the River Ouse at the mouth of the Wash 44mi/72km north of Cambridge. The train station is a 5-min walk east. The bus station is central.
☺ **Don't Miss:** At least one of the area's stately halls.
◷ **Timing:** Allow 4–6 hours; more for excursions.
🐾 **Walking Tours:** Depart 2pm Tue and Sat in summer (◒£3; ✆01553 774297; www.west-norfolk.gov.uk).

King Street presents a delightful succession of houses of varied dates and materials including **St George's Guildhall,** the largest surviving medieval guildhall in England, where Shakespeare is supposed to have acted.

The top of King Street opens into **Tuesday Market**, a large open space surrounded by well-preserved Georgian and Victorian buildings.

Head west from St James Rd (A 148) on St James Street to get to Saturday Market (street) and **Tales of the Old Gaol House** (⏱ *open Apr–Oct Mon–Sat 10am–5pm; Nov–Mar Tue–Sat and bank hols 10am–4pm;* ⌓£2.80; ℘01553 774 297; www.west-norfolk.gov.uk). Occupying the chequered flint **Guildhall** (1421), visitors pass through the old police station with its tiny cells and bleak history. In the **Regalia Room** are town charters, mayoral robes, civic silver and the **King John Cup** (1340).

Head further west from here to see the **Town House Museum of Lynn Life**, (⏱ *open May–Sept Mon–Sat 10am–5pm, Sun 2pm–5pm; Oct and Feb–Apr Mon–Sat, 10am–4pm;* ⏱ *closed bank hols, Dec 24–25, Jan 1;* ⌓£3; ℘01553 773 450; www.museums.norfolk.gov.uk), which displays period rooms from medieval times to the 1950s.

On the walk back to St James Rd, take a right on Church Street to see **St Margaret's Church** (⏱ *open year-round daily, 7.45am–5.45pm (7.45pm Sun);* &; ℘01553 772 858; www.stmargarets kingslynn.org.uk), a twin-towered church originally built in the 13C. It exhibits examples of most architectural styles. Surviving glories include 14C screens, a Georgian pulpit and a 17C moon clock.

Back on St James Rd, head north until you find a left turn onto North Street, home to **True's Yard** (⏱ *open year-round Tue–Sat 10am–4pm;* ⏱ *closed 25 Dec–3 Jan;* ⌓£3; & ✕; ℘01553 770 479; www.west-norfolk.gov.uk). Two cottages house a small museum illustrating the hardships of the former fishing community.

EXCURSIONS
Holkham Hall★★
31mi/50km northeast via the A 149.
⏱ *Open noon–4pm on varying days of the week.* ⌓£8 (combined ticket

Marble Hall, Holkham Hall

with Bygones Museum £10). & �� ✕. ℘01328 710 227. www.holkham.co.uk.
Seat of the Earls of Leicester and Coke of Norfolk (1754–1842) – the inventor of modern agriculture – Holkham Hall is palatial Palladian designed by **William Kent**. Most monumental of the interiors is the Marble Hall. The Grand Drawing Room has works by Claude and Poussin and the Saloon boasts Rubens and Van Dyck. In the South Sitting Room hang works by Titian, Guido Reni, Gainsborough and Battoni; the Landscape Room is devoted to Poussin and Claude.

Houghton Hall★★
13mi/21km east via A1076 and A 148.
⏱ *Open Easter–Sept, Wed, Thu, Sun, bank hols 1.30pm–5pm (grounds 11am–5.30pm).* ⌓£8.80 Grounds and park only, £5. & ⓟ ✕. ℘01485 528 569. www.houghtonhall.com.
Houghton Hall, which is transitional between Baroque and Palladian, was built (1722–35) for Sir Robert Walpole, Britain's first Prime Minister. Its main rooms by William Kent are dedicated to "taste, expense, state and parade". Its joys are its ceilings and Kent furniture, Sèvres porcelain, thrones by Pugin and 17C Mortlake tapestries.

Oxburgh Hall★★
NT. 18mi/29km southeast. **House:**
⏱ *Open 11am–5pm: mid-Mar–Jul and Sept–Oct Sat–Wed; Aug daily; bank hols and Good Fri.* **Garden:** ⏱*Open as*

house except Nov–Jan (Sat–Sun only), (Nov–Feb closes 4pm). ☞£6.75. *Garden only, £3.50.* ♿🅿✕. ✆01366 328528. *www.nationaltrust.org.uk.*

This was one of the first fortified manor houses (1482) to be built as a status symbol. Its **gatehouse** and flanking ranges are 15C; the hall range is 19C. The interior presents elaborate **embroideries** depicting mammals; letters from Henry VIII, Queen Mary and Queen Elizabeth I, and woodcarvings by Grinling Gibbons in the King's Room.

Sandringham★

8mi/13km northeast. 🕐 *Open Easter Sat–late Jul and Aug–late-Oct/early-Nov, daily 11am–5pm (4 pm Oct).* ☞£10 *(Grounds and museum only, £6.50).* ♿🅿✕. ✆01553 612 908. *www.sandringham-estate.co.uk.*

"Dear old Sandringham, the place I love better than anywhere else in the world", wrote George V of the Royal Family's country home, a neo-Jacobean house acquired in 1862. The large Saloon is hung with family portraits and 17C tapestries. The corridor is adorned with intricately-wrought Oriental arms and armour. In the main Drawing Room is Russian silver and Chinese jade.

FENLAND CHURCHES★

The glories of the Fens (🕐 *see ELY*) are its sunsets and churches, admirably complemented by the flat and featureless landscape.

St Clement's Church *(Terrington St Clement;* ✆01553 828 430*)* boasts a splendid west window and northwest tower. The interior has exquisite Georgian panelling and a 17C **font cover**.

St Peter's Church *(Walpole St Peter).* Huge plain glass windows illuminate the magnificent interior of the 14C "Cathedral of the Fens".

St Mary's Church *(West Walton.* ✆01945 780 252; www.ely.anglican.org/parishes/ westwalton)* is mid-13C Early English at its most profuse and extravagant.

All Saints' Church *(Walsoken;* ✆01945 583 740; www.allsaintswalsoken.com).* Dating from 1146, "the grandest Norman parish church in Norfolk" presents a hammerbeam tie-beam roof, an eight-sided **font** portraying the Seven Sacraments and Crucifixion, and a 16C wall painting, the Judgement of Solomon.

Norwich★★

Norfolk

In 1066 Norwich was the fourth most populous city in England, and later grew rich as the centre of the East Anglian wool trade. Today it is one of the country's best-preserved medieval cities and the surviving towers and spires of over 30 flint churches, many now redundant, etch the skyline. The city is dominated by the hill-top castle; below is the centre of old Norwich, where cobbled streets, lined with half-timbered houses, lead through stone gateways to the cathedral.

CATHEDRAL★★

Palace Street. 🕐 *Open daily 7.30am–7pm (6pm winter). Contribution requested.* 🚶 *Guided tour Mon–Sat*

▸ **Population:** 171, 304.

🕐 **Michelin Map:** Michelin Atlas p 31 or Map 504 Y 26.

🛈 **Info:** Millennium Plain. ✆01603 213 999. www.visitnorwich.co.uk.

▸ **Location:** 62mi/100km NE of Cambridge. Train station 10min from centre. Buses – Surrey Street Station (10mins from centre), or Castle Meadow (central). Tourist buses (✆01263 587 005. www. city-sightseeing.com).

😊 **Don't Miss:** Cathedral; Blickling Hall; Norfolk Broads boating in the summer.

🚶 **Walking Tours:** Apr–Oct from the tourist info centre.

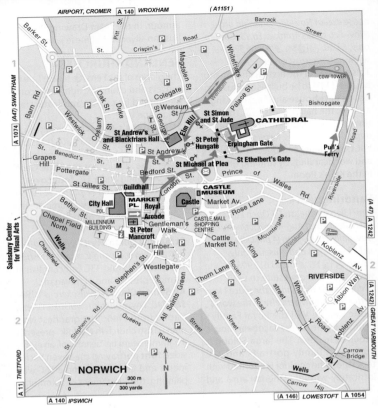

NORWICH

10.45am, noon, 2.15pm. ✆01603 218 300. *www.cathedral.org.uk.*

The Norman cathedral was begun in 1096 and consecrated in 1278. Its choir clerestory was rebuilt in Early English style in the 14C and Perpendicular vaults added in the 15C and early 16C. The 15C **spire** (315ft/96m) is the second-tallest in England after Salisbury.

Inside, above the steadfast Norman nave and transepts the 400 carved and painted bosses on the vaults portray "a strip cartoon of the whole story of God's involvement with man from creation to last judgement". Note the **misericords** of the choir stalls, the ambulatory, St Luke's Chapel (displaying the famous 14C five-panelled Despenser Reredos) and Jesus Chapel (displaying Martin Schwarz's *Adoration of the Magi*, painted in the 1480s).

The **Prior's Door**, leading from the nave to the cloisters, with its sculptured fig-ures of Christ flanked by two angels, two bishops and two monks, is one of the most beautiful doors of the early Decorated style. The unusual two-sto-reyed cloisters, the largest in England, were rebuilt (c. 1297–1430) and have superb tracery. The 400 roof bosses on the vaulted ceiling illustrate the Book of Revelations.

CITY
Norwich Castle Museum & Art Gallery★(Z)

Castle Meadow. 🕐 *Open Mon–Sat 10am–4.30pm (Sat 5pm/school hols 5.30pm), Sun 1pm–5pm.* £5.70. ⚹. *Guided tours daily.* ✆01603 493 625. *www.museums.norfolk.gov.uk.*

The castle was begun in 1160, built on a commanding hill-top. The high-walled stone **keep** has retained many of its orig-inal features – Norman arches, windows, chapel niche and the well (110ft/34m deep); the **battlements** and **dungeons** are included in a guided tour. tracing the history of Norwich through Norman and other local finds.

The art gallery *(ground floor)* displays an outstanding collection of works by the **Norwich School** of painters, greatly influenced by Dutch landscape artists. Also on display are works by 20C **East Anglian** artists – Alfred Munnings, Edward Seago – as well as Victorian and Dutch works. The porcelain section contains a fascinating collection of British teapots from 1720. The Ecology gallery includes remains of a 600,000-year-old Elephant, excavated in 1992.

Cloisters, Norwich Cathedral
©Linda Steward/iStockphoto.com

Market Place★ (Z)

The square, which is 900 years old and the largest in East Anglia, is occupied six days a week by market stalls mostly selling local produce. To the north is the chequered flint **Guildhall**, begun in 1407. To the west, is the modern **City Hall**, "probably the foremost English public building of between the wars").

The Forum

2 Millennium Plain, Bethel Street.
🕐 *Open year-round daily 7am–midnight.* ♿🅿✕. 𝒞*01603 727 920.*
www.theforumnorwich.co.uk.

This spectacular new glass building, the landmark Millennium project for the East of England, houses (among many other businesses) the tourist office.

To the south is Norwich's grandest parish church, **St Peter Mancroft**, Perpendicular par excellence, with a fine hammerbeam roof, a great east window with medieval glass, and a 15C font. To the east is the Art Nouveau **Royal Arcade**.

Elm Hill (Y)

This quaint cobbled street, formerly the centre of the weaving industry, is lined with medieval brick and timber houses. At the Tombland end stands the church of **St Simon and St Jude,** now put to commercial use. Farther along sits the thatched 15C restaurant, **Britons Arms** (right), and the medieval church of **St Peter Hungate**, re-built 1460 (🕐 *open Apr–Sept, Mon–Sat, 10am–5pm;* ♿;

𝒞*01603 667 231*), now a museum displaying embroidered vestments, church brasses and stained glass. Across the street can be seen the east window of **Blackfriars Hall**, which together with **St Andrew's Hall**, once formed the choir and nave of the Convent Church of the Blackfriars. Both halls, with fine hammerbeam roofs, are now used for public and civic functions. The 13C brick vaulted crypt is now a café.

Sainsbury Centre for Visual Arts★ (Z)

University of East Anglia. 3mi/5km west of the city centre. 🕐 *Open Tue–Sun*

Royal Arcade
S. Tesson/Michelin

Norfolk Broads

A. Williams/MICHELIN

10am–5pm (Wed 8pm). ♿✕.
℘01603 593 199. www.scva.org.uk.
This important regional gallery is housed in one of the most exciting buildings of the 1970s, designed by Norman Foster. The 19C and 20C European works by Degas, Seurat, Picasso, Epstein, Bacon, Modigliani, Moore and Giacometti are delightfully juxtaposed with African, Pacific, Oriental and American Indian art and high quality artefacts, both ancient and modern.

BLICKLING HALL★★
NT. 15mi/24km north on A140 (Y).
House: ◷ Open late Feb–Oct Wed–Sun and bank hols 11pm–5pm; mid-Jul–early Sept also open Mon. Oct–Nov Wed–Sun 1pm–4pm. **Gardens:** ◷ Same days/dates as house. **Park:** ◷ Open dawn–dusk. ⊜£8.85. ♿🅿✕. ℘01263 738 030. www.national trust.org.uk.
This splendid turreted and gabled brick mansion was built 1619–25 by Robert Lyminge, the architect of Hatfield House, and is one of the most intact of great Jacobean houses, famed for its long gallery, fine tapestries, paintings and rare books. There is a magnificent staircase; a plastered ceiling (120ft/37m) portraying the *Five Senses* and *Learning* in the Long Gallery; a splendid tapestry of Peter the Great defeating the Swedes; and paintings by Reynolds, Gainsborough and Canaletto. The present parterre and gardens date from the late 19C.

NORFOLK BROADS★
One of Britain's premier wildlife habitats, the Broads – large lakes formed out of medieval peat diggings – are the home of Chinese water deer, kingfishers, bitterns, herons and great crested grebes, and insect species such as the swallowtail butterfly and the Norfolk hawker dragonfly which are found nowhere else in Britain. Peaceful waterways wind their way through misty fens, cutting between lush woods and open marshes beneath a seemingly endless sky. The villages are famous for their churches, some of which have hammerbeam and thatched roofs. The navigable waterways (over 125mi/200km) and the 14 Broads are best explored by boat.

Wroxham
The "capital of the Broads" on the River Bure, and a centre for boat hire.

Ranworth
The Perpendicular tower and Decorated south porch of **St Helen's Church** (◷open daily, 9am–6pm; 4pm winter; ♿✕) give no hint of the splendour inside: the finest rood screen (15C) in East Anglia, a brightly painted (restored) array of saints, apostles and martyrs.

Potter Heigham
The capital of the northern Broads is on the River Thurne. **St Nicholas' Church** has a Norman tower and a hammerbeam and thatched roof.

Peterborough
Cambridgeshire

Peterborough began life as a village around a monastery. It became a town around a cathedral and then a city dominated by brickworks. It is now a high-tech centre for financial institutions but ancient survivals include the cathedral, the 17C arcaded guildhall, the church of St John the Baptist in Cowgate and some Georgian houses in Priestgate. A pedestrian zone has replaced the ancient city centre.

> ▶ **Population:** 134,788.
> ᵴ **Michelin Map:** Michelin Atlas p 29 or Map 504 T 26.
> ▤ **Info:** ℘01733 452 336. www.visitpeterborough.com.
> ▷ **Location:** 25mi/40km north of Cambridge. The city is linked directly to London by rail (45 min) and the train station is a short walk from the centre. Queensgate Bus Station is close by.
> ◈ **Don't Miss:** The cathedral's west front, 13C nave ceiling and fan vaulting.
> ◐ **Timing:** Allow half a day in Peterborough.
> ᵅᵅ **Kids:** One of the Specials Days at Nene Valley Railway.

CATHEDRAL★★

◐ *Open year-round Mon–Fri 9am–6.30pm, Sat 9am–5pm, Sun 7.30am–5pm.* ☞*£3.50 contribution requested.* ▢ *(wheelchair users only).* ᵴ✕. *℘01733 343 342. www.peterborough-cathedral.org.uk.*
Peterborough and Ely were the two great monasteries of the Fens. The present building is the third church on the site, started in 1118 and consecrated in 1238. In 1643 Cromwell's men destroyed the stained glass, the high altar, the cloisters and statues.

The Early English **west front** is most memorable and fascinating with its three giant arches and its rich early Perpendicular (14C) porch. The interior is a superb example of Norman architecture. The nave has an uninterrupted vista towards the altar. The transepts and choir with their **Norman elevations** are a robust expression of faith. The 13C **nave ceiling** is a wonderful example of medieval art with figures of bishops, saints and mythical beasts. The 15C wooden ceiling in the sanctuary is decorated with bosses and the superb **fan vaulting** at the east end (in the New or Eastern Building) is late 15C Perpendicular. In the north choir aisle Catherine of Aragon is buried and in the south choir aisle Mary Queen of Scots was temporarily laid to rest (1587–1612). The 14C Almoner's Hall (south of the Cathedral) houses the visitor centre where the history of the cathedral and the life of the monks is interpreted.

EXCURSIONS

Flag Fen Archaeology Park and Bronze Age Centre★★

3mi/4.8km east by A 47 and A 1130 (signs). The Droveway, Northey Road. ◐*Open Mar–Oct daily.* ◐*Closed Dec 24–Jan 2.* ☞*£5.* ᵴ▢✕. *℘01733 313 414. www.flagfen.org.*
Flag Fen is one of the most important prehistoric sites in Britain and home to a 3,500 year-old timber monument and causeway.

ᵅᵅ Nene Valley Railway★

8mi/13km west on the A 47 and south on the A 1. ◐ *Call or visit website for times and dates.* ☞*£12, child £6. Yard and station open all year.* ᵴ▢✕. *℘01780 784 4404 (timetable), 01780 784 444 (enquiries); www.nvr.org.uk.*
Steam locomotives puff between Wansford and Peterborough *(15mi/24km – 90min return).* The carriages are fitted out with shiny wooden fascia and the smoke billowing over the flat landscape makes for a ride from yesteryear. A **museum** at Wansford displays railway memorabilia, a **Thomas the Tank Engine** (children's book character) and old rolling stock, some from abroad.

THE MIDLANDS

The Midlands of England has many definitions and for foreign visitors it is a somewhat amorphous area, which is dipped into only occasionally: an excursion around the Cotswolds from Bath, a day trip to Stratford-upon-Avon from London; perhaps an overnight trip to Chatsworth House. This guide defines the Midlands to the west by the mountains of Wales, to the east by the flatlands of East Anglia, to the north by the southern end of the Pennines, and to the south by the broad vales north of the Thames.

Highlights

1 Discover the stately home and gardens of **Chatsworth House** (p284) in Derbyshire.

2 Stroll through dramatic Dovedale in the **Peak District** (p302)

3 See the origins of the Industrial Age at **Ironbridge Gorge** (p289) near Shrewsbury.

4 Pay homage to Shakespeare at **Anne Hathaway's Cottage** (p310) in Stratford-upon-Avon.

Heart of England and Shakespeare Country

At the geographical heart of the Midlands lies Birmingham. Often described as England's "second city" this former powerhouse of the Industrial Revolution has made huge strides from manufacturing centre to cultural hub. A short ride

from the buzzing modern metropolis are the beautiful timber-framed buildings of Warwick and Stratford-upon-Avon (birthplace of William Shakespeare) and the picture-perfect thatch of Anne Hathaway's Cottage. Shakespeare spent his early life in Stratford and married Hathaway there at the age of 18, some ten years before his plays are thought to have appeared on the London theatre scene. In his later years he returned to live in his home town. North of Stratford-upon-Avon is Coventry, famous for its magnificent modern cathedral.

- Birmingham
- Coventry
- Stratford
- Warwick

Southwest Midlands

Hereford and the Wye Valley butt up to the marches, or borderlands, of Wales. This is perfect walking territory with romantic ruined abbeys and castles recalling the area's rich history. Worcester was the site of the final battle of the

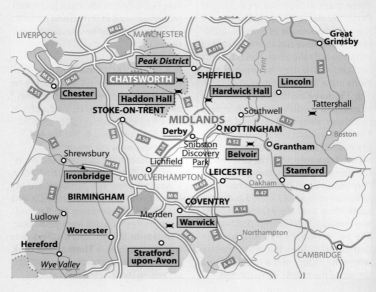

Warwick Castle and the River Avon

©Martin Lovatt/iStockphoto.com

Civil War, the result of which was England and Wales's first and last period as a republic. Worcester is also the home of Royal Worcester Porcelain.

- Hereford
- Wye Valley
- Worcester

North Midlands

Birthplace of the Industrial Revolution, the aptly-named Ironbridge Gorge in Shropshire is now a UNESCO site with fascinating living history museums, returned to its green and pleasant leafy natural state. Shropshire is one the Midland's most beautiful shires, quiet and relatively unexplored with the possible exception of Ludlow. In recent years this has acquired the mantle of England's most important provincial town for gourmets but is well worth a visit for non-foodies too.

The Peak District is a walkers' paradise, where the "right to roam" was born. It is also dotted with caves rejoicing in names such as the Devil's Arse, which tells you something about the straight-talking qualities of the local folk. Magnificent halls and country houses also abound; such as Haddon Hall and Hardwick Hall, perfect showcases for the lives of 16C and 17C country nobility. Finest of all is Chatsworth, "England's Versailles", (though much less stuffy).

- Chatsworth
- Lichfield
- Peak District
- Stoke-on-Trent
- Ironbridge
- Ludlow
- Shrewsbury

East Midlands

In the 9C–10C the East Midlands was controlled by Danish conquerors, whose kingdom was known as the Five Boroughs of the Danelaw. Its five principal towns are still the region's principal centres; Derby, Leicester, Lincoln, Nottingham and Stamford.

Derby to the west traces its past back to the Roman town of Derventio, built beside the River Derwent. It would later become a Daneburgh and was also the most southerly point reached by Bonnie Prince Charlie's army before its retreat to Culloden. The city's porcelain gained fame in the 18C, while today it is known as the home of Rolls Royce. Nearby, Nottingham is probably best known for Sherwood Forest and its connections with the legend of Robin Hood, but the city offers far more, as a modern gateway to the North.

Leicester, to the south of the region, was the seat of 8C East Mercian bishops and the capital of King Lear's kingdom. The city still looks to the gods through the eyes of the National Space Centre. East of here, Stamford has been called "as fine a town built all of stone" as you could wish to see. To the north of the region you will find Lincoln, a charming and picturesquely sited little city, its cathedral an architectural showpiece.

- Derby
- Lincoln
- Stamford
- Leicester
- Nottingham

Birmingham★
West Midlands

The "Second City of the Kingdom" and one of the centres of the Industrial Revolution, Birmingham still produces a high proportion of Britain's manufactured exports. Tourism is very much a priority of the city these days however.

A BIT OF HISTORY

Industry – Industrialisation began in the mid 16C, the city "swarming with inhabitants and echoing with the noise of anvils" (William Camden). Its 18C growth, marked by the miles of canals radiating from the centre (Birmingham has more miles of canal than Venice) attracted **James Watt** (1736–1819), inventor of the double-action steam engine, **William Murdock** (1754–1839), inventor of coal-gas lighting, and **Matthew Boulton** (1728–1809), whose Soho factory was the first to be lit by gas.

The grim conditions caused by the city's phenomenal growth in the 19C stirred the philanthropic cocoa manufacturer, George Cadbury (1839–1922), to create one of the world's first garden suburbs, **Bournville**.

Modern City – Though much crass post-war development was demolished in the course of enthusiastic redevelopment, enough fine late 19C/early 20C buildings remain to evoke the atmosphere of the city's civic heyday. The **Bull Ring**, an icon of insensitive mid-20C architecture, has now been re-developed into a new shopping centre boasting spectacular buildings and large-scale public art.

Today Britain's second city is determined to acquire a new image as a **European business and cultural centre**. A superb symphony hall in the **International Convention Centre** is home to the City of Birmingham Symphony Orchestra (CBSO), the refurbished Birmingham Hippodrome Theatre is the new headquarters for the Birmingham Royal Ballet, formerly Sadler's Wells, while the **National Exhibiton Centre** (NEC) and the **National Indoor Arena** (NIA) host important exhibitions and sporting events.

▶ **Population:** 965,928.

◉ **Michelin Map:** Michelin Atlas p 27 or Maps 403 or 404 O 26.

🗎 **Info:** The Rotunda (Tourism Centre and Ticketshop) 150 New Street. Welcome Centre, New Street/Corporation Street junction. National Exhibition Centre Convention and Visitor Bureau. Birmingham Airport Information Desk. ℘0844 888 3883 (all offices); ℘0121 202 5000 (ticket hotline). www.visitbirmingham.com.

▶ **Location:** Birmingham lies very close to the geographical centre of England, 117mi/188km NW of London. New Street Station in the heart of the city is where most train travellers arrive. The Digbeth bus station is a 10 min walk from the centre.

☺ **Don't Miss:** Birmingham Museum and Art Gallery, especially its Pre-Raphaelite collection; Barber Institute of Fine Arts; Black Country Living Museum; Dudley.

🕐 **Timing:** Allow two days.

🅿 **Parking:** Avoid driving in the city centre.

👫 **Kids:** Cadbury World, Bournville; Thinktank; National Sea Life Centre; Black Country Living Museum.

CITY CENTRE
Birmingham Museum and Art Gallery★★

🕐*Chamberlain Square. Open year-round daily, 10am (10.30am Fri, 12.30pm Sun)–5pm.* ♿. *℘0121 303 2834. www.bmag.org.uk.*

Bull Ring

Marketing Birmingham

Birmingham's municipal gallery is famed for its outstanding collection of **Pre-Raphaelite paintings**. The elaborate iron-work of the two-tiered Industrial Gallery is a late-Victorian marvel, a fascinating setting for its ceramics and stained glass. Beyond is the **Edwardian Tea Room**.

Among the extensive holding of European paintings are outstanding works, like the *Madonna and Child* by Bellini, Claude's *Landscape near Rome* and a *Roman Beggar Woman* by Degas. At the heart of the collection are the pre-Raphaelites: mostly key works like *The Last of England* by Ford Madox Brown, *The Blind Girl* by Millais, *Beata Beatrix* by Rossetti and *Two Gentlemen of Verona* by Hunt. Other rooms are devoted to local history, archaeology and natural history; there is a spectacular **fossilised skull** of a triceratops. The Pinto Gallery holds an amazing array of wooden objects.

Barber Institute of Fine Arts★★

University of Birmingham, Edgbaston. 2.5mi/4km south of the city centre on the A38. From the Bristol Road turn right up Edgbaston Park Road to the university south car park. ◷*Open year-round daily 10am (noon Sun)–5pm.*

◷*Closed Jan 1, Good Fri, Dec 25–26.* ♿🅿. ✆*0121 472 0962 (24hr info),* ✆*0121 414 7333 (enquiries).* *www.barber.org.uk.*

This small but lovingly-chosen collection was built up with the bequest of Lady MCH Barber (d. 1933) and displayed together with furniture and other *objets d'art*. Among the Italian Old Masters there are several Venetians including Bellini, Cima, and Guardi. Flemish painters include Brueghel the Younger and Rubens.

The French School is well-represented, with works by Poussin, Watteau, Delacroix, Ingres, Corot and Courbet and an outstanding group of Impressionists and Post-Impressionists, including Bonnard, Degas, Gauguin, Manet, Monet, Renoir, Vuillard and Van Gogh.

Among the English painters are Gainsborough, JMW Turner and Whistler.

👥 Thinktank (Millennium Point)

◷*Open year-round 10am–5pm (4pm last admission).* ◷*Closed Dec 24–26.* 💷*£7.95, child £5.85; inc IMAX £13.55, child £9.85.* ♿🅿*(charge)*✕. ✆*0121 202 2222. www.thinktank.ac.*

Three floors of interactive galleries (the past, the present, the city, the future) chart both local and global scientific and technological invention. Testimonies from people involved in the various activities which account for Birmingham's industrial progress give a historical perspective while the IMAX cinema and a state-of-the-art planetarium add a wow factor.

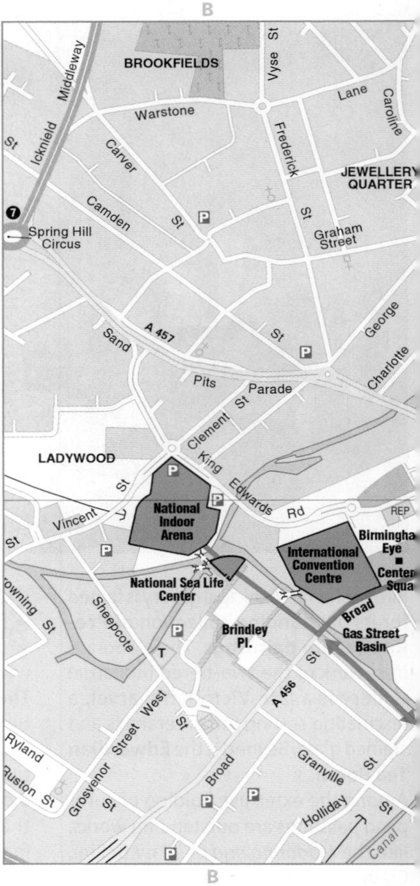

Canal Walk

1mi/1.6km.

The walk between Gas Street Basin and the Museum of Science and Industry passes the canals, locks, bridges and buildings spawned by the city's 19C expansion.

The **Gas Street Basin** is surrounded by both new and restored 18C and 19C buildings. The painted narrowboats moored along the quay are typical of the craft that once plied the Midlands' canal network.

OUT OF TOWN
Aston Hall★★

2mi/3km north of the city centre on A 38 (M). Closed until 2010. *0121 327 0062. www.bmag.org.uk.*

The "*noble fabric which for beauty and state much exceedeth anything in these parts*" was built 1618–35 by John Thorpe. The Jacobean **interior** is characterised by splendidly ornate ceilings and fireplaces. Its most gorgeous rooms are the Long Gallery, with its strapwork ceiling, arcaded oak panelling and de la Planche tapestries of the *Acts of the Apostles*, and the Great Dining Room, with more extravagant strapwork and paintings by Romney and Gainsborough.

Jewellery Quarter

1mi/1.2km northwest.

Something of the atmosphere of early industrial Birmingham with its countless workshops and specialist craftspeople survives in this densely built-up area just outside the city centre. The **Museum**

of the Jewellery Quarter (*75–79 Vyse Street;* open year-round Tue–Sun and bank hols 11.30am–4pm, Nov–Easter, closed Sun; closed Dec 25–27, Jan 1; *0121 554 3598; www.bmag.org. uk*), set up in the former premises of a jewellery business, tells the story of the area as well as demonstrating traditional skills and techniques. The splendid Georgian **St Paul's Church** forms the centrepiece of St Paul's Square, the only remaining 18C square in Birmingham.

National Sea Life Centre

Brindleyplace. Open year-round daily 10am–5pm. Closed Dec 25. £15.95, child £10.95 (buy online for significant savings). *0121 643 6777. www.sealife.co.uk.*

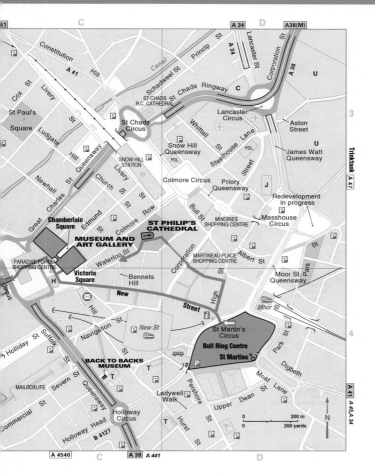

While boasting the usual features of this nationwide group of marine life centres, this new-wave aquarium also concentrates on the specific story of the River Severn. A pathway climbs up through the displays of sea and freshwater fish as the landscape changes from the oceans to the estuary and upriver to its source. From the top, with a view over the canals below, a lift takes visitors down to the "seabed" and an impressive transparent tunnel, to walk beneath rays and sharks. **Planet Earth: Shallow Seas** is a "4-D Experience" with special effects including wind, rain and snow supplementing the 3-D screen images. Dolphins, sea lions and other sea creatures leap from the screen as you feel the wind and salt spray on your face.

Bournville★

4mi/6km southwest of city centre on the A 38 and A 441.

In 1879 the Quaker Cadbury brothers moved their cocoa factory from the cramped conditions of the city centre to the rural surroundings of the Bournbrook estate. Cottages and community facilities for their workers were built around the Village Green where the stone Rest House, presented to Mr and Mrs George Cadbury in 1914 as a silver wedding anniversary gift from Cadbury employees worldwide, is now an information centre. To one side the Bournville School tower houses the **Bournville Carillon** which rings out every Saturday at noon and 3pm (⊙*open daily Wed–Sat 11.30am –4.30pm; www.bournville-web.*

281

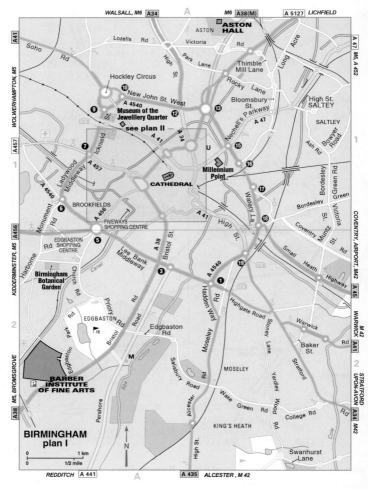

BIRMINGHAM
plan I

net) installed by George Cadbury after hearing the old Carillon in Bruges.

Selly Manor

Maple Road, northeast of the green. ◷*Open year-round Tue–Fri 10am–5pm, also Apr–Sept Sat–Sun and bank hols 2pm–5pm.* ◉*£3.50.* ℘*0121 472 0199. www.bvt.org.uk/sellymanor.*
Selly Manor and Minworth Greaves are two of the city's oldest houses, rescued by George and Laurence Cadbury. Relocated and restored, they are now home to a fine collection of 13C–18C vernacular furniture. A Tudor-style garden has been recreated featuring plants that would have been planted in home gardens.

♣♣ Cadbury World

South of the green. ◷*Open Feb–Dec 9am/10am–3pm/5pm. Call or see website for details; reservations advised.* ◷*Closed most of Jan, several days Nov and Dec.* ◉*£13.45, children £10.10 (book online).* ♿▣✕. ℘*0845 450 3599. www.cadburyworld.co.uk.*
This is the visitor centre of the famous chocolate company, though it should be emphasised that the factory itself is *not* open to visitors. It tells the story of chocolate and cocoa, gives an insight into production and packing methods past and present and offers a ride through fairytale Beanville and tasting opportunities.

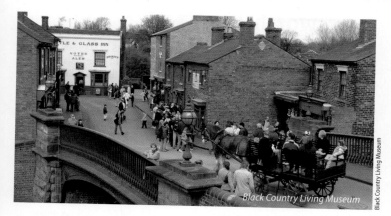

Black Country Living Museum

Black Country Living Museum

👥 Black Country Living Museum, Dudley★

Tipton Road, 10mi/15km northwest of Birmingham on the A 4123 or 3mi/4km from Junction 2 on the M 5. 🕐*Open Mar–Oct daily 10am–5pm. Nov–Feb Wed–Sun 10am–4pm.* 🕐*Closed Dec 25.* 👓*£12.50, child £6.75.* 👍📷✕. 📞*0121 557 9643. www.bclm.co.uk.*

The sprawling landscape of the South Staffordshire coalfield may have given rise to the name Black Country, which comprises Wolverhampton, Walsall, Dudley and Sandwell. Historic buildings from all around the area have been moved and authentically re-built to form this museum-village, which covers 26acres/11ha and presents the rich heritage of this industrial region. Coal mining is represented by a reconstructed pit-head and an impressive underground display of the conditions in a "Thick Coal" mine in the 1850s. Nearby is a working replica of the world's first steam engine (1712). The heart of the display, reached by an electric tramway and flanked by two canal arms, is the village: houses, a grocery, hardware shop, baker's, chemist's, sweet shop, glasscutter's, chainmaker's, nail shop, rolling mill, anchor forge, boatdock, Methodist chapel and pub. Spectacular limestone caverns beneath the adjacent Castle Hill can be visited by canal boat.

ADDRESSES

🍴 PUBS AND RESTAURANTS

Visit the Water's Edge and Brindleyplace developments in the Gas Street Basin area for lively wine bars, cafés, restaurants and traditional English pubs. There is a full choice of international cuisine of high standard on offer in Birmingham but the town is most famous for its Indian and Chinese restaurants and its Balti curry houses are renowned.

🛍 SHOPPING

Birmingham is the principal shopping centre for the Midlands with branches of famous London stores, such as Selfridges, in the Bullring centre, and Harvey Nichols, in the designer mall, The Mailbox. The Palisades and The Pavilions shopping complexes house most other major department stores and high street brands. Explore the Jewellery Quarter for shops selling hand-made gold and silver jewellery.

🎭 ENTERTAINMENT

The City of Birmingham Symphony Orchestra (CBSO), based at the splendid Symphony Hall, and Birmingham Royal Ballet, are internationally renowned. Pop and rock concerts, major sporting and other events (Blue Man Group, Cirque du Soleil etc.) are staged in the National Indoor Area (NIA), part of the National Exhibion Centre (NEC), just outside town. After dark, Broad Street, The Mailbox and the Water's Edge are hotspots for drinking, dining and dancing.

Chatsworth ★★★
Derbyshire

The original Chatsworth was begun in 1551 by Sir William Cavendish and Bess of Hardwick, that indomitable Elizabethan who was married four times and multiplied her wealth with each marriage. It was transformed 1686–1707 by the first Duke of Devonshire into a Baroque palace, and extended 1820–27 into "le second Versailles". Today, set amid magnificent countryside, it remains one of the very finest stately homes in the country and contains one of Europe's outstanding private art collections. The glorious verdant grounds are a delight in summer for their formal landscaping, family facilities and carefree atmosphere.

HOUSE
The Painted Hall, by Laguerre, is unashamedly Baroque; the ceilings and walls are a soaring profusion of colours. **Beneath the Great Stairs** is the grotto, with superb stone carvings. The two coronation chairs in the lobby were used by William IV and Queen Adelaide in 1830. The long landscape by Gaspard Poussin in the Green Satin Dressing Room is "among the finest landscapes in the world" (Gustave Waagen).
The State Rooms are characterised by unrestrained ceilings by Laguerre and Verrio and Louis XIV furniture; the gilt side tables in the Dining Room are by Kent; the Drawing Room tapestries (c. 1635), based on Raphael, were woven at Mortlake; the violin on the inner door of the Music Room is a remarkable *trompe l'oeil* by Jan van der Vaart.
The wrought-iron panels on the landings of the West Stairs are by Jean Tijou. The ceiling depicting the Fall of Phaeton is an early work by Sir James Thornhill (1675–1734) and the painting of Samson and Delilah is by Tintoretto (1518–94). In the corridor are two Egyptian memorial tablets which are 3,800 years old. The chapel is unaltered since 1694 and includes a fine work by Verrio and a gloriously Baroque altarpiece by Cibber.

Michelin Map: Michelin Atlas p 35 or Map 502 P 24.
Location: Bakewell, Derbyshire; in the Peak District, 8mi/13km north of Matlock.
Times and Charges: Open mid-Mar–Dec 23 daily 11am–5.30pm (6pm/dusk garden). All areas £16.50, child £10. House and garden £11.50, child £6.25; garden £7.50, child £4.50. Farmyard and adventure playground £5, child £5.50. Book online for savings. Tours of garden (all year) and house (May–Jun) 1hr each, noon and 2pm (charge). (charge). 01246 565 300. www.chatsworth.org.
Kids: Farmyard and Adventure Playground.

A Veronese hangs in the passage. **The Library** (90ft/28m) has some 17,000 books and a splendid gilded stucco ceiling by Edward Goudge (Wren's best pupil) framing Verrio's paintings. The 6th Duke built the **Sculpture Gallery** to house an incomparable collection of sculptures, including works by Antonio Canova. Hanging amid these is *King Uzziah* by Rembrandt.

PARK AND GARDEN ★★★
The genius of Capability Brown made this one of the grandest of 18C parks. The garden's most majestic feature is the Cascade, designed in 1696, each step a different height that varies the sound of the falling water that disappears into pipes, to reappear out of the Seahorse Fountain on the south lawn. The garden as we see it today is mostly the creation of Joseph Paxton (1803–65). More modern family-friendly additions are the farmyard which features milking demonstrations and daily animal-handling sessions, and the huge woodland adventure playground for children.

Coventry★
West Midlands

Coventry is known for its magnificent cathedral, Lady Godiva's legendary ride through the streets, and terrible devastation during the World War II.

A BIT OF HISTORY

Coventry's history stretches back to Saxon times. In its most famous legend, the city played host in 1043 to a Benedictine Priory founded by Leofric, Earl of Mercia, and his wife, **Lady Godiva**, who, according to legend, rode naked through the streets to persuade her husband to relieve the citizens from the burdensome taxes he had imposed. On 14 November 1940 the biggest bombing raid of its time destroyed most of the city, including the 13C church, which in 1918 had become a cathedral. The only remains of medieval Coventry are the timber-framed properties in **Spon Street (Y)**.

CATHEDRAL★★★ *1hr*

Fairfax Street. Open year-round daily (Sun noon) 9am–5pm. Old Cathedral Tower open daily except during bell ringing sessions. Check with the tourist information centre for opening times. New Cathedral £3.50 contribution requested, Old Cathedral Tower £2.50.

- ▶ **Population:** 299,316.
- **Michelin Map:** Michelin Atlas p 27 or Map 504 p 26.
- **Info:** Coventry Cathedral. ☎024 7622 5616. www.visitcoventry.co.uk.
- **Location:** Coventry is 19mi/30km east of Birmingham. Pool Meadow bus station is in the centre, the train station is a 5 min walk from town.
- **Kids:** Transport Museum.

☎024 7652 1200. www.coventry cathedral.org.uk.
Regarded by traditionalists as too modern and by modernists as too traditional, the **new cathedral** is one of the few post-war buildings to meet with the approval of the ordinary person. The architect was **Sir Basil Spence**.

The tower and spire, with restored bells, dominate the city centre of Coventry which is known as the city of the three spires. The flèche on the new cathedral (sometimes described as a TV aerial) has been both criticised and praised. Flanking the entrance steps is *St Michael Defeating the Devil* by **Jacob Epstein**. The majestic porch was designed to link the new cathedral with the ruins of the old and dramatically expresses

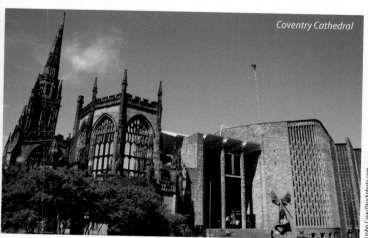
Coventry Cathedral

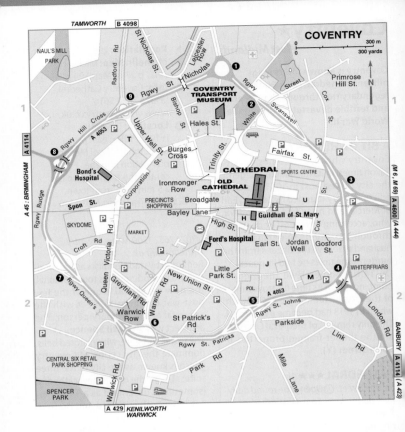

the meaning of death and resurrection. The overwhelming impression of the **interior** is of height, light and colour: height from the soaring slender nave pillars supporting the canopied roof; light from the great west screen, a wall of glass engraved with patriarchs, prophets, saints and angels by John Hutton; colour from the Baptistery window by John Piper, a symbol of the light of truth breaking through the conflicts and confusions of the world. The font is a great rough boulder from the hillside at Bethlehem. The ten great windows are set in recesses angled southwards to enable the sun to pour into the nave through the beautiful colours. The whole is dominated by the huge tapestry, *Christ in Glory*, designed by **Graham Sutherland**.

The **Old Cathedral**★ (Y) is late 13C with large-scale Decorated and Perpendicular additions. All that remains are the walls, the crypt and the tower (294ft/90m), and the spire, one of the architectural glories of England, exceeded in height only by Norwich and Salisbury. The east end is marked by a simple cross of charred timbers.

👥 COVENTRY TRANSPORT MUSEUM★ (Y)

Millennium Place, Hales Street. 🕐Open year-round daily 10am–5pm. 🕐Closed Dec 24–26. ♿✖. ✆024 7623 4270. *www.transport-museum.com.*
This museum is wholly appropriate for the city that was the birthplace of the British car industry and subsequently home to over 100 different manufacturers. Visitors walk through time, from 19C boneshakers into the future, while exploring the largest display of British road transport in the world.

Derby★

Derbyshire

The city of Derby is not one of England's most attractive county towns but it does provide a base for the picturesque Peak District and is surrounded by many outstanding country houses. In 1756 the Derby porcelain industry began here and the town is also famous as the birthplace of Rolls-Royce.

- ▶ **Population:** 223,836.
- **Michelin Map:** Michelin Atlas p 35 or Map 502 P 25.
- **Info:** Market Place. ℘01332 255 802. www.visitderby.co.uk.
- **Location:** 41mi/66km northeast of Birmingham. The train station is 1mi/1.6km southeast of the centre, the bus station is a 5 min walk from town.

CITY

At the heart of the city, west of the river Derwent on Queen Street is the **Cathedral** (◯open year-round Mon–Sat 9.30am–4.30pm. Sun for services only; ↝guided tours 10.30am second Mon each month, entrance to Tower on certain days; ◷£5 contribution; ♿; ℘01332 341 201; www.derbycathedral.org), a sublime blending of three eras – early 16C (the high tower), early 18C (James Gibbs' nave) and late 20C (retrochoir). The highlight is the magnificent Bakewell wrought-iron **screen and gates**, and the pedimented baldachin over the high altar. South of the chancel rests Bess of Hardwick.

Just southwest of the cathedral on The Strand is the **Derby Museum and Art Gallery**★ (◯open Mon 11am–5pm, Tue–Sat 10am–5pm, Sun and bank hols 1pm–4pm; ◯closed Christmas and New Year; ♿; ℘01332 716 659; www.derby.gov.uk/museums), home to two superb collections. The China Gallery contains the world's largest **collection of Derby Porcelain**★, while the Wright Gallery holds many of the finest paintings and drawings of **Joseph Wright of Derby** (1734–97).

A twenty minute walk south of here, near the Derbyshire Royal Infirmary, is the new works of **Royal Crown Derby Porcelain**★ (194 Osmaston Road; ◯Open Mon–Sat, 10am–5pm; ↝factory tours (booking essential) Tue–Fri 11am, 1.30pm; ◷museum and studio only, £2.95; full tour £4.95; ♿🅿✕; ℘01332 712 833; www.royal-crown-derby.co.uk). A collection dating from 1756 to the present day is on display. In the **Raven Room** a priceless mint collection of Royal Crown Derby is displayed as it would have been in a Victorian house.

EXCURSIONS

Kedleston Hall★★

NT. 4mi/6km northwest of Derby on Kedleston Road. **House:** ◯Open Mar–Oct, Sat–Wed noon–5pm. **Pleasure Grounds and Park:** Mar–Oct daily 10am–6pm, Park also Nov–Feb 10am–4pm. ◷£8.18. Park and pleasure grounds only, £3.63. ♿🅿✕. ℘01332 842 191. www.nationaltrust.org.uk.

This Palladian mansion is the work of three architects: Matthew Brettingham, James Paine and Robert Adam. They created one of the grandest 18C houses in England. The Curzon family have lived at Kedleston for over 500 years. The

Marble Hall, Kedleston Hall

©Richard Bryant/Arcaid/Corbis

rooms centre on the **Marble Hall**. The **State Drawing Room** shows Adam at his most colourful; note the Cuyp landscape and the Veronese Achilles. The **Saloon** or **Rotunda**, reaches to the coffered dome (62ft/19m). Adam's **Ante Room** and **Dressing Room** is graced by a neo-Classical screen with a segmental arch above the entablature, in a room hung with 17C and 18C Masters.

Sudbury Hall, National Trust Museumof Childhood★★

NT. 15mi/24km west of Derby via the A 516 and A 50. **Hall:** ○*Open mid-Feb–Oct Wed–Sun, bank hols and Good Fri 1pm–6pm.* **Museum:** ○*Open mid-Feb–Mar Wed–Sun, Mar–Oct daily, Nov–Dec Sat–Sun, 11am–5pm.* **Grounds:** ○*Open mid-Feb–Oct 10am–6pm.* ⊗*Hall £6.45, museum £6.90, both £12.* ♿🅿✕. ✆*01283 585 337. www.nationaltrust.org.uk.*

The **Jacobean exterior** (1660–1702) is deliberately conservative; the **interior** a radical combination of late Renaissance Classicism and Baroque.

The hall, which is densely hung with 18C paintings, is beautified by the work of Grinling Gibbons, Edward Pierce and

James Pettifer (all craftsmen who had worked with Wren on many of his London churches) and capped by Louis Laguerre's ceiling paintings.

The **Staircase** was built by Pierce and the exquisite plasterwork above it is by Pettifer; the finest ceiling of all is in the **Long Gallery**.

The **Museum of Childhood** covers a variety of childhood experiences from the 19C to the present day, in eight new galleries from Outdoor Adventure to Stories and Imagination, and Toys.

Denby Pottery

8mi/13km north of Derby by A 38 and B 6179. **Visitor Centre:** ○*Open year-round daily 9.30am (10am Sun)–5pm.* ○*Closed Dec 25–26 Dec.* ⌁*For tour times/prices see website.* ♿🅿✕. ✆*01773 740 799. www.denby visitorcentre.co.uk.*

All aspects of the production of the famous Denby earthenware are demonstrated to visitors with opportunities to try making and decorating pieces, plus food demonstrations and glassmaking.

Hereford★
Herefordshire

Seat of a bishop in AD 676, Hereford was a flourishing city and became capital of Saxon Mercia, with its own mint. In 1070 however a new market was created where the roads converged north of the town. Today Hereford is the prosperous centre for a rich agricultural region on the border with Wales. There are many outstanding half-timbered buildings preserved in the city.

CITY

In the heart of the city, just north of the river Wye, is the **Cathedral**★★ (*Cathedral:* ○*open year-round daily–Evensong;* ⌁*guided tour weekdays at 11am, 2pm* (⊗*£2.50; brass rubbing £1.50*);

▸ **Population:** 48,277.
⌖ **Michelin Map:** Michelin Atlas p 26 or Map 503 L 27.
ℹ **Info:** 1 King Street. ✆01432 268 430. www. visitherefordshire.co.uk.
▶ **Location:** Hereford is 56mi/91km southwest of Birmingham and 57mi/93km northeast of Cardiff.

⊗*requested donation £5;* ♿✕; ✆*01432 374 202; Mappa Mundi Exhibition and Chained Library:* ○*open year-round Mon–Sat 10am–5pm (4pm winter), Sun 11am–4pm;* ⊗*£4.50;* ✕; ✆*01432 374 209; www.herefordcathedral.org*), a mainly 12C red sandstone building. The massive tower was added in the 14C. The chantry to John Stanbury, Bishop from 1453–74, is a fine example of Perpendicular architecture.

Among the treasures is the **Mappa Mundi**★, a map of the world with Jerusalem at its centre, made by Richard of Haldingham in Lincolnshire. The **Chained Library**, one of the finest in the country, contains 1,400 books and over 200 manuscripts, dating from the 8C to the 15C, including the "Cider Bible" in which the "strong drink" of the authorised version has been translated as "cidir". There is a small 13C Limoges enamel reliquary, which used to contain a relic of St Thomas Becket, whose murder is depicted on the side.

Head west from here towards Eign Street and turn left down Ryelands Street until you arrive at number 21 and the **Cider Museum, King Offa Distillery** (🕐 open Tue–Sat bank hols and cider festival weekend Apr–Oct 10am–5pm, Nov–Mar 11am–3pm; ✆£3.50; ♿🅿✕; ✆01432 354 207; www.cidermuseum.co.uk). An old cider factory houses this museum, which tells the story of cidermaking through the ages, particularly during its heyday in the 17C.

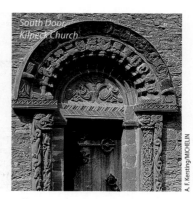
South Door, Kilpeck Church

A. F. Kersting/MICHELIN

EXCURSION
Kilpeck Church★★
8mi/13km southwest of Hereford via the A 465 and a minor road (right). 🕐*Open daily year-round dawn–dusk.* ✆*Contribution requested.* 🅿. ✆*01981 570 315.*
The Church of St Mary and St David was built in 1135. Nowhere else in Britain has such rich Norman **carving** and decoration survived. Only two of the 70 grotesques around the corbel have any religious significance. The gargoyle heads on the west wall are pure Viking. Look out for the notorious sheela-na-gig.

Ironbridge Gorge★★

Shropshire

The densely-wooded, mineral-rich Severn Gorge was the birthplace of the Industrial Revolution. In 1708 Abraham Darby (1678–1717), came to Coalbrookdale and revolutionised the industry by using coke as a fuel for smelting iron, replacing traditional charcoal. His experiments made it possible to use iron in transport, engineering, and construction (including the world's first iron bridge. A number of sites along the gorge now form one of the UK's most important, and most interesting industrial heritage complexes. The Ironbridge itself is one of the great symbols of the Industrial Revolution.

- **Michelin Map:** Michelin Atlas p 26 or Map 503 M 26 – 12mi/19km east of Shrewsbury.
- **Info:** ✆01952 884 391. www.ironbridge.org.uk.
- **Location:** 34mi/54km northwest of Birmingham.
- **Kids:** Blists Hill and Enginuity.

IRONBRIDGE GORGE MUSEUM★★
Coalbrookdale. 🕐*Open daily year-round 10am–5pm.* 🕐*Closed Dec 26–31.* ✆*Passport ticket valid at all 11 sites £14.95.* ♿🅿 *and* ✕ *at all sites.* ✆*01952 884 391 www.ironbridge.org.uk.*
The **Museum of Iron**★ illustrates the history of iron-making and the story

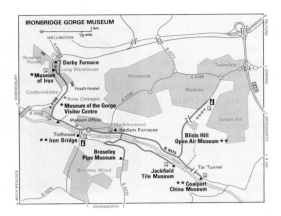

IRONBRIDGE GORGE MUSEUM

of the Coalbrookdale Company. It is housed in the great warehouse, built in 1838, which has cast-iron windows, sills and lintels. By the time of the Great Exhibition in 1851, the Coalbrookdale Company employed 4,000 men and boys and produced 2,000 tons of cast iron a week, for railway stations, bridges, fireplaces and a multitude of other uses. The **Museum of the Gorge and Visitor Centre**★ houses an exhibition and audio-visual introduction to Ironbridge Gorge. Alongside is **Enginuity**, a hands-on interactive exhibition designed to explain the principles of the manufacturing processes at Ironbridge in simple and fun terms.

The Iron Bridge★★ is a famous landmark bridge across the Severn Gorge at Coalbrookdale and was needed to

replace the hazardous ferry crossing, the only other bridges being at Buildwas and Bridgnorth. A design by Shrewsbury architect, Thomas Pritchard, was chosen and the Act of Parliament obtained in February 1776. Work began under **Abraham Darby III** in November 1777 and the Iron Bridge was opened on New Year's Day 1781. The bridge's single graceful span was a triumph of the application of new technology to the solution of a difficult problem. The ironwork weighs over 378t – the builders, unfamiliar with the new technology, undoubtedly erred on the side of caution. In the old **Tollhouse** *(free admission)* is an information centre with a display illustrating the history of the bridge.

The **Jackfield Tile Museum** is housed in an original gas-lit trade showroom, where galleries and period room settings show off the often magnificent colourful wall and floor tiles once manufactured here in immense quantities in the 19C.

The **Coalport China Museum**★★ dates from 1792 and manufacturing continued here until the works moved to Stoke-on-Trent in 1926. The old works, including the interior kiln of a bottle oven, have been restored as a museum of china, showing techniques of manufacture and particularly the products of Coalport. Nearby, you can walk through the **Tar Tunnel**, cut in 1786 to aid drainage from the Blists Hill Mine. It was found to ooze bitumen through the mortar of the brick lining (it still does today) and was turned

Iron Bridge at Coalbrookdale

©David Bailey/Dreamstime.com

into pitch, lamp-black and rheumatics remedies. Many visitors' favourite part of the site is **Blists Hill ★★**, a delightful reconstruction of a Victorian community of the 1890s, including a bank, pub, butcher's shop, school, mason's yard, mine and candle factory, as well as the inclined plane which carried boats from Blists Hill to the Severn and Coalport. Many of the buildings have been brought from elsewhere and re-built on site. More attractions are being built here, including a miners' railway *(visit www.blistshill.org for more details)*.

Leicester

Leicestershire

Leicester was once the capital of King Lear's kingdom, the seat of the 8C East Mercian bishops. The wealth of Leicester was based on the manufacture of hosiery from the medieval period until the mid 20C. Today Leicester is a cosmopolitan and increasingly fashionable town with two excellent family excursions.

- ▶ **Population:** 318,518.
- **Michelin Map:** Michelin Atlas p 28 or Map 504 Q 26.
- **Info:** 7–9 Every Street, Town Hall Square. ℘0844 888 5181. www.goleicestershire.com.
- **Location:** 43mi/69km east of Birmingham.
- **Kids:** National Space Centre; Snibston.

CITY

In the city centre, between the River Soar and St Martin's Square, is the **Guildhall★** *(Guildhall Lane. Open Feb–Nov Sat–Wed 10am (1pm Sun)–4.30pm; ℘0116 253 2569; www.leicestermuseums.ac.uk),* the site of the last stand of the Leicester Parliamentarians in the Civil War. Note the robust timber roof and uprights in the Hall, the c. 1500 glass in the Mayor's parlour, and one of the earliest public libraries in England.

Head southwest from the Guildhall to St Nicholas Circle, then turn down Castle Street for **St Mary de Castro Church★** *(open Easter–Oct Sat and bank hols 2pm–5pm; ℘ 0116 270 9995).* The shadowy and attractive interior goes back to 1107. The best Norman work is the sedilia. Head east from the Guildhall, then turn right onto Gallowtree Gate and continue to the railway station and beyond, then take a right onto New Walk for number 53 and the **New Walk Museum and Art Gallery★** *(open year-round daily 10am (11am Sun)–5pm; ℘0116 255 4900; www.leicestermuseums.ac.uk),* An excellent collection of works by English painters, including Wright of Derby, Hogarth, Bacon, Stanley Spencer and LS Lowry, and a large collection of German Expressionist works. There are also large-scale dinosaur skeletons and mummies in the Ancient Egypt section.

EXCURSIONS

National Space Centre★

just off the A6, 2mi/3km north. Open year-round Tue–Sun and Mon during school hols, 10am–5pm/4pm (last admission 90 mins before closing).

Rockets, National Space Centre

£11.74, child £9.79. ☐✕. ℘0116 261 0261. www.spacecentre.co.uk.

Six themed galleries include actual space hardware, hundreds of interactive hands-on activities and an exploration of the universe through the latest in audiovisual technology. The highlight for most visitors is the Space Theatre show, using the latest audiovisual, laser and animation techniques, inside the UK's largest planetarium. Space Now tells the story of the UK's involvement in cutting edge space exploration. Watch live demonstrations and meet scientists.

▲▲ Snibston ★

Ashby Road, Coalville. 16mi/26km northwest by A 50. ⏱*Open Apr–Oct.* £12.50. &☐✕. ℘01530 278 444. *www.leics.gov.uk/snibston.*

Coalville was a mining town from 1832 until the closure of its colliery in 1986. The pit and ancient colliery buildings have been transformed into landscaped

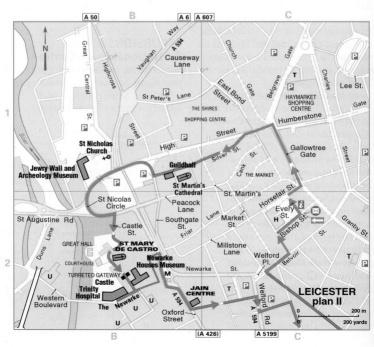

grounds, a country park, an underground tour, train rides and an impressive exhibition hall and museum containing over 90 hands-on stations telling the story of technology and design.

Bosworth Battlefield

Sutton Cheney, Market Bosworth. 14mi/22km west. ℘01455 290 429. www.bosworthbattlefield.com.
In 1485 Richard III was killed at the Battle of Bosworth and the first Tudor monarch, Henry VII, took the throne, ending years of dynastic war. An excellent new state-of-the-art visitor centre, on the edge of the rollling fields where the battle took place, interprets the event

Lichfield★

Staffordshire

This predominantly Georgian town lies just north of the Midlands industrial conurbation and is graced by its cathedral. This may be the smallest in the country but it is also one of the most beautiful and most picturesquely sited.

TOWN
Cathedral★★

🕐*Open year-round daily 7.30am (Sat 8am)–6.15pm (Sun winter 5pm, summer 6.30pm).* ☜*Contribution requested.* ♿✕. ℘01543 306 100. www.lichfield-cathedral.org.uk.
The present building, which replaced an earlier Norman church, was begun in 1195 and is a fine synthesis of the Early English and Decorated styles. During the Civil War the close was besieged three times, the cathedral was bombarded and the central spire collapsed in 1646. Repairs were made during the 1660s and the interior of the building was changed substantially by Wyatt in the 18C, but its medieval grandeur was restored by the sensitive work carried out by Sir George Gilbert Scott 1857–1901.
The three spires – unique among English cathedrals – are known as the **three**

and a re-enactment takes place on the weekend closest to 22nd August.

Boughton House★★

51mi/82km SE via the A 6. 🕐*Grounds May–Aug (house Aug only).* ℘01536 515 731. www.boughtonhouse.org.uk.*
Originally a monastic house owned by the Abbey of Edmundsbury, it was bought by Edward Montagu in 1528 and extended. More were made by the first Duke of Montagu, ambassador to Louis XIV, who built the north front and embellished the interior. Amongst its paintings are masterpieces by El Greco, Murillo, Teniers the Younger, Gainsborough, Van Dyck, Lelys and Knellers.

> ▶ **Population:** 28,666.
> ⚬ **Michelin Map:** Michelin Atlas p 27 or Map 502 O 25.
> ▯ **Info:** ℘01543 412 112. www.visitlichfield.co.uk.
> ◗ **Location:** 18mi/29km north of Birmingham.

sisters of the vale. On the west front the red sandstone is carved with saints.
The perfectly proportioned nave, adorned with wooden roof **bosses** and decorated capitals, leads the eye past the Transitional crossing and western choir to the Lady Chapel and the fine 16C Flemish glass at the east end. Among the many fine monuments are those to Samuel Johnson and David Garrick.

Samuel Johnson Birthplace Museum

Breadmarket Street. 🕐*Open daily Apr–Sept 10.30am–4.30pm; Oct–Mar 11am–3.30pm.* 🕐*Closed Jan 1, Dec 25–26.* ℘01543 264 972. www.lichfield.gov.uk.*
Samuel Johnson (1709–84), the famous **lexicographer**, was born in this house, built by his father. The exhibits illustrate his life from childhood to marriage, his move to London, the English dictionary and his friendship with Boswell.

Lincoln★★
Lincolnshire

Set high on a limestone plateau beside the River Witham and dominated by the triple towers of the cathedral, Lincoln is visible for miles around the Eastern English countryside. Much of the lower part of the town is a pedestrianised shopping area dotted with the occasional medieval church; steep narrow streets lead to the upper town with its imposing cathedral, castle and Roman remains.

A BIT OF HISTORY

Lindum Colonia, a settlement established since the Bronze Age and occupied by the Ninth Legion in about AD 60, was turned into a colonia in about AD 96 and confined to the plateau top (42 acres/17ha) surrounded by a wooden palisade. In the 3C Lincoln, now one of the four provincial capitals of Roman Britain, doubled in size. The city spread down the southern slopes to the river and was encased in a gated stone wall (4.5ft/1.5m thick) – offering a good view from the Bishop's Old Palace. The surviving **Newport Arch**, the only Roman arch in England through which traffic still passes, was the city's north gate. Lincoln survived the Roman decline, emerging as the capital of the Anglo-Saxon kingdom of Lindsey, and converted to Christianity in c. 630. After the Conquest, it gained in importance, with the building of the castle and cathedral, and became one of the most prosperous cities in medieval England, shipping its wool direct to Flanders. Many half-timbered buildings survive from this time.

CATHEDRAL★★★

Open summer Mon–Fri 7.15am–8pm (6pm weekends). Winter Sat 7.15am–6pm, Sun 7.15am–5pm. £4. Guided tours of cathedral, tower and roof, see website for details. ☏01522 561 600. www.lincoln cathedral.com.

The first cathedral, built by Remigius, was early Norman, the result of a short

▸ **Population:** 80,281.
▸ **Michelin Map:** Michelin Atlas p 36 or Map 502 S 24.
▸ **Info:** 9 Castle Hill, Cathedral Quarter. 21 The Cornhill, High Street. ☏01522 873256. ☏(both offices) 01522 873800. www.lincoln.gov.uk.
▸ **Location:** Northeast Midlands, 88mi/141km from Birmingham and 39mi/62km from Nottingham. The train station and bus station are almost opposite each other in the lower part of the city centre. It's easy to cover the centre on foot, albeit a steep walk from "downhill" to "uphill".
▸ **Don't Miss:** The cathedral, especially the roof tour (Sat only) on a clear day; the High Bridge; Belvoir Castle.
▸ **Timing:** Allow a full day to see the cathedral and town.
▸ **Walking Tours:** The Lincoln Guild of Guides operate several city centre tours on a daily basis. Ask at the tourist office.

and decisive programme between 1072 and 1092. Alexander, Lincoln's third bishop, builder of Newark Castle, re-roofed the cathedral following a fire in 1141. Hugh of Avalon, a French monk, built the present Early English cathedral following the earthquake of 1185 which virtually destroyed the original Norman building.

Few cathedrals have achieved such even proportions: the chancel is as long as the nave, the west towers almost as high as the crossing tower. The **west front**, the most famous view, consists of early Norman central sections, surrounded by a cliff-face of Early English blind arcading. The south side is graced by the intricate carving inside the **Galilee Porch** and **Judgement Porch** and the north side

Lincoln Cathedral

A. Williams/MICHELIN

provides a splendid and varied view of the buttressed Decorated **east end**, the north transept and the flying-buttressed chapter house.

Interior

Lincoln limestone and Purbeck marble shafts combine to create piers of contrasted texture which support the triforium, clerestory and vaults, showing Early English architecture at its best.

The **nave** is composed of seven bays; an exceptional font of Tournai marble stands in the second south bay; the windows are filled with Victorian stained glass. The crossing is flooded with light from the windows of the **Dean's Eye** (13C glass) in the north transept and the **Bishop's Eye** (14C leaf-patterned tracery, filled with fragments of medieval stained glass) in the south.

East of the magnificent 14C stone screen is **St Hugh's Choir**, furnished with 14C oak **misericords** and covered with the so-called "crazy vault of Lincoln", the first rib-vault of purely decorative intentions in Europe, curiously asymmetrical yet "easier to criticise than improve" (Pevsner). The **Angel Choir** is geometrical (late Early English), rich, light and spacious, so called after the 28 carved stone angels in the spandrels beneath the upper windows.

The soaring **East Window** of Victorian glass depicts Biblical scenes in the earliest Gothic eight-light window (1275). High on the first pier from the east end on the north side, the **Lincoln Imp**, the grotesque that has become the city's emblem, looks down on the shrine of St Hugh.

The 13C **cloister** is vaulted in wood (note the bosses: a man pulling a face, a man sticking out his tongue). Forming the north range is Christopher Wren's **Library**, above a classical loggia. East of the cloister is the **Chapter House** (early 13C) – the vaulting springing from a central shaft and externally supported by flying buttresses – where Edward I and II held some of the early English parliaments.

Precincts

Amidst the mostly Georgian and Victorian houses the **Vicar's Court (Y)** dates from 1300–400; the four ranges and mid-15C barn behind are a rare survival and among the prettiest examples of their kind in England.

The **Bishop's Palace (Y)**, *(EH; ⊙open Apr–Oct daily 10am–5pm, Nov–Mar Thu–Mon 10am–4pm; ⊙closed Jan 1, Dec 24–26; ⬤£3.90; P; ℘01522 527 468; www.english-heritage.org.uk)* is ruined but redolent of its former grandeur and gives an idea of the richness of Lincoln's medieval prelates. According to a description before its destruction in the Civil War, "the great hall is very fair, lightsome and strong… one large middle alley and two out alleys on either side with eight grey marble pillars bearing up the arches and free-stone windows very full of stories in painting glass of the Kings of this land."

CITY
Castle Hill

This street, which is lined by houses dating from the 16C to the 19C, links the 14C **Exchequer Gate** and the East Gate leading to the castle.

Castle★

⏱*Open daily May–Aug 10am–6pm, May and Sept 10am–5pm; Oct–Apr 10am–4pm.* ⏱*Closed Jan 1 and Dec 24–26.* ⬤*£4.* ☞*Guided tour Apr–Sept daily 11am and 2pm, also weekends in winter.* ✕. ✆*01522 511 068. www.lincolnshire.gov.uk.*

The construction of the Norman castle was begun by William the Conqueror in 1068, though nothing remains of the original. The keep's mound is now crowned by the late 12C **Lucy Tower**, once surrounded by a ditch (20ft/6m deep) and a drawbridge. At the top is a circular Victorian burial ground for prisoners, marked by rows of small gravestones. The **East Gate** was added in the 12C, **Cobb Hall** in the 13C. This was a defensive tower and in the 19C the roof was the scene of public hangings. Iron rings, still fixed to the walls, were used to attach prisoners' chains.

A Norman tower was enlarged in the 14C and added to in the 19C when it became known as the Observatory Tower, from which there is a splendid **view** of the cathedral and the surrounding countryside. It is possible to walk round the walls along the east, north and west sides (not recommended for vertigo sufferers). Although besieged in the wars of 1135–54 and 1216–17, the castle gradually lost its military significance but became a centre for the administration of justice which continues to this day; it is home to the Crown Court.

The Georgian **Prison Building**, constructed between 1787 and 1791, is now used to display one of the four surviving copies of **Magna Carta** (1215) in a darkened room accompanied by a voice intoning its contents in medieval Latin. The vellum document is preceded by a small exhibition explaining the document's history and importance to democracy.

In the **Victorian Prison Building** (1845/6), where prisoners were kept in solitary confinement, is a tableau showing oakum picking and the tiered **Prison Chapel** where a preacher addressed prisoners in their separate pews.

Jew's House★

The house and its beautifully designed Norman windows and doorway and original chimney buttress date from c. 1170; the adjoining **Jews' Court** was once used as a synagogue.

The Collection (Usher Gallery)★

Danes Terrace. ⏱*Open year-round daily 10am–4pm.* ⏱*Closed Dec 24–26 & 31.* ♿✕. ✆*01522 550 990. www.lincolnshire.gov.uk.*

This is a new space devoted to art and archaeology in Lincoln. The latter comprises artefacts from the Stone, Bronze and Iron Ages, Roman, Saxon, Viking and Medieval eras as well as fine, decorative and contemporary visual arts. Usher Gallery treasures are 16C–19C **miniatures**, 17C and 18C French and English clocks, Chinese, Sèvres, Meissen and English **porcelain** and English and Continental glass. A room is devoted to the watercolours of **Peter de Wint** (1784–1849) who painted views of the Lincolnshire countryside and of Lincoln Cathedral. In the **Tennyson** room are many of the poet's personal items including hats, pens, the warrant appointing him Poet Laureate, and photos of his funeral.

High Bridge★★

Medieval (though much restored), with the River Witham flowing through its Norman vaults (the Glory Hole), its timber-framed houses are a unique reminder of what Old London Bridge must have looked like. Upstream is **Brayford Pool**, Lincoln's medieval port,

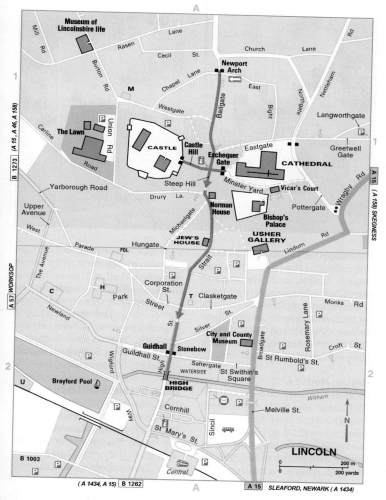

while downstream are two historic inns, the 14C Green Dragon and the 15C Witch and Wardrobe.

Museum of Lincolnshire Life

Burton Road. ⏰*Open year-round daily 10am–4pm (closed Sun Oct–Mar).* ⏰*Closed Dec 24–26 and 31, Jan 1.* 💷*£2.25.* ✗. ☎*01522 528 448.* *www.lincolnshire.gov.uk.*
Housed in the former barracks of the Royal North Lincoln Militia is a display on local domestic, social and industrial life over the last two centuries, with re-creations of traditional life.

EXCURSIONS
Belvoir Castle★★

35mi/56km southwest on the A 607 via Grantham; in Denton turn right (signs). ⏰*Open usually daily 11am–5pm (Sat 4pm), varies seasonally, see website for details.* ✎*Guided tours (free) Mon–Fri 12.30pm, 2.30pm.* 💷*£10 (garden only £5).* 🅿*(charge).* ♿✗. ☎*01476 871 002.* *www.belvoircastle.com.*
Built by John Webb (a pupil of Inigo Jones) in 1654–68, Belvoir (pronounced "Beever") was romanticised by James Wyatt into an early 19C "castle on a hill." The interior is part Gothic fantasy, part Baroque fantasy; the Ballroom contains

Belvoir Castle

Thomas Becket's illuminated breviary. The ceiling of the Elizabeth Saloon depicts Jupiter, Juno, Mercury and Venus. In the picture gallery are miniatures (Hilliard and Oliver) and paintings by Jan Steen, Cornelius Janssen, David Teniers II, Poussin and Gainsborough. The Regent's Gallery (131ft/40m long) is hung with vast Gobelins tapestries.

Belton House★

NT. 26mi/42km south on the A 607.
🕐 *Open mid-Mar–Oct Wed–Sun, Good Fri and bank hols 11am–5pm.* ☞£9.09 *(gardens only £7.27).* ♿🅿✕. ✆*01476 566 116. www.nationaltrust.org.uk.*
Belton is the fulfilment of the golden age of English domestic architecture from Wren to Adam. The classical simplicity of the Marble Hall provides the setting for paintings by Reynolds, Hoppner and Romney; the woodcarvings in the Salon are possibly the work of Grinling Gibbons; and in the Red Drawing Room is Fra Bartolomeo's *Madonna and Child.*

Doddington Hall★

5mi/8km southwest. 🕐*Open Easter Sun–Sept, Wed, Sun and bank hols. Garden also mid-Feb–Apr and Oct, Sun only. House 1pm–5pm, Gardens 11am–4pm.* ☞£7.75. *Gardens only, £5.* ♿🅿✕. ✆*01522 694 308. www.doddingtonhall.com.*
Doddington Hall is late Elizabethan and outward-looking, abandoning the traditional internal courtyard. With the exception of the parlour, all the interior was refurbished in 1764 by Thomas Lumby, a local builder. The **parlour** itself is in Queen-Anne style, its walls graced with paintings, including works by Sir Thomas Lawrence, Sir Peter Lely and Ghaerardt. The stairs are a masterpiece. The superb **Long Gallery** has displays of paintings and porcelain.

Gainsborough Old Hall★

18mi/29km west on A 57 (Z) and north on A 156. 🕐*Open year-round Mon–Sat 10am–4pm. Late Mar–Oct Sun 1–4 pm.* ☞*Guided tours by appt.* ☞£3.80. ♿🅿✕. ✆*01427 612 669. www.gainsborougholdhall.co.uk.*
One of the best-preserved late-medieval manor houses in England, this striking timber-framed hall was built between 1460 and 1480. Richard III visited it in 1483. It was originally all timber-framed, except for the brick kitchen, brick tower and stone bay window, but Elizabethan features were added to the two ranges. The Hall itself has a sturdy single-arched braced roof; the **kitchen** gives an excellent impression of medieval life in the servants' quarters. The east wing contains great chambers, while the west wing is a unique example of 15C lodgings. The tower is furnished as a late 15C bedchamber. There is a permanent exhibition about the Old Hall and the Mayflower Pilgrims.

Ludlow ★

Shropshire

Set in the rolling Shropshire Hills, close to the Welsh border, Ludlow is a Norman "planned town". One-time seat of the powerful Mortimer family, the castle passed into royal ownership with the accession of Edward IV. The town prospered in the 16C and 17C because of its role as seat of the Council for Wales and the Marches. The centrepiece of the Ludlow Festival (last week of June and first week of July) is a Shake-speare play performed in the inner bailey of the castle.

- ▶ **Population:** 9,040.
- **Michelin Map:** Michelin Atlas p 26 or Map 403 L 26.
- **Info:** Castle Square. ℘01584 875 053. www.ludlow.org.uk.
- ▷ **Location:** 41mi/66km west of Birmingham.

🐾 TOWN WALK

Ludlow Castle ★ *(Castle Square; ⓒopen Feb–Nov daily from 10am, closing times vary; ⓒclosed Dec 25; ⊛£4.50; &✗; ℘01584 874 465; www.ludlowcastle. com)* stands on a fine defensive site protected by the River Teme and low limestone cliffs. It was begun by Roger de Lacy shortly after the Domesday survey and built of locally-quarried stone. It was from here that Roger Mortimer, the most powerful and perhaps the richest man in all England, virtually ruled the country, after using his power to topple Edward II in 1326. He completed the block of buildings containing the **Great Hall** and Solar, one of the leading palaces of the day. **Arthur, Prince of Wales** brought his young bride **Catherine of Aragon** to honeymoon in Ludlow in the winter of 1501 and it was here that Arthur died early the following year (to be succeeded by his brother and future king Henry VIII). The chapel with its richly ornamented west door is one of only five round chapel naves still standing in Britain.

Heading east from the castle towards Bull Ring/Old Street, take a left onto College Street to find **St Laurence's Church** ★ *(ⓒopen Apr–Oct daily 10am–5.30pm, Nov–Mar 11am–4pm; ⊛£3 contribution requested; &; ℘01584 872 073; www.stlaurences.org.uk).* The tower dominates the surrounding countryside and is mentioned in the locally-famous collection of poems, *A Shropshire Lad,* by **AE Housman** (1859–1936), whose ashes are buried in the churchyard. Twenty eight **misericords** ★ in the choir stalls date from 1447.

On Bull Ring you will find the **Feathers Hotel** ★ *(www.feathersatludlow.co.uk).* The existing building was enlarged and re-fronted in 1619 to produce what Pevsner described as "the prodigy of timber-framed houses where everything of motifs that was available has been lavished on the façade".

EXCURSIONS

Stokesay Castle ★

EH. 6mi/10km north. ⓒ*Open late Mar–Sept daily 10am–5pm; rest of year opening times vary.* ⓒ*Closed Dec 24–26, Jan 1.* ⊛*£4.90.* &Ⓟ. ℘*01588 672544. www.english-heritage.org.uk.* Stokesay is the best-preserved example in England of a 13C fortified manor house. The hall has a fine roof of shaped and tapered tree trunks. The solar is furnished with a notable stone fireplace, peepholes into the hall below and 17C fittings.

Offa's Dyke

Offa's Dyke is a border earthwork, probably built by Offa, King of Mercia 757–96 AD. It gives its name to a long-distance footpath, one of Britain's National Trails, which runs from Sedbury in the south, near Chepstow, to Prestatyn in the north, through the varied and little-frequented landscapes of the Welsh Marches.

It would take an average of 12 days to walk the entirety, passing through the Black Mountains, Shropshire Hills, the Eglwyseg Mountains and the Clwydian Range.

Nottingham
Nottinghamshire

This East Midlands city is famous for its associations with Robin Hood, his arch enemy (the Sheriff of Nottingham) as well as lace-making and literary giants such as DH Lawrence and Lord Byron.

- **Population:** 270,222.
- **Michelin Map:** Michelin Atlas p 36 or Map 504 Q 25.
- **Info:** 1–4 Smithy Row. ℘08444 775 678. www.visitnottingham.com.
- **Location:** 51mi/82km north east of Birmingham. The train station is 10 min walk from the centre. There are two bus stations, Victoria and Broad Marsh, each a 5 min walk from town.
- **Kids:** Justice Museum.

CITY

Just west of Broad Marsh bus station on Castle Road is the **Castle Museum**★ (*open daily;* cave tours Mon–Sat; *closed Jan 1–2 and Dec 25–26;* £3.50, includes the Museum of Nottingham Life at Brewhouse Yard; caves £2.50; ; ℘0115 915 3700; www.nottinghamcity.gov.uk). Of the original Norman castle only the subterranean passage, **Mortimer's Hole**, from the castle to the **Brewhouse Yard**, and **Ye Olde Trip to Jerusalem** (allegedly the oldest inn in England) survive. Displays on the lower floors tell the history of Nottingham and include fine examples of medieval Nottingham **alabasters**★. Beneath the castle is a series of caves.

Just northeast of the bus station off Middle Hill on Weekday Cross/High Pavement is the **Galleries of Justice Museum** (; *open Tue–Sun and bank hols 10am–5pm (winter Tue–Fri 10am–4pm, Sat–Sun 11am–4pm);* £8.75, child £6.80; *closed Dec 24–28, Dec 31–Jan 1;* ℘0115 952 0555; www.galleriesofjustice.org.uk). Behind the elegant 18C façade the turnkey takes visitors on an entertaining tour featuring highwaymen (and women), unwholesome uses for this former courtroom, Great Train Robbers and executions that took place just ouside this cramped and squalid prison, dating back to the 15C.

EXCURSIONS
DH Lawrence Birthplace Museum

Eastwood, 10mi/16km NW on the A 610. 8A Victoria Street. Open year-round daily 10am–5pm (4pm Nov–Mar). £2 weekends and bank hols. Free on weekdays. . ℘01773 717 353. www.dhlawrenceheritage.org.

This tiny terraced cottage was the first of four Lawrence family homes in Eastwood. Exhibits and a video give a useful insight into the writer's early life and influences in this small mining town.

Newstead Abbey★

*11mi/18km north of Nottingham off A 60. **House:** Open Apr–Sept daily noon–5pm. **Gardens:** Open daily 9am–6pm or dusk. Closed last Fri Nov and Dec 25. £7 (gardens only £3.50). . ℘01623 455 900. www.newsteadabbey.org.uk.*

The medieval priory of the Abbey was converted in the 16C into a house, which became the ancestral seat of Lord Byron. The 19C rooms include the apartments of Byron and a selection of his manuscripts, memorabilia and portraits. Lakes, gardens and parkland make an attractive setting.

Sherwood Forest

Once one of the 65 Royal Forests which covered much of England, Sherwood was protected from agriculture and development by royal hunting laws: in this perfect environment for poaching, the outlaw bands became legends, and by the 15C **Robyn Hode** had become a composite folk-tale character embracing all their exploits. Some of the woodland was subsequently cleared and is now heathland; much has been replanted with conifers. The **Sherwood Forest Visitor Centre and Country Park**

(1mi/2km north of Edwinstowe Country Park; ⏱*open daily, dawn–dusk; visitor Centre closed until 2011;* ♿🅿✕*, picnic site;* ☎*01623 823 202; www.nottingham shire.gov.uk) stands where the supposed* marriage of Robin Hood and Maid Marian took place; from it paths lead to the 500-year-old **Major Oak** (33ft/10m in diameter).

Southwell Minster★★

14 mi/22km northeast. ⏱*Open daily 8am–7pm/dusk.* 💰*£3 donation requested.* ♿🅿✕*.* ☎*01636 812 649. www.southwellminster.org.uk.*
Southwell – pronounced Su'thel – is dominated by the Norman Minster, well-known for the foliage carving of its late 13C master masons. It is the only cathedral in England to boast a complete set of three Norman towers and dates from c. 1108. Smooth lawns and well-spaced graves frame the **west front**, pierced by a Perpendicular seven-light window. The intimate **interior** combines Norman severity with the glory of the mid-14C **screen**, depicting 286 images of men, gods and devils and the even more glorious Early English **choir** and **chapter house** (1288). The latter is the first single-span stone vaulted chapter house in Christendom, decorated with some of the finest medieval naturalism (late 13C) carved in stone.

Peak District★★
S. Yorkshire, Derbyshire, Staffordshire

The teeming northen industrial areas of Sheffield, Manchester, the Potteries and West Yorkshire have on their doorstep the unspoiled landscape of the Peak District National Park covering 555sq mi/ 1,437sq km. To the north the sombre moorlands and precipitous outcrops of the Dark Peak, culminate in Kinder Scout (2 088ft/636m); to the south is more pastoral White Peak, a plateau divided up by drystone walls and by spectacular steep-sided dales.
It was on Kinder Scout, on 24 April 1932, that a mass trespass by ramblers was organised. They were anxious to establish a right of access to these wild spots. The "trespass" resulted in the imprisonment of five of their number. In the end, however, it helped lead to the establishment of the National Parks. Today, disused railway lines have been turned into footpaths and there are rock faces to be climbed and pot-holes to be explored, particularly around Castleton, where the caves can be visited by the less energetic as well.

◔ **Michelin Map:**
Michelin Atlas p 35 or Map 502 O, P 23 and 24.
🛈 **Info:** Ashbourne ☎01335 343 666. Bakewell ☎01629 813 227. Buxton ☎01298 25106. Castleton ☎01629 816 558. Edale ☎01433 670 207. Matlock ☎01629 583 388. Matl. Bath ☎01629 55082. www.visitpeakdistrict.com.
▶ **Location:** The park extends from Holmfirth in the north to Ashbourne in the south and from Sheffield in the east to Macclesfield in the west.
👪 **Kids:** A cave visit; the cable cars at the Heights of Abraham; Gulliver's Kingdom.

NORTH
Buxton
The Romans discovered the warm springs and built baths here c. AD 79. In the 16C Mary Queen of Scots was occasionally permitted, during her long captivity at Sheffield Manor, to "take the waters". Buxton took on the aspect of a spa town in 1780 when John Carr of York built **The Crescent** which, with the

nearby **Opera House**, is still the centre of activity.

👥 Castleton Caves

The village of Castleton is still dominated by the ruined keep (mostly 12C) of the castle begun by William Peveril soon after the Norman Conquest. The local caves are natural cavities or lead-mining workings or a mixture of both. This important range of caverns presents lofty chambers with attractive mineral colourings and limestone formations.

Peak Cavern/Devil's Arse (🕐open Apr–Oct daily 10am–5pm, Nov–Mar Sat–Sun 10am–5pm; 💬guided tour (60 min); ⚉£7.25, joint ticket with Speedwell Cavern £12; 🅿✖; ✆01433 620 285; www.devilsarse.com) is entered at the foot of the hill below the castle.

Near the impressive entrance of the cave the roof is still blackened by soot from the chimneys of a community of ropemakers, who occupied and built houses in the cave for 300 years until 1974.

Speedwell Cavern (west on the B 6061; 🕐open year-round daily 10am–5pm; ⚉£7.75; joint ticket with Peak Cavern £12; 💬Guided tour (45min); 🅿✖; ✆01433 620 512; www.devilsarse.com) is reached by boat along an underground canal.

Blue John Cavern★ (off the A 625; 🕐open daily 9.30am–5.30pm/dusk (Jan times available by telephone; 🕐closed 25–26 Dec; ⚉£7.95; 💬guided tour (50min); ✆01433 620 642; www.bluejohn-cavern.co.uk) is the source of a purplish-blue form of fluorspar, called Blue John, a semi-precious mineral which is worked into jewellery and larger pieces. Blue John is also mined in **Treak Cliff Cavern** (🕐open daily 10am, call for tour times; 🕐closed 24–26 Dec, 1 Jan; ⚉£7.95; 💬guided tour (40min); 🅿✖; ✆01433 620 571; www.bluejohnstone.com). In 1926 the skeletons of Bronze Age miners with flint implements were found.

Derwent Reservoir

Created to supply water to the nearby cities, **Derwent**, **Howden** and **Ladybower Reservoirs** are today a "Lake District" enjoyed by yachtsmen, cyclists and walkers alike.

Eyam

Eyam (pronounced "eem") is known as "The Plague Village" because in 1665 the inhabitants, stricken by the disease, cut themselves off voluntarily from the outside world – only a quarter of them survived. Their story is told in the **Eyam Museum** (Hawkhill Road; 🕐open late-Mar–Oct, Tue–Sun and Bank Hols 10am–4.30pm; ⚉£2; ✆01433 631 371; www.eyammuseum.demon.co.uk).

Eyam Hall (Hope Valley; 🕐House open late Mar–early May Wed–Thu, Sun and bank hols noon–4pm ; Gardens open Jul–Aug, same days as house, noon–4.45pm; ⚉£6.25, gardens only £2; ♿; ✆01433 631 976; www.eyamhall.com) is still owned by the Wright family who built it in 1671. It has changed little: the rooms are furnished with portraits, costumes, silver and porcelain, 15C and 16C tapestries.

SOUTH
Arbor Low

The best-known of the Peak's prehistoric monuments, a circle of stones lies within a surrounding bank and ditch.

Bolsover Castle★

EH. 16mi/26km east of Matlock via Chesterfield on the A 632. 🕐Open daily May–Sept 10am–6pm (5pm Oct). Nov–Apr Thu–Mon 10am–4/5pm. 🕐Closed Dec 24–26, Jan 1. ⚉£6.90. ♿🅿✖. ✆01246 822 844. www.english-heritage.org.uk.

This Gothic folly of a castle is perched on a hill above the coal mines and pit-heads. Completed in 1633, its interior is rich in carved Jacobean fireplaces, panelling, strapwork and ceiling paintings.

Chatsworth House★★★

See CHATSWORTH.

Dovedale★★

A dramatic 2mi/3.2mi gorge in the Derbyshire hills where the River Dove has washed away the soft limestone, exposing cliffs, caves and crags. From its entrance between Thorpe

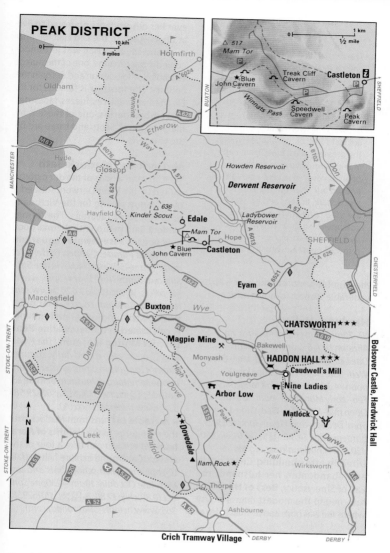

Cloud (942ft/287m) and Bunster Hill (1,000ft/305m), it meanders below the rocky outcrops of Lovers' Leap, The Twelve Apostles and **Ilam Rock**★.

Haddon Hall★★

🕐 Open noon–5pm; May–Sept daily; around Easter weekend Thu–Tue; Apr and Oct Sat–Mon; early–mid-Dec daily 10.30am–4pm. ∞£8.75. 🅿 (£1) ✗. ✆01629 812 855. www.haddonhall.co.uk.

Overlooking the River Wye since the 12C, rambling and very English, Haddon Hall was continually enlarged until the early 17C. The **interior**, like the exterior, is in a multitude of styles; the Hall (1370) is medieval, the Dining Room and Great Chamber are Tudor and the Long Gallery is Elizabethan. The rooms are matched in splendour by the Mortlake **tapestries**. The chapel boasts splendid **murals**. The terraced **gardens** date from the 17C or earlier. Lavishly planted with roses

Well Dressing

The annual Well Dressing is a unique Peak District tradition. Pagan thanksgivings to local water spirits have been transformed into Christian ceremonies, in some 20 Peak District villages. Eyam, Youlgreave, Wirksworth and Monyash are just some of the villages where the dressing takes place from early May to August each year. A large board is covered in clay, a design pricked out on it and then flowers, seeds, bark, lichens and grasses are used to fill out the design in colours. The board is then placed by the well or spring and blessed at a special open-air church service.

they tumble prettily to the river with its venerable stone packhorse bridge.

Hardwick Hall★★

NT. 20mi/32km east of Matlock via Alfreton by A 615 and A 61 north. Doe Lea. **Hall:** ◷*Open mid-Mar–Oct Wed–Sun, Good Fri and bank hols, noon–4.30pm.* ☞*Hall tours mid-Feb–early Mar 11am–noon.* **Gardens:** *Open mid-Mar–Oct, Wed–Mon 11am–5pm. Dec Sat–Sun 11am–3pm.* ☞*£9.09, gardens only, £4.54.* ▯✕*.* ☏*01246 850 430. www.nationaltrust.org.uk.*

Directly after building Chatsworth and abandoning her husband, the Earl of Shrewsbury, **Bess of Hardwick** returned to the modest manor house where she was born and re-built it. However her descendants preferred to live at Chatsworth so the Old Hall fell into ruins and the New Hall was left unoccupied, frozen in time, one of the purest examples of 16C design and decor in the country. The **interior** is famous for its Elizabethan fireplaces, friezes, tapestries and **embroideries**; one of these is by Mary Queen of Scots and three are by Bess herself.

Matlock and Matlock Bath

The cliffs and woods of the deep gorge carved by the River Derwent formed a picturesque setting for the Victorians to develop spa facilities. The former Matlock Bath Hydro, with thermal pool, now houses a **freshwater aquarium** *(110 North Parade;* ◷*open Easter–Oct daily 10am–5.30pm, Nov–Easter Sat–Sun and Xmas Hols 10am–5pm;* ☎*call for price;* ☏*01629 583 624; www.matlockbathaquarium.co.uk).* A far older Peak District industry, lead mining, is celebrated in the fascinating **Peak District Mining Museum** *(The Pavilion;* ◷*open year-round daily; summer 10am/11am–4pm/5pm; winter 11am/noon–3pm/4pm;* ☎*museum or mine £3, both £5;* ▯*(charge);* ♿✕*;* ☏*01629 583 834; www.peakmines.co.uk).*

A ▲▲**cable car** runs from Matlock over the river gorge to the **Heights of Abraham**, where you can take a tour of the Masson Cavern and explore hilltop trails *(*◷*open mid-Feb school hols and late Mar–late Oct daily 10am–4.30pm/5pm;* ☎*£10.80, child £7.80;* ♿▯✕*;* ☏*01629 582 365; www.heights-of-abraham.com).*

Shrewsbury
Shropshire

The medieval border settlement of Shrewsbury grew up around its Norman castle, which commanded the loop in the Severn. The modern county town has elegant Queen Anne and Georgian buildings, a wealth of black-and-white houses and "shuts" – medieval shortcuts and alleyways.

▸ **Population:** 64,219.
◔ **Michelin Map:** Michelin Atlas p 26 or Map 503 L 25.
▤ **Info:** Roweleys House, Barker Street. ☏01743 281200. www.visit-shrewsbury.com.
▻ **Location:** Shrewsbury is 44mi/71km north west of Birmingham.

ABBEY★

Open Mon–Sat 10.30am–3pm. Sun 9.30 am–2.30pm. &. ℘*01743 232 723. www.shrewsburyabbey.com.*

The Benedictine Abbey, founded in 1083, stands just outside the town, across the English Bridge. The 14C tower carries a statue of Edward III, in whose reign it was built, and there are Norman pillars in the nave dating from the 11C.

EXCURSIONS

Weston Park★★

17mi/27km east of Telford by A 5.
House: *Open late May– early Sept Sun–Fri (daily Jun–Aug) 1pm–5pm. Closed part of Aug.* £8 *(Garden only £5.50).* &PX. ℘*01952 852 100. www.weston-park.com.*

This 17C house is unusual in having been built by a woman, Lady Elizabeth Wilbraham. The splendidly furnished interior is remarkable for the quality of the portraits – from Holbein to Lely's likeness of Lady Wilbraham and a rare portrait by Constable.

Beyond the formal gardens is the park, designed by Capability Brown, grazed by deer and rare breeds of sheep. It contains many family attractions – a miniature railway, pets corner and adventure playground.

Wenlock Priory★

EH. 12mi/19km SE by A 458. Opening times vary. £3.40. P. ℘*01952 727 466. www. english-heritage.org.uk.*

The Cluniac priory was founded c. 690, pillaged by the Danes and later re-founded. The church, one of the longest monastic churches in England (the nave is 350ft/106m long), was built in the 1220s by Prior Humbert.

The delicate interlaced arcading of the chapter house is the work of the Normans. So too is the magnificent **lavatorium** (1180), where the monks washed before meals.

Wenlock Edge★

Southwest of Much Wenlock on B 4378. This massive limestone escarpment provides magnificent **views**.

Powis Castle★★

Opening times vary. £9.90 *(garden only £7.20).* &PX. ℘*01938 551 929. www.nationaltrust.org.uk.*

The town of Welshpool (Y Trallwng) lies at the northern end of the ridge on which Powis Castle is built. The massive twin towers of the gateway date from the late 13C. The Long Gallery, with its mid-17C *trompe l'œil* panelling, is dated 1592 while the Dining Room and Oak Drawing Room were remodelled in the early 20C. The castle houses the collections of the first **Lord Clive** (1725–74), founder of British India, and many fine paintings.

The Italianate **gardens**, created towards the end of the 17C have not been remodelled and are one of the rare remaining masterpieces of the period.

Stamford★★

Lincolnshire

Located half-way between the Midlands and East Anglia, Stamford has a long history, being one of the five Danelaw towns. "As fine a built town all of stone as may be seen" was the opinion of Celia Fiennes, late 17C traveller and writer. It has maintained its elegance and was the first town in England to be designated a Conservation Area.

▶ **Population:** 17,492.
⚭ **Michelin Map:** Michelin Atlas p 29 or Map 504 S 26.
▯ **Info:** Arts Centre, 27 St Marys Street. ℘01780 755 611. www.lincolnshire.gov.uk.
▷ **Location:** 44mi/70km northeast of Cambridge. The train station is a 5 min walk from the centre; the bus station is in town.

TOWN
St Martin's Church★
High Street St Martin's. ⏱*Open daily 10am–4pm.* ∞*Contribution requested.*
The church was rebuilt c. 1480 in the Perpendicular style. The north chapel is dominated by the alabaster monument to **William Cecil**, **Lord Burghley** (1520–98). In the nearby churchyard is the grave of Daniel Lambert (1770–1809, 52st 11lb when he died), reputed to be the fattest man in England, who, in spite of his size, was a keen horseman and "very partial to the female sex"..

Lord Burghley's Hospital★
Station Road and High Street St Martin's.
These charming late Elizabethan almshouses were built on the site of the medieval hospital of St John the Baptist and St Thomas the Martyr in 1597.

Browne's Hospital★
Broad Street. ⏱*Open May–Sept Sat–Sun and bank hols; Oct–Apr by appointment.* ℘*01780 763153.*
One of the best-preserved medieval hospitals in England, Browne's was built c. 1475, with cubicles for "ten poor men". Both the chapel and the audit room are lit by late 15C stained glass.

Stamford Museum
Broad Street. ℘*01780 766 317. www.lincolnshire.gov.uk.*
The story of Stamford embraces its Saxon origins and its starring role as *Middlemarch* in the BBC television serial of the novel by George Eliot. It includes a life-size model of Daniel Lambert (⏱*see above*), whose clothes have been displayed here ever since here died.

EXCURSIONS
Burghley House★★
Southeast. ⏱*Opening times vary.*
&⏹✗. ∞*£11.30 (gardens only, £6.50).*
℘*01780 752 451. www.burghley.co.uk.*
This is one of the country's finest Elizabethan mansions, built by **William Cecil**, **Lord Burghley**. The extensive late-17C re-decorations include Baroque ceilings painted by **Laguerre** and **Verrio**, at their most exuberant in the **Heaven and Hell Rooms**.
The distinguished collection of **paintings** includes works by Veronese, Bassano, Gainsborough, Kneller and Lawrence and Brueghel the Younger. Capability Brown (by Nathaniel Dance) looks out over the grounds he created. A fascinating recent addition to the grounds is **The Gardens of Surprise**.

Stoke-on-Trent
Staffordshire

The potteries that this area is world-famous for (and for which is it nicknamed) existed long before the time of England's most distinguished potter, **Josiah Wedgwood** (1730–95). Kilns date back to the early 14C but it was the opening of Wedgwood's Etruria factory in 1769, the exploitation of Staffordshire's coalfields and the digging of the Trent–Mersey Canal that turned a local industry into a national one and an industry into an art. Most of the great brick kilns (bottle, conical, squat, swollen, slender) have now disappeared. A few monumental survivors remain, particularly in Longton.

▶ **Population:** 266,543.
& **Michelin Map:** Michelin Atlas p 35 or Map 403 N 24.
▤ **Info:** ℘01782 236 000. www.visitstoke.co.uk.
◯ **Location:** 43mi/69km north of Birmingham. A car is best for getting around the "Five Towns" that make up Stoke-on-Trent.
☺ **Don't Miss:** The Wedgwood Visitor Centre; Little Moreton Hall.
◯ **Timing:** Allow 1–2 days including an excursion.
♦ **Kids:** Alton Towers; Trentham.

CITY MUSEUMS
Gladstone Pottery Museum★
Uttoxeter Road, Longton. ○*Open daily 10am–5pm.* ✆£5.95. ♿🅿✕. ✆01782 237 7076. www.stoke.gov.uk/museums. This unique surviving pottery factory or "potbank" retains its original workshops, cobbled yard and distinctive bottle ovens. It produced bone china from 1850 until the 1960s when it was converted into a museum of British pottery. The potters' traditional skills are demonstrated in the workshops.

The Potteries Museum and Art Gallery★
Bethesda Street, Hanley. ○*Open year-round.* ♿✕. ✆01782 23 23 23. www.stoke.gov.uk/museums. The city museum houses a superb ceramics collections from 14C English pottery right through to the modern studio movement and examples of current industrial production. There is a World War II Spitfire and an art and crafts collection, and major art exhibitions are staged.

EXCURSIONS
Alton Towers★★
12mi/19km east via the A 50, A 521 and B 5032. ○*Open Feb half-term and mid-Mar–early Nov, daily, gates open 9.30am. Rides start 10am, closing times vary.* ✆Prices vary; book online in advance. ♿🅿 (£4) ✕. ✆08705 20 40 60. www.alton-towers.co.uk. Britain's most famous theme park offers a great variety of spectacular rides, a waterpark and a spa as well as tranquil gardens. It is set in the beautiful grounds of Alton Towers, a 19C neo-Gothic mansion, now in ruins.

Biddulph Grange Garden★
NT. Grange Road, Biddulph. 7mi/11km north on the A 527. ○*Opening times vary.* ✆Mid-March–Oct £6.10, rest of year £3. Joint ticket with Little Moreton Hall (ⓘ see below) £11. 🅿✕. ✆01782 517 999. www. nationaltrust.org.uk. This unusual and exciting garden with themed sections devoted to different parts of the world was designed in the mid-19C by James Bateman to display specimens from his extensive plant collection.

Little Moreton Hall★★
NT. Congleton 10mi/16km north on the A 500 and A 34. ○*Open 11am–4pm/5pm.* ✆£6.10. Joint ticket with Biddulph Grange (ⓘ see above) £11 ✆Guided tour (free) most days main season. ♿🅿✕, picnic area. ✆01260 272 018. www. nationaltrust.org.uk. This beautiful moated half-timbered manor house is characterised by rich and intricate patterns on square panels, elaborate joinery and window tracery and 16C glass.

It was begun in the 1440s with the building of the Great Hall and completed some 140 years later with the addition of John Moreton's Long Gallery. Note the tracery in the bay window of the Great Hall, the painted panelling frieze in the parlour, the arch-braced roof trusses and plaster figures in the Long Gallery.

Wedgwood Visitor Centre★
7mi/11km south on the A 500, A 34 and a minor road (left) to Barlaston. ○*Open year-round daily, 9am (10am Sat–Sun)–5pm.* ✆Free. ✆Tours Mon–Fri. ✆£6.25 Fri–Sun, £8.25 Mon–Thu. ♿🅿✕. ✆01782 204 218. www.wedgwoodvisitorcentre.com. Established in 1938 the Wedgwood Factory offers the perfect overview of the pottery-making process, with a suitably excellent collection of Wedgwood ware (neo-Classical, Victorian, Art Nouveau, Art Deco and modern), and Wedgwood portraits by Stubbs, Reynolds, Lawrence and Wright of Derby.

👥 Trentham★
5mi/8km south of Hanley. ○*Open Easter–Sept 10am–6pm/dusk.* ✆01782 646 646. www.trenthamleisure.co.uk. Britain's most spectacular Italian Garden, designed by Capability Brown, covers 750 acres. It has recently become the region's second largest leisure centre, featuring a monkey forest, treetops walk, big wheel, garden centre; shopping and restaurants.

Stratford-Upon-Avon★★
Warwickshire

Stratford is not only Shakespeare Country but Forest of Arden country too. Its timber frames were hewn from the surrounding woods and its favourite son's mother was called Mary Arden. **William Shakespeare** (1564–1616) forsook his home town and his wife, Anne Hathaway, for London, where success came to him as a jobbing playwright, who was able to distil sex and violence, farce and philosophy into the most potent lines in the language. He returned to Stratford in 1611, rich and famous enough to acquire a coat of arms, and lived at New Place until his death. Today Stratford is one of England's most popular tourist destinations.

TOWN
Shakespeare's Birthplace★ (A)
🕐*Open daily Feb half-term, Apr–Oct 9am–5pm; Nov–Mar 10am–4pm.* 🕐*Closed 23–25 Dec.* 🚃*£9, includes entry to Hall's Croft and Nash's House. Joint ticket to all five houses £15.* ✆*01789 204 016. www.shakespeare.org.uk.*
The half-timbered house where the dramatist was born is part museum (including a First Folio), part shrine. Note the graffiti on the upstairs windows (Scott, Carlyle, Ellen Terry and Henry Irving). In the same complex is an exhibition illustrating Shakespeare's life and times.

Harvard House and Museum of British Pewter
🕐*Open early Jul–Aug and bank hols Wed–Sun and late May–early Jul and early Sept–Oct Fri–Sun, noon–5pm.* 🚃*£3.50 (free with joint ticket to Shakespeare properties (🕐see above and below).* ♿. ✆*01789 204 016. www.shakespeare.org.uk.*
This ornately-carved half-timbered house bears the date 1596, when it was home to Katharine Rogers. The Ameri-

▶ **Population:** 22,231.
⬡ **Michelin Map:** Michelin Atlas p 27 or Map 403 P 27.
▤ **Info:** Bridgefoot. ✆0870 160 7930. www.shake-speare-country.co.uk.
◗ **Location:** 24mi/38km south of Birmingham. Its train station is on the edge of town, a 10 min walk away, the regional Riverside bus station is a 5 min walk from the centre. Stratford is small enough to be able to comfortably cover most attractions on foot. A hop-on, hop-off City Sightseeing Bus covers the rest (🚃£10; ✆01789 412 680; www.city-sightseeing.co.uk).
🕿 **Don't Miss:** Hall's Croft; a night at the theatre; Mary Arden's House.
🕿 **Warning:** The town can be very congested during the summer months.
🕐 **Timing:** Allow two days; more for excursions.

can flag flies in honour of her son, **John Harvard** (b. 1607), founder of Harvard University, which owns the building today. Inside the house is displayed the Neish Collection of Pewter which ranges from Romano-Britain to the 19C.

Nash's House and New Place
🕐*Open daily Feb half-term and Apr–Oct 9am–5pm; Nov–Mar 10am–4pm.* 🕐*Closed 23–25 Dec.* 🚃*£9, includes entry to Hall's Croft and Shakespeare's Birthplace (joint ticket to all five houses £15).* ♿. ✆*01789 204 016. www.shakespeare.org.uk.*
Of New Place, Shakespeare's retirement home, built in 1483, only the foundations remain marked by a picturesque garden space. However, next door, **Nash's House**, home of Shakespeare's granddaughter, has been beautifully restored and houses exhibitions.

Shakespeare's eldest daughter, Susanna, married physician John Hall and the couple lived at **Hall's Croft**★ until some time after 1616. The restored house, part 16C, part 17C, contains furniture and paintings from Hall's time, notes about his patients and a small exhibition on medicine in his day.

Guild Chapel

🕐 *Open daily 10am–4.30pm.*
📞 *01789 204 671.*
The Chapel of the Guild of the Holy Cross (founded 1269), the ruling body of Stratford before the Reformation, is predominantly Perpendicular, with wall-paintings of Christ, Mary, St John, St Peter and the Last Judgement.

Grammar School

Exterior only.
Built c. 1417 as the Holy Cross Hall and turned into a school after the Reformation; amongst its pupils was William Shakespeare.

Holy Trinity Church

🕐 *Open (special services permitting) Apr–Sept Mon–Sat 8.30am–6pm. Mon–Sat rest of year 9am–4/5pm. Sun year-round 12.30pm–5pm. Last entry*
20 mins before closing time. ⛪*Church free. £1.50 donation requested to view Shakespeare's grave.* 🕐*Closed Good Fri, Dec 24–26, Jan 1.* 📞*01789 266 316. www.stratford-upon-avon.org.*
With an Early English tower and transepts and early Perpendicular nave and aisle, Holy Trinity would be notable even without **Shakespeare's grave** on the north side of the chancel. "Blessed be the man who spares these stones / And cursed be he that moves my bones."

Courtyard Theatre (Royal Shakespeare Company) (T1)

🕐*Courtyard Theatre guided tours (45 mins) are free. Several tours per week, inc. two on Sun, times vary according to performance and rehearsal schedule. Call for times and to book your place.*
🕐*Closed 24–25 Dec.* ⛪*£4.* ♿✖.
📞*0844 800 1114 (bookings). 01789 403444. www.rsc.org.uk.*
The 1,000-seat Courtyard Theatre opened in July 2006 and will be the home of the **Royal Shakespeare Company** (RSC) during the transformation of the Royal Shakespeare Theatre. When this is completed (scheduled for 2010), the Courtyard Theatre will be dismantled and The Other Place will re-open as

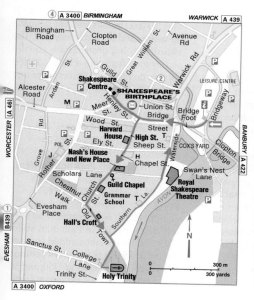

Mary Arden's House

the RSC's studio theatre. Tours include the chance to see the Royal Shakespeare Company Collection's paintings, sculpture and historical theatre material (backstage tours).

Adjoining it is the **Swan Theatre**, built in 1986 with a Jacobean-style apron stage and galleried seating within the shell of an earlier theatre largely destroyed by fire in 1926. It stages free exhibitions (⏰*open Mon–Fri 1.30 pm–6.30pm, Sat 10.30am–6.30pm, Sun 11.30 am–4.30pm; ☎01789 403444; www.rsc.org.uk*).

EXCURSIONS
Mary Arden's House ★
3mi/5km north, off A 3400 in Wilmcote. ⏰*Open daily Feb half-term and Apr–Oct 10am–5pm; Nov–Mar 10am–4pm.* ⏰*Closed 23–25 Dec.* ☜*£8; all five Shakespeare Houses £15 (♿see above and below). ✕. ☎01789 204 016. www.shakespeare.org.uk.*

Home of Shakespeare's mother, Mary Arden, featuring herring-bone timber framing and, mercifully, unrestored. Costumed characters re-enact the daily grind of Elizabethan times in the 16C farmhouse kitchen preparing and cooking food using traditional methods. Between the house and neighbouring Glebe Farm (preserved as a c. 1900 farmhouse) are dovecots, cowsheds, barns and outbuildings.

Anne Hathaway's Cottage
1mi/2km west via Shottery Road. ⏰*Open daily Feb half-term and Apr–Oct 9am–5pm; Nov–Mar 10am–4pm.* ⏰*Closed 23–25 Dec.* ☜*Guided garden tours summer. ☜£6, all five Shakespeare Houses £15 (♿see above and below). ✕(seasonal). ☎01789 204 016. www.shakespeare.org.uk.*

This much-loved picture-perfect building, where young William wooed his beloved Anne, is more a farmhouse than a cottage, and the rear was re-built after a fire in 1969. Upstairs are some dramatic tie-beams and the Hathaway bed. The award-winning grounds are equally picturesque featuring a herb-scented garden, orchard and Shakespeare tree garden.

Ragley Hall★
10mi/16km west off A 46, 2mi/3km beyond Alcester. ⏰*Open Feb–Oct weekends and school hols.* ***House:*** *Sun–Fri noon–4pm.* ***Park and Gardens:*** *10am–6pm (last admission 4.30pm).* ☜*£8.50. ♿🅿✕. ☎0800 093 0290, 01789 762 090. www.ragleyhall.com.*

This noble hall was designed and built by Robert Hooke in Palladian style, 1679–83. James Gibbs added some of the most perfect plasterwork **ceilings** he ever conceived around 1750, and 30 years later Wyatt built the gigantic portico. The walls are hung with paintings by Wootton, Van Loo, Reynolds, Hoppner, Lely and Cornelius Schut. The surprise is the **South Staircase Hall** decorated by Graham Rust between 1969 and 1983, with its ceiling of *The Temptation* and murals portraying classical gods, monkeys, birds and contemporary members of the Seymour family.

The grounds include a sculpture garden, adventure playground, woodland walks and an attractive lakeside picnic area.

Upton House★

NT. 14mi/22km southeast on A 422. **Garden:** ⏱*Open Apr–Oct daily 11am–5pm. Mar–Dec Sat–Wed 11am–5pm (Nov–Dec noon–4pm).* **House:** ⏱*Open Apr–Aug daily 1pm–5pm, Nov–Dec Sat–Sun 1pm–4pm.* ⏱*Guided tours house Apr and late Jul–Aug 11am–1pm.* ⏱*House and garden Mar–Oct £8.09, Nov–Feb £4.77; garden only,*

£4.77/£3.36. ♿🅿✕. ☎*01295 670 266. www.nationaltrust.org.uk.*

This late 17C house was bought by Viscount Bearsted, son of the founder of the Shell company and exhibits his spectacular collection of porcelain and paintings. In the **Hall** is a view of Venice by Canaletto and a landscape by Wootton. In the **Long Gallery** are Dutch paintings – note Jan Steen's *Four Senses* as well as the Chelsea and Bow porcelain. The **Boudoir** is reserved exclusively for French 18C and 19C works, including Boucher's *Venus and Vulcan*. The **Porcelain Lobby** is packed with Sèvres, Chinese, Chelsea and Derby china and porcelain. In the Games Room are Hogarth's *Morning* and *Night*. The pride of the collection is in the **Picture Gallery**, where among works by Holbein, Hogarth, Guardi, Tintoretto, Bruegel the Elder and Bosch hangs El Greco's *Christ taken in Captivity.*

ADDRESSES

🛏STAY

🛏 **Victoria Spa Lodge**, *Bishopton Lane, 2mi/3km northwest.* ☎*01789 227 985. www. victoriaspa. co.uk.* This beautiful Victorian lodge, a 20 min rural walk from the centre, was originally built as a spa and Princess (the future Queen) Victoria once stayed here. She gave her name to the hotel, and her coat-of-arms is built into the gables. Pretty public rooms and seven country-cottage style bedrooms.

🛏 **The Payton**, *6 John Street.* ☎*01789 266 442. www.payton.co.uk.* Set in a quiet area this listed Georgian town house offers five pale pastel-coloured bedrooms and a neat breakfast room.

🍽 EAT

🍽 **Golden Cross**, *Wixford Road, Ardens Grafton.* ☎*01789 772 420. www. thegoldencross.net.* Superior British pub food is on offer at this slickly-run inn 5mi/8km south of the town centre; the large garden and terrace is ideal for summer dining with a distinctly rural interior for less clement weather.

PUBLIC TRANSPORT

If you are travelling to Stratford from London, Oxford or the Chilterns you might like to consider a Shakespeare Explorer ticket from Chiltern Railways (*www.chilternrailways.co.uk*) which allows you to get out and about in Shakespeare Country with unlimited travel to and from all stations between Leamington Spa and Stratford-upon-Avon. These include Bicester (see below SHOPPING) and the pretty little spa town of Leaminton Spa.

🛒 SHOPPING

Shopping arcades include the **Minories**, the **Mulberry Centre**, **Bards Court**, **Red Lion Court** and **Bell Court**. The main shops are in **High Street** and **Henley Street**. **Sheep Street** is worth a visit for shoppers in search of something a bit different; a street market is held every Friday in **Rother Street**.

The best-value shopping in the region is at **Bicester Village** (35mi/56km southeast), a discount designer-outlet "village" with over 90 stores including the likes of Burberry, Polo Ralph Lauren and Dior

Warwick★

Warwickshire

"This perfect county town" (Pevsner), built mostly in the Queen-Anne style, contrasts and complements its 14C castle, "the most perfect piece of castellated antiquity in the kingdom" (Lord Torrington).

▶ **Population:** 22,476.

⚙ **Michelin Map:** Michelin Atlas p 27 or Map 403 P 27.

ℹ **Info:** Jewry Street. ℘01926 492 212. www.warwick-uk.co.uk.

◉ **Location:** 22mi/35km SE of Birmingham. The train station is a 10 min walk from town, the bus station is in the centre on Market St.

TOWN

Warwick Castle★★

🕐*Open daily 10am–6pm (Nov–Mar 5pm).* ✎*£16.95; save online.* ⚐🅿✗. ℘*0870 442 2000 (information). www.warwick-castle.co.uk.*

Britain's finest medieval castle occupies a picturesque location by the River Avon on the site of a Norman motte and bailey. The curtain walls and gatehouse are 14C, the Bear Tower and Clarence Tower date from the 15C. The castle was begun by Thomas de Beauchamp, 11th Earl of Warwick (1329–69). Now part of the Tussauds Group, the castle has been brought to life with wax models of historical characters, and popular summer events like jousts, falconry, character-actor talks and barbecues. Collections of paintings and furniture are displayed in the 17C and 18C **State Rooms** including works by Lely, Van Dyck and furniture by Boulle. The castle enjoys splendid grounds including a siege machine which fires twice daily, and its latest attraction is the **Castle Dungeon**, a horror house produced by those responsible for the London Dungeon.

Lord Leycester Hospital★

High Street. 🕐*Open Tue–Sun and bank hols 10am–5pm (4.30pm Oct–Mar and bank hols).* ✎*£4.90.* ℘*01926 491 422. www.lordleycester.com.*

This fine ensemble was founded in 1571 by Queen Elizabeth's favourite, Lord Leicester. The oldest parts of the timber-framed building, which surrounds a charming partly-cloistered courtyard, are the chapel (1383) and the guildhall (1450), built by Warwick "the king-maker".

Collegiate Church of St Mary★

Church Street. 🕐*Open 10am–4.30pm/ 6pm.* ✎*£2 contribution.* ⚐. ℘*01926 403 940. www.saintmaryschurch.co.uk.*

Re-built after a fire in 1694, though it originally dates from 1123. Its glory is the 15C Beauchamp (pronounced "beechum") Chapel containing the **tomb**★ and gilded bronze effigy of Richard de Beauchamp, Earl of Warwick.

Lord Leycester Hospital, Warwick

A. F Kersting/MICHELIN

Worcester★

Worcestershire

The great red sandstone cathedral rising above the bend in the River Severn, the wealth of timber-framed buildings and the Georgian mansions make Worcester among the most English of cities. The city name is also synonymous with its Royal Worcester porcelain and Worcester(shire) sauce. Worcester was the site of the final battle of the Civil War, where the New Model Army defeated Charles I's Cavaliers.

▶ **Population:** 82,661.
Michelin Map: Michelin Atlas p 27 or Map 503 N 27.
Info: High Street. 𝒞01905 726 311. www.visitworcester.com.
Location: 28mi/46km southwest of Birmingham. Foregate Street Station is 0.5mi/0.8km north of the centre. The bus station, to the rear of Crowngate shopping mall, is a little closer.

CITY
Cathedral★★

Open year-round daily 7.30am–6pm. £3 contribution requested. Tower Easter–Sept Sat, bank hols and school hols 11am–5pm (£3). Guided tours (£3) May–Oct Mon–Sat, Nov–Apr Sat only, 11am, 2.30pm. 𝒞01905 28854. www.worcestercathedral.co.uk.
In the late 11C an earlier church was re-built by Wulstan, the Saxon Bishop of Worcester, who thrived under his new Norman masters and was later canonised. His superb **crypt** survives but the greater part of his building, including the tower, was reconstructed in the 14C. The **choir** is an outstanding example of the Early English style. Monuments include **King John's tomb** in the choir, the **Beauchamp tomb** (14C) in the nave, and the alabaster effigy (c. 1470) of the Virgin and Child in the southeast transept. **Prince Arthur's Chantry** and its delicate tracery are late Perpendicular work. The Cloisters were re-built in 1374 with wonderful medieval bosses. The east walk leads to the **chapter house** (c. 1150), a very early example of central shaft vaulting. The **Edgar Tower**, once the main entrance to the medieval monastery and fortified against anti-clerical rioters, now opens into the serene cathedral precincts.

Royal Worcester Porcelain Works★

Severn Street. **Visitor Centre:** Open year-round Mon–Sat 9am–5.30pm, Sun 11am–5pm. Closed 25–26 Dec and Easter Sun. See website for tour details. Museum £5. 𝒞01905 21247. www.royal-worcester.co.uk.
Founded in 1751, Royal Worcester's historical success was due to the use of Cornish soaprock to simulate Chinese porcelain and the ability to adapt to changing fashions (Chinoiserie, Classicism, Romanticism), all of which are displayed here.

EXCURSIONS
Great Malvern

8mi/13km south on the A 449.
In the late 18C this small settlement which had grown up round a priory became fashionable owing to the medicinal properties of the local water; a Greek Revival-style **Pump Room** and Baths were built in 1819–23.
The highest of the **Malvern Hills**, which rise steeply above the town, is **Worcestershire Beacon** (1,395ft/426m), from which there is claimed to be a **view** of 15 counties and three cathedrals.

Elgar Trail★

40mi/65km circuit signed with "violins".
Much of the music of **Sir Edward Elgar** (1857–1934), that most "English" of composers, evokes this countryside of broad, tranquil vales and soaring hills.
A circular route includes the Elgar **Birthplace Museum** (open daily, 11am–5pm (4.15pm last admission); £6. 𝒞01905 333 224; www.elgar foundation.org).

Wye Valley★

England: Herefordshire, Worcester-shire, Gloucester-shire. Wales: Monmouthshire

The River Wye twists and turns through changing landscapes on its 135mi-/220-km course from Plynlimon on the west coast of mid Wales to the Bristol Channel. The final stretch, between Ross and Chepstow, has been popular since the late 18C and early 19C when it became one of the resorts of connoisseurs of Romantic scenery. The steep slopes of the deep and narrow valley are clothed in magnificent woodlands of oak, beech, yew and lime, pierced occasionally by limestone crags.

🚗 DRIVING TOUR

ROSS-ON-WYE TO CHEPSTOW
Ross-on-Wye

The **Market House**★, built in sandstone in the 1670s, bears a medallion of Charles II placed by John Kyrle, "Man of Ross", a benefactor of many of the buildings in the town. Tudor almshouses in Church Street were restored in 1575 by the Rudhall family, some of whose tombs are in the church.

▶ *Take the B 4228 south; after 3mi/5km turn right at the Wye Bridge and follow signs to Goodrich Castle.*

Goodrich Castle★

EH. Open Mar–Oct daily 10am–5pm (Jun–Aug 6pm). Nov–Feb Wed–Sun 10am–4pm £4.90. P (£1). 01600 890 538. www.english-heritage.org.uk. This picturesque sandstone ruin stands on a high spur commanding an ancient crossing of the Wye. Most of the castle dates from c. 1300 but the keep is Norman and the original entrance, now a window, was at first floor level.
During the Civil War the Royalist garrison was forced into surrender by the use of a large mortar, "Roaring Meg", which was specially cast by the besiegers nearby; it is now in Churchill Park in Hereford.

Info box

🚻 **Michelin Map:** Michelin Atlas p 16 or Map 503 L, M 28 and 29.

🗒 **Info:** 01989 562768. 01600 713 899. www.visitherefordshire.co.uk.

📍 **Location:** The part of the Wye Valley designated as an Area of Outstanding Natural Beauty is the 72mi/115km stretch just south of Hereford to Chepstow.

▶ *Continue south on the B 4228 and B 4229; turn left into a steep narrow road to Symonds Yat and Yat Rock; use the Forestry Commission car park.*

Symonds Yat★

From **Yat Rock** (473ft/144m) there is a famous vertiginous **view**★ of the extraordinary loop in the river and a fine prospect of the rich farmland of Herefordshire to the north.

▶ *Continue south on the B 4432 and B 4228. At the crossroads EITHER turn left into A 4136 to Monmouth OR continue south; in Coleford take the B 4226 east and the B 4227 south to Soudley.*

Forest of Dean

This "Queen of Forests All" has been a royal hunting preserve since Canute's day. The **Dean Heritage Centre** *(Camp Mill, Soudley; open Mar–Oct 10am–5pm, Nov–Feb 10am–4pm; closed Dec 24–26; £4.90; P; 01594 822 170; www.deanheritagemuseum.com)* presents an exhibition on the woodlands, featuring charcoal burning, an overshot waterwheel, a reconstruction of a cottage and the type of mine worked by the "Free Miners" of the Forest.

▶ *Return to Coleford; take the B 4431 and A 4136 west to Monmouth.*

Monmouth★

The 13C fortified **bridge-gate**, the emblem of Monmouth, leads into wide

Chepstow Castle

© John Page/SXC

Monnow Street. The town has retained much of its medieval street plan but little remains of the castle, where in 1387 **Henry V** was born. His statue is set in the handsome Georgian **Shire Hall**.

◗ *Detour west for 8mi/13km on A 40.*

Raglan Castle★

CADW. ◷*Open daily 9.30am– 4pm/5pm.* ∞*£3.* ✆*01291 690 228. www.cadw.wales.gov.uk.*
This striking fortress within a fortress, begun in 1435, may be ruined but is still a powerful reminder of lawless days on the Welsh frontier.

◗ *From Monmouth take A 466 south.*

Tintern Abbey★★

CADW. ◷*For hours see Raglan Castle above.* ∞*£3.60.* ⚐. ✆*01291 689 251. www.cadw.wales.gov.uk.*
The steep wooded slopes of the winding valley provide a picturesque setting for this Romantic ruin. In the latter part of the 18C the Abbey became a favoured destination of Romantic tourists, among them William Wordsworth. Only the 13C abbey church is recognisable as such.

◗ *Go south on the A 466 for 2.5mi/4km; turn right to the viewpoint.*

Wyndcliff

Access viewpoint either by 365 steps or easier approach from a car park 0.5mi/0.75km further south on the A 466.

From the **Eagle's Nest Viewpoint★** on top of the limestone cliff (800ft/240m), which dominates the loop in the river, the eye is led down the final reaches of the Wye to the mighty span of the **Severn Suspension Bridge**, completed in 1966. Farther downstream is the **Second Severn Crossing**, opened in 1996.

◗ *Continue (S) on A 466 to Chepstow.*

Chepstow★

The partly-walled town slopes down from the great Town Gate to the ancient crossing of the Wye, bridged by an elegant cast-iron structure (1816) which provides the best view of the castle.
Chepstow Castle★★ *(CADW;* ◷*hours and dates;* ⚐*See RAGLAN CASTLE;* ∞*£3.50;* ✆*01291 624 06; www.cadw.wales.gov. uk)* was begun in 1067 by William FitzOsbern, one of William the Conqueror's closest associates, then engaged in securing the western boundary of his domain. The site has excellent natural defences – a long narrow ridge, protected by cliffs dropping sheer into the river to the north and a deep declivity to the south. At the east end is the 13C Lower Bailey, guarded by the Outer Gatehouse and Marten's Tower. Beyond the Middle Ward rises the heart of the original castle, FitzOsbern's Great Tower, a hall-keep which is probably the earliest secular stone building in Britain. The Upper Ward leads to the castle's western extremity and highest point, the outer defence works of the Barbican.

Traditions die hard in Britain and while in many people's eyes there is still a North–South divide in lifestyle, it has evaporated in the cosmopolitan centres of Manchester, Liverpool and Leeds, and even in heritage-bound York. Here you will find the kind of shopping, eating and nightlife once only associated with London. Similarly while the Industrial Revolution took its toll on both the people and landscape of the North, its colourful history and heritage are now key to the region's tourist revival.

Yorkshire

The largest county in the UK, Yorkshire arouses more patriotism than any other region, described by its own people as "God's own country". For walkers the thought of the Yorkshire Dales and Moors is a heavenly, if often damp, prospect; fashion victims love Leeds; vampire hunters flock to Whitby; lovers of film and curry beat a path to Bradford; while more sedate tourists enjoy a nice cup of tea in genteel Harrogate and Richmond. But no trip to the county is complete without seeing York itself, where the glory of the Minster may convince you that God may indeed reside here!

- Beverley
- Fount. Abbey
- Haworth
- Leeds
- Bradford
- Harrogate
- Hull
- Richmond
- Ripon
- Sheffield
- York
- Yorks. Moors
- Scarborough
- Whitby
- Yorks. Dales

The Northeast

The northeast is most easily defined by the unmistakeable local Geordie accent. Like Yorkshire and Liverpool folk they have a fierce sense of place and a dry self-deprecating humour. Newcastle-upon-Tyne is the regional capital, famous for its bridges, its football team and raucous nightlife. The town is solidly Victorian with its quayside regenerated by new icons such as the Sage and Baltic music and arts centres. Durham is one of England's most perfectly sited towns, its magnificent cathedral set high above the gorge of the River Wear. Around here was mined much of the coal that pow-

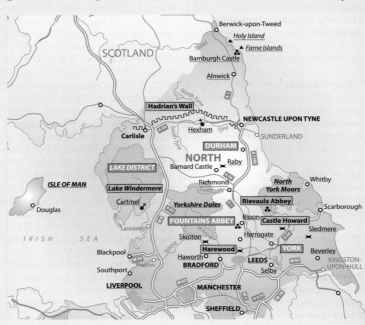

National Parks

Northumberland – Cheviot sheep graze the high open moorland that makes up most of this park. Part of Hadrian's Wall runs along the southern edge while Kielder Water, just beyond the western boundary, is a much-visited recreational area.

Lake District – Largest of the Parks, this is a combination of mountain and lake, woodland and farmland. Ice shaped the troughs and corries, while glacial rubble dammed the valleys and underlying rock dictated whether the hills were softly rounded, like Skiddaw, or wildly rugged, like Scafell Pike and Helvellyn.

Yorkshire Dales – Nearly half of the Dales is farmland. Over four centuries the monasteries' sheep walks developed into the start of a road system across the fells, the best known today being between Kilnsey and Malham Cove and Tarn. The unique limestone pavement "grykes" provide sheltered habitats for lime- and shade-loving plants. The "Dales" themselves, (Ribbles-, Swale-, Wensley- and Wharfe-) offer welcoming villages in rich valley pastures, while the limestone peaks of Ingleborough and Pen-y-Ghent present a more rugged face.

North York Moors – The moors rise sharply from the Tees in the north to Pickering and the Vale of York in the south. The eastern boundary is the sea. The park contains Whitby and its ruined abbey, plus Rievaulx and Rosedale abbeys.

Peak District – The deep dales and stone-walled fields of the White Peak are surrounded to east, west and north by the dramatic moors and peat bogs of the Dark Peak. Visitors come to walk, fish,cycle. rock-climb, go gliding or hang-gliding and windsurf on its lakes.

ered Britain. The northeast has always been an important frontier region, from the Romans' Hadrian's Wall (built to keep out the Scots Picts), still partially intact and interpreted in many places along its way, to Scots against English, perfectly demonstrated in the tug-of-war history of England's northernmost town, Berwick-upon-Tweed.

- 🚶 **Alnwick**
- 🚶 **Berwick-upon-Tweed**
- 🚶 **Durham**   🚶 **Hadrian's Wall**
- 🚶 **Newcastle-upon-Tyne**

The Northwest

The Lake District is regarded by many as England's most beautiful countryside. On a sunny day it is hard to beat the grandeur and sheer picture-postcard perfection of the hills reflected in the lakes. At most times of year it is a magnificent place for walking. Liverpool is famous for music, its football team, and the wry (often black) humour of its native "Scousers". It also possesses a classic Victorian city centre, a fascinat-ing dock history and some of the North's finest museums. For many visitors the Beatles Story is a must-see, as is a Beatles tour. Liverpool has also been boosted by the arrival of Tate Liverpool and being named European Capital of Culture 2008. Liverpool's traditional rival, Manchester, has an even more famous football team. It too has a monumental Victorian quality and has taken great cultural strides as witnessed by the dazzling waterside Lowry Centre and the stunning new city icon, Urbis. Both cities also boast a vibrant nightlife. By contrast Chester is more provincial, but is a perfect little black-and-white half-timbered walled town with important Roman heritage. Blackpool is England's most famous seaside resort complete with donkey rides, trams along the promenade, illu-minations and one of the country's best theme parks.

- 🚶 **Blackpool**   🚶 **Carlisle**
- 🚶 **Chester**   🚶 **Liverpool**
- 🚶 **Manchester**   🚶 **Isle of Man**
- 🚶 **Lake District**

Alnwick★
Northumberland

This attractive grey-stone town (pronounced "Annick") grew up around the great medieval castle whose stern walls still seem to bar the route from Scotland.

TOWN★

Though its streets were laid out in the Middle Ages, Alnwick's present sober and harmonious appearance dates from the 18C when much dignified re-building in stone took place.

▲▲ Castle★★

⏰ *Open daily Apr–Oct, Grounds 10am–6pm, Castle 11am–5pm.* ⏰ *Closed half-term hol Oct.* ☞ *£11.95, child £4.95.* 🅿✕. 📞 *01665 510 777, 01665 511 100 (information line); www.alnwickcastle.com.*

Among the many fortifications of this much-contested border country, Alnwick's castle is the most formidable. Begun in Norman times, it was acquired in 1309 by the **Percys**, the region's greatest family, and has remained in their hands ever since. Though much remodelled in the 19C, its basic features are all intact and, in an exquisite setting by the River Aln, it epitomises the romantic ideal of a mighty medieval fortress and was featured in the two *Harry Potter* films.

▲▲ Alnwick Garden

Denwick Lane. ⏰ *Open Apr–Oct daily 10am–6pm, Nov–Mar 10am–4pm.* ⏰ *Closed 24 Dec.* ☞ *Adult £9, up to four children free.* ♿🅿✕. 📞 *01665 511350. www.alnwickgarden.co.uk.*

Part of the castle estate, this 12-acre/5ha walled plot was rescued from dereliction in 2000 and has been turned into one of the most exciting contemporary gardens to be developed in the last century in Great Britain. Officially opened in October 2002 by its patron, the Prince of Wales, it features spectacular water displays, rose gardens and one of the largest **tree houses** in the world. Alnwick is unusual among British gardens for being very child-friendly.

▶ **Population:** 7,419.

🜚 **Michelin Map:** Michelin Atlas p 51 or Map 502 O 17.

🛈 **Info:** 2 The Shambles. 📞 01665 511 333. www. visitnorthumberland.com.

▶ **Location:** 30mi/50km N of Newcastle-upon-Tyne.

👁 **Don't Miss:** Castle; Alnwick Garden.

⏰ **Timing:** Allow at least half a day; Market days are Thu/Sat.

▲▲ **Kids:** The Castle (exploring in the footsteps of Harry Potter); Alnwick Garden, especially for its tree house.

EXCURSIONS

The skeletal ruin of **Dunstanburgh Castle** ★ *(8mi/13km northeast of Alnwick on the B 1340; after 3mi/5km turn right to Craster;* ⏰ *open late Mar–Oct daily 10am–5pm/4pm Oct, Nov–Mar Thu–Mon 10am–4pm;* ⏰ *closed 1 Jan, 24–26 Dec;* ☞ *£3.40;* ✕; 📞 *01665 576 231; www.eng lish-heritage.org.uk)* on its lonely crag of volcanic rock is one of the most stirring sights of the Northumbrian coast.

There are long **views** up and down this wonderfully unspoiled coastline of rocky headlands and sweeping sandy bays backed by dunes.

Nearby **Craster** is a fishing village built in dark stone, noted for its kippers (cured herrings).

Warkworth Castle and Hermitage★

EH. 7.5mi/12km east of Alnwick on the A 1068. ⏰ *Open late Mar–Oct daily 10am–5pm (4pm Oct). Nov–Mar Sat–Mon, 10am–4pm.* 🚶 *Guided tours of the Duke's Rooms on Wed, Sun and bank hols late Mar–Sept.* ⏰ *Closed 24–26 Dec, 1 Jan.* ♿🅿.
☞ *£3.90.* 📞 *01665 711 423. www.english-heritage.org.uk.*

Perched high above the river, the castle dates from the 12C and since 1332 has belonged to the Percys. Its general layout can be appreciated from the upper floor of the fine 13C **gatehouse**. The most prominent feature is the exceptionally beautiful restored **keep**, designed for comfort and convenience as much as for defence. From the castle the single street of the little planned town runs steeply downhill to the Norman **church of St Lawrence** and to the river crossing with its rare medieval bridge tower. Don't miss the **Hermitage**, half a mile upstream by hired boat or by footpath.

Cragside House★

NT. Rothbury, Morpeth. House: ◷ *Open mid-Mar–Oct Tue–Sun and bank hols 1pm–5pm, opens 11am Sat–Sun and certain weeks (see website). Estate and Gardens:* ◷ *Open same dates 10.30am–5.30pm; early Nov–late Dec Wed–Sun 11am–4pm.* ⊛*Estate closes once parking is full.* ◠*£12; gardens only £7.70 (Nov–Dec £3.80);* ◠*Cash only.* ⚫🅿✕. ℘*01669 620 333. www.nationaltrust.org.uk.*

The stupendous success of his engineering and armament works at Newcastle enabled **Lord Armstrong** (1810–1900), one of the greatest Victorian inventor/industrialists, to build this extraordinary country house in which Old English and Germanic styles are romantically combined. It was regarded as a wonder of the age and was the first house in the world to be lit by hydroelectricity. The many rooms of its well-preserved **interior**★ give a fascinating insight into the comforts and pretensions of late-Victorian domestic life. Cragside's gardens are home to the largest sandstone rock garden in Europe.

Berwick-Upon-Tweed★★

Northumberland

As a result of its location right on the border – facing northeast to the English, looking southeast to the Scots – the seaside town of Berwick (pronounced *"berrick"*) has been fought over many times, changing hands on no fewer than 14 occasions in the 12C alone. Founded under the kingdom of Northumbria, today it is England's northernmost city.

A BIT OF HISTORY

From 1558 onwards the **walls**★ were replaced with ramparts and bastions. The elegant 15-arch **Old Bridge**, built in 1611, is the fifth-known structure to have been built between Berwick and Tweedmouth. The castle has largely been demolished and the railway station was built on part of the site in the 19C. Some of the stone was used for Holy Trinity Church (1651), one of the few to have been built during the Commonwealth, and the remainder was "quarried" in 1720 to build **Berwick Barracks**, which now houses two museums.

- ▶ **Population:** 13,544.
- ◔ **Michelin Map:** Michelin Atlas p 57 or Map 502 O 16 – Local map Tweed Valley.
- ▯ **Info:** 106 Marygate. ℘01289 330 733. www.berwick-upon-tweed. gov.uk/guide. www.visit-northumberland.com.
- ▷ **Location:** Berwick-upon-Tweed is 70 mi/112km due north of Newcastle-on-Tyne. The train station is a 10 min walk from the centre. Some regional buses also stop here, while others go to Golden Square in town. Enjoy the views from the city walls to get your bearings.
- ◉ **Don't Miss:** Holy Island.
- ◷ **Timing:** Allow at least half a day to see the town.
- ♟ **Kids:** The arms and armour at Bamburgh Castle.
- ◎ **Cycling:** Follow the marked Coast and Castle Cycle Route.

TOWN
Berwick Barracks
EH. Clock Block, Ravensdowne.
🕐 *Open mid-Mar–Sept Wed–Sun
10am–5pm.* 🕐 *Closed Jan 1, Dec 24–26.
☎£3.50.* 📞*01289 330 430.
www.english-heritage.org.uk.*
Home to the King's Own Scottish Borderers Museum, the Contemporary Art Gallery and the Berwick Borough Museum, the highlights are the excellently crafted pieces collected by the "magpie millionaire" **Sir William Burrell**, which include Imari ware, brassware, medieval religious art, Chinese bronzes and glassware.

EXCURSIONS
Lower Tweed Valley★★
♿*See Scotland; TWEED VALLEY.*

Holy Island (Lindisfarne)★
*13mi/21km south on the A 1 and a
minor road east; the causeway to Holy
Island can be crossed only at low tide;
timetables posted at either end of the
causeway. Lindisfarne Centre:* 🕐
*Open Apr–Oct 10am–5pm, Nov–Mar
according to tides.* ☎£3.50. ♿. 📞*01289
389 004. www.holy-island.info.*
Here on this tiny island the **Lindisfarne Gospels** (now preserved in the British Museum) were written and magnificently illuminated in the Celtic tradition. They can be viewed both electronically

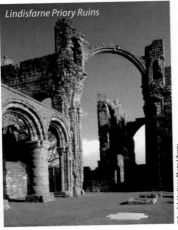
Lindisfarne Priory Ruins

© English Heritage Photo Library

and in facsimile format at the **Lindisfarne Centre**.

Lindisfarne Priory★(EH)
🕐*Opening times vary.* 🕐*Closed 24–26
Dec.* ☎£3.90. 📍. 📞*01289 389 200.*
The ruins visible today are those of a Benedictine house, founded from Durham in 1093.

Lindisfarne Castle★(NT)
Castle: 🕐 *Open third week Feb; mid
Mar–Oct times vary (call for details); Dec
27–29 Tue–Sun 10am–3pm, and bank
hols.* ***Garden:*** 🕐 *Open year-round
10am–dusk.* 🕐*Closed 1 Jan, 24–26 Dec.
☎£5.70 (garden only, £1).* 📍. 🚻 *Emergency WC only; nearest WC in village
1mi/1.6km from castle* 📞*01289 389 244.
www.nationaltrust.org.uk.*
This 16C castle was restored in 1902 by Edwin Lutyens as a holiday home for Edward Hudson, founder of *Country Life* magazine, The austere but beautiful interior is in inimitable "Lutyens" style.

Bamburgh Castle★
*20mi/32km south by A 1 and B 1342
east.* 🕐 *Open Mar–Oct daily 10am–
5pm.* ☎£7.50. 📍£1. ✗. 📞*01668 214
515. www.bamburghcastle.com.*
Beautifully sited next to a long sandy beach, the **Norman keep** still dominates this castle, which was restored in the Victorian era. Bought by Lord Armstrong (♿*see CRAGSIDE HOUSE*) in 1894, it houses a fine collection of arms and armour from the Tower of London, and much Sèvres, Crown Derby, Worcester and Chelsea porcelain. There are exquisite small collections of silver vinaigrettes, Fabergé carvings and jade

Farne Islands (NT)★
*NT. 15mi/24km south by A 1 and
B 1342/1340 east to Seahouses.*
🕐 *Landing permitted only on Inner
Farne and Staple Island. Open May–Jul
daily 10.30am–1.30pm (Staple Island).
1.30pm–5pm (Inner Farne); enquire
for other times of year.* ☎*Landing
fee May–Jul (breeding season) £5.70;
Apr, Aug–Sept £4.70. Access by boat
(separate charge), weather permitting)*

from Seahouses Harbour. ⓐ*Apr–Jul wear a wide-brimmed hat or baseball cap to protect against dive-bombing birds!* ⓖ *℘01665 721 099 (infoline), 01665 720 651 (warden). www.nationaltrust.org.uk, www.farne-islands.com (for boat information).*

The islands, 15 to 28 of them in total, depending upon the tide, provide nesting sites for 18 species of seabirds, and are home to the largest British colony of grey seals. The wildlife is generally very tame and it is possible to get very close-up views.

Beverley★

East Yorkshire

Georgian façades hide the ancient timber buildings of a town which in 1377 already boasted one of England's finest churches, a sizeable population of some 5 000 inhabitants and was the principal town of the area. The origins of Beverley can be traced back to the kingdom of Northumbria in the 7C.

- ▶ **Population:** 23,632.
- **Michelin Map:** Michelin Atlas p 41 or Map 502 S 22.
- **Info:** 34 Butcher Row. ℘01482 391 672. www.visiteastyorkshire.com.
- **Location:** 30mi/50km southeast of York. Once in town, let the landmark Minster be your guide.
- **Don't Miss:** The Percy Tomb and the misericords in the Minster.

TOWN
Beverley Minster★★
🕐 *Open Mon–Sat 9am–5pm (May–Aug 5.30 pm Nov–Feb 4pm). Sun noon–4.30pm (Nov–Mar 4pm).* Guided tours Mon–Sat 10.30am (£2), roof tours (£5) 11.15am, 2.15pm. ℘01482 868 540. www.beverleyminster.org.

The present Minster was begun about 1220 and at 332ft/101m long is of cathedral-like proportions. The **Great East Window**, a Perpendicular nine-lighted window containing all the fragments of medieval glass the Minster once possessed, was bequeathed in 1416.

The **Percy Tomb** (1340–49) and its canopy, with angels, symbolic beasts, and leaf carvings, is the most splendid of funerary monuments from the Decorated period. It probably commemorates Lady Eleanor Percy, who died in 1328. The early-16C **misericords** in the choir stalls are some of the finest in Britain.

St Mary's Church★
🕐 *Open Apr–Sept Mon–Fri 9.30am–4.30pm, Sat and bank hols 10am–4pm, Sun, 2pm–4pm. Oct–Mar Mon–Fri, 9.30am–noon and 1pm–4pm. Sun, before and after services only.* £2 min

contribution requested. ℘01482 881 437. www.stmarysbeverley.org.uk. Founded c. 1120, St Mary's was adopted by the wealthy trade Guilds. The tiny (36ft/11mx18ft/5.5m) Chapel of St Michael with its ingenious "telescopic" spiral staircase is contemporary with the Percy Tomb in the Minster.

The Perpendicular west front with slim shafts and fine mouldings is comparable with King's College Chapel in Cambridge. By 1524 the addition of the tower completed what is one of the finest parish churches in the north of England.

Look for the extensive collection of carvings of medieval musical instruments shared between the Minster and St Mary's at Beverley. All told there are 140 represented, on pew ends, choir stalls, ceiling bosses and in the south porch. The chancel ceiling, painted in 1445, with its pictorial record of 40 English kings, is unique.

Twenty-three misericords with extraordinary carvings of animals and men adorn the choir stalls, including a "Pilgrim Rabbit" carved c. 1325.

Blackpool
Lancashire

Since 1846 when the railway first made seaside holidays a possibility for the masses, Blackpool has been one of the most popular and typical British seaside resorts in all bar location. Thousands of holidaymakers from the industrial towns of the north and Midlands traditionally flocked here for their annual holiday, although short breaks are now more popular. About a third of all visitors to Blackpool now come in autumn to see the famous Blackpool illuminations.

RESORT
Blackpool Tower★
⏱ Open Feb–Nov, daily, 10am–11pm; Dec–Easter, Sat–Sun, 10am–11pm. £10. &✕. ☎01253 622 242. www.blackpooltower.com.
Inspired by the Eiffel Tower and opened in 1894, the 518ft/158m high tower is Blackpool's trademark. There is a splendid view from the top and the intervening levels provide a variety of entertainment.

Pleasure Beach
Ocean Boulevard. ⏱ Open Apr–Oct daily 10.30am–6pm or later (8pm school hols), mid-Feb–Mar and Nov, Sat–Sun only. Low season £15 (online price over 12 years old), child under 12 £13. High season (online) £21–£25, child £16–19. &✕. ☎0871 222 1234. www.blackpoolpleasurebeach.com.
With over 6 million visitors a year this huge theme park is Britain's most popular paid-admission tourist attraction boasting the very latest state-of-the-art rides and sideshows, for all ages.

▶ **Population:** 146,297.
⦿ **Michelin Map:** Michelin Atlas p 38 or Map 502 K 22.
◖ **Location:** 55mi/88km due north of Liverpool. The main train Station, Blackpool North, is around 440yds/400m from the centre on Talbot Road. The bus station is on the same road some 50yds/45m away.
⦿ **Don't Miss:** A trip up Blackpool Tower; a ride on an old-fashioned tram.
⦿ **Timing:** Allow at least one full day and one night; longer if the weather is good and/or you have children in tow.
⦿ **Kids:** The whole of Blackpool is geared to children.

Bradford★
West Yorkshire

Bradford prospered through the wool trade and by 1500 it was a bustling market town "*which already standeth much by clothing*". By 1850 there were 120 mills and Bradford had become the world's worsted capital. Among its famous sons are the author JB Priestley (1894–1984), composer Frederick Delius (1862–1934) and the contemporary painter David Hockney (b. 1937). The Bradford of today is essentially a Victorian city.

▶ **Population:** 289,376.
⦿ **Michelin Map:** Michelin Atlas p 39 or Map 402 O 22 .
▤ **Info:** ☎01274 433 678. www.visitbradford.com.
◖ **Location:** 9mi/14km west of Leeds. Bradford Interchange just south of the centre, off Bridge Street, is the terminus for buses and trains.
⦿ **Timing:** Allow one day.
⦿ **Kids:** An IMAX film at the National Media Museum.

CITY
👥 National Media Museum★
Prince's View. **Museum:** 🕐 *Open year-round Tue–Sun, bank hols and half term hols, 10am–6pm.* 🎫*Free.* **Cinema:** 🕐 *Open 10am–late.* 🎫*IMAX £6.95, child £4.95.* ✂. 📞*0870 70 10 200. www.nationalmediamuseum.org.uk.*

Part of the same family as London's famous Science Museum, this lively modern museum houses Britain's largest cinema projector and a curved screen (52ft/16m high and 64ft/20m wide), showing 2-D and 3-D IMAX films. The exhibitions trace the history and practice of photography, the cinema, television and all new media. There is also a conventional cinema showing arthouse and fringe films and hosting film festivals.

Wool Exchange
Market Street. 🕐*Open shopping hours.* Built 1867 in Italianate/Gothic style, this was once the centre of the world's wool trade. The statues at the entrance are those of St Blaize, patron saint of wool combers, and of Edward III, who did much to encourage the wool industry. It now houses shops and offices.

Bradford Cathedral
1 Stott Hill. 🕐 *Open year-round Mon–Sat 8am–5.30pm.* 🕐 *Closed Dec 25–Jan 1.* ♿. 📞*01274 777 720. www.bradfordcathedral.co.uk.*
The battlemented exterior does not give the impression of a building which, in parts, dates back to the 1440s; the west tower with battlements and pinnacles dates from 1493.

The chancel has some fine stained glass, c. 1862, by William Morris, Rossetti and Burne-Jones.

Little Germany
Near the cathedral.
This merchants' district, named after the booming mid-19C export trade with Germany, has been restored to show its fine Victorian architecture (1830–99).

EXCURSION
Saltaire
3mi/5km north.
With its cobbled streets and honey-coloured stonework, Saltaire village was built in the 19C by mill owner and philanthropist Sir Titus Salt for the spiritual, physical and moral welfare of his workers. Thanks to its outstanding state of preservation it has been designated a **Unesco World Heritage Site**.
The vast imposing mill complex, **Salt's Mill**, (🕐 *open year-round Mon–Fri 10am–5.30pm, Sat–Sun 10am–6pm; top floor inc Hockney's opera set and café closed Mon–Tue;* 🕐*closed Dec 25–26, Jan 1.* ♿📁✂; 📞*01274 531 163; www.salts mill.org.uk)* is still the key feature of the village and now houses **The 1853 Gallery**, containing the largest collection of art in Europe by renowned Bradfordian **David Hockney**, alongside a Saltaire history exhibition, more galleries, arty shops and a smart restaurant and cafe.

ADDRESSES

🍺 PUBS AND 🍴 RESTAURANTS
A booklet listing places to eat in Bradford city centre is available free of charge from the Tourist Information Centre. Bradford is famous for the quality and quantity of its curry houses.

😃 ENTERTAINMENT
A booklet containing all the information you will need for a night out in Bradford, including pubs, clubs, cinemas and theatres, is also available free of charge from the Tourist Information Centre.
Three cinemas at the National Museum of Photography show the latest releases and host film festivals. The city's principal festival is the Bradford Mela held in June. This is a British-Asian celebration of outdoor entertainment, foods, street theatre, market stalls, children's activities and funfair rides: visit *www.bradford.gov.uk/bradford_mela* for details.

Carlisle★

Cumbria

The centre of Carlisle is marked by the Market Cross, which stands on the site of the Forum of Luguvalium, founded by the Romans, whose occupation lasted 400 years. The following 500 years of decline and border warfare did not encourage the inhabitants to build grandly or for posterity. The Guildhall (1407) is a rare timber-framed survivor.

CITY
Cathedral★

🕐*Open year-round daily 7.30am–6.15pm (Sun 5pm).* ✆*£2 contribution requested.* ⬤*Guided tours.* ♿🅿✕ *(Mon–Sat).* ✆*01228 548 151. www.carlislecathedral.org.uk.*
Henry I created the See of Carlisle in 1133, though all that remains of the original Norman building is the truncated nave and the south transept. New work begun in 1225 and includes the Decorated east window, a fine example of tracery, containing much original 14C glass, and the choir, with its set of sculptured capitals. In the choir, too, is a magnificent **painted ceiling★**, completed in 1360, featuring golden suns and stars on a blue ground. The 16C Brougham Triptych in the north transept is a masterpiece of Flemish craftsmanship.

Tullie House Museum and Art Gallery

Castle Street. 🕐*Open year-round daily Jul–Aug 10am (11am Sun)–5pm; Apr–Jun and Sept–Oct, 10am (noon Sun)–5pm; Nov–Mar 10am (noon Sun)–4pm.* 🕐*Closed Dec 25–26 and Jan 1.* ✆*£5.20.* ♿✕. *✆01228 618 718. www.tulliehouse.co.uk.*
The original house, which dates from 1689 and contains its original oak staircase, has been extended to house the local museum, which presents the long and often turbulent history of the border town through well-presented and lively displays, including Roman occupation, Hadrian's Wall, border *Reivers* (raiders) and the Civil War siege.

▶ **Population:** 72,439.
⬤ **Michelin Map:** Michelin Atlas p 44 or Map 502 L 19 – Local map Hadrian's Wall.
▤ **Info:** Old Town Hall. ✆01228 625 600. www.visitcumbria.com.
▷ **Location:** 13mi/21km northeast of Calbeck, on the northwest tip of the Lake District and 10mi/16km south of the Scottish border. The compact town centre lies between Town Hall Square and the castle; get your bearings from the view from the ramparts.
⬤ **Don't Miss:** The painted ceiling of the choir in the cathedral.

Carlisle Castle

EH. 🕐*Open Apr–Sept daily 9.30am–5pm. Oct–Mar daily 10am–4pm.* 🕐*Closed Jan 1 and Dec 24–26.* ✆*£4.40, includes entry to Regimental Museum.* ⬤*Guided tours Apr–Oct (£2).* ✆*01228 591 922. www.english-heritage.org.uk.*
Established by William II in 1092, the castle served to block the passage of Scots raiders. Opposite the entrance to the keep is the shell of the medieval hall, now the museum of the King's Own Royal Border Regiment. All that remains of the tower, in which Mary Queen of Scots was held, is the staircase to the east of the museum building.

Church of St Cuthbert with St Mary

Church: 🕐 *Open year-round daily, dawn–dusk. Tithe Barn:* 🕐 *Open most mornings.* ✆*01228 521 982. www.stcuthbertscarlisle.org.uk.*
The galleried church dates from 1779. The unusual pulpit was installed in 1905 to enable the preacher to speak to the galleries. The great **Tithe Barn★** (115ft/34m long), which now serves as the church hall, was built c. 1502.

Chester★★

Cheshire

Set on the northeast border of Wales in the green and prosperous countryside of Chesire, Chester has been an important city since Roman times and retains many tangible reminders of this period. The lasting impression on most visitors however its classic black-and-white half-timbered buildings, which feature prominently in this well-preserved historic walled city.

A BIT OF HISTORY

Deva (or Dewa), the Roman legionary fortress and naval base built on a loop of the River Dee, was one of the largest in Britain and home to the XX Valeria Victrix Legion for 200 years. 1,900 years ago a Roman surveyor laid out the line of the Via Praetoria, now Bridge Street, and of the Via Principalis, now Eastgate Street and Watergate Street, which took over where Watling Street entered the fort. The legionary headquarters stood at the junction on the site now occupied by St Peter's Church.

The port of Chester is known to have been used by seagoing vessels during the Roman occupation. The period of greatest prosperity was 12C–14C; even until the end of the 16C, Chester regarded Liverpool as a "creek of the Port of Chester". But by the 15C the Dee estuary was silting up and ships had to

- ▶ **Population:** 80,110.
- ⌚ **Michelin Map:** Michelin Atlas p 34 or Map 403 L 24.
- ℹ **Info:** Town Hall, Northgate Street. ℘01244 402 111. www.visitchester.com.
- ▶ **Location:** Buses from out of town arrive at Vicar's Lane, just outside the city walls; the train station is a 10 to 15 min walk northeast.
  Almost everything of interest is inside the old city walls. Take a walking tour (from the Tourist Information Centre), or an open-top bus tour (℘01244 347457; www.city-sightseeing.com).
- 😊 **Don't Miss:** Shopping at The Rows; the horseracing at Chester's historic racecourse (℘01244 304 600; www.chester-races.co.uk).
- 🕐 **Timing:** A day minimum, more if you visit the zoo.
- 👥 **Kids:** Chester Zoo.

anchor some 12mi/19km downstream. The **Roodee** (Anglo-Saxon for "Island of the Cross") is a tract of land between the river and the city wall now occupied by Chester racecourse. Horse races has been held here since 1540.

The Rows

A. Williams/MICHELIN

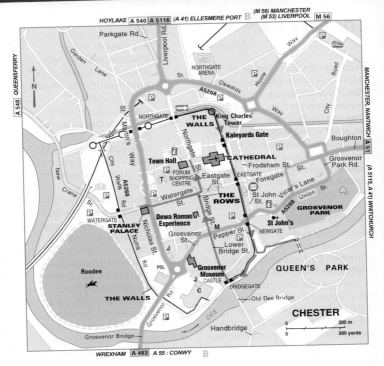

TOWN

The Rows★★

These shopping arcades, unique in Britain, first appear in the city records for 1331. They probably originated in the 14C when merchants erected shops at street level against the lower courses of the Roman buildings that had lined the streets or on top of the stone rubble and made steps and walkways to link them; upper storeys provided accommodation for the traders and their families.

Chester Cathedral★

⏱ *Open year-round Mon–Sat 9am–5pm, Sun 12.30pm–4pm.* ✆*£4 (inc audio tour).* ♿✖. ☎*01244 324 756. www.chestercathedral.com.*

The 14C gateway leads into Abbey Square, once the outer courtyard of the abbey; ahead are the cloisters.

The Norman abbey church was replaced between 1250 and 1540 by the present magnificent red sandstone building. Many of the original abbey buildings still stand round the 16C **cloisters**. The hammerbeam roof of the refectory has been superbly re-created. The Dean and Chapter still meet in the 13C **Chapter House** and the clergy and choir assemble in the vestibule before services.

The north transept contains the oldest part of the cathedral fabric, an 11C round-headed arch and arcade, and the oldest wooden ceiling, the **camber beam roof** (1518–24), which carries a splendid display of Tudor heraldry. The **stalls** and **misericords** in the choir date from 1390 and are among the finest in the country. The **Lady Chapel** has been restored to its 1250 appearance. Behind the High Altar is the 14C **shrine of St Werburgh**, daughter of the King of Mercia (d. c. AD 700).

City Walls★

No other city in Britain has preserved a continuous circuit of walls. From the Eastgate, by the Clock Tower, looking west to the spire of Holy Trinity Church (now the Guildhall) you can see the width of the Roman fortress. Parts of the Roman wall are visible between the northgate and **King Charles' Tower**.

Grosvenor Museum

27 Grosvenor Street. ☎ 01244 402 008.
www.chestercc.gov.uk.
This lively Chester history museum is
particularly strong on the Roman period
but all ages are covered. To the rear of
the museum is a town house which takes
you back to home life from the 17C to
the 1920s including a Victorian kitchen,
Georgian drawing room, a nursery and a
fully fitted Edwardian bathroom

Dewa Roman Experience

Pierpoint Lane. ♿. ☎ 01244 343 407.
www.dewaromanexperience.co.uk.
This walk-through "experience" moves
from Roman galley to a re-constructed
street, experiencing the sights, sounds
and smells of Dewa (Roman Chester).
There is an audio-visual presentation,
archaeological excavations and lots of
hands-on exhibits where you can try on
Roman armour, fire a catapult, handle
Roman-style artefacts and more.

CHESTER ZOO★

*3mi/5km north on the A 5116. Upton-
by-Chester. ◷ Open daily year-round
10am–5pm mid-Apr–Oct (6pm week-*

Eastgate Clock Tower

S. Sergent/Michelin

*ends, bank hols and school holidays),
Nov–mid-Apr 10am–4pm/4.30pm.
☙£10.86–£14.95, child £8.13–£11.30.
Monorail and waterbus £2 each.
♿ P ✕. ☎ 01244 380 280.
www.chesterzoo.org.*
A splendid zoo where the 7,000 or so
animals are housed and displayed in
spacious enclosures, separated from
the public by moats and flower borders
rather than cages.

Durham★★★

County Durham

The quiet streets of the little
medieval city with its castle are the
perfect foil for the great sandstone
mass of the Norman cathedral rising
above the deep wooded gorge of
the River Wear in a sublime fusion of
architecture and landscape, in what
is a truly remarkable setting★★★.

A BIT OF HISTORY

Christianity flourished early in the Saxon
Kingdom of Northumbria but conditions
were rarely stable in this border country
with its coastline exposed to raiders from
the east. In 875 the monks of Lindisfarne
fled south from Danish attacks, carrying with them the body of **St Cuthbert**
(d. 687) but it was not until more than
100 years later that his much-venerated

> ▸ **Population:** 36,937.
> ⚲ **Michelin Map:** Michelin
> Atlas p46 or Map 501 P 19.
> 🛈 **Info:** ☎ 0191 384 3720.
> www.durhamtourism.co.uk.
> ▷ **Location:** 18mi/28km S
> of Newcastle-upon-Tyne.
> The train station and bus
> station are almost opposite
> each other on North Rd,
> 10-mins from the centre.
> You can see this compact
> city on foot. Boat trips and
> rowing boats available.
> P **Parking:** Parking is difficult
> in the centre.
> ⚲ **Don't Miss:** Chapel of the
> Nine Altars; riverside views
> from or near Prebend's
> Bridge.

Durham Cathedral and the River Wear

B. Kaufmann/MICHELIN

remains found their final resting place on easily defended bluffs carved out by the Wear. From the 1070s the site's natural advantages were strengthened by the Normans, who built their castle to command the peninsula's narrow neck. In 1093 the cathedral's foundation stone was laid. Uniquely in England, Durham's bishop was not only spiritual leader but lay lord, the powerful Prince Palatine of a long-troubled province.

The city has remained compact, physically unaffected by the once intense industrial activity all around it. Its scholarly character was confirmed with the foundation in 1832 of the university, after Oxford and Cambridge England's oldest. It is also the county town, an important administrative and shopping centre. On the second Saturday in July, it is thronged with the thousands attending one of Britain's great popular festivals of modern times, the famous **Miners' Gala**.

CATHEDRAL★★★

🕐 *Mon–Sat 9.30am–6pm. Sun 12.30pm–5.30pm. Mid-Jul–Aug open daily until 8pm. For specific opening times of areas within cathedral see website.* 👐*Donation requested. Tower £3. Treasures of St Cuthbert £2.50. Audio-visual £1. Dormitory £1. Building the Church Exhibition £1.* 🎧Guided *tours (£4) Mon–Sat 10.30am, 11am, 2.30pm most weeks.* ♿.✕. ✆*0191 386 4266. www.durhamcathedral.co.uk.* Durham Cathedral's beauty lies in its unity: its fabric was mostly completed in the short period between 1095 and 1133 and though added to since, it remains a supremely harmonious achievement of Norman architecture on the grandest possible scale.

Exterior

The usual entrance is the northwest portal, which has many arches and is embellished with the celebrated lion's head **Sanctuary Knocker**★, a 12C masterpiece of expressive stylisation. **Palace Green** is dominated by the cathedral.

Interior

In the **nave**★★★ the first impression is one of overwhelming power. Huge deeply-grooved columns alternate with massive many-shafted piers to form an arcade supporting a gallery and clerestory. The pointed ribs of the beautiful vault are an important technical and aesthetic innovation, heralding the lightness and grace of Gothic architecture. The great weight of masonry, its arches enriched with various zig-zag patterning, is however so well proportioned that the final effect is one of repose, of great forces held in equilibrium. From the crossing there is a stupendous view up into the vault under the central tower, while in the south transept is an extraordinary brightly painted 16C clock. In the choir there are fine **stalls** and the splendidly vain **throne** and **tomb** of the 14C Bishop Hatfield. Beyond the 14C **Neville Screen** with its delicate stonework is the **Shrine of St Cuthbert**.

The 13C **Chapel of the Nine Altars**★★★, an earlier example of which is to be found at Fountains Abbey, is an Early English addition to the cathedral. The sunken floor, designed to gain as much height as possible, and the extravagantly tall lancet windows, which are separated by columns of clustered shafts, reveal a new preoccupation with lightness and verticality. The carved stonework of the bosses and capitals is extremely rich.

At the extreme western end of the building, perched on the very edge of the ravine, is the **Galilee Chapel**. Twelve slender columns, their arches profusely decorated with zig-zag carvings, sub-divide the interior, which contains the tomb of the **Venerable Bede** (d. 735), England's first historian. From the top of the cathedral's central tower (a long climb of 325 steps: access from south transept) spectacular **views**★ reinforce the full drama of Durham's site.

Monastic buildings

Around the much re-built cloisters are grouped the buildings of the former abbey. They include the monks' dormitory and the **Cathedral Treasury**★, with its collection of Anglo-Saxon embroideries, precious objects and manuscripts and, above all, the evocative relics associated with St Cuthbert – his tiny portable altar, his pectoral cross, fragments of his oak coffin… To the south is the tranquil precinct of the **College**, its mellow, mostly 18C buildings resting on medieval foundations.

From the **Market Place**, sited at the very neck of the peninsula, a streets descend steeply to the sloping Elvet Bridge on the east and to **Framwellgate Bridge** on the west. From here there is a fine **view**★★ upstream of the cathedral and the stern walls of the castle.

North Bailey and **South Bailey**, with their many pleasant 18C houses, follow the line of the town wall. Nearby is the church of St Mary-le-Bow, now housing the **Durham Heritage Centre** (North Bailey; ⏲ open Jul–Sept daily 11am–4.30pm, Easter–Oct Sat–Sun 2pm–4.30pm; &; ℘0191 384 5589; www.durhamheritagecentre.org.uk), telling the story of the city from medieval times to the present day. From here a lane leads downhill to Kingsgate footbridge of 1963, elegantly spanning the gorge to link the city with the uncompromisingly modern building of the University Students' Union, **Dunelm House**. South Bailey ends at the Watergate, from which a track leads down to **Prebend's Bridge**. From here, from the path on the far bank and from the riverside itself are those **views**★★★ which have long captivated writers and artists; a perfect composition of water, trees and humble mill buildings.

Oriental Museum★★ (Durham University)

From the city centre take the A 1050 and A 167 south towards Darlington. Elvet Hill, off South Road. ⏲ Open Mon–Fri 10am–5pm. Sat–Sun and bank hols noon–5pm. ⏲Closed 24 Dec–1 Jan. ⏲£1.50. &℗✕. ℘0191 334 5694. www.dur.ac.uk/oriental.museum. Changing displays range from Ancient Egypt via India and Southeast Asia to Japan; of outstanding interest are its ceramics, jade and other hardstone pieces and an extraordinary room-like bed, all from China.

CASTLE★

⏲ Open by guided tour only on most days out of university term time, and daily Easter–30 Sept 10am–noon and 2pm–4.30pm. In term time Mon, Wed,

Sat–Sun, 2pm–4pm. Closed Christmas holidays. £5. 0191 334 3800. www.durhamcastle.com.

University College, or Castle as it is known, is Durham University's oldest college, founded 1832, and located in a Norman fortress' keep. The present Castle began in 1072 as a simple defensive mound commissioned by William the Conqueror. The Norman architecture of the castle was much modified by successive Prince Bishops.

From the courtyard, protected by the much re-built gatehouse and overlooked by the keep on its great earth mound, the tour proceeds via the 15C **kitchen** into the imposing **Great Hall**, then to galleries built around the original castle wall, whose fine arched doorway is still intact. The upper floors are reached by the broad steps of the spectacular **Black Staircase** of 1662. There are two chapels, one of the 16C with humorous misericords including a bagpipe-playing pig and a nagging wife in a wheelbarrow. The **Norman chapel**★, deep below, dates from the castle's earliest days and evokes a more primitive world, with its capitals crudely ornamented with weird figures and savage faces.

Fountains Abbey★★★
North Yorkshire

Set in the wooded valley of the little River Skell amid glorious North Yorkshire countryside, these Cistercian ruins – the largest abbey ruins in England – are not only famously picturesque but also wonderfully evocative of monastic life.

A BIT OF HISTORY

In 1132 a small band of Benedictine monks, revolting against the slack discipline at their abbey in York, were

- **Michelin Map:** Michelin Atlas p 39 or Map 502 P 21.
- **Info:** Visitor Centre. 01765 608 888. www.fountains abbey.org.uk.
- **Location:** 27mi/43km NW of York.
- **Opening:** Daily. Mar–Oct 10am–5pm. Nov–Feb 10am–4pm or dusk. Mill open daily Mar–Oct 10am/10.30am–3.30pm/ 5pm. £7.10.
- Guided tour (free). £3.

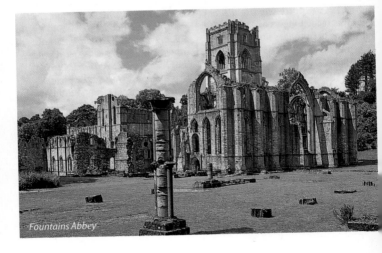
Fountains Abbey

granted land in this "place remote from all the world". They set about transforming their wilderness into the flourishing and productive countryside characteristic of Cistercian endeavour and, within a century, Fountains Abbey was the centre of an enormous enterprise, managing fish-farms and ironworkings, as well as forests and vast tracts of agricultural land, the profits from which paid for an ambitious building programme.

The great complex fell into decay following the Dissolution but in 1768 it was bought by the Aislabie family, who had long desired it as the ultimate in picturesque ruins to complete their lavish landscaping of the adjacent Studley Royal estate.

Façade, Fountains Hall

©Wojtek Buss/World Pictures/Photoshot

VISIT

Fountains Hall – Stone from the abbey was used to build the splendid five-storey Jacobean mansion (1598–1611). Behind the striking **façade**★ with its Renaissance details, the interior is laid out to the conventional medieval plan.

Fountains Abbey – The grassy levels of Abbey Green extend to the west front of the roof-less abbey church and the monastic buildings adjoining the south side. The scale and diversity of the monastic buildings suggest the varied activities of the great community of monks and lay brothers. The church's tall tower (c. 1500) rises above the stately Norman nave. At the east end is the spectacular 13C **Chapel of the Nine Altars** with soaring arches and a huge Perpendicular window.

The most complete and beautiful remains are those of the buildings grouped round the cloister in accordance with the standard Cistercian plan: in the western range is the **Cellarium**, with its astounding 300ft/90m vaulted interior below the lay brothers' dormitory; in the south range is the **Great Refectory**. In the east range is the **Chapter House**, entered through three fine Norman arches.

Studley Royal Water Garden – The gardens were designed to be visited starting from the Canal Gates: choose from a 45min, 1hr 45min, or 2hr route.

From 1720 until his death in 1742 John Aislabie, Chancellor of the Exchequer, devoted his vast personal fortune to create a garden at his Yorkshire estate. He remodelled the sinuous valley of the Skell into a spectacular landscape consisting of a series of formal water features and contrived views, embellished with garden buildings and flanked by woodland on the steeper slopes.

The canalised river, emerging from a dark grotto, is led past the **Moon Pond**, overlooked by a Classical **Temple of Piety**, and finally discharges into a lake over a grand cascade flanked by pavilions, known as fishing tabernacles.

Along the east side of the valley is a high-level walk which passes through a twisting tunnel, past the **Gothic Tower** and the elegant **Temple of Fame** to **Anne Boleyn's Seat** and the surprise view of the east end of the abbey ruins.

The **Seven Bridges Walk** follows the course of the Skell downstream from the lake, zig-zagging from bank to bank.

In the deer park stands **St Mary's Church** (🕐 *open year–round*), a masterpiece of High Victorian Gothic by William Burges, on the axis of a long avenue which extends east to the original entrance to the park from the village of **Studley Royal** and aligned on the twin towers of **Ripon Cathedral** (3.7mi/6km north).

Hadrian's Wall★★

Cumbria, Northumberland

In AD 122 the Roman Emperor Hadrian visited Britain and ordered the building of a defensive wall across the northernmost boundary of the empire from Wallsend on the Tyne, to Bowness on the Solway Firth (73mi/117km). Although Hadrian's Wall has come to represent the frontier between England and Scotland, it is well south of the modern border between the countries. Parts of this wall can still be seen today and museums, camps and settlements give a picture of military and civilian life on Rome's "Northwest Frontier".

A BIT OF HISTORY

The Wall – The wall was built by legionaries, citizens of Rome, and garrisoned by as many as 24,000 auxiliaries from conquered territories. It was defended by a ditch on the north side; on the south side it was paralleled by a military road and "vallum", defining the military zone. The wall was built in stone and turf, with forts, milecastles and turrets at regular intervals along its length. It follows the best strategic and geographical line and, at places such as Cawfields and at Walltown Crags, commands splendid

- **Michelin Map:** Michelin Atlas pp 50 and 51 or Map 502 L 19 M, N and O 18.
- **Info:** Hexham. ℘01434 652 220. Once Brewed Visitor Centre, Bardon Mill. ℘01434 344396. www.hadrians-wall.org. www.hadrianswall-northumberland.com.
- **Location:** Hadrian's Wall runs from the North Sea to the Solway Firth, from just beyond Carlisle in the west to just beyond Newcastle-upon-Tyne.

views. Milecastles along Hadrian's Wall have been numbered, from east to west, from Wallsend (0) to Bowness (80).

ALONG THE WALL

Follow the B 6318.

The main sites (listed below from east to west) all have car parks and are indicated by light brown signposts.

Corbridge Roman Camp★

EH. West of Corbridge. ⊙ Open late Mar–Oct, daily, 10am–5.30pm (4pm Oct); Nov–Mar, Sat–Sun, 10am–4pm. ⊙ Closed Jan 1 and Dec 24–26. ⊛£4.40. ♿. ℘01434 632 349. www.english-heritage.org.uk.

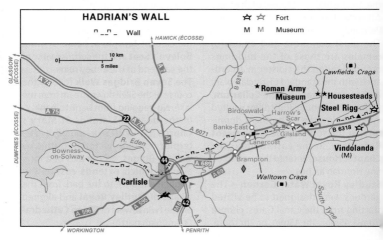

This site was occupied for longer than any other on the wall. The **museum** of the Corbridge Roman Camp presents the layout with its **granaries**, fountain, headquarters building and temples. From the elevated viewpoint there is a good overall **view** of the visible remains which represent only a small part of the base and settlement.

Hexham Abbey★

Hexham. ⏲Open daily, 9.30am–5pm. ⏲Closed Good Fri. ⚬ £3 contribution requested. ♿✕. ✆01434 602 031. www.hexhamabbey.org.uk.
Stones from the Roman settlement of Corbridge (Corstopitum) were used in the construction of Hexham Abbey, which was founded in AD 674. All that remains of the original abbey is the **Saxon Crypt★★**.
The fine Early English choir with imposing transepts belongs to the later church (1180–1250). The stone staircase in the south transept was the Night Stair, which led to the canons' dormitory. The **Leschman Chantry★** (1491) has amusing stone carvings on the base and delicate woodwork above.

Chesters Roman Fort★

EH. Near Chollerford. ⏲ Open daily 10am–6pm (4pm Oct–Mar). ⏲Closed Jan 1 and Dec 24–26. ⚬£4.40. ✕(Summer only). ♿. ✆01434 681 379. www.english-heritage.org.uk.

The fort lies just west of the point where the wall crossed the River Tyne and remains of the bridge can still be seen on the far bank. The four gateways, headquarters building and barrack blocks of this fort can be traced from their foundations. By the river are the remains of a **bath house★**. The **museum** contains a selection of sculptured stones collected from and around the wall in the 19C.

Temple of Mithras

Carrawburgh. 5 min walk from the car park.
This is an unexpected find in such a desolate stretch of moorland. Inside the lobby is a statue of the mother goddess (the original is reconstructed in the Museum of Antiquities in Newcastle). The temple was destroyed early in the 4C, probably by the Christians.

Housesteads Roman Fort★★

EH, NT. ⏲ Open daily 10am–6pm (4pm Oct–Mar). ⏲ Closed Jan 1 and Dec 24–26. ⚬£4.40. ♿✕. ✆01434 344 363. www.english-heritage.org.uk.
This large fort (5 acres/2ha) is perched high on the ridge and is the most complete example on the wall. Still clearly visible are the foundations of the large courtyard house of the commandant, the granaries, barracks, headquarters building, the four main gateways, the **hospital** and 24-seater **latrine block** as well as part of the civilian settlement.

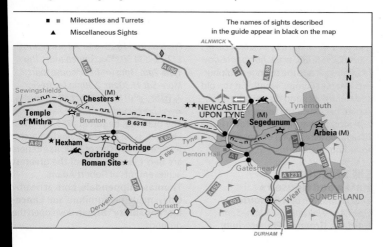

| | Milecastles and Turrets | The names of sights described |
| ▲ | Miscellaneous Sights | in the guide appear in black on the map |

Vindolanda

Chesterholm. ⏲ *Open daily early Feb–Dec 10am–6pm (5pm Feb–Mar and Oct–Nov.* ⏲ *Closed Dec 25.* ✎£5.20. *Combined ticket with Roman Army Museum £8.* ♿✕. ☎01434 344 277. *www.vindolanda.com.*

The fort and civilian settlement on the Stanegate, south of the wall, date from the period before the building of the wall. Full-scale replicas have been built of a stretch of the wall with a stone turret, as well as of the turf wall, which was the earliest barrier, with a timber milecastle. The **museum**★ holds a unique collection of writing tablets, leather goods, textiles and wooden objects

Roman Army Museum★

Carvoran. ⏲ *Open daily, as for Vindolanda.* ✎£4.20. ♿✕. ☎01697 747 485. *www.vindolanda.com.*

With an audio-visual presentation and examples of Roman armour, dress and weapons, this is the largest and most modern of the wall museums and presents a lively picture of the wall and its garrison. To the east the quarry viewing-point overlooks one of the finest sections of the Wall, **Walltown Crags.**

Harrogate★
North Yorkshire

Harrogate is a genteel little town. Its heyday as a famous 19C spa town has left a legacy of elegant buildings with fine shops and hotels, which make an excellent base for touring the Yorkshire Dales and Moors.

TOWN

The **Royal Pump Room**, built in 1842, and the **Royal Baths Assembly Rooms**, built in 1897, were the hub of this spa town at its height at the end of the 19C when some 60,000 people a year came to "take the waters" bubbling up from 36 springs within an area of an acre. At the **Royal Pump Museum** *(Crown Place;* ⏲*open year-round Mon–Sat 10am–5pm, 4pm Nov–Mar, Sun 2pm/Aug noon–5pm;* ⏲ *closed Jan 1 and Dec 24–26;* ✎£3; ♿; ☎01423 556 188; www.harrogate.gov. uk),* you can taste the strongest sulphurous water in Europe, wonder at the old spa treatments and discover how Harrogate became a spa town. An unusual and attractive aspect of the town is the **Stray**, 200 acres/80ha of grassland surrounding the centre.

EXCURSIONS
Harewood House★★

8mi/13km south by A 61. **House:** *Open Apr–Nov daily 10.30am–5pm.* **Gardens, Grounds, Planetarium:**

- ▶ **Population:** 66,178.
- ⛭ **Michelin Map:** Michelin Atlas p 40 or Map 502 P 22.
- ▤ **Info:** Royal Baths, Crescent Road. ☎0845 389 3223. www.harrogate.gov.uk.
- ◖ **Location:** Harrogate is 21mi/34km west of York. Both the bus and train stations are on Station Parade, in the town centre.
- ▲▪ **Kids:** Mother Shipton's Cave.

⏲ *Open Apr–Nov daily 10.30am–6pm; also Feb half-term daily; Mar and Nov–mid-Dec Sat–Sun. Planetarium Star Shows at 11am, 1pm, 2pm; book on arrival.* ✎*Grounds, bird garden, terrace gallery, Below Stairs and Planetarium £8.25–£10. All attractions £12.25–£14.30.* ↻*Garden tours Thu 1pm, 2pm, 3pm (*✎*free); house tours Mon–Sat 11.30am, 2.30pm (*✎*free).* ♿▣✕. ☎0113 218 1010 (24hr info). *www.harewood.org.*

The building, begun in 1759 by Edwin Lacelles, is an essay in Palladian architecture by John Carr of York; its interiors are neo-Classical, one of the greatest achievements of Robert Adam.

Thomas Chippendale, born at nearby Otley, made the furniture and **Lancelot "Capability" Brown** developed the grounds.

The **Entrance Hall** is the only room to retain its original form, complete with fine plaster-work ceiling. Old Master paintings are hung throughout; there is much rare Chinese porcelain, as well as Sèvres pieces collected at the beginning of the 19C. The **Gallery**★ is perhaps the pinnacle of Adam's work at Harewood. In the grounds is the **Bird Garden** with over a hundred species of threatened and exotic birds housed in sympathetic environments. The new **Yorkshire Planetarium** is an unexpected bonus.

Knaresborough

2mi/3km east of Harrogate on the A 59. Knaresborough is a small market town set on the north bank of the river Nidd. Its ruined **Castle** keep (*Castle Yard;* open *Good Fri–early Oct daily 10.30am–5pm; £2.70 including museum and sally-port; guided tour through the sallyport underground tunnel 11am, noon, 2.30pm, 3.30pm;* P(charge; 01423 556 188; www.harrogate.gov.uk/museums), now in ruins, was started in about 1130. After the murder of Thomas Becket in Canterbury Cathedral in December 1170, the four killers took refuge in the castle. In addition to its underground sallyport it has a rare surviving Tudor courtroom.

Beside the river is **Mother Shipton's Cave** (*High Bridge;* open *daily 10am –5.30pm Apr–Oct; Nov and Feb–Mar up to Easter school hols Sat–Sun; £6, child £4;* P; 01423 864 600; www. mothershiptonscave.com), where Mother Shipton, England's most famous prophetess, born c. 1488, was reputed to have lived and prophesied. Adjacent is the **Petrifying Well**, a geological phenomenon whose cascading waters seem to turn items into stone. In fact they are covering it with a stalactite deposit. It is said to be England's oldest visitor attraction, first opening its gates in 1630.

ADDRESSES

CRAFTY SHOPPING

Darley Mill Centre – *7mi/10km west via A 59.* Open *daily, 9.30am (11am Sun) to 5.30pm (5pm Sun).* 01423 780 857. A well restored flour mill in the Nidder valley has been converted into a craft shop selling glassware, gifts, household goods and linen. Its water wheel is still in working order.

Haworth

North Yorkshire

Haworth is an unpretentious Yorkshire hill village, its dark, gritstone cottages crowded together on the edge of the Pennine moors. The long, steep main street is lined with souvenir shops and tea rooms, all enjoying the benefits of association with the Brontë sisters, who lived in the parsonage at the top of the hill and wrote most of their stories there.

VILLAGE
Brontë Parsonage Museum★
Open *Apr–Sept daily 10am–5.30pm. Oct–Christmas and Feb–Mar daily 11am–4.30pm.* Closed *Dec 24–27. £6.* P. 01535 642 323. www.bronte.org.uk.

- **Population:** 4,956.
- **Michelin Map:** Michelin Atlas p 39 or Map 502 O 22.
- **Info:** 2–4 West Lane. 01535 642329. www.visitbradford.com/ bronte-country.
- **Location:** 19mi/30km west of Leeds, 8mi/13km west of Bradford.

The parsonage, where Patrick Brontë and his family lived, conserves furniture, paintings and fascinating memorabilia, such as the children's drawings and homemade books. Here they conceived imaginary kingdoms (Angria and Gondal) wrote poetry and created their masterpieces, and here too their brother,

Brontë Country

The Brontë sisters drew on their local knowledge for descriptions of the places in their novels. Two houses which appear in *Shirley* under other names can be visited near Batley. In the 19C the family of Mary Taylor, one of Charlotte's close friends, lived in an 18C red-brick house, now the **Red House Museum** *(Oxford Road, Gomersal, Cleckheaton;* 🕐*open daily 11am (noon Sat–Sun)–5pm;* 📞*01274 335 100; www.kirklees.gov.uk)*; the house appears in *Shirley* as Briarmains and is now furnished as it would have been in the 1830s. **Oakwell Hall**, *(Nutter Lane, Birstall, near Batley, on A 638;* 🕐*same as Red House Museum;* ✆*£1.40 Mar–Oct, free Nov–Feb;* ✗; 📞*01924 326 240; www.kirklees.gov.uk)* is a dark-stone Elizabethan manor, with impressive latticed windows, furnished as it was for the Batt family in the 1690s; it is surrounded by traces of a moat and a country park with a wildlife garden.

Brontë Family

Patrick Brontë was born Patrick Brunty in Northern Ireland and studied for Holy Orders at St John's College in Cambridge. He came to Haworth as curate in 1820, bringing his wife, Maria and their six children. His wife, who was consumptive, died the following year. In 1825 the two eldest girls, Maria and Elizabeth, fell ill at boarding school in Cowan Bridge and died. In 1846 appeared the first publication by the three surviving sisters, a joint volume of poems by "Currer, Ellis and Acton Bell", names chosen to preserve their initials but conceal that they were women. There followed *Wuthering Heights* (1847) by Emily and *The Tenant of Wildfell Hall* by Anne, who also drew on her experience as a governess for *Agnes Grey* (1847), and *Jane Eyre* (1847) by Charlotte. All died young: their brother, Branwell, aged 31 in September 1848, Emily (at 30) three months later and Anne (at 29) the following summer in Scarborough, where she is buried. Charlotte married her father's curate in 1854 and died in 1855, aged 39. Patrick Brontë outlived his wife and all six children.

Branwell, painted the three sisters, now in the National Portrait Gallery.

A gateway (now marked by a stone) led directly from the parsonage garden to the church, where five of the six Brontë children and their mother are buried.

Brontë Weaving Shed: Town End Mill

Town End Mill, North Street.
🕐 *Open Mon–Sat 10am–5.30pm, Sun 11am–5pm.* 🕐*Closed Easter Sun, Dec 25.* 📞*01535 646 217.*

Haworth was originally a weaving village, with over 1,200 handlooms in action at its peak in the 1840s. Here Victorian looms still produce "Brontë tweed" and visitors can try their hand at operating them. there is also an exhibition about Timmy Feather, known as Yorkshire's last handloom weaver. A shop sells knitwear made at the mill.

EXCURSIONS
Keighley and Worth Valley Railway

Oxenhope. 2mi/3km south on the A 6033. 🕐 *Operates Jul–Aug daily, see website for other times.* ✆*£9.40 return ticket, £14 Day Rover.* ♿📄✗. 📞*01535 647 777 (recorded information), 01535 645 214 (office). www.kwvr.co.uk.*

A re-created Edwardian station is the terminus of this railway, whose steam engines travel through moor scenery along a branch line linking Oxenhope with Haworth, Oakworth (where the film *The Railway Children* was set), Damems, Ingrow and Keighley. At Ingrow is a **Museum of Rail Travel** *(Halifax Road;* 🕐 *open year-round daily 11am–4.30pm;* ✆*£1.50;* 📞*01535 680 425; www.vintage carriagestrust.org)* operated by a local charity that preserves old-fashioned wooden rail carriages.

Kingston-Upon-Hull

England

Kingston-upon-Hull, commonly known as Hull, has a long maritime history. It was an important centre for fishing and particularly for whaling, and is still a major seaport. The **Old Town**, contained between the River Humber and the west bank of its tributary, the Hull, was once surrounded by walls and a moat and still presents the narrow cobbled lanes and ancient inns of medieval and 17C Hull. Its famous modern landmark is the Humber Bridge, built 1972–81 as the longest single-span suspension bridge in the world, measuring 4,626ft/1,410m).

> ▶ **Population:** 310,636.
> ◔ **Michelin Map:** Michelin Atlas p 41 or Map 502 S 22.
> ⓘ **Info:** Queen Victoria Sq. ℘01482 223 559. www.realyorkshire.co.uk.
> ▷ **Location:** Kingston-upon Hull is 38mi/61km south-east of York on the River Humber estuary which flows into the North Sea.
> ♟ **Kids:** The Deep.

CITY

Hull Maritime Museum

Queen Victoria Square. ◔ *Open Mon–Sat 10am–5pm, Sun 1.30pm–4.30pm.* ◔ *Closed Good Fri, Dec 25–26 Dec, Jan 1.* ℘01482 300 300. www.hullcc.gov.uk/museums.
Over seven centuries of Hull's maritime heritage is presented by models, artefacts and paintings.

Ferens Art Gallery

Queen Victoria Square. ◔ *Open Mon–Sat 10am–5pm, Sun 1.30pm–4.30pm.* ◔ *Closed Good Friday, Dec 25–26, Jan 1.* ♿. ℘01482 300 300. www.hullcc.gov.uk/museums.
The city art collection ranges from European Old Masters to contemporary art, including works by such artists as Franz Hals, Canaletto, David Hockney and Henry Moore. Another selection of works displays Hull's maritime history.

Wilberforce House Museum

High Street. ◔ *Mon–Sat 10am–5pm, Sun 1.30pm–4.30pm.* ♿. ℘01482 300 300. www.hullcc.gov.uk/museums.
The birthplace of **William Wilberforce** (1758–1833) houses a refurbished museum about slavery, the triangular trade and the plantations, and the life and work of the man who was instrumental in achieving its abolition. There is period furniture in certain rooms, as well as collections of costumes, clocks and Hull silver.

♟ The Deep★★

◔*Open year-round daily 10am–6pm (5pm last admission).* ◔ *Closed 24–25 Dec.* ☞£8.95, child £6.95 (save 10 % online). ♿✕; Ⓟ£3 (£2 refund against cafe/shop purchase). ℘01482 381 000. www.thedeep.co.uk.
In a stunning building on the Humber estuary, designed by Sir Terry Farrell, The Deep is one of the most spectacular aquariums in Europe, home to 40 sharks and over 3,500 fish.

EXCURSIONS

Burton Constable★

16mi/27km east. Skirlaugh Grounds. ◔ *Open Easter Sat–late Oct and last week Nov–first week Dec, Sat–Thu 1pm (grounds 12.30pm)–5pm (house 4pm Nov–Dec).* ☞£6. Grounds only, £2.50. ♿Ⓟ✕. ℘01964 562 400. www.burtonconstable.com.
The house was built about 1600 and its **east front**, brick with mullion windows and projecting wings, makes a strong impression. The **Entrance Hall**, the Great Hall of the Elizabethan house, dates from 1760. In the **Muniment Room**, the remodelling of the house in Georgian times can be followed. The **Long Gallery**, of noble proportions and decoration, contains many family portraits.

Lake District ★★★

Cumbria

William Wordsworth once said of the Lakes that "I do not know of any tract of country in which, in so narrow a compass, may be found an equal variety in the influences of light and shadow upon the sublime and beautiful." The Lake District can be appreciated in many ways – exploring the narrow rolling lanes by car (often congested in summer), taking a trip in a launch, sailing or windsurfing on the lakes. But, above all, this is a region to walk, from the fells to the glistening to water. Most of the area is incorporated in the Lake District National Park (880sq mi/2,280sq km) of which a quarter is part of the National Trust.

LANDSCAPE

The area takes its name from the beautiful stretches of water which occupy many of the glaciated valleys radiating out from a high central core of volcanic rocks, presenting abrupt cliffs, crags and precipices. Among the many famous peaks are the stony wastes of **Scafell Pike** (3,206ft/977m), the highest point in England. Elsewhere, much of the landscape has been formed by slate: to the north, in the gently-rounded but majestic heights of the Skiddaw group; to the south, in the more broken country reaching its highest point in the commanding presence of **The Old Man**, looming over Coniston Water. The most austere scenery is near the head of Wasdale, where awesome screes plunge to the shore of Wast Water, the deepest and most forbidding of the lakes. The wild drama of the fells is set off by the gentler, pastoral character of much of the lowland, particularly in the park-like surroundings of Lake Windermere. Rainfall is high and the many tarns and tumbling becks are well-fed. The peaks are often capped in cloud and the slopes shrouded in mist but the air is soft and the changing light plays continuously with the rich and subtle colour-mix of

- **Michelin Map:** Michelin Atlas p 44 Map 502 K, L 20.
- **Info:** www.golakes.co.uk.
- **Location:** In Cumbria in the northwestern-most part of England. It covers around 885sq mi/2,292sq km). Oxenholme Station, at Kendal, is the rail gateway to the Lakes with a branch line to Windermere. Buses from all over the northwest run to the main villages. Ambleside and Windermere make good touring bases; half-day and full-day guided tours in mini-coaches are available. Try Lakes Supertours (℘01539 442 751, 01539 488 133; www.lakes-supertours.com) or Mountain Goat tours (℘01539 445 161; www.mountain-goat.com).
- **Don't Miss:** A boat trip or walk.
- **Warning:** Motorists should note that some mountain roads are narrow with sharp bends and severe gradients. Walkers and fell climbers are advised to choose routes suited to their experience and to take the usual precautions.
- **Timing:** Three days min.
- **Kids:** Hill Top (Beatrix Potter's cottage) for little ones; The Aquarium of the Lakes.
- **Walking:** Ask at your tourist information office. It is worth investing in one of Wainwright's walking guides to the region.
- **Bicycle Trails:** Cycles are readily available for hire. Try Windermere station.
- **Sailing:** Lake Windermere has plenty of watersports. On Coniston, try Coniston Boating Ctr (℘015394 41366).

Lake Windermere

A. Williams/MICHELIN

rock and vegetation: coarse grasses, heathers and bracken clothing the mountainsides, bright-berried rowans and white-stemmed birches sheltering in mossy clefts, dark pines standing elegantly by the lakeside and bright green pastures interspersed with the luxuriant foliage of oak and sycamore. The rocks are used in the man-made structures of the countryside: in ancient bridges; in the drystone walls which climb high into the fells; in the rough-hewn stone of sturdy barns, cottages and whitewashed farmhouses with massive roofs of slate. Even the towns are mostly built of stone and slate. Until well into the 20C mining was an important activity in Cumbria; coal, iron-ore, lead, copper and graphite, some of which was transported to the coast by rail and made the coastal fishing villages thriving ports. Slate and granite are still quarried on a small scale.

🚗 DRIVING TOURS

1 LAKELAND POETS TOUR
30mi/48km. The more frequented area round Windermere evokes the memory of the Lakeland poets – **Wordsworth**, **Coleridge** and **Southey** – who were variously inspired by the landscape.

Lake Windermere★★
The longest lake in England (10mi/16km), attractively framed by wooded slopes and bare fells, is particularly lively and

popular for water sports. On the east shore stands the town of **Windermere**, created in the 19C tourist boom. **WindermereLake Cruises**, (🕐 *cruises daily;* ♿; *onboard catering;* ℘*01539 443 360; www.windermere-lakecruises.co.uk*), pass close to the many islets, including Belle Isle, and the unspoilt west bank. The **Windermere Steamboat Centre** (🕐*closed for refurbishment;* ℘*01539 445 565, www.steamboat.co.uk*), on the lake shore, has a collection of steam, motor and sail boats, some afloat, including the 19C *Dolly*, claimed as the world's oldest mechanically powered boat.

Bowness-on-Windermere
The pretty village is known for its promenade skirting the bay. A **ferry** carries cars and pedestrians across the lake to Sawrey.
The 🚻 **Aquarium of the Lakes**, (*Lakeside, Newby Bridge;* 🕐 *open daily 9am–6pm/5pm winter;* 🕐 *closed Dec 25;* 👓*£8.35, save ten percent online;* ♿🅿 *(charge)*✗; ℘*015395 30153; www. aquariumofthelakes.co.uk*) reveals the aquatic and animal life of the rivers, streams and lakes and also includes otters, piranhas and marmosets.

▶ *In Newby Bridge turn right to Sawrey.*

🚻 Hill Top
NT. Near Sawrey. 🕐 *Open mid-Feb–mid-Mar Sat–Thu 11am–3.30pm.*

Mid-Mar–Oct Sat–Thu (also Good Fri and last Fri Oct) 10.30am–4.30pm. Timed entry ticket system. Try to avoid peak periods when you may not get in at all. £6.20, child £3.10. (charge at peak times). 01539 436 269. www.nationaltrust.org.uk.

This tiny 17C house was the home of **Beatrix Potter** who created Peter Rabbit, Benjamin Bunny, Jemima Puddle-Duck and many more favourite characters. Unchanged since her death in 1943, it now attracts thousands of visitors seeking the inspiration for their childhood delight. Inside are Beatrix Potter's watercolours, her dolls' house and mementoes.

Hawkshead★

The narrow slate-walled lanes and paths of this traditional Lakeland village are bordered by flower-decked cottages. Wordsworth attended the local grammar school from 1779 to 1787.

The **Beatrix Potter Gallery**, *(NT; Main Street; same as Hill Top (above) admission by timed ticket; £4.20 discount for Hill Top visitors; ; 01539 436 355; www.nationaltrust.org.uk)* covers her work as artist, author and local farmer, and displays a selection of her watercolours.

Coniston Water★

The road from Hawkshead provides a fine view of the lake and the surrounding fells dominated by the form of **The Old Man of Coniston** (2,631ft/801m).

Brantwood★

East shore of Coniston Water. Open mid-Mar–mid-Nov daily 11am–5.30pm, mid-Nov–mid-Mar Wed–Sun 11am–4.30pm. Closed Dec 25–26. £5.95, grounds only, £4. 01539 441 396. www.brantwood.org.uk.

This house was the home of **John Ruskin**, one of the greatest figures of the Victorian age. On the walls are exquisite watercolours by himself and by Pre-Raphaelite contemporaries whom he championed. His study turret provides a splendid **view**★ of Coniston in its attractive lakeside setting with the form of The Old Man to the left, perfectly mirrored in the tranquil waters of the lake.

Coniston

The little slate-grey town is known for its associations with the author, artist and social reformer John Ruskin (1819–1900), who came to live at nearby Brantwood in 1872. He is buried in the churchyard. Near by, the **Ruskin Museum**, *(open daily 10am–5.30pm; mid-Nov–mid-Mar 3.30pm; £4.50; ; 01539 441 164; www.ruskinmuseum.com)*, holds drawings, manuscripts and other mementoes. The museum's new **Bluebird Wing** is dedicated to the world water-speed record-breaking boat *Bluebird*, and its driver, **Donald Campbell** who set four successive records in the late 1950s on Coniston Water. He was killed when *Bluebird* crashed on Coniston in 1967.

From Coniston take the A 593; in Skelwith Bridge turn left to Grasmere.

Grasmere

The village would be beautiful even if **William Wordsworth** had never existed. It was here that the family lived in two different dwellings between 1799 and 1850 – Dove Cottage and Rydal Mount. The churchyard of 13C St Oswald's is where Wordsworth, various members of the family and Coleridge's son David Hartley are buried.

Dove Cottage, The Wordsworth Museum and Art Gallery ★

Town End, just off the A 591. Open daily 9am–5.30pm. Closed Dec 24–26, second week Jan–first week in Feb. £7.50, joint ticket available with Rydal Mount. 01539 435 544. www.wordsworth.org.uk.

The home of William Wordsworth (1770–1850) and his sister Dorothy from 1799 to 1808, the cottage takes its name from being an early 17C inn (The Dove and Olive Bough) and became a magnet for early 19C literary Romantics such as Coleridge, Southey and De Quincey. In the kitchen, where Dorothy cooked the inhabitants' two meals per day (both

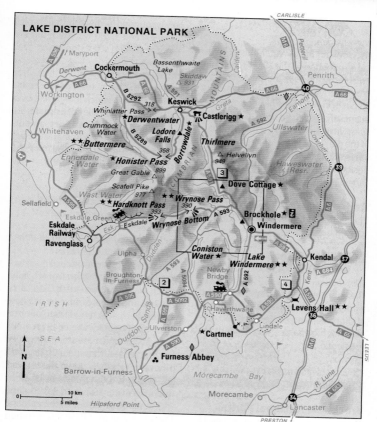

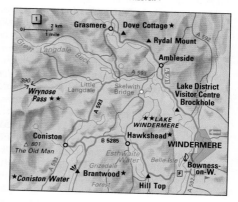

porridge) are three chairs embroidered by Dora Words-worth (the poet's daughter), Sara Coleridge and Edith Southey.

The room off it was first Dorothy's, then William's. Upstairs is the sitting room, looking out over the waters of Grasmere, the main bedroom, the Newspaper Room (wallpapered in newspaper to keep it warm), and the pantry-cum-spare room.

The cottage was for a short period home to De Quincey.

Behind is a museum containing manuscripts, memorabilia and Lakeland paintings.

The Jerwood Centre's romantic reading room presents many rare first editions. The centre was completed in 2004.

Rydal Mount and Gardens

Windermere–Keswick Road. 🕐 *Open Mar–Oct daily 9.30am–5pm, Nov–Dec 24 and Feb, daily Wed–Sun 11am–4pm.* 🕐 *Closed Dec 25–26* ⊜*£6, joint ticket available with Dove Cottage.*

🅿. 𝒫01539 433 002.
www.rydalmount.co.uk.
Overlooking Rydal Water, this 16C cottage, extended in the 18C into a farmhouse, became the home of William Wordsworth (1770–1850) from 1813 until his death in 1850. Here he wrote his most financially successful book, *Guide to the Lakes*. Inside, his library now forms part of the drawing room, and the study ceiling is still painted with the Renaissance design he copied from a visit to Italy. Outside is a beautiful garden.

Ambleside
This attractive little town makes a good touring base.

2 ESKDALE VIA WRYNOSE PASS
50mi/80km.
This route leads to the less-frequented, wilder and at times desolate expanses of Ulpha Fell and Furness Fell and goes over two high passes (severe bends and gradients).

▶ *From Windermere take the A 591 north.*

Brockhole National Park★
Get your bearings at the comprehensive and imaginative **Lake District Visitor Centre** (🕐 open mid-Feb–Oct daily 10am–5pm; ♿ 🅿 (charge)✗; 𝒫01539 446 601; www.lake-district.gov.uk), with an adventure playground, displays on the ecology and history of Lakeland, a Beatrix Potter exhibition and lakeside walk.

▶ *South of Ambleside; left on the A 593. Beyond Skelwith Bridge turn right.*

At first the road is enclosed by dykes and then starts to climb up the V-shaped valley between the bare slopes which are grazing grounds for hill sheep.

Wrynose Pass★★
From the pass (1,280ft/390m) there is a **view** back down to Little Langdale.
Wrynose Bottom – The road runs parallel with the River Duddon along Wrynose Bottom through the wild splendour and

gently rounded forms of the fells, which rarely exceed 3,280ft/1,000m but are scarred by steep scree slopes.

Hardknott Pass★★
At the southern end of the pass (1,289ft/393m), which looks west over the more pastoral valley of **Eskdale**, are the ruins of **Hardknott Fort**, an outstanding example of a Roman auxiliary fort built of stone in the 2C AD.

Ravenglass and Eskdale Railway
🕐 *Operates late-Mar–Oct daily. Oct–late-Mar reduced service, call or see website for schedule.* ⊜£5.40 single journey, £10.80 all-day ticket. ♿. 𝒫01229 717 171. www.ravenglass-railway.co.uk.
The narrow-gauge railway (7mi/11.3km), which was laid down in 1875 to carry iron ore and granite, now carries passengers in closed, semi-closed or open carriages drawn by one of 12 locomotives, six of which are steam engines. The line passes from the high fells and tributary waterfalls down the Esk valley, through the heather, bracken or tree-clad lower slopes to Ravenglass, where seabirds gather in the estuary. The tiny museum at Ravenglass station is devoted to the history of the railway and the local mines.

▶ *Either return by the same route or make a long detour via Ulpha, Broughton-in-Furness and Newby Bridge at the southern end of Lake Windermere.*

3 KESWICK AND NORTHERN LAKES
29mi/47km.
North of Dove Cottage the road runs parallel to the Rothay up to Dunmail Raise before descending into the valley overshadowed by "the dark brow of mighty" **Helvellyn** (3,114ft/949m). Wordsworth used to walk this route to visit Coleridge and Southey in Keswick.
Thirlmere – Originally two smaller water bodies, the lake (3.5 mi long, 1.2 mi wide), enclosed by mountains and

forests, is a reservoir, raised 50ft/15m by a dam, surrounded by plantations. **Castlerigg Stone Circle**★ – (*Signposts*). The circle is older than Stonehenge and its purpose is unknown. It is set on a grassy outcrop offering far-flung **views** south towards Thirlmere and Helvellyn and west to Derwentwater and Keswick.

Keswick

Keswick, a lakeland town of medieval origin, claims the world's first pencil factory (1832), using the graphite which was mined in Borrowdale as early as the mid-16C. The small but interesting **Pencil Museum**, (⏱ *open daily 9.30am–5pm;* ⏱ *closed Jan 1 and Dec 25–26;* ⬭*£3;* ♿ 🅿 *;* 📞 *01768 773 626; www.pencil museum.co.uk*) celebrates the town's 175-plus years of pencil making. The local **museum**, (*Station Road;* ⏱ *open Apr–Oct Tue–Sat and bank hols 10am–4pm;* ♿*;* 📞*01768 773 263; www.aller dale.gov.uk/keswick-museum*) is a real cabinet of curiosities including a 664-year-old cat, the remarkable Musical Stones "pianola", played by Royal Command for Queen Victoria, Napoleon's teacup, the skin of Britain's rarest fish and, more conventionally, manuscripts by both Wordsworth and Southey. Wordsworth used to visit Southey and Coleridge when they and their extended families lived together at Greta Hall (⟳ *private*).

▷ *From Keswick take the B 5289 south.*

Derwentwater★

This lake is 3mi/5km long, 1mi/0.5km wide and flanked by clerestories of crags. Southey called it the most beautiful of English lakes.

Lodore Falls

This most literary cascade (according to Southey) "comes thundering and floundering, and thumping and plumping and bumping and jumping and whizzing and hissing and dripping and skipping and grumbling and rumbling and tumbling and falling and brawling and sprawling" but only after heavy rain!

Borrowdale

The attractive valley, where graphite was mined in the mid 16C, leads to the tiny hamlet of Rosthwaite set in a clearing in characteristic Lakeland scenery.

Honister Pass

The road climbs over the pass (1,175ft /358m). To the south are two of the region's most prominent summits – **Great Gable** (2,949ft/899m) and **Scafell Pike** (3,206ft/977m).
Beyond the pass the road descends to Buttermere, which is separated by a glacial delta from Crummock Water, and continues to Cockermouth.

Wordsworth House

NT. Cockermouth. Main Street. ⏱ *Open Apr–Oct Mon–Sat 11am–5pm.* ⬭*£5.36.* ✗. 📞*01900 824805, 01900 820884 (infoline). www.nationaltrust.org.uk.*
The elegant neo-Classical Georgian house (1745), in which the poet **William Wordsworth** was born in 1770 and spent his early years, is furnished with his own or contemporary furniture and exhibits some of his work, documents and the Wordsworth family tree. The garden leads down to the Derwent.

▷ *From Cockermouth return to Keswick EITHER by the A 66 (the quicker route), OR by the slow steep scenic B 5292.*

The A 66 skirts the west shore of **Bassenthwaite Lake** whereas the slower road climbs over **Whinlatter Pass** (1,043ft/318m) revealing extensive and magnificent views of typical lakeland scenery.

④ KENDAL AND FURNESS
40mi/64km.

▷ *From Windermere take the A 591 east.*

Kendal

The "Auld Grey Town", built out of the local limestone, is the thriving regional centre. It was birthplace of Henry VIII's sixth wife, Catherine Parr, and before then was famous for its wool trade.

Today it is known for its **Mint Cake**, an essential energy-boosting sweet in the backpack of serious walkers.

The **Abbot Hall Art Gallery** and **Museum of Lakeland Life** (◐ *both open mid-Jan–mid-Dec Mon–Sat, 10.30am–5pm/4pm Nov–Mar;* ∞ *Art gallery free, museum £4.75.* 🅿 *(charge);* ✕. *℘01539 722 464; www.abbothall.org. uk),* share an 18C country house. The gallery, occupying the main house, features changing exhibitions, a collection of drawing-room paintings by George Romney (1734–1802), and a delightful coffee shop. The museum section, in a stable block, has permanent collections of the Arts and Crafts movement, *Swallows and Amazons* author Arthur Ransome, and the Victorian period.

▷ *Take the A 591 and then A 590 south.*

Levens Hall and Garden★
◐ *Open Apr–mid-Oct Sun–Thu 10am (noon house) to 4.30pm.* ∞ *£10.50. Gardens only, £7.50.* ☞ *Guided garden walks.* 🅿✕. *℘01539 560 321. www.levenshall.co.uk.*
An Elizabethan manor has been added to a 13C pele tower to give the present graceful residence. The Great Hall, with its panelling of local oak and ornate ceiling, is an introduction to equally outstanding carving and **plaster-work** throughout. The dining room, covered in Cordova leather in 1692, has a magnificent set of Charles II walnut dining chairs. The **Topiary Gardens** are unique in that the 1690 design has been preserved intact.

There is a small steam engine collection and beer connoisseurs might like to try the house's unique Morocco Ale.

▷ *Take the A 590 west to Lindale and then minor roads (signs) to Cartmel.*

Cartmel Priory★
◐ *Open daily, 9am–5.30pm (3.30pm in winter). No visits during services.* ♿. *℘01539 536 261. www.cartmelpriory.org.uk.*
Cartmel Priory survived the Dissolution of the Monasteries and is the grandest medieval building (mostly 12C) in the Lake District. It has a curious double tower, one set diagonally upon the other. Inside there is a fine east window and, above the droll misericords in the choir, a beautifully carved screen (1620). The **Priory Gatehouse** (*NT; Cavendish Street;* ◐ *open Easter–Oct Wed–Sun, Nov–Easter Sat–Sun 10am–4pm;* ∞ *£2; ℘02524 701178; www.nationaltrust.org. uk),* and the 17C and 18C houses give the market square an urbane air.

ADDRESSES

🛏 STAY

🍴🍴🍴 **Fair Rigg Guest House**, *Ferry View, Bowness on WIndermere, ℘01539 443 941. www.fairrigg. co.uk.* A traditional 19C property with views over the lake to the hills; all six rooms are modern, light and cheery, taking advantage of the vista.

🍴🍴🍴🍴 **Riverside Hotel**, *Under Loughrigg, Ambleside. ℘01539 432 395. www.riverside-at-ambleside.co.uk.* Beautiful Victorian country house beside the river on a quiet lane a short stroll from the village, with five attractive bedrooms, one with a four-poster bed and two with spa baths; all have views of river or garden.

🍷 EAT

🍴🍴 **Bull Inn**, *1 Yewdale Road, Coniston ℘01539 441 335.* A large 16C coaching inn of great character which takes its beers very seriously (there's a microbrewery on-site) and produces honest-to-goodness traditional Lakeland dishes such as trout with almonds and plum pudding.

🍴🍴🍴 **The Weary Sportsman**, *Castle Carrock. ℘01228 670 230. www.theweary.com.* The traditional whitewashed pub exterior hides a thoroughly contemporary interior with striking modern lighting and chic furnishings and fittings; the menu is similarly eclectic, from toffee pudding to vegetable tempura. The local area offers the usual outdoor pursuits, as well as nunnery walks at Armathwaite.

Leeds★

West Yorkshire

Set in the heart of northern England, Leeds is above all a great Victorian city; its population multiplied tenfold between 1800 and 1900 and it ranks third in size among England's provincial cities. Moreover it is Britain's fastest-growing metropolis. Heavy industry has been replaced by light engineering and offices, and clothing manufacture by retailers; the precincts and arcades attract shoppers from all over the North. The rich cultural life of this provincial capital ranges from acclaimed opera to the fashionable nightclubs, which bring in multitudes of weekend revellers.

▶ **Population:** 424,194.

◔ **Michelin Map:** Michelin Atlas p 40 or Map 502 P 22.

▯ **Info:** The Arcade, Leeds City train station. ℘0113 242 5242. www.leedsliveitloveit.com. www.leeds.gov.uk.

◖ **Location:** 25mi/40km SW of York. Leeds City train station, off City Square, and the bus station, behind Kirkgate market, are in the centre.

▲▲ **Kids:** Royal Armouries Museum. Nat. Coal Mining Museum.

CITY
Royal Armouries Museum★★★

Armouries Drive. ◔ *Open year-round daily 10am–5pm.* ◔ *Closed Dec 24–26.* ℘*08700 344 344 (infoline).* ♿✕. *www.armouries.org.uk.*

This purpose-built modern multi-million pound citadel in glass, grey brick and marble was inaugurated in 1996 to provide a worthy setting for part of the superlative collection of weaponry, formerly housed in the Tower of London. The quality of the exhibits is matched by an array of advanced and imaginative display techniques which set the items in their context and encourage visitor participation: interactive computers and video screens chatter and hum, and live demonstrations provide movement and drama. A splendid central space, the **Street**, rises between the six floors of the main part of the building to the glazed roof. It terminates in a glazed keep, known as the **Hall of Steel** (over 100ft/30m high), its interior walls hung with a stunning assortment of weaponry arranged in decorative patterns.

Five spacious galleries are devoted to War, Hunting, the Tournament, self-defence and to the weaponry of Asia. The countless treasures include a gro-

Oriental Gallery, Royal Armouries Museum

Royal Armouries Museum

tesque grinning face-mask presented to Emperor Maximilian (the museum's emblem), gorgeously inlaid sporting guns, a set of Japanese armour presented to King James I in 1614 and a near-complete set of elephant armour. Among the curiosities is a tiny cyclist's revolver designed to discourage dogs and a monumentally unwieldy punt gun once used by wildfowlers to fell dozens of ducks at a single discharge.

The **Tiltyard**, the first to be built in Britain for hundreds of years, is the setting for thrilling performances of jousting and combat of all kinds.

Town Hall and Victoria Square

The town hall was the winning design in a competition in 1853. External Corinthian columns, the Baroque tower (225ft/69m) and the splendour of the interior made it a symbol of civic pride when opened by Queen Victoria in 1858. On fine days, chess enthusiasts can be seen playing "Giant Chess" on the boards marked out in Victoria Square.

St John's Church

○ Open Tue–Sat 9.30am–5.30pm. ℘0113 244 1689.

The oldest church in central Leeds. Sensitive restoration in 1868 left the interior almost unchanged since the church was built in the 1630s.

City Art Gallery★

The Headrow. ○ Open Tue–Fri 11am–6pm (8pm Wed). Sat–Sun 11pm–5pm. ○Closed bank hols, Jan 1, Dec 25–26. &. ℘0113 224 3732. www.leeds.gov.uk/citymuseum.

This is one of the best provincial galleries in Britain, with international-class permanent and temporary exhibitions. Its strength lies in its collection of **19C and 20C British art**, particularly from the early to mid 20C, virtually all major artists of the period being represented. The dominance of British art is relieved by French paintings: a Courbet, several Impressionists and a brilliant Derain of 1905, *Barges on the Thames*. The greatest British sculptor of the 20C, **Henry Moore** (1898–1986), was a Yorkshireman; the

range of his achievement, from exquisite small-scale studies to the *Reclining Figure* of 1929 and the powerful post-war *Meat Porters*, is shown in the gallery and neighbouring **Henry Moore Institute** (○ open daily; ℘0113 246 7467; www.henry-moore-fdn.co.uk).

Kirkstall Abbey and Abbey House Museum★

2mi/3km northwest on the A 65. **Abbey Ruins:** ○ Open Apr–Sept Tue–Sun 11am–4pm, Oct–Mar Sat–Thu 11am–3pm. **Visitor Centre:** ○ Open Tue–Thu, Sat–Sun & bank hols from 10am; closes 5pm, Sat–Sun 6pm, bank hols and Oct–Mar 4pm. &PX. ⊜£3.50. ℘0113 230 5492. www.leeds.gov.uk.

Kirkstall was a traditional Cistercian Abbey, started in 1152. The austere ruins, which still stand almost to roof height, are dominated by the 16C crossing tower. Opposite, across the busy road, is the former abbey gatehouse, now **Abbey House Museum** (○ open Tue–Fri, Sun and bank hols 10am–5pm. Sat noon–5pm; ⊜£3.43; www.leeds.gov.uk/abbeyhouse), which re-creates the sights and sounds of life in Victorian Leeds in the year 1880.

EXCURSIONS

Temple Newsam★

Near Whitkirk, 4mi/6.4km east on the A 63. Temple Newsam Road. **Visitor Centre:** ○Open Tue–Sun and bank hols, 10.30am–5pm (4pm winter). **House and Farm:** ○Open Tue–Sun & bank hols (farm also open Mon in school hols) 10/10.30am–5pm (4pm winter). ⊜House £2.43, farm £3.19. &P (£3.60). X. ℘0113 264 7321. www.leeds.gov.uk. This was the birthplace of Lord Darnley, husband of Mary Queen of Scots. The brick Jacobean-style house, forming three sides of a court, was begun in the late 15C and substantially rebuilt in the first part of the 17C. The house is an attractive setting for a collection of English, European and oriental **decorative arts**★ and for many of the Old Master paintings owned by the City of Leeds. The park was once landscaped by Lancelot "Capability" Brown.

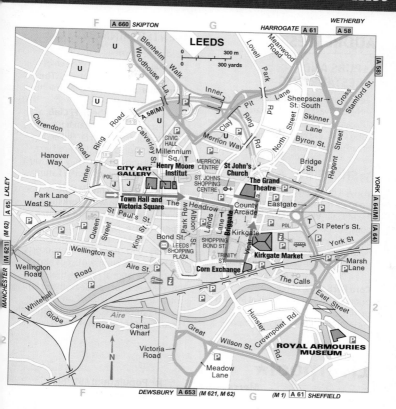

Nostell Priory★

NT. 18mi/29km southeast by A 61 and A 638. Doncaster Road. **House:** ⏱ *Open Mar–Oct Wed–Sun and bank hols 11pm–5pm; mid-Dec–Christmas 11am–4pm.* 👥*Guided tours 11am–1pm.* **Grounds:** ⏱ *Open Mar–Oct Wed–Sun and bank hols 11am–5.30pm. See website for winter times.* ⬥*£7.70. Garden only, £4.80.* ♿. ✆*01924 863 892. www.nationaltrust.org.uk.*

This Palladian mansion was begun in 1733 by James Paine, then only 19 years old. Robert Adam was commissioned in 1765 to complete the State Rooms and they are amongst his finest interiors. **Thomas Chippendale**, once an apprentice on the estate, designed furniture especially for the house.

♣♣ National Coal Mining Museum for England

South of Leeds; 6mi/10km W of Wakefield on the A 642. ⏱ *Open daily.*

⏱ *Closed Jan 1 and Dec 24–26.* ♿📦✕. ✆*01924 848 806. www.ncm.org.uk.*

Until its closure in the 1980s Caphouse Colliery contributed significantly to Britain's industrial might. There is an array of machinery around the pit-head buildings as well as displays and exhibits, but the highlight of a visit is the donning of helmet and lamp and the descent (450ft/140m) into the old workings in the company of a former miner (no children under-five).

Yorkshire Sculpture Park★

20mi/32km south by M 1 to Junction 38 and 1mi/1.5km north off A 637. West Bretton. ⏱ *Open year-round daily 10am–6pm (5pm Nov–Mar).* ⏱ *Closed Dec 23–25 Dec.* ⬥📦(£4). ✕, *picnic area.* ✆*01924 832 631. www.ysp.co.uk.*

Amid a parkland setting lies an outstanding array of modern sculpture, including works by Henry Moore and Barbara Hepworth.

ADDRESSES

🍴 PUBS AND 🍷 RESTAURANTS

Leeds Waterfront, once derelict, is now home to a vast array of restaurants, pubs and shops. The Exchange Quarter along Call Lane is one of the best areas for fashionable cafés and dining.

🛒 SHOPPING

Many of the main high street stores are to be found in **Briggate**, and the elegant **Victoria Quarter** which boasted the first Harvey Nichols store outside London. For hand-made goods head for **Granary Wharf**, which is open daily. For something special or eclectic pay a visit to the slightly bohemian **Corn Exchange**, which has over 50 outlets. **The Sunday Festival Market**, or Kirkgate market, is said to be the largest covered market in Europe.

😀 ENTERTAINMENT

Leeds is renowned for its vibrant club culture. If you are in search of more laid-back nightspots, try: **The Wardrobe** where the live jazz nights often attract both national and international stars; the **Hi Fi Club**, a '70s-inspired subterranean bar/club close to Call Lane with DJ-led and live music nights based around jazz, funk, soul and hip hop. They also run a popular comedy night every Saturday. .

The **City Varieties Music Hall**, (re-opens autumn 2010) the **West Yorkshire Playhouse** and the **Grand Theatre and Opera House** are the main perform-ing arts venues. Outdoor opera, ballet, pop, jazz and classical music concerts are held in the summer. Leeds also hosts International Film Festival, an International Concert Season and an International Pianoforte Competition. For listings buy a copy of the fortnightly *Leeds Guide* or visit www.leeds.gov.uk.

Liverpool★

Merseyside

Though its days of mercantile splendour are long over, Liverpool remains an eminently handsome city, with some glorious architecture and fine civic buildings, reflecting the energy, taste and philanthropy of the Victorian age. Today leisure developments lead the way in the revival of the city's fortunes. The Albert Dock revival and the Tate Liverpool gallery were city centrepieces as Liverpool celebrated its role as European Capital of Culture in 2008. The city's most famous sons, the Beatles, gave the city a new reputation in the 1960s; the Liverpool sound and the Mersey beat and their career are celebrated in Albert Dock and throughout the city.

A BIT OF HISTORY

On 28 August 1207 King John granted a charter for settlers to establish a port on the Mersey. Gradual silting up of the Dee estuary and the attendant

▶ **Population:** 481,786.
🧭 **Michelin Map:** Michelin Atlas p 34 or Map 502 L 23.
🚩 **Info:** The 08 Place, Whitechapel. Anchor Courtyard, Albert Dock. ☎0151 233 2008. www.visitliverpool.com. 112 Lord Street, Southport. ☎01704 533 333.
▶ **Location:** Liverpool is in northwest England, around 75mi/120km due south of the Lake District and 34mi/54km west of Manchester. Lime Street Station links to a small underground network; the bus station is just around the corner on Norton Street. Get to know the city's streets and the river Mersey in one tour with 🚌**Liverpool Duck Tours** (Gower Street Bus Stop; 🕐mid-Feb–Christmas

Waterfront with Royal Liver Building, Cunard Building and Port of Liverpool Building (from left to right)

A. Williams/MICHELIN

abandonment of Chester, a port since Roman times, turned the new village of Liverpool into England's second port. It centred around seven streets, which still exist today – Castle and Old Hall, Water and Dale, Chapel and Tithebarn, up to Hatton Garden – and the "Pool", an inlet following today's Canning and Paradise Streets and Whitechapel.

Liverpool started to expand when trade with the West Indies – sugar, rum, cotton and, until 1807, slaves – brought such prosperity that by 1800 there were more than 80,000 "Liverpudlians". In the 19C Liverpool, home to the Cunard and White Star liners, was Britain's gateway to the empire and the world. The Mersey Docks and Harbour Company handled the cargo traffic, employing some 20,000 men in the immediate post-war period. Today, with container ships and mechanical handling, only just over 2,500 men now work in the docks.

> every hour daily 10.30am–6pm; ⊜peak £11.95, off-peak £9.95, child £7.95/£9.95; ℘0151 708 7799; www.theyellowduck marine.co.uk). Open-top bus tours run every hour (🕐11am–2pm Mar–Oct, also 3pm in July) starting at Albert Dock.
>
> 🚻 **Don't Miss:** Walker Gallery; Liverpool Anglican Cathedral; Albert Dock museums.
>
> 🕐 **Timing:** Allow at least two days (to include one excursion).
>
> 🧍 **Kids:** Liverpool Duck Tour; hands-on fun at World Museum; sharks at Blue Planet Aquarium; animals at Knowsley Safari Park; World of Glass.
>
> 🥾**Walking Tours:** Daily in summer from the tourist office and Albert Dock.

ALBERT DOCK★ (CZ)

Massive brick warehouses enclose a dock basin (7acres/3ha). Completed in 1846, finally closed in 1972, the complex has now been revitalised with shops, cafés and apartments, museums and the northern extension of the Tate.

Merseyside Maritime Museum and International Slavery Museum★

Albert Dock. 🕐*Open daily, 10am–5pm.* 🕐*Closed Dec 24–26.* 🅿✕. ℘*0151 478 4499. www.liverpoolmuseums.org.uk.* Liverpool's seafaring past is presented through displays on the history of shipbuilding, the evolution of the port, navigation and the growth of maritime insurance, ship models and paintings

and the *Edmund Gardner*, a former
pilot cutter that can now be found
in dry dock (🕐*closed until 2010*).
The poignancy of the story of the
nine million emigrants to the New
World who passed through Liverpool between 1830 and 1930
is exceeded only by the sadness
of the history of the slave trade
show-cased in the **International
Slavery Museum**, only yards
away from the dry docks where
18C slave trading ships were
repaired and fitted out.

A second separate "museum
within the museum" is the **HM
Customs and Excise National
Museum** which charts the fight
against smuggling over the centuries as well as modern detec-
tion methods.

Museum of Liverpool

Albert Dock. 🕐*Open from 2010.*
*℘0151 478 4499. www.liverpool
museums.org.uk.*
This new museum will follow 800
years of Liverpool history, from
medieval "*Lyverpoole*" to 21C
"Livercool", featuring cultural
aspects such as the story of Liverpool music.

Tate Liverpool★

Albert Dock. 🕐 *Open daily
10am–5.50pm (closed Mon Oct–
Mar). Last Thu of every month
and Tue–Sat during Aug, closes
9pm.* 🕐 *Closed Jan 1, Good Fri,
Dec 24–26.* 👁*Charge for special
exhibitions only.* 👁 *Guided free
tour daily at 12.30pm, (family
tour) 2pm.* ♿🅿✖. *℘0151 702
7400. www.tate.org.uk/liverpool.*
The Tate family originated from
Liverpool and the choice of the
city to house part of the national
collection of 20C art was a happy one. This transformed warehouse will eventually showcase semi-permanent exhibi-
tions from the Tate's primary collections
of 20C art and world-class temporary
exhibitions.

The Beatles Story

Britannia Vaults, Albert Dock.
🕐 *Open year-round daily 9am–7pm
(last admission 5pm).* 🕐 *Closed 25–26
Dec.* 👁*£12.25.* ♿🅿*(charge).* *℘0151
709 1963. www.beatlesstory.com.*

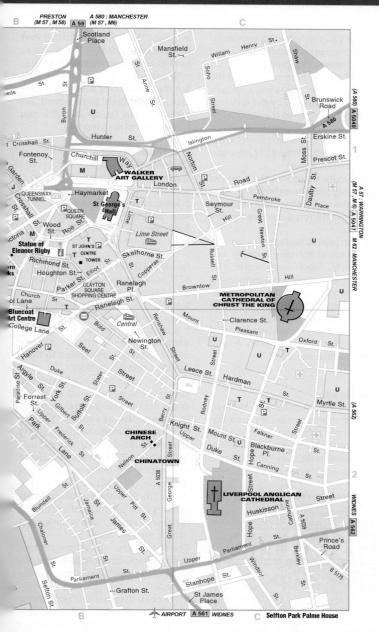

Relive or discover the decade of the Beatles, the 1960s, the new phenomena of rock'n'roll, teenagers, the Merseybeat and Beatlemania. The original Beatles group consisted of **John Lennon** (1940–1980), **Paul McCartney** (b. 1942), **George Harrison** (1943–2001) and **Ringo Starr** (b. 1940); their manager was Brian Epstein, "the Fifth Beatle" (1934–1967). The places (The Cavern, Strawberry Fields, Penny Lane, Hamburg) and the hits are presented in a lively and entertaining manner by a walk-through presentation plus a new "Fab4D cinema experience".

The **childhood homes** of two of the Beatles, Paul McCartney and John Lennon are now owned by the National Trust and are open to the public via a minibus tour (⏱*operates Mar–Nov most days, see website for details;* ✆£16, NT members £7.50; ✆0151 427 7231; www. nationaltrust.org.uk).

20 Forthlin Road was the home of McCartney and where the Beatles composed and rehearsed some of their earliest songs. **Mendips** is where Lennon grew up.

The most popular Beatles tour is the two-hour **Magical Mystery Tour** (⏱*year-round daily 2.30pm from the Gower Street Bus Stop, Albert Dock; extra tour noon on Sat, Sun and school hols, advance reservations recommended;* ✆£13.95; ✆0151 236 9091; www.cavernclub.org).

The whole city celebrates **International Beatle Week Festival** every August (www.liverpooltour.com).

CITY
Pier Head

The spirit of Liverpool and the Mersey is best appreciated by standing on the corner of Water Street and the Strand. The ferries on the Mersey have been part of the scene since the monks of Birkenhead Priory began rowing travellers across

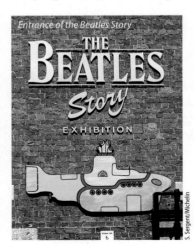
Entrance of the Beatles Story

in about 1150. The green-domed **Port of Liverpool Building** (1907) and its neighbour, the **Cunard Building** (1913), reflect the city's maritime connections but the **Royal Liver Building** (1908), with its "Liver Birds" (pronounced "lie-ver") on the cupolas, is probably the best known symbol of Liverpool.

Liverpool Anglican Cathedral★★

St James Mount. **Cathedral:** ⏱ *Open year-round daily 8am–6pm.* ✆*Contributions welcome.* **Tower:** ⏱ *Open Mon–Sat 10am–3.30pm.* ✆*Tower and Embroidery Gallery £4.25.* ⏱*Guided tour (1hr) 10am–3pm. Great Space Film and audio tour Mon–Sat 9am–4pm* (✆£4.75). P *(charge).* ✗. ✆0151 709 6271. www.liverpoolcathedral.org.uk. This monumental edifice in red sandstone is the largest Anglican church in the world. Work began in 1904 and it took most of the century to build, a triumphant reinterpretation of the Gothic tradition by its architect **Sir Giles Gilbert Scott** (1880–1960).

The first impression is of vastness, strength and height. Scott's unusual design includes double transepts and the central "**Great Space**" (15,000sq ft/1,400sq m) under the tower, giving an uninterrupted view of altar and pulpit. The tower (331ft/100m) extends the full width of the building and houses the heaviest ringing peal of bells in the world (31t). Set in the floor immediately below is the memorial to the architect, (a Roman Catholic) who is buried just outside the west door.

The **Baptistery**, with its marble font and a baldachin and font cover contains some of the finest wood carving in the cathedral.

In the **choir** there are liver birds on the steps leading into the stalls. Beyond is the **Lady Chapel**★ with a notable reredos and a 15C Madonna.

Metropolitan Cathedral of Christ the King★★

Mount Pleasant. ⏱ *Open year-round daily 8am–6pm (5pm Sun in winter).* ✆*Contribution requested.* ♿ P *(charge).*

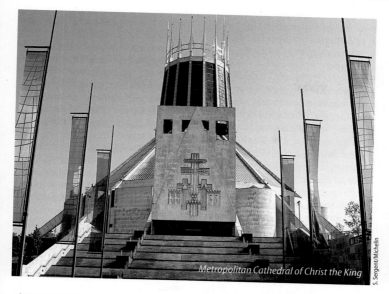

Metropolitan Cathedral of Christ the King

S.Sergent/Michelin

☎ *0151 709 9222. www.liverpool metrocathedral.org.uk.*

The cathedral stands on Brownlow Hill, occupied 1771–1928 by a home for Liverpool's destitute. **Sir Edwin Lutyens** was chosen as the architect and the foundation stone was laid in 1933. However the completed cathedral was not consecrated until 1967.

The distinctive **exterior** is an extraordinary buttressed circular concrete structure, culminating in the lantern (290ft/88m high) with its crown of pinnacles. From the inner porch the High Altar is immediately visible, at the centre of the circular nave (194ft/60m in diameter). The **tower**, its stained glass in the colours of the spectrum, rises above the **High Altar**, the architectural as well as liturgical focal point. The clever design of the baldachin candlesticks and crucifix ensure an uninterrupted view of the celebrant at the altar for every member of a full 2300-strong congregation.

The massive brick vaults crypt includes a venue for regular concerts, a museum recounting the story of the building of the cathedral and the burial place of the archbishops; its door is a six-tonne marble disc, which rolls back as did the stone traditionally sealing the tomb of Christ.

World Museum

William Brown Street. ◷ *Open year-round daily 10am–5pm. Timed ticket to planetarium (free) from information desk.* ◷ *Closed Jan 1, Dec 25–26.* ♿ ▣ ✕. ☎ *0151 478 439. www.liverpoolmuseums.org.uk.*

This eclectic museum whose subjects range from live bugs to space exploration, combines historic treasures from across the globe with the latest interactive technology. Its internationally important collections include archaeology, ethnology and the natural and physical sciences as well as Britain's only free planetarium. Its origins are the old Liverpool Museum and includes most of the of the collection of Joseph Mayer (a mid-19C local goldsmith and antiquarian) featuring Anglo-Saxon treasures, mummies and Wedgwood china.

Walker Art Gallery★★

William Brown Street. ◷ *Open year-round daily 10am–5pm.* ◷ *Closed Jan 1, Dec 25–26.* ♿✕. ☎ *0151 478 4199. www.liverpoolmuseums.org.uk/walker.*

The Walker's collection of British and European paintings is among the best in the country.

Numerous painters of the Italian school are represented, from the 14C to the

Renaissance and beyond. The extensive holdings of Northern European art include works by Rembrandt, Elsheimer and Cranach.

The range of British work is particularly complete, extending from Elizabethan and later portraits to key works by Stubbs, Wright of Derby and Richard Wilson; there are typically uncanny works by Fuseli and many **Pre-Raphaelites**, including Millais and Ford Madox Brown. Narrative paintings include WR Yeames' *When did you last see your Father?*

A small number of French Impressionists – Degas, Seurat and Monet – are juxtaposed with their British contemporaries like Sickert.

St George's Hall

"One of the finest neo-Grecian buildings in the world" (Pevsner) was completed in 1854; it contains a circular Concert Room and a vast Great Hall of more than Roman opulence. The hall dominates the neighbouring neo-Classical civic buildings which are a focal point of the city.

Statue of Eleanor Rigby

Stanley Street.
The statue is the work of Tommy Steele, a contemporary of The Beatles; a plaque behind her dedicates the statue "To all the lonely people." Round the corner in Mathew Street is the **Cavern Club**, where the Beatles first performed.

Sefton Park Palm House

Sefton Park, South Liverpool. Open year-round daily from 10.30am; Nov–Mar closes 4pm; Apr and Oct closes 5pm; May–Sept closes 6.30pm; may close for special events, see website. *&. ℘0151 726 2415. www.palmhouse.org.uk.*
This magnificent tiered octagonal Grade II-listed Victorian glasshouse showcases the Liverpool Botanical collection.

EXCURSIONS
Southport

20mi/32km north via the A 565.
This elegant and dignified seaside resort is distinguished by its tree-lined streets, attractive flowerbeds and famous gardens (its Flower Show is held late Aug). Broad and spacious **Lord Street**, where the shops have wrought-iron and glass-roofed canopies extending over the pavements, is the epitome of a Victorian promenade. Families enjoy the beaches (6mi/9km) and amusement parks. **Royal Birkdale** (south), is one of several first-class golf courses in the locality.

Rufford Old Hall★

*NT. 20mi/32km north on the A 59 (DY). **House:** Open mid-Mar–Oct Sun–Wed 11pm–5pm (Sat 1pm–5pm). **Garden:** Open as house, 11am–5pm, also Nov–Christmas noon–4pm. £6 (Garden only, £4.20). &.* ✕. *℘01704 821 254. www.nationaltrust.org.uk.*
This is one of the finest 15C houses in Lancashire. The **Great Hall**★ has a magnificent **hammerbeam roof** and ornate carved screen. The Carolean wing was reconstructed in brick in 1662. There is much original furniture, arms and armour, and a folk museum.

Martin Mere Wildfowl and Wetlands Centre

20mi/32km north on the A 59 to Rufford and west on the B 5246. Open daily, 9.30am–5.30pm (late Oct–Feb 5 pm). £8.75. & ✕. *℘01704 895 181. www.wwt.org.uk.*
This sanctuary provides hides and nature trails for birdwatchers and is a protected wildfowl habitat of 350 acres/140ha. The mere (lake) is home to home to over 100 species of rare and endangered ducks, geese, swans, flamingos and beavers and a winter haven to thousands of pink-footed geese, Icelandic Whooper swans and Bewick swans from Russia.

⚇ Knowsley Safari Park

8mi/13km east by A 5047 (and the eastbound carriageway of the A 58 (Prescot bypass). Open daily 10am/10.30am–3pm/4pm. £12, child £9. & ✕. *Rides £1.50 each. ℘0151 430 9009. www.knowsley.com.*
It was in the menagerie, established at Knowsley in the 19C by the Earl of Derby, that **Edward Lear** made many of his animal drawings; the tales he told

to Lord Derby's grandchildren became his *Book of Nonsense*. Today visitors can drive **safari**-fashion along a 5-mi/8-km route, passing herds of antelopes, camels, buffalo and white rhino, plus tigers, monkeys, giraffes and more. There is also an elephant paddock, a sealion show, an **Aerial Extreme** tree-top walkway and amusement rides.

The National Wildflower Centre

Just off junction 5 of the M62. Court Hey Park. ◐ *Open daily Mar–Aug 10am–5pm.* £3.50. ⚿ℙ✕. ℘0151 738 1913. www.nwc.org.uk. Set in a Victorian park within 35acres/ 14ha of parkland, this bucolic Millennium Commission attraction features seasonal wildflower displays, demonstration areas with events and activities, and a mix of old and new (award-winning) buildings.

👤👤 The World of Glass

12mi/18km east by A 5047 (EY) and A 57 to St Helens. ◐ *Open Tue–Sun and bank hols 10am–5pm, last admission 3pm.* ◐*Closed Dec 25–26, Jan 1.* £5.30, child £3.80. ⚿ℙ✕. ℘08700 114 466. www.worldofglass.com. Visitors pass through an inverted brick cone recalling the old furnaces into the modern building on the site of the pioneering Pilkington factory. There's live glass-blowing, a 3-D theatre and lots of interactive stations at this very family-friendly place.

Speke Hall★

NT. Near airport, 8mi/13km SE on the A 561. The Walk. **House:** ◐*Open mid-Mar–Oct Wed–Sun and bank hols 11am–5pm. Nov–mid-Dec and first two weeks Mar Sat–Sun 11am–4.30pm.* **Garden and grounds:** ◐ *Open Tue–Sun 11am–5.30pm (Oct–Mar dusk).* £7.27 (garden £4.31). ℙ✕. ℘0151 427 7231. www.nationaltrust.org.uk. This black-and-white Elizabethan manor house was built between 1490 and 1612 by successive generations of the Norris family. The **Great Hall** is the oldest part of the building; its panelling, including

Speke Hall

S. Sergent/Michelin

the Great Wainscot of 1564, is particularly fine. The many smaller rooms reflect the Victorian preference for privacy and comfort. In the courtyard two ancient yews possibly pre-date the house.

Port Sunlight

West-side of the Mersey, south of Birkenhead. The model village was established in the late 19C by William Hesketh Lever for the workers of his soap factory, giving them a style of life very different from that of the crowded slums of the period. Lord Leverhulme's company became Unilever, one of the world's largest manufacturers of consumer goods. The **Lady Lever Art Gallery**, (◐*open Mon–Sat 10am–5pm, Sun noon–5pm;* ⚿ℙ✕; ℘0151 478 4136; www.ladylev erartgallery.org.uk) also founded by Lord Leverhulme and opened in 1922, contains British paintings including Pre-Raphaelite works, period furniture, and a fine Wedgwood collection.

👤👤 Blue Planet Aquarium

Take the M6, the M56 at J20, then the M53 at junction 15. Cheshire Oaks. ◐*Open 10am–5pm/6pm.* £14.50, child £10.50. ⚿ℙ✕. ℘0151 357 8804. www.blueplanetaquarium.co.uk. This claims to be the largest "aquarium adventure" of its kind and has more types of shark (10 species) than anywhere else in Britain. Its shark-infested Aquatunnel is one of the longest in the world at 70m/230ft.

Isle of Man★

This mountainous island in the Irish Sea was settled by Celts, then by Norsemen, ruled by Scotland, then by England. Its own language, Manx, akin to Gaelic, is now extinct, though the famous tailless cat survives. The island, a British dependency but not part of the United Kingdom, has its own laws, presented each year to an open-air parliament of the people; this 1,000-year-old descendant of the Norse *Thingvollr* ("assembly field") is held at a central point on the island, Tynwald Green, a site with prehistoric associations. The lowland pattern of unspoiled farmland, small fields bounded by stone walls or high hedgebanks, gives way as the land rises to wild open moorland, bright in late summer with gorse and heather. The highest summit is Snaefell (2,036ft/621m), from which England, Scotland, Ireland, and Wales can be seen. Most of the coastline (100mi/160km) is untouched by modern intrusions.

ISLE
Manx transport
The island still attracts multitudes of holidaymakers, mainly from the north of England. Its halcyon days of mass tourism were, however, the late 19C and early 20C and from this time dates an extensive network of vintage transport. Horse trams – nicknamed "toast racks" – ply the Douglas promenades, narrow-gauge steam railways serve the south and, most remarkable of all, double-track electric tramways lead from Douglas along the high cliffs to the northern resort of Ramsey and to the very summit of Snaefell.

Isle of Man TT Races
May/Jun. www.iomtt.com
Motorcyclists flock to the island each year as they have done since the first Tourist Trophy races was held here in 1907. Road closure and speed limits on the mainland made organisers turn to

- **Population:** 69,788.
- **Michelin Map:** Michelin Atlas p 42 or Map 402 G 21.
- **Info:** ℰ01624 686801. www.gov.im/tourism.
- **Location:** The Isle of Man Steam Packet Company runs ferries to Liverpool, Heysham (Morecambe) Dublin and Belfast. The island also has an airport.

the Isle of Man. The race course remains one of the world's most dangerous.

Douglas
The great sweep of Victorian and Edwardian hotels facing promenades and the sandy bay give the island's capital an unmistakable identity. The **Manx Museum** (○*open Mon–Sat 10am–5pm;* ○*closed Dec 25–26 Dec, Jan 1;* ▣✕; ℰ01624 648 000; www.gov.im/mnh), "the treasure house of the island's story" displays good examples of early Christian sculpture; the Folk-Life Galleries include a reconstructed Manx farmhouse.

Laxey Wheel★★
Take the Manx Electric Railway north along the coast. Walk up the valley (0.6mi/1km). ○*Open Easter/late-Mar–late Oct daily 10am–5pm.* ◎£3.30. ▣. ℰ01624 648 000. www.gov.im/tourism. This giant water wheel, a splendid monument of the industrial age, was built in 1854 when the Laxey Valley was the scene of intense lead and silver mining activity.

Snaefell Mountain Railway★
Take the Manx Electric Railway via Laxey on the east coast. ○*Operates (weather permitting) Laxey to summit May–Sept, daily, 10.30am–3.30pm.* ◎£7.80. ▣✕. ℰ01624 662525. A vintage tramcar climbs up the side of the glen and on to the mountain slopes to the terminus at the café just below the summit. On a clear day there are stupendous **views★★★** of the lands fringing the Irish Sea.

Manchester ★
Greater Manchester

Though the smoking chimneys of the cotton mills in this north-west metropolis have long gone, Manchester still retains many fine historical buildings erected by the Victorian successors to those hard-headed Georgian merchants. Today the city has developed into a major provincial centre of finance and has recently added a number of high-profile visitor attractions in visually stunning state-of-the-art buildings. It has long been renowned for its nightlife, the local music scene and the most famous football club in the world.

A BIT OF HISTORY

Thanks to trade with the American colonies, Manchester became the centre of the rapidly expanding cotton industry. However its principles of free trade led to tragedy on 16 August in 1819 when a crowd assembled on St Peter's Fields to demand Parliamentary reform and repeal of the Corn Laws; 11 died and many were injured by the cavalry sent in to disperse them in what came to be known as the **Peterloo Massacre**. The **Free Trade Hall** was constructed on the site of this outrage.

CASTLEFIELD URBAN HERITAGE PARK ★
South end of Deansgate.
Britain's first urban heritage park, Castle-field traces the development of Manchester from Roman times. The remains of the **Roman fort** – "the castle in the field" – and the north gate and part of the west wall have been reconstructed on their original site.
In the 18C Castlefield became the centre of a canal system, which started in 1761 with the Duke of Bridgewater's canal. In 1830, the world's first passenger station, Liverpool Road Station, was opened by the Liverpool and Manchester Railway. The tow-path is open to pedestrians and a walkway (*1mi/1.5km*) beside the River Irwell links Castlefield with the

- ▶ **Population:** 402,889.
- **Michelin Map:** Michelin Atlas p 39 or Map 502 N 23.
- **Info:** Town Hall Extension building, Lloyd Street. ℘0871 222 8223. www.visitmanchester.com.
- ◗ **Location:** Manchester is 34mi/54km east of Liverpool and 42mi/67km southwest of Leeds. Manchester has three main stations, Piccadilly is the main one, a 10 min walk east of the city centre. The two coach stations, Chorlton Street and Piccadilly Gardens are close to each other, a 5 min walk east. The city centre is compact and can be covered on foot. Public transport links to suburban sights are good, or take a City Sightseeing hop-on hop-off tour bus (*operate late May–late Sept daily; £8; ℘01253 473 003; www.citysightseeing.co.uk*).
- **Don't Miss:** Lowry; Imperial War Museum North.
- **Timing:** Allow at least two days to visit Manchester.
- **Kids:** Get hands-on at the MOSI, Urbis and Jodrell Bank; Manchester United's Old Trafford stadium tour for football-mad kids. The bright colours and activities of the Lowry.

PUBLIC TRANSPORT

A modern tram system, Metrolink, runs frequent services connecting the main railway stations. For further details ℘0161 205 2000. For information on bus timetables and services visit the Greater Manchester Passenger Transport Executive website (*www.gmpte.com*).

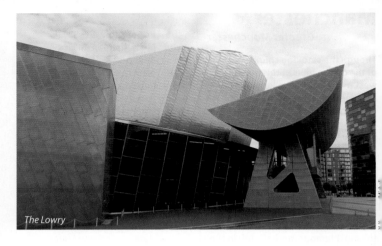
The Lowry

Ship Canal and Salford Quays. Cruises are now offered along the waterways that once carried goods across the Pennines: **Manchester Ship Canal Cruises** (🕐 operate late Apr–mid-Oct, see website for schedule and fares; ♿; ✆0151 330 1444; www.merseyferries.co.uk), along the route opened by Queen Victoria in 1894 (6hr/36mi/58km), and the **Irwell and Mersey Packetboat Company** (🕐 call for times; ✆0161 736 2108), along the River Irwell and Ship Canal to Salford Quays (50min).

The big attraction is the city's largest museum, the 👥 **Museum of Science and Industry** ★ (Liverpool Road; 🕐 Open daily 10am–5pm; 🕐 Closed Dec 24–26; ♿ 🅿 (£5)✕; ✆0161 832 2244; www.mosi.org.uk). **MOSI**, as it is known, gives a fascinating view of Manchester's industrial heritage. Exhibition galleries are devoted to printing, machine tools, gas and electricity, locomotives, the history of flight and a science centre.

CITY
Urbis
Cathedral Gardens. 🕐 Open Tue–Sun (shop and café daily) 10am–6pm. ♿✕. ✆0161 605 8200. www.urbis.org.uk.
This eclectic arty post-Millennium project is housed in a stunning glass triangular building that has become a new city icon. It houses an exhibition centre and Interactive galleries which explore the culture and dynamism of cities around the world, covering photography, design, architecture, music and contemporary art.

Cathedral★
🕐 Open daily. ♿✕. ✆0161 833 2220. www.manchestercathedral.org.
The church, refounded as a chantry college in 1421, became the cathedral of the new diocese in 1847. Six bays form the nave – the widest of any church in England – and six the choir. The **choir screen** is a unique piece of medieval carving. In the choir itself the **stalls and canopies**★ are beautifully carved. The **misericords** (c. 1500) are a comic depiction of medieval life.

Royal Exchange
Manchester owes its prosperity to "King Cotton". Raw cotton imported via the port of Liverpool and the canal network, a pure water supply from the Pennines, a high degree of humidity in the air and a large available working population were the factors responsible for the rapid growth of the cotton and ancillary industries. English cotton was sold throughout the world and the Manchester cotton exchange was the very nerve centre of this trade.
Inside the exchange the prices of cotton on the day the market last traded are still shown on the board high up near the roof (west end). Today this immense hall is partly occupied by the 700-seat

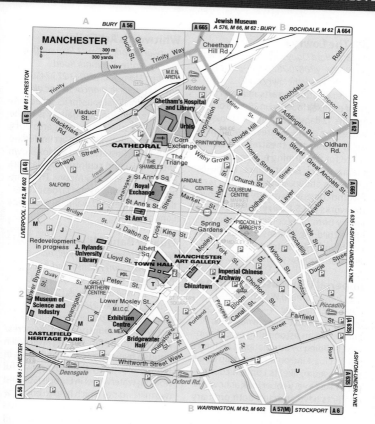

Royal Exchange Theatre, a seven-sided, glass-walled capsule, literally suspended from huge marble pillars.

John Rylands University Library

&. 𝒫0161 275 3751.
www.library.manchester.ac.uk.
The beautiful John Rylands Library at Deansgate is one of the finest examples of modern Gothic architecture in Europe, designed by Basil Champneys, opened in 1900 and founded in memory of a successful textile manufacturer. The library possesses many early printed books and rare and valuable manuscripts.

Town Hall★

Designed in Gothic style by Alfred Waterhouse and built from 1868 to 1877, the town hall is one of the greatest civic buildings of the Victorian era. Its tower with octagonal top stage rises 286ft/87m above the pedestrian area of Albert Square. Two staircases lead from the low vaulted entrance hall to the **Great Hall**, with its hammerbeam roof and twelve Pre-Raphaelite style murals by Ford Madox Brown 1876–88.

Manchester Art Gallery★

Moseley Street. ⏱ *Open Tue–Sun and bank hols, 10am–5pm.*
⏱ *Closed Jan 1, Good Fri, Dec 24–26 and 31.* &.✕. 𝒫0161 235 8888.
www.manchestergalleries.org.uk.
The interior, recently restored to its 19C glory, displays an interesting Pre-Raphaelite collection with works by Millais, Hunt and Rossetti and Ford Madox Brown's *Work* (1852) illustrating the various classes of a developing industrial society. Note the works of Stubbs, Turner and Constable and the industrial landscapes of the North, captured with sensitivity by LS Lowry (1887–1976).

⚲⚲ The Lowry★

Pier 8, Salford Quays. 🕐 *Opening times vary.* ♿.✖. ☏*0870 787 5780,* ☏*0161 876 2000. www.thelowry.com.*

This visually stunning arts and entertainment complex, opened in 2000 as one of Britain's 12 flagship Millennium projects, graces the docks of Greater Manchester. It houses two theatres and studio space for performing arts, presenting drama, opera, ballet, dance, musicals, children's shows, popular music, jazz, folk and comedy. Its gallery space shows the works of **LS Lowry** (1887–1976), a locally born painter nationally famous for his child-like "matchstick" figures and northern England street scenes, alongside contemporary exhibitions.

Imperial War Museum North★

The Quays, Trafford Wharf. 🕐 *Open daily.* 🕐 *Closed Dec 24–26.* ☐£4. ♿✖. ☏*0161 836 4000. www.iwm.org.uk.*

Located in an astonishing award-winning building by international architect Daniel Libeskind on the city's ship canal, this museum, like its London counterpart, takes a very sober look at how 20C conflicts have affected both ordinary combatants and the people at home. A highlight is the **Big Picture Show**, a 360° audio-visual show which immerses visitors into the IWM's world-renowned collections of war-related images and sound. Continually changing images are projected onto the gallery walls, floor and visitors themselves, accompanied by music, sounds and reminiscences from the oral history archives.

⚲⚲ Manchester United Tour and Museum

Old Trafford. Matt Busby Way, North Stand. 🕐 *Opening times vary.* ⚲ 9.40am–4.30pm on non-match days (pre-booked). ✆Museum and tour £11.74, child £7.83 (museum only, £8.32, child £6.61). ☐✖. ☏*0161 868 8000. www.manutd.com.*

Take a look behind-the-scenes inside "The Theatre of Dreams" to see what makes the most famous football club in the world tick from the Trophy Room to the pitch.

Whitworth Art Gallery★

Whitworth Park. 1.5mi/2.5km south of the city centre. Denmark Road. 🕐 *Open Mon–Sat.* ☏*0161 275 7450. www.whitworth.manchester.ac.uk.*

Internationally famous for its collections of art and design, the gallery is home to an impressive range of watercolours, prints, drawings, modern art (including Paula Rego, Rossetti, Ford Madox Brown and Millais) and sculpture by Barbara Hepworth and Henry Moore. The Whitworth also features the largest collections of textiles and wallpapers outside London.

Quarry Bank Mill★

NT. 10mi/16km south. Styral, nr. Wilmslow. Quarry Bank Road. Mill. 🕐 *Opening times vary.* ✆Mill and house £9 (Mill only, £6). ♿☐ (£2.70) ✖. ☏*01625 527 468, 01625 445 896. (Infoline). www. nationaltrust.org.uk.*

In a wooded country park (284 acres/ 11ha) beside the fast-flowing River Bollin stands a five-storey cotton mill, built in 1784, powered by the most powerful working waterwheel in Europe (50t) and two mill engines which help to bring the past to life. The production of cotton cloth from the cotton plant to the bolt of calico on sale in the mill shop is traced in a fascinating exhibition including live demonstrations of hand-spinning and loom weaving. The Apprentice House presents the spartan lifestyle of the pauper children that worked here.

⚲⚲ Jodrell Bank Visitor Centre

Bomish Lane. 🕐 *Opening times vary.* ✆£2, child £1, 3-D theatre £1. ☐✖. ☏*01477 571 339. www.jodrellbank. manchester.ac.uk/visitorcentre.*

A discovery centre, 3-D theatre, arboretum and outdoor play areas are just some of the fun places you'll find at this science complex attached to Britain's most famous radio telescope.

Macclesfield

19mi/31km south. For over 200 years Macclesfield was synonymous with silk production; explore its history at the two museums.

ADDRESSES

🍴 PUBS AND
🍽 RESTAURANTS

Chinatown in the city centre is the largest 'Chinatown' city centre enclave of Chinese shops and restaurants in the UK, with numerous places to eat. There is a wide range of eating options in the **Northern Quarter** and **Princess Street**. Rusholme, outside the city centre, is the area for Indian restaurants. Pick up a copy of the *Manchester Food and Drink Guide* (*www.citylife.co.uk*).

🛒 SHOPPING

Along **Market Street** and in the **Arndale Centre** you will find all the main high street department stores. For boutiques and designer shops visit **King Street** and **St Ann's Square**. Bargain hunters should head towards the **Northern Quarter**, **Afflecks Palace** and the **Coliseum Centre**.

☺ NIGHTLIFE

See the local *Manchester Evening News*, visit the official tourist information website or *www.citylife.co.uk*.

Newcastle-Upon-Tyne★
Tyne and Wear

Newcastle is an important hub on the busy east-coast route to Scotland. Its dramatic site, rich history and the distinctive dialect spoken by its population of "Geordies" give this undisputed capital of the northeast of England an exceptionally strong identity. Despite recent decline Newcastle retains great vigour as a commercial, educational, entertainment and cultural centre. The city centre shopping complex in Eldon Square was one of the most ambitious of its kind when built, while the gargantuan MetroCentre on the outskirts of Gateshead is billed as one of the largest shopping and leisure complexes in Europe. Post-Millennium, the BALTIC Centre for Contemporary Arts and The Sage music venue are powerful symbols of the city's new cultural ambitions.

A BIT OF HISTORY

The easily defended bridging point where the Tyne enters its gorge was exploited by the Roman founders of Pons Aelius, one post among many along Hadrian's Wall, then by the Normans, whose "New Castle" dates from 1080. Later, abundant mineral resources, particularly coal, stimulated trade, man-

▶ **Population:** 189,150.

🗺 **Michelin Map:** Michelin Atlas p 51 or Map 502 P 19.

ℹ **Info:** Central Arcade, Market Street. ☎0191 277 8000. Guildhall, Newcastle Quayside. ☎0191 277 8000. The Sage, St Mary's Place. ☎0191 478 4222. www.newcastlegateshead.com. www.visitnewcastlegateshead.co.uk.

▶ **Location:** 84mi/134km due north of York. Central (railway) Station is just that, with a Metro station attached. Haymarket Bus Station is north of the city centre, also linked to the Metro network which offers fast, efficient travel around Newcastle and Tyneside. Newcastle-upon-Tyne is the city north of the river while the separate town of Gateshead begins as soon as you cross any of the town-centre bridges. The city centre is best seen on foot.

👁 **Don't Miss:** The BALTIC Centre; views from the city bridges.

🕐 **Timing:** Two days minimum.

👪 **Kids:** Centre for Life; Beamish Open-Air Museum.

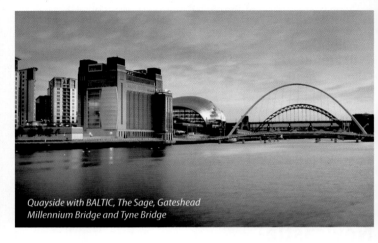

Quayside with BALTIC, The Sage, Gateshead Millennium Bridge and Tyne Bridge

ufacturing and engineering. The great railway inventor **George Stephenson** (1781–1848) was born nearby, as was his son Robert, and in the 19C Tyneside became one of the great centres of industrial Britain, dominated by figures like **William Armstrong**, later Lord Armstrong (1810–1900), whose engineering and armament works at Elswick helped equip the navies of the world.

CITY

The approach from the south through **Gateshead** reveals an astonishing **urban panorama**★★. The city of Newcastle has spread slowly from the north bank of the Tyne via steeply-sloping streets and precipitous stairways up to the flatter land to the north. Buildings of all periods and materials are dominated by the castle and the cathedral tower.

Quayside★

Newcastle and Gateshead are linked by seven bridges, which make an outstanding **composition**★ extending upstream. The oldest is the unusual **High Level Bridge (CZ)** (1848), designed by **Robert Stephenson** with railway tracks above and roadway below. The **Swing Bridge (CZ)** (1876) designed by Lord Armstrong, brightly painted and nautical-looking, follows the alignment of the original crossing. The monumental stone piers of the great **Tyne Bridge (CZ)** (1928) add drama to the townscape. Among the tightly-packed Victorian commercial buildings are a few much older survivors: the 17C Guildhall **(CZG)**, the remarkable timber-framed **Bessie Surtees' House** and the 18C Classical **All Saints Church**★. The riverside walkways with sculpture, pubs, bars and hotels are a popular place for a stroll.

PRACTICAL INFORMATION

PUBLIC TRANSPORT

The Tyne and Wear Metro runs from 5.30am–11.30pm, linking Newcastle city with Tyneside and the coast. Trains run every seven minutes to the airport and the coast, and every three minutes at peak times within the city. For full details on bus and Metro travel contact Nexus (℘0191 203 3333; www.nexus.org.uk).

SIGHTSEEING

For sightseeing on the River Tyne, regular cruises run from Newcastle Quayside and North and South Shields during the summer months. Contact **River Escapes** (℘01670 785666; www.tyneleisureline.co.uk) Travel through once thriving maritime heritage, to landmarks likesuch as the Gateshead Millennium Bridge, Tyne Bridge, The Sage and BALTIC Centre.

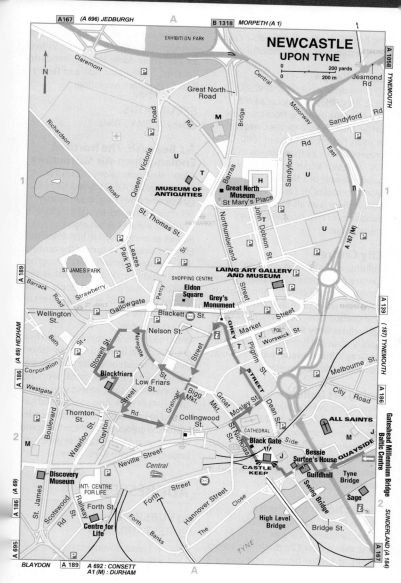

BALTIC Centre

Gateshead Quays. ⏲ *Open daily.* .
☎ *0191 478 1810. www.balticmill.com.*
Housed in a landmark former flour mill
on the River Tyne in Gateshead, this is
the biggest gallery of its kind in the
world – presenting an ever-changing
international programme of contemporary visual art. The views from the top
are fantastic.

The Sage

⏲ *Open daily.* ♿ 🅿 *(charge).* 🍴 ☎ *0191
443 4661. www.thesagegateshead.org.*
This amazing new addition to the riv-
erfront, likened to a giant stainless
steel armadillo, was built 1994–2004,
designed by Sir Norman Foster and Mott
MacDonald. It is home to the Northern
Sinfonia but hosts all kinds of musical
performances taking in every genre. Like

the BALTIC it offers fashionable cafés, bars, restaurants and wonderful views.

Castle Keep★
🕐 *Open daily.* £2.50. 📞*0191 232 7938, http://museums.ncl.ac.uk/keep.*
The city took its name from the 'new castle' built by William the Conqueror's son, Robert Curthose in 1080. The present keep is all that remains of its 12C successor and is a particularly good example of a Norman keep. From the roof of this massive stone edifice there is an all-embracing panorama of city, river and distant countryside.

City Centre★
Enlightened planning gave 19C Newcastle a new centre of classical dignity, comprising fine civic buildings, great covered markets and shopping arcades and spacious streets, of which the most splendid is **Grey Street★**, curving elegantly downhill from the high column of **Grey's Monument**, past the great portico of the Theatre Royal.

Laing Art Gallery★
New Bridge Street. 🕐 *Open daily.* 🅿*(charge).* 📞*0191 232 7734. www.twmuseums.org.uk*
The gallery's collection of English art emphasises the 19C, notably with the apocalyptic works of the visionary **John Martin**.

Great North Museum★
Barras Bridge. 📞*0191 222 6765. www.twmuseums.org.uk.*
This major new £26 million museum looks at global history and matters closer to home too. Highlights include a large-scale, interactive model of Hadrian's Wall, the wonder and diversity of the animal kingdom, life and death in Ancient Egypt, and spectacular objects from the Ancient Greeks. There will also be a planetarium and much more…

👥 Centre For Life
Times Square. 🕐 *Open daily.* £8. 🅿*(charge).* 📞*0191 243 8223. www.lifesciencecentre.org.uk.*

This new science centre, based on the theme of "life" offers live science shows, an interactive dome theatre, hands on displays, a simulator ride and family-based laboratory workshops.

EXCURSIONS
See HADRIAN'S WALL.

👥 Beamish, The North of England Open-Air Museum★★
10mi/16km south by any of the river bridges and the A 692 towards Consett. 🕐 *Opening times vary.* £16 (winter £6), child £10 (winter £6). 🅿✕. 📞*0191 370 4000. www.beamish.org.uk.*
As well as re-creating life in the north of England around the turn of the century this popular museum in its attractive countryside setting also evokes the environment of ordinary people at the start of the 19C, just as the full effect of the Industrial Revolution began to be felt in the region.
Preserved tramcars, supplemented by a pre-World War II motorbus, take visitors through the extensive site to the **town**, whose shops, houses, bank, working pub, sweet factory, newspaper office and printer's workshop, stocked and furnished authentically, and inhabited by costumed guides, evoke the urban scene of yesteryear. Visitors can also penetrate underground into a real mine.

ADDRESSES

🍴 PUBS AND RESTAURANTS
Jesmond Road, Shieldfield Road and Shields Road offer a variety of pubs. The *Evening Chronicle* gives details of pubs with live music, and of what is playing where. The Bigg Market area and Newcastle Chinatown offers a wide range of Indian and Chinese restaurants respectively, but for more details of restaurants see the tourist board website. For nightlife, Bigg Market, with over 160 pubs is popular with the youth of Newcastle. A young crowd flocks to the Quayside area for riotous nights out at the various bars and clubs.

SHOPPING

MetroCentre in Gateshead is open daily, and boasts over 300 shops and services. **Eldon Square**, a shopping mall, houses high street shops and department stores. **Eldon Garden** has a more fashionable range. Also worth a visit is **Northumberland Street**. **Monument Mall**, accessible directly from Monument Metro station. The **Vine Lane Antiques Market**, (Northumberland Street), the **Newcastle Antiques Centre** held in Grainger Street, or the southern area of Jesmond are musts. The finest traditional markets is the **Grainger Market** while Sunday shoppers can visit the new Quayside market, held on the Quayside under Tyne Bridge or the Jesmond Armstrong Bridge Arts Market.

ENTERTAINMENT

Listings can be found in the *Evening Chronicle* and *The Crack*. The Sage, the Theatre Royal, Northern Stage and the Journal Tyne Theatre host drama, music, opera and dance. **Metro Radio Arena** is the venue for major bands and spectacular shows and sporting events. **St James' Park** (www.nufc.premiumtv.co.uk) stadium, the home of Newcastle United football team, also welcomes visitors.

Richmond ★

North Yorkshire

This attractive country market town enjoys a beautiful location set at the foot of Swaledale on the north east edge of the Yorkshire Dales National Park.

> **Population:** 7,862.
> **Michelin Map:** Michelin Atlas p 45 or Map 502 O 20.
> **Info:** ℘01748 828 743. www.yorkshiredales.org.
> **Location:** 47mi/75km northwest of York.

TOWN

Richmond Castle ★

Opening times vary. £4. ℘01748 822 493. www.english-heritage.org.uk. The castle, begun 1071, stands on a cliff edge high above the river. The entrance is through the **keep**, built of grey Norman masonry (100ft/30m), stout enough to stand comparison with the White Tower in the Tower of London. An 11C arch leads into the courtyard. **Scolland's Hall**, built in 1080, is the second -oldest such building in England. From the roof of the keep there is a splendid **view** across the cobbled marketplace and over the moors.

The Georgian Theatre Royal and Museum ★

Victoria Road. Open Mon–Sat. £2.75. ℘01748 823 710. www.georgiantheatreroyal.co.uk. The only Georgian theatre in the country with its original form and features, it was opened in 1787 but fell "dark" in 1848 until being reopened in 1963.

EXCURSION

The Bowes Museum ★

Barnard Castle. Open year-round daily 10am–5pm. £7. Guided tours late May–Oct. ℘01833 690 606. www.bowesmuseum.org.uk. A French-designed château, set in landscaped gardens (20 acres/9ha) is an unexpected surprise in this area. It was built, from 1869 onwards, to house the extraordinary array of ceramics, pictures, tapestries, furniture and other *objets d'art* amassed by John Bowes and his French wife, Josephine.

Their treasures include novelties like an automated silver swan (*demonstrations once or twice a day; times displayed in the foyer*); its rippling neck, as it swoops to catch a wriggling fish in its beak, is remarkably lifelike. There are also paintings of the first rank: a magnificent St Peter by El Greco, part of an extensive collection of 15C–19C Spanish work; two Goyas, two Canalettos and works by Boudin and Courbet.

Ripon★

North Yorkshire

Ripon's cathedral qualifies its status as one of the smallest cities in England. The cathedral and large thriving market square (Thursday is the main market day) are the focus. At nine o'clock every night, a horn is blown to "set the watch", an ancient custom commemorates the responsibility of the medieval *Wakeman* for the safety of the citizens at night.

> **Population:** 13,806.
>
> **Michelin Map:** Michelin Atlas p 40 or Map 502 P 21.
>
> **Info:** Minster Road. ℘01765 604 625. www.ripon-internet.com. www.yorkshire dales.org/ripon.html.
>
> **Location:** Ripon is 11mi/ 18km north of Harrogate.

CITY

Ripon Cathedral★

Minster Road. Open daily 7.30am (8am Sat–Sun)–6.30pm. £3 contribution requested. Guided tour. ℘01765 604 108. www.riponcathedral.org.uk.

The cathedral was started in 1254 on the Saxon crypt of St Wilfrid's Church (AD 672). The imposing Early English west front has been called "the finest in England" (Pevsner). The medieval font stands near the west door in the south aisle. Above it are the remains of the great 14C east window shot out in 1643 by the Roundheads. The tiny **Saxon Crypt** (11ft x 8ft x 9ft high) was built by St Wilfrid on his return from Rome. **Misericords** and exquisite **choir stalls** were carved at the end of the 15C. The **Chapel of the Holy Spirit** has a striking modern metal screen, symbolising the Pentecostal "tongues of flame". The **Treasury** displays silverware given to the cathedral, as well as the "Ripon jewel", a Saxon gold brooch set with amber and garnets.

Market Square

This is one of the largest (2 acres/1ha) in the north of the country. The **Town Hall**, built by Wyatt in 1801, has an Ionic portico and carries along its frieze the motto "Except ye Lord Keep ye Cittie ye Wakeman Waketh in Vain." The **Wakeman's House**, a 14C two-storeyed, timber-framed house, was the home of the last holder of the office, Hugh Ripley, who in 1604 became first Mayor of Ripon.

Yorkshire Law and Order Museums

Open Apr–Oct and school hols daily 11am–4pm. £6 joint ticket. ℘01765 690 799. www.riponmuseums.co.uk.

Three museums in separate historic buildings in very close proximity to each other – the Courthouse Museum (*Minster Road*); the Prison Museum (*St Marygate*), and the Workhouse Museum (*Allhallowgate*) – together provide a fascinating interwoven insight into law and order and the harsh conditions in bygone days in this part of the world.

EXCURSIONS

See FOUNTAINS ABBEY.

Lightwater Valley

North Stainley, 3mi/5km N of Ripon, off A 6108. Open mid-Mar–Oct. Over 1.3 m tall £17.95. ℘0871 720 0011. www.lightwatervalley.co.uk.

This is one of the biggest theme parks in the north of England, with over 40 rides and attractions for all ages. The Ultimate is still the longest rollercoaster in Europe.

The adjacent **Lightwater Country Village** (open year-round from 10am) is a very popular complex of factory outlet **shops** and eating places, also home to a **Bird of Prey Centre** (open Apr–Sept 10am–5pm, Mar and Oct 10am–3pm, Nov 11am–3pm, Dec 10am–1pm; £3.50, child £2.50, £1.50 all tickets if booked with theme park ticket; ℘01765 635 010; www.lightwaterbirdsofprey.com), home to over 50 birds of prey, wallabies, pythons, tarantulas, dragons, lizards and 'creepy crawlies'.

Black Sheep Brewery

Masham, 8mi/13km north of Ripon by A 6108. ☐✕. *📞01765 680 101. www.blacksheep.co.uk.*

The Theakston family has maintained a long brewing tradition in Masham, and when the firm was taken over in 1989 Paul Theakston built this brewhouse in a former kiln. The tour shows the "tower" system, whereby the raw materials enter at the top and progress by gravity to the brew itself, at the bottom. A shop sells gifts on the black sheep theme.

The World of James Herriot

23 Kirkgate, Thirsk. 12mi/20km north-east by A 61. ☜£5.75. ☐✆. *📞01845 524 234. www.worldofjamesherriot.org.*

A tour of the house and surgery reveals the dedication of the vet-turned-author, who won the hearts of millions of viewers of the popular television series *All Creatures Great and Small*, based on a series of semi-autobiographical novels.

Newby Hall★

4mi/6km SE via the B 6265 and a minor road. ☜£11 (garden only, £8). ☐✕. *📞0845 450 4068. www.newbyhall.com.*

The original 17C mellow brick mansion, extended and remodelled during the 18C by John Carr and Robert Adam, is renowned for its Adam interiors, Gobelins **Tapestry Room**★ and gallery designed for a rare collection of Classical sculpture brought from Italy by William Weddell in 1765. From the south front of the house, **gardens** descend to the River Ure. A miniature passenger railway runs beside the river. There are also adventure gardens for children and a woodland walk.

Scarborough

North Yorkshire

Incongruously located on the chilly northeast coast, Scarborough claims to be Britain's first seaside resort. It reached its fashionable zenith in the late 19C/early 20C, and despite recent developments remains one of the best places in Britain to savour the Victorian seaside.

- ▶ **Population:** 38,809.
- ◔ **Michelin Map:** Michelin Atlas p 47 or Map 502 S 21.
- 🛈 **Info:** Brunswick Shopping Centre, Westborough. *📞01723 383636. www.discoveryorkshirecoast.com.*
- ▶ **Location:** 41mi/65km NE of York.

RESORT

Along the **seafront**, there are promenades, cliff railways, bridges spanning deep denes, pavilions, cafés, chalets, pretty little shelters and the great bulk of the refurbished **spa**, now an entertainment and conference centre. The elegant early 19C **Crescent** is home to **Scarborough Art Gallery**, (☜£2; ☐(charge); *📞01723 374 753; www.scarboroughmuseums.org.uk.*).

Just off North Bay Beach the ♟♟**Sea Life and Marine Sanctuary** (*Scalby Mills Road; ☜£12.95, child £9.95;* ☐☐(charge); ✕; *📞0871 423 2110; www.sealife.co.uk*), an underwater safari plus rescued animals, is one of the town's more interesting and educational family attractions.

EXCURSIONS

◔*See WHITBY.*

Flamborough Head★

20mi/32km southeast along the coast. The headland (215ft/66m), from which there are spectacular **views** out to sea and along the coast, is marked by a lighthouse. **North along the coast** (*Cleveland Way footpath*) is some outstanding chalk-cliff scenery; near **Bempton** the cliffs soar to 427ft/130m.

Robin Hood's Bay★

16mi/26km north on the A 171, then a minor road to the right (signposted). The little village in this picturesque bay was once the haunt of smugglers.

Sheffield

South Yorkshire

The fourth largest provincial city in England has been known since the 14C for the production of steel and fine cutlery. Today Sheffield remains an important manufacturing centre and the commercial and cultural focus of a wide region with splendidly revitalised art galleries, excellent night life and shopping.

- **Population:** 431,607.
- **Michelin Map:** Michelin Atlas p 35 or Map 502 P 23 – Local map Peak District.
- **Info:** 14 Norfolk Row. ℘0114 221 1900. www.yorkshiresouth.com.
- **Location:** Sheffield is 54mi/86km south of York.
- **Kids:** Weston Park Museum.

CITY
Millennium Galleries

Arundel Gate. ⏰ Open daily 10am (11am Sun)–5pm. ⚏Charge for temporary exhibitons only. ⏰ Closed Dec 24–26 and Jan 1. ℘0114 278 2600. ♿✕. www.museums-sheffield.org.uk.
Flanked by a **Winter Garden** and a **Peace Gardens** the Millennium Galleries form the new cutural heart of the post-millennium city. A light and spacious glass-and-white concrete building is home to three permanent galleries. **Craft and Design** showcases new work by contemporary makers and designers. The **Ruskin Gallery** includes over 900 paintings, watercolours and drawings. A fourth space is devoted to world-class **touring exhibitions**.

Graves Gallery
Surrey Street. ⏰Open year-round Mon–Sat 10am–5pm. Other details as Millennium Galleries, ♿above. ♿.
This attractive suite of galleries is known for its holding of 19C and 20C British and European art including works by famous names from Pablo Picasso and Pierre Bonnard to Sir Stanley Spencer and Helen Chadwick.

👥 Weston Park Museum
1 mi/1.6km from centre. Western Bank. ⏰ all details same as Millennium Galleries, ♿see above. ♿.
This eclectic new gallery showcases the city's varied and unusual treasures in a popular "fascinating histories and incredible facts" style with lots of hands-on exhibits ranging from Egyptian Mummies to living ants and bees.

Whitby

North Yorkshire

Once a centre for ship-building and whaling, Whitby is now a fishing port and holiday resort at the mouth of the River Esk. The east side is overlooked by the abbey ruins on the headland (the first few chapters of **Bram Stoker's** *Dracula* are set here. Whitby's beaches are popular for windsurfing.

- **Population:** 13,640.
- **Michelin Map:** Michelin Atlas p 47 or Map 502 S 20.
- **Info:** ℘01723 383 636. www.discoveryorkshirecoast.com.
- **Location:** 47mi/75km NE of York.

TOWN
Whitby Abbey★
EH. ⏰ Opening times vary. ⚏£4.90. ♿⊞✕. ℘01947 603 568. www.english-heritage.org.uk.

in AD 657 **St Hilda**, Abbess of Hartlepool, founded the first abbey and earned Whitby an outstanding reputation as a holy place. In 867 however, it was sacked by the Danes. Two centuries later it was re-founded by one of William the Conqueror's knights, Reinfrid, though the present ruins belong to a second re-building that took place between 1220 and 1320. It was finally suppressed under Henry VIII in 1539. All that now remains to be seen of this once-great abbey is the east front with typical early Gothic lancet windows, the grand Early English presbytery, the north transept and north wall of the nave with a door and windows in ornate 14C Decorated style and part of the west front, once surmounted by a large Perpendicular window.

Captain Cook Memorial Museum

Grape Lane. ⏰ *Open daily Mar, Apr–Oct.* ⊜£4. ♿. ✆*01947 601 900. www.cookmuseumwhitby.co.uk.*
The late-17C house of shipowner John Walker, where James Cook served as an apprentice, is now a museum celebrating

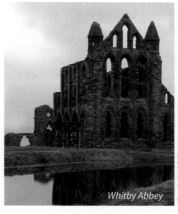

Whitby Abbey

© Timothy Smith/SXC

the years Cook spent in Whitby and his achievements as one of the world's greatest navigators. The tour ends in the attic where the young seaman had his quarters.

York★★★

North Yorkshire

York first came to prominence as a Roman capital, became capital of eastern England under the Danes and later became rich on the wool trade. York is marked by many elegant Georgian buildings that reflect the wealth of those moving from the north into what had become an important centre of social and cultural life. It is the survival of these and many much older buildings that draws hundreds of thousands of visitors here every year and has established the city as the tourist capital of northeastern England. It is famous for its Minster, its wonderful railway museum and its many ghost walks.

A BIT OF HISTORY

In AD 71 the Roman Ninth Legion built a fortress, **Eboracum**, later capital of the northern province, and here in AD 306 Constantine the Great was proclaimed Emperor. After the departure of the Romans the Anglo-Saxons made

▶ **Population:** 123,126.
⚲ **Michelin Map:** Michelin Atlas p 40 or Map 502 Q 22.
🛈 **Info:** York Railway Station; De Grey Rooms, Exhibition Square. Both: ✆01904 55 00 99. www.visityork.org.
◖ **Location:** 84 mi/134 km S of Newcastle-upon-Tyne; 25mi/40km NE of Leeds. The train station is just outside the city walls. Buses call in the vicinity. Most attractions are within the old walls, easily explored on foot. Try a York City Sightseeing hop-on open-top bus tour (✆*01904 655 585; www. yorktourbuses. co.uk*).
☺ **Don't Miss:** The stained glass in York Minster; National Railway Museum; The Shambles; Castle Howard.
⏰ **Timing:** Two–three days.
👪 **Kids:** National Railway Museum; JorvikViking Centre.

Eoforwic the capital of their Kingdom of Northumbria. In AD 866 the Vikings captured the city and made it **Jorvik**, one of their chief trading bases.

The prosperity of medieval York, a city of 10,000 people and 40 churches, was based on wool. York was once the richest city in the country after London. With the decline of the wool trade after the Wars of the Roses (1453–87) and following the Dissolution of the Monasteries (16C) the city's prosperity waned.

YORK MINSTER★★★

Minster, Undercroft, Treasury, Crypt: Open Mon–Sat 9am (9.30am November–March)–5pm (last entry). Sun noon–3.45pm (last entry). ○ *Closed for sightseeing Good Fri, Easter Sun, 24–25 Dec.* ⊜*Minster £6; Undercroft, Treasury and Crypt £4; Tower £4; Minster plus either of above £8; combined ticket all areas £9.50.* ⬩⬩ *Guided tours Mon–Sat (free).* ⬩✗. ℘*01904 557 200. www.yorkminster.org.*

The Minster is the largest Gothic church north of the Alps (534ft/160m long; 249ft/76m wide across the transepts; 90ft/27m from floor to vault; 198ft/60m to the tops of the towers).

The nave, built 1291–1350, is in Decorated style; the transepts of the mid-13C are the oldest visible parts of the present building. The **Chapter House**★★,

octagonal with a magnificent wooden vaulted ceiling, is late 13C. The late-15C **Choir Screen**★★ is by William Hyndeley. Its central doorway is flanked by statues of English kings from William the Conqueror onwards. The finest monument in the Minster is the **tomb** (1) of the man who began the present building, **Archbishop Walter de Gray**.

Stained Glass★★★

The Minster contains the largest single collection of medieval stained glass to have survived in England. The **West Window** (2) was painted in 1339 by Master Robert. It was the largest in the Minster at the time but was surpassed by the **East Window** (3) in the Lady Chapel, painted by John Thornton of Coventry 1405–08. It is the largest expanse of medieval glass in the country and revitalised the York school of glass painting. The **Five Sisters Window** (4), lancets of grisaille glass from c. 1250, is the oldest window still in its original place in the Minster.

The **Pilgrimage Window** (5), c. 1312, shows grotesques, a monkey's funeral and scenes of hunting. Next to it is the **Bellfounders Window** (6), given by Richard Tunnoc, buried in the Minster in 1330. He is depicted presenting his window to the Archbishop, amongst scenes of casting and tuning a bell. The

Choir Screen, York Minster

Jesse Window (7), depicting Jesus' family tree, dates from 1310.

A real insight behind the scenes of maintaining the cathedral is provided by two new visitor attractions unveiled in 2009. **Bedern Glaziers' Studio**, built in the 13C as the chapel of the College of Vicars Choral, is a new workshop space for the **York Minster Glaziers**, the team of craftspeople who are responsible for the preservation and conservation of the stained glass. Here for the first time they will go about their delicate work in full view of the public, (⏰ *open by guided tour only, Wed and Fri 2pm, depart from from the group desk in the Minster; tours last 1hr and are limited to max 10 people so booking advisable;* ♿; ✆ *01904 557 216;* 👁*£5).*

Just as fascinating and with a chance to literally explore the face of the Minster is the **Stoneyard Tour**. The Stoneyard is where the Minster's stonemasons and carvers repair the widespread erosion of the stonework. As well as a tour of the workshop in full flow, visitors can ascend the east front scaffolding in the workmen's lift, wearing hard hats, and get a bird's eye view of both the stonework, before and after repair, and the city of York way down below (⏰*open by booked guided tour only, call* ✆*01904 557 216 for all details).*

The more conventional way of ascending the tower is internally via 275 steps.

Treasurer's House

NT. Minster Yard. ⏰ *Open Mar–Nov Sat–Thu 11am–4.30pm (Nov 3pm).* 👁*£5.90 house, £7.20 house and cellar.* 👁*Ghost tours of cellar daily* 👁*£2.05.* ♿✕. ✆ *01904 624 247. www.nationaltrust.org.uk.*

Re-built in the 17C and 18C, this features a magnificent series of rooms with furniture and pictures from many periods. The **Great Hall** has had its false ceiling removed, and has an unusual staircase c. 1700. The early 18C ceiling in the **Dining Room** has decorated beams and panels.

A fascinating collection of 18C drinking vessels illustrates the skill and ingenuity of the glass-maker.

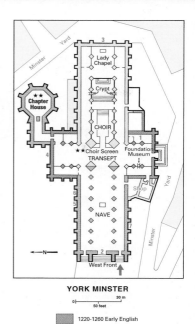

YORK MINSTER

0 ————— 30 m
0 ————— 50 feet

▨ 1220-1260 Early English
▦ 1280-1350 Decorated
▢ 1361-1472 Perpendicular

THE WALLED TOWN
The Walls★★

The walls (3mi/5km) embrace virtually the whole of medieval York. The **Multangular Tower**, western corner of the Roman fort, still stands in the Yorkshire Museum Gardens (👁*see below*). The 13C walls follow the course of the Roman wall to the north of the Minster and are built atop the earthen bank raised by the Anglo-Danish kings. Where roads entered the city through the earthen bank the Normans built fortified gateways, now known as "bars". **Bootham Bar** is on the site of the Roman gateway. The walls lead around the Deanery Garden to **Monk Bar** and on to Aldgate; here a swampy area and the River Foss constituted the defences. Brick-built walls, c. 1490, run from **Red Tower**, pass **Walmgate** around the south of York Castle to **Fishergate Postern**, built in 1505 on what was then the riverbank. Here York Castle took up the defences. Beyond Skeldergate Bridge and **Baile Hill**, the walls resume to **Micklegate**

YORK

0 — 200 m
0 — 200 yards

WHERE TO STAY

Acer.................................. ②
Crook Lodge.................... ④

WHERE TO EAT

Blackwell Ox Inn.............. ①
Melton's Too.................... ③
The Tasting Room........... ⑤

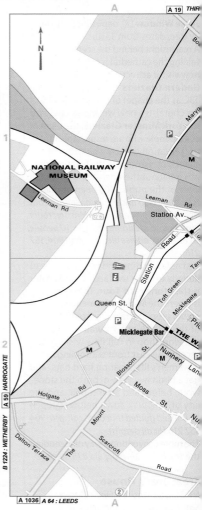

N

A 19 THIR

NATIONAL RAILWAY MUSEUM

Leeman Rd

Leeman Rd

Station Av.

Station Road

Queen St.

Micklegate Bar

THE W

A 59 HARROGATE
B 1224 : WETHERBY

Holgate Rd

Blossom St.

Moss St.

Nunnery Lane

Dalton Terrace

The Mount

Scarcroft

Road

A 1036 A 64 : LEEDS

Bar, traditional point of entry of the monarch into York, and where the severed heads of traitors were exposed after execution. From here the walls turn northeast and lead to the North Street Postern (BY), where the ferry crossed the Ouse before Lendal Bridge was built.

York Castle Museum★

🕐 Open daily 9.30am (10am Fri school term)–5pm. 🕐 Closed Jan 1 and Dec 25–26. ✆£7.50. ♿✗. ☎01904 687 687. www.yorkcastlemuseum.org.uk.
In what was the **Debtors Prison** and the **Female Prison**, two striking build-

ings from 1705 and 1777 respectively, there is now a museum of everyday life. The highlight is its recreated Victorian street, which combines real shop fittings and stock, with sound and light effects which evoke the period atmosphere. Half Moon Court is an authentic reproduction of an Edwardian street.
A prize exhibit is the **Coppergate Helmet**, a Saxon relic (c. AD 750), made of iron with brass fittings. It probably belonged to a Northumbrian noble. There are costumes, period rooms, pubs and shops as well as the actual cell in which legendary highwayman

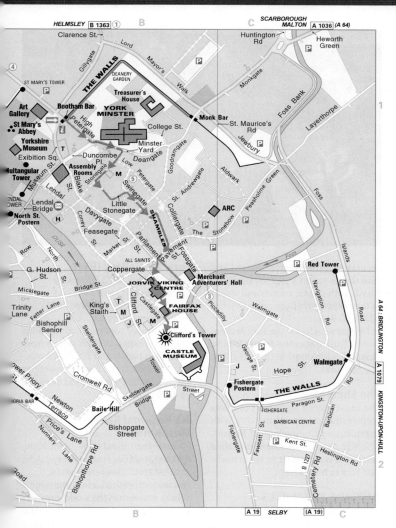

Dick Turpin was held before execution in 1739.

Fairfax House★

Castlegate. ◷ *Open mid-Feb–Dec Sat–Thu 11am (1.30pm Sun)–4.30pm. Fri by guided tour only 11am and 2pm.* ◷*Dec 24–26.* ✆£6. ☎01904 655 543. *www.fairfaxhouse.co.uk.*

Perhaps the finest Georgian town house in England, Fairfax House was built by in 1755. It houses a collection of Georgian furniture, paintings, clocks and porcelain, and there are displays of eating and dining in 18C England.

Jorvik Viking Centre★

Coppergate. ◷ *Open daily. Apr–Oct 10am–5pm. Nov–Mar 10am–4pm.* ◷*Closed 25–26 Dec.* ✆£8.50, child £6. *Pre-booking recommended in peak season to avoid queues (charge).* ☎01904 543 400, ☎01904 615 505. *www.jorvik-viking-centre.co.uk.*

During building work in the late 1970s archeologists uncovered four rows of buildings from the Viking town, with remarkably well-preserved items, including boots and shoes, pins, plants and insects. Two rows now illustrate an archeological "dig" and two have been

National Railway Museum

National Railway Museum

accurately reconstructed. "Time Cars" take the visitor on a journey back into Jorvik, with sights, sounds and smells as they would have been on an October day in AD 948.

In February each year the York Archeological Trust stages the **Jorvik Viking Festival**, with longship races, feasting and fireworks.

The Shambles★

The most visited amongst the many picturesque streets of the city, with overhanging timber-framed houses. Also visit nearby **Pavement**, so called because it was the first street in medieval York to be paved.

OUTSIDE THE WALLS

Immediately outside the line of the old walls, west of the Minster next to the River Ouse, is **Museum Gardens**, home to the ruins of **St Mary's Abbey** and the 14C **Hospitium** (⊶ no public access); one of the oldest surviving half-timbered buildings in York, this was originally a guest house for the abbey. By contrast is the Classical 19C building housing the **Yorkshire Museum** (⊙ open year-round daily 10am–5pm; ⊙ closed Dec 25–26 Dec and Jan 1; ⊜£5; ₺; ℘ 01904 687687; www.yorkshiremuseum.org.uk) which displays some of the city's finest Roman, Viking and medieval treasures. It also has an observatory (⊙ open 11.30am–2.30pm; ₺).

York Art Gallery (BY)

Exhibition Square. ⊙ *Open daily 10am–5pm.* ⊙ *Closed 1 Jan and 25–26 Dec.* ₺✕. ℘ 01904 687 687. *www.yorkartgallery.org.uk.*

This extensive collection of paintings spans over 600 years and ranges from 14C Italian panels and 17C Dutch masterpieces to Victorian narrative paintings and 20C century works by LS Lowry and David Hockney.

▲▲ National Railway Museum★★★

⊙ *Open year-round daily 10am–6pm.* ⊙ *Closed 24–26 Dec. Parking (charge).* ₺✕. ℘ 08704 214 001. www.nrm.org.uk.

This magnificent collection, the largest railway museum in the world, presents the history of the railways in the country of their invention. The Great Hall, a wonderfully spacious former locomotive shed, houses an array of locomotives from clunky early 19C machines to the sleek super-trains of the 21C.

However the museum's brief extends beyond the glamour of machines like these to the whole technology and culture of the railway, demonstrated by an extraordinarily rich and varied array of other related objects. The South Hall recreates the atmosphere of a mid-20C mainline station, allowing close inspection of engine cabs, the interiors of coaches, both primitive and luxurious, dining and sleeping cars, goods wagons and road vehicles. Outside are more treasures undergoing or awaiting restoration, plus a miniature railway.

EXCURSIONS
Castle Howard★★

15mi/24km northeast via the A 64.
Castle: Open mid-Mar–early-Nov and late Nov–Christmas hols daily 10am (11am house)–4pm (last admission).
Grounds: Open 10am–6.30pm (winter 4.30pm/dusk). £11 (Gardens only £8.50; low season £4.50). Guided tours house and garden Mar–Nov daily 11am–3pm (free). 01653 648 333. www.castlehoward.co.uk.

Remarkably Castle Howard, **Sir John Vanbrugh's** tour de force, was the first building he had ever designed.

The landscaping of the surrounding **park**★★★ is one of the most grandiose landscaping projects ever; it consists of a series of compositions focused on some of the most ambitious and beautiful garden structures ever built, notably the **Temple of the Four Winds**, and, crowning a distant rise, a colossal colonnaded **Mausoleum** by Hawksmoor. The woodland garden presents rare trees, shrubs, rhododendrons and azaleas.

The striking entrance to the house, topped by a painted and gilded dome (80ft/24m), is familiar to many as the castle was used as the principal location for the TV series *Brideshead Revisited*.

The **statuary** in the **Grand Entrance** is remarkable, particularly the **altar** from the Temple of Delphi.

The heart of the house is the **Great Hall**, which rises through two storeys into the painted dome. In the **Long Gallery** and its **Octagon** are pictures by Lely, Kneller and Van Dyck and two **Holbeins** – the portrait of **Henry VIII** shows a stricken monarch, painted in 1542, just after the execution of Catherine Howard. The magnificent stained-glass windows in the **Chapel** are by the 19C artist Sir Edward Burne-Jones. The **Stable Court** presents period costume (17C on).

ADDRESSES

STAY

Acer, *52 Scarcroft Hill.* 01904 653 839. www.acerhotel.co.uk. This pretty, terraced Victorian house a few minutes walk from the city centre offers immaculate traditional rooms and a warm welcome.

Crook Lodge, *26 St Mary's, Bootham.* 01904 655 614. http://crooklodge.yorkwebsites.co.uk. Pretty bedrooms in an attractive Victorian house enjoying a quiet city centre location, with private car park.

EAT

The Tasting Room, *13a Swinegate Court East.* 01904 627 879. www.thetastingroom.co.uk. Nestled in a quaint courtyard, try fresh home-prepared food within a spacious and contemporary funky, chatty environment.

Melton's Too, *25 Walmgate.* 01904 629 222. www.melton-stoo.co.uk. Cafe-bistro offspring of York's famous Melton's restaurant set in a charming 17C building and specialising in tapas and other eclectic good-value dishes.

Blackwell Ox Inn, *Huby Road, Sutton-on-the-Forest (8mi/13km north of York).* 01347 810 328. www.blackwelloxinn.co.uk. Worth the journey for the food in either the restaurant or the bar of this country house-like pub.

PUBS AND RESTAURANTS

The Riverside between the Lendal Bridge and Ouse Bridge, Micklegate Bar, Stonegate Walk and Swinegate are all worth exploring.

SHOPPING

Browse elegant Edwardian shops and beautiful Mulberry Hall for china and crystal in Stonegate.

ENTERTAINMENT

The Grand Opera House, the Theatre Royal and the Barbican Centre host dance, opera, musicals and drama.

Yorkshire Dales★

North Yorkshire

Northwest of the great manufacturing towns of Leeds and Bradford lie the Yorkshire Dales (valleys), featuring dramatic limestone scenery, crags, caves, and swallow holes in which streams disappear. In the broad dales such as Airedale, Wensleydale and Wharfedale the stone-built villages are set harmoniously in an ancient pattern of stone-walled fields. Most of the area is preserved in the **Yorkshire Dales National Park** (680sq mi/1,760sq km).

⚓ WALKING

The Dales are a walker's paradise crisscrossed with paths and a specially designated cycleway. The four main recognised routes are: the **Nidderdale Way** (53mi/85km) starting and finishing in Pateley Bridge; the **Dales Way** (80mi/129km), from Ilkley to Bowness-on-Windermere in the Lake District, passing through Wharfedale, Langstrothdale and Dentdale; the challenging **Yorkshire Three Peaks Way** (24.5mi/39km), taking in Penyghent, Whernside and Ingleborough; and the **Pennine Way**, at 268mi/429km the ultimate Yorkshire route, which passes through Airedale, Malhamdale, and the Three Peaks. The idea is not to complete any of these, but to dip in and out for as little or as long as you wish, using public transport to get you back to the start. All four have dedicated websites (*www.yorkshiredales.org/walking.html*) which offer good advice. Or simply pick up walking information at your nearest tourist information office which will be well-used to walkers' requests.

SIGHTS

Skipton is a good base from which to explore the Yorkshire Dales, perhaps by boat, on the trans-Pennine **Leeds–Liverpool Canal** (*operates daily Easter–Oct; ℘01756 790829; www.canaltrips.co.uk*).

- ⓘ **Michelin Map:** Michelin Atlas pp 39 or Map 502 N, O 21 and 22.
- ⓘ **Info:** There are 19 information centres in the Dales. For full details visit www.yorkshiredales.org.
- ⓘ **Kids:** White Scar Caves; Yorkshire Dales Falcony Centre.

Skipton Castle★ (*open daily Mar–Sept 10am–6pm; Oct–Feb 10am–4pm; Sun (year-round) open noon; £6; ℘01756 792 442; www.skiptoncastle.co.uk*) is one of the most complete and best-preserved medieval castles in England. The beautiful **Conduit Court** was built by the 10th Earl. Its present appearance owes much to mid-17C restoration.

Just outside Skipton, **Bolton Priory★** (*open daily 8am–dusk or 4-4.30pm; ℘01756 710 238*) was founded by the Augustinians c. 1154, in a setting of great beauty on a bend of the River Wharfe. At the Dissolution, the lead was stripped from all the roofs except for the gatehouse and the nave of the church, which still functions as a thriving parish church.

Further afield, **White Scar Caves** (*Ingleton; open from 10am by guided tour (80 min, 1mi/1.6km) daily Feb–Oct, weekends Nov–Jan, weather permitting; last tour 4pm; £7.95, child £4.95; ℘01524 241 244; www.whitescarcave.co.uk*) is a vast show-cave, the longest in England. It includes a massive ice-age cavern, underground waterfalls and streams and stalactites galore.

The **Yorkshire Dales Falconry and Conservation Centre** (*Crows Nest, near Giggleswick, northwest of Skipton on the A 65 via Settle; open year-round daily 10am–4.30pm. closed Jan 1 and 25–26 Dec; £5.90, child £3.90; ℘ 01729 822 832.;www.dalesfalconry.f9.co.uk*) overlooking dramatic dales scenery. Eagles, vultures, hawks, falcons, owls and kites give regular flying demonstrations.

Yorkshire Moors★

North Yorkshire

The beauty of this expanse of open moorland lies in its wildness. The heather-covered high ground stretches southeast from industrial Middlesbrough to Whitby and Scarborough on the coast and to Pickering and Helmsley in the south. Much of the land is embraced by the **North York Moors National Park.**

◣ WALKING

Four regional walking routes have been designed by the National Park Authority with a short holiday/long weekend in mind, and are an easy and enjoyable way to explore the North York Moors National Park. These are the **Esk Valley Walk**, the **Tabular Hills Walk**, the **Hambleton Hillside Mosaic Walk** and the **Newtondale Horse Trail**. These avoid roads wherever possible and link with local services such as bus routes. Maps and specialist guidebooks are available from the park shop or online. You don't have to complete any of these, just dip in and out for as little or as long as you wish. Serious walkers may also llike to consider the **Cleveland Way National Trail** and The **North Sea Trail**, both of which have their own websites (*access via www.visitnorthyorkshire-moors.co.uk*)

SIGHTS

The southern gateway to the North York Moors, **Hemlsley** is an attractive village boasting the impressive 12C–13C ruins of **Helmsley Castle** *(EH; ◯open summer daily 10am–6pm. Thu–Mon Oct 10am–5pm & Nov–Mar 4pm; ☜£3.90; ♿▣(charge); ℘01439 770 442; www.english-heritage.org.uk)*. Below it, **Helmsley Walled Garden** (◯ *open Good Fri–Oct daily 10.30am–5pm; Nov–Mar visit website for times; ☜£4; ♿▣✕; ℘01439 771 427; www.helmsleywalledgarden.co.uk)*, has fruit trees and herbaceous borders herb and ornamental gardens

---

⚜ Michelin Map: Michelin Atlas pp 46 and 47 or Map 502 Q, R, S 20 and 21.

▯ Info: Danby. ℘01439 772 737. Old Town Hall, Market Place, Helmsley. ℘01439 770173; 58 Market Place, Malton. ℘01653 600048. The Ropery, Pickering. ℘01751 473791. www.yorkshirevisitor.com. www.visitnorthyorkshire moors.co.uk. www.york shiremoorsandcoast.com.

---

glasshouses, ponds and fountains. 3mi/5km northwest of Helmsley on the B1257 lie the majestic ruins of **Rievaulx Abbey★★** *(EH; ◯ open Apr–Sept daily 10am–6pm. Oct Thu–Mon 10am–5pm, Nov–Mar Thu–Mon 10am–4pm; ☜£4.90; ▣✕; ℘01439 798 228; www.english-heritage.org.uk.* Pronounced "ree-voh", this was the first major monastery built by the Cistercian, founded c. 1132, with the monastic buildings ompleted in the late 12C. A complex of monastic buildings – infirmary, chapel, kitchens and a warming house – give an idea of the community's work and house an exhibition on the abbey's history.

Nearby **Rievaulx Terrace and Temples** *(NT; ◯open daily Mar–Oct 11am–5pm; ☜£4.50; ℘01439 798 340, 01439 748283 (winter); www.nationaltrust.org.uk)* is one of Yorkshire's finest 18C landscape gardens, featuring classical Georgian temples and a long curving grass terrace with fine views.

Some 12 mi/19km east, sheep nibble the grass verges in the charming village of **Hutton-le-Hole**. The **Ryedale Folk Museum** (◯*open year-round daily. 10am–5.30pm, Nov–Mar dusk; ◯closed early Dec–mid-Jan. ☜£5.25; ♿; ℘01751 417 367; www.ryedalefolkmuseum.co.uk)* houses a collection of rural bygones.

The ruins of **Rosedale Abbey** (12C) lie at the bottom of the steep (1:3) north slope which gives a magnificent panoramic **view**★ across the moors.

SCOTLAND

This fiercely patriotic nation entered the 21C bearing a new identity, most vigorously represented by the new Scottish Parliament, a symbol of a country intent on self-rule, if not independence. The old cultural trappings of shortbread and tartan, tweed and heather, kilts and bagpipes, haggis and whisky remain, but are joined by modern icons like the "Armadillo" concert centre at Glasgow. Perthshire is a European adventure sports capital, while the country as a whole has become a fashionable get-away-from-it-all holiday destination.

Highlights

1. Ascend **Cairn Gorm** and walk or ski its slopes (p387).
2. Stroll **Edinburgh**'s Royal Mile from castle to palace (p393).
3. Discover the secrets of the **Burrell Collection** (p411).
4. Traverse the **Caledonian canal** in search of Loch Ness (p417).
5. Take in the scenery from **Kyle of Lochalsh** to **Gairloch** (p437).

Edinburgh, Lothians and Fife

You may hear as many English as Scottish voices in the nation's most beautiful and cultured city, but this is the gateway to Scottish history. The ancient kingdom of Fife is the ancestral home of Scottish monarchs, and is of course world-famous for its golf.

- **Dunfermline**
- **Edinburgh**
- **St Andrews**

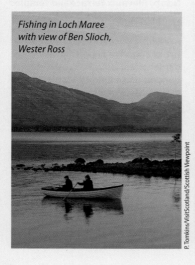

Fishing in Loch Maree with view of Ben Slioch, Wester Ross

P. Tomkins/VisitScotland/Scottish Viewpoint

Borders and Southwest

The gentle rolling countryside of the Borders makes an easy transition from England but the many (now-Romantic) ruins and castles tell of a turbulent history.

To the west, unspoiled Dumfries and Galloway is best known for its Robert Burns connections and golf. A short ferry trip away, the Isle of Arran is the tonic for the stresses of modern life.

- **Isle of Arran**
- **Ayr**
- **Dumfries**
- **Inveraray**
- **Jedburgh**
- **Tweed Valley**

Argyll and the Western Isles

Scotland's west-coast islands have a magic and identity all their own with elemental beauty and equally elemental weather, well-known to walkers and nature watchers. This is not an easy land to visit or inhabit but discovery brings lasting rewards.

- **Isle of Iona**
- **Isle of Mull**
- **Oban**
- **Isle of Skye**
- **Western Isles**

Glasgow and Central Scotland

Glasgow is a buzzing city; an exciting mix of year-round arts and culture, stylish places to eat and stay and some of the best shopping in the UK.

In Stirlingshire, Perthshire and particularly the Trossachs you will find the picture-postcard Scotland of mountains and glens, stags and eagles and the Highland Games. William Wallace, Robert the Bruce, Mary Queen of Scots and Rob Roy made the history of this region, while Sir Walter Scott mythologised it.

- **Dundee**
- **Glamis**
- **Glasgow**
- **Perth**
- **Pitlochry**
- **Stirling**
- **Trossachs**

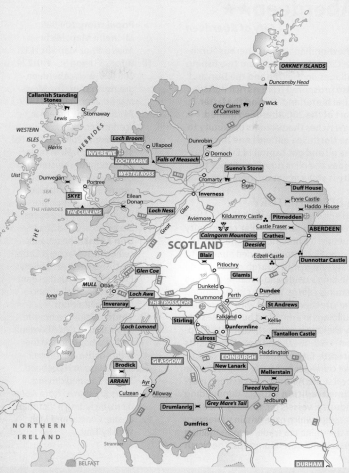

Highlands and Islands

Picture-postcard Scotland comes to life in the Highlands with majestic scenery, awesome wilderness, towering mountains, and broad expanses of shimmering water, none more famous than Loch Ness. John O'Groats may feel like the end of the world but beyond lie the 70 or so scattered islands that make up the Orkneys. Northernmost of all, the Shetland are a blend of Scotland and Norway, surprisingly varied for such a small area and often truly spectacular. Both island groups have a deep sense of history and boast some of Europe's oldest prehistoric monuments.

🜨 **Cairngorms** 🜨 **Inverness**

🜨 **Orkney Isl** 🜨 **Shetland Isl.**
🜨 **Wester Ross** 🜨 **Wick**

Aberdeen and Grampians

The beautiful Grampian region, famous for its turreted castles, malt whisky distilleries, dramatic mountains rugged coastlines, and Royal Deeside, beloved of Queen Victoria, has long been a firm favourite with visitors. Less well known, largely on account of its relative isolation is Aberdeen, Scotland's third city, grown wealthy and sophisticated on oil wealth.

🜨 **Aberdeen**
🜨 **Banff** 🜨 **Elgin**
🜨 **Grampian Castles**

Aberdeen★★

City of Aberdeen

The dignified and prosperous "Granite City", developed from two fishing villages on the Dee and the Don and also prospered from its rich agricultural hinterland. During the latter part of the 20C Aberdeen gained new riches thanks to its proximity to the North Sea oilfields and became the oil and gas capital of Europe. Today the oil is running out but the city is still a major offshore centre.

A BIT OF HISTORY

An episcopal city by the 12C, Old Aberdeen had a large secular community outside its precincts; in the late 15C Bishop Elphinstone founded a university. A second distinct burgh grew around the King's castle and became an active trading centre. As the city expanded the streets were lined with impressive buildings in a dignified but simple style by the native architect, Archibald Simpson (1790–1847), who gave Aberdeen its **Granite City** nickname and its distinctive character by his masterly use of the local stone. Aberdeen has a strong **maritime tradition** with its shipbuilding industry: vessels for whaling, the Clipper ships which gave Britain supremacy in the China tea trade, wooden sailing vessels and iron steamships. The North

▶ **Population:** 204,885.

Michelin Map: Michelin Atlas p 69 or Map 501 N 12.

Info: 23 Union St. ℘01224 288 828. www.aberdeen-grampian.com. The Mews, Mar Rd, Braemar. ℘01339 741 600. www.braemar scotland.co.uk.

Location: 126mi/203km NE of Edinburgh. Most major attractions are clustered in Old Aberdeen and the city centre. The train station and the bus station (for local and inter-city buses) are both on Guild Street.

Don't Miss: The heraldic ceiling in St Machar's Cathedral; Aberdeen Art Gallery; Pitmedden Gardens, Grampian castles; a Highland Games gathering.

Timing: Allow an hour to stroll around Old Aberdeen. and two hours to see the sights of the city centre.

Kids: Maze at Hazlehead.

Trails: Themed driving tours are signed from Aberdeen, including a Victorian, Castle, Coastal and Malt Whisky Trail.

Union Street at night

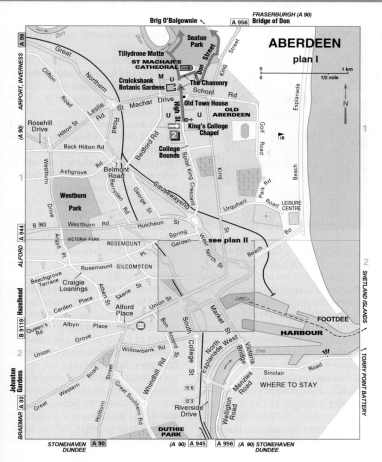

ABERDEEN
plan I

FRASERBURGH (A 90)
Bridge of Don A 956

Brig O'Balgownie
Seaton Park
Tillydrone Motte
ST MACHAR'S CATHEDRAL
Cruickshank Botanic Gardens
The Chanonry
Old Town House
OLD ABERDEEN
King's College Chapel
College Bounds

Sea has brought prosperity with the growth of fisheries – whaling from the 1750s, the herring boom in the 1870s and white fishing in the present day. More recently Aberdeen has become the "offshore capital of Europe" for the North Sea oil industry and exploration and supply base activities continue to play an important role.

WALKING TOURS

2 OLD ABERDEEN★★

Aberdeen's medieval streets capture the essence of the old town, which became a burgh of barony in 1489, a status retained until 1891. The North Sea provided growth in the 18–19C in the form of fisheries.

Start at **King's College Chapel**★ *(Admission by door in Quadrangle; 25 High Street;* open Mon–Fri; *closed Christmas and New Year;* ; *01224 272 137; abdn.ac.uk).* The only original building left of Bishop Elphinstone's university in its campus setting. Outstanding features are a delicate Renaissance **crown spire**★★★, the tinctured arms on the west front buttresses (including those of James IV and his queen, Margaret Tudor) and rare, richly carved **medieval fittings**★★★. At the crossroads stands the **Old Town House** (Y), an attractive 18C Georgian house. Beyond is The Chanonry, a walled precinct for the residences of the bishop and other clerics. From the Chapel, walk up the High Street past the **Old Town House**, **Chanonry** and **Cruickshank Botanic Gardens** to

Crown spire, King's College

B. Kaufmann/MICHELIN

get to **St Machar's Cathedral**★★ *(The Chanonry;* ⏱*open Apr–Oct daily;* ♿*;* ℘*01224 485 988; www.stmachar.com),* whose twin spires have long been one of the landmarks of Old Aberdeen.

The cathedral which dates from the 14C and 15C was built "overlooking the crook of the Don" in compliance with instructions from St Columba. The impressive exterior is complemented by a splendid 16C **heraldic ceiling**★★★.

The brightly-coloured coats of arms present a vision of the European scene around 1520. The early 14C **Brig o'Balgownie**★ (approach via Don Street – V), with its pointed Gothic arch and a defensive kink at the south end, is one of Aberdeen's most important medieval structures.

1 CITY CENTRE

Start at the **Maritime Museum**★ *(Provost Ross's House, Shiprow;* ⏱*open daily;* ♿*;* ℘*01224 337 700; www.aagm.co.uk).* The museum is located in two 16C town houses bordering Shiprow, a medieval thoroughfare winding up from the harbour. Ship models, paintings, artefacts and interactive displays trace local maritime industries.

Follow Shiprow round to Union Street and turn right towards **Castlegate**. The medieval market place was situated here. Notable features are the Mannie Fountain (1706), a reminder of the city's first water supply, and the splendid **Mercat Cross**★★ dating from 1686 and decorated with a unicorn, a frieze, and royal portrait medallions and coats of arms. It was the place for public punishment and proclamations.

Behind the 19C **Town House** on Castle Street rises the tower of the 17C **Tolbooth** *(*⏱*open early Jul–mid-Sept Tue–Sat, Sun;* ♿*;* ℘*01224 621 167; www.aagm.co.uk),* which houses exhibits on the history of crime and punishment within the city.

Handsome **Marischal Street** extends south from Castle Street. It was laid out in 1767–68 with houses built to a uniform three storeys and attic design.

Return to Castle Street and turn left, then right on Broad Street for **Marischal College**★, founded in the 16C by and amalgamated with the older King's College to form Aberdeen University; it has a striking 20C granite façade. **Marischal Museum** *(*⟲*closed until summer 2010;* ℘*01224 274 301; www.abdn.ac.uk)* tells the history and prehistory of Northeast Scotland with fine ethnographical collections.

At the end of Broad Street turn left onto Upper Kirkgate for **Provost Skene's House**★ *(Guestrow, between Broad Street and Flourmill Lane;* ⏱*open year-round Mon–Sat 10am–5pm;* ⏱*closed 1–2 Jan and 25–26 Dec;* ✕*;* ℘*01224 641 086; www.aagm.co.uk),* a 17C town house containing tastefully furnished period rooms and elaborate plasterwork ceilings and panelling. The chapel

Aberdeen "The Flower of Scotland"

Aberdeen's parks and gardens are justly famous. Try to see: **Union Terrace Gardens** (YZ – off Union Street) with their celebrated floral displays including Aberdeen's coat of arms; the splendid **Winter Gardens** in Duthie Park (X); the rose garden and maze at **Hazlehead**▲▲; the delightful **Johnston Gardens** and the university's **Cruickshank Botanic Gardens** (V).

Balmoral Castle

©Louise McGilvray/Fotolia.com

boasts an outstanding 17C painted **ceiling**★★ of New Testament scenes. Continue on Upper Kirkgate towards the **Aberdeen Art Gallery**★★ *(Schoolhill;* 🕐 *open daily;* 👨‍🦽✕; ℘*01224 523 700; www.aagm.co.uk),* whose permanent collection has a strong emphasis on contemporary art. Various works of art are displayed in its elegant marble-lined interior. The **Scottish Collection** includes important works by local artists. The **Macdonald Collection**★★ of British artists' portraits is a survey of the art world in the 19C.

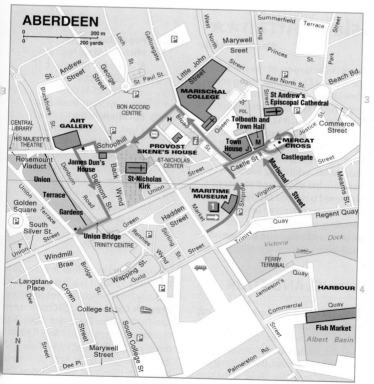

EXCURSIONS
Deeside★★

Deeisde may be explored by following the A 93 west from Aberdeen. Allow at least a day to see the splendid valley of the salmon-rich Dee, which penetrates deep into the Grampian Mountains (*see GRAMPIAN CASTLES*).

30mi/48km west of Aberdeen, the green at **Aboyne** forms the setting for colourful **Highland Games** in August. About 19mi/30km further on you come to **Balmoral Castle** (*open Apr–Jul daily 10am–5pm; £7; guided tours of garden (free) Wed 2pm; 01339 742 334; www.balmoralcastle.com*), which has been the summer residence of the Royal Family since Queen Victoria's reign.

Continuing on the A 93 for 10mi/16km you will find **Braemar**. Like neighbouring Balmoral, Braemar has its own **castle**, (*open Easter–Oct Sat–Sun 11am–5pm; £5; 013397 41600 www.braemarscotland.co.uk*), but is better known for the **Braemar Highland Gathering**, held annually in September and normally attended by royalty. At the road's end is the famous beauty spot of Linn o'Dee, where, in season, salmon may be seen leaping.

Pitmedden Garden★★

NTS. 14mi/22km north by A 92 (V).
Open May–Oct daily 10am–5.30pm (grounds year-round). £5. 0844 4932177. www.nts.org.uk.
Sir Alexander Seton (c. 1639–1719), possibly influenced by designs of Le Nôtre or the gardens of Sir William Bruce at Holyrood, laid out the original formal gardens. The garden is seen at its best in July and August, when 30–40,000 annuals are in bloom. Within this walled garden a belvedere provides the best viewing point.

Isle of Arran★★
North Ayrshire

Arran is the largest of the islands in the Firth of Clyde, measuring some 20mi/32km long by 10mi/16km wide; cut in two by the Highland Boundary Fault, it is said to present "Scotland in miniature". A mountainous northern part (Goat Fell 2 866ft/874m) has deep valleys and moorlands, whilst the southern half consists of lowland scenery. Sheltered bays and sandy beaches, together with ample facilities for yachting, swimming, golf, sea-angling and fishing, make tourism the island's principal industry.

ISLAND TOUR

56mi/90km – allow about half day, not including visiting time.
Mainly a coastal route, the road affords views of the diversity of scenery; but as well as the coast road, try the 10mi/16km String Road across the "waist" of the island,

- ▶ **Population:** 4,726.
- **Michelin Map:** Michelin Atlas p 53 or Map 501 E 17.
- **Info:** The Pier, Brodick. 0845 225 5121. www.ayrshire-arran.com.
- **Location:** In the Firth of Clyde, just off Scotland's southwestern point.
- **Don't Miss:** Brodick Castle's rhododendron garden in bloom (late spring).
- **Petrol:** Make sure the fuel tank is full before setting out as there are few filling stations.

between Blackwaterfoot and Brodick. The first highlight is outside the port and bay from which it takes its name. **Brodick Castle★★** (*Castle: open Apr–Oct Sun–Thu 11am–4pm (3pm Oct) Grounds: open year-round daily 9.30am–dusk; £10; 0844 4932 152 www.nts.org.uk*) is the historic stronghold of the Hamiltons, Earls of Arran. The

13C red sandstone castle was extended by Cromwell in 1652 and again in the baronial style in 1844. The Hamilton and Beckford treasures comprise a fine collection of silver, porcelain, furniture and family portraits as well as paintings by Watteau, Turner and Herring. The gilded heraldic ceiling is remarkable. An 18th Century formal walled garden and a 65acre/26ha rhododendron garden, one of the finest in Britain, benefit from the mild local climate. 1.5mi/3km inland off the road north of Blackwaterfoot lie the **Machrie Moor**

Stone Circles. Moorland backed by mountains makes an impressive setting for these remnants of Bronze Age stone circles, built about the same time as the later parts of Stonehenge. Arran was on the main migration route for Neolithic agriculturalists up the western seaboard of Scotland. As the road swings round Arran's southern tip the granite island of **Ailsa Craig** (1,000ft/300m high) can be seen to the south. The road from Lamlash Bay, sheltered by Holy Island, to Brodick gives a spectacular view of Brodick Castle dominated by Goat Fell.

South Ayrshire

Ayr is a pleasant market town that has grown up around a medieval core. Today it is a thriving resort on Scotland's southwest coast with splendid sandy beaches as well as a famous racecourse and golf courses which host international competitions. It is probably most notable, however, as the hub of **Burns Country**.

BURNS COUNTRY
Alloway★

3mi/5km south of Ayr by B 7024.
Alloway is famed as the birthplace of the poet Robert Burns (1759–96), whose birthday on 25 January is celebrated throughout the world. Within the **Burns National Heritage Park** are a number of sites: the spartan **Burns Cottage and Museum★** (⏰*open daily Apr–Sept 10am–5.30pm, Oct–Mar 10am–5pm;* ⏰*closed Jan 1–2, Dec 25–26;* ▨*£4; combined ticket to all other Burns attrac-*

> ▸ **Population:** 47,872.
> ⏱ **Michelin Map:** Michelin Atlas p 48 or Map 501 G 17.
> ▯ **Info:** 22 Sandgate. ☏0845 225 5121. www.ayrshire-arran.com.
> ▶ **Location:** Ayr is 36mi/57km SW of Glasgow. Ayr station is 1mi/1.6km from the town centre. The bus station is at Sandgate in the centre.
> ☺ **Don't Miss:** Culzean Castle for its cliff-top setting.

tions; ▣✖; ☏*01292 443700; www.burns-heritagepark.com) evokes* his humble origins and displays an extensive collection of manuscripts and relics; the **Burns Monument** overlooks the River Doon and the 13C **Brig o'Doon**; The **Tam O'Shanter Experience** (⏰*admission details as Burns Cottage and Museum;* ▨*£2) presents* the bard's life and times as well as an introduction to southwest Scotland. **Alloway Kirk** also has Burns associations.

Culzean Castle★
NTS. 16mi/25km southwest of Ayr by A 719. **Castle:** ⏰ *Open Easter/Apr–Oct, daily 10.30am–5pm; Nov–Mar Thu–Sun 11am–4pm.* **Country Park:** ⏰ *Open daily 9.30am–dusk.* ▨*Castle and country park £12, country park only £8.*

A moving landmark

According to tradition, Ayr's Auld Brig (13C), a narrow cobbled bridge immortalised by the Scottish bard, Robert Burns, was financed by two sisters who lost their fiancés when they drowned trying to ford the river in spate.

Culzean Castle

E. Morris/Michelin

&PX. ℰ0844 4932149. www.nts.org.
uk. www.culzeanexperience.org.
Culzean Castle (pronounced Cullane)
enjoys a dramatic cliff-top **setting-
★★★**. The castle was the work of **Robert
Adam** (1728–92). Though a classicist,
Adam added arrow slits and battlements to this most spectacular castle,
to complete the mock-medieval touch.
The harmonious interior is enhanced by
friezes, chimney-pieces and delicately
patterned ceilings. The elegant **Oval
Staircase★★** and **Saloon** are good

examples of the architect's original
style. He also designed the splendid
furnishings. The Eisenhower exhibition
traces the castle's connection with the
former American President. The grounds
include a Victorian walled garden comprising the Pleasure Garden with extensive herbaceous borders, the restored
Victorian Vinery and Peach House), a
Fountain Court Garden (including the
Orangery), a herb garden, wildlife garden and an adventure playground.

Banff★

Aberdeenshire

This small royal burgh town, set on
the coast at the mouth of the River
Deveron, boasts attractive 18C
buildings. Banff is an excellent base
for excursions along the splendid
coastline, with magnificent views of
cliffs and headlands, to the picturesque fishing villages of **Portsoy**,
Cullen and **Buckie** to the west, and
Macduff, **Gardenstown**, **Crovie** and
Pennan to the east.

▸ **Population:** 4,402.
○ **Michelin Map:** Michelin
Atlas p 69 or Map 501 M 10.
🛈 **Info:** Collie Lodge. ℰ01261
812419. www.aberdeen
-grampian.com.
◗ **Location:** 40mi/65km
north of Aberdeen. Banff
Bridge is the nearest train
station, 1.2mi/2km from
town. There is no bus
station though the town is
serviced by the Aberdeen–
Elgin line.

DUFF HOUSE★★

*Overlooking the Duff House Royal
Golf Club beside the river Deveron.*
○*Open Apr–Oct daily 11am–5pm.
Nov–Mar Thu–Sun 4pm.* ⬭*£6.20.*
&PX. ℰ*01261 81 81 81.
www.duffhouse.org.uk.*
This splendid Baroque mansion designed
by William Adam has been restored to
its former glory. A double curving stair-

case rises up to the great central block
and Corinthian pilasters support a richly
decorated pediment. Small intimate
rooms surround the spacious vestibule
dominated by a grandiose painting by
William Etty, and the Great Drawing
Room hung with Gobelins tapestries
and pastoral paintings by Boucher.

Cairngorms★★
Highland and Moray

This granitic range between the Spey Valley and Braemar features some of Britain's wildest and most dramatic mountain scenery. Much of its lies above 3,000ft/almost 1,000m, with Ben Macdui (4,296ft/1,309m) as its highest point even though the region is named for the lower peak of Cairn Gorm (4,084ft/1,245m).

CAIRNGORMS NATIONAL PARK

Cairngorms National Park covers 64,000 acres/26,000ha, making it the biggest national park in Britain, with the largest area of arctic mountain landscape in the UK at its heart. The severe climate of the windswept summits allows only an Arctic-Alpine flora to flourish. The mountains are the home of the golden eagle, ptarmigan, snow bunting, dotterel and of the rare osprey (RSPB observation hide at Loch Garten).

The only reindeer herd in Britain is to be found in the Glenmore Forest Park. From here the **Speyside Way** (♿ *see ELGIN for more on Speyside*) long-distance path winds northwards. This area is famous for its salmon fishing and there is an exhibition on salmon fisheries at the **Tugnet Ice House** (*Spey Bay, near Fochabers;* ⏰ *open May–Sept daily 11am–4pm;* ♿🅿️; ℘*01309 673 701*).

Cairn Gorm ★★★

The modern funicular railway (⏰ *every 15–20min (last train 4.30pm/5pm depending on weather);* ♿✕; ℘*01479 861 261; www.cairngormmountain.com*) provides visitors with an easy way of appreciating something of the magic and beauty of this mountain peak.

The northern and western slopes of Cairngorm are ideal for skiing, and the construction in the 1960s of the **Aviemore Centre** – a complex of shops, hotels and entertainment facilities with an "après-ski" flavour – transformed the **Aviemore**★ village into Britain's first winter sports resort. There are ice-rinks

- ⓖ **Michelin Map:** Michelin Atlas pp 61, 62, 67, 68 or Map 501 I, J, K 11 and 12.
- ⓘ **Info:** 14 The Square, Grantown-on-Spey. ℘01479 873 535. www.cairngorms.co.uk. www.visitcairngorms.com (for Eastern Cairngorms).
- ⓒ **Transport:** Aviemore train station is 2.6mi/4.2km from the centre. Buses run from Aviemore to the Cairngorm Mountain Railway.
- ⓢ **Don't Miss:** The view from Cairn Gorm (on a clear day) and perhaps a sunset meal in their award-winning Ptarmigan restaurant at 3540 ft/1079m.
- ⓢ **Warning:** The mountains are remote and can be a treacherous place to all but well-equipped and experienced walkers and mountaineers.
- 👥 **Kids:** Landmark Forest Theme Park; Strathspey Steam Railway.

for skating and curling, a dry ski slope and a swimming pool. Winter sports facilities are also available at Grantown-on-Spey, an elegant 18C town.

The **Strathspey Railway** (👥; *Dalfaber Road;* ⏰ *daily service Easter–Sept, times vary rest of year;* ♿🅿️✕ *(on-board train);* ℘*01479 810 725; www.strathspeyrailway.co.uk*) operates a steam service from Aviemore to Boat of Garten and Broomhill.

EXCURSIONS

12mi/19km south of Aviemore is Kincraig and the **Highland Wildlife Park**★ (⏰ *open, weather permitting year-round.* ⓔ*£9.45, child £7.20.* ♿🅿️✕; ℘*01540 651 270; www.highlandwildlifepark.org*), home to Scottish wildlife as well as internationally endangered animals including tigers, bison and deer. Those seeking respite from the Cairngorms' rugged scenery should head to Kingussie a further 6mi/9.6km south, and the **Highland Folk Museum** (*Duke Street;* 🕐 *open Easter–Aug;* ♿📱; 📞*01540 661 307; www.highland folk.com*), which relates the life of the Highlanders (dress, musical instruments, farm implements, old crafts) and includes a "black house" typical of the Western Isles, and a clack mill. Kingussie is also a pony-trekking centre.

6mi/10km north of Aviemore is the **Landmark Forest Theme Park** (👥👤, *Landmark, Carrbridge;* 🕐 *open daily; certain rides closed in winter;* 🎫*Admissions vary seasonally;* ♿📱✗; 📞*0800 731 3446, www.landmark-centre.co.uk*), a favourite family day out with lots of adventure climbs, three watersplash rides, a high-wire challenge course and nature-themed activities.

Dumfries★
Dumfries and Galloway

Dumfries, "Queen of the South", has long been the chief town of Scotland's southwest and is probably best-known for its historical associations. Robert the Bruce (1306–29) started his long campaign to free Scotland from Edward I in Dumfries by killing John Comyn, one of the competitors for the crown, and having himself crowned at Scone in 1306. Eight years later, his victory at Bannockburn was crucial in achieving Scotland's independence. The poet Robert Burns, who epitomized the national spirit, is Dumfries' most famous citizen.

EXCURSIONS
Drumlanrig Castle★★
18mi/29km northwest on the A 76. 🕐 *Open Good Fri–Aug (gardens Sept) daily 11am (gardens 10am)–5pm.* 🎫*Castle £8. Gardens only, £4.* ♿📱✗. 📞*01848 600 283. www.drumlanrig.co.uk.*
The castle was a 14C–18C Douglas stronghold and stands impressively with four square towers quartering the courtyard structure. Innovation comes with the main façade and its terraces, horseshoe staircase, dramatic turreted skyline and rich sculptural detail. The interior holds a superb collection of paintings (including a Holbein and a Rembrandt), fine furniture and clocks. In the oak-panelled Dining Room, carved panels attributed to Grinling Gibbons alternate with 17C silver sconces and family portraits.

> ▸ **Population:** 21,164.
> ⚉ **Michelin Map:** Michelin Atlas p 49 or Map 501 J 18.
> ▤ **Info:** 📞*01387 253 862.* www.visitdumfriesand galloway.co.uk.
> ⬯ **Location:** Southwest Scotland, 33mi/53km NW of Carlisle across the border. Both the train station (Station Road, off English Street) and the bus station (Whitesands) are in the town centre.
> 🕐 **Timing:** Allow two days.

Sweetheart Abbey★
HS. 8mi/13km southwest by the New Abbey Road, A 710. 🕐 *Open late Mar–Oct daily, Nov–Mar Sat–Wed.* 🎫*£2.94.* 📱. 📞*01387 850 397. www.historic-scotland.gov.uk.*
Sweetheart Abbey, which was founded in 1273 by Dervorgilla, was the last Cistercian foundation in Scotland. Its name derives from the fact that the foundress was laid to rest together with a casket containing the embalmed heart of her husband. The beauty and charm of the ruins are enhanced by the contrast between warm red sandstone and the clipped green of surrounding lawns.
On the way back to Dumfries turn left just out of New Abbey for the **National Museum of Costume** (*Shambelli House, New Abbey;* 🕐 *open Apr–Oct daily 10am–5pm;* 🎫*£3;* 📱✗; 📞*0138 850 375; www.nms.ac.uk*), which displays

Robert Burns (1759–96)

The bard lived and farmed in and around Dumfries and a statue stands at the north end of the High Street. The **Robert Burns Centre** (Mill Road; ⏰ open Apr–Sept Mon–Sat 10am–8pm, Sun 2pm–5pm; Oct–Mar Tue–Sat, 10am–1pm, 2pm–5pm; ⊠charge for audio-visual theatre only, £1.60; ♿🅿✕; ☏01387 264 808; www.dumfriesmuseum.demon.co.uk), is an excellent introduction to Burns who spent the last few years of his life at **Burns House**, now a museum (⏰ open Apr–Sept daily, 10am (2pm Sun) to 5pm; Oct–Mar, Tue–Sat, 10am–1pm, 2pm–5pm; ☏01387 255 297; www.dumfriesmuseum.demon.co.uk), after giving up his farm at **Ellisland** (Hollywood Road; ⏰ open Apr–Sept daily 10am–1pm, 2pm–5pm (Sun 2pm–5pm), Oct–Mar Tue–Sat, 10am–5pm; ⏰ closed early Dec–early Jan; ⊠£3.50; ☏01387 740 426; www.ellislandfarm.co.uk), outside Dumfries, and taking up a post with the Excise. Behind the old red sandstone church is a **mausoleum** where Burns, his wife (Jane Armour) and several of their children are buried. **Alloway** (3mi/5km south of Ayr), his birthplace, is also on the **Burns Trail** (leaflets from tourist information centres).

both historical and modern costumes in the charming setting of a small country house.

Caerlaverock Castle★

HS. 9mi/15km southeast on the B 725, bear right at Bankend. ⏰ Open daily late Mar–Sept 9.30am–4.30pm/5.30pm. ⊠£5.09. ♿🅿. ☏01387 770 24. www.historic-scotland.gov.uk.
Overlooking the Solway Firth, this imposing medieval castle is girt by a moat and earthen ramparts. Its formidable machicolated exterior with a keep gatehouse and curtain walls is in contrast to the harmonious **Renaissance courtyard façade★★**. The castle, which was besieged by Edward I in 1300 and later became the principal seat of the Maxwells, was abandoned in the 17C.

Ruthwell Cross★

HS. 16mi/26km on the B 725; fork left at Bankend. ☏01387 870249 for details of opening times.
In the church stands the 7C Ruthwell Cross which depicts the Life and Passion of Christ; it is an outstanding example of **early Christian art**.
The tracery, animals and birds, together with runic inscriptions, are a credit to the artistry and skill of the sculptor. The cross was demolished in 1642 by the General Assembly; the pieces were re-assembled and installed in the church in 1887.

Dundee★

City of Dundee

Dundee is Scotland's fourth city, a busy seaport, an educational centre and the capital of Tayside. Dundee and the surrounding area has been continuously occupied since the Mesolithic. Traditional historic activities (such as whaling and jute milling) have given way to modern high-tech industries. The city centre blends fine Victorian buildings and modern shopping facilities, while the city has a thriving cultural scene.

▸ **Population:** 165,873.
● **Michelin Map:** Atlas p 62 or Map 501 K, L 14.
▯ **Info:** ☏01382 527 527. www.angusanddundee.co.uk.
◖ **Location:** East coast, on the northern shore of the River Tay, backed by the Sidlaw Hills. Trains arrive at Taybridge Station on South Union Street; inter-city buses arrive at Seagate station: both centrally located.

CITY WALK

Just east of the Tay Bridge in Victoria Dock is **The Frigate Unicorn**★ (*open Apr–Oct, daily 10am–5pm, Nov–Mar Wed–Fri noon–4pm, Sat–Sun 10am–4pm; closed 1 Jan and 24–26 Dec; £4; (charge); 01382 200 900; www.frigateunicorn.org*), which was launched in 1824 as a 46-gun frigate for the Royal Navy. She is now the oldest British-built ship still afloat. Visitors can explore the main gun decks, with their 18-pounders and the Captain's and officers' quarters, and discover the flavour of life in the Royal Navy in the golden age of sail.

West of the Tay Bridge near the railway station you will find **Discovery Point**★ (; *Discovery Quay, Craig Harbour; open Apr–Sept daily 10am (11am Sun)–6pm, Oct–Mar 10am (11am Sun)–5pm; closed Dec 25–6, Jan 1–2; £7.50, child £4.50, joint ticket with Verdant Works (see below) £11.25, child £8.50; 01382 201 245; www.rrsdiscovery.com*) and the pride of the city, the **RRS Discovery**★, which was custom-built in Dundee in 1901 for scientific exploration. The ship forms the centrepiece of an exciting exhibition, with a spectacular audio-visual presentation devoted to Captain Scott's Antarctic Expedition (1901–04), the vessel's dramatic rescue and other journeys.

On the other side of the tracks, on Greenmarket, is **Sensation** (; *open daily Apr–Oct 10am–5pm; closed 1 Jan; £6.95, child £4.95; 01382 228800; www.sensation.org.uk*), Dundee's award-winning hands-on science centre with over 80 interactive stations. Just north of here is the Universty of Dundee and beyond on West Henderson's Wynd is **Verdant Works**★ (*open Apr–Oct daily 10am (11am Sun)–6pm, Nov–Mar Wed–Sat 10.30am–4.30, Sun 11am–4.30pm; £6.25, child £3.85, joint ticket with Discov. Point (above) £11.25, child £8.50; 01382 225 282; www.verdantworks.com*), featuring original working machinery alongside the latest hands-on exhibits to tell the entertaining story of the jute industry in Dundee and worldwide.

Northwest of the Tay Bridge by the Forum is a fine Victorian Gothic building, which houses the **McManus Galleries**★ (*Albert Square; closed for renovations until late 2009; 01382 432 350; www.mcmanus.co.uk*), the city's art gallery and museum.

Dunfermline★

Fife

Dunfermline, the former capital of Scotland, lies immediately north of the present capital, Edinburgh, across the Firth of Forth. Its great abbey and royal palace figure frequently in Scottish history. The town has long been a thriving industrial centre, with coal mining and linen weaving, and new industries maintain this tradition today.

A BIT OF HISTORY

Royal residence – Malcolm Canmore (c. 1031–93) sheltered the heir to the English throne, **Edgar Atheling** and his family, fleeing from William the Conqueror after Hastings (1066). Edgar's sister **Margaret** married the Scots king in 1070.

> **Population:** 29,436.
>
> **Michelin Map:** Michelin Atlas p 56 or Map 501 J 15.
>
> **Info:** 01383 720 999. www.visitfife.com.
>
> **Transport:** From Edinburgh trains run to Dunfermline Town station and buses to Queen Anne Street station.
>
> **Don't Miss:** Abbey Church; Culross Village.
>
> **Timing:** Half day for the city, full day for excursions.

She was a devout Catholic and was largely responsible for introducing the ideas which gradually supplanted the rituals of the Celtic church. The Benedictine abbey was founded by **David I**, son

Culross Village

VisitScotland Fife

of Queen Margaret. **Robert the Bruce** (1274–1329) helped with the reconstruction of the Abbey in 1034 and is buried here. James VI (James I of England) gave the palace to his Queen, Anne of Denmark, and Charles I was born here.

There were fleeting royal visits, after the Union of the Crowns in 1603, but the palace was never again a regular royal residence.

TOWN WALK

Northwest of the train station lies **Dunfermline Abbey**★ (HS; ☉ open late Mar–Oct daily 9.30am–12.30pm and 1pm–5.30pm (Oct 4.30pm), Nov–Mar Mon–Thu and Sat 9.30am–12.30pm and 1pm–4.30pm (closed Thu pm, Sun am); ☞£3.62; ℗; ℰ01383 739 026; www.historic-scotland.gov.uk), an 11C Benedictine abbey founded on the site of a Celtic church. The Norman nave of the **abbey church**★★ with its massive pillars and round-headed arches is one of the finest in Scotland. The east end (re-built in the early 19C) serves as the parish church; a memorial brass marks the tomb of Robert the Bruce. There are few remains of the great monastic ensemble.

Nearby, **Abbot House** (Maygate; ☉ open year-round daily 10am–5pm (Nov–Feb Sun–Fri closes 4pm); ☉closed Jan 1, Dec 25–26; ☞£4; ♿℗✕; ℰ01383 733 266; www.abbothouse.co.uk) is now an attractive heritage centre. Head south from here on St Margaret

Street, which leads to Moodie Street and the **Andrew Carnegie Birthplace** (☉ open Apr–Oct daily 11am (2pm Sun)–5pm; ♿; ℰ01383 724 302; www.carnegiebirthplace.com). The self-made steel baron and great philanthropist, Andrew Carnegie (1835–1919) was born in this house before emigrating to America with his family in 1848. An exhibition traces his life and work.

EXCURSIONS
Culross★★

13mi/21km east on the A 944 andB 9037. According to legend St Mungo, patron saint of Glasgow, was born in this small burgh (pronounced "Coo'ross") on the north shore of the Firth of Forth.

A Cistercian house was founded here in the 13C. Trade with the Low Countries, salt panning and coal mining brought prosperity to the town.

Today Culross is famous for its fine examples of Scottish vernacular architecture of the 16C and 17C in all its rich detail. The small buildings in the **village**★★★ feature inscribed lintels, decorative finials, skewputts, crow-stepped gables, forestairs, harling and rubble stonework with door and window trims. The **Town House** (NTS; same ticket to Study and Palace; ☉ Apr–May and Sept Thu–Mon noon–5, Jun–Aug daily noon–5, Oct Thu–Mon noon–4; Study and Town House by guided tour only, from palace reception every 30 mins, first tour 12.30pm, last tour

4pm/Oct 3pm; Garden all year 10am–6pm or dusk; ☜£8.50; 🅿&✗; ✆0844 493 2189; www.nts.org.uk) is a stone-and-slate building erected in 1625 in Flemish style; it contrasts with the white harling and red pantiles of the surrounding buildings. The Back Causeway, behind, has a central line of raised paving stones for the exclusive use of local notables. Opposite, The **Study**★, which has a 17C painted ceiling (restored) and original panelling, is the oldest house in Culross with a replica of the 1588 mercat cross in front of its gable end. The **Palace**★★, a comfortable house built (1597–1611) by George Bruce, a rich merchant and coalmine owner, boasts pine-panelled rooms and 21 fireplaces which burnt coal rather than logs. Dutch tiles carried as ballast in his ships were used for flooring and roofing.

Falkland Palace★

NTS. 31mi/48km northeast by the M 90, A 91 and A 912. ⏱ Open Mar–Oct Mon–Sat. ☜£10.50. ✆0844 493 2186. www.nts.org.uk.

In 1425 this hunting–seat of the earls of Fife passed to the crown and became one of the Stewarts' favourite royal palaces. The gatehouse and street façade built in Gothic style by James IV, a Renaissance monarch who entertained a splendid court, is in sharp contrast with the Renaissance ornament of the courtyard façade of the south range added by his son, James V who took a French bride. A tour of the interior includes the Keeper's gatehouse apartments, adorned with royal portraits, coats of arms and elegant furnishings. The east range contained the royal apartments. At the rear of the **gardens**★ is a Real (Royal) Tennis court.

Edinburgh★★★

City Of Edinburgh

Edinburgh, capital of Scotland, lies on the Firth of Forth, a deep inlet gouged into the east coast. The city is located on a series of volcanic hills, each giving a different and often spectacular vantage point. Most famous of these is Arthur's Seat (823ft/251m), overlooking Holyrood Park. Edinburgh boasts a colourful history; the Old Town, huddled for years on the ridge running down from the Castle Rock, contrasts with the New Town, with its elegant Georgian streets and squares.

PUBLIC TRANSPORT

Bus services are frequent and usually run on time. A new tram service in the city centre was installed in 2009. Visit the Tourist Information Centre or the Transport Information Centre at 1 Cockburn Street for timetables. The two main operators are Lothian Buses (✆0131 555 6363) and First Buses (✆08708 72 72 71).

▸ **Population:** 418,914.

🜢 **Michelin Map:** Michelin Atlas p 56 or Map 401 K 16.

🛈 **Info:** 3 Princes Street, south of Waverley Station. ✆0845 2255 121. www.edinburgh.org.

◔ **Location:** Edinburgh is compact. You can visit all the Old Town and much of the New Town on foot. Waverley Station, at the very heart of the city, accommodates all main bus and train services. Haymarket station is 2mi/3km west of the centre and also services Glasgow, Fife and the Highlands.

🅿 **Parking:** Difficult and expensive.

☺ **Don't Miss:** The Royal Mile; a walking tour; the Scottish Parliament Building; the views from the Nelson Monument and Arthur's Seat; Charlotte Square; the

Edinburgh International Festival ★★★

This prestigious festival *(three weeks in August)* has provided a quality programme of performances in all the art forms since its inception in 1947. The **Military Tattoo** presents a spectacle rich in colour, tradition, music and excitement, under the floodlights of the Castle Esplanade. Also a part of festival time, **The Fringe** spills out onto the streets and squares of Edinburgh, with performers from all over the globe presenting over a thousand productions, often avant-garde, sometimes just plain eccentric. The **Jazz** and **Film Festivals** are also of note.

A BIT OF HISTORY

The Castle Rock had been a secure refuge for generations when in the late 11C Malcolm Canmore and Queen Margaret chose the site for their residence. Their son, David I, favoured the site by founding the Abbey of the Holy Rood. During the reign of the early Stuarts Edinburgh gradually assumed the roles of royal residence, seat of government and capital of Scotland. With the Union of the Crowns (1603) and subsequent departure of James VI of Scotland and I of England for London, Edinburgh lost much of its pageantry and cultural activity. In 1707 self-rule came to an end with the Union of the Parliaments.

It was in the late 18C during the Enlightenment, a period of intellectual ferment, that plans were mooted for a civic project of boldness and imagination: the creation of the Georgian New Town. The town has gained further status as the seat of the Scottish Assembly, which sits in the new Parliament building next to the Palace of Holyroodhouse.

OLD TOWN

1 THE ROYAL MILE ★★

The principal thoroughfare of Old Edinburgh runs from the castle down the ridge through Castle Hill, Lawnmarket, High Street and Canongate to the abbey and Palace of Holyroodhouse. For two centuries the city's Flodden Wall (16C) restricted the spread of Edinburgh, confining expansion to the ten-and twelve-storey "tenements", with narrow wynds and closes, so typical of the Old Town. The few original buildings which remain can still today give the impression of what medieval and 17C Edinburgh must have looked like.

Fringe Festival; Royal Museum and Museum of Scotland; Royal Yacht Britannia; Forth Bridges, view from South Queensferry.

🕐 **Timing:** Three days min.

👫 **Kids:** Edinburgh Zoo; Our Dynamic Earth; Deep Sea World (North Queensferry).

🚶 **Walking Tours:** The Edinburgh Literary Pub Tour (☎0800 169 7410; www.edinburghliterarypub tour.co.uk); Mercat Tours (☎0131 225 5445; www.mercattours.com) City of the Dead Tour (☎0131 225 9044; www.black*hart*.uk.com; (not for children).

Bus Tours: Bus tours of the city depart daily every 15–20 mins from Waverley Bridge next to the station (🚌£10. ☎0131 220 070. www.city-sightseeing.co.uk).

Castle ★★

HS. ♿🕐*Open daily (subject to state and military events and the Tattoo) daily 9.30am–5pm/6pm.* 🎫*£10.77 (buy online to save waiting in line).* 🚶*Guided tour (free).* ✗. ☎0131 225 9846. www.edinburghcastle.gov.uk.

The impressive silhouette of the castle and its **rock** ★★ is probably the best-known view of Edinburgh. Though a royal residence since the 11C, the castle and most of the buildings today are basically those resulting from its use as a military garrison over recent centuries.

EDINBURGH

WHERE TO STAY

WHERE TO EAT

The esplanade, an 18C parade ground, is the setting for the Edinburgh Festival's most popular event, the Military Tattoo. The fortifications afford splendid **views** across Princes Street to the New Town. The one o'clock salute is fired from one of the batteries. The main points of interest include the **Honours of Scotland**★★★ (the Scottish Crown Jewels), the **Stone of Destiny** on display in the Crown Room, **Mons Meg**, one of the oldest and most spectacular cannons in the world, and the **Royal Scots Regimental Museum**, the senior regiment in the British Army, raised in 1633, (Ⓞclosed Sat–Sun winter. ✆0131 310 5014. www.theroyalscots.co.uk/museum.html) and the oldest Infantry Regiment of the Line. The 12C St Margaret's Chapel is dedicated to Malcolm's Queen. Around Crown Square are the Scottish National War Memorial the Scottish United Services Museum, the 16C **Great Hall** with its hammerbeam roof, and 15C Palace.

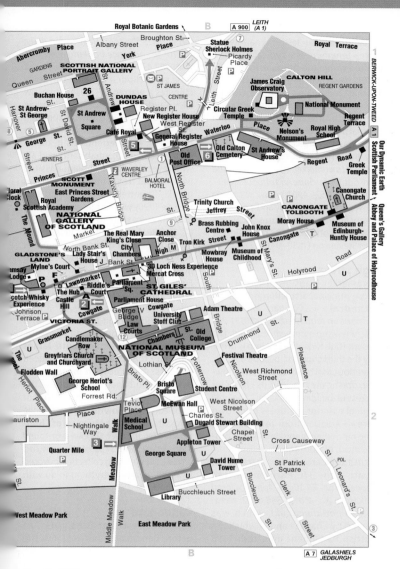

Castle Hill

Proceed down Castle Hill past the **Scotch Whisky Experience** *(354 Castlehill;* ⏰ *admission by tour only, Jun–Aug daily 9.30am–6.30pm. Sept–May daily 10am–6pm;* ⏰ *closed 25 Dec;* 🎟️*£7.50;* ♿✕; ☎ *0131 220 0441; www.whisky-heritage.co.uk)*, with an exhibition and film on whisky distilling. Opposite stands the Outlook Tower housing Edinburgh's **Camera Obscura and World of Illusions** *(549 Castlehill;* ⏰ *open year-round daily; last camera presentation 1hr before closing;* 🎟️*£8.50;* ♿; ☎ *0131 226 3709; www.camera-obscura.co.uk)*, which affords a fascinating ever-changing live window on the city.

Lawnmarket

Castle Hill leads into Lawnmarket. Here you will find **Gladstone's Land**★ *(NTS; 477B Lawnmarket;* ⏰ *open year-round daily;* 🎟️*£5.50;* ♿; ☎ *08444 932 120; www.*

nts.org.uk) on your left. This narrow six-storey tenement is a typical building erected within the city walls in the 17C; in 1617 it was acquired and extended by Thomas Gledstanes, a wealthy merchant. The restored premises comprise a shop with living quarters above, complete with original painted ceilings and furnishings. A few yards downhill, up a narrow alleyway, the **Writers' Museum** *(Lady Stair's Close, off Lawnmarket;* ⏰*open year-round Mon–Sat 10am–5pm; Aug also Sun noon–5pm;* ✆*0131 529 4901; www.cac.org.uk)* showcases three of Scotland's greatest literary figures: Robert Burns (1759–96), Sir Walter Scott (1771–1832) and Robert Louis Stevenson (1850–94).

High Street

Lawnmarket leads into High Street, whose principal attraction is **St Giles' Cathedral**★★ (⏰*open daily;* 💷*£3 contribution requested;* ✕*;* ✆*0131 225 9442; www.stgilescathedral.org.uk).* The present High Kirk of Edinburgh is probably the third church to occupy this site. Alterations and restorations have, however, drastically changed its character since its re-building in the 14C. The only original exterior feature is the crown **spire**★★★ dating from 1495. Inside, it is the monuments and details that provide much of the interest.

Behind the cathedral on Parliament Square is the 17C **Parliament Hall** (⏰*open Mon–Fri 10am–4pm;* ⏰*closed Bank Hols;* ♿*;* ✆*0131 348 6852; www.scottish.parliament.uk),* which was decreed by Charles I and in which the Scottish Parliament met from 1693 to 1707. It is now behind a Georgian façade. Its magnificent **hammerbeam roof** is an original feature. Nearby is a 17C equestrian statue of Charles II. At the east end of the square stands the **Mercat Cross**, formerly the hub of Edinburgh life, meeting place of traders and merchants and scene of royal proclamations, demonstrations and executions. Opposite the cathedral are the **City Chambers**, formerly the Royal Exchange built in 1753. Adjacent, part of the same complex is the entrance to **The Real Mary King's Close** *(Warris-*

ton's Close; ➤*tours year-round daily;* 💷*£10;* ✕*; advance booking essential.* ✆*08702 430 160. www.realmarykingsclose.com).* Hidden beneath the Royal Mile lies a warren of "closes" (narrow alleyways) where people lived, worked and died. As the Old Town expanded ever upwards these closes became built over, or as legend has it, deliberately sealed up, inhabitants and all, whenever the dreaded plague visited (which it did frequently). For centuries they lay forgotten and abandoned until the late 1990s when tours were licensed to reintroduce them to the general public. The Real Mary King's Close is now the most popular of these. Paranormal activity has been frequently recorded down here.

Further down High Street is the picturesque **John Knox House** (⏰*open year-round Mon–Sun;* 💷*£2.25;* ♿✕*;* ✆*0131 556 2647/9579)* built in about 1490, is associated with both John Knox, the religious reformer, and with James Mossman, the goldsmith to Mary Queen of Scots. An exhibition incorporates details on both men and re-creates the atmosphere of 16C Edinburgh. Nextdoor is the early-17C **Mowbray House**, while across the road is the **Museum of Childhood** *(42 High Street;* ⏰*open year-round Mon–Sat;* ♿*;* ✆*0131 529 4142; www.cac.org.uk),* a fascinating collection devoted to anything and everything to do with childhood.

Canongate

High Street leads into Canongate. Just before Canongate Church stands the attractive 16C **Canongate Tolbooth**★ **(BY)**, home to the **People's Story** *(163 Canongate;* ⏰*open year-round Mon–Sat 10am–5pm; also Aug Sun noon–5pm;* ♿*;* ✆*0131 529 4057; www.cac.org.uk)* which uses oral history, reminiscence and written sources to tell the story of the lives, work and leisure of the ordinary people of Edinburgh, from the late 18th century to the present day.

Opposite stand three 16C mansions known as Huntly House occupied by the **Museum of Edinburgh**, *(142 Canongate;* ⏰*open Mon–Sat, 10am–5pm; also*

Palace of Holyroodhouse
©Philip Coblentz/Brand X Pictures

Aug Sun noon–5pm; &; ℰ0131 529 4143; www.cac.org.uk) offering some fascinating local exhibits including the true story of the famous dog, "Greyfriars Bobby".

Just before you arrive at the Parliament, take a right on Reid's Close to find **Our Dynamic Earth** (⚐; ⏰open Apr–Oct daily, Nov–Mar Wed–Sun 10am–5pm; last admission 1hr 30 min before closing; ⊜£9.50; child £5.95; &✕; ℰ0131 550 7800; www.dynamicearth.co.uk) tucked away behind it. Occupying what appears to be a giant marquee just below the dramatic Salisbury Crags, Edinburgh's major Millennium visitor attraction gallops through the natural and geological history of the earth via a series of often spectacular exhibits, experiences and hands-on displays.

At the end of Canongate on the right is Britain's most controversial post-Millennium building, the **Scottish Parliament** (⏰meetings year-round Tue–Thu 9am–6.30pm; book tickets (free) in advance; ☛guided tours on non-business days (⊜£5.85; booking essential); &✕; ℰ0131 348 5200. www. scottish.parliament. uk). The new parliament building was designed by the Spanish architect Enric Miralles (1955–2000) who died before its completion in 2005, four years late and ten times over budget. Its unusual design and outlandish features make it a must-see for students of modern architecture and recommended viewing for anybody else.

Palace of Holyroodhouse★★

Palace: ⏰ *Open Apr–Oct daily 9.30am–6pm; Nov–Mar daily 9.30am–4.30pm.* *Gardens:* ⏰ *Open daily summer only.* ⏰*Closed mid-May–first week Jun; third week Jun 26–early Jul; Dec 25–26 and during Royal and State visits, see website.* ⊜£10 (joint ticket with Queen's Gallery £13). &. ℰ0131 556 5100. www.royalcollection.org.uk

At the east end of the Royal Mile, amid the green slopes of Holyrood Park, leading up to Arthur's Seat, stands the Palace of Holyrood, official residence of the monarch in Scotland. The abbey was founded by David I, in 1128. James IV started to transform the guesthouse of the abbey into a royal palace but it was Charles II's architect Sir William Bruce who created a magnificent building in the Palladian style.

On arrival you will find the **Queen's Gallery** (⏰same hours as Palace with separate entrance; ⊜£5; joint ticket with Palace £13; &) **on your right, which** offers a programme of changing exhibitions of works of art from the Queen's private Royal Collection.

The inner court elevations are outstanding Renaissance work of the Stuart period and among Scotland's earliest examples. The decoration and craftsmanship in the **State Apartments** is outstanding, particularly the **plasterwork ceilings★★★**, the fruit of ten years' labour by "gentlemen modellers".

The **Historic Apartments** in the 16C round tower have close associations with Mary Queen of Scots and contain tapestries from the Mortlake workshop founded by her son; the painted ceilings are magnificent. In the small room adjoining the bedchamber Mary's secretary, Rizzio, was murdered in 1566.

The roofless nave is all that is left of this once-great **Abbey** (⏱ *same opening times as the palace; visitors are free to visit on their own at the end of the guided tour)*, dating from the late 12C and early 13C. Here are buried the remains of David II, James II, James V and also of Lord Darnley, father of James VI of Scotland, who united the Crowns in 1603.

②/③ SOUTH OF THE MILE

Grassmarket, just south of the Royal Mile, was once one of Edinburgh's main markets, as well as the setting for public executions. Today it is a popular area for student accommodation. Off of Grassmarket you can see the remains of the **Flodden Wall**. Follow the route marked on the map to see **Edinburgh University**, laid out around George Square, before continuing to the Royal Museum of Scotland.

Royal Museum of Scotland★★

Chambers Street. ⏱ *Open year-round daily 10am–5pm* ⏱*Closed 25 Dec.* ♿✕. ☎*0131 247 4422. www.nms.ac.uk.*

Details of a sculpture of Weituo from Henan Province, China (18C), National Museum of Scotland

National Museums of Scotland

The elaborate Venetian Renaissance-style façade of the main building contrasts with the interior. The spacious, well-lit Main Hall is a masterpiece of Victorian cast-iron and plate-glass construction. The collections devoted to the arts and sciences range from natural history to sculpture, decorative arts and Asiatic, European and Middle Eastern art. A major project is underway to transform the museum and parts of it are shut until 2011; nonetheless there is still an awful lot to enjoy here.

A sandstone drum tower highlights the innovative design of the **Museum of Scotland** part of the collection, which traces the story of the country from 3,500 years ago to the present day with the unique collections placed in their historical perspective and with the help of an interactive computer system. The exhibits *(start in the basement galleries)* explain the natural landscape and geological foundation, the peopling of the country, the independent kingdom (1100–1707), the modern state (18C–19C) and various other aspects of Scotland.

NEW TOWN★★

When the decision had been taken to extend the Royalty of Edinburgh, the development was organised by a then unknown architect, James Craig, whose design had won the competition. The **North Bridge** was thrown across the valley and the New Town was laid out on a grid-iron pattern, with vistas and focal points. The wealthy soon took up residence in these splendid squares and elegant streets.

④ GEORGE STREET

The principal street of Craig's plan is closed at either end by Charlotte and St Andrew Squares. From the street intersections there are good views away to the Forth or down to Princes Street Gardens with the castle as backdrop. George Street ends at St Andrew Square. Head north from this square on St Andrew Street for the **Scottish National Portrait Gallery**★ (*1 Queen Street;* ⏱*Same as National Gallery (*⏱*see below);* ♿*). The museum, which is housed

North Bridge, Edinburgh

W.Buss/MICHELIN

in a fine Victorian building, "illustrates Scottish history by likeness of the chief actors in it". On display are masterpieces of portraiture of royalty, statesmen, politicians, literary figures, sportsmen and musicians past and present with some superbly innovative modern works.

It was Robert Adam who was commissioned in 1791 to design **Charlotte Square**★★★, New Town's most elegant square. The National Trust for Scotland have magnificently refurbished two properties. At No 7, the **Georgian House**★ (NTS; 7 Charlotte Square; ◷open daily; ⊜£5.50; ⅋; ℘0131 226 3318; www.nts.org.uk) is filled with Georgian treasures: furniture, silver, porcelain and fine paintings, while its lower floors give a good impression of domestic life in the period 1790–1810. At **No. 28 Charlotte Square** is a beautiful café/bistro and picture gallery of Scottish Colourists (NTS; ◷open year-round: café Mon–Sat 9.30am–5pm; gallery Mon–Fri 11am–3pm; ◷closed Dec 25–Jan 2; ⅋).

⑤ PRINCES STREET

Princes Street has grown from a totally residential street, looking out onto gardens in the newly filled-in Nor'Loch, into Edinburgh's prime shopping street. The gardens, famous for the **Floral Clock** composed of 20,000 annuals, opened to the public in 1876.

Following Sir Walter Scott's death in 1832, a public appeal was launched and the foundation stone of the **Scott Monument**★ (Princes Street; ◷open daily 9am (Sun 10am) – 3pm/6pm; ⊜£3; ℘0131 529 4068; www.cac.org.uk) was laid in 1840. The 200ft/61m tall Gothic spire shelters a marble statue of **Scott** and is surrounded by 64 characters from his novels and by the busts of 16 Scottish poets. A viewing platform (287 narrow stairs to the top) affords a magnificent **view**★ over central Edinburgh.

Dividing Princes Street Gardens into East and West are two imposing classical buildings, the National Gallery and the Royal Scottish Academy. The recently refurbished **Royal Scottish Academy** (RSA) is used for special temporary exhibitions. The adjacent **Weston Link** is a new space containing a restaurant, café and IT gallery.

National Gallery of Scotland★★

The Mound. ◷Open year-round daily 10am–5pm (Thu 7pm). ◷Closed Dec 25–26. ⅋✕. ℘0131 624 6200. www.nationalgalleries.org.

An imposing Classical building houses the collection of paintings. Masterpieces of European art (15C–19C) include Raphael, Rembrandt, Vermeer, Poussin, Claude Lorrain, Boucher, Monet and Van Gogh. The British tradition is represented by Turner, Gainsborough and Constable, among others. There is a fine collection of **Scottish paintings**, including Ramsay, Raeburn, McTaggart and the Glasgow School.

.

6 CALTON HILL

East of Princes Street, beyond elegant Waterloo Place, rises **Calton Hill** crowned by Classical monuments which gave rise to the name "Edinburgh's acropolis": the porticoed **National Monument**, a Greek **temple** and the 18C **Old Observatory**. There are wonderful views from here but for the very best **panorama**★★★ climb to the top of the **Nelson Monument**, a folly in the shape of an upturned telescope (*open Apr–Sept Mon–Sat; £3; 0131 556 2716; www.cac.org.uk*). The harmonious sweep of **Regent**, **Calton** and **Royal Terraces** (19C) is enhanced by architectural and iron-work features.

EXCURSIONS
Scottish National Gallery of Modern Art★

West of the centre, on Belford Road beyond the Belford Bridge over the Water of Leith. Open year-round daily 10am–5pm (6pm during the Edinburgh Festival). Closed Dec 25–26. 0131 624 6200, 0131 624 6336 (recorded information). 0131 624 6200, 0131 332 2266 (recorded info). www.nationalgalleries.org.

In a garden setting with sculptures by Epstein, Hepworth and Moore, among others, the SNGMA has fine examples of 20C art ranging from Fauvism and Cubism—with highlights by Matisse and Picasso—to Russian Primitivism, Nouveau Réalisme, Pop Art and a collection of Scottish art, in particular by the Scottish Colourists and Edinburgh School. Immediately across the road is the **Dean Gallery** (*same opening details and facilities as SNGMA*), famous for its giant *Vulcan* sculpture by Edinburgh-born Eduardo Paolozzi (among other works by him) and a world-class collection of Dada and Surrealist featuring works by Dalí, Miró, Ernst, Magritte and Picasso.

Royal Yacht Britannia

Port of Leith, 2mi/3km north of city centre. Ocean Terminal Centre. Open daily. £10. Closed Dec 25, Jan 1. (charge). 0131 555 5566 (book online). www.royalyachtbritannia.co.uk.

The Royal Yacht was launched from a Clydebank shipyard in 1953. By the time she was de-commissioned in 1997 she had sailed more than a million miles on nearly one thousand official engagements, carrying Queen Elizabeth II and her family all over the world. Aboard visitors can see the royal apartments, crew's quarters, bridge and wheelhouse and engine room. The facinating audio tour and visitor centre brings it to life.

Edinburgh Zoo

2mi/3km west on Corstorphine Road. Open daily. £11.20. Child £7.60. £3.50. 0131 334 9171. www.edinburghzoo.org.uk.

One of Britain's finest and most successful zoo parks (in terms of breeding), Edinburgh is home to over 1,000 animals and is famous for the largest penguin colony in captivity. Its collection of big cats and the African Plains Experience are other highlights.

Dalmeny★★

6mi/10km west by A 90.
The village is famous for its parish **St Cuthbert's Church**★ (*open Apr–Sept Sun 2pm–4pm, otherwise key obtainable at post office or 5 Main Street, opposite church; 0131 331 1479*), an exceptionally fine example of Norman ecclesiastical architecture, with an intricately carved south **doorway**★★. To the east of the village is **Dalmeny House**★ (*South Queensferry; open late May–late Jul, Sun–Tue by guided tours only at 2.15pm, 3.30pm; £5; 0131 331 1888; www.dalmeny.co.uk*), home of the Earls of Rosebery. Of particular interest are the Rothschild collection of 18C French furniture, porcelain and tapestries.

Forth Bridges★★

Best viewed from the esplanade at South Queensferry, 9mi/15km west on the A 90.
The first ferry across this, the narrowest part of the Forth, was operated around 1070 by the monks of Dunfermline, for pilgrims travelling to the abbey. By the 17C it was the busiest ferry crossing in Scotland. The **Forth Rail Bridge** was begun in 1883 and was opened in 1890.

Forth Rail Bridge

A. Williams/MICHELIN

he **Road Bridge**, a slim-line elegant uspension bridge with its amazing curve", was built 1958–64.

On the north side of the bridge stands **Deep Sea World** (☉open year-round aily 10am–5pm/6pm; ✆£11.75, child £8; ⏳▣✕; ✆01383 411 880; www.deepsea world.com), a spectacular aquarium oasting the longest underwater viewng tunnel in Britain.

Hopetoun House★★

1mi/18 km west on the A 90 and A 904. outh Queensferry. ☉ Open Good ri–Sept daily 10.30am–5pm. ✆£8. rounds only, £3.70. ⏳▣✕. ✆0131 31 2451. www.hopetounhouse.com. mansion of contrasts set in beautiful andscaped grounds, the house (built 699–1707) displays the mature clasicism of **Sir William Bruce**, its main taircase richly embellished with carving eading the eye upwards to the painted upola. The flamboyant extensions and rontage (1721–67) are the work of Wilam Adam, completed by his son John. he grandeur of the State Apartments is omplemented by the original furnishngs, magnificent plaster ceilings and a otable art collection.

Linlithgow Palace★★

HS) 19mi/31km west by the A 8 and 1 9. ☉ Open year-round daily .30am–5.30pm (Oct–Mar 4.30pm). ✆£5.09 ▣✕. ✆01506 842 896. /ww.historic-scotland.gov.uk.

The history of the town is that of its royal palace, around which it grew from the 12C. Following the re-building of the palace in 1424 it enjoyed over a century of grandeur as the centre of Scotland's court until the Union of the Crowns (1603). The roofless and forbidding four-square ruin still shelters several delicate features, notably the 1530s **fountain**★ in the courtyard and a superbly carved **fireplace**. Alongside the palace stands the 15C–16C late Gothic **St Michael's Church**★ (☉open daily 10.30am–4pm (Oct–Apr 1pm). ✆01506 842 188. www. stmichaelsparish.org.uk) with its controversial defiantly modern spire (1964).

Rosslyn Chapel★★

7mi/11km south. Roslin village (signposted). ☉ Open year-round Mon–Sat 9.30am–6pm (Oct–Apr 5pm), Sun noon–4.45pm. ✆£7.50. ☛Guided talks throughout the day. ✆0131 440 2159. www.rosslynchapel.org.uk.
One of the most mysterious and mythologised sites in Britain, famously starring recently in Dan Brown's *The Da Vinci Code*, Rosslyn Chapel stands on the edge of the Esk Valley and is a bewildering example of craftsmanship. It was built at the orders of Sir William St Clair, third and last Prince of Orkney (1396–1484). Work lasted from 1446 until 1486, just after Sir William's death. Amongst the intricate, rich decoration, perhaps the best known single item is the **Apprentice Pillar**★★★. Legend

has it that while the master mason was abroad, his apprentice carved the pillar. On his return, when seeing the quality of craftsmanship, the master mason is said to have killed his too-gifted apprentice in a fit of jealousy.

Haddington★
18 mi/29km east.

This handsome market town grew up in the 12C around a royal palace and by the 16C it was the fourth-largest town in Scotland. In the 18C it entered a golden age based on agricultural wealth. Follow The Sands past the 16C **Nungate Bridge** with its pointed cutwaters up to the **High Street**★ and its continuous line of frontages, often gable-ended. The 14C–15C **St Mary's Parish Church** enjoys a peaceful riverside setting. Its

impressive dimensions are a reminder of its history as a great burgh church. The historic house of **Lennoxlove**★ (*1mi/0.5km south on the B 6369;* ⟶ *visit by guided tour only, Easter Sun–Mon and Apr–Oct Wed, Thu and Sun;* £5; ♿🅿✕; 01620 828 605 www.lennoxlove.com) has associations with Mary Queen of Scots, and boasts several fine **portraits** and **furniture**.

Cairnpapple Hill★
24mi/39km west by A 8, M 9 to Linlithgow and A 707 to Torphichen. Cairnpapple is a mile beyond. Apr–Sept 9.30am - 5.30pm. 01506 634 622. www.historic-scotland.gov.uk. Cairnpapple was used from about 3,000–1400 BC, firstly as a ceremonial site, then later as a burial site.

ADDRESSES

🛏 STAY

⊖⊜⊜⊜ **Balmoral**, *1 Princes Street.* 0131 556 2414. www.thebalmoral hotel.com. The haunt of visiting royalty, rock stars and presidents who enjoy richly furnished rooms in baronial style at this most central of all city landmarks.

⊖⊜⊜⊜ **The George**, *19–21 George Street.* 0131 225 1251. www.principal-hayley.com. Beautifully appointed classic New Town hotel that makes the most of Robert Adams listed 18C design. Tempus restaurant (⊖⊜⊜) sits beneath a magnificent glass dome.

⊖⊜⊜⊜ **The Glasshouse**, *2 Greenside Place.* 0131 525 8200. www. theetoncollection.com. The city's most unusual and trendy boutique hotel mixes ultramodern styling (glass themes with great views onto park and city) and all the latest gadgets behind the façade of a 19C church.

⊖⊜⊜⊜ **The Scotsman**, *20 North Bridge Street.* 0131 556 5565. www. theetoncollection.com. The grand marble offices of Edinburgh's principal newspaper now host this stunning modern hotel. Its beautiful North Bridge Brasserie (⊖⊜⊜) is recommended.

⊖⊜⊜⊜ **Prestonfield**, *Priestfield Road.* 0131 225 7800. www. prestonfield.com. This superbly-restored elegant 17C country house on the edge of Holyrood Park is just a few minutes' walk from the city centre and offers 22 rooms. Excellent restaurant (⊖⊜⊜).

🍴 EAT

⊖⊜⊜ **Atrium**, *Traverse Theatre, 10 Cambridge Street.* 0131 228 8882. www.atriumrestaurant.co.uk. Ultra-stylish, beautifully furnished friendly restaurant with an adventurous food repertoire, set inside a popular modern theatre.

⊖⊜⊜ **The Tower**, *Museum of Scotland, Chambers Street.* 0131 225 3003. www. tower-restaurant. com. Expect top-class game, grills and seafood at this very stylish contemporary restaurant on the top floor of the Museum of Scotland; stunning views from window tables and the terrace.

⊖⊜⊜ **Oloroso**, *33 Castle Street.* 0131 226 7614. www.oloroso.co.uk. Very stylish third-floor restaurant with great views of the castle, serving up Modern Asian-influenced dishes.

⊖⊜ **Blue**, *10 Cambridge Street.* 0131 221 1222. www.bluescotland. co.uk. Long-established with a very

ashionable elegant modern inte-
ior, Blue serves up superb simply-
rafted Modern Scottish cuisine.

⊜⊜ **Le Café Saint-Honoré**, *34 North
West Thistle Street Lane*. ✆*0131 226
211. www.cafesthonore.com*. A bustling
tmospheric, typically-French bistro
elebrating the Auld Alliance between
cotland and France. Booking essential.

⊜⊜ **Nargile**, *73 Hanover Street*.
✆*0131 225 5755. www.nargile.co.uk*.
imple light and airy decor, typical
urkish hospitality, *mezes* and tasty
vell-prepared authentic cuisine brings
he real taste of Turkey to Edinbugh.

🛒 SHOPPING

rinces Street boasts Edinburgh's
amous department store, **Jenners**,
nd many popular UK high-street
ames. The best-quality shops however
re to be found on George Street.

ashion boutiques and music shops
re to be found in Rose Street (parallel
o Princes Street). Antique shops are
nainly in the area around the Royal
lile, Victoria Street and Grassmarket
 the Old Town and in Dundas and
histle Streets in the New Town.

uality garments in tweed, tartan,
ashmere and wool are sold in Jenners,
urberry, the Scotch House, Romanes
atterson (Princes Street) and Kinloch
nderson. The Cashmere Store in the
oyal Mile and Kinloch Anderson's Retail

Shop on the corner of Commercial
Street and Dock Street in Leith are also
worth a visit. **Edinburgh Crystal** in
Penicuik (free shuttle bus from Waverley
Bridge) has a huge array of crystal
articles on sale in its factory shop.

In the Royal Mile there are gourmet
food shops selling smoked salmon,
kippers, cheese, haggis, oatcakes, shortbread and Dundee cake as well
as malt whiskies.

🍺 PUBS

The best way to sample the local
brews is on a pub crawl starting at
the **Abbotsford** in Rose Street or the
Café Royal (D), the haunt of literary
celebrities, in Register Place. The latter
boasts an oyster bar. **Deacon Brodie's**
in Lawnmarket or **Greyfriars Bobby**
in Candlemaker Row are also popular
establishments. There are pubs with
a lively atmosphere popular with students in Grassmarket, and fashionable
pubs and bars by the riverside in Leith.

🎭 ENTERTAINMENT

The List, a fortnightly magazine, lists
films, plays and concerts on offer in
town. Certain hotels hold "Scottish
Evenings" including traditional
entertainment, and pubs like the Ensign
Ewart in Lawnmarket and Bannerman's
in Niddry Street are regular venues for
jazz, folk, Scottish and world music.

Elgin★

Moray

gin stands on the banks of the
ossie just off the northeast coast.
he original town plan has been well
reserved, with the main street link-
g the two mainstays of a medieval
urgh – the cathedral and castle.

ATHEDRAL★

S. ♿🕐 *Open late Mar–Oct
aily 9.30am–5.30pm. (Oct 4.30).
ct–Mar Sat–Wed 9.30am–4.30pm.
£4.60.* ✆*01343 547 171.
ww.historic-scotland.gov.uk.*

▸ **Population:** 11,855.
♿ **Michelin Map:** Michelin
Atlas p 68 or Map 501 K 11.
ℹ **Info:** 17 High Street
✆01343 542 666. www.
aberdeen-grampian.com.
www.elginscotland.org.
⊙ **Location:** Elgin is
38mi/61km northeast
of Inverness.
The train station, at Station
Road, on the Aberdeen–
Inverness line, is just
south of the centre.

The diocese dates back to 1120, but the ruins here are those of a cathedral built in 1270. In 1390 Alexander Stewart, the **Wolf of Badenoch**, second son of King Robert II, destroyed both cathedral and town. Both were repaired, and the 13C **chapter house★★** was re-constructed in the 15C. The cathedral suffered further deterioration after conservation was begun in the early 19C.

SPEYSIDE

A signposted tour *(70mi/112km)* through the glens of Speyside includes several famous distilleries which offer a fascinating glimpse into the production of the "sovereign liquor". Essential stops are: **Glenfiddich Distillery** *(0.5 mi/0.8km) north of Dufftown; ⚓🕐 open year-round Mon–Sat 9.30am (noon Sun)–4.30pm; Nov–Mar Mon–Fri 9.30am–4pm. ℘01340 820 373. www.glenfiddich.co.uk/distillery);* picturesque **Dallas Dhu Distillery** *(HS; 1.25mi/2km south of Forres; ⚓🕐 open Apr–Oct daily 9.30am–5.30pm, Oct–Mar Wed–Sat 9.30am–4.30pm; ⚓£5.09; ℘01309 676 548; www.historic-scot land.gov.uk; and* **Speyside Cooperage** *(Dufftown Road; ⚓🕐 open year-round Mon–Fri 9am–4pm; ⚓£3.30; ℘01340 871 108; www.speysidecooperage.co.uk)*

which relates the story of the ancient craft of barrel making.

EXCURSIONS
Sueno's Stone★★
Forres. 12mi/19km west on the A 96 and B 9011.
This superbly carved Pictish stone, probably a funerary monument commemorating a battle, stands on the outskirts of Forres. The large 9C sandstone slab (20ft/6m high) is unique in Britain. Three sides are decorative – one carved with a wheel cross. The fourth side, the most spectacular, shows horsemen, warriors and headless corpses.

Brodie Castle★
NTS. 20mi/32km west on the A 96. ⚓ 🕐 Open daily Apr, Jul–Aug 10.30am–5pm. May–Jun, Sept–Oct Sun–Thu 10.30am–5pm. ⚓£8.50. 🅿✗. ℘08444 932 156. www.nts.org.uk.
The seat of the Brodies since the 11C, the castle developed from a 16C tower-house to the present building. Interiors of various periods are the setting for a splendid collection of paintings, exquisite timepieces and French **furniture**. The ornate **plasterwork ceilings** date from the 17C.

Glamis★

Angus

This pleasant village (pronounced "Glarms") was made famous by Shakespeare, its castle the residence of the character Macbeth. Set in the rich agricultural Vale of Strathmore in the Angus Glens countryside of eastern Scotland. The area around Glamis abounds with stones carved by the Picts.

SIGHTS
Glamis Castle★★
Dundee Road. 🕐 Open mid-Mar–Oct daily 10am–6pm (last tour 4.30pm). Nov–Dec daily 10.30am–4.30pm (last tour 3pm). ⚓£8.50. Grounds only, £4.20. 🚶Guided tour (50min) every

> ▸ **Population:** 648.
> ⚓ **Michelin Map:** Atlas p 62 or Map 501 K, L 14.
> ▷ **Location:** 12mi/19km north of Dundee.

10–15min. ⚓🅿✗. ℘01307 840 393. www.glamis-castle.co.uk.
Glamis is the archetypal Scottish castle, its massive sandstone pile bristles with towers, turrets, conical roofs and chimneys. It has a fascinating history, including a ghost (Lady Glamis, burnt as a witch), literary associations (Macbeth was Thane of Glamis) and Royal Family connections since the 14C; most recently it was the childhood home of the late Queen Mother.

Glamis Castle

B. Kaufmann/MICHELIN

xterior – The 15C L-shaped core of the
astle has been added to and altered,
pparently at random through the
enturies. Statues of James and his son,
harles I, flank the driveway. To the side
a beautiful Italian Garden.

terior – Family and other portraits,
acobean armour and furniture, Mort-
ke tapestries and interiors of many
eriods are on display. The chapel has
series of paintings of the Apostles and
cenes from the Bible by Jacob de Wet
695–1754), a Dutch artist who also
orked at Blair and Holyroodhouse.
he splendid **Drawing Room** is adorned
y a **plasterwork ceiling** (1621) and a
agnificent fireplace.

ngus Folk Museum★

rkwynd. Open weekends only
aster, Apr–Jun & Sept noon–5pm.
l–Aug daily noon–5pm, Sun. All
ank hols noon–5pm. £5.50. .
°0844 4932141. www.nts.org.uk.
attractive row of 18C cottages houses
is fascinating collection of domestic
ad agricultural bygones, including a
hoolroom and Victorian parlour.

XCURSIONS

berlemno Stones★

'mi/20km northeast via the A 94 and
9134. Open May–Oct. The stones
e boarded up from Nov–Apr.
ur sculptured stones, with animal
ad abstract symbols, hunting and
attle scenes and a cross with flanking

angels, stand at the roadside and in the
churchyard.

Meigle Sculptured Stone Museum★★

7mi/11km west by A 94. Meigle.
Open Apr 1 or Easter–Oct daily
9.30am–5.30pm (Oct 4.30pm).
£3.13. . 01828 640 612.
www.historic-scotland.gov.uk.
The former village school displays
an outstanding collection of early
Christian monuments★★ in the
Pictish tradition, all found locally. The
carving is full of vitality and shows a
high degree of skill.

Edzell Castle★

(25mi/40km northeast by A 94 and
B 966 to Edzell village. Open Easter
or Apr–Oct daily 9.30am–5.30pm (Oct
4.30pm). Nov–Mar Sat–Wed 9.30am–
4.30pm. £4.60. . 01356 648
631. www.historic-scotland.gov.uk.
The ruined castle is an early 16C tower
house but the highlight here is the
formal walled garden known as **The
Pleasance**★★★ which is without equal
in Scotland. Sir David Lindsay (c. 1550–
1610) created this garden in 1604; it is a
product of the Renaissance ideas he had
absorbed on his wide travels. The blaze
of summer colour against the rich red of
the walls diverts attention from the rich
heraldic and symbolic **sculptures** on
the surrounding walls, but these, too,
reward closer inspection.

Glasgow★★★
City of Glasgow

Scotland's most populous city is an important industrial centre and port, lying 44 miles/70km west of Edinburgh, just a few miles inland. Many of Scotland's leading businesses make Glasgow their home. In recent years the city has had a renaissance as a cultural centre.

A BIT OF HISTORY

It was to this part of the embattled Kingdom of Strathclyde that **St Mungo** came in the mid 6C: he set up his wooden church on the banks of the Molendinar Burn, and became the first bishop of the city. In the 17C, Glasgow became the centre of the Protestant cause. By the 18C the city was rich from trade in textiles, sugar and tobacco, her wealth increasing in the 19C through banking, ship-building and industry.

The arts prospered amid the wealth: neither the **Glasgow Boys** (WY MacGregor, James Guthrie, George Henry and John Lavery, who advocated realism in an age of romanticism), nor the pioneer Modern movement led by **Charles Rennie Mackintosh**, could have so flourished in any other city. The realist and radical traditions have been adopted by the Glasgow painters of the 1980s (Steven Campbell, Ken Currie, Peter Howson, Adrian Wisniewski and Stephen Conroy). Today Glasgow is the home of the Scottish Opera, Scottish Ballet and several notable **art collections**.

▶ **Population:** 662,853.

Michelin Map: Michelin Atlas p 55 or Map 501 H 16.

Info: 11 George Square. *℘*0141 566 0800. www.seeglasgow.com.

Location: Glasgow is on the east coast of Scotland, 46 mi/73km west of Edinburgh via the M 8. Trains from England arrive at Central Station; from Edinburgh at nearby Queen Street Station. Neighbouring Buchanan Street Bus Station is the terminus for regional, inter-city and local buses. Since Glasgow's main sights are well scattered about, it is advisable to use public transport. The underground stations are indicated on the town plan below. Open-topped bus tours leave from George Square. (*℘*0141 204 0444. http://citysightseeing glasgow.co.uk).

Don't Miss: The Burrell Collection, Glasgow Cathedral; Hunterian Art Gallery Mackintosh Wing; Museum of Transport; an excursion to New Lanark.

Timing: Allow at least three days in the city.

Kids: Glasgow Science Ctr.

PUBLIC TRANSPORT

Buchanan Bus station (*℘*0141 332 3708) gives information on travel passes for the metro, bus and trains. The **SPT** (Strathcyde Partnership for Transport) **Discovery** ticket valid for one day allows visitors to discover the varied aspects of Glasgow starting from different metro stations. Their range of tickets (*www. spt.co.uk/tickets*) also includes the **Charles Rennie Mackintosh Trail Ticket** (*£12*) offering combined entry to all paying Mackintosh attractions in the city, the Hill House in Helensburgh, as well as unlimited travel on Subway and FirstBus services in Greater Glasgow.

SIGHTSEEING

PDG Helicopters, (*℘0870 607 9000; http://tours.pdg-helicopters.co.uk*) offer helicopter rides which afford spectacular views of the city and of Loch Lomond.

Boat trips "doon the watter" along the Firth of Clyde are also very popular.

CATHEDRAL–THE BARRAS

Start at the **Cathedral**★★★ (🕐open Apr–
Sept Mon–Sat 9.30am–5.30pm, Sun 1pm–
5.30pm; rest of year closes 4pm; free
guided tours May–Sept; 🕐closed Jan 1–2
Jan and Dec 25–26; ♿ ; ℰ 0141 552
8198; www.glasgowcathedral.org.uk), the
fourth church on the site of St Mungo's
original building. The site is best viewed
from the heights of the nearby Necropo-
lis. The cathedral is mostly 13C and 14C
with 15C additions. The **nave** is late
Gothic; its elevation of richly moulded
and pointed arches, more numerous
at each level, rises to the timber roof.
Beyond the 15C stone screen is the **choir**,
mid-13C in the finest early pointed style.
Beyond the ambulatory, through one of
the four chapels leading off from it, is
the upper chapter-room (re-built in the
15C) where the medieval university held
its classes. The lower church is another
Gothic delight, where light and shade
play effectively amidst the piers enshrin-
ing the **tomb of St Mungo**, Glasgow's
patron saint, whose legend is illustrated
on the St Kentigern Tapestry (1979). The
15C **Blacader Aisle** is an extension by
Glasgow's first archbishop with ribbed
vaulting and carved bosses.
South of here on the High Street you
will find the **Glasgow Cross**. The heart
of Glasgow until Victorian times; the
Tolbooth Steeple★ is the last reminder
of its faded elegance. Further on you
will come to the **People's Palace and
Winter Gardens** (Glasgow Green; 🕐
open year-round Mon–Thu and Sat
10am–5pm, Fri and Sun 11am–5pm;
♿🅿✕; ℰ 0141 271 2962; www.glas-
gowmuseums.com). This social history
museum with exotic gardens is sited on
Glasgow Green, a place used for grazing,
jousting, parades, public hangings and
above all, free speech. From the gardens, follow the route marked on the
map to see **The Barras** (**CZ**), a famous
century-old colourful weekend street
market.

CITY CENTRE HIGHLIGHTS

Suggested tour routes marked on map.

George Square

Though started in 1782 George Square
is magnificently Victorian. Of special
interest are the 1869 **Merchants'
House** and, opposite, the **City Chambers**★ (♿🕐guided tour, official functions permitting, Mon (excl Bank Hols)–Fri
10.30am, 2.30pm; ℰ0141 287 4018; www.
glasgow.gov.uk) where the grandeur and
opulence of the loggia, council and banqueting halls are reminders that Glasgow was the second city of the Empire
in Victorian times.

Gallery of Modern Art★

Royal Exchange Square. 🕐Open daily
10am/11am–5pm (Thu 8pm). Free
guided tours. ♿✕. ℰ 0141 229 3050.
www.glasgowmuseums.com.
This great 18C neo-Classical mansion
houses a wide-ranging collection of
contemporary art. It has a massive
Corinthian portico and a magnificent
main hall with a barrel-vaulted ceiling.
British artists include Beryl Cook and,
David Hockney while European artists
represented include Vasarely (pioneer of
Op Art) and Nicky de Saint-Phalle.

Charles Rennie Mackintosh (1868–1928)

The city's famous architect, designer and artist developed his original style
combining the Scottish vernacular tradition and Art Nouveau influences. Glasgow
takes great pride in its legacy of fine buildings and interiors by Mackintosh:
Glasgow School of Art, the **Mackintosh House**, **The Willow Rooms** (217
Sauchiehall St), **Queens Cross Church** (270 Garscube Rd) and **Scotland Street
School** (225 Scotland St) as well as the offices of the Daily Record (Renfield Lane)
and the **Glasgow Herald** (Mitchell St). **Hill House** in Helensburgh is a must for
fans of domestic architecture. An unusual recent addition is the **House for an Art
Lover** (Bellahouston Park) built to Mackintosh's original design for a competition.
See also the recently redesigned **Kelvingrove** collection.

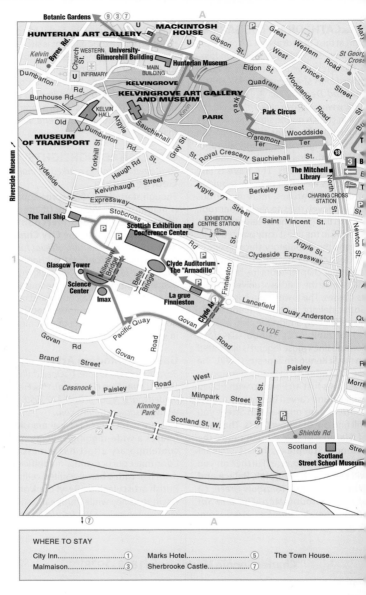

Glasgow School of Art★

167 Renfrew Street. Mackintosh Gallery.
Visit by guided tour only. £7.75.
0141 353 4526. www.gsa.ac.uk.
The building was designed 1897–1909
by Charles Rennie Mackintosh and is his
masterpiece.

It holds his acclaimed library with three-
storey-high windows and suspended

ceiling, plus the furniture gallery wit[h]
items from Miss Cranston's Tea Rooms

Tenement House

NTS. 145 Buccleuch Street. Open
Mar–Oct daily 1pm–5pm. £5.50.
0844 4932197. www.nts.org.uk.
A piece of important Glasgow social his[-]
tory, this two-room flat with kitchen an[d]

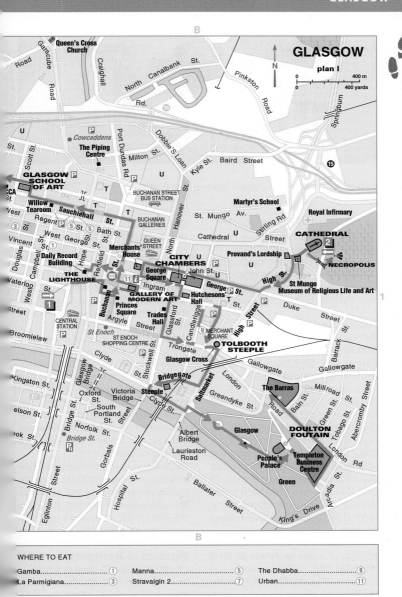

bathroom, portrays turn-of-the-century tenement life.

👥 Glasgow Science Centre

By the Clyde, 50 Pacific Quay. 🕐 *Open Apr–Sept daily 10am–6pm. Oct–Mar Tue–Sun 10am–3pm/5pm.* 🎫 *£6.75, child £4.95.* ♿ 🅿 *(£3)* 🍴 📞 *0871 540 1000. www.glasgowsciencecentre.org.*

Housed in three stunning modern buildings of real architectural merit this new hands-on Science Centre contains hundreds of interactive exhibits in its Science Mall, a Science Show Theatre, a Climate Change Theatre plus a planetarium and an IMAX cinema.

Visitors can also take a ride to the top of the rotating landmark 416ft/127m-high

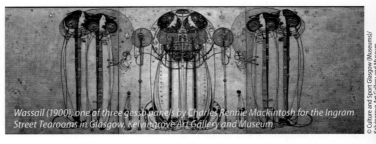

Wassail (1900), one of three gesso panels by Charles Rennie Mackintosh for the Ingram Street Tearooms in Glasgow, Kelvingrove Art Gallery and Museum

© Culture and Sport Glasgow (Museums)/
Kelvingrove Art Gallery and Museum

Glasgow Tower for a splendid view of the city.

KELVINGROVE HIGHLIGHTS

The area around Kelvingrove Park is home to three impressive museums. The park, with its famous bandstand, takes its name from the river Kelvin, which flows past the university and gave scientist William Thomson his title, Lord Kelvin.

Hunterian Museum, Art Gallery and Mackintosh House★★

🕐 *Open Mon–Sat 9.30am–5pm.* 🎫*Mackintosh House £3 (free Wed after 2pm), other areas free.* ♿✗. ✆*0141 330 4221 for Museum;* ✆*0141 330 5431 for Art Gallery and Mackintosh House;* ✆*0141 330 4772 Zoology Museum. www.hunterian.gla.ac.uk.*

These University of Glasgow museums hold an eclectic and fascinating collection including medicine and anatomy, one of the world's great **coin** collections, and Roman and Egyptian artefacts. There is also a separate zoology museum.

The art gallery includes an important holding of works by **James McNeill Whistler** (1843–1903), as well as portraits and 19C and 20C Scottish art. The **Mackintosh House**★★★ is a reconstruction of the home of Charles Rennie Mackintosh.

Kelvingrove Art Gallery and Museum★★

🕐 *Open year-round Mon–Thu and Sat 10am–5pm, Fri and Sun 11am–5pm.* 🕐*Closed Jan 1–2 and Dec 25–26. Free guided tours.* ♿🅿✗. ✆*0141 276 9599. www.glasgowmuseums.com.*

The building opened in 1902, financed by the 1888 Glasgow International Exhibition. The European art section is displayed in the first-floor galleries. The Dutch and Flemish holding includes works by Jordaens, Rubens, Bruegel the Elder and Rembrandt, as well as Ruisdael landscapes. French 19C and early 20C movements are represented by Millet, Fantin-Latour and Courbet; and the Impressionists by Monet, Pissarro, Renoir and Sisley.

Van Gogh's 1887 portrait depicts the Glasgow art dealer, Alexander Reid, with whom he shared a flat in Paris. The British section includes portraits by Ramsey, Raeburn, Reynolds and Romney and the work of the Pre-Raphaelites. William McTaggart's outdoor scenes and the highly distinctive works of the Scottish Colourists are enjoying a growing reputation.

The recently refurbished **Glasgow Style** gallery provides a permanent home for the city's extensive collection of Charles Rennie Mackintosh exhibits, including the spectacular interior of Kate Cranston's **Ingram Street Tea Rooms**.

Museum of Transport★★

1 Bunhouse Road. 🕐 *Open as Kelvingrove (♿see above).* 🔊*Free guided tours.* ♿🅿✗. ✆*0141 287 2720. www.glasgowmuseums.com.*

The museum has comprehensive displays of trams and trolleybuses from 1872–1967, vintage cars with the emphasis on **Scottish-built cars**★★★, fire vehicles and bicycles.

The **Clyde Room of Model Ships**★★★ displays the varied and impressive output of Scottish shipyards, in particular those of Clydeside.

BURRELL COLLECTION★★★

3mi/5km southwest on the M 77 Pollok Park. ⏰ *Open 10am/11am–5pm Mon–Thu, Sat 10am–5pm, Fri and Sun 11am–5pm.* 🚶*Guided tour (free).* ♿🅿✕. *℘0141 287 2550. www.glasgowmuseums.com.*

The collection of ship-owner **Sir William Burrell** (1861–1958) is spaciously laid out in a custom-built gallery, surrounded by parkland. The **Ancient Civilisations** section includes items from Egypt, Mesopotamia, Italy and Greece. **Oriental Art** incorporates ceramics, bronzes and jades from the third millennium BC to the 19C, and features the enamelled Ming figure of a **lohan**, or disciple of Buddha, which is dated to 1484. Burrell's particular interest was in **Medieval** and **Post-Medieval European Art** and there are some outstanding examples. Of the early works to be found in **Paintings**, **Drawings and Bronzes**, Bellini's *Virgin and Child* is notable. The **Hutton Castle Rooms** are complete with medieval and antique furnishings.

EXCURSIONS
Pollok House★

Off the M 77 just south of the city centre. Pollokshaws Road. 💷£5.50. ♿🅿✕. *℘0844 4932202. www.nts.org.uk.*

The highlight of this 18C mansion is the collection of **Spanish paintings**★★ acquired by Sir William Stirling Maxwell (1818–78). These include portraits by El Greco and etchings by Goya as well as works by Tristan, Alonso Cano and Murillo.

Hill House, Helensburgh★

NTS. 21mi/34km northwest by A 82 and A 814. Upper Colquhoun Street. ⏰*Open Mar–Oct 1.30pm–5.30pm.* 💷£8.50. *℘0844 493 2208. www.nts.org.uk.*

On a hillside overlooking the Clyde, this is a first-rate example of pioneer modern domestic architecture (1902–04) and interior design by Charles Rennie Mackintosh.

New Lanark★★

20mi/32km southeast by M 74 and A 72. ⏰ *Open daily 10.30am (Oct–Mar 11am) –5pm.* 💷£6.95. ♿🅿✕. *℘01555 661 345. www.newlanark.org.*

In the deep gorge of the River Clyde, an 18C planned industrial village comprising four cotton mills, housing and amenities for the workforce was the acclaimed achievement of the Glasgow manufacturer and banker David Dale and his son-in-law Robert Owen, a social reformer. In 1986, the village was nominated a World Heritage Site. Among the interesting buildings are the Nursery Buildings for pauper apprentices, the store, the counting house and tenements *(Caithness Row)*, and the Institute – a social centre. **Mill no. 3 (Annie McLeod Experience, exhibition, visitor centre)** is the most handsome of the four units. The riverside **Dyeworks** has displays on the wildlife of the Falls of Clyde Reserve.

The **Falls of Clyde** framed by woods are a popular beauty spot. It has inspired painters (including Turner) and poets (such as Scott and Wordsworth) alike.

ADDRESSES

⊜⊜⊜ **Malmaison**, *278 West George Street.* *℘0141 572 1000. www.malmaison.com.* Visually-striking former Masonic chapel with ultra-stylish rooms in bold patterns and colours. The French-themed Brasserie restaurant (⊜⊜⊜) is recommended. The hotel is named after the Château de Malmaison in Rueil-Malmaison, outside Paris, once the home of Bonaparte's first wife, José-phine de Beauharnais and headquarters of the French government (1800-1802).

⊜⊜⊜ **City Inn**, *Finnieston Quay.* *℘0141 240 1002. www.cityinn.com.* Wide range of prices and good-value deals available in this smart functional contemporary-styled hotel.

⊜⊜⊜ **Marks Hotel**, *110 Bath Street.* *℘0141 354 7705. www.marks hotels.com.* The spacious attractive rooms in this ultra-trendy 103-bedroom hotel (with a stunning penthouse) include satellite plasma TV and are excellent value

⊜⊜⊜ **Sherbrooke Castle**, *11 Sherbrooke Avenue, Pollokshields.* ℘*0141 427 4227. www.sherbrooke. co.uk.* A celebration of late-19C Baronial style with Romantic and rich imposing furnishings, country house refinement and a panelled dining room just 5mins from the city centre.

⊜⊜ **The Town House**, *4 Hughenden Terrace.* ℘*0141 357 0862. www.thetownhouseglasgow.com.* Elegant personally-run town house with nice Victorian touches, spacious rooms and an inviting lounge with a real fire.

⧖/EAT

⊜⊜⊜ **Gamba**, *225a West George Street.* ℘*0141 572 0899. www.gamba. co.uk.* Smart stylish long-established but very modern restaurant, with a strong claim to being the best seafood restaurant in Glasgow.

⊜⊜⊜ **Manna**, *104 Bath Street.* ℘*0141 332 6678. www.mannarestaurant.co.uk.* Attractive fashionable city-centre restaurant, serving some of the best steaks in the city with top-quality Scottish beef. Good value.

⊜⊜ **The Dhabba**, *44 Candleriggs.* ℘*0141 553 1249. www.thedhabba.com.* Stylish modern North Indian restaurant serving authentic and accomplished dishes; try one of their unusual Dum Pukht specials, sealed in its own dish.

⊜⊜ **La Parmigiana**, *447 Great Western Road, Kelvinbridge.* ℘*0141 334 0686. www.laparmigiana.co.uk.* Compact traditional establishment serving a sound repertoire of tasty Italian food.

⊜⊜ **Stravaigin 2**, *8 Ruthven Lane.* ℘*0141 334 7165. www.stravaigin. com.* "Think Global Eat Local" is the message of this long-established but trend-setting unfussy bistro, offering a contemporary menu with an eclectic range of original dishes.

⊜⊜ **Urban**, *23–25 St Vincent Place.* ℘*0141 248 5636. www.urbanbrasserie. co.uk.* This stunning grand new brasserie is set in the former Bank of England's Scottish headquarters, serving Modern British cuisine using seasonal and, wherever possible, locally sourced products.

⦿ PUBS AND ⧖/RESTAURANTS

The lively atmosphere of Glasgow pubs is famous: **Rab Ha's** in Hutcheson Street, **Times Square** in St Enoch's Square, **Curlers** and **Bonhams** in Byres Road and **Dows** in Dundas Street among many other venues, are well worth a visit. Glasgow also offers a wide range of restaurants to suit all tastes.

For a light meal or afternoon tea visit the delightful **Willow Rooms** at 217 Sauchiehall Street, designed by Mackintosh for Miss Cranston.

⛒SHOPPING

Sauchiehall, Buchanan and Argyle Streets are pedestrian shopping precincts. The glass-roofed Princes Street shopping centre in Buchanan Street is a pleasant haven where Scottish items are on offer. The Italian Centre on the corner of John and Ingram Streets offers the finest Italian fashion plus stylish bars, brasseries, restaurants and cafés.

Scottish Crafts in Princes Street displays fine items by Scottish craftsmen.

The Barras, a large indoor and outdoor market, is the place to visit not only for a bargain but also for the spectacle.

⦿ ENTERTAINMENT

Glasgow has a dynamic cultural scene with avant-garde theatre staged by the Citizens Theatre, the Centre for Contemporary Arts, the Tramway Theatre and the Tron Theatre. Other venues include The Mitchell Theatre, the King's Theatre and the Theatre Royal. Exhibitions are held at the McLellan Galleries, The Lighthouse and The City Halls – recently converted at great expense and including The Old Fruitmarket.

The List magazine, published fortnightly, is the best guide to what's on in the Greater Glasgow area. Tickets for many events are on sale at the Ticket Centre, City Hall, Candleriggs.

Football is a city passion, and it is essential to book well in advance for the "Old Firm" matches between Rangers and Celtic, but be warned that strong sectarian feelings are aroused at these engagements.

Grampian Castles★★

Aberdeenshire

Aberdeen's hinterland is rich in castles, from Norman to the Scottish baronial style which characterises the golden age of castle-building (16C–17C).

CASTLES

Haddo House★

NTS. 26mi/42km north of Aberdeen by A 92 and B 9005. House: 🐾 *Visit by guided tour only. Good Fri–Jun and Sept–early Nov Fri–Mon noon–5pm. Jul–Aug daily 11am–5pm. Garden and country park:* 🕐 *Open year-round daily 9am–dusk.* ⌖*£8.50.* ♿🅿✗. *☏08444 932 179. www.nts.org.uk.*

The present house was designed by William Adam in 1469. George Hamilton Gordon (1784–1860), Prime Minister during the Crimean War, still found time to repair the house and to landscape the parkland. Elegant rooms with coffered ceilings and wood panelling are a perfect setting for family portraits and mementoes. The country park offers splendid vistas.

Fyvie Castle★

NTS. 26mi/42km north of Aberdeen by A 947. Castle: 🕐 *Open Apr–Jun and Sept–Oct Sat–Wed noon–5pm; Jul–Aug*

🐚 **Michelin Map:** Atlas p 69 or Map 401 L, M and N 12 and 13.

daily 11am–5pm. ⌖*£10.50.* ♿🅿✗. *☏08444 932 182. www.nts.org.uk.*

Alexander Seton, Lord Chancellor (c. 1639–1719), remodelled Fyvie creating the spectacular **south front** (150ft/46m long), an impressive example of 17C baronial architecture, and the **wheel stair**. In the late 19C Fyvie was refurbished in opulent Edwardian style, decorated with portraits by the Scottish master of this art, **Henry Raeburn**.

Crathes Castle★★

NTS. 15mi/24km southwest of Aberdeen by A 93. 🕐 *Open Apr–Oct daily 10.30am–5.30pm (Oct 4.30pm). Nov–Mar Sat–Sun 10.30am–3.30pm.* ⌖*£10.50.* ♿🅿✗. *☏08444 932 166. www.nts.org.uk.*

The wonderfully crowded and detailed skyline of this 16C tower house is a striking example of the inventive baronial tradition. The interiors include some fine early vernacular furniture as well as some outstanding examples of **painted ceilings**. Stone pendants and armorial paintings adorn the barrel-vaulted **High Hall** where the **Horn of Leys** – the original token of tenure dating from 1322 – has pride of place above the fireplace.

Dunnottar Castle

P. Tomkins/VisitScotland/Scottish Viewpoint

The oak-panelled roof decorated with armorial devices and the horn motif is a unique feature of the **Long Gallery**. The series of **separate gardens**★★★ are a delight in the wealth and colour of the planting.

Castle Fraser★

NTS. 15mi/24km west of Aberdeen by A 944 and B 993 at Dunecht. ⟶Visit by guided tour only. **Castle:** ◷Open Apr–Jun and Sept–Oct Thu–Sun and bank hols noon–5pm; Jul–Aug daily 11am–5pm. ⟶£8.50. ⟶ ⟶ ⟶, woodland trails, adventure playground. ✆08444 932 164. www.nts.org.uk.

Castle Fraser, built 1575–1636, is a traditional tower house with highly individual decoration. The **exterior**★★ is remarkable. The local style with its harmonious combination of traditional features – turrets, conical roofs, crow-stepped gables, chimney stacks, decorative dormers and gargoyles – was Scotland's unique contribution to Renaissance architecture. The **central block** of this Z-plan castle is distinguished by a magnificent heraldic achievement. The refurbished interiors bring to life the simple lifestyle of a 17C laird.

Dunnottar Castle★★

18mi/29km south of Aberdeen via the A 92. ◷ Open Easter Monday–late Jun, Mon–Sat 9am–6pm, Sun 2pm–5pm. Late Jun–late Sept, daily 9am–6pm. Late Sept–Easter Sunday, Fri–Mon 10.30am–sunset. ⟶£5. ✆01569 762 173.www.dunnottarcastle.co.uk.

Set on an almost inaccessible **promontory**★★★ with sheer cliffs on three sides, the castle dates from the 14C and was the last castle remaining in Royalist hands during the Commonwealth. Here the Honours of Scotland (royal regalia) were held during an eight-month siege by Cromwell's troops in 1651–52, being finally smuggled out and hidden in a nearby church. The fortified **gatehouse** and **keep** contrast with the 17C **Waterton's Lodging** and the **16C–17C buildings** arranged around a quadrangle.

Inveraray★★
Argyll and Bute

This delightful white-washed township lies roughly halfway along Scotland's west coast on the shores of Loch Fyne, a short distance from its castle, the seat of the chief of Clan Campbell.

INVERARAY CASTLE★★

Just north of town. ⟶◷ Open Apr–Oct daily 10am (Sun noon)–5.45pm. ⟶£6.80. ⟶ ⟶. ✆01499 302 203. www.inveraray-castle.com.

The exterior is in Gothic Revival style. The 5th Duke refurbished the interiors in the neo-Classical style after the fashion of Carlton House in London. In particular, the **dining room** is a masterpiece of delicately detailed plasterwork and painting. The Tapestry Drawing Room reveals an Adam-designed compartmented ceiling, decorative panels and

- ▶ **Population:** 770.
- ◔ **Michelin Map:** Michelin Atlas p 54 or Map 501 E 15.
- ▯ **Info:** Front Street. ✆01499 302 063. www.inveraray-argyll.com.
- ◑ **Location:** 37mi/60km southeast of Oban.

overdoors by Girard. The **armoury hall** with its decorative display of pole-arms, Lochaber axes and broadswords is where the duke's personal piper plays a medley of Campbell tunes to awaken the household.

In the Saloon, Pompeo Batoni's 8th Duke of Hamilton faces Gainsborough's Conway. Among the portraits in the northwest hall and staircase note the re-building 3rd Duke (Allan Ramsay), the re-decorating 5th Duke (Gainsborough) and his duchess, Elizabeth Gunning.

🚗 DRIVING TOUR

LOCH FYNE TO LOCH AWE

The great sea-loch of **Loch Fyne**★★ stretches from the heart of the Argyll mountains down the arm of Loch Gilp where it turns due south to reach the open sea. In the 19C this was a successful herring fishery. Loch Fyne is notable for its oyster fishery and the Loch Fyne Oyster.

5.6mi/9km south of Inveraray on the A 83 is Auchindain, home to the **Auchindrain Museum**★ (*6mi/10km on the A 83; ⊙open Apr–Sept daily 10am–5pm; ⊜£4.50; ♿🅿; ✆01499 500 235; www.auchindrain-museum.org.uk*), an open-air folk museum evoking life in the communal-tenancy farms.

Follow the loch south and round the headland to Lochgliphead, then follow A 816 and B 841 to **Crinan**★, a delightful hamlet at the western end of the Crinan Canal. From Crinan, picturesque roads (*the A 819 north to Cladich and the lochside B 840*) lead to scenic **Loch Awe**★★, the third largest freshwater loch in Scotland and the site of two hydroelectric projects. The loch is famous for trout fishing, while its islands include several ruined castles (♿*see OBAN for more on the loch*).

Inverness★

Highlands

Standing at the northern end of the Great Glen, astride the River Ness flowing from Loch Ness, Inverness is the traditional capital of the Scottish Highlands and the legendary Loch attracts many boating visitors.

👣 CITY WALKING TOUR

Just east of Young Street bridge on Castle Wynd is the **Museum and Art Gallery**★ (⊙*open Mon–Sat 10am–5pm;* ⊙*closed Dec 25–26 and Dec 31–Jan;* ♿✕; ✆01463 237 114; http://inverness. highland.museum*), an imaginative wellpresented exhibition interpreting the region's rich heritage, including the Great Glen, the Picts, General Wade's roads and Telford's Caledonian Canal. Immediately to the south is 19C **Inverness Castle** (*Castle St*), the most recent of a series, sitting on a low cliff overlooking the River Ness and the cathedral on the opposite bank. A good **view** of the town and the River Ness may be enjoyed from the esplanade. Across the bridge, follow the road to Ardross Street and take a left for **St Andrew's Cathedral** (⊙*open daily;* ✕; ✆01463 233 535; www.invernesscathedral.com*), a richly decorated neo-Gothic church of 1866–69. Its nave piers are of polished Peterhead granite.

- ▶ **Population:** 62,186.
- ⏱ **Michelin Map:** Michelin Atlas p 67 or Map 501 H 11.
- ▯ **Info:** Castle Wynd. ✆01463 234 353. www.inverness -scotland.com.
- ◖ **Location:** 156mi/250km north of Edinburgh and 119mi/190km southwest of John O'Groats. The town services much of northern Scotland and trains and buses arrive at the central stations off Academy Street.
- 👥 **Kids:** Loch Ness Exhibition Centre at Drumnadrochit.

EXCURSIONS

Cawdor Castle★

13mi/21km northeast on the A 96 and B 9090. ⊙ *Open May–mid-Oct daily 10am–5.30pm.* ⊜*£8.50. Gardens and grounds only, £4.50.* ♿🅿✕. ✆01667 404 401. www.cawdorcastle.com.

Built in the late 14C by the Thanes of Cawdor (the title Shakespeare's witches promised to Macbeth), the castle was added to in the 17C. Note the lovely 17C Flemish and English tapestries and amidst the many portraits one of the 18C thane, splendidly dressed in an assortment of tartans. Outside, there are three gardens to enjoy.

Nessie

The initial sighting of a large snake-like, hump-backed monster with a long thin neck in Loch Ness was made in the 8C by a monk. Despite various expeditions, some highly equipped with submarines, helicopters and sonar electronic cameras, the loch has failed to reveal its secret (the true identity of Nessie). The tradition is hardly surprising in a country where the kelpie or water-horse was common in the tales and legends of the past.

Fort George★

HS. 20mi/32km northeast on the A 96 and B 9006. ○ *Open daily 9.30am–4.30pm/5.30pm.* ⊘£6.56. 🔥🅿️✕. ℘01667 460 232.
Set on a peninsula jutting out into the Moray Firth, this impressive artillery fortress was built between 1745 and 1746 on the orders of George II, to preserve his law and order from being disrupted by the Highland clans. Sights include the fort, its elaborate defences and several exhibitions including the **Queen's Own Highlanders Regimental Museum** (○*closed winter Sat–Sun and third week Dec–early Jan*).

Cromarty★

26mi/42km northeast by A 9 and A 832.
On the northern tip of the Black Isle at the mouth of the Cromarty Firth guarded by the Sutors Stacks, the tiny port of Cromarty has been aptly described as "the jewel in the crown of Scottish vernacular architecture". Pay a visit to the fine 18C **Cromarty Courthouse Museum** (*Church Street;* ○*open May–Sept Sun–Thu daily 11am–4pm;* ℘*01381 600 418; www.cromarty-court house.org.uk*).

Dornoch★

55mi/88km northeast on the A 9.
The scenic route cuts across the Black Isle, passes along the north bank of the Cromarty Firth, near the pretty little town of **Tain**, formerly an important pilgrimage centre, and crosses the Dornoch Firth to reach this charming burgh which boasts miles of sandy beaches and famous golf courses. The medieval cathedral dominates the town.

Culloden

NTS. 6mi/10km east by A 9 and B 9006. Culloden. Visitor Centre: ○ *Open Apr–Oct daily 9am–6pm. Nov–Mar daily 10am–4pm.* ○*Closed mid-Jan–late Jan.* ⊘£12. 🔥🅿️✕. ℘08444 932 159. www.culloden.org.uk.
Here on 16 April 1746 the Jacobite army under Bonnie Prince Charlie was slaughtered by Government troops under "Butcher Cumberland", George II's younger son, finally ending the hopes of a Stuart restoration to the British throne. A major new **visitor centre** interprets the battle and its significance.

Urquhart Castle by Loch Ness

🚗 DRIVING TOUR

GREAT GLEN★
65mi/105km SW on the A 82.
The geological fault of the Great Glen cuts across the Highlands, linking the Atlantic Ocean with the North Sea through a series of narrow lochs joined together by part (22mi/35km) of Thomas Telford's **Caledonian Canal** (1803–22). The lochs and canals are now used principally for pleasure craft (operators offer "Monster Hunting" trips on Loch Ness). At the southern end of the glen, **Fort William**★ marks the northern tip of Loch Linnhe, sitting in the shadow of Britain's highest mountain, **Ben Nevis** (4 406ft/1 344m). The town makes an ideal touring centre.
Heading north from here on the A 82 you come to Torlundy, where cable cars (🚡; *return trip £9.50;* 🅿 ✕; ☎ *01397 705 825. www.nevis-range.co.uk),* rise to the Nevis Range ski resort with great **views**★★ en route. From here the A 82 will take you past Loch Lochy and Loch Oich until you arrive at Loch Ness.

Loch Ness★★
The dark waters of this loch (754ft/230m deep) are renowned the world over as the home of the elusive **Nessie**. First spied in the 8C by a local monk, Nessie has continued to captivate and mystify and, despite modern technology, preserve her true identity.
From Fort Augustus and its canal lock, travel north on the west side of the loch on the A82 to see the much-photographed ruins of **Urquhart Castle** *(HS;* 🕐 *open daily Apr–Oct 9.30am–6pm (5pm Oct), Nov–Mar 9.30am–4.30pm);* ☞*£6.36;* 🅿; ☎*01456 450 551; www.historic-scotland.gov.uk).* This former stronghold was one of a chain of defences controlling this natural route. It is strategically set on a promontory jutting into the loch
Next stop on the A 82 is the pretty little village of **Drumnadrochit**. Here you can satisfy your curiosity in all things Nessie at the **Loch Ness Exhibition Centre**★ (👪 🕐 *open daily;* ☞*£6.50, child £4.50;* 🚻 🅿 ✕; ☎ *01456 450 573; www.loch ness-scotland.com),* an entertaining multi-media visitor centre.

Isle of Iona★
Argyll and Bute

St Columba established his monastic settlement here 1,400 years ago. It remains one of the most venerated places in Scotland.

ISLE
The Saint's community flourished until brought to an end by the Norse raids of the 8C and 9C. Intricately carved crosses and grave slabs are a testament to its prior artistic accomplishments. A Benedictine monastery was re-established in the early 13C but disappeared at the Reformation. In 1938 a third religious brotherhood – now an ecumenical community – came to the isle and a major restoration programme was completed in 1966. The abbey today is a place of hospitality, reflection and worship, while a small community of crofters inhabits the fertile island.

▶ **Population:** 268.
⊙ **Michelin Map:** Atlas p 59 or Map 501 A 14 and 15.
ℹ **Info:** Main Street, Tobermory, Isle of Mull. ☎08707 200 625. www.isle-of-iona. com. www.visitscottish heartlands.com.
▶ **Location:** West coast, off southwesterly tip of the Isle of Mull. CalMac ferries (www.calmac.co.uk) make the short jurney between the islands.

Take the road from the old Benedictine **Nunnery** with its medieval church and conventual buildings. Go through the gate past the intricately-carved 15C **Maclean's Cross**★ and the early Christian burial ground, **Reilig Odhrian** (where Scotland's kings from Kenneth

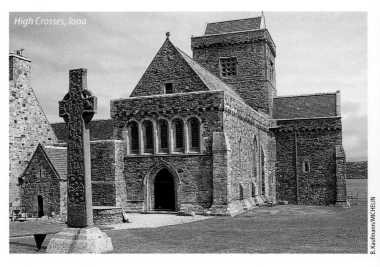

High Crosses, Iona

B. Kaufmann/MICHELIN

MacAlpine to Malcolm III were buried) to the 12C **St Oran's Chapel**★, the oldest building on the island, with a fine Norman west door. Walk down the **Street of the Dead**, where three **High Crosses** catch the eye (an 8C **Cross of St Martin**★, a 9C–10C truncated shaft of St Matthew and a replica of the 8C St John's Cross). On the other side of the Street of the Dead is St Columba's cell, Tor Abb. The **abbey** (HS; ⏱open daily 9.30am–4.30pm/5.30pm; ☞£4.70;

&.; ℘01681 700 512; www.historic-scotland.gov.uk), stands on the site of its Columban predecessor. To the north of the west front is St Columba's shrine. Beyond the abbey is the **Infirmary Museum**★, (⏱ Open daily 9am–5pm. ℘01681 700 404) with an outstanding collection of early Christian and medieval stonework including the ornate 8C **Cross of St John**★ (restored), medieval effigies and grave slabs.

Jedburgh★

Borders

The royal burgh of Jedburgh, spanning the Jed Water with a mid-12C triple-arched bridge, was once a much fought-over border post. Today it is a peaceful market town on one of the main routes into Scotland.

TOWN WALKING TOUR

Just off the A 68 on Abbey Bridge End is **Jedburgh Abbey**★★ (HS; ⏱open daily 9.30am–5.30pm (Oct–Easter 4.30pm); ☞£5.09; &.🅿; ℘01835 863 925; www.historic-scotland.gov.uk), founded in 1138 for the Augustinian order. It was one of the many Border abbeys founded

▸ **Population:** 4,053.
&. **Michelin Map:** Michelin Atlas p 50 or Map 501 M 17.
🛈 **Info:** Murray's Green ℘01835 863 170. www.scot-borders.co.uk.
◖ **Location:** 10mi/16km north of the border.

by David I to spread monasticism in 12C Scotland and witnessed the coronation of Malcolm IV in the 12C and many royal events. The abbey was often plundered and attacked before the final destructive raid in 1545. The ruined abbey church is a majestic example of 12C architecture and has a powerful **west front**, while the rhythm and design of the **nave** display the assurance of an art well-mastered. The mid-12C **east end** is notable for the massive pillars rising to the clerestory and buttressing the arches of the main arcade. Continue north on Abbey Bridge End to the B 6358.

To your right down High Street, then right onto Queen Street is the **Mary Queen of Scots Visitor Centre**★ (◔ open Easter–Nov daily 10am (11am Sun)–4.30pm; ⊜£3.50; ℘01835 863 331; www.discovertheborders.co.uk), a fine 16C tower house where Mary Queen of Scots stayed in 1566. Engraved glass panels, paintings and documents relate the life of this tragic queen.

Head back down High Street and continue on Castle Gate for **Jedburgh Castle Jail and Museum** (◔ open late-Mar–Oct Mon–Sat 10am–4.30pm; Sun 1pm–4pm; ⊜£2.25; ℘01835 864 750; www.discovertheborders.co.uk). Built in 1823 on the site of the original castle, this prison was considered one of the most modern jails of its day. There are exhibits interpreting Jedburgh's local and industrial history.

EXCURSIONS
Bowhill★★
19mi/31km northwest by A 68, A 699, A 7 and A 708. **House:** ◔Open Jul daily 11pm–5pm; Aug daily by tour only 2pm, 3.30pm. **Country Park:** ◔Open Easter–Aug. ⊜£7. Park only, £3. ℘01750 22204. www.bowhill.org.

Among the many treasures which grace Bowhill are fine pieces of French **furniture**, Mortlake tapestries, relics of the Duke of Monmouth and an important collection of paintings including works by Leonardo da Vinci, Canaletto, Claude, Wilkie (George IV in Highland Dress), Reynolds (Winter, The Pink Boy), Gainsborough and other masters. There is also a collection of **miniatures**.

Hermitage Castle★
26mi/42km SW on B 6358, A 698, B 6399. ◔ Open Easter–Oct 9.30am–5.30pm (Oct 4.30pm). ⊜£3.62. 🅿. ℘01387 376 222. www.historic-scotland.gov.uk.

In its isolated moorland setting this massive ruin has a history of torture, treason and romantic trysts and evokes the Borders' troubled past. A strategic stronghold of the Wardens of the March, it guarded the old reivers' routes. It was here that Mary Queen of Scots came on her dash to the injured Earl of Bothwell, her future husband. The uniform appearance of Hermitage is deceptive as the original fortified manor-house dating from the mid 14C was converted into a late 14C tower house with four corner towers added at a later stage. The castle is enclosed by tall outer walls with loopholes, parapets and pointed arches. The Border Abbeys were King David I's main achievement, the development of monasticism in 12C Scotland: Kelso 1128 (original foundation 1113), Melrose 1136, Jedburgh 1138 and Dryburgh 1150.

Isle of Mull★
Argyll and Bute

This narrow island (nowhere more than 26mi/42km across) sits at the mouth of Scotland's Great Glen. It is dominated by the mountain Ben More (3 169ft/966m), with a deeply-indented coastline (some 300mi/480km long) ranging from rocky cliffs to sandy beaches; the sea views are superb. Inland, pastoral crofting landscapes contrast with desolate moorlands.

▶ **Population:** 2,838.
⬩ **Michelin Map:** Atlas p 59 or Map 501 B, C 14.
▤ **Info:** Craignure ℘08707 200 610; Tobermory ℘08707 200 625; visitscot tishheartlands.com.
◖ **Transport:** CalMac ferries (www.calmac.co.uk) connect Mull with Oban (40mins), Iona, Kilchoan and Lochaline on the mainland.

ISLE

The main town and ferry port, **Tobermory**, fringes the yachting centre of Tobermory Bay, 22mi/35km north along the coast from Craignure, the island's main ferry terminal.

1.5mi/2.5km south of Craignure is **Torosay Castle** (🕐 open Easter–Oct daily 10.30am–5pm; gardens also open Nov–Easter 9am–dusk: ☞£6.50, gardens only, £5 (£2.50 winter); ✕; 📞01680 812 421; www.torosay.com), a superb example (1856) of David Bryce's fluency in Scottish Baronial style, perfected by Robert Lorimer's **gardens★**, which have spectacular **views★**.

About 1.6mi further south along the coast is **Duart Castle** (🕐 open Apr, Sun–Thu 11am–4pm; May–mid-Oct, daily 10.30am–5.30pm; ☞£5.30; 🅿✕; 📞01680 812 309; www.duartcastle.com),

home of the Chief of the **Clan MacLean**, perched on a rocky crag guarding the Sound of Mull, with magnificent views. The keep dates from c. 1250 but the 13C castle was burnt in the late 17C. Sir Fitzroy MacLean, the 26th Chief, restored the stronghold to its present appearance in 1911.

ISLE OF STAFFA

National Nature Reserve; 🕐 open daily. Ferries Apr–Oct from Iona, Fionnphort Ulva and Mull, see website for operators. 📞08444 932 237. www.nts.org.uk.

This basaltic island, with its amazing rock formations and spectacular caves owes its fame to Mendelssohn's overture Fingal's Cave, composed following his visit in 1829. Its awesome beauty has inspired poets and painters alike.

Oban

Argyll and Bute

A busy tourist centre and service town for the hinterland and islands, Oban lies opposite the Isle of Mull at the southern end of the Great Glen. It owes its development to the railways and steamboats; hence the dominating Victorian aspect to the town. The outstanding landmark is **McCaig's Tower** (1897), a replica of the Colosseum, built to relieve unemployment, but never finished.

▶ **Population:** 8,203.
　Michelin Map: Michelin Atlas p 60 or Map 501 D 14.
　Info: Argyll Square. 📞01631 563122. www.oban.org.uk.
　Location: 44mi/71km south of Fort William. The train and bus stations are by the ferry terminal on Station Square.

LOCH AWE★★

18mi/29km east by A 85. The road follows the narrow defile of the **Pass of Brander** overlooked to the north by the lower slopes of **Ben Cruachan** (3,689ft/1,126m). Scotland's longest lake (over 25mi/40km long), lies in the heart of Campbell country. **Kilchurn Castle** juts out on the northern shore. The 15C stronghold, built by Sir Colin Campbell, with 1693 extensions, was abandoned in the mid 18C.

GLEN COE★★

The dramatic approach to Glen Coe (11mi/18km long) – the stark and grandiose setting where the infamous **Glen Coe massacre** occurred – is heralded by the **Meall a Bhuiridh** (Hill of the Roaring Stags, 3,636ft/1,108m), the **Buachaille Etive Mor** (Big Herdsman of Etive 3,345ft/1,022m) and the glacial valley, Glen Etive, between them. The flat-topped rock, the Study pinpoints the head of Glen Coe. Beyond the waterfall rise mighty rock-faces the **Three Sisters**, the outliers of **Bidean nam Bian** (Peak of the Bens) soaring to 3,766ft/1,141m, stretch to one side, the serrated ridge of **Anoach Eagach** to the other; Loch Achtriochtan spreads out on the valley floor. **Glencoe and Dalness Visitor Centre**

NTS. Ⓒopen Mar–Oct daily 9am–6pm; Jan–Feb and Nov–mid-Dec Thu–Sun 10am–4pm; ☞£5.50; ☕; ☎0844 4932222; www.nts.org.uk) provides information on and guides for local walks and climbs.

On the shores of Loch Leven nestles the village of **Glencoe** (population 315) which houses the small **Glencoe and North Lorn Folk Museum** (Ⓒopen Easter week and mid-May–Sept Mon–Sat 10am–5.30pm; ☞£2; ♿Ⓟ; ☎01855 811 664). The picturesque road south (A 82, 828) skirts the south shore of Loch Leven and descends along the east coast of **Loch Linnhe**, the largest sea loch in Scotland, and cuts across to Loch Creran and back to Oban passing the **Scottish Sea Life Sanctuary** (Ⓒ open Mar–Oct daily 10am–5pm, reduced hours in winter;

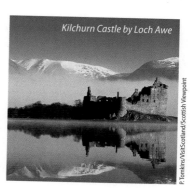

Kilchurn Castle by Loch Awe

P. Tomkins/VisitScotland/Scottish Viewpoint

Ⓒ closed Dec 25; ☞£10.95 (save by booking online); ♿✕; ☎01631 720 386; www.sealsanctuary.co.uk), a busy rescue and rehabilitation facility for both common seals and grey seals.

Orkney Islands★★

Orkney

 ing off the northeast tip of mainland Scotland, the Orkney archipelago comprises 67 islands of which less than 30 are inhabited. The cliffs are home to countless seabirds, and seals and otters are common. The first Neolithic settlers came in the 4th millennium BC. Some of their dwellings remain and their fine stone tombs can be seen throughout the islands. From the early Iron Age – around the 5C BC – fortified villages grew up round the massive stone buildings known as *brochs*. The Vikings came to Orkney from the late 8C AD, sweeping away the culture of the Pictish Orcadians. Orkney's culture still has Scandinavian elements, though the islands were returned to King James III of Scotland in 1468, as part of the dowry of his Danish bride.

- ▶ **Population:** 19,612.
- ♦ **Michelin Map:** Atlas p 74 or Map 501 K, L, M 6 and 7.
- ℹ **Info:** West Castle Street, Kirkwall. ☎01856 872 856. www.visitorkney.com.
- ▷ **Location:** The main island of Orkney is divided into the Eastern Mainland and the Western Mainland. Several British airports service Orkney and mainland ferries run here from Aberdeen (6hrs), Scrabster (90mins), Gills Bay (1hr) and John O'Groats (40mins) which is 10mi/16km south of the islands. Orkney Ferries (☎01856 872044) and Loganair (☎01856 872494) service the other islands.
- ☺ **Don't Miss:** St Magnus Cathedral, Kirkwall; Skara Brae; Old Man of Hoy.

KIRKWALL★★

Capital since Viking days, Kirkwall stands on the isthmus separating the eastern and western parts of the island. Handsome town houses (now shops), some emblazoned, line the stone-flagged main street and pends (alleyways) lead to attractive paved courtyards.

St Magnus Cathedral★★ dominates the skyline of Kirkwall (&⌚*open Apr–Sept daily 9am–5pm, Oct–Mar Mon–Fri 9am–5pm;* 🚶*guided tour including tower;* 🅿; 📞*01856 874 894).* Built by Earl Rognvald,1137–1152, and dedicated to his murdered uncle, Earl Magnus, the cathedral is an outstanding example of Norman architecture. The red stone exterior is severe and plain. The three west front **doorways** added later show confident originality in their combination of red and yellow sandstone.

Inside carefully controlled proportions create a sense of vastness belying the building's modest dimensions. The square pillars on either side of the organ screen enshrine the relics of St Magnus *(right),* and Earl Rognvald *(left).*

Opposite on Broad Street in the fine 16C townhouse of Tankerness House is **The Orkney Museum**★ (⌚ *open Apr–Sept Mon–Sat 10.30am–5pm, Sun 2pm–5pm, Oct–Mar Mon–Sat 10.30am–12.30pm, 1.30pm–5pm;* 📞*01856 873 191; www. orkney.org),* with excellent displays on the islands' prehistory.

Walk south from here on Broad Street and go left on Palace Road for **Earl's Palace**★ (&⌚*open Easter–Oct daily 9.30am–5.30pm (Oct 4.30pm);* ⌚*closed Dec 25–26, Jan 1–2;* 💷*£3.62;* 📞*01856 871 918; www.historic-scotland.gov.uk.* The remains of this early Renaissance palace have splendid corbelling on the windows, chimney breast and corbel course, and sculptured panels above the main entrance and oriel windows. It was built c. 1600–07 by **Earl Patrick Stewart**. The vaulted chambers on the ground floor hold exhibitions of Orkney history from the early Middle Ages to the present, while the grand staircase leads to the Great Hall and apartments.

🚗 DRIVING TOUR

WESTERN MAINLAND★★

Leave Kirkwall west by A 965 for the **Rennibister Earth House** *(behind the farmhouse, access by trapdoor and ladder),* by the south-eastern shore of Bay o' Firth. The oval chamber has five wall recesses and an entrance passage. Human bones were found in it, though its purpose remains uncertain. Further west, approximately 500 metres from the south-eastern shore of the Harray loch is **Maes Howe**★★ (⌚*open Apr–Sept daily 9.30am–5pm, Oct–Mar 9.30am–4pm;* ⌚*closed Dec 25–26, Jan 1–2;* 💷*£5.20.* 🅿🍴; 📞*01856 761 606; www.historic-scotland.gov.uk).* This Neolithic burial cairn dates from pre-2700 BC and was covered by a mound (26ft/8m high and 115ft/35m wide). The cairn was broken into in the 12C by Norsemen, who left runic marks.

Maes Howe is part of the Heart of Neolithic Orkney World Heritage Site. West of Maes Howe, the **Stones of Stenness** sit at the base of a neck of land separating the lochs of Stenness and Harray. The **Ring of Brodgar** Stone Age circle stands on this neck. It still has 27 of its original 60 stones standing. Two entrance causeways interrupt the encircling ditch. West of the Stones of Stenness on a promontory jutting into the loch is **Unstan Cairn**, a Stone Age chambered tomb from the mid-fourth millennium.

Further west on the A 965 is **Stromness**★, the second-largest town and principal port. Stromness grew from its original Norse settlement to become a whaling station in the 18C and the last port of call for the Hudson Bay Company ships sailing to Canada. The **Pier Arts Centre** *(Victoria Street;* &⌚*Open year-round Mon–Sat 10.30am–5pm;* 📞*01856 850 209; www.pierartscentre. com)* has a permanent collection of abstract art based on the work of the St Ives artists, Ben Nicholson and Barbara Hepworth. Aspects of Orkney's natural and maritime history are presented in the **Stromness Museum** *(52 Alfed Street;* &⌚*open Apr–Sept daily 10am–5pm; Oct–mid-Feb and mid-Mar Mon–Sat, 11am–3.30pm;* 💷*£3;* 🅿; 📞*01856 850 025; www.scfb.co.uk).*

North of Stromness on the A967 is **Skara Brae**★★ (&⌚*open Apr–Sept daily 9.30am–5.30pm, Oct–Mar 9.30am–4pm,* 💷*£5.58 (winter: site partially closed),* 🅿🍴, *picnic area;* 📞*01856 841 815; www. historic-scotland.gov.uk)* on the southern

re of the Bay o' Skaill. This 5 000-year
settlement was buried in sand for a
g period. The seven best-preserved
he Age dwellings are rectangular
h coursed flagstone walls and a
rth in the middle, and are connected
subterranean sewer system.

her north, separated from the main-
d by the waters of Brough Sound is
Brough of Birsay★ *(access on foot
oss causeway at low tide;* ⊙ *open
-Jun–Sept 9.30am–5.30pm, when
s permit;* ⊛£3.13; ℘*01856 841 815 or
56 721 205; www.historic-scotland.
uk).* The earliest remains are Pictish.
he 10C Norse farmers occupied the
d and Earl Thorfinn the Mighty (c.
9–65) built a church after a pilgrim-
to Rome. It became a cathedral and
the initial resting place of St Mag-
before the construction of Kirkwall
hedral. Excavations show a small
ong nave, short narrow choir and
aded apse, surrounded by a Norse
veyard. A little to the southwest is
llection of stone-and-turf **Norse
g houses**.

urn to Kirkwall. About 10mi/16km
h by A 961, past St Mary's is **Scapa
v**. From the **Churchill Barriers**, built
ne Second World War by Italian pris-
rs of war to link the four islands with
mainland, there is a good view of
naval base where the German Grand
t scuttled itself in 1919. Beyond the

Old Man of Hoy
B. Kaufmann/MICHELIN

first barrier is the **Italian Chapel**★, a
unique and moving testament to faith
in adversity, built by the same prisoners
inside two Nissen (prefabricated corru-
gated iron) huts.

Pentland Firth Crossing

The crossing (a very choppy two-hour
car ferry journey operating between
Stromness and Scrabster) is an ideal way
of seeing the outstanding cliff scenery of
Hoy. The name means high island and its
highlights are the sheer cliffs of St John's
Head (1,140ft/347m) and the famous
Old Man of Hoy★★★, a breathtaking
red sandstone sea stack (450ft/137m)
rising sheer out of the turbulent waters.
It is the domain of myriad screeching
and hovering seabirds.

erth★

Perthshire and Kinross

former Royal Burgh retains the
osphere of a country town and
ideal touring base, situated
he River Tay, noted for salmon
ing and for freshwater mussels
ch produce beautiful pearls.

IT OF HISTORY

"Fair City" has played a prominent
in Scottish history and might well
become the capital had not James
en assassinated here in 1457. Other
ing events included the murderous

> ▶ **Population:** 41,916.
> ⌖ **Michelin Map:** Michelin
>   Atlas p 62 or Map 501 J 14.
> ⓘ **Info:** Lower City Mills,
>   West Mill Street.
>   ℘01738 450600.
>   www.perthshire.co.uk.
> ◐ **Location:** 42mi/67km due
>   north of Edinburgh. The
>   train station (direct con-
>   nections to Edinburgh and
>   Glasgow) is on Kings Place,
>   the bus station a few yards
>   away at Leonard Street.

The Stone of Destiny

According to legend, the Stone of Destiny was Jacob's pillow which eventually reached Ireland by way of Egypt and Spain and is believed to have served as a coronation stone for the High Kings at Tara. Kenneth MacAlpine was the first king to be crowned on the stone at Scone and it subsequently served for the coronation of all Scottish kings until 1296 when the Scots were defeated by Edward I. He carried off the stone, which was placed beneath the Coronation chair in Westminster Abbey, where for 700 years it played an integral part in the Coronation rituals. It was stolen in 1950 but was later recovered in Arbroath Abbey. From early days controversy has raged about the authenticity of the stone. Some believe the original stone never left Scotland. In 1996 the people of Scotland greeted the return of the Stone of Destiny, which is the symbol of Scottish nationhood, with great emotion. It is now on display with the Honours of Scotland in Edinburgh Castle but will be returned (temporarily) to Westminster Abbey for use in future coronations.

Clan Combat of 1396 and the destruction of its monasteries following John Knox's inflammatory sermon of 1559. There are many fine examples of **Georgian architecture**★.

TOWN

The **Black Watch Regimental Museum**★ *(Balhousie Castle, Hay Street; ◷ open May –Sept Mon–Sat 10am–4.30pm, Oct–Apr Mon–Fri 10am–3.30pm; ◷ closed third week Dec–5/6 Jan;* 🅿️; *℘0131 310 8530; www.theblackwatch.co.uk)* is well signed on all approach routes into the city. In the early 18C General Wade enlisted and armed independent companies of Highlanders which became known as the **Black Watch**, for the "Watch" they kept on the Highlands and for their dark

tartan. The museum traces their often turbulent history.

Spanning the river Tay is the Perth Bridge. On the west bank, just to the south along Bridge Lane then George Street is the **Perth Museum and Art Gallery**★ *(78 George Street;* ♿ ◷ *open year-round Mon–Sat 10am–5pm (May–Aug also Sun 1pm–4.30pm); ◷ closed Christmas–New Year;* ℘*01738 632 488, www.perthshire.com).* There are interesting displays of local glass, silver and clock-making and natural history. In the art gallery hang works by Scottish artists.

EXCURSIONS
Scone Palace★★

2mi/3km northeast by A 93. ♿◷*Open Apr–Oct daily 9.30am–5.30pm (Sat 4.30pm).* ⬚*Palace £8.50. Grounds only, £4.80.* 🅿️✕*.* ℘*01738 552 300. www.scone-palace.co.uk.*

One of Scotland's most hallowed historic sites, Scone was the centre of Kenneth MacAlpine's Scotto-Pictish kingdom from the mid-9C and, from 1120, the first Augustinian priory in Scotland. **Moot Hill** (now occupied by a 19C chapel) was where Scottish kings were enthroned on the **Stone of Destiny** (Stone of Scone). Wrecked in the wave of destruction of 1559, the abbey eventually became the seat of the Earls of Mansfield.

The present neo-Gothic palace dates from 1808. Its richly furnished apartments contain a splendid array of porcelain and ivories, unusual timepieces, busts and portraits, and collection of papier-mâché objets d'art. The grounds include a maze, children's playground and 50-acre pinetum.

Dunkeld★

14mi/23km north on the A 9.

Dunkeld was the site of a monastic establishment from AD 700 and later a majestic Gothic **cathedral** *(Cathedra Street;* ◷ *open Apr–Sep, daily, 9.30am– 6.30pm; Oct–Mar, daily, 10am (2pm Sun) to 4.30pm;* 👄*guided tours (free, summer;* ℘*01350 727 249; www.dunkeld cathedral.org.uk)* now set in an attractive riverside precinct.

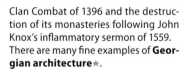

Pitlochry★
Perthshire and Kinross

This attractive town, set in the Tummel Valley, makes a fine touring centre to enjoy the magnificent scenery of mountains, lochs and moors. It hosts a famous festival of drama, music and art in summer and has recently become the adventure sports capital of Scotland with a wide range of activities.

- ▶ **Population:** 3,126.
- **Michelin Map:** Michelin Atlas p 61 or Map 501 I 1.
- **Info:** 22 Atholl Road. ℘01796 472215. www.perthshire.co.uk.
- **Location:** PItlochry is 28mi/45km northeast of Perth. Its train station, on the main line to Inverness, is on Station Road. The bus station is nearby.

EXCURSIONS
Queen's View★★
10mi/16km west by B 8019.
This beauty spot was named after Queen Victoria's visit in 1866, and commands a wonderful view up Loch Tummel.

Blair Castle★★
7mi/12km north on the A 9. Blair Atholl. ◷ *Open Apr–late Oct daily 9.30am–4.30pm (last admission). Nov–Mar Tue and Sat 9.30am–12.30pm (last admission).* ◉*£7.50.* ♿ ₧ ✕. ℘*01796 481 207. www.blair-castle.co.uk.*
Blair Castle was the centre of the ancient kingdom of Atholl and the home of the Duke of Atholl until the death of the last of the line in 1996. It is still home to the only private army left in the British Isles, the **Atholl Highlanders**, sole survivor of the clan system. A large part of the tower built here in 1269 still remains, and the castle with its turrets and parapets continues to command a strategic route into the Central Highlands.
The 18C interiors include sumptuous stucco ceilings, family **portraits** (by Lely, Jacob de Wet, Hoppner, Zoffany, and Landseer), collections of armour and porcelain, Jacobite and other historic relics. The grounds include nature trails and a deer park.

Shetland Islands★

There are 100 or so Shetland Islands but less than 20 are inhabited. Shetland is hilly and has many inlets (voes), the most famous of which, **Sullom Voe** is home to Europe's largest oil and gas terminal. Nonetheless, the oil industry still takes second place to fishing in importance, while the area directly affected by oil and gas exploration is bordered by beautiful, wild spaces. The islands also hold important evidence of early human settlement.

- ▶ **Population:** 22,522.
- **Michelin Map:** Atlas p 75 or Map 501 P, Q, R 1 to 4.
- **Info:** ℘08701 999 440. www.visitshetland.com.
- **Transport:** Daily sailings from Aberdeen to Lerwick and regular flights from Aberdeen, Edinburgh, Glasgow, Inverness and London to Sumburgh. The capital, Lerwick, is on the east coast of Mainland which is 50mi/81km long north to south, and 20mi/32km across at its widest.

LERWICK
The Shetlands' capital sits in a natural harbour sheltered by the Island of Bressay. Local attractions include the ruined **Clickhimin Broch**★ and the

Up Helly Aa★★★

This colourful and rousing fire festival is the most spectacular reminder of the Viking heritage. Explanations for the pageant held on the last Tuesday in January are various, from spring rites to placating the Norse gods, or up-ending of the holy days. The principal figure, the **Guizer Jarl** (earl) and his warriors, all clad in the finery of Viking war dress, head the great torch-lit procession in their Viking longship. A thundering rendering of the *Galley Song* precedes the burning of the galley and the final song, *The Norseman's Home*. Celebrations continue throughout the night.

©Jeff J. Mitchell/Reuters/Corbis

Shetland Museum and Archives

(Hay's Dock; &⊙open year-round Mon–Sat 10am–5pm, Sun noon–5pm. ✕; ℘01595 695 057; www.shetland-museum.org.uk).

This new waterfront centre, opened in May 2007 is the perfect starting point to learn about Shetlands heritage and culture. As well as museum displays there is a lively programme of events including storytelling, a popular islands' tradition.

EXCURSIONS
Jarlshof★★

Mainland. 25mi/40km south of Lerwick by A 970. HS. ⊙ Open Easter–Oct daily 9.30am–5.30pm (Oct 4.30pm).

Mousa Broch

B. Kaufmann/MICHELIN

⊚£4.70. 🅿. ℘01950 460 112. www.historic-scotland.gov.uk.

The site of Jarlshof has been occupied from the middle of the 2nd millennium BC until the 17C.

There are six Bronze Age houses, and a late Iron Age broch with other dwellings clustered around it. Numerous Viking longhouses tell of several centuries of occupation. There was a farmstead here in the 13C, the New Hall was built in the 16C.

Mousa Broch★★★

HS. Mousa Island. 12mi/19km south on the A 970. Motor boat (15min) from Sandwick jetty. ⊙ Open Apr–Sept daily 9.30am–5.30pm (4.30pm winter), call ℘01856 841 815 (Skara Brae) to confirm. ⊙ Closed 24–25 Dec. ⊚Ferry charge around £12. ℘01950 431 367 (ferry operator). 01856 841 815 (Historic Scotland).www.historic-scotland.gov.uk.

Small fortified farms, brochs, were peculiar to Scotland, the culmination of a tradition stretching back to 500 BC. Most have crumbled, but Mousa, probably dating from the first or second century AD, still stands to a height of over 43ft/13.3m and is the finest surviving Iron Age broch tower.

A staircase, chambers and galleries were built into the thickness of the walls of this imposing kiln-shaped **tower** which is more than 40ft/15ft across at its base. In the courtyard are a hearth and lean-to structures.

Isle of Skye★★
Highland

In Norse and Gaelic tales, Skye is known as the "Island of Cloud", or the "Winged Isle". Mystery and enchantment still lie heavy here. Skye is the largest of the Inner Hebrides group, just off the north west mainland. Crofting, tourism and forestry are the principal occupations of the islanders, 85 percent of whom still speak Gaelic.

▸ **Population:** 8,868.
Michelin Map: Atlas p 65 or Map 401 A, B 11 and 12.
Info: The Car Park, Bradford; Bayfield House, Bayfield Rd, Portree. ℘(both) 01845 225 5121. www.visithighlands.com/skye.
Location: Skye is joined to the mainland by the Skye Bridge at Kyle of Lochalsh and has two mainland ferry (www.calmac.co.uk) connections, from Mallaig and Glenelg to Armadale.

ISLE
The Cuillins★★★
The scenic splendour of the Cuillins makes these peaks the isle's most famous feature.
The **Black Cuillins**, a six-mile arc of sharp peaks, encircle Loch Coruisk; many of these peaks are over 3 000ft/914m in height, with Sgurr Alasdair (3 309ft/993m) the highest. On the other side of Glen Sligachan the softly-rounded forms of the pink granite **Red Cuillins** contrast with their neighbours.

Portree★
Skye's pleasant little capital, arranged around a sheltered bay, is a popular yachting centre.

Kilmuir
The town stands on the north coast of the **Trotternish Peninsula★★**, the most northerly of Skye's peninsulas, with lovely seascapes and a basalt rock pinnacle. The small churchyard has a monument to **Flora MacDonald** (1722–90), known for her part in the escape of Bonnie Prince Charlie after the collapse of the Jacobite cause at Culloden. She brought the Prince, disguised as her maid, from Benbecula in the Outer Hebrides to Portree. From here he left for France and lifelong exile.

Skye Museum of Island Life★
🕐 *Open Easter–Oct Mon–Sat 9.30am–5pm. ≋£2.50.* ♿ 🅿. ℘*01470 552 206. www.skyemuseum.co.uk.*
Preserves a township of thatched cottages, with a crofter's house, a weaver's house, a smithy and a ceilidh house giving an idea of crofting life in the 19C.

Trotternish Peninsula, Isle of Sky
© B.Perousse/MICHELIN

Dunvegan Castle

🕐 *Open Apr–mid-Oct 10am–5.30pm. mid-Oct–Mar 11am–4pm (call to confirm).* 🔒£7.50. ♿🅿✕. ✆01470 521 206. www.dunvegancastle.com.
Until 1748 the only entrance to this Hebridean fortress, the seat of the MacLeods, was by a sea gate. The castle is set on a rocky platform overlooking Loch Dunvegan. Most notable of the treasures kept here is the fragment of silk, known as the **Fairy Flag**. Legend has it that the flag given to the 4th Chief by his fairy wife has the power to ward off disaster to the Clan and has twice been invoked.
Seal spotting trips depart from the castle (🕐*operate May–mid-Oct;* 🔒£7; ✆01470 521 500).

St Andrews★★

Fife

This Fife coast resort is most famous as the home of golf, but is also known for its cathedral, castle and long-established university.

- ▶ **Population:** 11,136.
- 🧭 **Michelin Map:** Michelin Atlas p 56 or Map 501 L 14.
- ℹ **Info:** 70 Market Street. ✆01334 472 021. www.visitstandrews.co.uk, www.visitfife.com.
- ▷ **Location:** St Andrews is 54mi/86km northeast of Edinburgh. The nearest train station is 5mi/8km northwest at Leuchars, linked to St Andrew by bus. Buses from Edinburgh and Dundee terminate at the central City Road bus station.

A BIT OF HISTORY

In the 12C a priory, and later a cathedral were established, leading to the foundation of the University. By 1472 St Andrews was the ecclesiastical capital of Scotland. Its importance declined in the 17C, owing to the switch in trade from the Baltic to the American colonies, and after the Act of Union in 1707.
The 19C, however, saw St Andrews return to prominence as a tourist and golfing centre, an importance it has kept to this day.

CATHEDRAL★

At the eastern end of St Andrews' two main streets. 🕐 *Open year-round daily 9.30am–5pm (4.30pm Oct–Easter).* 🔒*£4.11, combined ticket with castle £7.05.* ♿ *.* ✆01334 472 563. www.historic-scotland.gov.uk.
The imposing **St Regulus Church** may have been originally intended to house the relics of St Andrew. Robert of Scone built the church, with its lofty tower, between 1127 and 1144. The tower *(151 steps)* affords a magnificent **panorama**★★ across St Andrews and its main monuments. St Regulus's was replaced from 1160 by the later cathedral, the largest church ever built in Scotland. After the Reformation this once-noble building was used as a stone quarry, and reduced to the ruin on view

The Saltire

The St Andrews cross (white on a blue ground) was adopted as the Scottish flag in the 13C. **St Andrew**, who was the patron saint of Angus, King of the Picts, later became the patron saint of Scotland. The cross with diagonal beams (saltire) recalls the saint's martyrdom in c. 69: the saint thought himself unworthy of being crucified on an upright cross. According to legend his relics of St Andrew were brought to Scotland in the 8C by St Rule (Regulus).

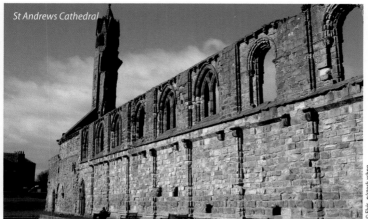
St Andrews Cathedral

© Elvis_p/stock.xchng

today. The **museum** has a good collection of early Christian sculptured stones. The ruined 13C **castle**, *(HS; ⊙open same hours as cathedral; ⊛£5.09; combined ticket with cathedral £7.05; ⅙; ℘01334 477 196; www.historic-scotland.gov.uk)*, overlooking the foreshore, was once a part of the palace of the archbishop.

EXCURSIONS
Scotland's Secret Bunker
10mi/16km southeast on the B 9131 and B 940. Crown Buildings Troywood. ⅙⊙ Open mid-Mar–Oct daily 10am–6pm (last admission 5pm). ⊛£8.90. ▣✗. ℘01333 310 301. www.secretbunker.co.uk.

Around 130ft/40m below the surface of Fife's farmlands, this now-not-so-secret bunker was built as an early warning radar station and later converted to a nuclear command centre. Protected by 10ft/3m of reinforced concrete, all stages of operational life are brought hauntingly to life with audio-visual displays evoking the menace of the Cold War era.

East Neuk★★
Leave St Andrews by the A 917.
The East Neuk, or East Corner, is a stretch of coastline dotted with picturesque fishing villages, each clustered around its harbour and with a wealth of vernac-

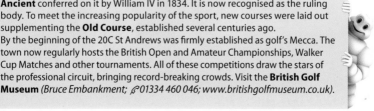

Golf: A Royal and Ancient Game
Since the 15C St Andrews links – with its swards of springy turf and sand bunkers – has been a place for playing golf or at least the early ball and stick version of this sport. So popular was the game that by 1457 an Act of Scottish Parliament was passed requiring that *"futeball and the golfe be utterly cryit down"* in favour of kirk attendance and archery practice. Mary Queen of Scots was an occasional player; her son James VI popularised the game in England.

Founded in 1754, the Society of St Andrews Golfers had the title **Royal and Ancient** conferred on it by William IV in 1834. It is now recognised as the ruling body. To meet the increasing popularity of the sport, new courses were laid out supplementing the **Old Course**, established several centuries ago.

By the beginning of the 20C St Andrews was firmly established as golf's Mecca. The town now regularly hosts the British Open and Amateur Championships, Walker Cup Matches and other tournaments. All of these competitions draw the stars of the professional circuit, bringing record-breaking crowds. Visit the **British Golf Museum** *(Bruce Embankment; ℘01334 460 046; www.britishgolfmuseum.co.uk).*

ular architecture. These were the ports to which once came the wealth of the fisheries, and Baltic and Dutch trade.

Crail is the most attractive village. In **Anstruther** is the **Scottish Fisheries Museum**★★, (St Ayles Harborhead; ○ open Apr–Sept Mon–Sat 10am–5.30pm, Sun 11am–5pm; Oct–Mar daily, Sun noon–4.30pm; ○ closed Jan 1–2 and Dec 24–25. ☜£6; ♿🅿✕; ✆01333 310 628; www.scotfishmuseum.org).

In **Pittenweem** is **Kellie Castle**★(NTS; *Castle:* open Apr–May & Sept–Oct Fri–Tue 1pm–5pm, Jun–Aug daily 1pm–5pm; *Gardens and Grounds:* ○ open daily 9.30am–5.30pm; ☜£8.50; ♿🅿 £3; ✕; ✆0844 4932184; www.nts.org.uk), a fine example of unspoilt 16C–17C traditional Scottish architecture featuring corbelled turrets with conical roofs, pedimented dormers, and crow-stepped gables. The 17C **plasterwork ceilings** are notable.

Stirling★★

Stirling

Controlling the route between Edinburgh and the Highlands and the crossing of the Forth at its tidal limit, Stirling has been strategically important from time immemorial, and its long history has been essentially that of the castle and former royal residence perched on its well-nigh impregnable crag. Today it is an ideal touring centre.

A BIT OF HISTORY

From its magnificent site Stirling has seen many battles, the most important being Stirling Bridge in 1297 and Bannockburn in 1314. Stirling became a permanent royal residence with the accession of the **Stewarts**, and its Golden Age came under **James IV**. After his death at Flodden (1513), his queen

▷ **Population:** 30,515.
⌖ **Michelin Map:** Atlas p 55 or Map 501 I 15.
▯ **Info:** 41 Dumbarton Road. ✆08707 200 620. www. visitscottishheartlands.com.
◑ **Location:** Stirling is 43mi/70km northwest of Edinburgh. The train station is on Station Road, while the bus station is close by on Goosecroft Road; both are in the centre of town.

(Margaret)brought her son to Stirling, where he was crowned as James V. His daughter **Mary Queen of Scots** was crowned in the Chapel Royal, and her infant son, the future **James VI** of Scotland and I of England, was baptised here in 1566. It was with his departure

Stirling Castle at night

o Whitehall that Stirling's role as a royal residence ended.

CITY
Stirling Castle★★

NS. &⏰ *Open year-round daily
9.30am–6pm (5pm Oct–Easter).*
☞£8.32, includes Argyll's Lodging.
▶ Guided tours (free). 🅿 *(£2,
max stay 4 hrs)*✕*.* ☏*01786 450 000.
www.historic-scotland.gov.uk.*

The approach to the castle is up through
the old town. A statue of Robert the
Bruce stands guard on the esplanade.
In the **Casemates** there is an interesting exhibition with models and life-size
figures.

Begun by James IV in 1496, the palace is
a masterpiece of Renaissance ornamentation, completed by his son in 1540.
Its outstanding feature is the elaborate
design of the **external elevations**★★★
best admired from the Upper Square.
The façade of the **Great Hall** (1460–88)
is lit by four pairs of embrasured windows; the noble interior is notable for its
hammerbeam oak roof, minstrels' gallery and dais flanked by oriel windows.
In contrast the **Palace** itself (1496–1540)
is decorated with original figure carvings in recessed arches and above the
cornice; the **royal apartments** boast
the 16C oak medallions known as the
Stirling Heads★★. The early Renaissance **Chapel** (1594) features round-
headed windows framing the elaborate doorway and an ornate interior.
The King's Old Building houses the
**Argyll and Sutherland Highlanders
Regimental Museum**★ *(closes 45min
before castle)*, presenting 200 years of
regimental history.

Old Town
The medieval town, with its narrow
wynds and steep streets, spills downhill from the castle. **Argyll's Lodging**★
NS; ⏰*open year-round daily 9.30am–
5.30pm; 5pm Oct–Easter 4.30pm; entry
by guided tour only and must be pre-
booked at the castle or by calling 01786
450 000;* ☞*£8.32, same ticket as Stirling
Castle;* ☏ *01786 431319; www.historic-
scotland.gov.uk)* was built in 1632 by
Sir William Alexander, founder of Nova
Scotia and contains wonderful examples of fine **Scottish Renaissance
decoration**★.

In the **Church of the Holy Rude**★,
(⏰*open daily Easter–Oct 11am–4pm;
☞contribution requested;* ☏*01786 475
275; www.holyrude.org)* the infant James
VI was crowned, in 1567, with John Knox
preaching the sermon. It retains its 15C
oak **timberwork roof**.

Beyond **Bothwell House** *(39 St John's
Street)* with its projecting tower, stands
the **Old Town Jail** (⏰*Open daily.
Apr–May and Oct 10am–5pm, Jun–Sept
9.30am–5.30pm, Nov–Mar 10am–4pm;*
⏰*closed 1 Jan, 25–26 Dec; ☞£5;* ▶
*actor guided tours, summer daily, winter
weekends, Christmas hols, 95p extra;* 🅿*;*
☏*01786 450 050; www.oldtownjail.com)*,
where the harshness of prison life can
be experienced courtesy of lively actor
guides.

At the bottom of Broad Street, formerly
the centre of burgh life, with its mercat
cross and tolbooth, is **Darnley's House**,
a town house where Mary's husband,
Lord Darnley, is said to have stayed.

EXCURSIONS
Dunblane★
6mi/10km north on the A 9.

A mainly residential town of some 6,000
inhabitants, modern Dunblane gained
tragic notoriety in 1996 for a massacre
of 16 school children. The old town is
grouped round its beautiful 13C Gothic
cathedral★★ *(HS;* ☏ *01786 825 388;
www.historic-scotland.gov.uk).*

An ecclesiastical centre since Celtic
times, the cathedral dates from David
I's creation of the bishopric in 1150. It
survived the Reformation intact, and
remains a fine example of 13C Gothic
architecture. The vigorous carving of
the canopied 15C **Chisholm stalls** and
their misericords is remarkable. In the
glorious **choir** is the ornate **Ochiltree
stalls**. The **Lady Chapel**, the oldest part
of the building, has ribbed vaulting and
carved bosses. Adjoining the south side
of the nave is a 12C tower, and the magnificent **west front**★★, overlooking the
Allan Water.

Doune Castle★

HS. 10mi/16km on the A 84. ○ *Open Apr–Oct daily, Nov–Mar Sat–Wed.* ♿*£4.11.* 🅿. ✆*01786 841 742. www.historic-scotland.gov.uk.*
This late 14C fortress with its four-storey **keep-gatehouse** (95ft/29m-high), stands apart from the village.
With elaborate accommodation on a semi-royal scale, it is an example of a truly self-contained, secure residence of its period.

Bannockburn Heritage Centre

NTS. 2mi/3km south by the A 9. ○ *Site open daily (heritae centre Mar–Oct).* ♿*£5.50.* ♿🅿✕. ✆*0844 4932139. www.nts.org.uk.*
An equestrian statue of **Robert the Bruce** marks the king's command post on the eve of the battle. By 1313 Bruce had retaken most of the kingdom lost to Edward I, who had died in 1307. On 24 June 1314, he routed a numerically superior English army, ineptly led by Edward II. After Bannockburn, independence for Scotland was assured. An audio-visual presentation tells the dramatic story.

National Wallace Monument

1mi/1.5km northeast by the A 9 and B 998. ♿*£6.50.* 🅿✕. ✆*01786 472 140. www.nationalwallacemonument.com.*
Sir William Wallace (1270–1305) rallied Scottish forces against English rule.
He recaptured the castle from Edward I's forces after his victory at Stirling Bridge in 1297. Following the Scots' submission in 1304, Wallace was captured and died a traitor's death in London in 1305.
An audio-visual presentation depicts Wallace and his place in Scottish history. From the viewing platform (246 steps) atop Abbey Craig (362ft/110m) there is a **panorama**★★ of Stirling surroundings.

Trossachs★★★
Stirling

Occupying Scotland's midriff area, the Trossachs is one of Scotland's most famous scenes, with rugged mountains and wooded slopes reflected in the waters of many lochs. Sir Walter Scott's romantic poetry and novels did much to popularise the Trossachs, reinforced by Wordsworth and Coleridge, who followed in his footsteps in 1830.

SIGHTS
Callander★

This busy summer tourist centre became known to millions as the Tannochbrae of television's *Dr Finlay's Casebook.*
Callander has been popular with visitors for over a century and is the main eastern gateway to the Trossachs.

Loch Venachar

The Trossachs road *(A 821)*, skirts the lower slopes of **Ben Ledi** (2 882ft/879m) overlooking the banks of Loch Venachar, before reaching the scattered settlement

---

⌖ **Michelin Map:** Michelin Atlas p 55 or Map 501 G 15.

🛈 **Info:** Ancaster Square, Callander. ✆08707 200 628.; The Old Station, Balloch Road, Balloch. ✆08707 200 607. www.lochlomond-trossachs.org. www.visitscottish heartlands.com.

◖ **Location:** The Trossachs stretch between Loch Venachar in the east to the shores of Loch Lomond. The principal town, Callander (16 mi/25km north west of Stirling), is a good base. Outdoor explorers should make the National Park Headquarters their first stop. A regular train service runs between Balloch and Glasgow.

○ **Time:** Two to three days.

👪 **Kids:** Aquarium.

Loch Lomond
©Achim Prill/iStockphoto.com

of **Brig o'Turk**. The village has artistic, associations, favoured by Ruskin and Millais and, later, the **Glasgow Boys**.

Loch Katrine★★

1mi/1.5km from A 821 to the pier, visitor centre and car park.
A good way to see this lovely loch is to take a **boat trip** (◯operates from Trossachs Pier Apr–early Sept daily, see website or call for times; ⊜1-hr scenic cruise £10; &; ℰ01877 332 000; www.lochkatrine. com) on the *SS Sir Walter Scott*. The loch isles, Ellen's Isle and Factor's Isle figure respectively in works by Sir Walter Scott's *The Lady of the Lake* and *Rob Roy*. To the south of Loch Katrine looms the twin-peaked form of **Ben Venue** (2,393ft/727m). Beyond, a hilltop viewpoint affords a magnificent **panorama-★★★** across the Trossachs.

Aberfoyle

The attractive village, busy now with tourists every summer, was made famous as the place from where Rob Roy abducted Baillie Nicol Jarvie. A road leads west through the forest park to Loch Lomond.

Loch Lomond★★

The blue waters of this loch (653ft/200m deep) are flanked by rugged mountains in the north and pastoral woodlands in the south. **Loch Lomond Shores**, a state-of-the-art visitor centre (&◯open daily 10am–4pm; ⊜£6.50 combined ticket for audiovisual presentations and *access to rooftop terrace or separate charge for each.* ⊞; ✕; ℰ0845 345 4978; www.lochlomondshores.com) offers spectacular views, an audio-visual presentation of the area, interactive family attractions and shops. Two attractions that explore the waters in different ways are the ♨♨**Loch Lomond Aquarium** (&◯open daily from 10am, closing times vary. ⊜£10.95, child £8.95, savings online; ℰ01389 721500; www.sealifeeurope.com) and **Sweeney's Cruise**, who offer loch voyages (&◯operates Easter–Sept; call for times and prices; ℰ01389 752 376; www.sweeney.uk.com) calling at the attractive village of **Luss**★ with its mellow stone cottages.

The **West Highland Way** follows the east shore northwards to Fort William passing on the way the lower slopes of **Ben Lomond**★★ (3,192ft/974m), the most southerly of the Highland "Munros" (mountains over 3,000ft/912m).

Rob Roy MacGregor (1671–1734)

Much of the rugged terrain of the Trossachs is closely associated with the daring exploits of the outlawed clan leader and hero of Sir Walter Scott's novel, *Rob Roy* (1818). Rob was a real person; Glen Gyle at the head of Loch Katrine was his birthplace and he and his wife and two of their sons lie in the churchyard of Balquhidder on Loch Voil.

Tweed Valley★★

Borders

The Tweed Valley has long been a favoured area of settlement. Ancient forts and monastic houses are found all over the region. It was much fought over and the troubled times are remembered in many a Border ballad and poem. Today, the valley is primarily agricultural, though the traditional woollen and knitwear industries are the mainstay of the towns. On its long and beautiful course the Tweed flows past several famous landmarks – castles, abbeys and great houses – making the exploration of its banks a delight.

⊕ DRIVING TOUR

130mi/210km

Moffat

At the head of the Annan Valley, the small town of Moffat makes a good base from which to explore the area.

▷ *Take the A 708 Selkirk road.*

Grey Mare's Tail★★

At the head of Moffat Water Valley is the Grey Mare's Tail, a spectacular waterfall (200ft/60m drop). The road leads on up the now narrow V-shaped valley to cross the pass and then descends the valley of the Little Yarrow Water. Here, by St Mary's Loch, is Tibbie Shiel's Inn, meeting place of **James Hogg** (1770-1835), "the Ettrick Shepherd" and his friends.

▷ *Take the road to the left, signposted Tweedsmuir, past Megget Water; turn right into A 701.*

Broughton

In this trim roadside village is the **John Buchan Centre** *(Old Church;* ⊙*Open Easter weekend and May– Sept daily 2pm–5pm;* ⊕*£1.50;* P*;* ℰ *01899 221 050; www.john-buchansociety.co.uk),* a tribute to

- ⊛ **Michelin Map:** Michelin Atlas p 50 or Map 501 K, L and M 17.
- ⊞ **Info:** ℰ0870 608 0404. www.scot-borders.co.uk.
- ▷ **Location:** The River Tweed rises in the Tweedsmuir Hills to the west of the Borders and flows eastwards acting as the frontier with England for the latter part of its journey, ending at Berwick-upon-Tweed, some 97mi/155km east.
- ⊙ **Timing:** Allow three days.

the author and statesman **John Buchan**, Lord Tweedsmuir (1875-1940).

▷ *Take the B 7016 east and the B 712 north, parallel to the Tweed. At the junction, turn right into the A 72.*

One mile short of Peebles, on a rocky outcrop overlooking the river is **Neidpath Castle**, (⊙*privately owned, no admission)* a 14C L-plan tower house,

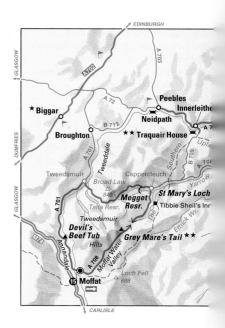

typical of the fortified dwellings needed in the days of border and clan warfare.

Peebles

The former spa town is a good centre from which to explore the Tweeddale countryside, or to fish for salmon. The author **Robert Louis Stevenson** and the explorer **Mungo Park** lived in the town. **William Chambers**, publisher of the famous Dictionary, who was born here, donated the Chambers Institute, a library and a museum to the town.

◗ 6mi/10 km down river, by A 72. Cross the Tweed at Innerleithen.

Traquair House★★

◔ Open Jun–Aug daily 10.30am–5.30pm; Good Fri–May and Sept daily noon–5pm; Oct daily 11pm–4pm; Nov Sat–Sun 11am–3pm. ✎£7, grounds only, £3.50. ♿🅿✕. ✆01896 830 323. www.traquair.co.uk.

There was a royal hunting lodge here as early as 1107, which was transformed into a Border "peel", or fortified tower house, during the Wars of Independence. The wings were added in the late 17C. This typical tower house has

a wealth of relics, treasures and traditions and many Jacobite associations and personal belongings of Mary Queen of Scots. Also of interest are the **vaulted chamber** where cattle used to be herded in times of raids, a priest's room and a **brew-house** whose ale is highly regarded. In the grounds are a maze and craft workshops.

◗ Return to the A 72; head east on the B 7060, then the A 7 left to Abbotsford.

Abbotsford★★

♿◔ Open mid-Mar–Oct daily 9.30am–5pm (Sun Mar–May and Oct 11am–4pm) ✎£7. 🅿✕. ✆01896 752 043. www.scottsabbotsford.co.uk.
A fantasy in stone, typical of **Sir Walter Scott** (1771–1832), the man who did so much to romanticise and popularise all things Scottish. He bought the house in 1812 and transformed it.
Visitors can see his massive writing desk and a collection of some 9,000 rare books and many items relating to Scotland and its history, collected throughout his life.

◗ Take the A 7 to the A 72, turn right.

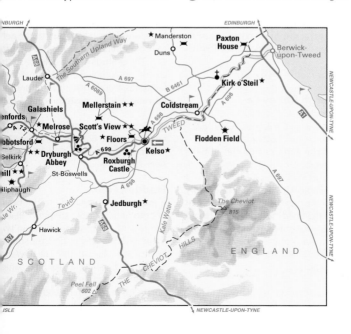

Melrose★

The pleasant town, grouped around the abbey ruins, is overshadowed by the **Eildon Hills**. Their strange triple peak – of volcanic origin – was believed to have been the work of Michael Scott, a 13C wizard, who is buried in the abbey. David I founded **Melrose Abbey★★** (🕐 *open year-round daily 9.30am–5.30pm/Oct–Mar 4.30 pm;* 👓*£5.09;* 🅿; 📞*01896 822 562; www.historic-scotland. gov.uk*) in 1136. Once one of the richest abbeys in Scotland, the original buildings were damaged in the 14C, notably in 1322 by Edward II's retreating army. Robert the Bruce, whose heart is buried here, ensured their rebuilding. The ruins date from the late 14C to the early 16C and are distinguished by a profusion of **decorative sculpture★★★**: delicate tracery, canopied niches, intricate vaulting and ornate gables.

▷ *Leave Melrose by the B 6361 running along the Tweed. Past the viaduct, turn left onto the A 68, then, once over the river, right on a minor road to Leaderfoot, then up Bemersyde Hill and turn right onto the B 6356.*

Scott's View★★

The magnificent viewpoint (593ft/181m) faces west across the winding Tweed to the three conical peaks of the Eildons.

▷ *Local road to Dryburgh Abbey.*

Dryburgh Abbey★★

🕐 *Open daily 9.30am–5.30pm (4.30pm Oct–Mar).* 👓*£4.60.* ♿🅿. 📞*01835 822 381.www.historic-scotland.gov.uk.*
One of the group of Border abbeys founded by David I, begun in 1150, Dryburgh was repeatedly attacked by the English in the 1300s and badly damaged when the town was razed in 1544. A sheltered meander of the Tweed provides a splendid **setting★★★** for the majestic ruins of the abbey in mellow red stone. Sir Walter Scott is buried in the east chapel.

▷ *Return to B 6356; take B 6004 to St Boswells; left on A 699 by the Tweed.*

Kelso★

Standing at the confluence of the Tweed and the Teviot, Kelso grew from a fording place into a thriving market town. Here again are the ruins of a fine **abbey**, founded 1128, but many times destroyed. The town has some remarkable Georgian architecture and the cobbled town **square★★** features an elegant 19C **Town Hall**. The graceful bridge was built in 1803 by John Rennie.
On the outskirts of Kelso is **Floors Castle★** (🕐*open Easter weekend and May–Oct daily 11am–5pm;* 👓*£7.50; ground only, £3.50;* ♿🅿✕; 📞*01573 223 333 www. floorscastle.com).* The distinctive pinnacled silhouette stands on a terraced site overlooking the Tweed. The main block, built to the designs of William Adam, was extended in the 19C when William Playfair added the wings. Many of the rooms were refurbished early this century to accommodate an outstanding collection of **tapestries** and **furniture**.

Mellerstain★★

6mi/10km northwest of Kelso via the A 6089. 🕐 *Open Easter weekend, May–Sept, Oct Sun only.* 👓*£7. Gardens only, £4.* ♿🅿✕. 📞*01573 410 225. www.mellerstain.com.*
The glory of this 18C mansion is the delicacy of Robert Adam's interior decoration. The **ceilings★★★** in delicate pastel colours are complemented by matching fireplaces, woodwork and furniture. The **Library★★★** is a masterpiece.

▷ *Return to Kelso and continue down river on A 698 to Coldstream. Follow A 697 across the Tweed to Cornhill-on-Tweed then Branxton.*

Flodden Field

A monument inscribed "To the brave of both nations" marks Pipers Hill, the centre of the English positions. In two hours, on 9 September 1513, the smaller English army slaughtered the flower of Scotland's chivalry and their King, James IV, who had led them into battle in support of his recently renewed "Auld Alliance" with the French.

Wester Ross ★★★

Highland

The Atlantic seaboard of Wester Ross is wild and dramatic, with magnificent mountains and placid lochs.

🚗 DRIVING TOURS

KYLE OF LOCHALSH TO GAIRLOCH★★★

120mi/192km if visiting Eilean Donan Castle – allow a whole day.

The route covers some of the finest scenery in the Wester Ross region – Loch Maree studded with islands, the Torridon area and the Applecross peninsula. Some of the roads will be busy in high season, but many stretches will allow the luxury of enjoying the scenery in solitude. **Kyle of Lochalsh** is the ferry port for Skye and a busy place in summer.

Eilean Donan Castle★

9mi/15km east of Kyle of Lochalsh by A 87. ⏲ *Open Easter–Oct daily 10am (9am Jul and Aug)–6pm.* 👓*£5.50.* 🅿✕. 📞*01599 555 202. www.eileandonancastle.com.*

The castle enjoys an idyllic **setting**★★ on an island in the loch and is now linked to the shore by a bridge. It was completely reconstructed in the 20C after 200 years disuse following an abortive Jacobite attack, with Spanish support in 1719. The ramparts afford **views** of three lochs.

▶ *Return to Kyle and leave by the road running along the coast to the north.*

Plockton★

Once a "refugee" settlement at the time of the Highland clearances, Plockton, with its palm-lined main street and sheltered bay, is a sailing centre.

▶ *At Achmore, take A 890 to the left, and at the junction with A 896, go left again, towards Lochcarron. At Tornapress, the visitor can elect to continue on A 896 to Shieldaig, but the minor road across the peninsula, via*

- 🚻 **Michelin Map:** Michelin Atlas p 66 or Map 501 D, E 10, 11 and 12.
- ℹ **Info:** Gairloch. 📞01445 712 130. Kyle of Lochalsh. 📞01599 534 276. Ullapool. 📞01854 612 135. www.visithighlands.com.
- ▶ **Location:** The touring centres are Kyle of Lochalsh, Gairloch and Ullapool, respectively, 78mi/125km, 69mi/110km and 57mi/91km west of Inverness.

Bealach-na Bo well repays the effort. It has hairpin bends and 1:4 gradients, and is not recommended for caravans or learner drivers.

Bealach-na-Bo

2 053ft/626m.

On the way up to the pass the hanging valley frames spectacular vistas of lochs and mountains, while from the summit car park, the **views**★★★ westward of Skye and its fringing islands are superb.

▶ *Either continue north along the coast, via Fearnmore, to Torridon, or return to Tornapress, for Torridon by A 896.*

Torridon Countryside Centre

NTS. ♿⏲*Open Apr–Sept daily 10am–5pm.* 👓*£3.* 🅿. 📞*0844 4932 229. www.nts.org.uk.*

The centre interprets the area's spectacular geology and nature and includes a deer enclosure. Information is available on walking and climbing.

▶ *At Kinlochewe, take A 832 to the left.*

Loch Maree★★★

Loch Maree epitomises the scenic beauty and grandeur of the west coast. It lies between Beinn Eighe and the towering **Ben Slioch** (3,217ft/980m) to the north. To the north is the **Letterewe Estate**, one of Scotland's great deer forests.

Victoria Falls★

A platform and the riverside path give good views of these falls, named after Queen Victoria's visit in 1877.

Gairloch

The ideal centre for touring the Torridon area, exploring the hills and enjoying the sandy beaches of this part of the west coast, and admiring the splendid views of the Hebridean Islands. The pier at the head of the loch still has all the bustle of a fishing port.

GAIRLOCH TO ULLAPOOL★★

56mi/90km – about 4hr.
This route runs along the coastline with its bays, beaches and headlands all backed, inland, by breathtaking mountain scenery.

> *Take the A 832 across the Rubha Reidh peninsula.*

Stop before descending to the River Ewe and look back from the roadside **viewpoint**★★★ at the superb view of Loch Maree with its forested islands.

Inverewe Garden★★★

NTS. ⏱ Open daily Apr–Oct 9.30/10am–9pm/sunset; visitor centre closes 5/6pm; Jan–Mar 10am–3pm, visitor centre 4pm.

£8.50. Guided walks May–Sept. ♿▣✕. ✆0844 4932 225.
These outstanding gardens enjoy a magnificent coastal setting on the same latitude as Leningrad. Their profusion so far north, is only possible by the influence of the Gulf Stream. Colour is found at most seasons, from azaleas and rhododendrons in May to heathers and maples in the autumn.

> *Continue on A 832; left onto A 835.*

Falls of Measach★★

The waters of the River Droma make a spectacular sight as they drop over 150ft/45m in the wooded cleft of the **Corrieshalloch Gorge**★. The road follows the north shore of **Loch Broom**★★ in a particularly attractive setting.

> *Continue northwest on the A 835.*

Ullapool★

The village was laid out in the 18C and flourished during the herring boom. Fishing still plays an important part in the local economy. Ullapool is an ideal touring centre; the car ferry terminal for Stornoway, a haven for yachtsmen and an unrivalled centre for sea angling. Various boats sail to the **Summer Isles** and their seals and sea birds.

Western Isles

Outer Hebrides

The chain of islands known as the Western Isles extends around 130mi/200km north–south. The Outer Hebrides share a history of Norse control with the Isle of Man much further south. Traditional activities include peat working and the weaving of Harris tweed. Buffeted by Atlantic waves, the islands are treeless and windswept, but rejoice in glistening *lochans* (small lochs), superb sandy beaches, and crystal-clear waters. The islands' isolation has helped to preserve the Gaelic culture that flourishes even

> ▶ **Population:** 23,224.
> ⚖ **Michelin Map:** Atlas p 71 or Map 501 Z, A 8, 9 and 10.
> ▤ **Info:** Lewis: Stornoway, ✆01851 703 088. Harris: Tarbert, ✆01859 502 011. www.visithebrides.com.

today; special events and festivals of Gaelic art and music (Mods) are held all year round. Gatherings (ceilidhs), concerts, highland games and agricultural shows are joyful community occasions with music, dance and poetry among other performances. Gaelic is still widely spoken.

ISLE OF LEWIS
Stornoway

Stornoway, the capital and only sizeable town, is the base for excursions inland where hotels (and petrol) are scarce. The land-locked harbour is over-looked by a 19C castle. Eye peninsula to the north has some fine sandy beaches.

Callanish Standing Stones★★

16mi/26km west of Stornoway, well signposted off A 858.
Over 4,000 years old and contemporary with Stonehenge, the stones, of Lewisian gneiss, form a circle, while approach avenues form the points of the compass. It is generally assumed that the stones were used for astronomical observations.

Carloway Broch★

5mi/8km beyond Callanish Standing Stones, signposted off A 858.
This is an incomplete example of a broch (small fortified farm c. 500BC), though

GETTING THERE

Lewis and Harris are actually one island. A ferry makes the short journey to the southern chain (North Uist, Benbecula, South Uist, Eriskay and Barr) which are linked by bridges and causeways. There are boat services to the mainland: Stornoway–Ullapool and Lochboidsale/Castle Bay–Oban, and also between Uig and Skye.

enough remains of the galleried walls and entrance chamber for the builders' skill to be admired.

Arnol Black House

6mi/10km beyond Carloway, signposted off A 858. Open year-round Mon–Sat, 9.30am–6.30pm (4.30pm Oct–Mar). £2.80. 01851 710 395.
This typical basic dwelling has been preserved as a reminder of island life as it was until half a century ago.

Wick

Highland

Wick is a thriving market town that was once the country's premier herring port. Only a small fishing fleet now operates, a far cry from its heyday when over 1,000 boats sailed out of Wick and neighbouring Pulteneytown.

EXCURSIONS
John O'Groats

19mi/31km north on the A 9.
Traditionally this is the northeastern-most point in mainland Britain, some 876mi/1,410km from the southeastern most point, Land's End.
The settlement takes its name from a Dutchman, Jan de Groot, who started a ferry service to the Orkneys in the 16C. The eight-sided tower of the hotel recalls the tale of this ferryman who, to settle disputes amongst his seven descendants, built an octagonal house, with eight doors and an octagonal table.

> ▶ **Population:** 9,713.
> ⚫ **Michelin Map:**
> Atlas p 74 or Map 501 K 8.
> **Info:** Wick: 0845 225 5121. County Road John O'Groats: 01955 611 373. www.visithighlands.com.
> **Location:** Near the northeastern tip of the Scottish mainland, Wick is 16mi/26km south of John O'Groats. The bus and train station are next to each other in the centre of town.

Duncansby Head★

2 mi/3.2km east of John O'Groats.
The northeastern headland of mainland Scotland, Duncansby Head, overlooks the treacherous waters of the Pentland Firth. The **scenery** is spectacular. Standing just offshore, the **Stacks of Duncansby**★★, pointed sea stacks, rise 210ft/64m up from the water. A variety of sea birds flock to the rocks.

There are many traditional Welsh icons: male voice choirs, rugby, coal pits, slate mines, medieval castles, Mount Snowdon and of course, sheep, which still outnumber people over three to one. Since around the turn of this century many new icons have added to and updated Wales's offering to the world: outstanding national museums in stunning new buildings that interpret past industries; the striking new Welsh Senned (parliament) building and redevelopment of Cardiff's docks; pioneering coastal adventure activities such as coasteering and RIBs (rapid inflatable boats) in Pembrokeshire; Cardiff's Millennium Stadium and Mount Snowdon's 21C visitor centre. Add to this near-deserted roads, wild walks, charming little seaside towns, some of Britain's most beautiful beaches and the ultimate folly of Portmeirion, and it's easy to see why Wales is back on the tourist map.

Highlights

1. Brave the miners' underground tour at **Big Pit Museum** (p451).
2. Explore the ultimate architectural folly, **Portmeirion** (p460).
3. Climb the walls of mighty **Caernarfon Castle** (p446).
4. Ascend **Snowdon** (p462) – by whichever means suit you best!
5. Chill out on glorious **Gower Peninsula** beaches (p465).

North Wales

North Wales is a land of picture-book castles: Harlech, Caernarfon, Conwy and Beaumaris, built by Edward I in the 13C as part of his Iron Ring to prevent rebellion in the region.

Towering above all is mighty Snowdon, the kingpin of an area unequalled in Britain for its majestic scenery. Snowdonia is not only a magnet for walkers, its railway and the small-gauge railways of Ffestiniog are evergreen attractions, as is nearby Portmeirion. The relatively

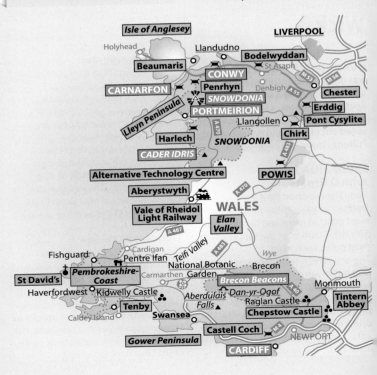

National Parks

Snowdonia – The Snowdon massif, heartland of the park, and Cader Idris are the most popular areas – with half a million people reaching Snowdon's summit each year and only a quarter of them admitting to using the railway. The Aran Mountains in the south and the rugged Rhynogydd are less crowded.

Pembrokeshire Coast – For much of its length this narrow park is less than three miles wide. Steep cliffs display spectacularly folded and twisted rock formations; sheltered bays invite bathing and scuba-diving. Offshore islands such as Skomer and Skokholm support huge colonies of seabirds.

Brecon Beacons – High red sandstone mountains divide the ancient rocks of mid-Wales from the coalfields and industrialisation farther south. Along the southern edge of the park, a limestone belt provides a dramatic change in scenery and there are hundreds of sink-holes and cave systems.

mote golden sands of the Lyn Peninsula have a real charm while the Isle of nglesey is mostly pastoral. Last-stop est, before Ireland, is Holy Island's ectacular coast.

- **Isle of Anglesey**
- **Caernarfon**
- **Conwy**
- **Llandudno**
- **Llangollen**
- **Portmeirion**
- **Snowdonia**

id-Wales

e Brecon Beacons is one of the least plored parts of Wales but highly pular with walkers. Nonetheless, off e beaten track, they are more likely to eet sheep, or the odd mountain pony an fellow humans. By contrast, buzz-g sociable Aberystwyth (in summer at ast) is the Principality's most likeable liday resort, maintaining an elegant d unspoiled air.

- **Aberystwyth**
- **Brecon Beacons**

uth Wales

e south is the heartland of Welsh dustry with the Valleys, just north of rdiff, providing coal to Britain and the rld, and the iron and steel works of rt Talbot, adjacent to Swansea, power-g British imperialism and Industrialisa-n from the 1830s–mid-20C.

day where there was once over 0 mines, only one working pit now mains, but Big Pit and the Rhondda eritage Park still remember the miners.

By contrast the port cities that grew rich on coal and metal are enjoying something of a renaissance and Cardiff in particular – "Europe's newest capital" (since 1955) – boasts cultural attractions, shopping, entertainment, restaurants and nightlife commensurate with that status. Swansea has a less obvious appeal; after seeing its splendid National Waterfront Museum make your way out to the Gower Peninsula and beautiful golden sands.

- **Cardiff**
- **Swansea**

Pembrokeshire

Travelling the inland roads of the westernmost part of the Principality, even in high summer, can feel like a step back to a quieter time. And in the lonelier places dolmens, megaliths and Celtic crosses remain. The Pembrokeshire Coast attracts most visitors. Its coastline varies from ragged rocks to glorious beaches with a rich bird and animal life including puffins, seals and dolphins. Tiny St David's is not only home to Wales' finest church but in and around here a number of young adventure tour operators are bringing a whole new, and very different, set of pilgrims to this part of the world. Tenby is an established and deserved favourite with families seeking classic bucket-and-spade holidays, but is just one of many beaches to choose from on this stretch of coast.

- **Pembrokeshire Coast**
- **St David's**
- **Tenby**

Aberystwyth★★
Ceredigion

Set roughly halfway along the west coast, Aberystwyth successfully combines the difficult balancing act of being the liveliest seaside resort in the Principality with being a prestigious university town and maintaining its unspoiled Victorian appearance. Despite its popularity with "foreign" (English) visitors the town retains a real sense of Welshness.

▶ **Population:** 8,636.
Michelin Map: Atlas p 24 or Map 503 H 26.
Info: ℘01970 612 125. www.tourism. ceredigion.gov.uk.
Location: 121mi/194km due west of Birmingham. The railway station and bus station are a 10min walk from the centre of town.
Don't Miss: the Light Railway to Devil's Bridge Falls.

☛ TOWN WALK

Arriving in Aberystwyth by train, you may spot a puff of smoke from the **Vale of Rheidol Light Railway**★ (mid-Jun–mid-Sept daily, reduced timetable at other times; return £13.50; ⊞✕; ℘ 01970 625 819; www.rheidolrailway.co.uk), which shares the station with National Rail services. This narrow–gauge steam railway hauls from Aberystwyth through the wonderfully wooded Vale of Rheidol to the waterfalls at **Devil's Bridge**★. The journey (12mi/19km) takes an hour as the train climbs slowly up to the terminus (639ft/195m). The line was built in 1902 to service the lead mines in the Vale of Rheidol. The engines and rolling stock are all original.

Terrace Road leads from the railway station to the seafront via the **Ceredigion Museum** (Open year-round Mon–Sat 10am–5pm; ; www.ceredigion.gov.uk), next to the tourist office. The restored Edwardian Coliseum Theatre is now one of the most unusual and striking museum interiors in Britain. Objects of all ages from the county of Ceredigion (Cardiganshire) are on display with the focus on the Victorian period and later. Continuing on to the **seafront**★, you will find few modern intrusions to mar the Victorian harmony of Marine Terrace. To the north, the **Cliff Railway** of 1896 (Cliff Terrace; operating times vary; £3.20 return; ℘01970 617 642; www. aberystwythcliffrailway.co.uk) still scales the heights of Constitution Hill, which is home to the world's largest **Camera Obscura** (opening times vary; ℘01970

617 642 to confirm times and days; £1). On the promontory beyond the sadly shortened pier to the south is the ruin of the castle begun in 1277 by Edward I. To the east of the centre, follow Penglais Road (A 487) past Bronglais General Hospital and take a right for the **National Library of Wales** (Reading Room: open Mon–Sat 9.30am–5pm/6pm; guided tour weekly Mon 11am; ⊞✕; ℘01970 632 800; www.llgc.org.uk). Set on top of Penglais Hill commanding a magnificent **view**★ across town, this is one of the United Kingdom's most important libraries. Its **permanent collection**★ houses a priceless collection.

EXCURSION
Elan Valley★★

34mi/55km east via the A44 to Rhayader; circuit of lakes 25mi/40km.

Reservoirs were built in the Elan Valley, 1892–1904, to supply water to Birmingham. The Claerwen Dam, built to increase the supply, was opened in 1952. The **Elan Valley Visitor Centre** (Rhayadrer; open mid–Mar–Oct daily 10am–5.30pm; ⊞ (£1)✕; ℘01597 810 898 or 01597 810 880 (winter); www.elanvalley.org.uk) at the foot of the Cabancoch dam, has displays explaining the construction and operation of this great engineering feat, as well as the ecology of the surrounding woods and high moorlands, habitat of the rare red kite. The reservoirs have created a landscape of great beauty. The dams are best seen in flood conditions.

Isle of **Anglesey** ★★

Ynys Môn – Anglesey

Anglesey is an island off the north-west tip of Wales, separated from the mainland by the **Menai Strait**; its landscape of low undulating hills, rich in prehistoric remains, is a perfect spot for walkers and yachtsmen.

🚗 DRIVING TOUR

Thomas Telford (1757–1834) built the **Menai Suspension Bridge** (A 5) to carry his road to Holyhead. The Admiralty insisted upon a clearance of 100ft/30m between water and roadway, and the bridge, with its span of 579ft/176m between towers, was the longest iron bridge in the world when it was opened in 1826. It gives its name to the small town on the other side. Modern traffic also flows to the island over the Britannia Bridge (A 55).

Head 4mi/6.4km northeast from Menai Bridge on the A 545 to **Beaumaris**★★. One of the fortress towns founded in the late 13C by Edward I, Beaumaris is now a peaceful little resort, with a wonderful prospect across the Menai Strait to Snowdonia. Its **Castle**★, *(CADW; ⏰open Apr–Oct daily 9am–5pm, Nov–Mar daily 9.30am/Sun 11am–4pm; ⏰closed Dec 24–26, Jan 1; ⬧£3.70; ✆01248 810 361; www. beaumaris.com)* was the last and the largest of Edward's Welsh strongholds. Though never finished, Beaumaris is the

- 🔆 **Michelin Map:** Atlas p 32 or Map 503 G, H 23, 24.
- ℹ️ **Info:** Station Site, Llan-fairpwll. ✆01248 713 177. Port Terminal, Holyhead. ✆01407 762 622. www. islandofchoice.com.
- ◗ **Location:** Bangor and Holyhead are on the main rail route with connections and services from most parts of the UK. Beaumaris is a good base on Anglesey.
- 🙂 **Don't Miss:** Beaumaris Castle, Plas Newydd.
- 🕐 **Timing:** Allow at least one full day.

finest example in Britain of a concentric castle. A moat surrounds it and there was once a defended dock, capable of taking ships of up to 40t. The Great Hall, impressive enough as it stands, would have risen to twice its present height. Heading southwest from Menai Bridge on the A 5, turn left in **Pentre Uchaf** onto the A 4080 and continue for 1.5mi/1.6km to **Plas Newydd**★★ *(NT; ⏰open Apr–Oct Sat–Wed and Good Friday, noon–5pm. Garden same dates (rhododendron garden open early Apr) 11am–5.30pm; guided tour (free) 11.15am; ⬧£7.50, garden only, £5.50; ⬧🅿️✕; ✆01248 714 795, 01248 715272 (Infoline); www.national trust.org.uk).* This magnificently sited late-18C mansion in extensive parkland and gardens (169 acres/68ha),

View of Anglesey from the Mainland

© Gareth Jones/stock.xchng

443

once home to the Marquess of Anglesey, looks over the Strait to the mountains of Snowdonia. In 1936 the artist **Rex Whistler** decorated the long dining room with a whimsical masterpiece of *trompe l'œil*.

Head west from Menai Bridge on the B 5420 to Llangefni and turn right onto B 5111 for Rhosmeirch and the **Oriel Ynys Môn**★ (open year-round daily 10.30am–5pm; ; 01248 724 444; www.angleseyheritage.org). This modern museum and gallery succeeds admirably in explaining the island's special identity. As well as imaginative displays evoking Anglesey's rich past, there are explanations of current issues and a reconstruction of the studio of **Charles Tunnicliffe** (1901–79), perhaps the foremost 20C British wildlife painter.

Brecon Beacons ★★

Carmarthenshire, Merthyr Tydfil, Monmouthshire, Powys, Rhondda Cynon Taff

These red sandstone mountains culminate in a spectacular north-facing escarpment overlooking the lesser uplands of mid-Wales. South from this great barrier (highest point Pen-y-Fan, 2,907ft/886m) extend high rolling moorlands cut by lush valleys, the broadest of them formed by the River Usk. Downstream from Brecon, centrally placed for exploring the Brecon Beacons National Park, the river is accompanied by the most delightful of waterways (33mi/53km), the Monmouthshire and Brecon Canal.

BLACK MOUNTAINS

To the east lie the **Black Mountains**, forming a natural border with Herefordshire. The quiet market town of **Hay-on-Wye** (*16mi/30km northeast of Brecon via the A 470, A 438 and B 4350*) at the northern end of the Black Mountains has become internationally known for its numerous second-hand bookshops and its annual literary festival. South of the town is **Hay Bluff**★★ (*4mi/6km by B 4423 and a single-track road*), an escarpment of the Black Mountains offering imcomparable **views** over the Wye Valley and far into central Wales.

8mi/13km south of Hay-on-Wye by B 4423 is **Llanthony Priory**★★ (open Apr–Oct Mon–Sat from 11am, Sun from

- **Michelin Map:** Atlas pp 15, 16 or Map 503 I, J, K 28.
- **Info:** Brecon: 01874 622 485. Hay-on-Wye: 01497 820144. http://tourism.powys.gov.uk. www.brecon-beacons.com.
- **Location:** The main centres are Aberdare, Abergavenny, Brecon, Crickhowell and Hay-on-Wye. For outdoor types the best starting point is the National Park Visitor Centre at Libanus, 5mi/8km southwest of Brecon (01874 623 366; www.brecon-beacons.com), which provides a wide range of information and other facilities.
- **Don't Miss:** Dan-yr-Ogof Caves; Llanthony Priory; hire a narrowboat on the Monmouthshire and Brecon Canal (details from tourist office).
- **Warning:** Walking is the best way to discover the Brecons, these are real mountains, so take sensible precautions.
- **Timing:** Two days minimum.
- **Kids:** Dan-yr-Ogof Caves.
- **Bicycle trails:** Routes are marked at the Garwnant Forestry Commission Visitor Centre (6mi/9km north of Merthyr Tydfil by A 470 and a side road - follow signs).

noon (see website); Nov–Mar Fri 6–11pm, Sat 11am–11pm, Sun noon–4pm; 🄿✕; ℘01873 890 487). The ruins of this late-12C Augustinian priory stand in the Vale of Ewyas beside the River Honddu. Eight splendid arches, topped by the ruined triforium, still stand beside the remains of the crossing tower and the east end of the church; parts of the monastic quarters now house a small hotel. The monks, whose numbers had sunk to four by the Dissolution, lasted longer than later communities who were attracted by the seclusion and tranquillity – the poet, **Walter Savage Landor**, who vainly tried to restore the ruined priory, the charismatic preacher, **Father Ignatius** and his adherents at the turn of the 19C, and **Eric Gill** and his followers in the 1920s.

CENTRAL BEACONS

The **Central Beacons** dominate the skyline south of **Brecon** (Aberhonddu; population 7,166), rising to 886m at Pen y Fan, the highest point in southern Britain. The Normans constructed a castle at Brecon, the ruins of which overlook the meeting of the rivers Honddu and Usk; they also built a priory whose church is now the cathedral. The stone-built former county town has kept its intricate medieval street pattern and numerous dignified 18C houses. The **Brecknock Museum and Art Gallery** (🕘 open year-round Tue–Sat and bank hols (Sun in Apr–Sept); 🕘 closed Jan 1, Good Fri, Dec 25; ⚇£1; ♿🄿 (limited); ℘01874 624 121; www.powys.gov.uk) is one of the region's best small collections with lively local displays on rural life and natural history.

FFOREST FAWR GEOPARK

Continuing west is the sandstone massif of **Fforest Fawr** (www.fforestfawr geopark.org.uk) and the hills known as 'Fans' (Fan Fawr is 734m). Water run-off from these hills formed steep river valleys with spectacular waterfalls. The park is known for its waterfalls, including the 27-metre **Henrhyd Waterfall** and the falls at **Ystradfellte★**, and its caves, such as **Ogof Ffynnon Ddu**.

Dan-yr-Ogof cave

GeoPictures.net/National Showcaves for Wales

The **Black Mountain, Y Mynydd Du**, is the most westerly block of sandstone, culminating in the summit of **Fan Brycheiniog** at 802m and the glacial lakes of **Llyn y Fan Fach** and **Llyn y Fan Fawr**.

👥 National Showcaves Centre for Wales★

19mi/30km southwest of Brecon via the A 40 and A 4067. 🕘 *Open Apr–Oct 10am–3pm (last admission). Extended hours in high season, call for details.* ⚇£11.50, child £7. 🄿✕. ℘01639 730 284. www.showcaves.co.uk.

This underground complex includes the largest as well as the longest single-chamber cave open to visitors in Britain. **Dan-yr-Ogof** is an 11mi/17km long cave system. The first section of the cave system is open to the public, more to cavers. Bones of humans and animals have been found in nearby chambers and human occupation of the caves dates back to the Bronze Age. The caves have been formed in the permeable limestone which underlies this southern part of the Beacons. The results include swallow-holes and underground rivers, examples of which can be seen in the "waterfall country" around the village of **Ystradfellte★**. There are archaeological displays, an interpretive exhibition and several areas themed for children including a dinosaur park.

ADDRESSES

⌂ STAY

▱▱ **The Old Post Office**, Llanigon. ℘01497 820 008. www.oldpost-office. co.uk. This small, beautifully converted characterful former 17C inn, 2mi/3km from Hay-on-Wye, mixes smart modern ambience with exposed beams and antique fittings.

▱▱▱ **Plough Inn**, Rhosmaen, Llandeilo. ℘01558 823 431. www.plough-rhosmaen.com This former farmhouse has been very smartly converted, with picture windows offering fine views of the countryside. The patron/chef serves Modern British cuisine (▱▱).

℘/ EAT

▱▱ **Old Black Lion**, Lion Street, Hay-on-Wye. ℘01497 82 0841. www.oldblacklion co.uk. Parts of this 17C inn date back to the 1300s with original exposed timbers. The changing menu uses the best of British produce including locally reared meat, seasonal vegetables and herbs from the pub's own gardens. Ten attractive bedrooms (▱▱▱) with special rates in winter.

▱▱ **Nantyffin Cider Mill Inn**, Brecon Road West, Crickhowell. ℘01873 810775. www.cidermill.co.uk. Originally a drovers inn dating back to the 16C and then a cider mill during the 19C, the building has been stunningly restored and serves Modern British cooking.

Caernarfon★★
Gwynedd

The strategic importance of Caernarfon (Welsh for "fort on the shore"), has long been appreciated. It was the most westerly position of the Roman Empire in Wales, who built their fort of Segontium nearby. The Normans chose the castle's present site for their wooden stronghold, which was probably replaced by a stone castle even before Edward I began his mighty structure, bristling with towers and turrets and designed as a seat of power whose walls imitated those of mighty Constantinople. The town today, still watched over by the castle and partly encircled within its walls, is a centre for visitors to Snowdonia and for yachtsmen eager to make use of its proximity to the waters of the strait and Caernarfon Bay. There are good beaches nearby.

CAERNARFON CASTLE★★★
Overlooking the Menai Strait. CADW. ☾ Open Apr–Oct daily 9.30am–5pm. Nov–Mar Mon–Sat 9.30am–4pm, Sun 11am–4pm. ☾ Closed Jan 1, Dec 24–26. ⊛£5.10. ℘01286 677 617. www.caernarfon.com.

- **Population:** 9,271.
- **Michelin Map:** Michelin Atlas p 32 or Map 503 H 24.
- **Info:** Oriel Pendeitsh, Castle Street. ℘01286 672 232. www.gwynedd.com. www.visitcaernarfon.com.
- **Location:** On the northwest tip of mainland Wales. The nearest railway station is Llanfairpwll 8.5mi/13.6km north. Climb the castle walls and battlements to get your bearings across town.
- **Don't Miss:** The view of the castle from the water if possible.
- **Timing:** Allow two hours.

Building work on this impressive structure started in 1283 under Master James of St George (c. 1235-1308), who built for his royal patron a castle with walls decorated with bands of coloured stone and polygonal towers like those of Constantinople. Grandiose in design, it was to serve as the seat of English government in the Principality. The appearance of the castle today is due to the vision of

Caernarfon Castle

A. Williams/MICHELIN

the constable in the 1840s, **Sir Llewelyn Turner** (1823-1903), who cleared, restored, re-roofed and renewed, in the teeth of local opposition. Massive curtain walls link the towers to form a figure of eight with the lower bailey to the right and the upper to the left. The great twin-towered gatehouse, **King's Gate**, was defended by five doors and six portcullises.

The **Eagle Tower**, crowned by triple turrets, each, as in Constantinople and *The Mabinogion*, crested with an eagle, had accommodation on a grand scale. Currently it houses the exhibition "A Prospect of Caernarfon", re-creating the investiture of **Charles, Prince of Wales**, in July 1969.

It was here that the first English Prince of Wales was born in April 1284, Edward of Caernarfon, later Edward II. The **Queen's Tower** houses the Regimental Museum of the Royal Welch Fusiliers. In **Castle Square**, opposite the balcony from which Charles, Prince of Wales, greeted his subjects, is the statue of **David Lloyd George** (1863-1945), Liberal MP for Caernarfon for 55 years and Prime Minister 1916-22.

OLD TOWN

The old town hugs close to Edward I's castle, occupying the land just north. The circuit (800yd/734m) of **town walls** and towers encircling the medieval town was built as a single operation at the same time as the castle. The walls are punctuated at regular intervals by eight towers and two twin-towered gates.

SEGONTIUM ROMAN FORT

Southeast of Caernarfon on A 487. Beddgelert Road. Open 12.30pm–4.30pm. Closed Jan 1, Dec 24–26. . 01286 675 625. *www.segontium.org.uk.*

The remains of the Roman auxiliary fort of Segontium overlooks Caernarfon town and the remains of Roman buildings in a large area of the fort are on view to the public. An exhibition in the site **museum** tells of the conquest and occupation of Wales by the Roman army, the military organisation of the day, the garrisons of Segontium and the history of the fort as seen in its remains; it also displays selected finds excavated on the site which reveal much about daily life in this remote Roman outpost.

St Peblig's Church

Llanbeblig. Near the Roman fort of Segontium. Open by appointment. . 01286 674 181. Fax 01286 673 750.

Situated outside the town, near to Segontium, is the parish church of Caernarfon. Peblig, reputed to have been the son of Magnus Maximus, is said to have returned to introduce Christianity. The church is mainly 14C, and contains a striking 16C alabaster tomb in the Vaynol Chapel.

Cardiff★★★

CAERDYDD – Cardiff

Cardiff, capital of Wales, arose around the Roman fort guarding the crossing of the Taff, on the road between Caerleon and Carmarthen. By the start of the 20C it was the world's principal coal port and much of its appearance today can be directly attributed to this era. At the end of the 20C a series of major projects – most notably the Welsh National Assembly Building, the redevelopment of the Cardiff Bay dockside, and the magnificent **Millennium Stadium** – have helped revitalise the city.

CITY CENTRE

Cardiff Castle★

Kingsway. ○ *Open year-round daily 9.30am–6pm (Nov–Feb 5pm), last admission/tour 1hr before closing.* ○ *Closed Jan 1, Dec 25–26.* ⊚£8.95, *or with personal 50 min guided tour of additional apartments £11.95.* ✕*.* ✆*029 2087 8100. www.cardiffcastle.com.*
The first known fortifications at Cardiff Castle were built by the Romans at the end of the 50s AD. After Hastings (1066), William the Conqueror gave Robert Fitz-Hamon a free hand in the southern borderlands, and he built a timber motte and bailey castle here within the ruins. The twelve-sided stone keep is 12C. It was the third **Marquess of Bute**

- ▶ **Population:** 262,313.
- ⚷ **Michelin Map:** Michelin Atlas p 16 or Map 503 K 29.
- 🗓 **Info:** ✆0870 1211 258. ✆029 2046 3833. www.visitcardiff.com.
- ◖ **Location:** In the southern-most part of Wales. High-speed InterCity trains link most cities with Cardiff. Both the train and bus station are on/just off Central Square. The sights are spread over quite a large area so the City Sightseeing (hop-on-hop-off) bus tour is a good way to get around (○Feb–Oct daily; ⊚£9; ✆029 2047 3432; www.city-sightseeing.com).
- ◔ **Don't Miss:** National Museum Cardiff; Cardiff Castle's exotic interiors; sports and music events at the Millennium Stadium.
- ◮ **Warning:** Big events at the Millennium Stadium will mean heavy congestion on the roads and booked-up central accommodation.
- ○ **Timing:** Two days minimum.
- ❢ **Kids:** The National Museum and Techniquest. The Dr Who Exhibition; Rhondda Heritage Park.

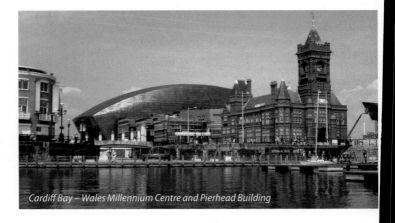

Cardiff Bay – Wales Millennium Centre and Pierhead Building

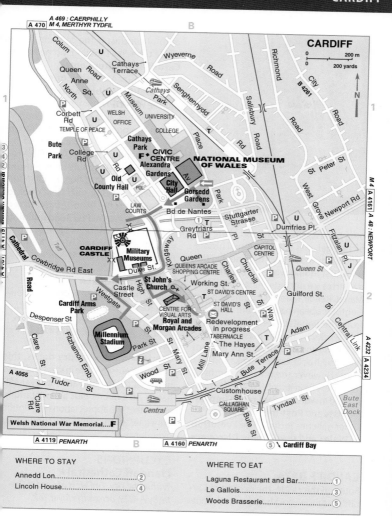

1847–1900), reputedly the richest man in Britain at the time, who in 1868 commissioned the architect **William Burges** (1827–81); his romantic imagination was given free rein in an extraordinary series of exotic **interiors** – Arab, Gothic and Greek – to create the unique monument to the Victorian age we see today.

A new **interpretation centre** explains the history of the castle with a film presentation. From its open-air roof terrace, there are fine views of the castle and city skyline. Also in the grounds are the **Welch Regiment Museum** and the **Queen's Dragoon Guards Museum**.

National Museum Cardiff ★★★

Museum Avenue, Cathays Park.
🕐 *Open year-round Tue–Sun and most bank hols 10am–5pm. Audio guide (most European languages).* ✕.
📞 *029 2039 7951. www.nmgw.ac.uk.*
The magnificently refurbished and extended headquarters of the National Museum and Gallery of Wales is situated in **Cathays Park**, the spacious early 20C civic centre, which is the outstanding example in Great Britain of Beaux-Arts planning and architecture. There are impeccably arranged displays of arche-

Welsh Landscape Gallery,
National Museum Cardiff

Amgueddfa Cymru – National Museum Wales

ology, glass, silver and porcelain; the picture galleries and the natural history collections are among the finest in the UK. Outstanding works in the **picture galleries**★★, include masterpieces by Manet, Renoir, Monet, Cézanne and Van Gogh; European painting and sculpture from the Renaissance onwards, with fine works by Claude and Poussin; and by modern greats such as Oskar Kokoschka and Max Ernst. However the great strengths of the gallery lie in its collections of **British art** and in works by the **French Impressionists** and **Post-Impressionists**. Other galleries include **The Evolution of Wales** and the **Glanely Discovery Gallery**, a popular hands-on space.

CARDIFF BAY★

South of the castle, the decline of Cardiff's extensive docklands, once the outlet for much of the coal dug from the South Wales Valleys, has been largely reversed by an ambitious programme of conservation and restoration and by the creation of major new cultural and recreational facilities. The project's keystone is the barrage constructed across the estuary of the Taff to create a freshwater lake (500 acre/200ha) with a 8mi/13km waterfront.

Butetown, named after the first promoter of the docks, the Second Marquess of Bute, was the core of the harbour area; its buildings, slowly being rescued from dilapidation, include the huge neo-Renaissance pile of the **Coal Exchange**, completed in 1866. By way

of total contrast is the contemporary white tube-like building, home to the **Cardiff Bay Visitor Centre**.

Pride of place bayside goes to the **National Assembly (Senedd)** building, the Welsh Government's new debating chamber and commitee rooms. This stunning construction of timber, steel, slate and glass was opened by the Queen on St David's Day 2006. Visitors can watch Assembly debates from the public viewing gallery (*&0845 010 5500; www.wales.gov.uk*) Next door to the Senedd is the historic strident red brick and terracotta **Pierhead Building** of 1896 which contains an interactive exhibition on the role of the National Assembly (*&0845 010 5500*).

♣♟ Techniquest★

Stuart Street. ⏰ *Open year-round Mon–Fri 9.30am–4.30pm (5pm school hols), Sat–Sun and bank hols 10.30am–5pm.* *£6.20.* ♿✖. *&029 20 475 475. www.techniquest.org.*

Overlooking the old dry docks, this ultra-modern structure in steel and glass houses a compelling array of over 150 hands-on exhibits plus a planetarium, and makes the appreciation of scientific principles an enjoyable and stimulating experience.

EXCURSIONS
Llandaff Cathedral★

Within the city, 7mi west of Cardiff Castle by A 4119, across the River Taff. ⏰*Open daily 9am–6pm.* 🅿 *(limited). &029 2056 4554. www.llandaffcathedral.org.uk.*

Tradition has it that St Teilo founded a community here in about AD 560, naming his church (*Llan*) after the Taff river nearby. The cathedral was built between 1120 and 1280 but fell into decay after the Reformation and it was not until the 18C that John Wood was chosen to restore the cathedral. Almost the whole of his work was destroyed by a land-mine which fell to the south of the cathedral on 2 January 1941. The chancel is now divided from the nave by a concrete arch embellished with some of the 19C figures from the choir stalls and by a huge aluminium *Christ in Majesty* by Epstein. In the Memorial Chapel of the Welch Regiment is Rosetti's *The Seed of David*.

South Wales Valleys

Immediately to the north of Cardiff and the other ports of South Wales lie **The Valleys**, once one of Britain's greatest coalfields. The whole area is rich in the relics of an industrial age but the essence of The Valleys seems particularly concentrated in the Rhondda Fawr and Rhondda Fach. Near Pontypridd, the **Rhondda Heritage Park**★ *(Trehafod, Lewis Merthyr Colliery; open year-round daily, except Mon Oct–Mar, 10am–6pm; children's "Energy Zone" play area open Apr–Sept daily 10am–5pm; guided tours daily 11am, 1pm and 3pm, booking advised; £5.60, child £4.30, Energy Zone £2 per child extra; simulator riders must be 1.1m tall; ; ℘01443 682 036; www.rhonddaheritagepark.com)*, developed around the old Lewis Merthyr mine, tells the fascinating and often poignant story of coal mining in these valleys and includes a dramatic "underground" train ride. Retired miners act as genial guides – as they also do in the far east of the coalfield, at **Blaenafon** *(28mi/45km northeast by M 4, A 4042 and A 4043)*, a town that played a vital part in the Industrial Revolution and has recently been awarded UNESCO World Heritage Status. The centre of activities today is **Big Pit: National Coal Museum**★ *(open Feb–Nov daily 9.30am–5pm, 3.30pm last admission, call for Dec and Jan times; underground tour (1hr) must be 1m tall); ; ℘01495 790 311; www.nmgw.ac.uk)*. Mining may have ceased in 1980 but the former pitmen still descend deep underground, in fact some 300ft/100m below the surface, accompanied by fascinated visitors. In the pithead buildings there are displays recalling the harsh realities of work in this ancient industry.

St Fagans National History Museum★★

St Fagans, 4mi/6.4km west. Open year-round daily 10am–5pm. Closed Dec 24–26. (£2.50) . ℘029 2057 3500. www.nmgw.ac.uk.

One of the finest collections of vernacular buildings in Britain stands in the parkland of St Fagans Castle, an Elizabethan mansion. Re-erected buildings from all over Wales include cottages, farmhouses, a chapel, bakehouse, school, corn mill, woollen mill, tannery, a village store and unusual edifices like a toll house and a cockpit. A unique collection of coracles, a working farmstead and an award-winning terrace of miners' cottages add to the variety of the exhibits, while a number of traditional craftsmen demonstrate their skills in their craft workshops. Modern galleries present the traditional domestic, social and cultural life and there are displays on costume and agriculture.

St Fagans Castle itself was built c. 1580 on the site of an earlier castle. It has been restored to its 19C appearance and furnished appropriately. Its fine formal gardens include a mulberry grove and there are fishponds, stocked as in the 17C with carp, bream and tench.

Caerphilly Castle★★ *(Caerffili)*

CADW. 7mi/11km north by A 470 (Y) then A 469. Open Apr–Oct daily 9am/9.30am–4pm/5pm. £3.60. ℘029 2088 3143. www.cadw.wales.gov.uk.

This massive stronghold sits threateningly behind its extensive water defences, reducing the busy town gathered round the outer limits of its vast site to relative insignificance.

Begun in 1268 by the powerful baron Gilbert de Clare, the castle was the first in Britain to be built from new on a regular concentric plan; the design of its walls, towers and gateways embodied many innovative features too and it served as a model for the castles of Edward I shortly to be built in North Wales (see INTRODUCTION: Architecture).

The castle's decay was accelerated in the Civil War by deliberate destruction, of which the half-ruined "leaning tower" in the southeast corner of the main ward is a poignant reminder. The present state of the impressive complex is largely due to the general restoration carried out in the 19C and 20C. The approach to the castle is via the great gatehouse; this is set in the immensely long **East Barbican**, a fortified dam separating the outer moat from the inner moat and its flanking lakes to north and south. Behind these defences is the castle's core, an outer ward with semi-circular bastions and an inner ward with drum towers, mighty gatehouses and the **Great Hall**, the last rebuilt c. 317. Protecting the western gatehouse, the original entrance, is an extensive western outwork and beyond this, the 17C redoubt on the site of a Roman fort.

Castell Coch★★

CADW. 5mi/8km north on the A 470.
🕐 *Open as Caerphilly Castle, above.*
👓*£3.60.* 𝄢*029 2081 0101. www.cadw. wales.gov.uk.*
A pseudo-medieval stronghold, created, as was Cardiff Castle, by the wealth of the Marquess of Bute and the imagination of William Burges, who in 1875 started to build a fantasy 13C castle, with turrets inspired by Chillon and Carcassonne in France and complete with drawbridge, portcullis and "murder holes". French, Gothic and Moorish influences combine in the interior decorations.

Caerleon★

12mi/19km northeast by M 4 to Junction 25, then follow signs.
Caerleon, ("City of the Legions" in Welsh), was home to between 5,000 and 6,000 men of the Legio II Augusta, from AD 75 until AD 300. At the **Caerleon Amphitheatre,Barracks and Baths★★** *(CADW;* 🕐*open as Caerphilly Castle, above;* 𝄢*01633 422 518; www. cadw.wales.gov.uk)* you can see the remains of the enormous **Fortress Baths★**. On the High Street in the **Roman Legion Museum★** (🕐*open daily 10am (2pm Sun)–5pm;* 🕐*closed Jan 1, Dec 24–26 and 31;* ♿*;* 𝄢*01633 423 134; www.nmgw.ac.uk)* are the remains of the fortress, which includes the most complete **amphitheatre★** in Britain and the only remains of a Roman Legionary barracks on view anywhere in

Europe. The amphitheatre, just outside the fortress walls, was built about AD 90. The **barrack buildings** are in pairs, with verandahs onto a central street, accommodating eight men to a room, with the centurion at the end of the block.

Tredegar House★★

11mi/18km east via the M 4.
🔭 *Visit by guided tour Easter–Sept, Wed–Sun and bank hols, 11am–4pm (last admission).* 👓*£6.25.* ♿🅿✕.
𝄢*01633 815 880. www.newport.gov.uk.*
One of the finest houses in England and Wales to be built in the expansive years following the Civil War, this great mansion of 1664–72 was the residence of the fabulous wealthy Morgan family – landowners, entrepreneurs and the developers in the 19C of the docks in Newport. Many of the interiors have been re-furnished, in part with original pieces; among the most striking are the Brown Room with its exuberant carving, the Gilt Room and the Cedar Closet with its scented panelling. The **grounds★** retain something of their original formal layout, with superb ironwork gates and geometric parterres.

ADDRESSES

🛏STAY

👓👓 **Annedd Lon**, *157 Cathedral Road.* 𝄢*029 2022 3349. www.anned dlon.co.uk.* Friendly centrally located guest-house in a very elegant Victorian-Gothic building in a conservation area. Good value.

👓👓👓 **Lincoln House**, *118 Cathedral Road.* 𝄢*029 2039 5558. www.lincoln hotel.co.uk.* Beautifully renovated and sympathetically furnished 23-bedroom Victorian house in an ideal central location. Friendly owners, good service.

🍴EAT

👓👓 **Le Gallois**, *6–10 Romilly Crescent.* 𝄢*029 2034 1264. www.legallois-ycymro.com.* Long-established bright cheery restaurant combining Gallic and Welsh flavours.

⬤🍽 **Laguna Restaurant and Bar**, ʌrk Plaza Hotel, Greyfriars Road. ℘029 2011 1103. www.parkplaza.com. ᵐart modern restaurant serving teresting mix of local and international food.

⬤🍽 **Woods Brasserie**, *Pilotage Build-*g, Stuart Street, Cardiff Bay. ℘029 ⁾49 2400. www.woods-brasserie.com. ᵒdern brasserie dishes are served ᵒm an open kitchen with full-length ᵢndows offering bay views.

🛒 SHOPPING

ᵉ **Capitol Shopping Centre**, : **David's Centre** and **Queen's Arcade** ᵉ modern shopping malls. ᵉgant Edwardian and Victorian ᵣcades house speciality shops.

ᵣaft in the Bay *(The Flourish, Cardiff ʌy)* is the shop window for the Makers ᵤild of Wales – ceramics, glass, textiles, ᵉwellery, wood and basketware. ℘029 2048 4611. www.makersguildin ᵃles.org.uk.

🍺 PUBS AND 🍴 RESTAURANTS

Visit the **Café Quarter** *(Mill Lane)* and the area around Cardiff Bay for a wide choice of establishments.

🎭 ENTERTAINMENT

Cardiff has a lively cultural scene, including the Welsh Proms, Welsh National Opera, the Cardiff Singer of the World opera competition (June), the Gŵyl Ifan Folk Dance Festival (June) and Cardiff Festival (July and August) comprising comedy, street entertainment, children's events, free open-air concerts and fairground fun. Popular concert and performing arts venues include the Wales Millennium Centre, St David's Hall, New Theatre, Cardiff International Arena (also an exhibition venue), Sherman Theatre, and Chapter Arts Centre. The **Red Dragon Centre** (Hemingway Road) is a themed leisure complex with a cinema, bowling alley, bars, restaurants, nightclub and shops and a 👥 **Dr Who Exhibition** *(℘02920 489257; www. doctorwhoexhibitions.com)*

Conwy★★
Aberconwy and Colwyn

ᵢewed from the east bank, the ᵃlled town and massive castle, ᵣistling with towers, make a breath-ᵃking sight against the mountain ᵃckground. Astride the River ᵒnwy (pronounced Con-oo-ee) is the ᵃmous Conwy Suspension Bridge ᵉsigned and built by Thomas Tel-ᵒrd in 1826, fitting seamlessly into ᵉ defensive ensemble.

ᴄONWY CASTLE★★

ADW. ⊙ *Open daily 9am/9.30am–*ᵖm /5pm. ⊕£4.60, joint ticket with *ᵃs Mawr (see below)* £7. ℘01492 592 ⁵8. www.conwy.com.
ʰis masterpiece of medieval architec-ᵤre (1283–87) was supplied from the ᵉa, as were Edward I's other Welsh ᵃstles. Eight massive drum towers with ᵢnnacled battlements protect the two

▶ **Population:** 3,649.
🗺 **Michelin Map:** Atlas p 33 or Map 503 1 24.
ℹ **Info:** Castle Buildings, Conwy. ℘01492 592 248. www.visitconwy.org.uk.
◐ **Location:** 5mi/8km south of Llandudno on the northeastern tip of Wales, 47mi/75km west of Chester.
◉ **Don't Miss:** Conwy Castle.
👥 **Kids:** Butterfly Jungle.

wards of the castle, set on its rocky ridge. The inner ward with the royal apartments was approached by water and the large outer ward from the town.

TOWN

The 13C **town walls**★★ (35ft/11m high and 6ft/2m thick) girdle the town on three sides, and were built at the same

Conwy Castle

time as the castle. The circuit is defended by 22 towers and three gateways and provides a good wall-walk between Upper Church Gate and Berry Street.

The original founder of Conwy, Llywelyn the Great, dominates all from his column in Lancaster Square.

Farther down the High Street at the corner of Crown Lane is **Plas Mawr**★★ (CADW; ⏰ *open Tue–Sun and bank hols: Apr–Sept 9.30am–5pm, Oct 9.30am–4pm;* ♿£4.90, joint ticket with Conwy Castle £7; ♿; ✆01443 336 000; www.cadw.wales.gov.uk), a mansion built in 1577 by Robert Wynne, a true Elizabethan adventurer. Its rooms still evoke the more gracious moments of the age in which it was built.

At the junction with Berry and Castle Streets is **Aberconwy House**, (NT; ⏰ open late Mar–Oct Wed–Mon 11am–5pm; ♿£3; ✆01492 592 246; www.nationaltrust.org.uk) a medieval town house c. 1300. A few minutes walk away at ♟**Conwy Butterfly Jungle** (Bodlondeb Park; ⏰open Wed–Mon: late Mar–early Sept 10am–5.30pm and Sept–early Nov 10am–4pm; ♿£5, child £3.50; ♿✗; ✆01492 593 149; www.conwy-butterfly.co.uk) you can see many of the world's most beautiful butterflies in free flight in a large jungle garden.

EXCURSIONS
Bodnant Garden★★
8mi/13km south of Conwy by the A 470. ⏰*Open late Feb–Oct daily 10am–5pm. First two wks Nov daily 10am–4pm.* ♿£6.80. ♿🅿✗. ✆01492 650 460. www.bodnantgarden.co.uk.

The garden (99 acres/40ha), laid out largely in the late 19C and early 20C, comprises formal terraces around the house and The Dell, an area for woodland walks. Noted for rhododendrons, camelias and magonlias, it is also justly famed for its golden Laburnum Arch, which flowers in late Spring.

Penrhyn Castle★★
NT. Bangor, 17mi/27km west of Conwy by the A 55. ⏰ *Open Apr–Oct Wed–Mon noon (11am Jul–Aug)–5pm. Grounds open 1hr earlier.* ♿£9; grounds and stable-block only, £5.60. 🅿✗. ✆01248 353 084. www.nationaltrust.org.uk.

This extraordinary evocation of the Middle Ages was built in the 1820s and 1830s for George Dawkins Pennant, heir to the enormous wealth produced by the Penrhyn slate quarries. Its mighty keep (124ft/38m high) gives it the very image of an impregnable Norman fortress, but in fact it was a country home of the utmost luxury, providing hospitality to the members of the Anglo-Irish Ascendancy on their way to and from the port of Holyhead. The décor of the interior is a *tour-de-force* of traditional craftsmanship, filled with furniture of an opulence seldom seen since. The paintings on show in the Dining Room include an array of Old Masters (Rembrandt, Canaletto, Jan Steen, Van der Velde…) unparalleled in North Wales. Its grandiose outbuildings house a railway museum, a dolls museum and large Victorian kitchens. Its extensive parklands include a walled garden with many unusual plants.

Llandudno★
Aberconwy and Colwyn

Safe sandy Blue-Flag beaches with views of Snowdonia, Punch and Judy shows, a Victorian pier and other traditional British seaside trappings make Llandudno an evergreen family summer holiday resort.

RESORT

The Victorian **Pier**★ of 1875, a delicious confection in the Anglo-Indian style, is, unlike many contemporary structures of its kind, splendidly shipshape.

The family of Alice Liddell, inspiration for Lewis Carroll's immortal *Alice in Wonderland,* spent most of their holidays in Llandudno and a delightful statue of the White Rabbit stands on the West Shore. The hill above town, known as the **Great Orme** (679ft/207m), can be reached by the 1903-vintage cable-hauled **Great Orme Tramway**★ (*Victoria Station, Church Walks; operates late Mar–late Oct daily 10am–6pm/Mar and Oct 5pm; £5.40 return; 01492 879306; www. greatormetramway.com);* by the **Llandudno Cable Car**★ *(Happy Valley; operates mid-Mar–Oct daily 10am–5pm; £6.50 return; 01492 877205; www. llandudnoattractions.com);* or by road. It offers superb views across the water, town and Snowdonia.

Far underground are the caves and passageways of the **Great Orme Ancient Copper Mines** (*open mid-Mar–Oct daily 10am–5pm; £6; 01492 870 447. www.greatormemines.info),* first worked by Bronze Age miners.

EXCURSIONS
Bodelwyddan★★

11mi/18km east on the A 470 and A 55. Bodelwyddan. Open late Mar–Oct Sat–Thu (also Good Fri and Aug daily) 10.30am–5pm. Nov–Mar Sat–Sun and Thu 10.30am–4/5pm. £5. 01745 584 060. www.bodelwyddan-castle.co.uk. Transformed in the course of the 19C to resemble a medieval stronghold, **Bodelwyddan Castle** has become a superb setting for a magnificent selection of

- **Population:** 13,202.
- **Michelin Map:** Michelin Atlas p 33 or Map 503 I 24.
- **Info:** Library Building, Mostyn Street, Llandudno. 01492 577 577. Castle Buildings, Conwy. 01492 592 248. www.visitconwy.org.uk.
- **Location:** The north-easternmost tip of Wales, 47mi/75km west of Chester. To get your bearings from on high take a ride on the tramway, or for a birds eye view jump aboard the longest passenger cable car system in Britain.
- **Don't Miss:** The ascent to the Great Orme; Bodelwyddan castle.

Victorian portraits from London's **National Portrait Gallery**. The paintings are hung in rooms whose fittings and furniture have been carefully and entertainingly chosen and arranged to evoke various themes. Thus the Billiard Room celebrates the masculine life of field, turf and boxing; the Library highlights eminent intellectuals and men of science; the Drawing Room has many female portraits. The gardens have been restored to their Edwardian character.

Rhuddlan Castle★★

16mi/26km east by A 470, A 5 and A 547. Castle Street. Open Apr–Sept daily 10am–5pm. £3.10. 01745 590 777. www.cadw.wales.gov.uk.
Diggers from the Fens (*see CAMBRIDGESHIRE*) and elsewhere laboured for three years during the war of 1277 to divert the River Clwyd, so that a castle which could be supplied from the sea could be built. A town grew up which, in the war of 1282, replaced Chester as the main base of operations against the Welsh in Snowdonia. In 1284 the "Statute of Wales" was issued here, "securing to the Principality of Wales its judicial rights and independence".

Rhuddlan Castle

©Christopher Moncrieff/Dreamstime.com

The castle was partly demolished after the Civil War. Entry to the remains is by the **west gatehouse**, the best surviving feature.

First and second floors provided comfortable apartments with fireplaces. Similar suites must have existed in the east gatehouse. The concentric plan of the castle within its wide dry moat, with lower walls to the outer ward and a defended river wall and dock, can still be traced on the ground.

St Asaph Cathedral★

15mi/24km east on the B 5155 and A 55. High Street. ◷ *Open Mon–Sat 9am–6.30 pm, Sun 7.30 am–4.30 pm.* ♿🅿*(charge).* ✆*01745 583 429, 583 597. www.stasaphcathedral.org.uk.*

This is the second-smallest cathedral city in the country, after St David's. St Kentigern founded a monastic community here in AD 560. The present cathedral, mainly 13C, houses the Bible used at Prince Charles' investiture in 1969.

Llangollen★
Denbighshire

The verdant Vale of Llangollen and the valley of the Dee have long formed a convenient route for travellers from England on their way to North Wales.

▸ **Population:** 2,546.
♿ **Michelin Map:** Michelin Atlas p 33 or Map 503 K 25.
▸ **Location:** 12mi/19km south of Wrexham.

TOWN

This little market town, dominated by the dramatically sited ruins of the 12C Castle Dinas Brân, is still a popular stopping place. Llangollen hosts the **International Eisteddfod** (Festival) and many other events in and around the spectacular tent-like structure of the **Royal International Pavilion**.

Plas Newydd★ *(10 min on foot from the town centre, Hill Street;* ◷ *open Easter–Oct daily 10am–5pm;* ✆*£3.50;* ♿🅿✕*; ✆01978 861314; www.nationaltrust.*

org.uk.) was the home of **The Ladies of Llangollen** from 1780 when they arrived from Ireland and set up house together. The lesbian relationship of Lady Eleanor Butler and Miss Sarah Ponsonby caused considerable comment in Regency Britain's high society, though they entertained a constant stream of distinguished visitors at their home. They began the transformation of a humble cottage into the eccentric "black and white" building it is today. They are buried together in nearby St Collen's Church.

XCURSIONS

langollen Railway

Operates daily service Jun–Oct
d most weekends throughout the
ar, see website for schedule.
£10 Dayrover ticket. &🖭🅿✕.
01978 860 979 (enquiries).
ww.llangollen-railway.co.uk.
is is the only standard-gauge pre-
rved steam railway in Wales; the
gular services are perhaps the best
ay of exploring the Vale of Llangollen
stream as far as Glyndyfrdwy.

anal Trips

angollen Wharf. ◷ Operate daily
ster–Oct 11am. Times may vary,
ll ahead. ◷ Sometimes closed Oct
d Thu–Fri, except in school hols.
£5. &. ℘01978 860 702.
ww.horsedrawnboats.co.uk.
rhaps the most relaxing way of
joying the scenery around Llan-
ollen is to take a 45-min ride on a
orse-drawn barge, on the winding
angollen branch of the Shropshire
ion Canal built by Telford. The
wpath follows the narrowing canal
estward to join the Dee at Telford's
orseshoe Falls, a curving elegant
eir in a romantic setting. You can
so hire a barge from here to cross
e spectacular Pont Cysyllte "stream
the sky" ((◷ see below).

rddig★★

2mi/3km south of Wrexham, off A
5. **House:** ◷ Open Mar–Oct Sat–Wed
d Good Fri 11am–5pm (4pm Mar and
t, also open Thu in Aug). Nov–Christ-
as Sat–Sun 11am–4pm. **Garden:**
Open similar dates (see website
r details, closes 1hr later Apr–Oct.
£8.90, garden and outbuildings only,
.80. 🅿✕. ℘01978 355 314,
978 315 151 (infoline).
ww.nationaltrust.org.uk.
is late-17C house was rescued in
73 from dereliction due to mining
bsidence. It contains much furniture
outstanding quality, supplied for it in
e 1720s, as well as magnificent por-
lain, tapestries and paintings. There
also a unique collection of portraits,

photographs and poetic descriptions of
staff. The restored joiner's shop, sawpit,
laundry, bakehouse, kitchen and servants' hall all furnish an insight into the
complex running of a country estate.
The **State Bedroom** with 18C Chinese
wallpaper contains a magnificently
restored bed from 1720. The early 18C
formal garden survives, at least in outline, and has now been restored.

Chirk Castle★★

NT. 7mi/11km east on the A 5.
Castle: ◷ Open mid-Feb–Oct Wed–
Sun and bank hols 11am–5pm
(4pm Feb–Mar and Oct), also open Tue
during Jul–Aug. **Gardens and Tower:**
◷ Open same days as castle 10am–6pm
(5pm Mar and Oct). ☞Guided tours of
State Rooms 11am–noon daily on open
days. ◿£8.28. Gardens only, £5.85.
&🅿✕. ℘01691 777 701.
www.nationaltrust.org.uk.
Chirk Castle, or Castell y Waun, was built
to a design similar to that of Beaumaris
((◷ see Isle of ANGLESEY), started the same
year, 1295. It has been in continuous
occupation from then until the present
day and shows the adaptation of a great
fortress to the changing needs of later
times. The **State Rooms** in the north
wing are the great glory of Chirk.
The castle stands in a landscaped park of
great splendour and extent, in part laid
out in the late 18C by William Emes, a
follower of Lancelot "Capability" Brown.
Close to the house, topiary and hedging
recall the formal gardens swept away by
Emes, but the most distinctive feature
of the grounds are the **wrought-iron
gates**★, a Baroque masterpiece made
at the nearby Bersham iron works.

Pont Cysyllte★★

4mi/7km east on the A 539.
One of the great monuments of the
industrial age, this magnificent aque-
duct was built 1795–1810 by the great
engineer Thomas Telford to carry the
Ellesmere Canal over the River Dee.
Throughout its length (1,007ft/307m)
it is accompanied by a towpath protected from the drop (121ft/23m) by
iron railing.

Pembrokeshire Coast ★★

Pembrokeshire

The Pembrokeshire Peninsula, the most western part of Wales and part of the old Kingdom of Dyfed, abounds not only in the dolmens and megaliths of prehistory but also in the splendid stone crosses of Celtic Christianity. In 1952 the coastline was designated the Pembrokeshire Coast National Park, the smallest and, as it comprises mostly coastal scenery, the least typical

- **Michelin Map:** Michelin Atlas p 14 or Map 503 E, F 27, 28 and 29.
- **Info:** Tenby, ☎01834 842402. Haverfordwest, ☎01437 763110. Fishguard Town, ☎01437 776 636. Fishguard Harbour, ☎01348 872037. Pembroke, ☎01646 622388. Saundersfoot, ☎01834 813672. www. visitpembrokeshire.com. www.pcnpa.org.uk.

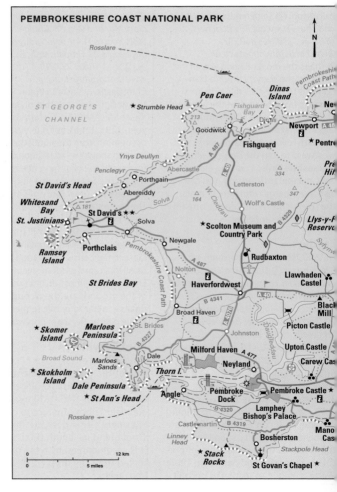

PEMBROKESHIRE COAST NATIONAL PARK

of the National Parks of Wales and England; its wonderful variety of beaches is backed by a cliff-line revealing a complex and sometimes spectacular geology and harbouring a rich bird-life.

Also see: Tenby

SOUTH COAST *85mi/135km*
Manorbier (Maenorbyr)

"The most delectable spot in Wales", according to Giraldus Cambrensis, traveller and historian born here c. 1146. When seen from the bay, the mighty walls of **Manorbier Castle** (*open Easter–Sept daily, also Oct Sat–Sun and during half-term 10.30am–5.30pm; £3.50; P; 01834 871 394; www.manorbiercastle.co.uk*), which belonged to his family, recall the great Crusader strongholds of the Levant. The spectacular stretch of coastline between St Govan's Head and Linney Head features high cliffs, arches (including the **Green Bridge of Wales**), sea-caves, blow-holes and stacks, including two impressive pillars, **Stacks Rocks**★ (Elegug Stacks). Near Bosherston, the **chapel**★ first established as a hermit's cell by St Govan in the 6C seems almost a part of the cliff face (*note: this area is part of the Castlemartin artillery range; check locally in advance to see if it is accessible*).

Pembroke Castle★★
Open Apr–Sept 9.30am–6pm, Oct and Mar 10am–5pm Nov–Feb 10am–4pm. Closed Dec 24–26, Jan 1. £3.50. Guided tour (1hr) daily May–Aug 11am, 12pm, 15pm. (Summer only). 01646 681 510. www.pembrokecastle.co.uk.

This powerful and ancient castle has for centuries guarded the strategically sited town of Pembroke and its safe anchorage. Soon after the Battle of Hastings in 1066 the Normans looked to Wales, but not until 1093 did Earl Roger of Montgomery build the first Pembroke Castle. The castle we see today was built in the 1190s and enlarged a century later. The massive **keep**, 70ft/21m high with walls 19ft/6m thick at the base, is the crowning glory of the castle. The **Wogan Cavern**, below the Norman Hall, is unparalleled in British castles; a natural vaulted cavern, 60ft/18m by 80ft/24m, probably used as a store and boathouse.

Marloes Sands
This broad sandy beach separates the Dale and Marloes Peninsulas. On the beach, note the **Three Chimneys**, Silurian rocks up-ended by powerful earth movements. Visits can be made to the bird sanctuary islands of **Skomer**★, Skokholm and Grassholm, with their colonies of sea birds, including the charming puffin, the emblem of this National Park.

Haverfordwest (Hwlffordd)

The former county town with its hill-top castle ruin is still the regional urban centre.

Newgale

One of several holiday villages on this coast, its splendid two-mile stretch of sand, backed by a storm ridge of shingle, makes this a favourite family holiday spot.

Solva (Solvach)

The picturesque harbour at Lower Solva was built to be out of sight of sea-raiders. Today it shelters pleasure boats as well as fishing craft.

NORTH COAST (55mi/85km)
St David's (Ty Ddewi)★★

See ST DAVID'S.
Beyond is **Strumble Head**★ and its light, the nearest point to Ireland.

Fishguard (Abergwaun)

The lower town offers a pretty haven for pleasure craft. Brunel planned to make Fishguard a transatlantic port to rival Liverpool and for a brief period great liners like the *Mauretania* did berth here, but today only the ferries sail from the eastern side of the bay towards Rosslare.

East of Fishguard the landscapes grow wilder and the cliffs more precipitous.

Pentre Ifan★

This massive *cromlech* (dolmen), over-looking Newport Bay, consists of four great upright stones, three of which support a massive capstone. It stands on the lower slopes of the rounded, heather-clad **Presely Hills** (Mynydd Preseli), from whose eastern crests came the bluestones of Stonehenge, probably transported across from Newport Bay.

Nevern

Among the yews in the churchyard of St Brynach's Church stands a splendid 11C Celtic wheelhead **cross** (13ft/4m high), richly carved in interlacing patterns.

Castell Henllys

Meline. ◷ *Open Apr–Oct daily 10am–5pm. Nov and Mar daily 11am–3pm.* ◷ *Closed 3 weeks over Christmas and New Year.* £3.50. Guided tours daily 1.30am, 2.30pm. ✗. ✆01239 891 319. www.castellhenllys.com.
This hill-top fort is the setting for a re-creation of an Iron Age community with storage pit, cultivated areas and a fine trio of conical thatched huts with smoky interiors.

Portmeirion ★★★

Gwynedd

Built on a wooded peninsula, with wonderful views over the shining waters and sweeping sandbanks of Traeth Bach, and with the mountains of Snowdonia as a backdrop, this dream village was the creation of the ever-fertile imagination of the architect and pioneer preservationist, Sir Clough Williams-Ellis (1893–1978). It has often been used as the setting for films and TV programmes, the most famous of which, *The Prisoner* (1966–67), has cult status. The village is run as a hotel, as originally intended, but is accessible with a small admission fee.

▸ **Population:** 4,187.
Michelin Map: Atlas p 32 or Map 503 H 25.
Info: Station Square, Pwllheli. ✆01758 613 000.
◷ **Opening Times:** Daily 9.30am–5.30pm (Nov–Mar 10am–5pm). £7 (Nov–Mar free with website voucher). ♿🅿✗. ✆01766 770 000. www.portmeirion-village.com.
Location: 20mi/32km south of Mt Snowdon.
Don't Miss: The beaches of the Lleyn Peninsula; Harlech Castle.

Central Piazza, Portmeirion

© Shayne Rex/www.portmeirion-village.com

ILLAGE

he Village" is an extraordinary mixture
fantasy, theatrical effects and visual
cks; Sir Clough claimed that it was
serve "no useful purpose save that
looking both handsome and jolly",
fficient incentive to attract the large
mber of visitors who come for the day
to stay in the hotel or in one of the
ray of delightful buildings, most of
em with a Baroque, Rococo or Medi-
rranean flavour.

chways lead to **Battery Square** with
me of Portmeirion's earliest buildings,
ile the Citadel area is dominated by
e **Campanile**, which looks much
ler than its actual height (80ft/24m)
cause of Sir Clough's mastery of illu-
nism. In the valley leading down to
e shoreline is the **Piazza**, the green
art of the village, with shops and res-
urants and views to the Pantheon and
e Bristol Colonnade, one of the many
uctures rescued from demolition and
-erected here.

XCURSIONS

arlech Castle★★

DW. 18mi/29km east by A 487
Maentwrog then south by A 496.
Open Apr–Oct daily 9am–5pm,
v–Mar daily 9.30am (11am Sun)–
m. £3.70. 01766 780 552.
vw.cadw.wales.gov.uk.

rlech Castle was built 1283–89, during
ward I's second campaign in Wales.
impressive outline rises on a rocky
g, 200ft/60m above the plain; with
noramic views to Snowdonia, across

the Lleyn Peninsula and out to the open
sea. Pause to look at the massive east
front with its daunting **Gatehouse**, and
solid drum towers, which confronted
would-be attackers. Enter by the modern wooden stairs, at the spot where a
second, inner drawbridge pivoted to
come down. Inside, the strength and
importance of the gatehouse becomes
apparent.

Lleyn (Llyn) Peninsula★★

West by the A 487 and A 497.
Geologically a continuation of the
mountains of Snowdonia, this remote
peninsula with its wild scenery and
splendid coastline is one of the strongholds of Welshness. At the base of the
peninsula is the charming Victorian seaside resort of **Criccieth** with the ruins of
its 13C Welsh **castle** *(CADW; open as
Harlech Castle; £3.10; 01766 522 227;
www.cadw.wales.gov.uk),* and the resort
of **Pwllheli**. Near the end of the peninsula, sheltered from the winds among
the trees of the westernmost woodland,
are the gardens of **Plas-yn-Rhiw**★ *(NT;
Rhiw; NT; call for opening times; £4;
; 01758 780 219; www.national
trust.org.uk),* an endearing little country
house, part Tudor, part Georgian, with
spectacular bay views.
The other attractions of the peninsula
are mostly natural, ranging from the
strangely shaped trio of hills named Tre'r
Ceiri, to wonderful golden sandy beaches
and, in the far southwest, the rugged
height of **Mynydd Mawr**a, overlooking
the pilgrims' island of **Bardsey**★.

Snowdonia★★★

Gwynedd

Snowdonia National Park covers 840sq mi/2,180sq km of wild beauty amongst the scenic mountains of North Wales. Mount Snowdon, at 3,560ft/1,085m, is the highest mountain in England and Wales, dominating the north. Cader Idris at 2,930ft/830m towers south. In all there are 96 peaks over 2,000ft/600m here.

NATIONAL PARK AREA
Betws-y-Coed★

Beautifully set amid tree-clad slopes at the junction of the Rivers Conwy and Llugwy, Betws-y-Coed (Chapel in the Woods) is the gateway to Snowdonia. A sturdy stone bridge, Pont y Pair, spans the Llugwy downstream from its romantically wooded ravine, where cascades form the famous **Swallow Falls**. Telford's ornate cast-iron bridge over the Conwy proclaims that it was "Constructed in the same year the Battle of Waterloo was fought."

Llanberis★

This little slate-quarrying town is the starting point for the **Snowdon Mountain Railway** (ⓒ see below) but has attractions of its own such as the excellent **Welsh Slate Museum**★ (ⓒ open Easter–Oct daily 10am–5pm, Nov–Easter Sun–Fri 10am–4pm; ♿ 🅿 ✕; ℘01286 870 630; www.nmgw.ac.uk), housed in the engineering workshops of the great Dinorwig Quarry.

Snowdon Mountain Railway

© Snowdon Mountain Railway

- ⚓ **Michelin Map:** Michelin Atlas p 32 or Map 503 I 24.
- ▤ **Info:** Royal Oak Stables, Betws-y-Coed, ℘01690 710 426. Unit 3, Stryd Fawr, Blaenau Ffestiniog, ℘01766 830360. Canolfan Hebog, Beddgelert, ℘01766 890615. www.snowdonia-npa.gov.uk.
- ▶ **Location:** Betws-y-Coed, Beddgelert, Blaenau Ffestiniog and Llanberis all make good bases.
- ⬡ **Don't Miss:** Snowdon Mountain Railway and the view from the summit; Llechwed Slate Caverns; Centre for Alternative Technology.
- ⏱ **Timing:** Three days min.

Visitors can penetrate far into the depths of the mountain itself, to see where the turbines of the **Dinorwig Power Station** are housed in great man-made caverns. The starting point for exploring this is the **Electric Mountain Visitor Centre** (ⓒ open year-round daily 10am–4.30pm, Jun–Aug and all school hols 9.30am–5.30pm, tours Easter–Oct 👓 visitor centre free, underground tour £7.50, booking advisable; ♿ 🅿 ✕ ℘01286 870 636; www.electricmountain.co.uk).

Snowdon★★★

The easiest ascent of the mountain is from Llanberis aboard the **Snowdon Mountain Railway**★★ (ⓒ operates weather permitting, late Mar– early Nov 9am–5pm every 30min; summit train early May onwards; 👓 summit £23 return £16 one way; ♿ 🅿 ✕; ℘0871 720 0033 www.snowdonrailway.co.uk), a rack-and-pinion line built in 1896 and the only one of its type in Britain; its centenarian steam locomotives still soldier on.

Principal footpaths are fully described in the leaflets and maps published by the Park Authority. The most straightforward path follows the ridge used by the rail way, while the most scenic begins at the Pen-y-Pass car park on Llanberis Pass. For experienced walkers, the scramble along the knife-edge of Crib Goch is an exhilarating experience. In fine weather, the **panorama**★★★ from the summit of Snowdon takes in all Anglesey, the Isle of Man, and the Wicklow Mountains in Ireland. Take it all in from the comfort of Hafod Eyri, the striking £8.3million **Snowdon Summit Visitor Centre**, completed in 2009.

Blaenau Ffestiniog★

Slate is still quarried here albeit on a lesser scale than in the past. In the 👥👤 **Llechwedd Slate Caverns**★

🕐open year-round daily, tours 10am–4.15pm/4.15pm Oct–Mar, Victorian Village Apr–Sept only; 🕐closed Jan 1 and Dec 25–26; ⊙one tour £9.45, child £7.15; two tours £15.20, child £11.60; 🅿✕; ℘01766 830 306; www.llechwedd-slate-caverns.co.uk) the story of Welsh slate is told in film and visitors are carried by train through two individual sets of caverns, where tableaux depict working conditions. A pub shop and houses above ground replicate Victorian and early-20C village life.

Blaenau Ffestiniog is linked to Porthmadog on the coast by the **Ffestiniog Railway**★★ (🕐 operates Apr–Oct daily 9am–5pm; ♿🅿✕; Nov–Mar certain days only, 10.15am–5pm, see website for timetable and fares; ⊙£17.50 all day rover; ℘01766 516 000; www.festrail.co.uk), built in 1836 to haul slate from quarry to port. The traditional narrow-gauge

Beddgelert

Three valleys meet here and the village looks south to the Pass of Aberglaslyn. The dramatic scenery is enough to attract the tourist, but in the 18C the local innkeeper, anxious to encourage trade, embroidered an old legend, and created "Gelert's Grave". The tale has it that Llywelyn the Great had a hound called Gelert. He left Gelert guarding his baby son and returned to find the child missing and the dog covered in blood. Llywelyn, believing Gelert had killed his son, slew the poor beast before he discovered that it had in fact saved the boy from a wolf, whose body was discovered nearby.

line (13mi/21km) now takes tourists through the splendidly wooded scenery of the Vale of Ffestiniog, past lakes and waterfalls, to the "city of slate" among the mountains. A new and equally scenic Ffestiniog line, the **Welsh Highland Railway** (www.welshhighlandrailway.net) was completed in late 2009, retracing the original 40-mi/64-km route to Caernarfon; see website for details.

Centre for Alternative Technology★★

3mi/5km north of Machynlleth on the A 487. 🕐 *Open daily.* ⊙£8.40. ♿🅿✕. ℘01654 705950. www.cat.org.uk. Pioneers in inventing and promoting ecologically friendly ideas since 1973.

St David's★
Tyddewi – Pembrokeshire

The cathedral is the centrepiece of this tiny city. St David's today is a thriving tourist-oriented community, at the westernmost point of the Pembrokeshire Coast Path.

A BIT OF HISTORY

There has been a Christian community and daily worship on this site for more

▶ **Population:** 1,428.
🕐 **Michelin Map:** Atlas p 14 or Map 503 E 28 – Local map Pembrokeshire Coast.
🛈 **Info:** Oriel y Parc, Landscape Gallery. ℘01437 720392. www. visitpembrokeshire.com.
⊙ **Location:** Saint David's peninsula, SW Wales

Offshore Exploration

A boat trip is an essential part of exploring the Pembrokeshire Coast There are several boat excursions that depart from St Justinian, a few minutes drive from St David's in search of the local wildlife. There is usually a choice of taking a conventional boat or a ride in a jet-powered rigid inflatable which can be a bit bumpy but is also a great thrill. The main opertors are **Thousand Islands Expeditions** (Cross Square, St David's; ☏01437 721 721; www.thousandislands. co.uk) and **Voyages of Discovery** (1 High Street, St David's; ☏01437 720 285; www.ramseyisland.co.uk).

than fourteen centuries and since the decree of Pope Callixtus II in the 12C, two pilgrimages to St David's are the equivalent of one to Rome – a privilege shared only with Santiago de Compostela in Spain.

RELIGIOUS SIGHTS
Cathedral★★
◷ Open year-round daily, 7.30am (12.45pm Sun)–6pm. ☞£2 Contribution requested. ☞ Guided tours Aug Mon 11am Fri 2.30pm, ☞£4 donation requested. ♿🅿✕. ☏01437 720 691. www.stdavidscathedral.org.uk.
Wales' greatest church, built in lichen-encrusted purple stone, sits in a secluded

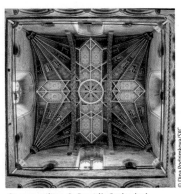
© Dina Podzimkova/SXC

Ornate ceiling, St David's Cathedral

hollow, revealing itself with dramatic suddenness to the visitor passing through the gatehouse into the precinct containing both Cathedral and Bishop's Palace.
The present building was started in 1180 by Peter de Leia (1176–98), Florentine monk and third Norman bishop. Up to the wall behind the high altar, what we see today is substantially his cathedral The whole building slopes upwards from west to east (approx 14ft/3.5m) and presents a unique and striking impression to a visitor entering the south porch, at the western end of the nave The late 15C **nave roof** is a magnificent piece of work, in Irish oak, incorporating the dragon of Wales on the pendants. In the south choir aisle is the tomb of the historian **Gerald of Wales** (1146–1223). Before the high altar is the table tomb of **Edmund Tudor**, grandfather of Henry VIII, who ordered it to be moved here from Greyfriars at Carmarthen after the Dissolution. The remains of St David's shrine, built in 1275, are on the north side of the presbytery.

Bishop's Palace★
CADW. ◷Open Apr–Oct daily 9am–5pm. Nov–Mar daily 9.30am (Sun 11am)–4pm. Last admission 30min before closing. ◷ Closed Jan 1 and Dec 24–26. ☞£3. ☏01443 336000. www.cadw.wales.gov.uk.
The close wall surrounding the cathedral and palace probably dates from c. 1300 The surviving buildings date chiefly from the thirteenth and fourteenth centuries particularly the work of Bishop Thomas Bek (1280-93) and Bishop Henry de Gower (1328-47).
The latter added the south porch and the decorated windows to the cathedral The palace consists of three long buildings, surrounding a courtyard, which is completed by a wall pierced by a buttressed gateway. The **Bishop's Hall** and **Solar**, with kitchen and chapel, appear to have been the main residence, the **Great Hall** to the south, with its elaborate porch and stairs from the courtyard being reserved for the entertainment of important guests.

Swansea ★

Abertawe – Swansea

Swansea is the lively urban centre for southwest Wales and after Cardiff, the country's second city. Three centuries of industrial activity in the **Lower Swansea Valley** resulted in one of Britain's most spectacularly derelict landscapes. Since the late 1960s however a thoroughgoing programme of reclamation has succeeded in transforming the area, which now consists of parkland, light industrial units and commercial and retail developments, with few traces left of its industrial past. Swansea city centre is undergoing a £1bn restoration programme due to complete in 2015 with a vastly improved retailing centre at its core. The Tower, Meridian Quay is Wales's tallest building (351ft/107m).

▶ **Population:** 172,433.

Michelin Map: Michelin Atlas p 15 or Map 503 I 29.

Info: Plymouth Street. &01792 468 321. www.visitswanseabay.com.

Location: Swansea is 40mi/64km west of Cardiff. Frequent trains run direct from London, Bristol, Manchester and Cardiff. The train station is a 10-min walk north, the bus station is in the centre by the Quadrant Shopping Centre.

Don't Miss: The Maritime Quarter and the Gower Peninsula beaches.

Timing: Allow one day to see Swansea.

Kids: Seaside attractions at The Mumbles; the beaches of the Gower Peninsula.

CITY

Glynn Vivian Art Gallery ★

Alexandra Road. Open Tue–Sun and bank hols 10am–5pm. & &01792 516 900. www.swansea.gov.uk.
Built on the fortune made from copper-smelting, this gallery is one of the best places in which to survey a wide variety of Welsh art, as well as a fine collection of Swansea pottery.

Maritime Quarter ★

The mid-19C South Dock has been renovated as a marina, the centrepiece of a new "inner-city village" of spruce apartments, public squares and quayside walks, one of which hosts a statue of local-born poet **Dylan Thomas** 1914–53). The jewel in the crown is the **National Waterfront Museum** ★ *(Oystermouth Road;* open year-round daily 10am–5pm; Closed 1 Jan and 25–26 Dec; & ✗; &01792 638950; www.museumwales.ac.uk) housed in a magnificent building, opened 2005, that elegantly combines old and new architecture. Its varied exhibits include a complete, re-erected woollen mill; several retired vessels, among them a lightship, are moored at the quayside,

and historic vehicles of the Mumbles Tramway can be seen in the tramshed. Beyond simple displays, the museum explores the whole way of life for ordinary people at the time of the Industrial Revolution in Wales.

EXCURSIONS

Gower Peninsula ★★

West of Swansea a chain of superb beaches and magnificent cliffs extends along the south coast of the peninsula (14mi/22km), Britain's first designated Area of Outstanding Natural Beauty.
The Mumbles, Swansea's own seaside resort overlooked by Oystermouth Castle, was the terminus of the Mumbles Railway, the world's first scheduled passenger railway, which opened for horse-drawn traffic in 1804 and closed only in 1960.
The approach to the tiny village of **Rhossili** ★★ in the far southwestern corner of the peninsula hardly prepares the visitor for the breathtaking **views** which open up from the coastguard cottages housing the National Trust visitor centre. The cliffs fall dramatically away

to the great arc (3mi/5km) of **Rhossili Bay** with the surf crashing on its wonderful sandy beach. High above is Rhossili Down (633ft/193m); to the south is **Worms Head**, a mile-long sea-serpent in rock, accessible only at low tide.

Aberdulais Falls★

NT. 11mi/17km northeast by A 483, A 48 and A 465. 🕐 *Open Good Fri–late Oct daily 10am–5pm. Late Oct–Good Fri Sat–Sun and bank hols 11am–4pm.* ⊜*£3.63.* ♿🅿✕. ✆*01639 636 674. www.nationaltrust.org.uk.*

In a pretty wooded gorge, the waters of the River Dulais crash down among huge boulders and past the remains of the works of the Aberdulais Tinplate Co., founded 1830. The site's industrial history goes back to 1584, when copper smelting began and a new exhibition and interpretation project shows how the falls played an important role in the industrialisation of South Wales. It was also frequented by artists (including Turner) who found it an appropriately picturesque subject.

Kidwelly★ (Cydweli)

CADW. 21mi/34km northwest via the A 483, A 4070 and A 484. 🕐 *Open Apr–Oct daily 9am–5pm. Nov–Mar daily 9.30am (Sun 11am)–4pm.* 🕐 *Closed 1 Jan and 24-26 Dec.* ⊜*£3.* ♿🅿. ✆*01554 890 104. www.cadw.wales.gov.uk.*

Bishop Roger of Salisbury's first ring-work was complete by the foundation of the priory c. 1130, though the present **castle** dates from the 1280s. The walls enclosed the Norman town to form a "bastide" such as are found in North Wales at Conwy and Caernarfon. St Mary's Church, built c. 1320, in Decorated style, originally served a Benedictine monastery.

National Botanic Garden of Wales★

🕐 *Open daily 10am–6pm (4.30pm Nov–Mar).* ⊜*£8 (£5 winter).* ♿🅿✕. ✆*01558 668 768. www.gardenof wales.org.uk.*

The **Great Glasshouse**, the largest single-span glasshouse in the world, creates a perfect Mediterranean landscape in miniature where 10,000 plants, numbering 1,000 species, can flourish in their native environment. The surrounding grounds were laid out in the Regency period with five lakes, herbaceous borders and a double-walled garden, which have been rescued from dereliction as a Millennium project.

The house, **Middleton Hall** (destroyed by fire in 1931), was designed by Samuel Cockerell for Sir William Paxton.

ADDRESSES

🎭 ENTERTAINMENT

Nightclubs, bars and restaurants are to be found in the Maritime Quarter on the waterfront. Some pubs offer live music.

Concerts by international orchestras and soloists are held at the **Brangwyn Hall,** opera and ballet at the **Grand Theatre.** Other venues include **Dylan Thomas Theatre** and the **Taliesin Centre.**

In addition to the local festivals – the **Swansea Bay Summer Festival** (May–Sept), **Swansea Festival of Music** (Oct), the **Margam Festival of Music and Arts** (July), the **Gower Festival** of small classical concerts takes place in the churches of the area (July) – visitors may also attend the rehearsals of the famous **Welsh Male Voice Choirs** *(see http://visitswanseabay.com for details).*

🤸 OUTDOORS/SPORTS

Outdoor activities include canoeing, sailing, surfing (Bay Caswell and Langland Bay or Llangennith for the Atlantic rollers), windsurfing (Oxwich, Port Eynon), waterskiing (Swansea Bay, Oxwich Bay), hang-gliding and parascending (Rhossili Bay).

LC, Swansea's biggest leisure complex, is home to Wales' largest waterpark, a four-storey aquatic-themed play-area for young adventurers, a 30-ft/9-m climbing wall, and one of the largest exercise and wellness arenas in the Principality. For more details visit *www. thelcswansea.com.*

Tenby★★

*Dinbych-y-pysgod –
Pembrokeshire*

This little medieval town on its rocky
promontory, near the country's
southwestern most point, combines
all the ingredients of a popular seaside resort in a compact and pleas-
ing pattern. During the Victorian
era Tenby was eagerly visited for its
"restorative qualities"; walkways
were built here for seaside strolls.

HARBOUR AND SEAFRONT★★

A perfect composition of jetty, massive
retaining walls, Fishermen's Chapel and
rugged warehouses, backed by Georgian and Regency houses crowded
prettily together and rising to crown
the low cliff. Superb sandy beaches
extend north and south. On Castle Hill
Tenby Museum and Art Gallery (○
open year-round daily 10am–5pm (winter
Mon–Fri only); ✕ ; ○ closed Christmas
period; ⇒£4; ☎01834 842 809; www.
tenbymuseum.org.uk) with paintings
by Augustus and Gwen John and other
Tenby artists.

TOWN

A good stretch of the **town walls**
encloses a characteristically intricate
web of medieval streets, widening out
at **St Mary's** (○ Open daily 9am–5pm;
☎01834 842 068), one of Wales' most
substantial parish churches, with a spire
over 150ft/45m tall. The **Tudor Merchant's House** (NT; ○ open Apr–Oct
Sun–Fri and Sat during bank hol weekends 11am–5pm; ⇒£2.70; ☎01834 842

279; www.nationaltrust.org.uk), is a late-
15C town dwelling, virtually unchanged
externally and well preserved inside,
with period furniture.

EXCURSIONS
Carew Castle and Tidal Mill★
*5mi/8km west of Tenby just off A 477.
○Open (both) Apr/Easter–Oct daily
10am–5pm, castle also open Nov–Mar
(daily see website for closed dates)
11am–3pm. ⇒Castle and mill £3.50,
castle only £2.50. Guided tours castle
daily summer 2.30pm. �. ☎01646 651
782. www.carewcastle.com.*
Much of what still stands today dates
from the late 13C–early 14C. The magnificent Elizabethan architecture, with
rows of tall mullioned windows reflected
in the mill pool, recaptures some of the
elegance of the period.
The **tidal mill**, the only one of its kind
remaining in Wales, is a restored late-
18C building and has an audio-visual
presentation to explain its workings to
visitors. The heavily ornamented **Celtic
cross** near the entrance to the castle is
one of the earliest Christian monuments
in Wales, erected shortly after 1035.

Population: 5,226.
Michelin Map: Michelin Atlas p 14 or Map 503 F 28.
Info: Unit 2, Upper Park Road. ☎01834 842 402. www.visit-pembrokeshire.com.
Location: 53mi/85km west of Swansea.

Tenby
© Fotosearch

INDEX

INDEX

INDEX

INDEX

MAPS AND PLANS

THEMATIC MAPS

TOWN PLANS AND SIGHTS

LOCATOR MAPS

PLANS OF MONUMENTS

LOCAL MAPS

Great Britain Maps: Based upon Ordnance Survey of Great Britain with the Permission of the Controller of Her Majesty's Stationery Office © Crown Copyright 100000247.

MAPS OF GREAT BRITAIN

Michelin maps 501, 502, 503, 504 – Scotland; Northern England, The Midlands; Wales, The Midlands, South West England; South East England, The Midlands, East Anglia (Scale 1: 400 000 -1cm = 4km - 1in: 6.30miles) cover the main regions of the country, the network of motorways and major roads and some secondary roads. they provide information on shipping routes, distances in miles and kilometres, major town plans, services, sporting and tourist attractions and an index of places; the key and text are printed in four languages.

COUNTRY MAPS

The Michelin Tourist and Motoring Atlas - Great Britain & Ireland (Scale 1: 300 000 - 1cm = 3km - 1in: 4.75 miles) covers the whole of the United Kingdom and the Republic of Ireland, the national networks of motorways and major roads. It provides information on route planning, shipping routes, distances in miles and kilometres, over 60 town plans, services, sporting and tourist attractions and an index of places; the key and text are printed in six languages.

ONLINE

Michelin is pleased to offer a route-planning service on the Internet: **www. ViaMichelin. com.** Choose the shortest route, a route without tolls, or the Michelin recommended route to your destination; you can also access information about hotels and restaurants from The Red Guide, and tourist sites from The Green Guide.

MAP LEGEND

Highly Recommended	★★★
Recommended	★★
Interesting	★

Tourism

⦿ →	Sightseeing route with departure point indicated	AZ **B**		Map co-ordinates locating sights
♦ ⚓ ♦ ⚓	Ecclesiastical building	🛈		Tourist information
✡ ☪	Synagogue – Mosque	⊶ ❖		Historic house, castle – Ruins
⬒	Building (with main entrance)	◡ ✿		Dam – Factory or power station
■	Statue, small building	☆ ⌂		Fort – Cave
⚐	Wayside cross	᚛		Prehistoric site
◎	Fountain	▾ ♈		Viewing table – View
●━━■	Fortified walls – Tower – Gate	▲		Miscellaneous sight

Recreation

🏇	Racecourse	🏃	Waymarked footpath
⛸	Skating rink	◆	Outdoor leisure park/centre
♒ ♒	Outdoor, indoor swimming pool	🎢	Theme/Amusement park
⛵	Marina, moorings	♈	Wildlife/Safari park, zoo
⌂	Mountain refuge hut	⚙	Gardens, park, arboretum
◻━■━◻	Overhead cable-car	🕊	Aviary, bird sanctuary
🚂	Tourist or steam railway		

Additional symbols

═══ ══	Motorway (unclassified)	⊗ ◉	Post office - Telephone centre
❶ ❶	Junction: complete, limited	✉	Covered market
═══ ══	Pedestrian street	⚔	Barracks
꞊꞊꞊꞊꞊	Unsuitable for traffic, street subject to restrictions	△	Swing bridge
▦▦▦ -----	Steps - Footpath	◡ ✕	Quarry - Mine
🚂 🚌	Railway - Coach station	Ⓑ Ⓕ	Ferry (river and lake crossings)
◻+++++◻	Funicular - Rock-railway	🚢	Ferry services: Passengers and cars
━ ◉	Tram - Metro, underground	⛴	Foot passengers only
Bert (R.)…		③	Access route number common to MICHELIN maps and town plans

Abbreviations and special symbols

C	County council offices	**T**	Theatre
H	Town hall	**U**	University
J	Law courts	🅿	Park and Ride
M	Museum	M 3	Motorway
POL.	Police	A 2	Primary route

Michelin Apa Publications Ltd

A joint venture between Michelin and Langenscheidt

58 Borough High Street, London SE1 1XF, United Kingdom

No part of this publication may be reproduced in any form
without the prior permission of the publisher.

© 2010 Michelin Apa Publications Ltd
ISBN 978-1-906261-82-5
Printed: November 2009
Printed and bound in Germany